the foreign policy of the soviet union

THE FOREIGN POLICY OF THE SOVIET UNION

edited with introductory essays by ALVIN Z. RUBINSTEIN

University of Pennsylvania

third edition

Random House   New York

Library of Congress Cataloging In Publication Data.

Rubinstein, Alvin Z.   ed.
  The foreign policy of the Soviet Union.

  Includes bibliographies.
  1. Russia—Foreign relations—1917–1945.
2. Russia—Foreign relations—1945–   I. Title.
DK63.3.R8 1972   327.47   71–38820
ISBN 0–394–31699–1

Typography by Jack Ribik

Manufactured in the United States of America. Composed by Cherry Hill
Composition, Pennsauken, N.J. Printed and bound by The Kingsport
Press, Inc., Kingsport, Tenn.

Third Edition
987

To Frankie

Preface to the Third Edition

To the generation coming of political age, Stalin and Khrushchev, the Cold War, Berlin, Korea, the Twentieth Congress of the CPSU, the Sino-Soviet split, and other salient features of the recent past are but names and happenings whose significance for today and relationship to tomorrow are not readily understood. Indeed, in the historical consciousness of many students they are as remote as are Wilson, Clemenceau, Lenin, and Hitler; Sarajevo, Petrograd, and Versailles. Untouched by the "old" Cold War, the new generation wonders at the meaning of, or need for, the "new" Cold War. Knowledge of the past cannot illumine the future, but it can alert us to the pitfalls of the present. In the decade ahead the Soviet-American relationship—whether conflictive or cooperative—will overshadow all other international relationships in importance; it will shape the evolution of the international system and that of the internal political systems of the two countries as well.

In this revised and expanded edition greater attention has been devoted to developments of the past two decades. Two new chapters have been added: one on the Brezhnev period, the other on Soviet policy in the United Nations. The chapters dealing with ideology, the origins of the Cold War, the later Stalin period, the Khrushchev years, disarmament, the role of developing areas in Soviet thought, Soviet penetration of the Third World, and the problems and prospects facing Soviet leaders have been revised. More than a third of the Soviet documents and readings are new, and more than half of the book deals with the Khrushchev and Brezhnev periods of Soviet foreign policy.

The Soviet materials cover topics such as COMECON, Sino-Soviet relations, the Brezhnev Doctrine, peacekeeping, attitudes toward the United Nations, proposals for curbing the arms race, the national-democratic state, the Middle East, Latin America, and psychological aspects of the Cold War. The introductory essays analyze recent developments, including the German problem, nationalism in Eastern Europe, Soviet policy toward India, the Middle East, the Vietnam war, the Strategic Arms Limitation Talks, and Communist China. The bibliographies at the ends of the chapters list the major works in the field and are intended to assist those who seek in-depth knowledge of the various aspects of Soviet policy.

I would like to express my appreciation to Barry L. Rossinoff and Jane Cullen of Random House for the skill and care with which they shepherded this edition to press.

Philadelphia, Pa.   Alvin Z. Rubinstein
December 20, 1971

Preface to the First Edition

Science has brought the dream of a more abundant world within the realm of the possible. It has also given rise to fears of incomprehensible disaster. In seeking to master nature, man is in danger of bringing about his own self-destruction. The ultimate test for mankind will be the ability of statesmen, scientists, and citizens of contending political systems to master themselves. Specifically, the crucial question facing us today is: Can the Soviet and Western worlds peacefully coexist given their incompatible goals? Can the irreconcilable be reconciled? Can there, in fact, be an acceptable and continuing accommodation between them?

The purpose of this study is to provide an analytical and historical examination of Soviet foreign policy since 1917—its origins and evolution, its character and objectives—thus increasing the student's understanding of the nature of the contemporary Soviet challenge. Careful attention has been devoted to the historical, ideological, and political determinants influencing Kremlin policy. Each chapter treats a particular aspect or period of Soviet foreign policy. Essays on the key developments affecting Soviet behavior and the changing and varied character of Soviet objectives are followed by excerpts from important writings and official pronouncements, designed to familiarize the student with the Soviet rationale for its own actions, as well as with Soviet views on the motivations and behavior of its antagonists. The interrelationship between Soviet policy in Europe and in Asia is discussed and an attempt is made to trace the threads of continuity between Czarist and Soviet foreign policy objectives. It is hoped that this introduction to the subject will stimulate the student to further exploration. An extensive bibliography is included for the benefit of those who desire to pursue various phases of Soviet foreign policy in greater detail.

It is a pleasure to express my appreciation to my colleagues and friends who have given so generously of their time and knowledge. I am grateful for their encouragement and patience. This study has benefited from their criticisms and suggestions.

Dr. Garold W. Thumm, of the University of Pennsylvania, read the entire manuscript, and I am indebted to him for his penetrating comments. Professors David J. Dallin, Philip E. Jacob, and Norman D. Palmer, of the University of Pennsylvania, and Dr. Gene D. Overstreet, of Swarthmore College, contributed greatly of their specialized knowledge. My thanks to the Editors of *Current History* for their permission to use parts of my articles which appeared in the February 1957 and January 1959 issues (Copyright, 1957, 1959, by Events Publishing Co.,

Inc.). Grateful acknowledgment is also made to all the publishers and organizations whose permission to reprint specific material is indicated in the footnote at the beginning of each reading.

I wish also to thank the editors, artists, and staff of Random House for their cooperation and counsel in the making of this book. I wish particularly to express my appreciation to Leonore C. Hauck for patiently and skillfully editing the manuscript.

Alvin Z. Rubinstein

Contents

the foreign policy of the soviet union

1
the ideological bases of soviet foreign policy

In 1871 the Russian philosopher and noted Slavophile Nicholas Danilevsky forecast a clash between Russia and the West for supremacy in Europe. He held that Russian civilization, being more dynamic and progressive, would overwhelm Western civilization and emerge to universal preeminence. If we substitute the word "Soviet" for "Russian," then Danilevsky's prognostication assumes uncanny relevance. More than one hundred years later, two hostile worlds confront each other not only in Europe, but in all areas of the world. Given the military power and imperial ambitions of the Soviet Union, Soviet foreign policy may be expected to remain the most crucial problem confronting the United States. An understanding of the nature of Soviet policy, its assumptions, objectives, and operating procedures, is therefore essential.

The establishment of Soviet power since 1945 in the heart of Europe and the emergence of the Soviet Union as a superpower possessing the nuclear and missile capability to destroy the United States have been the outstanding determinants of the pervasive and irreconcilable antagonism between East and West. The resulting insecurity has been further heightened by a fundamental ideological hostility. Other factors have been involved as well: the escalation of the arms race as a consequence of rapid technological change; the decreased power of Western Europe; the rise of Communist China to international prominence; the phoenix-like emergence of Japan as an industrial giant; and the difficulties and uncertainties occasioned by decolonization and nationalism in the Third World. These factors have all served to exacerbate international tension and give to the Cold War its all-inclusive quality.

3

The foreign policy of the Soviet Union, like that of any great power, is an amalgam of discrete elements. It is the result of an often unfathomable ordering of history, of fundamental, generally understandable historical forces, and, finally, of the influence of dynamic personalities endowed with a thirst for power and empire. Thus Soviet foreign policy can be seen as the end product of a complex interaction of many determinants, which, though always changing, are ever present. Throughout Russia's history, from the ninth century on, the physical attributes—geography, climate, population, and resources—have played important roles. They have influenced the unique features of Russia's economic, social, and political growth; its religion and culture; its reaction to external events; and the key figures in its history.

With this myriad of determinants it is apparent that many interpretations of present-day Soviet policy are possible. Each has some validity; each can be supported by evidence that is often impressive. None can claim exclusiveness. By way of illustration, we may distinguish several approaches.

One interpretation views present Soviet policy as a mere continuation of traditional Czarist objectives. Its proponents realize that recent Soviet aggrandizement has been aided by an impressive economic and military growth, by Moscow's emergence as a superpower, and by the availability for manipulation of disciplined, Moscow-controlled, foreign communist parties. But they argue that the increments of strength have served only to promote the attainment of traditional strategic objectives. Foremost among these is the quest for strategically secure frontiers. This explains the urge to the sea—the age-old Russian desire for ports on the Baltic, the Mediterranean, and the Yellow Seas—one of the most basic trends in Russian history, one that has persisted regardless of modifications of doctrine, method of rule, or governmental structure. This approach also stresses the importance of the Eastern motif in Soviet policy—the expansion of Russia into Asia as well as into the center of Europe. When thwarted in one direction, Russia has moved in the other. This long-term orientation of expansion is considered a constant of Soviet policy.

Another school of thought sees in Soviet foreign policy a blueprint for world domination, for the establishment of world communism. Its adherents point to the revolutionary character of Bolshevik declarations and to an ideology committed to unremitting hostility toward the noncommunist world. Just as Hitler set forth in amazing clarity his plan for world conquest, so too have contemporary Soviet leaders made clear their global pretensions. The writings of the Soviet deities have never been repudiated. Marxist-Leninist ideology conditions its followers to view noncommunist nations as hostile, separated by an unbridgeable gulf from the communist world. The spread of communism as a social system is seen as inevitable. Add to such an ideology the conspiratorial background of the original Bolsheviks and a tradition of secretive, elite rule inherited from the past and refined by modern techniques of mass manipulation and, some analysts argue, we can expect Soviet rulers to use all available means of deceit and diplomacy to attain their global objectives.

As knowledge of the Soviet political process has increased, Western analysts have adopted more sophisticated approaches. For example, they seek to establish the interrelationship between foreign policy positions, on the one hand, and the domestic struggle for power and competition among bureaucratic elites over the allocation of scarce economic resources, on the other. Though foreign policy differences are rarely aired publicly, these differences presumably do exist. Kremlinology seeks to illuminate the factional alignments and the substantive issues around which these struggles revolve. Thus, whether Moscow will facilitate an agreement on the Middle East crisis or in the Strategic Arms Limitation Talks (SALT) depends in large measure, it is argued, on the outcome of the struggle in the Soviet hierarchy between those who favor increased investment in military and military-related industries and those who press for greater attention to nonmilitary priorities. Such an approach is time consuming and difficult, but it promises to place analyses of Soviet foreign policy making within a systematic analytical framework.

The elements of continuity in Russian and Soviet foreign policy aims suggest that, notwithstanding rivalries among Kremlin factions, there are concrete, widely shared objectives among the Soviet elite and that Soviet options are shaped and limited as much by capabilities as by consensus. In a broadcast on October 1, 1939, Winston S. Churchill offered this explanation for the behavior of the Soviet Union in joining with Nazi Germany to partition Poland: "I cannot forecast to you the action of Russia. It is a riddle wrapped in a mystery inside an enigma; but perhaps there is a key. That key is Russian national interest." In March 1971, at the Twenty-fourth Congress of the Communist Party of the Soviet Union (CPSU), Leonid Brezhnev stated, "We shall never forsake the national interests of the Soviet state." But the question remains: What combination of factors is considered crucial by each set of Soviet leaders as it acts to define and implement Soviet national interest?

Any explanation of Soviet foreign policy must consider ideological and nonideological determinants. Mindful of the fact that history, in the words of Max Beloff, "above all is the study of the imperfect, the contingent and the unique,"[1] let the interpreter remain alert to all the more important influences on Soviet policy formulation: the geographic position of the Soviet Union; the traditional Russian quest for strategically secure frontiers; the economic and military capability of the Soviet Union; the changing perceptions in the Kremlin of Western cohesiveness and "contradictions"; the seriousness of Soviet domestic difficulties; the impact of the changing international system; and the influence of a Marxian world outlook whose historical antecedent consisted of deep-rooted Russian messianism.

The ideological ingredient tends to compound and confuse the already hazardous task of interpreting Soviet foreign policy. Just as no explanation of Soviet policy can afford to ignore ideology, so would it be the height of naïveté to accept all ideological pronouncements at face value. But in view of Lenin's oft-repeated dictum that "without revolutionary theory there can be no revolutionary movement," it is essential that students of Soviet affairs study carefully the ideological treatises of Marx, Lenin, Stalin, Khrushchev, and their disciples. These writings attempt to present and justify theory and practice as an integrated whole. Action is always explained in terms of ideology; ideology is used to justify action. It is not possible to tell to what extent such ideological justifications influence the formulation of policy or serve merely to cloak in an aura of infallibility and inevitability the tactical maneuvers of the moment. But it would be folly to assume that because the relationship between ideology and behavior is neither readily apparent nor easily determined, it is therefore nonexistent; and that ideology and the perceptions and assumptions that derive from it do not affect the ultimate choice of policy alternatives. It is important that the fundamental tenets be understood, for not only do they underlie the Soviet view of the noncommunist world, but they also provide us with an indispensable key to interpreting the explanations that are given for adopted courses of policy.

In general, Soviet ideology may be regarded as a systematic body of goals, ideas, and assumptions shared by the elite and affecting their attitudes and behavior. It helps to shape the mode of their response to social, economic, and political phenomena; conditions their perception of reality; and provides the terminology and the methodological tools for an allegedly "scientific" interpretation of history, as well as the categories for dialectically viewing, assessing, and rationalizing events. "Facts"—that is, propositions of known, accepted, or verifiable character—are selected and ordered according to the leadership's evaluation of any particular situation, and developments are related to one another within a rationalistic system. Soviet practitioners have never pretended that ideology could mark each path, crossroad, or detour on the international landscape, but the general direction of history is purportedly revealed through the Marxist-Leninist time-telescope, which enables one to "look into the future and see the outlines of impending historical changes." Ideology provides the key to "the unshakable laws of social development." Thus, though Soviet foreign policy is rooted in Russian history, it is conditioned by a dynamic world outlook.

Karl Marx provided many of the fundamental principles of Soviet ideology, but it was Lenin who adapted Marx's approach to the international arena and gave it contemporary validity. Lenin was above all a revolutionary strategist. His theoretical writings resulted usually from an effort to explain specific developments in terms of Marxist thought. A case in point is *Imperialism: The Highest Stage of Capitalism*, one of Lenin's important works (reading 1). Published in Switzerland in 1916 during Lenin's exile, it is primarily an attempt to extend the Marxian concept of the class struggle to the international arena and to show thereby that World War I stemmed from the avarice of monopoly capital and the big financial interests. The importance of Lenin's work can scarcely be overestimated, for it has conditioned the Soviet view of the capitalist world. It purports to explain the "inevitability" of capitalism's demise. In addition, it links the inevitability of war to capitalism as a social system. Its appeal is strengthened by the converse proposition: that only through socialism can permanent and universal peace be assured. Though written more than fifty years ago, Lenin's interpretation of imperialism remains an integral part of communist ideology and helps account for the continuing and complete hostility of the Soviet Union toward the capitalist world.

For his new analysis of capitalist society, Lenin relied heavily upon two earlier works, *Imperialism* (1902), by the English economist J. A. Hobson, and *Das Finanzkapital* (1910), by the Austrian Marxist Rudolf Hilferding. Previously, Marx had explained the coming doom of capitalism in terms of the social forces it itself created—the simultaneous trends toward monopoly and ever greater concentration of economic (and hence, political) power, on the one hand, and a growing proletarianization and impoverishment of society, on the other. The resultant insoluble contradictions and conflicts, accompanied by a heightened class consciousness on the part of the proletariat, precipitate the downfall of capitalism. But events did not follow Marx's prognosis. By 1914 it had become apparent that his concept of capitalism did not approximate the reality existing in Western Europe. The proletariat had not come to power, nor had revolution occurred in the most highly developed countries. Indeed, world capitalism was strong, seemingly stable, and expanding. Why, then, had Marx's predictions about the collapse of capitalism not proved true? Lenin gave his answer.

According to Lenin, in a maturing capitalist economy there is a fundamental disequilibrium between production and consumption that makes profitable employment of capital increasingly difficult. To overcome the declining rate of profit, the capitalists compel their compliant, controlled governments to seek relief for them abroad in the form of colonies and spheres of influence. These acquisitions are exploited by the capitalists as sources of cheap labor and raw materials, as well as markets for excess capital and for surpluses of manufactured goods. The quest for colonies was the outstanding characteristic of the period from 1870 to 1914. Through this expansion capitalism was able temporarily to postpone revolution and disaster. It should be emphasized that this expansion of capitalism is what Lenin meant by imperialism. To Lenin, imperialism was not a "policy," since that would imply an element of choice, but rather a matter of compulsion (i.e., inevitability).[2]

However, once the available underdeveloped areas of the world have been absorbed, the persistent pressure for profit, an essential of capitalism, drives the capitalist states into competition over the redistribution of the spoils. Their conflicts can be settled only by war, the ultimate "contradiction of capitalism." According to Lenin, World War I represented the initial convulsions of a moribund world capitalism. Subsequently, this imperialist war would be transformed into a global war, out of which would come the final triumph of socialism.

Marx analyzed capitalist society within a national framework and, specifically, in terms of Western European industrial development. Lenin, on the other hand, considered capitalism as a global phenomenon. The more capitalism develops, "the stronger the need for raw materials is felt, the more bitter competition and the hunt for raw materials become throughout the world, the more desperate the struggle for the acquisition of colonies becomes." This competition is a struggle between nations and national oligarchies, not between individual capitalists. For Lenin, the imperialist nation assumes the role previously held in Marx's analysis by the individual capitalist. This struggle among the capitalist nations stems from the uneven development of capitalism —the fact that some nations develop later than others and that these newcomer imperialists are left with barren pickings, others having preempted the choice colonies. But the newcomers, more aggressive, ambitious, and dissatisfied with the existing distribution of colonies, strive to redress this inequality of empire by *force*. "There can be *no other* conceivable basis, under capitalism, for partition of spheres of influence, of interests, of colonies, etc.," said Lenin. And the clash arising out of these basic inequalities cannot long be avoided. In modifying Marxist theory, Lenin held that, even though competition *within a nation* may be controlled, the struggle *among sovereign capitalist nations* cannot be similarly regulated. Imperialist wars are merely the clash of capitalists transplanted to the international arena. They will shake the foundations of capitalism and usher in an era of revolutionary change, in which world capitalism will break, as does a chain, at its weakest link. Lenin and his successors explained the unexpected success of the Bolshevik revolution in backward Russia in these terms. The previously held Marxist expectation that revolution would occur first in a highly developed country was dropped from the Soviets' doctrinal baggage. No longer is it considered "un-Marxist" for communists to seize power in a backward country. "Where will the chain break in the near future? Again, where it is weakest," said Stalin. Thus does "creative" Marxism tailor theory to reality.

Marxist thought holds that the historical process is governed by objective laws, functioning as inexorably as the laws of nature. These laws contain and allow for the "subjective factor," that is, the conscious, human element, "not merely as the obedient servant and executor of the law, but as the medium through whose actions and thoughts alone the historical laws become laws."[3] In the dialectical process the interaction of these two factors, of the objective and subjective forces, determines the course of history. Though human will cannot materially change the unalterable design of these historical forces, man must understand their character and direction, for he can facilitate and promote the realization of this design. Soviet ideologists insist that an understanding of the laws of historical development is possible through the conceptual tools provided by Marx's philosophical system, "dialectical materialism." "It is, in effect, revolution writ large into the cosmos; its basic postulates are so many reasons why 'the bourgeoisie' are on the way down and 'the proletariat' on the way up, why 'capitalism' must inevitably give way to 'socialism' everywhere, and why this must occur by violent revolution."[4]

Very briefly, dialectical materialism is believed to afford a "scientific" basis for determining historical development. Nature is regarded as a single, interrelated whole, which is in a constant state of change. This change derives from contradictions "inherent in things and phenomena" and from the struggle of opposites stemming from these contradictions. Thus, the proletariat, though produced by the capitalist system, is at the same time antagonistic toward it and is the vehicle for its eventual downfall. Each social system gives rise to mutually antagonistic social classes. Through the ensuing class struggle, an inherent feature of all societies, a higher form of society evolves, with communism considered as the highest stage of human development. As mentioned previously, the imperialist stage of capitalism actually denotes the transference of the class struggle from a particular society to the world at large. The basic incompatibility and hostility between capitalism and socialism are *inevitabilities* of historical development, the result of operative "objective forces." Coexistence for long is unthinkable; inevitably, socialism must supplant capitalism. This helps account for the continuing policy assumption, by the Soviet leaders, of unmitigated hostility between the two systems. Ideologically, it serves to rationalize the "necessity" for the Cold War. As the "objective" contradictions between capitalism and socialism intensify, a period of revolutionary crises develops. These crises differ in intensity and come in rhythmic cycles of ebb and flow. In a speech in 1925, Stalin held that whereas World War I constituted a crest in this unfolding drama of revolution, the subsequent period was one of decline, in which a "partial and temporary stabilization of capitalism" had set in.[5] This evaluation of Stalin's was linked to the struggle between Stalin and Trotsky for the mantle of Lenin's leadership. It derived from the controversy over two ideas: Stalin's formulation that socialism could be built in one country versus Trotsky's view that only a policy of "permanent revolution" could ensure the preservation of socialism in the Soviet Union.

In April 1924, shortly after the death of Lenin, Stalin delivered a series of lectures at Sverdlov University, Moscow, in which he enunciated the essential guides to Soviet political behavior. According to Stalin, the "strategy and tactics of Leninism constitute the science of leadership in the revolutionary struggle of the proletariat." *Strategy* deals with the main forces of the revolution; it is "the determination of the direction of the main blow of the proletariat at a given stage of the revolution, the elaboration of a corresponding plan for the disposition of the revolutionary forces (main and secondary reserves), the fight to carry out this plan throughout the given stage of the revolution." Strategy is changed in response to the objective conditions characterizing a particular historical epoch or stage of revolution. In the period of the temporary stabilization of capitalism, the Soviet Union must concentrate on building socialism in one country in order to strengthen the base from which world revolution is to be organized and generated, when conditions are ripe. Defense of the Soviet Union is the primary concern of all foreign communist parties.

Tactics "are a part of strategy, subordinate to it and serving it." They are the methods used to achieve the directives of strategy. They require constant evaluation of existing political potentialities, within both the capitalist and socialist camps, and must be adjusted according to the flow or ebb, that is, the rise or decline of revolutionary forces. It is the responsibility of the most politically advanced element, that is, the Communist Party, to gauge the direction and intensity of the tide and then to devise tactics best able to promote the overall objectives of Soviet strategy. Thus, calls for "peaceful coexistence" can be reconciled with the ultimate objective of subverting the capitalist world if they are viewed as nothing more than a tactic.

One of Lenin's outstanding qualities was his readiness to accept temporary setbacks, to make concessions, to contemplate coexistence with any antagonist—especially stronger ones—if he could derive some advantage. Lenin argued that dealing with capitalist states was justifiable if it weakened anti-Soviet forces. In *"Left-Wing" Communism, an Infantile Disorder,* he castigated the German communists for adopting the counterproductive and politically sterile position of "no compromises" with any bourgeois parties or institutions. Had the Bolsheviks followed such a purist course the Russian revolution would have been stillborn. Lenin stressed the need for tactical flexibility:

> The more powerful enemy can be vanquished only by exerting the utmost effort, and *without fail,* most thoroughly, carefully, attentively and skillfully using every, even the smallest, "rift" among the enemies, every antagonism of interest among the bourgeoisie of the various countries and among the various groups or types of bourgeoisie within the various countries, and also by taking advantage of every, even the smallest, opportunity of gaining a mass ally, even though this ally be temporary, vacillating, unstable, unreliable and conditional. . . .
>
> To accept battle at a time when it is obviously advantageous to the enemy and not to us is a crime; and the political leader of the revolutionary class who is unable to "tack, maneuver, and compromise" in order to avoid an obviously disadvantageous battle, is absolutely worthless.

It is never really possible to say where tactics leave off and strategy begins. Political leaders tend to respond to day-to-day problems, usually to the neglect of long-term planning. Early Soviet foreign policy *behavior* was shaped more by weakness than by revolutionary drives, more by the international system than by Kremlin machinations.

At the Fourteenth Congress of the CPSU in December 1925, Stalin formalized peaceful coexistence as a policy intended to provide a weak and isolated Soviet Union with a measure of defensive insurance:

> There has been established a certain temporary balance of power; a balance which has determined the current phase of peaceful coexistence between the land of the Soviets and the countries of capitalism. That which we once believed to be a short respite after the war has turned out to be a whole period of respite. Hence a certain balance of power and a certain period of "peaceful coexistence" between the world of the bourgeoisie and the world of the proletariat.

In December 1927, at the Fifteenth Congress of the CPSU, Stalin emphasized that as long as the Soviet Union was weak it was necessary "to postpone war by 'buying off' the capitalists and to take all measures to maintain peaceful relations . . . the maintenance of peaceful relations with the capitalist countries is an obligatory task for us. Our relations with the capitalist countries are based on the assumption that the coexistence of two opposite systems is possible. Practice has fully confirmed this."

Prior to 1945, the Soviet Union intermittently used the policy of peaceful coexistence to buttress its essentially defensive strategy. It was the tactic of an elite whose capability for pursuing a "forward strategy" was severely limited. However, since the late 1950s and early 1960s the cut of peaceful coexistence has been tailored to suit the foreign policy of a confident, powerful, assertive Soviet Union. To Moscow, peaceful coexistence today implies a strategy of global rivalry with the West short of nuclear war; far from avoiding conflict, it is an affirmation of the Soviet belief that through ideological, economic, political, and cultural activities the struggle against the West can be waged, and won (reading 2).

Contravening the statements of Soviet leaders calling for peaceful relations with the capitalist world have been the more frequent and prominent pronouncements of hostility. This dualism in Soviet policy has plagued relations with the West since 1917. It is a source of unresolved controversy among Western analysts: what are the *real* intentions of the Soviet Union, and what is the significance of ideology for Soviet leaders?

In his report to the Eighth Congress of the Communist Party, on March 18, 1919, Lenin had stated:

We are living not merely in a state but in a system of states, and the existence of the Soviet Republic side by side with imperialist states for a long time is unthinkable. One or the other must triumph in the end. And before this end supervenes, a series of frightful collisions between the Soviet Republic and the bourgeois states will be inevitable.[6]

This classic statement of the irreconcilability of capitalism and socialism and the inevitability of their clash remained central, though varying in prominence, to Stalin's pronouncements on the subject until the Nineteenth Party Congress of October 1952, at which time he formulated a rather interesting modification.

After 1917, and especially before World War II, the Soviet government stressed the theory of "capitalist encirclement," partially out of a genuine sense of insecurity, but primarily to justify the suffering and sacrifice demanded of its people by Stalin's decisions to embark on a program of rapid industrialization and collectivization of agriculture. This theory reflected the pervasive fear of an "imperialist" attack against the Soviet Union and implied a type of war quite distinct from Lenin's "inevitable" *inter-capitalist* wars stemming from the nature and contradictions of twentieth-century capitalism. No systematic attempt was ever made, however, to link Lenin's theory of "inevitable" inter-capitalist wars with the subsequent Stalinist corollary of the "inevitable" capitalist war against the Soviet Union. Thus there were, in fact, two distinct communist doctrines on war, though the impression that they were one and the same was encouraged:[7] first, the Leninist theory of imperialism, with its focus on inter-capitalist wars and rivalries; second, the theory of "capitalist encirclement," with its focus on the inevitability of war between socialist and capitalist camps. Although both doctrines were retained in the Soviet ideological arsenal, after World War II the emphasis was on the first one.

Shortly before the Nineteenth Party Congress Stalin published his *Economic Problems of Socialism in the USSR* (reading 3). In this final appraisal of the world scene and effort to ensure his prominence as an architect of communist theory, Stalin held that, as an aftermath of the war, capitalism had suffered grievous wounds and no longer embraced a global market. Economically, the world had split into two parallel trading systems. Politically, capitalism had lost much of its former awesome power and therefore was not likely to attack the Soviet Union, although the contradictions and antagonisms between the two systems continued to exist. A capitalist attack on the Soviet Union was unlikely because "war with the USSR . . . is more dangerous to capitalism than war between capitalist countries; for whereas war between capitalist countries puts in question only the supremacy of certain capitalist countries over others, war with the USSR must certainly put in question the existence of capitalism itself." On the other hand, Stalin maintained that wars between capitalist countries would inevitably result from the intensified competition for shrinking world markets that attended the division of the world into two camps and the end of capitalism's era of expansion. Finally, though implying that *armed* conflict between the socialist and capitalist systems was not probable, Stalin did stress their continued and fundamental hostility.

This orthodox Leninist position was reaffirmed by Nikita S. Khrushchev at the Twentieth Party Congress of February 1956. But he also reinforced the prevailing political strategy of the post-Stalinist period—the theme of peaceful coexistence—by introducing an important modification of Marxist-Leninist doctrine (reading 4): the noninevitability of war. Khrushchev's contention that "war is not fatalistically inevitable" marks a retreat, if not a categorical shift, from the deterministic notion that war between the two systems is inevitable and, as such, constitutes a significant change in ideology. He suggested, in effect, that the altered balance of world power makes it possible for the "camp of peace" (socialist camp) to offer the hope of permanent peace to all peoples. Wars, whether between capitalism and socialism or within the capitalist world itself, may be not only forestalled but prevented—provided that the "progressive social and political forces" within the capitalist world actively check "the schemes of the war-makers." Khrushchev called for popular pressure against those parliamentary governments which are opposed to Soviet policy. If "progressive" groups can capture a stable parliamentary majority or force their governments to accede to Soviet wishes, war can be avoided. Thus the formula for peace is based upon Soviet-determined ingredients. Nonetheless, Khrushchev's thesis that (nuclear) war is not inevitable is of crucial importance, for it connotes the recognition by Soviet leaders of the mutually catastrophic character of an all-out nuclear war. Having struggled and suffered to develop an advanced, stable, and gradually prospering society, they are not likely to jeopardize all this by provoking a nuclear showdown with the United States. The technological revolution in military weaponry has induced a significant change in Soviet ideology and strategic thinking.

In addition, the concept of "capitalist encirclement" was largely abandoned during the Khrushchev period for a number of reasons— *inter alia,* the emergence in the mid-1950s of the USSR as a superpower, the unpalatability of total war as a solution to *political* problems in view of the development of thermonuclear weapons, and the emergence of the "system of socialist states" existing side by side with the "system of capitalist states." Further, "capitalist encirclement" was a self-isolating concept; by implication it regarded the entire noncommunist world as hostile to the USSR and contradicted post-1955 Soviet efforts to encourage neutralism and nonalignment in the "zone of peace"—the areas of Afro-Asia and Latin America not committed militarily or politically to either of the two major power blocs. By 1958, the Soviet leadership explained that the danger of "capitalist encirclement" in a geographical sense had been ended by the emergence of communist political systems in Eastern Europe and China. They also asserted that since the balance of international forces was shifting to the socialist camp, it was now "capitalism" that was being encircled by "socialism." Nevertheless, Soviet writers continue to talk of "capitalist encirclement" as a political threat and to emphasize the need for vigilance and strength because of the ever-present danger of "aggression" from the capitalist world, particularly the United States, which is increasingly disturbed over its progressively eroding power and political influence.

The ideological innovations of the Khrushchev period (1954–1964) did not mean that Soviet leaders relinquished any of their principal political objectives. What they did signify was the recognition, in a period of nuclear stalemate, of the need to attain these objectives by essentially nonmilitary means. Soviet leaders are as convinced today as ever of communism's eventual victory. As long as they believe that their interests can benefit most through a "policy of peace," not only as a positive propaganda device but also as a useful additive to Soviet power, they will retain such an approach.

Most specialists on Soviet affairs today agree that important, far-reaching changes have been made since 1955 in those elements of Soviet ideology that have particular relevance for the formulation of foreign policy. There is also agreement on what these doctrinal changes have been: for example, abandonment of the Zhdanov "two-camp thesis" (see Chapter VI); virtual abandonment of the concept of "capitalist encirclement," which was enunciated by Stalin in the late 1930s; introduction of Khrushchev's thesis that war is no longer "fatalistically inevitable"; and the promulgation at the Twentieth Party Congress of the "zone of peace" concept relative to developing areas (see Chapter XIII). There is widespread disagreement, however, over the significance of these changes.

Certain Western analysts offer the comforting notion that for Soviet leaders, ideology is less and less a determinant of foreign policy. This study, it may be noted, reflects the view that Soviet ideology plays an important role in conditioning the Soviet "image" of the outside world and, consequently, in influencing the range and choice of policy alternatives.

Soviet leaders may indeed no longer believe in impending world revolution or in the necessity of using force to bring about the downfall of capitalism (though they justify its relevance in "just wars" of national liberation), but it is reasonable to assume that they continue to believe in the inevitable triumph of communism, in the growing ascendancy of Soviet power and influence, and in the validity of their analyses of developments in the noncommunist world. Their meteoric rise to world power can only make them more confident that the balance of power is shifting in their favor, and this confidence may be presumed to reinforce the belief of the Soviet elite in the essential validity of their Marxist-Leninist evaluation of international developments.

Soviet foreign policy accepts change as a permanent feature of the historical process. It affirms the ideological conviction that through the dialectical method future trends can be anticipated. If ideology is in fact one of the important influences shaping the outlook and choice of alternatives of Soviet decision-makers, we can agree that "the belief system which the Soviet leadership has inherited has served to condition, if not to determine, its every move."[8] Thus, for example, the Soviet attitude toward the Western Powers derives in important measure from Soviet *perceptions* of their motivations, policies, and objectives. These perceptions, which are significantly fashioned by ideology, lead the Soviets to see Western actions and motivations in the worst possible light.

Soviet writers postulate the inevitable continued "ideological struggle" of the camp of communism and the camp of capitalism until communism triumphs. Ideology conditions the Soviet leaders to view the outside world with hostility and mistrust. The analyses presented by Leonid Brezhnev, General-Secretary of the CPSU at the International Meeting of Communist and Workers' Parties in Moscow in June 1969 (reading 5) and at the Twenty-fourth Congress of the CPSU in March 1971 (reading 6) may be regarded as typical. Accordingly, the leaders take actions to safeguard the security of the Soviet Union. These actions, in turn, arouse responses in the West that confirm in the minds of Soviet leaders their inherited and ingrained prejudices about the innate hostility of the outside world. Once the circle is completed and self-interest becomes the overriding concern, it is futile to argue whether a particular development is a cause or an effect.

From what we know of political infighting in Soviet decision-making circles, it is clear that the engineers of the Soviet state are not rigid determinists. Their sharing of a Marxist-Leninist heritage does not signify unanimity on all major policy questions. Though they may agree at a given time in their evaluation of the "objective" conditions controlling the ever-shifting pattern of international forces, they may disagree on which of several policy alternatives to adopt. A common perception of reality does not necessarily produce uniform answers to specific policy problems. Debate and discord in the inner circles of the Party are probably as intensive as that found in the decision-making circles of any government, though they are not aired publicly. The range of possible alternatives is limited by ideology, but we do not know how stringently or how loosely any faction adheres to accepted doctrine to formulate its position, or to what degree naked power considerations and personality factors affect these calculations.

NOTES

1. Max Beloff, *The Foreign Policy of Soviet Russia, 1936–1941* (New York: Oxford University Press, 1949), Vol. II, p. 395.

2. Alfred G. Meyer, *Leninism* (Cambridge, Mass.: Harvard University Press, 1957), p. 241.

3. From an essay by Herbert Marcuse, "Dialectic and Logic Since the War," in Ernest J. Simmons (ed.), *Continuity and Change in Russian and Soviet Thought* (New York: Columbia University Press, 1955), p. 353.

4. Historicus, "Stalin on Revolution," *Foreign Affairs,* 27 (1949), 181.

5. *Ibid.,* p. 195.

6. V. I. Lenin, *Selected Works* (New York: International Publishers, 1943), Vol. VIII, p. 33.

7. U.S., Department of State, *The 20th CPSU Congress and the Doctrine of the "Inevitability of War,"* Intelligence Report No. 7284 (June 22, 1956), pp. 9–10.

8. John S. Reshetar, Jr., *Problems of Analyzing and Predicting Soviet Behavior* (New York: Random House, 1955), p. 13.

1/Imperialism: The Highest Stage of Capitalism

V. I. LENIN

While capitalism remains capitalism, surplus capital will not be used for raising the standard of living of the masses in a given country, for this would mean a decrease in profits for the capitalists; rather, it will be exported abroad to backward countries in order to increase profits. In these backward countries profits are usually high, for capital is scarce, the price of land is comparatively cheap, wages are low, and raw materials are cheap. The possibility of exporting capital is created by the fact that a number of backward countries are drawn into the system of world capitalism; main railway lines either have been built or are being built there, the basic conditions for the development of industry have been assured, and so forth. The need to export capital arises from the fact that in a few countries capitalism has become "overripe," and capital cannot find (due to the backward state of agriculture and the impoverishment of the masses) field for "profitable" investment . . .

The Division of the World Among the Capitalist Combines

The monopolistic corporations of the capitalists—cartels, syndicates, trusts—divide among themselves first of all the internal market, seizing control more or less completely of the production of a given country. But the internal market, under capitalism, is inevitably linked with the foreign market. Capitalism long ago created a world market. As the export of capital increased and as foreign and colonial relations and "spheres of influence" spread in every possible way by the biggest monopolistic corporations affairs "naturally" tended toward a global agreement among them, toward the establishment of international cartels . . .

The capitalists do not divide the world out of personal malice, but because the degree of concentration that has been reached impels them to adopt this course in order to obtain profits; they divide the world according to "capital" and according to "strength," for there can be no other method of division under the system of commodity production

V. I. Lenin, *Sochinenia,* 2d ed. (Moscow: State Publishing House, 1929), Vol. XIX, pp. 120–175, *excerpts.* Editor's translation.

and capitalism. Power varies with the degree of economic and political development; in order to understand what is taking place, it is necessary to know what questions are solved by such changes in power; whether these changes are "purely" economic or *non*economic (e.g., military) is a question of secondary importance that cannot in the least affect the basic views on the latest epoch of capitalism. To substitute for the question of the *content* of the struggle and agreement among capitalist combines, the question of the form of the struggle and agreement (today peaceful, tomorrow not peaceful, the day after tomorrow again not peaceful) is a peaceful way to descend to the role of the sophist.

The epoch of modern capitalism shows us that certain relations are established among combines of capitalists *based* on the economic division of the world; parallel with these relations and in connection with them certain relations are established among political alliances, among states, on the basis of the territorial division of the world, of the struggle for colonies, and of "the struggle for economic territory.". . .

The Division of the World Among the Great Powers

Colonial policy and imperialism existed before the latest stage of capitalism, and even before capitalism. Rome, founded on slavery, conducted a colonial policy and carried out imperialism. But "general" arguments about imperialism, which ignore or put into the background the fundamental difference of socioeconomic systems, inevitably degenerate into empty banalities or bragging, such as the comparison of "greater Rome with greater Britain." Even the capitalistic colonial policy of the *previous* stages of capitalism is essentially different from the colonial policy of finance capital.

The basic feature of contemporary capitalism is the domination of monopolist combines by the biggest entrepreneurs. These monopolies are most durable when *all* the sources of raw materials are controlled by one group, and we have seen with what zeal the international capitalist combines exert their effort to make it impossible for their rivals to compete with them; for example, by buying up mineral rights, oil fields, and so forth. Only possession of colonies provides a complete guarantee of success to the monopolies against all competitors, including the possibility that the competitors will defend themselves by means of a law establishing a state monopoly. The more capitalism develops, the stronger the need for raw materials is felt, the more bitter competition and the hunt for raw materials become throughout the world, the more desperate the struggle for the acquisition of colonies becomes. . . .

Imperialism, as a Particular Stage of Capitalism

Imperialism emerged as a development and direct continuation of the basic characteristics of capitalism in general. But capitalism became capitalist imperialism only at a definite, very high stage of its development, when certain of the basic characteristics of capitalism began to change into their opposites, when the features of a period of transition from capitalism to a higher socioeconomic system began to take shape and reveal themselves in all spheres. Economically, the replacement of capitalist free competition by capitalist monopolies is of key importance. Free competition is the fundamental characteristic of capitalism and of commodity production generally; monopoly is exactly the opposite of free competition, but we have seen the latter being transformed into monopoly before our eyes, creating large-scale industry, squeezing out small-scale industry, replacing large-scale industry by still larger-scale industry, and finally bringing about such a concentration of industry and capital that monopoly has become and is the result. . . . At the same time, the monopolies growing out of free competition do not eliminate it, but exist over it and alongside of it, thereby giving rise to a number of particularly acute and intense antagonisms, frictions, and conflicts. Monopoly is the transition from capitalism to a higher order.

If it were necessary to give the briefest possible definition of imperialism, we should have to say that imperialism is the monopoly stage of capitalism. Such a definition would include, on the one hand, that finance capital is bank capital of the few biggest monopolist banks, merged with the capital of the monopolist combines of industrialists; and on the other hand, that the division of the world is the transition from a colonial policy, which has spread without opposition to territories unoccupied by any capitalist power, to a colonial policy of monopolistic possession of the territories of the world.

But too brief definitions, although convenient, since they summarize the main points, are nevertheless inadequate. . . . Therefore, without forgetting the conditional and relative value of all definitions in general, which can never include all facets of a phenomenon in its complete development, we must give a definition of imperialism that will include the following five essential features: (1) the concentration of industry and capital, pushed to such a high stage of development that it has created monopolies that play a decisive role in economic life; (2) the merging of bank capital with industrial capital and the creation, on the basis of this "finance capital," of a financial oligarchy; (3) the export of capital, as distinguished from the export of commodities, acquires particular importance; (4) international monopoly combines of capitalists are formed that divide up the world; (5) the territorial division of the world by the largest capitalist powers is completed.

Imperialism is capitalism in that stage of development in which the domination of monopolies and finance capital has been established, in which the export of capital has acquired outstanding importance, in which the division of the world by the international trusts has started, and in which the partition of all the territory of the earth by the largest capitalist countries has been completed. . . .

The Parasitism and Decay of Capitalism

We now have to examine another very important aspect of imperialism. . . . We refer to parasitism, which is inherent in imperialism. . . . Imperialism is the immense accumulation of money capital in a few countries. Hence, the extraordinary growth of a class, or rather of a stratum, of *rentiers*, that is, people who live by "clipping coupons," who do not engage at all in production, whose profession is idleness. The export of capital, one of the most essential economic bases of imperialism, isolates this rentier group still further from production and sets the seal of parasitism on the entire country. . . .

The Critique of Capitalism

The question of whether it is possible to change the bases of imperialism by reforms, whether to proceed to a further aggravation and deepening of the contradictions that it engenders, or backward toward allaying them, is a fundamental question in the critique of imperialism . . . Let us take India, Indochina, and China. It is well known that these three colonial and semicolonial countries, inhabited by six- or seven-hundred million souls, are subjected to the exploitation of the finance capital of several imperialist powers: England, France, Japan, the United States, and so on. Let us assume that these imperialist countries form alliances against one another in order to protect or expand their possessions, interests, and "spheres of influence" in these Asiatic countries. These will be "interimperialist" or "ultraimperialist" alliances. Let us assume that *all* the imperialist powers conclude an alliance for the "peaceful" partition of these Asiatic countries; this alliance would be "internationally united finance capital." There have been actual examples of such an alliance in the twentieth century, for example, in the relations of the powers with China. We ask, is it "conceivable," assuming the preservation of capitalism . . . that such alliances would not be short-lived, that they would preclude frictions, conflicts, and struggles in any and every possible form?

It is enough to state this question clearly in order to make any reply other than a negative one impossible. For, under capitalism, there can be *no* other conceivable basis for partition of spheres of influence, of interests, of colonies, and so forth, than a calculation of the *strength* of the participants, their general economic, financial, military, and other strength. But the relative strength of these participants is not changing uniformly, for under capitalism there cannot be an *equal* development of different enterprises, trusts, branches of industry, or countries. Half a century ago, Germany was a pitiful nonentity if its strength was compared with that of England; the same was true with Japan as compared with Russia. Is it "conceivable" that in ten or twenty years the relative strength of the imperialist powers will have remained *un*changed? Absolutely inconceivable.

Therefore, "interimperialist" or "ultraimperialist" alliances, given the realities of capitalism . . . no matter what form the alliances take, whether of one imperialist coalition against another or of a general alliance embracing *all* the imperialist powers, are *inevitably* only "breathing spells" between wars. Peaceful alliances prepare the ground for wars, and in turn grow out of wars; one is the condition of the other, giving rise to alternating forms of peaceful and nonpeaceful struggle on *one and the same basis,* namely, that of imperialist connections and relationships between world economics and world politics.

2/The Soviet View of Peaceful Coexistence

The inevitability of the coexistence of two social systems stems from the law of uneven economic and political development of capitalism, formulated by Lenin. Having discovered this law, Lenin arrived at the conclusion that it was possible for the proletarian revolution to be victorious initially in one or several countries, but that it was impossible for such a victory to occur simultaneously in all or the majority of capitalist countries. This means that at this given stage of development

"Peaceful Coexistence," *Diplomaticheskii Slovar* [*Diplomatic Dictionary*] (Moscow: State Publishing House for Political Literature, 1961), Vol. II, pp. 297–300, *excerpts.* Editor's translation.

in human society, there will simultaneously exist (coexist) new, socialist states and old, capitalist states.

The period of coexistence of the two systems began with the victory of the socialist revolution in Russia and the creation of the Soviet state. After World War II a number of states were detached from the system of capitalism. The camp of socialist states emerged, and socialism was transformed into a world system. Therefore, at this time there is not simply the coexistence of two social systems, but the coexistence of two world social systems. . . .

The possibility of peaceful coexistence is conditioned by the real possibility, proved through experience, of settling international questions by peaceful means on the basis of an agreement. States do not exist in isolation. Each of them is in a system of states. Coexistence inevitably gives birth to different international problems, the settlement of which depends on the necessary cooperation forthcoming from the interested states. If such cooperation is absent and the emerging international problems are not solved by means of an agreement, the contradictions among states sharpen. This situation is pregnant with the danger of war, and it makes peaceful coexistence transitory and unstable.

Of the greatest significance for securing peaceful coexistence are equal and mutually profitable economic cooperation and the development of cultural and other ties between states of the two systems. . . .

Peaceful coexistence constitutes the general line of the foreign policy of the Soviet state. The struggle of the Soviet Union for the establishment of diplomatic relations with the capitalist countries in the early years of the existence of the Soviet state; the struggle against aggression and a new world war; the active participation in the creation of the United Nations as an international organization of peaceful coexistence; the struggle for strengthening peace in the postwar period; the program of general and complete disarmament advanced by the Soviet Union in 1959—these have been the most significant stages in the struggle of the Soviet Union for peaceful coexistence. . . .

The steadfast growth of the power and cohesiveness of the states of the socialist camp, whose foreign policy corresponds to the innermost aspirations of all peoples, is the powerful basis for peaceful coexistence. Given the existing relationship of power, imperialism cannot count on a victory in a war against the socialist states, and this represents an important guarantee of peace. . . .

Peaceful coexistence is a specific form of class struggle between socialism and capitalism. In peaceful competition with capitalism, the socialist system will win, that is, the socialist method of production has decisive advantages over the capitalist system. There is no contradiction between the Marxist-Leninist formulation concerning the inevitability of the victory of communism in the whole world and the policy of peaceful coexistence. Peaceful coexistence concerns relations between states. It does not touch upon relations within states; it does not touch upon the revolutionary struggle for the transformation of society.

Peaceful coexistence among the states of the two systems does not mean compromise in ideological questions. The bourgeois and communist world outlooks cannot be reconciled; moreover, this is not necessary for peaceful coexistence among states. Each can maintain its own position on ideological questions without having this serve as a roadblock preventing cooperation in economic questions and in questions concerning international peace and security.

Naturally, the concept of peaceful coexistence as a condition of relations among states is inapplicable to the internal relations of a state. Therefore, the attempts of the revisionists to extend the concept of peaceful coexistence to class relations within a state are absurd. The recognition of the necessity and possibility of peaceful coexistence does not signify rejection of the class struggle, of the idea of the inevitability of the victory of communism over capitalism.

3/The Crisis of Capitalism

JOSEPH STALIN

The disintegration of the single, all-embracing world market must be regarded as the most important economic sequel of the Second World War and of its economic consequences. It has had the effect of further deepening the general crisis of the world capitalist system.

The Second World War was itself a product of this crisis. Each of the two capitalist coalitions which locked horns in the war calculated on defeating its adversary and gaining world supremacy. It was in this that they sought a way out of the crisis. The United States of America hoped to put its most dangerous competitors, Germany and Japan, out of action, seize foreign markets and the world's raw material resources, and establish its world supremacy.

But the war did not justify these hopes. It is true that Germany and

Joseph Stalin, *Economic Problems of Socialism in the USSR* (Moscow: Foreign Languages Publishing House, 1952), *excerpts.*

Japan were put out of action as competitors of the three major capitalist countries: the USA, Great Britain, and France. But at the same time China and European People's Democracies broke away from the capitalist system and, together with the Soviet Union, formed a united and powerful socialist camp confronting the camp of capitalism. The economic consequence of the existence of two opposite camps was that the single all-embracing world market disintegrated, so that now we have two parallel world markets, also confronting one another.

It should be observed that the USA and Great Britain and France, themselves contributed—without themselves desiring it, of course—to the formation and consolidation of the new, parallel world market. They imposed an economic blockade on the USSR, China, and the European People's Democracies, which did not join the "Marshall Plan" system, thinking thereby to strangle them. The effect, however, was not to strangle, but to strengthen the new world market.

But the fundamental thing, of course, is not the economic blockade, but the fact that since the war these countries have joined together economically and established economic cooperation and mutual assistance. The experience of this cooperation shows that not a single capitalist country could have rendered such effective and technically competent assistance to the People's Democracies as the Soviet Union is rendering them. The point is not only that this assistance is the cheapest possible and technically superb. The chief point is that at the bottom of this cooperation lies a sincere desire to help one another and to promote the economic progress of all. The result is a fast pace of industrial development in these countries. It may be confidently said that, with this pace of industrial development, it will soon come to pass that these countries will not only be in no need of imports from capitalist countries, but will themselves feel the necessity of finding an outside market for their surplus products.

But it follows from this that the sphere of exploitation of the world's resources by the major capitalist countries (USA, Britain, France) will not expand, but contract; that their opportunities for sale in the world market will deteriorate, and that their industries will be operating more and more below capacity. That, in fact, is what is meant by the deepening of the general crisis of the world capitalist system in connection with the distintegration of the world market.

This is felt by the capitalists themselves, for it would be difficult for them not to feel the loss of such markets as the USSR and China. They are trying to offset these difficulties with the "Marshall Plan," the war in Korea, frantic rearmament, and industrial militarization. But that is very much like a drowning man clutching at a straw.

This state of affairs has confronted the economists with two questions:

(a) Can it be affirmed that the thesis expounded by Stalin before the Second World War regarding the relative stability of markets in the period of the general crisis of capitalism is still valid?

(b) Can it be affirmed that the thesis expounded by Lenin in the spring of 1916—namely, that, in spite of the decay of capitalism, "on the whole, capitalism is growing far more rapidly than before"—is still valid?

I think that it cannot. In view of the new conditions to which the Second World War has given rise, both of these theses must be regarded as having lost their validity.

Inevitability of Wars Between Capitalist Countries

Some Comrades hold that, owing to the development of new international conditions since the Second World War, wars between capitalist countries have ceased to be inevitable. They consider that the contradictions between the socialist camp and the capitalist camp are more acute than the contradictions among the capitalist countries; that the USA has brought the other capitalist countries sufficiently under its sway to be able to prevent them going to war among themselves and weakening one another; that the foremost capitalist minds have been sufficiently taught by the two world wars and the severe damage they caused to the whole capitalist world, not to venture to involve the capitalist countries in war with one another again—and that, because of all this, wars between capitalist countries are no longer inevitable.

These Comrades are mistaken. They see the outward phenomena that come and go on the surface, but they do not see those profound forces which, although they are so far operating imperceptibly, will nevertheless determine the course of developments.

Outwardly, everything would seem to be "going well": the USA has put Western Europe, Japan, and other capitalist countries on rations; Germany (Western), Britain, France, Italy, and Japan have fallen into the clutches of the USA and are meekly obeying its commands. But it would be mistaken to think that things can continue to "go well" for "all eternity," that these countries will tolerate the domination and oppression of the United States endlessly, that they will not endeavor to tear loose from American bondage and take the path of independent development.

Take, first of all, Britain and France. Undoubtedly, they are imperialist countries. Undoubtedly, cheap raw materials and secure markets are of paramount importance to them. Can it be assumed that they will endlessly tolerate the present situation, in which, under the guise of

"Marshall Plan aid," Americans are penetrating into the economies of Britain and France and trying to convert them into adjuncts of the United States economy, and American capital is seizing raw materials and markets in the British and French colonies and thereby plotting disaster for the high profits of the British and French capitalists? Would it not be truer to say that capitalist Britain, and, after her, capitalist France, will be compelled in the end to break from the embrace of the USA and enter into conflict with it in order to secure an independent position and, of course, high profits?

Let us pass to the major vanquished countries, Germany (Western) and Japan. These countries are now languishing in misery under the jackboot of American imperialism. Their industry and agriculture, their trade, their foreign and home policies, and their whole life are fettered by the American occupation "regime." Yet only yesterday these countries were great imperialist powers and were shaking the foundations of the domination of Britain, the USA, and France in Europe and Asia. To think that these countries will not try to get on their feet again, will not try to smash US domination and force their way to independent development, is to believe in miracles.

It is said that the contradictions between capitalism and socialism are stronger than the contradictions among the capitalist countries. Theoretically, of course, that is true. It is not only true now, today; it was true before the Second World War. And it was more or less realized by the leaders of the capitalist countries. Yet the Second World War began not as a war with the USSR, but as a war between capitalist countries. Why? Firstly, because war with the USSR, as a socialist land, is more dangerous to capitalism than war between capitalist countries; for whereas war between capitalist countries puts in question only the supremacy of certain capitalist countries over others, war with the USSR must certainly put in question the existence of capitalism itself. Secondly, because the capitalists, although they clamor, for "propaganda" purposes, about the aggressiveness of the Soviet Union, do not themselves believe that it is aggressive, because they are aware of the Soviet Union's peaceful policy and know that it will not itself attack capitalist countries.

After the First World War it was similarly believed that Germany had been definitely put out of action, just as certain Comrades now believe that Japan and Germany have been definitely put out of action. Then, too, it was said and clamored in the press that the United States had put Europe on rations; that Germany would never rise to her feet again, and that there would be no more wars between capitalist countries. In spite of this, Germany rose to her feet again as a great power within the space of some fifteen or twenty years after her defeat, having broken out of bondage and taken the path of independent development.

And it is significant that it was none other than Britain and the United States that helped Germany to recover economically and to enhance her economic war potential. Of course, when the United States and Britain assisted Germany's economic recovery, they did so with a view to setting a recovered Germany against the Soviet Union, to utilizing her against the land of socialism. But Germany directed her forces in the first place against the Anglo-French-American bloc. And when Hitler Germany declared war on the Soviet Union, the Anglo-French-American bloc, far from joining with Hitler Germany, was compelled to enter into a coalition with the USSR against Hitler Germany.

Consequently, the struggle of the capitalist countries for markets and their desire to crush their competitors proved in practice to be stronger than the contradictions between the capitalist camp and the socialist camp.

What guarantee is there, then, that Germany and Japan will not rise to their feet again, will not attempt to break out of American bondage and live their own independent lives? I think there is no such guarantee.

But it follows from this that the inevitability of wars between capitalist countries remains in force.

It is said that Lenin's thesis that imperialism inevitably generates war must now be regarded as obsolete, since powerful popular forces have come forward today in defense of peace and against another world war. That is not true.

The object of the present-day peace movement is to rouse the masses of the people to fight for the preservation of peace and for the prevention of another world war. Consequently, the aim of this movement is not to overthrow capitalism and establish socialism—it confines itself to the democratic aim of preserving peace. In this respect, the present-day peace movement differs from the movement of the time of the First World War for the conversion of the imperialist war into civil war, since the latter movement went further and pursued socialist aims.

It is possible that in a definite conjuncture of circumstances, the fight for peace will develop here or there into a fight for socialism. But then it will no longer be the present-day peace movement; it will be a movement for the overthrow of capitalism.

What is most likely, is that the present-day peace movement, as a movement for the preservation of peace, will, if it succeeds, result in preventing a *particular* war, in its temporary postponement, in the temporary preservation of a *particular* peace, in the resignation of a bellicose government and its supersession by another that is prepared temporarily to keep the peace. That, of course, will be good. Even very good. But, all the same, it will not be enough to eliminate the inevitability of wars between capitalist countries generally. It will not be enough, because, for all the successes of the peace movement, imperialism will remain, continue in force—and, consequently, the inevitability of wars will also continue in force.

To eliminate the inevitability of war, it is necessary to abolish imperialism.

4/Some Fundamental Questions of Present-day International Development—Report of the Central Committee of the CPSU to the Twentieth Party Congress *February 1956*

N. S. KHRUSHCHEV

Comrades, I should like to dwell on some fundamental questions concerning present-day international development, which determine not only the present course of events, but also the prospects for the future.

These questions are the peaceful coexistence of the two systems, the possibility of preventing wars in the present era, and the forms of transition to socialism in different countries.

Let us examine these questions in brief.

The Peaceful Coexistence of the Two Systems

The Leninist principle of peaceful coexistence of states with different social systems has always been and remains the general line of our country's foreign policy.

It has been alleged that the Soviet Union advances the principle of peaceful coexistence merely out of tactical considerations, considerations of expediency. Yet it is common knowledge that we have always, from the very first years of Soviet power, stood with equal firmness for peaceful coexistence. Hence, it is not a tactical move, but a fundamental principle of Soviet foreign policy.

N. S. Khrushchev, *Report of the Central Committee of the CPSU to the Twentieth Party Congress* (Moscow: Foreign Languages Publishing House, 1956), pp. 38–47, *excerpts.*

This means that if there is indeed a threat to the peaceful coexistence of countries with differing social and political systems, it by no means comes from the Soviet Union or the rest of the socialist camp. Is there a single reason why a socialist state should want to unleash aggressive war? Do we have classes and groups that are interested in war as a means of enrichment? We do not. We abolished them long ago. Or, perhaps, we do not have enough territory or natural wealth, perhaps we lack sources of raw materials or markets for our goods? No, we have sufficient of all those and to spare. Why then should we want war? We do not want it; as a matter of principle we renounce any policy that might lead to millions of people being plunged into war for the sake of the selfish interests of a handful of multi-millionaires. Do those who shout about the "aggressive intentions" of the USSR know all this? Of course they do. Why then do they keep up the old monotonous refrain about some imaginary "communist aggression"? Only to stir up mud, to conceal their plans for world domination, a "crusade" against peace, democracy, and socialism.

To this day the enemies of peace allege that the Soviet Union is out to overthrow capitalism in other countries by "exporting" revolution. It goes without saying that among us Communists there are no supporters of capitalism. But this does not mean that we have interfered or plan to interfere in the internal affairs of countries where capitalism still exists. Romain Rolland was right when he said that "freedom is not brought in from abroad in baggage trains like Bourbons." (*Animation*) It is ridiculous to think that revolutions are made to order. We often hear representatives of bourgeois countries reasoning thus: "The Soviet leaders claim that they are for peaceful coexistence between the two systems. At the same time they declare that they are fighting for communism, and say that communism is bound to win in all countries. Now if the Soviet Union is fighting for communism, how can there be any peaceful coexistence with it?" This view is the result of bourgeois propaganda. The ideologists of the bourgeoisie distort the facts and deliberately confuse questions of ideological struggle with questions of relations between states in order to make the Communists of the Soviet Union look like advocates of aggression.

When we say that the socialist system will win in the competition between the two systems—the capitalist and the socialist—this by no means signifies that its victory will be achieved through armed interference by the socialist countries in the internal affairs of the capitalist countries. Our certainty of the victory of communism is based on the fact that the socialist mode of production possesses decisive advantages over the capitalist mode of production. Precisely because of this, the ideas of Marxism-Leninism are more and more capturing the minds of the broad masses of the working people in the capitalist countries, just as they have captured the minds of millions of men and women in our country and the People's Democracies. (*Prolonged applause*) We believe that all working men in the world, once they have become convinced of the advantages communism brings, will sooner or later take the road of struggle for the construction of socialist society. (*Prolonged applause*) Building communism in our country, we are resolutely against war. We have always held and continue to hold that the establishment of a new social system in one or another country is the internal affair of the peoples of the countries concerned. . . . Indeed, there are only two ways: either peaceful coexistence or the most destructive war in history. There is no third way. . . .

The Possibility of Preventing War in the Present Era

Millions of people all over the world are asking whether another war is really inevitable, whether mankind which has already experienced two devastating world wars must still go through a third one? Marxists must answer this question taking into consideration the epoch-making changes of the last decades.

There is, of course, a Marxist-Leninist precept that wars are inevitable as long as imperialism exists. This precept was evolved at a time when (1) imperialism was an all-embracing world system, and (2) the social and political forces which did not want war were weak, poorly organized, and hence unable to compel the imperialists to renounce war.

People usually take only one aspect of the question and examine only the economic basis of wars under imperialism. This is not enough. War is not only an economic phenomenon. Whether there is to be a war or not depends in large measure on the correlation of class, political forces, the degree of organization and the awareness and resolve of the people. Moreover, in certain conditions the struggle waged by progressive social and political forces may play a decisive role. Hitherto the state of affairs was such that the forces that did not want war and opposed it were poorly organized and lacked the means to check the schemes of the warmakers. Thus it was before the First World War, when the main force opposed to the threat of war—the world proletariat—was disorganized by the treachery of the leaders of the Second International. Thus it was on the eve of the Second World War, when the Soviet Union was the only country that pursued an active peace policy, when the other Great Powers to all intents and purposes encouraged the aggressors, and the right-wing Social-Democratic leaders had split the labor movement in the capitalist countries.

In that period this precept was absolutely correct. At the present time, however, the situation has changed radically. Now there is a world camp of socialism, which has become a mighty force. In this camp the peace forces find not only the moral, but also the material means to prevent aggression. Moreover, there is a large group of other countries with a population running into many hundreds of millions which are actively working to avert war. The labor movement in the capitalist countries has today become a tremendous force. The movement of peace supporters has sprung up and developed into a powerful factor.

In these circumstances certainly the Leninist precept that so long as imperialism exists, the economic basis giving rise to wars will also be preserved remains in force. That is why we must display the greatest vigilance. As long as capitalism survives in the world, the reactionary forces representing the interests of the capitalist monopolies will continue their drive towards military gambles and aggression, and may try to unleash war. But war is not fatalistically inevitable. Today there are mighty social and political forces possessing formidable means to prevent the imperialists from unleashing war, and if they actually try to start it, to give a smashing rebuff to the aggressors and frustrate their adventurist plans. To be able to do this all anti-war forces must be vigilant and prepared, they must act as a united front and never relax their efforts in the battle for peace. The more actively the peoples defend peace, the greater the guarantees that there will be no new war. (*Stormy, prolonged applause*)

Forms of Transition to Socialism in Different Countries

In connection with the radical changes in the world arena new prospects are also opening up in respect to the transition of countries and nations to socialism.

As far back as the eve of the Great October Socialist Revolution Lenin wrote: "All nations will arrive at socialism—this is inevitable, but not all will do so in exactly the same way, each will contribute something of its own in one or another form of democracy, one or another variety of the dictatorship of the proletariat, one or another rate at which socialist transformations will be effected in the various aspects of social life. There is nothing more primitive from the viewpoint of theory or more ridiculous from that of practice than to paint, 'in the name of historical materialism,' this aspect of the future in a monotonous grey. The result will be nothing more than Suzdal daubing." (*Works*, Vol. 23, p. 58)

Historical experience has fully confirmed Lenin's brilliant precept. Alongside the Soviet form of reconstructing society on socialist lines, we now have the form of People's Democracy. . . .

It is probable that more forms of transition to socialism will appear. Moreover, the implementation of these forms need not be associated with civil war under all circumstances. Our enemies like to depict us Leninists as advocates of violence always and everywhere. True, we recognize the need for the revolutionary transformation of capitalist society into socialist society. It is this that distinguishes the revolutionary Marxists from the reformists, the opportunists. There is no doubt that in a number of capitalist countries the violent overthrow of the dictatorship of the bourgeoisie and the sharp aggravation of class struggle connected with this are inevitable. But the forms of social revolution vary. It is not true that we regard violence and civil war as the only way to remake society . . .

Leninism teaches us that the ruling classes will not surrender their power voluntarily. And the greater or lesser degree of intensity which the struggle may assume, the use or the nonuse of violence in the transition to socialism depends on the resistance of the exploiters, on whether the exploiting class itself resorts to violence, rather than on the proletariat.

In this connection the question arises of whether it is possible to go over to socialism by using parliamentary means. No such course was open to the Russian Bolsheviks, who were the first to effect this transition. Lenin showed us another road, that of the establishment of a republic of Soviets, the only correct road in those historical conditions. Following that course we achieved a victory of history-making significance.

Since then, however, the historical situation has undergone radical changes which make possible a new approach to the question. The forces of socialism and democracy have grown immeasurably throughout the world, and capitalism has become much weaker. The mighty camp of socialism with its population of over 900 million is growing and gaining in strength. Its gigantic internal forces, its decisive advantages over capitalism, are being increasingly revealed from day to day. Socialism has a great power of attraction for the workers, peasants, and intellectuals of all countries. The ideas of socialism are indeed coming to dominate the minds of all toiling humanity.

At the same time the present situation offers the working class in a number of capitalist countries a real opportunity to unite the overwhelming majority of the people under its leadership and to secure the transfer of the basic means of production into the hands of the people. The Right-wing bourgeois parties and their governments are suffering bankruptcy with increasing frequency. In these circumstances the working class, by rallying around itself the toiling peasantry, the intelligentsia, all patriotic forces, and resolutely repulsing the opportunist elements who are incapable of giving up the policy of compromise with the capitalists and landlords, is in a position to defeat the reactionary forces opposed to the popular interest, to capture a stable majority in parliament, and transform the latter from an organ of bourgeois democracy into a genuine instrument of the people's will. (*Applause*) In such an event this institution, traditional in many highly developed capitalist countries, may become an organ of genuine democracy, democracy for the working people.

The winning of a stable parliamentary majority backed by a mass revolutionary movement of the proletariat and of all the working people could create for the working class of a number of capitalist and former colonial countries the conditions needed to secure fundamental social changes.

In the countries where capitalism is still strong and has a huge military and police apparatus at its disposal, the reactionary forces will of course inevitably offer serious resistance. There the transition to socialism will be attended by a sharp class, revolutionary struggle.

Whatever the form of transition to socialism, the decisive and indispensable factor is the political leadership of the working class headed by its vanguard. Without this there can be no transition to socialism.

5/Imperialism in the Present Epoch—Speech at the International Meeting of Communist and Workers' Parties *June 7, 1969*

LEONID BREZHNEV

Many important features of modern imperialism can be explained by the fact that it is compelled to adapt itself to new conditions, to the conditions of struggle between the two systems.

First and foremost, we cannot afford to ignore the fact that the imperialism of our day still has a powerful and highly developed production mechanism. We cannot afford to ignore the fact that modern

Leonid Brezhnev, "For Greater Unity of Communists, for a Fresh Upsurge of the Anti-imperialist Struggle," Speech at the International Meeting of Communist and Workers' Parties, Moscow, June 7, 1969 (Moscow: Novosti Press Agency, 1969), pp. 8–12, *excerpts.*

imperialism makes use also of the possibilities placed before it by the increasing fusion of the monopolies with the state apparatus. The programming and forecasting of production, state financing of technological progress and scientific research and steps aimed at achieving a certain restriction of market anarchy in the interests of the biggest monopolies are becoming more and more widespread. In some countries this is leading to a certain enhancement of the effectiveness of social production. . . .

To meet the challenge of socialism and strengthen their positions, the imperialists are combining their efforts on an international scale and having recourse to various forms of economic integration. International monopoly associations are being set up with the support and participation of bourgeois governments. Imperialist military and political alliances are becoming more active.

It goes without saying that today, despite all this, the ineradicable inter-imperialist contradictions remain a vital law governing capitalist society. These contradictions are made all the more acute by the circumstance that the reciprocal penetration of capital of these countries is intensifying and the interdependence of their national economies is increasing. The growth of contradictions between the imperialist powers finds expression particularly in the weakening of aggressive military blocs, chiefly NATO. . . .

The influence of the so-called military-industrial complex, i.e., the alliance of the largest monopolies with the military in the state apparatus, is growing rapidly in the most developed capitalist states. This sinister alliance is increasingly pressuring the policy of many imperialist countries, making it still more reactionary and aggressive.

Where the exploiters find themselves unable to ensure the "order" required by them within the framework of bourgeois democracy, power is placed in the hands of openly terrorist regimes of the fascist type. There are many examples of this in our day. These regimes enjoy the financial and political support of the ruling circles of imperialist powers and of the top monopolies. . . .

The policy of military gambles, combined with the stockpiling of weapons of mass annihilation by the principal imperialist powers, makes the imperialism of our day a constant menace to world peace, a threat to the lives of many millions of people, to the existence of whole nations. . . .

We hold that it would be a gross error to underrate the threat of war created by imperialism, above all US imperialism, the main force of world reaction. Millions of people must be made to understand what is being brought to mankind by the imperialist policy of unleashing wars, by the existence of aggressive blocs, by the policy aimed at revising existing state frontiers, and by subversive activities against the socialist countries and the progressive regimes in the young national states. Our task is to see to it that the peoples not only appreciate the entire danger of this policy of the imperialists, but also multiply their efforts in the struggle to frustrate the aggressive designs of imperialism.

6/Imperialism, Enemy of the Peoples and Social Progress—Report of the Central Committee of the CPSU to the Twenty-fourth Party Congress

March 1971

LEONID BREZHNEV

The features of contemporary capitalism largely spring from the fact that it is trying to adapt itself to the new situation in the world. In the conditions of the confrontation with socialism, the ruling circles of the capitalist countries are afraid more than they have ever been of the class struggle developing into a massive revolutionary movement. Hence, the bourgeoisie's striving to use more camouflaged forms of exploitation and oppression of the working people, and its readiness now and again to agree to partial reforms in order to keep the masses under its ideological and political control as far as possible. The monopolies have been making extensive use of scientific and technical achievements to fortify their positions, to enhance the efficiency and accelerate the pace of production, and to intensify the exploitation and oppression of the working people.

However, adaptation to the new conditions does not mean that capitalism has been stabilised as a system. *The general crisis of capitalism has continued to deepen.*

Even the most developed capitalist states are not free from grave economic upheavals. The USA, for instance, has been floundering in one of its economic crises for almost two years now. The last few years have also been marked by a grave crisis in the capitalist monetary and financial system. The simultaneous growth of inflation and unemploy-

Leonid Brezhnev, *Report of the Central Committee of the CPSU to the Twenty-fourth Party Congress* (Moscow: Novosti Press Agency, 1971), pp. 19–21, *excerpts.*

ment has become a permanent feature. There are now almost eight million unemployed in the developed capitalist countries.

The contradictions between the imperialist states have not been eliminated either by the processes of integration or the imperialists' class concern for pooling their efforts in fighting against the socialist world. By the early 1970s, the main centres of imperialist rivalry have become clearly visible: these are the USA—Western Europe (above all, the six Common Market countries)—Japan. The economic and political competitive struggle between them has been growing ever more acute. The import bans imposed by official US agencies on an ever growing number of products from Europe and Japan, and the European countries' efforts to limit their exploitation by US capital are only some of the signs of this struggle.

In the past five-year period, imperialist foreign policy has provided fresh evidence that imperialism has not ceased to be reactionary and aggressive.

In this context, one must deal above all with US imperialism, which in the last few years has reasserted its urge to act as a kind of guarantor and protector of the international system of exploitation and oppression. It seeks to dominate everywhere, interferes in the affairs of other peoples, high-handedly tramples on their legitimate rights and sovereignty, and seeks by force, bribery and economic penetration to impose its will on states and whole areas of the world. . . .

Another fact, comrades, that should also be borne in mind is that since the war militarism in the capitalist world has been growing on an unprecedented scale. This tendency has been intensified in the recent period. In 1970 alone, the NATO countries invested 103 thousand million dollars in war preparations. Militarisation has acquired the most dangerous nature in the USA. In the last five years, that country has spent almost 400 thousand million dollars for military purposes. . . .

The imperialists are prepared to commit any crime in their efforts to preserve or restore their domination of the peoples in their former colonies or in other countries which are escaping from the grip of capitalist exploitation. The last five-year period has provided much fresh evidence of this. The aggression against the Arab states, the colonialist attempts to invade Guinea, and the subversive activity against the progressive regimes in Latin America—all this is a constant reminder that the imperialist war against the freedom-loving peoples has not ceased.

And the continuing US aggression against the peoples of Vietnam, Cambodia and Laos is the main atrocity committed by the modern colonialists; it is the stamp of ignominy on the United States.

FOR FURTHER STUDY

Aspaturian, Vernon V. *Process and Power in Soviet Foreign Policy.* Boston: Little, Brown, 1971.

Barghoorn, Frederic C. *Soviet Russian Nationalism.* New York: Oxford University Press, 1956.

Brzezinski, Zbigniew K. "Communist Ideology and International Affairs," *The Journal of Conflict Resolution,* Vol. 4, No. 3 (1960).

Burin, Frederic S. "The Communist Doctrine of the Inevitability of War," *The American Political Science Review,* Vol. 57, No. 2 (June 1963).

Dallin, Alexander (ed.). *Soviet Conduct in World Affairs.* New York: Columbia University Press, 1960.

Diplomaticus. "Stalinist Theory and Soviet Foreign Policy," *The Review of Politics,* Vol. 14 (1952).

Garthoff, Raymond L. "The Concept of the Balance of Power in Soviet Policy-Making," *World Politics,* Vol. 4 (1951).

Historicus. "Stalin on Revolution," *Foreign Affairs,* Vol. 27, No. 2 (1949).

Hunt, R. N. C. *The Theory and Practice of Communism.* 5th ed. New York: Macmillan, 1957.

_____. "The Importance of Doctrine," *Problems of Communism,* Vol. 7 (1958).

Kase, Francis J. *People's Democracy: A Contribution to the Study of the Communist Theory of State and Revolution.* Leyden: Sijthoff, 1968.

Kennan, George F. "The Sources of Soviet Conduct," *Foreign Affairs,* Vol. 25, No. 4 (1947).

Leites, Nathan. *The Operational Code of the Politbureau.* New York: McGraw-Hill, 1951.

Mayer, Peter. *Cohesion and Conflict in International Communism: A Study of Marxist-Leninist Concepts and Their Application.* The Hague: Nijhoff, 1968.

Meyer, Alfred G. *Leninism.* Cambridge, Mass.: Harvard University Press, 1957.

Moore, Barrington, Jr. *Soviet Politics: The Dilemma of Power.* Cambridge, Mass.: Harvard University Press, 1950.

Mosely, Philip E. "Soviet Foreign Policy: New Goals or New Manners?" *Foreign Affairs,* Vol. 34, No. 4 (1956).

_____. "The Meanings of Coexistence," *Foreign Affairs,* Vol. 41, No. 1 (1962).

Pachter, Henry. "The Meaning of 'Peaceful Coexistence,'" *Problems of Communism,* Vol. 10 (January–February 1961).

Plamenatz, John. *Ideology.* New York: Praeger, 1971.

Reshetar, John S., Jr. *Problems of Analyzing and Predicting Soviet Behavior.* New York: Random House, 1955.

Riefe, R. H. "Moscow and the Changing Nature of Communist Ideology," *The Journal of International Affairs,* Vol. 12, No. 2 (1958).

Rubinstein, Alvin Z. "Ideology and Behavior," in his *The Soviets in International Organizations: Changing Policy Toward Developing Countries, 1953–1963.* Princeton, N.J.: Princeton University Press, 1964.

Sharp, Samuel L. "National Interest: Key to Soviet Politics," *Problems of Communism,* Vol. 7 (1958).

Ulam, Adam B. "Soviet Ideology and Soviet Foreign Policy," *World Politics,* Vol. 11 (1959).

Wetter, Gustav A. "The Soviet Concept of Coexistence," *Soviet Survey,* No. 30 (1959).

Wolfe, Bertram D. "Communist Ideology and Soviet Foreign Policy," *Foreign Affairs,* Vol. 41, No. 1 (1962).

Zimmerman, William. *Soviet Perspectives in International Relations 1956–1967.* Princeton, N.J.: Princeton University Press, 1969.

Zinner, Paul E. "Ideological Bases of Soviet Foreign Policy," *World Politics,* Vol. 4 (1952).

2 the formative years, 1917-1921

The revolutionary turned ruler confronts a galaxy of unknowns. When the Bolsheviks took power on November 7, 1917, they faced challenges for which their experiences as underground revolutionaries and exiled members of an obscure political faction had not prepared them. Expecting world revolution, they had no appreciation of the complexity of their problems. Trotsky tells of Lenin's comment: "What foreign affairs will we have now?" Time and events soon provided the answer.

Burdened with the Czarist legacy of a dispirited, disorganized army, a population weary of war and suffering, and an internal order on the brink of breakdown, the Bolsheviks considered that their initial task was to take Russia out of the war. "Peace" had been one of the main slogans in their drive for power. The promise of peace represented a major political commitment, one which they neither dared nor desired to break. The undoubted popularity of such a move attracted the Bolsheviks as a means of gaining popular support. Furthermore, viewing the struggle as an "imperialist" war, they were predisposed to regard the traditional methods of international law and diplomacy as alien to a proletarian state. Accordingly, on November 8, the day after the Bolsheviks seized power, the All-Russian Congress of Soviets of Workers', Soldiers', and Peasants' Deputies unanimously approved a "Decree of Peace," proposing "to all warring peoples and their Governments to begin immediately negotiations for a just and democratic peace" (reading 7). The Congress defined such a peace as "an immediate peace without annexations (i.e. without seizure of territory, without the forcible annexation of foreign nationalities) and without indemnities." Since this appeal was directed to the peoples of Western

Europe, as well as to their respective governments, it was the first use by the Bolsheviks of what was later to be known as "demonstrative diplomacy." George F. Kennan has explained this as "diplomacy designed not to promote freely accepted and mutually profitable agreement as between governments, but rather to embarrass other governments and stir up opposition among their own peoples."[1] The declaration caught Russia's allies unawares, and their reaction was one of concern and confusion. This initial excursion into the realm of diplomacy presaged ill for future relations with the Bolsheviks.

It soon became apparent that the Bolsheviks were serious about their decision to remove Russia from the war. The issue for them was survival. Negotiations with the Germans resulted in a preliminary armistice agreement on December 15, 1917, the first step toward taking Russia out of the "imperialist" war. Russia's allies—France, Great Britain, and the United States—expressed alarm and sought to dissuade the Bolsheviks from their course. The "Decree of Peace" had also announced the Bolsheviks' intention to publish the secret treaties entered into by the Czarist government. This they proceeded to do, to the further consternation of the Allies. Publication in November and December of 1917 of these documents, which outlined the division of future spoils, caused a sensation in the United States and stimulated demands in Western circles for a redefinition of peace aims. It led President Wilson to issue his celebrated Fourteen Points, the open declaration of Allied aims, on January 8, 1918.[2] Referring directly several times to the German-Bolshevik negotiations at Brest-Litovsk, Wilson declared that "the treatment accorded Russia by her sister nations in the months to come will be the acid test of their good will, of their comprehension of her needs as distinguished from their own interests, and of their intelligent and unselfish sympathy." Noble words. But subsequent events, particularly the Allied intervention, made a mockery of them. Indeed, there is little to indicate that Wilson's address ever had the remotest effect on Allied policy toward Russia.[3]

Meanwhile, the unorthodox delaying tactics of the Bolsheviks at the Brest-Litovsk negotiations irritated the Germans, who were eager for a speedy conclusion of peace. Only then could they transfer the bulk of their formidable army from the Eastern Front to the West and deal a knockout blow to the Allies before American strength was felt. The Bolshevik negotiators, unable to obtain any assurance of Allied support in the event of a rupture with Germany, attempted to prolong the discussions. The impatient German military commander, Hoffmann, drawing a blue line on a map marking German demands, gave the alternatives: an unequivocal answer or an immediate resumption of the German offensive. Leon Trotsky, the chief Russian negotiator, requested a few days in which to consult with Party leaders. He returned to Petrograd

(Leningrad) on January 20 to find that the Constituent Assembly, only recently convened, had been dissolved and that the Bolsheviks had assumed absolute power. Russia's fleeting flirtation with democracy had ended.

Now began the first momentous Bolshevik debate on foreign policy. The Bolsheviks had hitherto assumed that, after appropriate agitation and propagandizing, the German troops would revolt against their "imperialist" government and thereby spark a proletarian revolution in Germany, which would spread, in turn, to Western Europe, signifying the start of a new era. Indeed, most Bolsheviks shared the ideological assumption that the revolution in Russia could prove successful only if accompanied by revolutions elsewhere in Europe.

Lenin, ever the realist and tactician, though accepting this assumption, felt, nevertheless, that the situation required a different tactical approach. In his *Theses on the Question of the Immediate Conclusion of a Separate and Annexationist Peace* (reading 8), Lenin argued, with force and clarity, that the preservation of the revolution in Russia must outweigh the more uncertain prospects of world revolution: that, at least for the immediate future, the interests of the international proletariat must be subordinated; and, indeed, that the best way to ensure the eventual success of the world socialist revolution was first to safeguard the revolution in Russia. Therefore, he called for an immediate end to hostilities. Trotsky, on the other hand, argued that the German demands should be summarily rejected and no peace signed; other "Left Communists," including Radek, Pokrovsky, and Kollantai, went even further and called for a "holy war" against the Germans. In an attempt to reconcile these diverse approaches, the Central Committee agreed upon Trotsky's formula of "no war, no peace." This was designed to prolong the negotiations and was expected, along with the continued dissemination of propaganda, to arouse the proletariat and precipitate a revolution in Germany. However, in recognition of Lenin's objections, the Central Committee agreed that, should the Germans resume their advance, a peace treaty would be signed. Lenin concurred, adding facetiously that "for the sake of a good peace with Trotsky, Latvia and Estonia are worth losing."[4] On January 30, Trotsky returned to Brest-Litovsk. He found the Germans in a far less patient mood and in the process of recognizing as spokesman for the Ukraine a splinter anti-Bolshevik group, with whom they signed a separate peace treaty on February 9, thereby obtaining badly needed grain and raw materials.[5]

Confronted with German annexational demands, Trotsky, to the astonishment of the Germans and Austrians, put his "no war, no peace" policy into effect by announcing Russia's immediate withdrawal from the war, her refusal to sign any terms of peace, and her decision to end all negotiations.[6] The Germans responded quickly, determined now to force Russia to accede. On February 18, the Central Powers launched a general offensive, advancing rapidly against feeble Russian resistance. In Petrograd the Central Committee hurriedly convened and, after some heated discussion, voted to sue for peace. But the Germans rolled onward, eager for more conquest and, seemingly, for the capture of Petrograd itself and the overthrow of the Bolshevik regime.[7] The Bolsheviks were thoroughly alarmed. Trotsky proposed that aid be sought from the Allies. Lenin, though not present, gave his approval to seeking "potatoes and arms from the bandits of Anglo-French imperialism."[8] But Allied policy toward the Bolsheviks remained a jumble of suspicion, ignorance, and misunderstanding. The efforts of several junior Allied diplomatic representatives—Raymond Robins (American), Bruce Lockhart (British), and Jacques Sadoul (French)— received little encouragement from their respective governments and were either ignored or misinterpreted.

In the face of mounting German victories, the Bolshevik plenipotentiaries signed a "Carthaginian" peace on March 3, 1918. For the Germans, the fruits of victory represented a third of Russia's population, of her cultivated land, and of her industry. Meanwhile, Raymond Robins, the American Red Cross representative, tried to prevent the ratification of the Brest Treaty by promising Allied support. The Allies' growing hostility toward the Bolsheviks, however, intensified an already developed Bolshevik distrust, which was further aggravated by reports of an impending Japanese intervention in Siberia. At this vital moment, the Allied embassies moved to the small town of Vologda to avoid capture during the threatening German advance on Petrograd. There they remained, diplomatic orphans, isolated from the maelstrom of events in Petrograd and Moscow (the Bolsheviks moved the capital to Moscow on March 11). Thus, the essentials of policy were being formulated in the Allied capitals virtually without the benefit of reports from knowledgeable personnel at the scene.

On March 5, Trotsky handed a note to Robins in which he asked what Allied policy would be: (a) if the Soviets refused to ratify the peace treaty with Germany; (b) if the Soviets decided to renounce the treaty; or (c) if the Germans continued to advance despite the treaty. The key questions asked were:

1. Can the Soviet Government rely on the support of the United States of North America, Great Britain, and France in its struggle against Germany?
2. What kind of support could be furnished in the nearest future and on what conditions—military equipment, transportation supplies, living necessities?
3. What kind of support would be furnished particularly and especially by the United States?

Should Japan . . . attempt to seize Vladivostok and the Eastern-Siberian Railway . . . what steps would be taken by the other Allies, particularly and especially by the United States . . . ?[9]

After an unavoidable three-day delay, the dispatch was forwarded to Washington. Meanwhile, David R. Francis, the American ambassador, cabled a report indicating support of Robins and adding that a Japanese landing in Siberia at this time would be a gross mistake. On March 14, 1918, the fourth All-Russian Congress of Soviets gathered to ratify the treaty. Lenin, who had agreed to a forty-eight hour delay at the urgent request of Robins, could wait no longer. After reading a telegram of greeting from President Wilson, which was dated March 11 but which did not answer Trotsky's questions, Lenin turned to Robins and Lockhart and asked what they had heard from their governments. Each could only answer "nothing." In the early hours of the morning of March 15, Lenin outlined the economic, military, and political necessity for taking Russia out of the war. Soon afterward, the Congress ratified the treaty, and Russia was out of the war. Whether a favorable reply from Washington could have prevented the ratification at that late date is, of course, open to conjecture. Describing these events, Kennan writes: "Once again, as so often in the course of these rapidly moving events, Washington—troubled, hesitant, and ill-informed—had spoken, reluctantly, into the past."[10]

The shape of the future was not long in developing.

For the Bolsheviks, the Brest-Litovsk crisis served as a crucible from which emerged the outlines of a foreign policy. During their early days in power they were busy consolidating the regime and had no real understanding of the nature of foreign policy. Trotsky, in his autobiography, offers an interesting commentary on this prevailing naïveté. Upon assuming the position of Commissar of Foreign Affairs, he states, the expectation was that "I will issue a few revolutionary proclamations to the peoples of the world and then shut up shop." The Bolshevik leaders, expecting the socialist revolution to spread throughout the world, saw no need to adhere to the traditional ways of international politics. But Brest-Litovsk convinced them that an adjustment had to be made. Three factors were paramount in their thinking. First, they recognized that military weakness left them prey to foreign attack and increased the likelihood of their deposition. Second, the absence of expected revolutions in Germany and Western Europe meant that they could not depend on world revolution to strengthen the socialist revolution in Russia; therefore, though continuing to anticipate world revolution as the only ultimate security, the Bolsheviks undertook the creation of a Red Army to provide for their short-term safety. Finally, the policies both of the Central Powers and of the Entente buttressed the Bolsheviks' conviction, held to this day, that the capitalist world, irrespective of its competing internal alliances, was hostile and would persist in its efforts to overthrow the Bolshevik regime. Only world revolution could guarantee national security; yet national security was essential for the eventual success of world revolution.[11] This dualism—the furthering of world revolution and the quest for national security—has remained a salient feature of Soviet foreign policy.

Soviet behavior in the international arena represents a unique adaptation to the existing pattern of world politics: it tends to rationalize actions of national self-interest in terms of the transcendent concerns of the international proletariat; and while using traditional balance-of-power politics to protect the revolution, it spares no effort to undermine this system and replace it with "an international proletarian community." The stress on fomenting world revolution developed out of initial military weakness and, having proved its effectiveness as a weapon, has remained an integral part of the Soviet diplomatic arsenal. (Note: After the Allied intervention and the subsequent civil war, the use of subversion and revolutionary propaganda became increasingly important as a technique to defeat the enemy and consolidate the power of the regime.)

The landing of Japanese troops at Vladivostok on April 5, 1918, triggered by the murder of three Japanese shopkeepers, began the intervention. Before it ended, British, French, and American troops would be involved, a bitter, all-out civil war would run its course, and Bolshevism would emerge triumphant in Russia.

From the ratification of the Brest-Litovsk Treaty in March to the resumption of official German-Soviet relations in May, the Bolsheviks had toyed with the possibility of accepting Allied aid and continuing in the war against Germany. However, as relations with the Allies deteriorated and as it became apparent that the Germans, engrossed in the struggle on the Western front, had neither the intent nor the strength to overthrow the Bolshevik regime, this alternative lost whatever likelihood it may have had. On the other hand, the Allies, confused and uncertain, were not yet committed to intervention against the Bolsheviks. Reasonable justification soon replaced this initial Allied hesitancy. The catalyst was the Czecho-Slovak revolt, one of the strangest episodes of the entire period.[12]

The Czechs and Slovaks, originally part of the Austro-Hungarian armies, had deserted by the thousands and looked forward to the establishment of an independent state. Their sentiments were unmistakably pro-Allies. Shortly after the overthrow of the Czar, Thomas Masaryk, the future president of Czechoslovakia, had journeyed to Russia to negotiate for the organization of the Czechs and Slovaks into a unified force and for their removal (by way of Siberia) to the Western front for use in fighting the Germans and Austrians. The Provisional Government approved and took measures to transport this force. However, with the Bolshevik decision to leave the war and the increasingly obvious anti-Bolshevik trend of Allied policy, the Czech Legion's position became untenable. The Bolsheviks feared that the Legion would be used to overthrow them; indeed, they believed that the Czechs were acting in concert with the recently landed Japanese forces toward this end. The Legion, on the other hand, fearing imprisonment, refused to surrender its weapons during the trip across Siberia for transshipment to the Western front. Earlier, in March, the British had landed a small detachment at Murmansk, with the tacit consent of the Bolsheviks, to safeguard substantial Allied stores. The German advance heightened concern for the safety of these supplies, and the Allied command decided to employ part of the Czech Legion to strengthen the British force. The intricate pattern of subsequent events need not concern us here. Suffice it to note that the Allied decision to intervene was precipitated by the chance outbreak of fighting between the Czech Legion and the Bolsheviks.

The confusions of these months were many. But isolated events have a way, in periods of great stress and confusion, of encouraging certain policy decisions that seem for the moment to characterize the entire situation. The Allies had not planned to use the Czechs to overthrow the Bolsheviks, but the plight of the Czechs helped provide the necessary impetus for what was at best a haphazardly conceived policy. According to Kennan, the immediate reasons for the Czech-Bolshevik fighting lay:

> . . . primarily in the general climate of confusion and suspicion that prevailed at this culminating moment of war and revolution; in the extremely complex situation in which the Czech Corps then found itself; in the complicating factor of the presence of large numbers of the war prisoners of the Central Powers, partly Bolshevized and partly not so, all along the Siberian line; in the abundant rumors of German instigation of Soviet actions. . . .
>
> Had the Corps succeeded in making its way peacefully through the vast tinderbox of central Siberia during the spring of 1918, striking no sparks and raising no crucial issues as it went along, this—rather than what actually occurred—would have been the true wonder.[13]

In late June, additional British forces landed at Murmansk, followed by British and French landings at Archangel. A few weeks later, American troops also came to North Russia; and in early August they joined the Japanese in Siberia. The intervention was now a reality, nourished by the seeming success of anti-Bolsheviks in these areas and by the desire of Allied strategists to re-create an Eastern front against the Germans. There was no longer any possibility of compromise. The mold of hostility hardened. Increasingly, Bolshevik statements reflected desperation. The summer of 1918 was their darkest hour. Hope of survival depended on their ability to sow discord among the Allies and foment world revolution (reading 9). As the intervention spread, Soviet relations with Germany improved—notwithstanding the assassination of German Ambassador Mirbach, on July 6, 1918, by a disgruntled left-wing Socialist Revolutionary who hoped to precipitate a break with Germany and thereby force Russia back into the war on the side of the Allies. Both the German and Soviet governments desired friendly relations, though for different reasons (the Germans were preoccupied with the fighting on the Western front and welcomed the respite in Russia; the Bolsheviks, increasingly threatened by the Allied intervention, were content to let the Brest boundaries remain in effect for the time being). Thus German-Soviet relations improved as Allied-Soviet relations deteriorated. This was to be a recurring pattern from 1918 to 1941—as Soviet relations with one deteriorated, a rapprochement was effected with the other.

World War I ended on November 11, 1918. Whatever rationale the intervention originally had was no longer valid. But conflicting national interests and growing British and French commitments to anti-Bolshevik forces precluded any immediate disengagement. The intervention had become involved in the civil war. An eminent student of the period has described the situation thus: "One searches in vain in the records of the time not only for a consistent Allied policy, but even for a steadfast policy on the part of the individual Allied powers."[14] Fear of Bolshevism's spread to the rest of Europe, resentment over the Bolshevik repudiation of the prewar Czarist debts, the growing influence of émigré and pro-White groups—all sustained the resolve of the interventionists.

On November 13, the Bolsheviks abrogated the Brest-Litovsk Treaty, declaring its provisions null and void. During the autumn and winter a Red Army was conscripted, trained, and toughened for battle. Under the driving leadership of Leon Trotsky, this organization proved itself superior to the smorgasbord of armies and leaders that comprised the White Guard interventionists. A centralized military command, a compact geographical base and internal lines of communication, effective appeals to patriotism against foreign enemies, and the inability of the Whites to coordinate their military activities or agree on a common political program, all worked to Bolshevik benefit. In addition, the Bolshevik promise of self-determination, including the right of secession, induced the national minorities in Armenia, Georgia, Central Asia, etc., to resist attempts by the White armies to reimpose *Russian* control. During the crucial 1918 to 1920 period, the unrest and revolts in these areas weakened the interventionists' attempts at a restoration, thus inadvertently aiding the Bolsheviks. Needless to add, once the

Bolsheviks defeated the Whites, they proceeded to reincorporate the minorities in the Caucasus and Central Asia into the Russian orbit and suppress all separatist movements.

The year 1919 was crucial. At Versailles a treaty was summarily handed to the Germans and with it were sown the seeds of the next war in a Europe weakened beyond its realization; in Germany, revolution met defeat at the hands of the military, and the fledgling Weimar republic started its tragic, short life; in America, Wilson's dream was defeated in the Senate and soon gave way to a "return to normalcy"—a phrase symbolizing America's abdication of international responsibility for two decades; the "Balkanized" area of central and southeastern Europe had not yet been linked with France in the unstable network of military alliances that was to give the French an illusion of security; in Paris fear of Bolshevism dominated French policy, and émigré Russians pushed for all-out war against the Bolsheviks; and in Russia, after the excesses and suffering of the period of "War Communism," Bolshevism emerged victorious. The Allies, forced to compromise by the unwillingness of their armies to fight in Russia in a struggle they did not understand, reluctantly abandoned their interventionist adventures.

Bolshevik behavior strengthened the cause of the prointerventionists. By their cynicism, lack of sincerity, and revolutionary agitation, they made negotiation in good faith virtually impossible. Encouraged by revolution in Hungary and Germany, unrest in France, and the illusions of ideology, they continued to anticipate world revolution. To hasten this objective, the Bolsheviks in March 1919 established the Communist International, thus providing the interventionists with an added pretext for military action. By the end of 1919, however, it was apparent that the anti-Bolshevik elements could neither defeat the Red Army by force, nor match Bolshevism's emotional appeal.

> To the great mass, Bolshevism was part promise and part fulfillment. From the revolution had come peace, land, and a new form of ownership. But it also painted a glorious future which attracted and provoked. The enemies of Communism had nothing thrilling or inspiring to offer. Lenin operated on credit. His capital was a promissory note on coming years. The Whites on the other hand could appeal only to the record of the past which they wished to enthrone again. Psychologically, the position of the Bolsheviks was therefore stronger.[15]

Each generation must learn anew the adage that it is not by bread alone that man lives.

A confident Lenin delivered the key address to the Seventh All-Russian Congress on December 5, 1919 (reading 10). His report marked a turning point in the period of War Communism. The danger from the Allied intervention had been successfully met, and the civil war had passed its most acute phase. The principal White Guard armies, under Kolchak and Denikin, had been defeated, and the pressures for peace had increased, particularly among the small nations bordering on European Russia—in 1920, Finland, Latvia, and Estonia concluded peace treaties with the Bolsheviks. Cogently presenting his analysis of the main stages of the intervention and the civil war, Lenin set forth the underlying assumptions of Soviet foreign policy, assumptions significant to the future of Soviet relations with the capitalist world and valid, in great measure, to this day: the fundamental antagonism between the capitalist and socialist systems; the expectation that the capitalist countries would attempt another intervention (a factor leading the Soviet leaders to orient their foreign policy along traditional balance-of-power lines); and the inevitable linking of Soviet national security with the necessity for world revolution.

Tactically, Soviet policy was learning to emphasize the importance of the international proletariat as an instrument to safeguard the Soviet Union; to exploit antagonisms within the capitalist world, not only between the "great" and "lesser" powers but within the respective countries themselves; and to capitalize on the conciliatory, frequently sympathetic, tendencies of the petty bourgeoisie and intelligentsia toward the Soviet Union. Soviet leaders appealed to the workers in the Allied countries to defend the socialist revolution by bringing pressure to bear on their governments to stop the intervention. Propaganda assumed an increasing importance in the policy of a *militarily* inferior Soviet Russia.

The last serious military threat came from the Poles. On April 25, 1920, Marshal Pilsudski launched an offensive and advanced rapidly into the Ukraine. By May 6 the Poles were in Kiev. By mid-May, however, the Red Army had counterattacked and the Poles in turn were in rapid retreat. By late July and early August the Soviet armies were at the gates of Warsaw. The Bolshevik leaders, stressing the class character of the struggle, expected revolution at any moment. (Ironically, Pilsudski had refused to act in concert with the White general, Denikin, the previous year, under conditions offering greater promise of victory. His anti-Russianism recognized no distinction between Red or White, since both groups favored a strong Russia, an unquestioned anathema to Pilsudski.)

In Moscow the Second Congress of the Communist International met from July 23 to August 7 in a buoyantly optimistic atmosphere stimulated by the continuous advance of the Red Army into Poland. Zinoviev later described the scene and the mood:

In the hall of Congress hung a large map. Every day we marked on it the advance of our forces, and every day with breathless interest the delegates examined the map. . . . All of them understood that if the military objectives of our troops were reached it would mean an immense acceleration of the international proletarian revolution. All of them understood that on every step forward of our Red Army depended in the literal sense of the word the fate of the international proletarian revolution.[16]

Hopes ran high for the International. No longer was it to be a mere propaganda association, as at its foundation in March 1919; it was now to be tempered into a "fighting organ of the international proletariat." To ensure a high degree of centralization and discipline, the Congress revised its structure and adopted new operating procedures (reading 11). The Congress also prescribed conditions of admission to the Comintern. These "21 conditions" made certain that the Comintern would, in fact, be "a single Communist Party having branches in different countries."

The emergence of the Kremlin as the undisputed spokesman and policy-maker for world communism can be traced to this Congress. First, it established a world-wide system of Moscow-controlled communist parties; second, it laid down the fundamentals of communist policy on all significant questions. Other important resolutions adopted at the Second Congress, particularly theses concerning the national and colonial question, will be discussed in a future chapter. By the late 1920s the struggle for power *within* the Kremlin having ended, all foreign communist parties acknowledged the primacy of the Communist Party of the Soviet Union and accepted Kremlin injunctions without question; the Comintern became a docile instrument of Soviet foreign policy.

Shortly after the Congress adjourned, the Poles, aided by the French, launched a powerful counteroffensive, and the overextended Red Army retreated in haste. Contrary to Lenin's expectations, the Polish proletariat did not revolt, but fought as Poles against the historic and hated enemy—Russia. With this defeat of the Red Army, Russian expectations of an imminent world revolution ended. An armistice, negotiated on October 12, 1920, led to a treaty of peace signed on March 18, 1921, at Riga,* which governed Polish-Soviet relations until the partition of September 1939. After the armistice the Soviets threw the bulk of their forces against von Wrangel, the last of the White generals, and by mid-November 1920 successfully ended this campaign. Subsequently, the intervention collapsed in Siberia and the Caucasus. The Bolsheviks now turned to the problems of reshaping Russian society and "coexisting" in a hostile world.

Lenin outlined the essentials of Soviet policy in two speeches de-

* The Soviets, imperiled by von Wrangel's White army in southern Russia, agreed to Polish demands and ceded part of Byelorussia, as well as a strip of territory serving to separate Russia from Lithuania.

livered in the fall of 1920 (readings 12 and 13). Tracing the phases of the intervention and the civil war, he reaffirmed the belief in the inevitability of world revolution and the triumph of communism, but held that a period of accommodation with the capitalist world, Party reorganization, and economic development was first necessary. By the time of the Tenth Party Congress (March 1921), the need for a temporary truce with the capitalist world was accepted and a rapprochement sought in the economic and political spheres.

Thus ended Bolshevism's first period of trial. A civil war and a foreign intervention had been successfully fought. The Communist Party was firmly entrenched. Thenceforth, Soviet foreign policy focused on the preservation of the Soviet Union, the improvement of its international position, and the spread of communist influence and power. With the end of War Communism, one period of Soviet foreign policy came to a successful conclusion. A second was about to begin.

NOTES

1. George F. Kennan, *Russia Leaves the War* (Princeton, N.J.: Princeton University Press, 1956), pp. 75–76.

2. Edward Hallett Carr, *The Bolshevik Revolution, 1917–1923* (New York: Macmillan, 1953), Vol. III, p. 13.

3. Louis Fischer, *The Soviets in World Affairs* (London: Cape, 1930), Vol. I, p. 42.

4. Leon Trotsky, *My Life: An Attempt at an Autobiography* (New York: Scribner, 1930), p. 383.

5. Robert D. Warth, *The Allies and the Russian Revolution* (Durham, N.C.: Duke University Press, 1954), p. 225.

6. *Ibid.,* p. 226.

7. Fischer, *op. cit.,* pp. 60–61.

8. Warth, *op. cit.,* p. 231.

9. U.S., Congress, *Congressional Record,* January 29, 1919, p. 2336.

10. Kennan, *op. cit.,* p. 517.

11. Carr, *op. cit.,* p. 57.

12. Fischer, *op. cit.,* p. 108.

13. George F. Kennan, *The Decision to Intervene* (Princeton, N.J.: Princeton University Press, 1958), p. 165.

14. William Henry Chamberlin, *The Russian Revolution, 1917–1921* (New York: Macmillan, 1935), Vol. II, p. 151.

15. Fischer, *op. cit.,* pp. 234–235.

16. Jane Degras, *The Communist International, 1919–1943, Documents* (New York: Oxford University Press, 1956), Vol. I, pp. 110–111.

7/Decree of Peace   *November 8, 1917*

The Workers' and Peasants' Government, created by the revolution of October 24th and 25th [November 6th and 7th] and based on the Soviet of Workers', Soldiers', and Peasants' Deputies, proposes to all warring peoples and their Governments to begin immediately negotiations for a just and democratic peace.

An overwhelming majority of the exhausted, wearied, and war-tortured workers and the laboring classes of all the warring countries are longing for a just and democratic peace—a peace which in the most definite and insistent manner was demanded by Russian workers and peasants after the overthrow of the Tsar's monarchy. Such a peace the Government considers to be an immediate peace without annexations (i.e. without seizure of foreign territory, without the forcible annexation of foreign nationalities) and without indemnities.

The Government of Russia proposes to all warring peoples immediately to conclude such a peace. It expresses its readiness to take at once without the slightest delay, all the decisive steps until the final confirmation of all terms of such a peace by the plenipotentiary conventions of the representatives of all countries and all nations. . . .

The Government considers it to be the greatest crime against humanity to continue the war for the sake of dividing among the powerful and rich nations the weaker nationalities which were seized by them, and the Government solemnly states its readiness to sign immediately the terms of peace which will end this war, on the basis of the above-stated conditions, equally just for all nationalities without exception. At the same time the Government announces that it does not consider the above-stated conditions of peace as in the nature of an ultimatum, that is, it is ready to consider any other terms of peace, insisting, however, that such be proposed as soon as possible by any one of the warring countries and on condition of the most definite clarity and absolute exclusion of any ambiguousness, or any secrecy when proposing the terms of peace.

The Government abolishes secret diplomacy and on its part expresses the firm intention to carry on all negotiations absolutely openly before all the people, and immediately begins to publish in full the secret treaties concluded or confirmed by the Government of landowners and capitalists from February up to November 7th, 1917. The Government

U.S., Congress, House Committee on Un-American Activities, *The Communist Conspiracy*, 84th Cong., 2d sess. (1956), H. Rept. 2241, Part I, pp. 8–10, *excerpts.* The "Decree of Peace" was adopted at a Meeting of the All-Russian Congress of Soviets of Workers', Soldiers', and Peasants' Deputies on November 8, 1917.

abrogates absolutely and immediately all the provisions of these secret treaties in as much as they were intended in the majority of cases for the purpose of securing profits and privileges for Russian landowners and capitalists and retaining or increasing the annexations by the Great Russians.

While addressing the proposal to the Governments and peoples of all countries to start immediately open negotiations for the conclusion of peace, the Government expresses its readiness to carry on these negotiations by written communications, by telegraph, as well as by parleys of the representatives of various countries, or at a conference of such representatives. To facilitate such negotiations the Government appoints a plenipotentiary representative in neutral countries.

The Government proposes to all the Governments and peoples of all the warring countries to conclude an armistice immediately; at the same time, it considers desirable that this armistice should be conducted for a period of not less than three months—that is, a period during which it would be fully possible to terminate the negotiations for peace with the participation of the representatives of all peoples and nationalities drawn into the war or compelled to participate in it, as well as to call the plenipotentiary conventions of people's representatives of all countries for the final ratification of the terms of peace.

While addressing this proposal of peace to the Governments and peoples of all warring countries, the Provisional Workers' and Peasants' Government of Russia appeals also in particular to the class-conscious workers of the three most forward nations of the world and the largest states participating in the present war—England, France, and Germany. The workers of these countries have been of the greatest service to the cause of progress and socialism. We have the great example of the Chartist movement in England, several revolutions which were of universal historic importance accomplished by the French proletariat, and finally the heroic struggle against the *exclusive* law in Germany and the prolonged, stubborn, disciplined work—a work setting an example for the workers of the whole world—of creating mass proletarian organizations in Germany. All these examples of proletarian heroism and historic creative work serve as a guarantee that the workers of the above-mentioned countries understand the duties which devolve upon them now in the cause of the liberation of humanity from the horrors of war and its consequences, a cause which these workers by their resolute and energetic activity will help us to bring to a successful end —the cause of peace, and together with this, the cause of the liberation of the laboring and exploited.

The Brest-Litovsk Crisis

8/Theses on the Question of the Immediate Conclusion of a Separate and Annexationist Peace

January 20, 1918

V. I. LENIN

1. The position of the Russian revolution at the present moment is that almost all the workers and the vast majority of the peasants undoubtedly support the Soviet government and the socialist revolution that it has started. To that extent the success of the socialist revolution in Russia is assured.

2. At the same time, the civil war, provoked by the frantic resistance of the wealthy classes, who fully realize that the last and decisive fight for the preservation of private ownership of the land and means of production is before them, has not yet reached its climax. The victory of Soviet power in this war is assured, but some time must inevitably pass, no little exertion of effort will inevitably be demanded, and a period of acute devastation and chaos, usually associated with all wars and with civil war in particular, is inevitable before the resistance of the bourgeoisie will be crushed.

3. Besides, this resistance, in its less active and nonmilitary forms—sabotage, corruption of the deposed groups and of agents of the bourgeoisie, who worm their way into the ranks of the socialists in order to ruin their cause, and so on and so forth—has proved so stubborn and capable of assuming so many diversified forms that the struggle to counter it will inevitably take some time and, in its main forms, is scarcely likely to end before several months. And without a decisive victory over the passive and covert resistance of the bourgeoisie and its supporters, the success of the socialist revolution cannot be possible.

4. Finally, the organizational problems of the socialist transformation of Russia are so great and difficult that their solution . . . will demand a fairly long time.

5. All these circumstances taken together are such as to make it perfectly clear that for the success of socialism in Russia a certain amount of time, not less than several months, will be necessary, during which time the socialist government must have a completely free hand

V. I. Lenin, *Sochinenia,* 2d ed. (Moscow: State Publishing House, 1930), Vol. XXII, pp. 193–199, *excerpts*. Editor's translation.

for first vanquishing the bourgeoisie in our own country and for taking care of the widespread and far-reaching mass organizational work.

6. The situation of the socialist revolution in Russia must be understood in terms of the international tasks of our Soviet state, for the international situation in the fourth year of the war is such that the probable moment of the outbreak of revolution or overthrow of any of the European imperialist governments (including the German) is quite impossible to estimate. That the socialist revolution in Europe must come and will come is beyond doubt. All our hopes for the *final* victory of socialism are based on this certainty and on this scientific prediction. Our propagandist activities in general and the organization of fraternization in particular must be intensified and broadened. But it would be a mistake to predicate the tactics of the socialist government in Russia on attempts to determine whether the European, and especially the German, socialist revolution will take place in the next six months (or a similarly short period) or not. As it is impossible to determine this, all such attempts, objectively speaking, would be but a blind gamble.

7. The peace negotiations in Brest-Litovsk have by this date—January 20, 1918—made it perfectly clear that in the German government (which leads the other governments of the Quadruple Alliance by the halter) there is no doubt that the upper hand has been gained by the military party, which has virtually presented Russia with an ultimatum (and it is expected, it is necessary to expect, that any day now it will be presented formally). The ultimatum is as follows: either the continuation of the war or an annexationist peace, that is, peace on the condition that we surrender all the territory we occupy, while the Germans keep *all* the territory they occupy and impose upon us an indemnity (outwardly disguised as payment for the maintenance of prisoners), an indemnity of about three thousand million rubles, payable in several years.

8. The demanding question of whether to accept this annexationist peace now, or immediately to wage a revolutionary war, faces the socialist government of Russia. Actually, no middle course is possible. No further delay is feasible, for we have *already* tried everything possible and impossible artificially to protract the negotiations.

9. Examining the arguments for an immediate revolutionary war, we encounter first of all the argument that a separate peace now would be, objectively speaking, an agreement with the German imperialists, an "imperialist deal," and so forth, and that, consequently, would be at complete variance with the basic principles of proletarian internationalism.

But this argument is clearly incorrect. Workers who lose a strike and resume work on terms that are unfavorable to them and favorable to the capitalists do not betray socialism. Only those betray socialism who barter advantages for part of the workers in exchange for advantages to the capitalists, only such agreements are in principle impermissible.

Whoever calls a war with German imperialism a defensive and just war, but actually receives support from the Anglo-French imperialists and hides from the people secret treaties concluded with them, betrays socialism. Whoever does not conceal anything from the people and does not conclude any secret treaties with the imperialists, but agrees to sign terms of peace unfavorable for the weak nation and favorable to the imperialists of one group, if at the given moment he has no strength to continue the war, he does not betray socialism in the slightest degree.

10. Another argument for immediate war is that, by concluding peace, we, objectively speaking, become agents of German imperialism, for we give it the opportunity to release troops from our front, surrender to it millions of prisoners, and the like. But this argument is also clearly incorrect, for a revolutionary war at the present moment would make us, objectively speaking, agents of Anglo-French imperialism, by giving it subsidiary forces. The British bluntly offered our commander-in-chief, Krylenko, one hundred rubles per month for every one of our soldiers provided we continued the war. Even if we did not take a single kopek from the Anglo-French, we would all, objectively speaking, be helping them by diverting part of the German army.

From this point of view, we would not entirely escape some sort of imperialist tie, and it is evident that it is impossible to do so entirely without overthrowing world imperialism. The correct conclusion from this is that with the victory of a socialist government in any one country questions must be decided, not from the point of view of whether this or that imperialism is preferable, but exclusively from the point of view of the best conditions for the development and consolidation of the socialist revolution that has already begun.

In other words, the underlying principle of our tactics must not be which of the two imperialisms is it now more profitable to assist, but rather, how can the socialist revolution most faithfully and reliably ensure the possibility of strengthening itself, or, at least, of maintaining itself in one country until it is joined by other countries.

11. It is said that the German Social-Democratic opponents of the war have now become "defeatists" and are requesting us not to surrender to German imperialism. But we recognized defeatism only in respect to *one's own* imperialist bourgeoisie, and victory over an alien imperialism, which is achieved in formal or actual alliance with a "friendly" imperialism, we have always rejected as a method intolerable in principle and unworthy in general.

The present argument is therefore only a modification of the previous one. If the German Left Social-Democrats were proposing that we delay negotiating a separate peace for a *definite* period, guaranteeing revolutionary action in Germany in this period, the question *might* become a different matter for us. Not only do the German leftists not say this, but, on the contrary, they formally declare: "Hold out as long as you can, but decide the question from the standpoint of the state of affairs in the *Russian* socialist revolution, for it is impossible to promise you anything positive regarding the German revolution."

12. It is said that we definitely "promised" a revolutionary war in a series of party declarations and that by concluding a separate peace we would be betraying our word.

This is untrue. We spoke of the *necessity* for a socialist government in an era of imperialism *"to prepare for and wage"* a revolutionary war; we said this in order to fight abstract pacifism and the theory of "defense of the fatherland" and, finally, to counter the purely selfish instincts of part of the soldiers; but we never gave any pledge to start a revolutionary war without taking into consideration the extent to which it is possible to wage such a war at any given moment.

Unquestionably, we must *prepare* for a revolutionary war. We are carrying out this promise, as we have in general carried out all our promises that could be carried out at once; we abrogated the secret treaties, offered all nations a just peace, and several times tried to prolong the peace negotiations in order to give other nations a chance to join us.

But the question whether it is possible to wage a revolutionary war *now and at once* should be decided only from the standpoints of whether material conditions permit it and of the interests of the socialist revolution that has already begun.

13. Having considered the arguments in favor of an immediate revolutionary war, we are forced to the conclusion that such a policy might perhaps answer the human craving for the beautiful, the dramatic, and the vivid, but it would certainly ignore the objective relation of class forces and material factors at the present moment of the socialist revolution.

14. There can be no doubt but that our army at the present and for the next few weeks (and probably for the next few months) is absolutely in no condition to resist a German offensive successfully: first, due to the extreme fatigue and weariness of the majority of the soldiers and the incredible confusion relating to supply and replacement problems; second, due to the utter unfitness of our horses, which dooms our artillery to inevitable destruction; and third, due to the utter impossibility of defending the coast from Riga to Revel, which gives the enemy a great opportunity of capturing the rest of Livonia, then Estonia, and of outflanking a large part of our forces, and finally, of capturing Petrograd.

15. Further, there is no doubt that the peasant majority of our army would at the present time unreservedly favor an annexationist peace and not an immediate revolutionary war; for the socialist reorganization of the army and the merging of the Red Guard detachments with it have only just begun.

With the complete democratization of the army, to wage war against the wishes of the majority of the soldiers would be sheer adventurism, while the creation of a really staunch and ideologically strong socialist workers' and peasants' army will require months and months, at least.

16. The poor peasantry in Russia is able to support a socialist revolution led by the working class, but it is presently incapable of a serious revolutionary war. It would be a fatal mistake to ignore this objective relation of class forces at this time.

17. The present situation in regard to a revolutionary war is as follows:

If the German revolution would break out and triumph in the coming three or four months, then, perhaps, the tactics of an immediate revolutionary war would not ruin our socialist revolution.

If, however, the German revolution does not occur in the next few months, the course of events, given the continuation of the war, will inevitably be such that a smashing defeat will force Russia to conclude a far more disadvantageous separate peace, a peace that would be concluded, not by a socialist government, but by some other . . . For the peasant army, which is unendurably exhausted by the war, will, after the first defeats—and probably, even within a matter not of months but of weeks—overthrow the socialist workers' government.

18. In such a situation it would be absolutely intolerable tactics to stake the fate of the socialist revolution that has already begun in Russia on the mere chance that the German revolution may begin in the near future, within a period estimated in weeks. Such tactics would be reckless. We do not have the right to gamble thusly.

19. And the German revolution will not be made more difficult, as far as its objective foundations are concerned, if we conclude a separate peace. Probably, the chauvinist intoxication will weaken it for a time, but the position of Germany will remain extremely grave, the war with Britain and America will be a prolonged one, and the aggressive imperialism of both sides will be fully exposed. A Socialist Soviet Republic in Russia will stand as a living example to the peoples of all countries, and the propaganda and revolutionary effect of this example will be enormous. There—the bourgeois system and a naked war of aggrandizement by two groups of plunderers. Here—peace and a socialist republic of Soviets.

20. In concluding a separate peace, we free ourselves *as much as is possible at the present time* from both hostile imperialist groups,

exploiting their hostility and war—to thwart concerted action on their part against us—and use this period to advance and consolidate the socialist revolution. The reorganization of Russia on the basis of the dictatorship of the proletariat and on the basis of the nationalization of the banks and large-scale industry, coupled with the exchange of goods in kind between the towns and the small peasants' societies, is economically possible, provided we are assured a few months peace in which to work. And such a reorganization will make socialism invincible both in Russia and all over the world, creating with that a solid economic basis for a mighty workers' and peasants' Red Army.

21. A really revolutionary war at the present time would mean a war waged by the socialist republic against the bourgeois countries, with the aim, clearly defined and completely approved by the socialist army, of overthrowing the bourgeoisie in other countries. We *obviously* are unable to achieve this objective at this *given* moment. We would be fighting now, objectively speaking, for the liberation of Poland, Lithuania and Courland. But no Marxist, without flouting the principles of Marxism and of socialism generally, can deny that the interests of socialism are higher than the interests of the right of nations to self-determination. Our socialist republic has done all it could, and continues to do so, for the realization of the right of self-determination for Finland, the Ukraine, and so forth. But if the concrete position of affairs is such that the existence of the Socialist republic is endangered at the present moment because of the violation of the right of self-determination of several nations (Poland, Lithuania, etc.), then, naturally, the preservation of the socialist republic has the higher priority.

The Allied Intervention and the Beginnings of "War Communism"

9/Report on Soviet Foreign Policy to the Fifth All-Russian Congress of Soviets *July 4, 1918*

GEORGI V. CHICHERIN

During the period following the conclusion of the Brest treaty, Russia's foreign policy has gone along lines different from those followed in the first months after the October Revolution. At the end of 1917 and the beginning of 1918 the basic feature of our foreign policy was the revolutionary offensive. It took its bearings from the immediate prospect of the world revolution, for which the Russian revolution was to serve as the signal. It was directed, over the heads of Governments, to the revolutionary proletariat of all countries, and both in its actions, sharply opposed to the entire nature of existing capitalist Governments, and in its words, its strongly agitational offensives were calculated to stir up the revolutionary proletariat of all countries to an international revolutionary struggle against imperialism, against the capitalist system.

When the failure of any immediate support from the proletariat of other countries led to the defeat of the revolutionary Russian forces by Austro-German imperialism, to the occupation of Finland, the Ukraine, the Baltic provinces, Poland, Lithuania, and White Russia by the armed forces of German and Austro-Hungarian imperialism, the setting of Soviet Russia's foreign policy changed radically. For the last four months it has been compelled to pursue the aim of pushing off and postponing the dangers threatening it from all sides, trying to gain as much time as possible, both in order to give the growing proletarian movement in other countries time to ripen, and to gain more time for the new forms of political and social relationships established by the Soviet Government to take root among the popular masses of Russia, and to tie them more closely to the Soviet program.

Not having yet succeeded in creating adequate fighting forces for the defense of the country, surrounded by enemies awaiting its ruin, suffering from the incredible destruction brought about by war and tsarism, Soviet Russia in its foreign policy had all the time to keep in mind the

Jane Degras, *Soviet Documents on Foreign Policy* (New York: Oxford University Press, 1951), Vol. I, pp. 83–85, *excerpts.* Published by permission of the Oxford University Press and the Royal Institute of International Affairs.

need of avoiding the dangers threatening its destruction at every step. This policy of delay was possible thanks to the conflict of interests not only between the two coalitions, but also within each of them, and even within the imperialist camp of each belligerent country. The struggle on the western front has for the present tied up the forces of both coalitions so much that neither has decided to go all out openly for the destruction of Russia. Some imperialists in both coalitions think of the future after the war, of economic relations with Russia, this world market most capable of expansion. Instead of a policy of robbery, these elements in both coalitions would prefer a policy of trade, of concessions and economic conquests. Some of the military elements think of the part Russia could play, even in the present war. The hope of dragging Russia into war, at a time when it is re-creating its military power, is a factor entering into the calculations of both coalitions. So, side by side with the war parties in both coalitions who advocate an offensive to crush Soviet Russia, there are other elements supporting this policy.

The Soviet Government, having decided to conduct a policy of waiting, of maneuvering, for it is not anxious for military revenge, but is convinced that the social changes called forth by the war will lead to new relations between the nations, was compelled to yield, even after Brest, to force of arms, and also to take into account in its foreign policy the influence of elements acting against the war parties. These elements are weak, and we are not yet in a position to reinforce their influence with our own military power; the revolutionary proletarian movement, which is growing everywhere, has not yet reached the point of explosion, and therefore the report which we have to give is a grave report, a report on our retreats, a report of great sacrifices made in order to give Russia the opportunity of recuperating, of organizing its forces, and awaiting the moment when the proletariat of other countries will help us to complete the socialist revolution we began in October.

10/Report to the Seventh All-Russian Congress of Soviets of Workers', Peasants', Red Army, and Cossack Deputies   *December 5, 1919*

V. I. LENIN

We have always said, both before the October Revolution and during the October Revolution, that we consider ourselves, and can consider ourselves, only as one of the detachments of the international army of the proletariat, a detachment that assumed an advanced position not only because of the development and training it had received, but because of the unique conditions existing in Russia; and that, therefore, the victory of the socialist revolution can be regarded as final only when the proletariat has triumphed at least in several of the advanced countries. And it is in this respect that we experienced most difficulty . . . We found out that the development of the revolution in the more advanced countries is much slower, much more difficult, and much more complex. This should not astonish us, for it was naturally far easier for a country like Russia to begin the socialist revolution than it is for advanced countries. But, at any rate, this slower, more complex, more zigzag type of development of the socialist revolution in Western Europe has confronted us with incredible difficulties. And first of all, one is inclined to ask: How can we explain the miracle that Soviet authority has managed to maintain itself in power for two years in a backward, poverty-stricken, and war-weary country, in spite of the obstinate struggle waged against it first by German imperialism, which was then considered as omnipotent, and then by the imperialism of the Entente, which a year ago settled accounts with Germany, knew no competitors, and lorded it over every country of the world without the smallest exception? Considered from the point of a simple calculation of forces, from the point of military strength, that is indeed a miracle, because the Entente was, and is, immeasurably more powerful than we. Nevertheless, what more than anything else distinguished the year under review is the fact that we gained a gigantic victory—so great a victory that one might perhaps, without exaggeration, say that *our main difficulties are already behind us.* However great may be the dangers and difficulties that still lie before us, the greatest are apparently behind us. We must clearly understand the reason for this and, what is more

V. I. Lenin, *Sochinenia,* 4th ed. (Moscow: Institute of Marx-Engels-Lenin, 1950), Vol. XXX, pp. 185–197, *excerpts.* Editor's translation.

important, correctly define our policy in the future, for the future will no doubt see other attempts by the Entente to repeat its intervention and, perhaps, there will again appear the old predatory alliance between international and Russian capitalists for the restoration of the power of the landlords and capitalists and for the overthrow of Soviet authority in Russia—in a word, an alliance whose aim will be to extinguish the hearth of the world socialist conflagration that the RSFSR has become.

When the history of the Entente intervention and the political lesson that we received are considered from this point of view, I can say that this period of history is divided into three main stages, in each of which we secured a profound and lasting victory.

The first stage, and the one that was naturally most accessible and easy for the Entente, was its attempt to defeat Soviet Russia by means of its own troops. Of course, after the Entente had defeated Germany it had armies of millions of men at its disposal, armies that had not yet openly declared for peace and had not yet recovered from the bugbear of German imperialism with which they had been frightened in every Western country. Of course, at that time, from the military point of view and from the point of view of foreign policy, it meant nothing for the Entente to take a tenth of its armies and send it to Russia. You must note that it had complete control over the seas, complete control over the navy. The transport of troops and supplies was entirely in its hands. Had the Entente, which hated us as only the bourgeoisie can hate a socialist revolution, succeeded at that time in throwing one-tenth of its armies against us, there is not the slightest doubt that the fate of Soviet Russia would have been sealed and would have had the same fate as befell Hungary.*

Why did the Entente fail to do this? It landed troops in Murmansk. The campaign in Siberia was undertaken with the aid of Entente troops, and Japanese troops still occupy a remote part of eastern Siberia, while the troops of all the states of the Entente were to be found, although not in large numbers, in every part of western Siberia. Then French troops landed in the south of Russia. This was the first stage of the international intervention in our affairs, the first attempt, so to speak, to strangle Soviet power with troops that the Entente took from its own armies, that is, the workers and peasants of the more advanced countries; these troops, moreover, were well-equipped, and, in general, as regards the technical and material conditions of the campaign, there was no demand that the Entente was not in a position to satisfy. There were no obstacles in its way. How then is one to explain the failure of this attempt? In the end the Entente was obliged to withdraw its troops from Russia, because these troops proved unfit

* [An attempted communist coup failed in 1919.—Ed.]

to carry on a struggle against revolutionary Soviet Russia. That, comrades, has always been our chief and fundamental argument. From the very beginning of the revolution we have said that we represent the party of the international proletariat and that, no matter how great the difficulties of the revolution were, a time would come—and at the most crucial moment—when the sympathy and the solidarity of the workers oppressed by international imperialism would make themselves felt. For this we were accused of utopianism. But experience has shown that if we cannot always depend on action being taken by the proletariat and if we cannot always depend on all the actions it takes, it can nevertheless be said that these two years of world history have proved that we were a thousand times right . . . in spite of our backwardness, in spite of the difficulties accompanying our struggle, the workers and peasants of England and France have shown themselves incapable of fighting us on our soil. . . .

After this first victory came the second stage in the intervention of the Entente in our affairs. At the head of every nation is a group of politicians who possess splendid experience, and who therefore, having lost one card, put their stakes on another, utilizing their domination over all the world. There is not a single country, there is not a single corner of the globe left where British, French, and American finance capital is not in fact in complete control. On this was based their new attempt. They attempted to compel the small states surrounding Russia, many of which had emancipated themselves and had received the opportunity of declaring their independence only during the period of the war—Poland, Estonia, Finland, Georgia, the Ukraine, and so forth —to wage war on Russia with the assistance of British, French, and American money. . . . The Entente met resistance bringing pressure on the small countries. The Finnish bourgeoisie (for example), which has stifled tens of thousands of Finnish workers during the White terror and knows that it will never be forgiven for having done so and that it is no longer supported by the German bayonets that gave it the opportunity to do so—this Finnish bourgeoisie hates the Bolsheviks with all the passion with which a plunderer of workers hates those who have thrown him off. Nevertheless, the Finnish bourgeoisie said to itself: "If we follow the instructions of the Entente, it means losing absolutely all hope of independence." And this independence had been granted them by the Bolsheviks in November 1917, when there was a bourgeois government in Finland. Thus, wide circles of the Finnish bourgeoisie wavered. We won the contest against the Entente because it had counted upon the small nations, yet, at the same time it had antagonized them . . . the small countries acted as we wanted them to act not because the Polish, Finnish, Lithuanian, and Latvian bourgeoisie derived any satisfaction in conducting their policy to the advantage of the Bolsheviks—that, of course, is nonsense—but because we were right in our definition of the universal-historical forces, namely, that either bestial capital would triumph and that, in such circumstances—no matter how democratic the republic—it would strangle every small nation of the world; or else the dictatorship of the proletariat would triumph, and only in this was there hope for the toilers and for all small, downtrodden, and weak nations. We showed that we were right not only in the theory, but also in the practice of world politics. . . .

This, comrades, the second stage of the international intervention, was our second historic triumph. In the first place, we deprived England, France, and America of their workers and peasants. Their troops would not fight against us. In the second place, we deprived them of these small countries, which are all against us and in every one of which a bourgeois government and not a Soviet government rules. . . .

But our successes did not stop with this . . . thirdly, within the Entente countries themselves we have started to deprive the Entente of the petty bourgeoisie and the educated middle classes that were formerly entirely hostile to us. [Lenin then read a declaration, signed by several leading French intellectuals, calling for an end to the Allied intervention in Russia.] . . . This is perhaps but a verbal expression of feeling on the part of a representative of the intelligentsia; but it may be said that this is our third victory over imperialist France, a victory won on French territory. That is what is shown by this declaration, a faltering and pitiful declaration in itself, but a declaration of the intelligentsia, who, as we have seen in tens and hundreds of instances, can make a million times more noise than their strength warrants, and who possess the ability of serving as a good barometer and of indicating whither the petty bourgoisie is tending.

Organizing for World Revolution

11/Statutes of the Communist International

Adopted at the Second Comintern Congress, August 4, 1920

The Communist International fully and unreservedly upholds the gains of the great proletarian revolution in Russia, the first victorious socialist revolution in the world's history, and calls upon all workers to follow the same road. The Communist International makes it its duty to support with all the power at its disposal every Soviet Republic, wherever it may be formed.

The Communist International is aware that for the purpose of a speedy achievement of victory the International Association of Workers, which is struggling for the abolition of capitalism and the establishment of Communism, should possess a firm and centralized organization. To all intents and purposes the Communist International should represent a single universal Communist Party, of which the parties operating in every country form individual sections. The organized apparatus of the Communist International is to secure to the toilers of every country the possibility at any given moment of obtaining the maximum of aid from the organized workers of the other countries.

For this purpose the Communist International confirms the following items of its statutes:

1. The new International Association of Workers is established for the purpose of organizing common activity of the workers of various countries who are striving towards a single aim: the overthrow of capitalism; the establishment of the dictatorship of the proletariat and of the International Soviet Republic; the complete abolition of classes; and the realization of socialism—the first stage of Communist society.
2. The new International Association of Workers has been given the name of The Communist International.
3. All the parties and organizations comprising the Communist International bear the name of the Communist Party of the given country (section of the Communist International).
4. The World Congress of all parties and organizations which form

U.S., Congress, House Committee on Un-American Activities, *The Communist Conspiracy,* 84th Cong., 2d sess. (1956), H. Rept. 2242, Part I, Section C, pp. 25–28, *excerpts.*

part of the Communist International is the supreme organ of this International. The World Congress confirms the programs of the various parties comprising the Communist International. The World Congress discusses and decides the more important questions of program and tactics, which are connected with the activity of the Communist International. . . .

5. The World Congress elects an Executive Committee of the Communist International which serves as the leading organ of the Communist International in the interval between the convention of World Congresses, and is responsible only to the World Congress.

6. The residence of the Executive Committee of the Communist International is every time decided at the World Congress of the Communist International.

7. A special World Congress of the Communist International may be convened either by regulation of the Executive Committee, or at the demand of one-half of the number of the parties which were part of the Communist International at the last World Congress.

8. The chief bulk of the work and greatest responsibility in the Executive Committee of the Communist International lie with the party of that country where, in keeping with the regulation of the World Congress, the Executive Committee finds its residence at the time. . . .

9. The Executive Committee is the leading organ of the Communist International between the conventions; the Executive Committee publishes in no less than four languages the central organ of the Communist International [the periodical *The Communist International*]. The Executive Committee makes the necessary appeals on behalf of the Communist International, and issues instructions obligatory on all the parties and organizations which form part of the Communist International. The Executive Committee of the Communist International enjoys the right to demand from the affiliated parties the exclusion of groups of members who are guilty of the infringement of international proletarian discipline, as well as the exclusion from the Communist International of parties guilty of the infringement of the regulations of the World Congress. In the event of necessity the Executive Committee organizes in various countries its technical and auxiliary bureaus, which are entirely under the control of the Executive Committee.

10. The Executive Committee of the Communist International enjoys the right to include in its ranks representatives of organizations and parties not accepted in the Communist International, but which are sympathetic towards communism; these are to have a consultative vote only.

11. The organs of all the parties and organizations forming part of the Communist International as well as of those which are recognized sympathizers of the Communist International, are obliged to publish all official regulations of the Communist International and of its Executive Committee.
12. The general state of things in the whole of Europe and of America makes necessary for the Communists of the whole world an obligatory formation of illegal Communist organizations along with those existing legally. The Executive Committee should take charge of the universal application of this rule.
13. All the most important political relations between the individual parties forming part of the Communist International will generally be carried on through the medium of the Executive Committee of the Communist International. In cases of exigency direct relations will be established, with the provision, however, that the ECCI shall be informed of them at the same time.
14. The Trade Unions that have accepted the Communist platform and are united on an international scale under the control of the ECCI, form Trade Union Sections of the Communist International. . . .

The End of Intervention: The Beginning of Coexistence

12/Speech at the Moscow Gubernia Conference

November 21, 1920

V. I. LENIN

When we raised the question of the tasks and conditions needed for the victory of the proletarian revolution in Russia three years ago, we always categorically stated that there could be no permanent victory unless it was followed up by a proletarian revolution in the West, and that a correct appraisal of our revolution was only possible from the international point of view. In order to achieve a permanent victory

V. I. Lenin, *On the Foreign Policy of the Soviet State* (Moscow: Progress Publishers, n.d.), pp. 294–297, *excerpts*.

we must achieve the victory of the proletarian revolution in all, or at any rate in several, main capitalist countries. After three years of desperate, stubborn struggle, we can see in what sense our predictions were or were not justified. They were not justified in the sense that there was no swift or simple solution of this problem. None of us, of course, expected that such an unequal struggle as the struggle of Russia against the whole of the capitalist world could drag on for three years. It turned out that neither side, the Russian Soviet Republic or the rest of the capitalist world, gained victory or suffered defeat, and at the same time it turned out that while our forecasts were not fulfilled simply, swiftly and directly, they were fulfilled insofar as we achieved the main thing—the possibility has been preserved for the existence of proletarian power and the Soviet Republic even in the event of the world socialist revolution being delayed. And in this respect it must be said that the Republic's international position is now such that it has provided the best and most precise confirmation of all our plans and all our policy.

That the military strength of the R.S.F.S.R. does not stand comparison with that of all the capitalist powers is obvious. In this respect we are very much weaker than they, but, nevertheless, after three years of war we forced nearly all these states to abandon the idea of further intervention. This means that what we conceived as being possible three years ago, while the imperialist war was still on, namely, a long drawn-out situation, without any final decision in favour of either side, has come about. And the reasons for this? It has not come about because we proved to be militarily stronger, and the Entente weaker, but because, throughout this period, the internal disintegration in the Entente countries intensified, whereas we, on the contrary, internally gained in strength. This has been confirmed and proved by the war. The Entente was unable to fight us with its own forces. The workers and peasants of the capitalist countries could not be forced to fight us. The bourgeois states managed to retain their bourgeois status at the end of the imperialist war. They managed to hold off and delay the crisis directly threatening them, but basically they so undermined their own position that, despite all their gigantic military forces, they had to acknowledge after three years that they were unable to crush the Soviet Republic with its almost non-existent military forces. It turned out, therefore, that fundamentally our policy and our predictions proved correct in everything and that indeed the oppressed people in any capitalist country were our allies, for it was they who stopped the war. We are in the position of not having gained an international victory, which for us is the only sure victory, but of having won conditions enabling us to coexist with capitalist powers who are now compelled to enter into commercial relations with us. In the course of the struggle we have won the right to an independent existence.

When we cast a glance at our international position as a whole, we see, therefore, that we have achieved tremendous successes, that we not only have a breathing-space but something much more significant. A breathing-space, as we understand it, is a brief period during which the imperialist powers have many times had an opportunity to make an attempt at renewing the war against us with greater strength. And today, too, we do not allow our attention to be distracted and do not deny the possibility of a future military intervention in our affairs by the capitalist countries. It is essential for us to maintain a state of military preparedness. But if we take a glance at the conditions under which we defeated all attempts by Russian counter-revolution and achieved the formal conclusion of peace with all Western states, it will be clear that we have more than a breathing-space—we have entered a new period in which we have, in the main, won the right to our international existence in the network of capitalist states. Internal conditions did not allow a single powerful capitalist state to hurl its army against Russia; this was due to the revolution having matured inside those countries which prevented them from conquering us as quickly as they might have done. There were British, French and Japanese armies on Russian territory for three years. There is no doubt that the most insignificant concentration of forces by these three powers would have been quite enough to win a victory over us in a few months, if not in a few weeks. We were able to hold that attack off only on account of disintegration among the French troops and the ferment that began among the British and Japanese. It is this divergence of imperialist interests that we have made use of all the time. We defeated the intervention only because their own interests kept them divided but consolidated and strengthened us. It was in this way that we obtained a breathing-space and made impossible the complete victory of German imperialism at the time of the Brest peace. . . .

We made a correct appraisal of the tension of the imperialist competition and said to ourselves that we must make systematic use of the discord between them to hamper their struggle against us.

13/On Foreign Trade Concessions   *December 21, 1920*

V. I. LENIN

Comrades, the question of concessions (to foreign countries) has created considerable excitement and even apprehension everywhere, not only in party circles and among the workers, but among the peasants as well. . . .

I think we must realize that on the question of concessions we cannot be guided only by revolutionary instinct. Weighing all sides of the question, we shall be convinced of the correctness of the policy that we have adopted—which consists of a continuation of concessions. . . .

If we look back at the past three years, from the point of view of the international situation of the Soviet republic, then we shall see clearly that we have been able to hold on and to win victories over the unprecedentedly powerful alliance of the Entente powers, supported by the White Guards, only because unity has never existed among these powers. We have been able to triumph till now only thanks to the serious disagreements among the imperialist powers and only because these disagreements have not been accidental party and domestic disagreements, but the result of deep-rooted, permanent differences of economic interests between the imperialist countries, which, standing firmly on the principle of private ownership of land and capital, cannot but follow a predatory policy designed to overthrow Soviet Russia. . . .

Our policy is to use the differences of the imperialist powers in order to make agreement difficult, or to make such agreement temporarily impossible. This has been the basic line of our policy for the past three years, which necessitated the signing of the Brest peace and an agreement with Bullitt—treaties concerning the peace and the armistice that were both extremely disadvantageous to us. This is the same policy line that has determined for us the decision to continue to use concessions. We are now giving America concessions in Kamchatka, which is not actually ours at present since it is occupied by Japanese troops. At the present moment we are not in a position to fight Japan. We are giving America a territory for economic utilization that is useless to us and where we lack naval and armed forces. By

V. I. Lenin, *Sochinenia*, 2d ed. (Moscow: State Publishing House, 1930), Vol. XXVI, pp. 5–14, *excerpts*. From Report on Concessions to the Communist Party Faction at the Eighth Congress of Soviets of the RSFSR, December 21, 1920. Editor's translation.

giving this we set American imperialism against Japan and the Japanese bourgeoisie, which are nearest to us and which still control the Far Eastern Republic.*

Our main interests in negotiating concessions are political. And recent events have shown that we have profited greatly from these concessions. . . .

We have a whole line of information showing that some capitalist countries are taking preparatory steps (to launching an attack against us), and one might say that the White Guards are laying the preliminary groundwork in all nations. Therefore, our main task is to reestablish trade relations, and to do this we must have at least part of the capitalists on our side.

In England the struggle has been going on for a long time. We have already profited, for representatives of this worst of all capitalist exploiting countries have come out in favor of a trade agreement with Russia . . . Our direct interest and our immediate duty is to support in every way the parties and groups that seek the negotiation with us of this agreement. . . .

Experience has shown only too well that only a socialist revolution can put an end to eternal wars. Thus, our policy does not attempt to incite war. We have done nothing, either directly or indirectly, that would justify war between Japan and America. All our propaganda and newspaper articles continually emphasize the truth, that war between America and Japan will be an imperialist war, as was the war between the English alliance and the German alliance in 1914; and that the socialists should not be concerned with the defense of the fatherland, but with the overthrow of the power of the capitalists and with the workers' revolution. But if we, who are doing all that we can to accelerate this revolution, find ourselves a weak socialist republic attacked by imperialist brigands, is it not correct to utilize the differences between them in order to make it difficult for them to unite against us? Of course such a policy is correct. We have followed it during the course of the past four years. The Brest treaty was the main manifestation of this policy. While German imperialism was fighting, we, utilizing the antagonisms among the imperialists, were able to hold on even when the Red Army had not been created. . . .

* [The Far Eastern Republic consisted of what are now the Maritime and Khabarovsk provinces of the Soviet Union and existed from April 1920 to November 1922. It was controlled by the Communist Party and was designed to serve as a buffer state between communist Russia and the noncommunist powers in the Far East, particularly the United States and Japan. With the end of the Allied intervention and the departure of Japanese troops from Vladivostok the Far Eastern Republic was dissolved and reincorporated into the RSFSR.—Ed.]

Our objective now is to obtain a trade agreement with England and start regular trade in order to purchase as soon as possible the machinery needed for our broad plan to rehabilitate our national economy. The sooner we do this, the greater will be our bases for becoming economically independent of the capitalist countries. Precisely now, when they burned themselves in the military invasion against Russia, they cannot think of quickly resuming the war; we must use the moment and direct our energy toward the objective of obtaining trade relations with the imperialist powers, even if the terms are high. We do not for a second believe that this will be but a temporary interruption. The experience of the history of revolutions, of large-scale conflicts, teaches us that wars, a series of wars, are inevitable. Such a question, as the existence of the Soviet republic side by side with the capitalist countries—the Soviet republic, surrounded by capitalist states —is so inadmissible from the capitalist viewpoint that all these countries will seize the first opportunity to resume the war. The peoples are now tired of the imperialist war, they threaten to revolt when a continuation of the war is suggested; but this does not preclude the possibility that the capitalists may resume their plan in a number of years. For this reason we must apply all our efforts to using the opportunity presented to us to conclude trade agreements. . . .

Our foreign policy, while we are alone and the capitalist world is strong, consists in utilizing existing antagonisms (of the capitalist world).

FOR FURTHER STUDY

Bradley, John. *Allied Intervention in Russia, 1917–1920.* New York: Basic Books, 1968.

Brinkley, George A. *The Volunteer Army and Allied Intervention in South Russia, 1917–1921.* Notre Dame, Ind.: University of Notre Dame Press, 1966.

Carr, Edward Hallett. *The Bolshevik Revolution, 1917–1923.* 4 vols. New York: Macmillan, 1950, 1952, 1953, 1954.

Carroll, E. Malcolm. *Soviet Communism and Western Opinion, 1919–1921.* Chapel Hill: University of North Carolina Press, 1965.

Chamberlin, William Henry. *The Russian Revolution, 1917–1921.* 2 vols. New York: Macmillan, 1935.

Deutscher, Isaac. *The Prophet Armed: Trotsky, 1879–1921.* New York: Oxford University Press, 1954.

Farnsworth, Beatrice. *William C. Bullitt and the Soviet Union.* Bloomington: Indiana University Press, 1967.

Gankin, Olga H., and Harold H. Fisher. *The Bolsheviks and the World War: The Origin of the Third International.* Stanford, Calif.: Stanford University Press, 1940.

Hulse, James W. *The Forming of the Communist International.* Stanford: Stanford University Press, 1964.

Kennan, George F. *Russia Leaves the War.* Princeton, N.J.: Princeton University Press, 1956.

_____. *The Decision to Intervene.* Princeton, N.J.: Princeton University Press, 1958.

Luckett, Richard. *The White Generals: An Account of the White Movement and the Russian Civil War.* New York: Viking, 1971.

Page, Stanley W. *The Formation of the Baltic States: A Study of the Effects of Great Power Politics upon the Emergence of Lithuania, Latvia, and Estonia.* Cambridge, Mass.: Harvard University Press, 1959.

Pipes, Richard. *The Formation of the Soviet Union: Communism and Nationalism, 1917–1923.* 2d ed. Cambridge, Mass.: Harvard University Press, 1964.

Reed, John. *Ten Days That Shook the World.* New York: Modern Library, 1935.

Reshetar, John S., Jr. *The Ukrainian Revolution, 1917–1920.* Princeton, N.J.: Princeton University Press, 1952.

Smith, C. Jay, Jr. *Finland and the Russian Revolution, 1917–1922.* Athens: University of Georgia Press, 1958.

Thompson, John M. *Russia, Bolshevism, and the Versailles Peace.* Princeton, N.J.: Princeton University Press, 1967.

Trotsky, Leon. *The History of the Russian Revolution.* Ann Arbor: University of Michigan Press, 1955.

Ullman, Richard H. *Anglo-Soviet Relations, 1917–1921.* 2 vols. Princeton, N.J.: Princeton University Press, 1961, 1968.

Wandycz, Piotr S. *Soviet-Polish Relations 1917–1921.* Cambridge, Mass.: Harvard University Press, 1970.

Warth, Robert D. *The Allies and the Russian Revolution.* Durham, N.C.: Duke University Press, 1954.

Wesson, Robert G. *Soviet Foreign Policy in Perspective.* Homewood, Ill.: Dorsey, 1969.

Wheeler-Bennett, John W. *The Forgotten Peace: Brest-Litovsk, March 1918.* New York: Morrow, 1939.

White, John Albert. *The Siberian Intervention.* Princeton, N.J.: Princeton University Press, 1950.

Zeman, Z. A. B. (ed.). *Germany and the Russian Revolution, 1915–1918: Documents from the Archives of the German Foreign Ministry.* New York: Oxford University Press, 1958.

3 accommodation and consolidation, 1921–1934

In the spring of 1921, the new period of Soviet foreign policy was initiated by three crucial events:

> . . . one affecting the domestic policy of the RSFSR, the second its foreign policy, and the third the prospects of revolution in the country where they had hitherto appeared brightest and most certain. In March 1921, after the Kronstadt rising, Lenin introduced the New Economic Policy; a trade agreement was concluded between the RSFSR and Great Britain; and a communist rising in Germany was heavily and ignominiously defeated.[1]

Desperately in need of time to rebuild their disrupted economy and frustrated by the failure of the communist uprising in Germany, the Bolsheviks conceded that the revolutionary tide in Europe had ebbed and that capitalism was entering an era of stabilization. They hoped to use this interregnum to develop Russia's strength for the uncertain future. To promote economic development, the New Economic Policy was instituted, foreign capital welcomed, and trade pacts negotiated. On the diplomatic level, Lenin sought to safeguard Russia from a feared coalition of capitalist powers intent upon another intervention and the overthrow of the Bolshevik regime. To end Russia's isolation therefore became a paramount concern of Bolshevik diplomacy. This was accomplished, first in Europe, then in Asia. The Bolsheviks accepted their new frontiers (see map).

A beginning had been made through the negotiation of the British-Russian trade agreement of March 16, 1921. Germany, however, offered even greater promise. On May 6, 1921, a trade agreement was con-

ARCTIC OCEAN

0   400 miles

Murmansk

NORWAY

SWEDEN

FINLAND

Leningrad

ESTONIA

BALTIC SEA

LATVIA

DENMARK

E. PRUSSIA

LITHUANIA

Moscow

G E R M A N Y

Berlin

Warsaw

POLAND

UNION OF SOVIET SOCIALIST REPUBLICS

CZECHOSLOVAKIA

AUSTRIA

HUNGARY

BESSARABIA

ROMANIA

ADRIATIC SEA

YUGOSLAVIA

BLACK SEA

BULGARIA

KARS

ITALY

ALBANIA

TURKEY

GREECE

SYRIA

IRAQ

MEDITERRANEAN SEA

PALESTINE

TRANS-JORDAN

SAUDI ARABIA

Russia and Europe, 1921

Areas of the Former Russian Empire Lost as a Result of World War I:
Finland, Estonia, Latvia, and Lithuania; the Russian Province of Poland
(Which Became Part of the Reestablished Nation of Poland);
Bessarabia (to Romania); and Kars Province (to Turkey)

cluded and soon supplemented by secret military discussions.* The German High Command desired to circumvent the restrictions of the Versailles Treaty and to train military personnel on Soviet territory; the Soviets, in turn, desired the help of German experts in building up Russia's military and industrial strength.

Russia and Germany had been invited to the Genoa Economic Conference, called by British Prime Minister Lloyd George in an effort to restore Europe's shattered economy. While there, on Easter Sunday, April 16, 1922, the Soviet and German foreign ministers—Chicherin and Rathenau—met at Rapallo, near Genoa, and signed an agreement of far-reaching import for European politics. Initial British and French surprise gave way to dismay. Rapallo marked the first significant diplomatic triumph achieved by the Bolsheviks through the astute use of traditional balance-of-power techniques. This rapprochement between the two pariahs of Europe ended their isolation and enhanced immeasurably their diplomatic bargaining position. For France and Britain it signified, though they were not then aware of it, the end of political preeminence on the continent of Europe. The scale was shifting toward a new balance of power.

By the Treaty of Rapallo the Kremlin obtained de jure recognition from Germany, a mutual cancellation of existing financial claims, and the regularization and expansion of German-Soviet trade (reading 14). Clandestine military collaboration followed.[2] German missions experimented in Russia with advanced techniques of war forbidden them by the Versailles Treaty. The Soviets benefited from military information, from loans, and from the construction of modern tank and plane factories. Within the broader diplomatic struggle, Rapallo enabled the Soviets to forestall the anticipated capitalist coalition against them, their principal bogy in the interwar period.

The Versailles Treaty system had left both Germany and Russia isolated, the French-inspired cordon sanitaire (which consisted of French alliances with the small nations of Eastern Europe) being directed as much against the one as against the other. Each felt a strong need for an ally. At Rapallo each found a measure of strength and security. German-Soviet relations remained friendly until the rise of Hitler in 1933, though with fluctuating degrees of cordiality. For the Soviets in the 1920s Rapallo was particularly significant: in addition to ending their diplomatic isolation and ensuring their security against attack from a united capitalist world, it provided tangible economic and military benefits. For the Germans, bitter over the restrictive provisions

* There is an interesting parallel between the events of 1921–1922 and those of 1939. For just as the commercial agreement of May 1921 was the forerunner of the Rapallo Treaty, so did the discussions for an economic accord in the summer of 1939 serve to veil the preliminary conversations which culminated in the Nazi-Soviet Nonaggression Pact of August 23.

of the Versailles Treaty, the loss of territory in the east, the harsh schedule of reparations, and the "war guilt" clause, it was a means of developing economic and military strength. General von Seeckt's secret negotiations during the crucial 1920–1922 period received the support of various influential factions and even the tacit approval of the anti-militaristic Social Democrat President, Ebert. Power politics outweighed ideological and political differences and made the Rapallo agreement a necessity for both.

Rapallo also spotlighted ideological differences between the left and right wings of the Russian Communist Party—between the school of permanent revolution and that of temporary stabilization. Both schools believed that a communist Germany was necessary for Soviet survival, but differed over the tactics to be used. The Comintern, headed by Zinoviev, who was supported by Trotsky and Kamenev, advocated a more aggressive policy of promoting revolution by the German Communist Party, with a concomitant de-emphasis of the Rapallo Treaty. Lenin, Chicherin, and Radek, on the other hand, favored more elaborate negotiations with the German government and reliance on Rapallo. The German Communist Party's failure at revolution in 1923 split that party and laid it open to unquestioned domination by the Kremlin-controlled Comintern. It also contributed to Zinoviev's downfall in his power struggle with Stalin. The once powerful German Communist Party became, as other foreign communist parties were to become under Stalin, a docile, expendable instrument to be manipulated by Moscow.

On October 5, 1925, with the signing of the Locarno Treaty, a pact of mutual security with France and Britain, Germany embarked on Foreign Minister Stresemann's pro-Western policy of "fulfillment." To quiet Moscow's alarm, specifically her fears of German entry into an anti-Soviet bloc, Germany signed the Berlin Treaty of April 24, 1926, with Russia. It ran for five years and was subsequently extended for an additional three-year period. Friendship with the USSR continued to have a strong attraction for the German military and the big Ruhr industrialists. The Soviets, however, insisted on according to Rapallo an importance unwarranted in view of Europe's fluctuating politics. For them, it seemed to provide the firmest guarantee for their national security among the available political alternatives. It did remain a vital security link, but only until the advent of Hitler's aggressive expansionist policies.

In addition to relying upon friendly relations with Germany, the Soviet leaders endeavored to establish close relations with other nations on a bilateral basis. Shunned by the League of Nations, they did not rest their security upon that organization's ability to preserve the peace. On the contrary, the Soviets regarded the League as a "masked league of the so-called Great Powers, who have appropriated to themselves the right of disposing of the fate of weaker nations" and as serving as "a cover for the preparation of military action for the further suppression of small and weak nationalities" (reading 15). Even after joining the League in 1934, the Kremlin appeared to base its principal hopes for a viable collective security system on direct agreement with France and Britain, rather than on any multilateral League action.

In quest of allies, two approaches were utilized. First, the Soviet Government sought to obtain diplomatic recognition. Of particular significance was the de jure recognition granted by Britain's first Labour Cabinet on February 2, 1924.* This set off a chain reaction, and by late 1924 every major power except the United States had recognized the Soviets. Second, to ensure that the nations on her western borders would not serve as a staging ground for an interventionist-minded capitalist coalition, the Soviet government sought to neutralize them by treaties of nonaggression and nonintervention. It desired, in effect, to undermine the French alliance system in Eastern Europe. Aided by Poland's grandiose pretensions to great power status and the fears these engendered among the Baltic countries, Moscow succeeded in negotiating a treaty of friendship and neutrality with Lithuania in 1926 and a trade pact with Latvia in 1927. Not until after the Kellogg-Briand Pact of 1928 outlawing war, however, were the Soviets also able to induce Poland, Romania, and Estonia to agree to treaties of nonaggression. On February 9, 1929, the East Pact, or oft-called Litvinov Protocol, was signed with these nations in Moscow. At the time Soviet diplomats considered it a signal achievement, for it ensured that no aggressive bloc would use Eastern Europe as a base for an invasion of the Soviet Union. The East Pact, however, did little in a positive sense to promote Soviet power in the area.

Soviet influence in Eastern Europe was of little consequence prior to 1939. The countries of Eastern Europe were united in their mistrust and fear of Bolshevik policy, ideology, and objectives, but in little else. The Versailles system of economic and political fragmentation in Eastern Europe did little to encourage cooperative approaches to mutual problems; and since the USSR did not pose any immediate military threat, being preoccupied with grave internal problems, the nations of the area took no important measures to improve relations with the neighboring colossus. Trade between the USSR and Eastern Europe remained insignificant; political ties were weak and proved incapable of fostering a common front against the resurgence of an aggressive Ger-

---

* In November of the same year, a successor Conservative Party Cabinet temporarily broke off diplomatic relations and denounced all existing treaties with the USSR over an alleged plot by Zinoviev to take advantage of British labor troubles and foment revolution. Though the "Zinoviev letter" was never proven to be authentic, it took a return to power of the Labour Party to bring about a resumption of diplomatic relations in December 1929.

many. Russia's traditional interests in Eastern Europe were ignored in the councils of Europe, and all major steps affecting the area in the interwar period were taken without Soviet participation. This exclusionist policy Stalin was to overturn after World War II, with momentous consequences for all of Europe.

The Soviets also sought to strengthen their national security through use of the Comintern. Local communist parties tried to undermine legitimate governments, agitate against groups deemed hostile by Moscow, and promote revolutionary activities. At times this presented the Kremlin with a basic policy dilemma: Soviet diplomacy sought to take advantage of divisions within the capitalist world and to produce such splits where possible and, at the same time, to acquire allies in the very capitalist countries it was alienating through the revolutionary activities of the Comintern.

In this fashion the goal of ultimate and complete security, to be gained after the victory of the proletarian revolution in the more important capitalistic countries, came into conflict with the goal of immediate security, to be obtained only with the acceptance of questionable allies.[3]

In Asia, meanwhile, revolutionary developments attracted Bolshevik attention, particularly to China. The Bolshevik revolution and communist ideology introduced a new, dynamic force into the Far Eastern scene. Its impact was widespread and profound, especially in China where the breakdown of central government authority and the mushrooming political ferment among intellectuals assured an eager receptivity for ideas promising national independence, rapid industrialization and transformation of society, and liberation from foreign domination. Bolshevik propaganda sedulously cultivated these aspirations.

In July 1919 the Bolsheviks in a general declaration to the Chinese people had solemnly renounced all former Czarist privileges in China.* Because of unsettled conditions in Siberia, the declaration did not reach China until March 1920, but its impact then was enormous, especially among the intelligentsia and students who were openly disgruntled over the arbitrary assignment at Versailles of former German interests in Shantung to Japan.[4]

Contact between Sun Yat-sen, founder of the Kuomintang, who had established a regime in Canton rivaling that of Peking, and the Comintern was effected briefly in 1921. Bolshevik efforts to obtain diplomatic recognition from Peking had foundered in the previous year over Soviet reluctance to relinquish all claims to Outer Mongolia and northern

* However, the Bolsheviks were careful to remain vague about the future status of the Chinese Eastern Railway, which had been Russian owned since the 1890s. For an excellent article on this issue see Allen S. Whiting, "The Soviet Offer to China of 1919," *Far Eastern Quarterly* (August 1951).

Manchuria, areas of former Czarist interest and control over which Moscow had succeeded in reestablishing a semblance of authority.[5] The Bolsheviks therefore directed closer attention to the revolutionary Sun Yat-sen and the Kuomintang, which offered the promise of a richer political harvest. Accordingly, it was in China that cooperation with bourgeois national movements, a policy advocated by Lenin at the Second Comintern Congress in 1920, was given its first test.

By 1923 the Soviet position in the Far East had been improved, albeit inadvertently, as a consequence of the Washington Conference (November 12, 1921–February 6, 1922). Though not invited, despite its protest that as a Far Eastern Power it should have a voice in matters affecting the area's future, Moscow, in a twist of irony for which history is often noted, emerged as the principal beneficiary. The Conference persuaded the Japanese to withdraw their remaining troops from Siberia and also effected the termination of the Anglo-Japanese alliance. The result was a shift in the Far Eastern balance of power in Russia's favor.

In January 1923 Moscow sent A. A. Joffe, the peripatetic Comintern agent, to Sun Yat-sen. They met in Shanghai and issued a Joint Manifesto (reading 16). This marked the start of the period of collaboration between the Soviet Union and the Kuomintang. The Manifesto acknowledged that "because of the nonexistence of conditions favorable to their successful application in China, it is not possible to carry out either Communism or even the Soviet system in China . . . and [China's] most pressing problems are the completion of national unification and the attainment of full national independence." It also postponed final disposition of the Chinese Eastern Railway and Outer Mongolia. In general, the Joffe-Sun agreement guided Soviet policy in China until 1927, and, at the behest of Stalin and Bukharin, Moscow henceforth supported Canton against Peking. Soviet advisers flocked to aid the Kuomintang (known as the KMT): General Blucher (Galen) helped found the Whampoa Military Academy; and Michael Borodin, perhaps the most important of all the Soviet agents in China, revitalized the Kuomintang party apparatus along Bolshevik lines. The organizational and political techniques introduced by the Soviets overshadowed their meager financial and material aid. In a preview of the future "popular front" tactic, Moscow sanctioned membership by Chinese communists in the Kuomintang, but only as individuals. The communist party preserved its identity and continued to exist as a party within a party.* Though the partnership

---

* The Chinese communist movement was founded by two Peking University professors, Chen Tu-hsiu and Li Ta-chao, who were attracted to Marxism and Lenin's doctrine of imperialism because they provided the means of "judging and criticizing the capitalist West from a western point of view." For a superb, sophisticated discussion see Benjamin L. Schwartz, *Chinese Communism and the Rise of Mao* (Cambridge, Mass.: Harvard University Press, 1951). The Chinese Communist party itself was officially established in July 1921.

proved to be fleeting, Russia succeeded in entering the mainstream of the Chinese revolution.

In May 1924, Moscow and Peking negotiated a series of diplomatic agreements, covering a wide range of issues, which were later upheld by the Kuomintang when it extended its control over North China. They called among other things for Soviet troop withdrawal from Outer Mongolia, recognition of the area as an integral part of China, and joint administration of the Chinese Eastern Railway pending a permanent settlement.* The Soviets also renounced extraterritoriality and other formerly held special privileges. Notwithstanding these concessions, the Soviet Union forced Chinese recognition of autonomy for Outer Mongolia, thus giving new expression to former Czarist interests in the area. (Indicative of Kremlin control was the fact that after 1928 Outer Mongolia was included in the Soviet Five Year Plan.) A Moscow-sponsored "People's Republic" was proclaimed shortly thereafter. In addition, "by providing the sole military and financial support for the fledgling regime, Russia assured itself of a loyal area on its vastly extended, poorly protected Asian flank."[6] Hence, Moscow's policy in Outer Mongolia, as in Manchuria, was an amalgam of security considerations and imperialist ambitions.

A vital conciliatory link with the Kuomintang disappeared when Sun Yat-sen died on March 12, 1925, and was quickly succeeded by Chiang Kai-shek. A year later, concerned over the growing influence of the left and communist wings of the Kuomintang and intent upon ending the confusion of competing factions, Chiang Kai-shek acted suddenly, arresting and executing several key communists. Within a month he moved in a similar fashion against the right. Throughout this purge of the opposition, he took care to reaffirm his continued fidelity to the alliance with Moscow. Despite the open plight of the Chinese communists, Stalin did nothing. Thus local communist party interests were once again sacrificed, as they had been in Germany, in order to promote Soviet interests and security. The possibility that China's national renaissance and "1917" might be at hand and the decidedly pro-Marxist sympathies of many Kuomintang leaders encouraged Stalin to consider the situation more favorable to the cause of communism than it actually was. This self-imposed myopia could no longer be justified, however, after the even harsher crackdown on the communists in April and May

---

* The Soviets, in implementing this phase of the agreement, managed to obtain operational control of the Chinese Eastern Railway and thus preserved their interests in Manchuria. Fighting broke out in 1929 along the railroad between Soviet and Chinese troops in a test of Soviet determination to remain in North China. Finally, in 1935, Moscow sold its interest in the Railway to Japan as part of its policy of appeasement in the Far East.

1927, which presaged the eclipse of Soviet influence in China for more than a generation.*

In his military campaign to unify China, Chiang Kai-shek captured Nanking and Shanghai in April 1927. A few days later he arrested local Shanghai communist leaders and brutally suppressed the attempt of the city's proletariat to establish a communist government. Moscow maintained its silence and persisted in efforts to continue the alliance with the Kuomintang. Mass revolutionary action was discouraged. But new suppressions in May finally ended the collaboration. Thus Moscow's initial attempt to communize China was thwarted, as had been earlier similar efforts in Turkey and Iran.

The Peking Government, meanwhile, suspecting Soviet intrigue, had searched the Soviet embassy compound in April and discovered a number of highly subversive documents, which spelled out in great detail the scope of Comintern conspiratorial activities. They contained a list of Comintern agents, a resolution relating to the Chinese question passed earlier in the year by the Executive Committee of the Comintern (reading 17), and an analysis of the Chinese situation as viewed by Moscow. According to the Chinese government, the captured documents proved: (a) that the Soviet embassy had an extensive political and military secret service organization in China, which conducted espionage everywhere, even in the foreign legations in Peking; (b) "that the so-called Soviet advisers and military instructors in the south are members of the various Councils of the Kuomintang and the Communists . . . and that they were paid by the Soviet Government through the Military Attaché in Peking"; and (c) that the Soviet government with its embassy in Peking acting as an intermediate agency was furnishing arms and munitions to the enemies of the (Peking) government to which its embassy was accredited. Publication of these documents occasioned sharp Soviet protests and denials concerning their authenticity.

By November Chiang Kai-shek had consolidated his control over the various dissident KMT factions, including the communists. The Soviet Government responded by breaking off diplomatic relations with Chiang's government in December 1927. Stalin, whose alliance with the Kuomintang not only had brought disaster to the party in China but threatened to undermine his position in the struggle for power with

---

* The story of the Soviet decline in China is a complex one, involving a number of interrelated conflicts—"the conflict between Chiang Kai-shek and Borodin, the conflict between the left and the right wings of the Kuomintang, the conflict between the Kuomintang as a whole and the Chinese Communists, the conflicts between the Comintern agents in China (notably Borodin and Roy), the conflict between Peking and Moscow, the conflict between Stalin and Trotsky, and the conflict between Soviet Russia and the Western Powers in China." Henry Wei, *China and Soviet Russia* (Princeton, N.J.: D. Van Nostrand Company, 1956), p. 64.

Trotsky, declared to a surprised Fifteenth Party Congress that capitalism's period of "stabilization" had come to an end and that the period of peaceful coexistence had been replaced by one of ominous and increased imperialist intervention against the USSR (reading 18). This interpretation, adopted and expanded by the Sixth Congress of the Communist International in September 1928, signified a return to a revolutionary line by the Comintern and to a lesser extent by the Soviet Union.

Soviet historians have since adjusted the pattern of events to cast Stalin's policy in a "correct" light, but whatever the interpretation, the fact remains that Comintern policy in China, as well as in other areas of Asia, was a failure. The year 1929 witnessed outbreaks of fighting in Manchuria, and war with China came dangerously close. By the end of the 1920s the Kremlin was on the defensive in Indonesia, India, Japan, and French Indochina, and communist influence in these areas remained marginal until the outbreak of World War II.

After the disappointments in China and elsewhere in Asia and the rupture with Great Britain, the Soviets searched abroad for new means of assuring their security. Internally they intensified the drive to develop "socialism in one country" and to accelerate industrial growth. Interpretations of international events continued to be presented (and formulated) within the Leninist framework, but "the Soviet Union proceeded to follow the typical balance of power pattern of cooperating with one power or group of powers against an opposing group, and shifting its alliances in accord with obvious national interests."[7]

Successive setbacks abroad, coupled with economic and party demands at home, led Stalin to adopt a cautious foreign policy for the Soviet Union, though at the same time he launched the Comintern on an ultrarevolutionary tack. These seemingly contradictory and confusing approaches were designed to promote Soviet security at a moment of increasing isolation. In September 1928, the Comintern elaborated the "hard" line at its Sixth Congress, which formulated the position of international communism in relation to the world situation (reading 19). The main principles enunciated remain in effect to this day. Specifically, they held that: (1) the Soviet Union is the citadel of world revolution— "she is the international driving force of proletarian revolution that impels the proletariat of all countries to seize power . . . she is the prototype of the fraternity of nationalities in all lands united in the World Union of Socialist Republics and of the economic unity of the toilers of all countries in a single world socialist economic system that the world proletariat must establish when it has captured political power"; (2) the preservation of the Soviet Union must be the primary concern of the international proletariat—"In the event of the imperialist states declaring war upon and attacking the USSR, the international proletariat must retaliate by organizing bold and determined mass action and struggle for the overthrow of the imperialist governments"; (3) all communist parties owe exclusive allegiance to Moscow. Local interests must be subordinated to the line set forth by the Comintern and the Soviet Union. The Congress concluded on an uncompromising note:

The Communists disdain to conceal their views and aims. They openly declare that their aims can be attained only by the forcible overthrow of all the existing social conditions. Let the ruling class tremble at a Communist revolution. The proletarians have nothing to lose but their chains. They have a world to win.

By eschewing all cooperation with reformist Social Democratic parties, now labeled "fascist" and considered the most dangerous foes of communism, Stalin introduced a disastrous exclusiveness which mortally split the German left and helped bring Hitler to power. His policy "paralyzed the political strength of the German working class when it alone could have barred Hitler's road to power."[8] Stalin, failing completely to comprehend the destructive dynamism of the Nazi movement, must bear considerable responsibility for what happened in Germany.

Militarily weak, and burdened with serious internal difficulties, the Soviet Union sought security in various ways. In the early 1930s, the USSR attempted to draw closer to the nations of Eastern Europe by negotiating nonaggression pacts with them. It also signed one, on November 29, 1932, with a France alarmed at the rising temper of German nationalism. These accords, however, did not provide any real measure of security for the Soviets; they merely provided the illusion of better relations. None ever developed into significant instruments of collective security. Russia still needed peace and this often-proclaimed desire was undoubtedly genuine. Though not a member of the League until 1934, it participated in several League-sponsored commissions seeking ways to decrease international tension.[9] At the Sixteenth Party Congress in June 1930, Stalin expressed what probably remained the *leitmotif* of his policy until 1939:

. . . a result of this policy (of negotiating nonaggression and trade pacts) is the fact that we have succeeded in maintaining peace, in not allowing the enemy to draw us into conflicts, in spite of a number of provocative acts and adventurist attacks on the part of the warmongers. We will continue to pursue this policy of peace with all our might and with all the means at our disposal. We do not want a single foot of foreign territory; but of our territory we will not surrender a single inch to anyone.

The desire for peace encompassed not only the absence of war but an expansion of economic relations as well. Having launched an ambitious

Five Year Plan that involved collectivization and industrialization crises, the Soviet Union looked to the West for the machinery and material required to build up its military and industrial strength. But the world depression bred an egocentric economic nationalism that militated against any really rational analysis of Soviet needs by the powers best equipped to help. Unable to rely on the United States, Great Britain, or France for expanded trade or loans, the USSR turned increasingly to Germany during the 1931–1934 period. But two events beyond the control of the Soviet leadership shaped its future and its foreign policy— the Japanese invasion of Manchuria and the triumph of Hitler in Germany. The latter was particularly crucial for it was to threaten the very existence of the Soviet state.

Faithful to the 1928 Comintern line, the German communists joined the ultranationalists in denouncing all efforts by the Weimar government to effect a rapprochement with the Western Powers. They aimed their heaviest fire at the Social Democrats and assisted the Nazis in undermining the operation of constitutional government by obstructionism and rowdyism in the Reichstag. Indeed, according to Max Beloff, "There is some evidence that early in 1931 a deliberate decision was taken to cooperate in the country with the Nazis in order to accelerate the destruction of the Social-Democratic Party and its organizations."[10] Hitler came to power, in great measure, through the assistance of the communists. After January 30, 1933, the policy of friendship with the Soviet Union was abandoned by Hitler until August 1939.

Moscow at first viewed Hitler's victory with mingled uncertainty, misunderstanding, and self-deception. It deluded itself as to the nature of Hitler's objectives and their implications for German foreign policy. While the Comintern talked of the imminence of proletarian revolution, Moscow carefully avoided giving the slightest provocation. The German Communist party was meekly surrendered as a sacrificial offering in a vain and costly attempt to convince Hitler of Russia's intent to remain aloof from any interference in German affairs. Rapallo was still formally operative, but German ratification, on May 5, 1933, of the protocol prolonging the 1926 Berlin Treaty was only partially reassuring. Stalin waited in silence and with growing anxiety, refraining for almost a year from any comment about events in Germany, thus adding to the confusion of an already sorely bewildered Comintern.

The German ambassador in Moscow, Herbert von Dirksen, favored friendship with the Soviet Union and repeatedly urged Berlin to allay Moscow's rising insecurity by a forthright statement of peaceful intent. In a secret dispatch to the Foreign Ministry on February 20, 1933, he wrote:

An attitude of watchful waiting is being taken toward the new German Cabinet here. Basically it is hoped that the strength of their mutual interests will make possible the continuance of the present friendly policy. But the foundations of their mutual relations are felt to be unstable, both in a juridical and in a political respect; in a juridical respect, because the Berlin Treaty and the Conciliation Convention are not in force because they were not ratified; in a political respect because there have for some time been no statements of political intention on the part of the Reich Government with respect to its Russian policy, while toward France very positive statements have been made by Germany in the past year. They are still haunted here by the story of the military alliance offered to France. The statements made by influential Germans privately to Soviet politicians regarding the unaltered course of Germany's Russian policy have, it is true, assuaged the strongest fears. But they could not take the place of the positive effect of a public statement by the German Government. There is also disappointment here over the fact that even the substitutes for such official government statements, such as friendly telegrams on special occasions or interviews of a positive nature on the part of Germany, have been omitted.[11]

His successor, Rudolf Nadolny, similarly urged cooperation with the Soviet Union—in vain. By late 1933 the Soviet Union had become sufficiently disenchanted and concerned over German policy to begin exploring ways of moving closer to the West. It signed a treaty of friendship with Italy, established diplomatic relations with the United States (which finally accorded recognition in November), and developed more cordial contacts with the French; and Foreign Minister Maxim Litvinov increasingly appeared at international conferences. Japanese expansion in the Far East and indications of Hitler's uncompromising anti-Soviet attitude had led the Kremlin to turn to the West.

At the Seventeenth Party Congress in January 1934, Stalin at last commented publicly on developments in Germany as well as on the over-all international situation (reading 20). His analysis, however, stopped far short of the harsh conclusions demanded by the events of the previous year. He appeared insensitive to the inherent threat posed by Nazism, preferring to regard it as likely to be short-lived. Throughout his speech, Stalin proffered the olive branch to Germany and tried to make unmistakable his desire for continued relations in the tradition of Bismarck and Rapallo.

In this connection some German politicians say that the USSR has now taken an orientation towards France and Poland; that from an opponent of the Versailles Treaty it has become a supporter of it, and that this change is to be explained by the establishment of the fascist regime in Germany. That is not true. Of course, we are far from being enthusiastic about the fascist regime in Germany. But fascism is not the issue here, if only for the reason that fascism in Italy, for example, has not prevented the USSR from establishing the best relations with that country. Nor is it a question of any alleged change in our attitude towards the Versailles Treaty. It is not for us, who have experienced the shame of the Brest Peace, to sing the praises of the Versailles Treaty. We merely do not agree to the world being flung into the abyss of a new war on account of that treaty. The same must be said of the alleged new orientation taken by the USSR. We never had any orientation towards Germany, nor have we any orientation towards Poland and France. Our orientation in the past and our orientation at the present time is towards the USSR, and towards the USSR alone. . . . And if the interests of the USSR demand rapprochement with one country or another which is not interested in disturbing peace, we adopt this course without hesitation.

But events soon compelled the Soviet Union to follow another path. The course of the next five years was determined not in Moscow or Paris or London, but in Berlin.

Hitler ignored Stalin's overtures. He proceeded to conclude a non-aggression pact with Poland, thus laying the diplomatic groundwork for the Nazi expansion of 1938–1939. This treaty bred suspicion and sharpened tension between France and Poland, between Czechoslovakia and Poland, and between Poland and the Soviet Union (which feared that Hitler was tempting the Poles with the old Pilsudski dream of annexing the Ukraine). It accelerated the increasingly evident withdrawal of France from Central Europe. In mid-1934, Hitler's purge of Roehm, his former co-conspirator; the death of Marshal Hindenburg, that senile fragment of Weimar legitimacy; and the Nazi assassination of the Austrian Chancellor Dollfuss, all denoted Hitler's growing dictatorial power. The shadows darkened ominously over Europe, and in the Kremlin fear of Germany forced Stalin to reappraise the course of Soviet foreign policy.

NOTES

1. Edward Hallett Carr, *The Bolshevik Revolution, 1917–1923* (New York: Macmillan, 1953), Vol. III, p. 225. The Riga Peace Treaty with Poland and a friendship pact with Turkey were also concluded at this time.

2. John W. Wheeler-Bennett, *The Nemesis of Power* (New York: St. Martin's, 1954), p. 130.

3. Barrington Moore, Jr., *Soviet Politics: The Dilemma of Power* (Cambridge, Mass.: Harvard University Press, 1950), p. 215.

4. Henry Wei, *China and Soviet Russia* (Princeton, N.J.: D. Van Nostrand Company, 1956), p. 18.

5. David J. Dallin, *The Rise of Russia in Asia* (New Haven, Conn.: Yale University Press, 1949), pp. 187–199.

6. Allen S. Whiting, *Soviet Policies in China, 1917–1924* (New York: Columbia University Press, 1954), pp. 250–251.

7. Moore, *op. cit.,* p. 214.

8. Isaac Deutscher, *Stalin: A Political Biography* (New York: Oxford University Press, 1949), p. 406.

9. The Soviet attitude toward the problem of disarmament is treated separately; see Chapter XI.

10. Max Beloff, *The Foreign Policy of Soviet Russia, 1929–1936* (New York: Oxford University Press, 1947), Vol. I, p. 62.

11. *Documents on German Foreign Policy: The Third Reich: The First Phase* (Washington, D.C.: Government Printing Office, 1957), Vol. I, p. 64.

The Soviet-German Rapprochement

14/Treaty Regarding Solution of General Problems

Rapallo, April 16, 1922

The German Government, represented by Reichsminister Dr. Walther Rathenau, and the Government of the RSFSR, represented by People's Commissar Chicherin, have agreed upon the following provisions:

I. The two Governments agree that all questions resulting from the state of war between Germany and Russia shall be settled in the following manner:

(a) Both Governments mutually renounce repayment for their war expenses and for damages arising out of the war, that is to say, damages caused to them and their nationals in the zone of war operations by military measures, including all requisitions effected in a hostile country. They renounce in the same way repayment for civil damages inflicted on civilians, that is to say, damages caused to the nationals of the two countries by exceptional war legislation or by violent measures taken by any authority of the state of either side.

(b) All legal relations concerning questions of public or private law resulting from the state of war, including the question of the treatment of merchant ships which fell into the hands of the one side or the other during the war, shall be settled on the basis of reciprocity.

(c) Germany and Russia mutually renounce repayment of expenses incurred for prisoners of war. The German Government also renounces repayment of expenses for soldiers of the Red Army interned in Germany. The Russian Government for its part, renounces repayment of the sums Germany has derived from the sale of Russian Army material brought into Germany by these interned troops.

II. Germany renounces all claims resulting from the enforcement of the laws and measures of the Soviet Republic as it has affected German nationals or their private rights or the rights of the German state itself, as well as claims resulting from measures taken by the Soviet Republic or its authorities in any other way against subjects of the German state or their private rights, provided that the Soviet Government shall not satisfy similar claims made by any third state.

III. Consular and diplomatic relations between Germany and the

Leonard Shapiro, *Soviet Treaty Series* (Washington, D.C.: Georgetown University Press, 1950), Vol. I, pp. 168–169, *excerpts*. Reprinted by permission of the Georgetown University Press.

Federal Soviet Republic shall be resumed immediately. The admission of consuls to both countries shall be arranged by special agreement.

IV. Both Governments agree, further, that the rights of the nationals of either of the two Parties on the other's territory as well as the regulation of commercial relations shall be based on the most favored nation principle. This principle does not include rights and facilities granted by the Soviet Government to another Soviet state or to any state that formerly formed part of the Russian Empire.

V. The two Governments undertake to give each other mutual assistance for the alleviation of their economic difficulties in the most benevolent spirit. In the event of a general settlement of this question on an international basis, they undertake to have a preliminary exchange of views. The German Government declares itself ready to facilitate, as far as possible, the conclusion and the execution of economic contracts between private enterprises in the two countries.

VI. Article I, Paragraph (b), and Article IV of this Agreement will come into force after the ratification of this document. The other Articles will come into force immediately.

The USSR and the League of Nations

15/Press Statement on the Soviet Union and the League of Nations   *November 23, 1925*

MAXIM LITVINOV

We regard the League of Nations, as before, not as a friendly association of peoples working for the general good, but as a masked league of the so-called Great Powers, who have appropriated to themselves the right of disposing of the fate of weaker nations. The fact that Germany, a defeated country that is in the military sense weak, is now entering the League, does not imply a change in the character of the League; it only

Jane Degras, *Soviet Documents on Foreign Policy* (New York: Oxford University Press, 1952), Vol. II, pp. 65–66, *excerpts*. Reprinted by permission of the Oxford University Press and the Royal Institute of International Affairs.

means that certain Powers are counting on using Germany to assist in carrying out their plans in general, and their hostile designs against the USSR in particular.

More than any other Government, the Soviet Government is interested in strengthening peace, on the basis of independence and self-determination for all nations. That is why it would welcome the creation of an international organization in which and through which every nation could realize its national sovereign rights and all nations could settle the differences arising between them by peaceful and friendly means. But less than any other Government does the Soviet Government see in the existing League of Nations an approximation to such an organization. Up to now the League of Nations has not in the slightest degree justified the hopes and expectations placed in it by its protagonists. It has not only failed even once to protect the rights and security of a small or weak nationality against coercion and the military verdict of stronger Powers, but on the chief question which is of vital interest to all mankind, and in particular to us, on the question of disarmament, it has not yet taken one single serious step.

The League is a cover for the preparation of military action for the further suppression of small and weak nationalities. To a considerable degree it is only a diplomatic *bourse,* where the strong Powers arrange their business and conduct their mutual accounts behind the back and at the expense of the small and weak nations. The USSR, as a state of the working masses, cannot take responsibility for the League of Nations, which sanctifies the enslavement and exploitation of foreign nations. Inspired solely by the desire to avoid any complications which might break the general peace, and in particular the progress of its great work of internal construction, and pursuing its policy of nonintervention in the internal affairs of other nations, the USSR does not feel the slightest desire to enter an organization in which it would have to play the part either of hammer or of anvil. In particular, the Soviet Government knows that it would then be confronted, in the form of partners or even of judges, with states, many of which have not even recognized it, and consequently do not even conceal their enmity toward it, and with others, even among those which have recognized it, which even now behave toward it with ill-concealed hostility.

You may therefore inform the public in your country that all the rumors of some kind of change in the Soviet Government's attitude to the League of Nations, and incidentally to Locarno, are without foundation, and that the Government of the USSR, like the Government of the United States, is firmly determined in the future as in the past, to stand aside from such organization.

Promise and Failure in China

16/Joint Manifesto *January 26, 1923*

SUN YAT-SEN AND A. A. JOFFE

1. Dr. Sun is of the opinion that, because of the nonexistence of conditions favorable to their successful application in China, it is not possible to carry out either Communism or even the Soviet system in China. M. Joffe agrees entirely with this view; he is further of the opinion that China's most important and most pressing problems are the completion of national unification and the attainment of full national independence. With regard to these great tasks, M. Joffe has assured Dr. Sun of the Russian people's warmest sympathy for China, and of (their) willingness to lend support.

2. In order to eradicate misunderstandings, Dr. Sun has requested M. Joffe to reaffirm the principles enunciated by Russia in its Note to the Chinese Government of September 27, 1920. M. Joffe accordingly reaffirmed these principles, and categorically declared to Dr. Sun that Russia is willing and ready to enter into negotiations with China on the basis of Russia's abandonment of all treaties, and of the rights and privileges (conceded by China) under duress, secured by the Tsarist Government from China. Among the above-mentioned treaties are included the treaties and agreements concerning the Chinese Eastern Railway.

3. Dr. Sun holds that the Chinese Eastern Railway question in its entirety can be satisfactorily settled only by a competent Sino-Russian Conference. But the key to the current situation lies in the fact that a *modus vivendi* ought to be devised for the administration of the said railway at present. Dr. Sun and M. Joffe are of the same opinion that the administration of this railway should be temporarily reorganized after an agreement has been reached between the Chinese and Russian Governments, but (on condition) that the real rights and special interests of either party are not injured. Dr. Sun also holds that the matter should be discussed with Chang Tso-lin.

4. M. Joffe categorically declares to Dr. Sun (and Dr. Sun is entirely satisfied with regard to this point): that it is not, and never has been,

Reprinted by permission of the publishers from *A Documentary History of Chinese Communism* by Conrad Brandt, Benjamin Schwartz, and John K. Fairbank (Cambridge, Mass.: Harvard University Press, 1952), pp. 70–71, *excerpts.*

the intention or the objective of the present Russian Government to carry out imperialistic policies in Outer Mongolia, or to work for Outer Mongolia's independence from China. Dr. Sun therefore does not deem the immediate evacuation of Russian troops from Outer Mongolia to be urgently necessary or to the real advantage of China. This is due to the fact that, the present Peking Government being weak and impotent, after the withdrawal of the Russian troops it would most likely be unable to prevent the activities of the Russian Whites from causing fresh difficulties for the Russian Government, thereby creating a situation even graver than that which exists at present.

17/Resolution Relating to the Chinese Question Carried at the Seventh Extended Plenary Session of the Executive Committee of the Communist International *Moscow, March 1927*

1. Imperialism and the Chinese Revolution

1. The Chinese revolution is one of the most important and powerful factors which disturbs the stabilization of capitalism. During the last two years imperialism has suffered in China considerable defeats, the results of which will produce a considerable influence on the exacerbation of the crisis of world capitalism. In consequence of the victorious advance of the National Army towards North China, the domination of the imperialists was practically undermined in half of the country. . . .

2. The fundamental power of imperialism in China consists in the actual monopoly of everything that concerns the financial and industrial life of the country (the salt tax, the mortgage of the customs revenues, railways, waterways, mines, heavy industry—all this belongs chiefly to foreign capital). Should capitalism keep this solid base, it will find in China a serious support in the matter of stabilization of capitalism. Owing to its huge population, China is a market with boundless

This document was received by the Soviet Military Attaché in Peking on March 28, 1927. The translation was made from a copy not damaged by fire, which was discovered after photographs of the damaged document had been made. See *Chinese Social and Political Science Review*, 11 (1927), Public Documents Supplement, pp. 169–177, *excerpts*.

possibilities. It may become a most profitable field for the investment of capital, provided the necessary political guarantees are secured. The enormous resources of raw materials are hardly touched in China. Therefore imperialism will make desperate efforts to crush the Chinese revolution which threatens to overthrow it. If it does not succeed in crushing the latter by means of its traditional method—the provocation of civil war—or possibly by means of armed intervention, imperialism will try to frustrate the national movement of liberation which develops alongside the revolution. . . .

3. From the international point of view the Chinese revolution, be it but for its anti-militaristic character, is an essential part of the international revolution. This fact is connected in China with the following most important circumstances which favor the further development and deepening of the Chinese revolution:

(a) The competition of the imperialistic powers in China which weakens the position of world imperialism.
(b) The crisis of world capitalism.
(c) The growth of the proletarian movement in Western Europe. . . .
(d) The development of the national-revolutionary movement in the colonies which doubtless will still more increase under the influence of the further development of the Chinese revolution.
(e) The fact that proletarian dictatorship exists in the USSR in connection with close geographical proximity of the latter to China and the geographical remoteness of China from the basic centers of the economic and military-political power of the imperialistic powers.

4. Parallel with the rapid development of the national revolutionary movement, the social forces participating in it are involved in a no less rapid process of regrouping.

The national revolution in China develops under such peculiar conditions that it differs substantially from the classical bourgeois revolutions of the Western European states of the past century, as well as from the revolution of 1905 in Russia. The chief of these peculiarities is the semi-colonial position of China, which is dependent on foreign imperialism. . . .

5. The consecutive stages of development of the revolutionary movement in China are characterized by serious regrouping of the social forces. During the first stage one of the chief motive powers consisted of the national bourgeoisie and the bourgeois intelligentsia who sought the support of the proletariat and the petty bourgeoisie.

In the second stage the character of the movement changes and its social base is shifted to another grouping of classes. New and more revolutionary forms of the struggle are developing. On the Chinese area a new factor of the highest order appears in the person of the laboring class.

The economic strikes grow into a political struggle against imperialism and become most important from the historic point of view. The proletariat forms a bloc with the peasantry, which enters into an active struggle for its interests, as well as with the petty town bourgeoisie and a part of the capitalistic bourgeoisie. This combination of forces brought about a politically corresponding grouping of parties in the Kuomintang and the Canton Government. At present the movement is on the threshold of the third stage and on the eve of a new regrouping of the classes. At this stage of the development the motive forces of the movement will be a bloc—of a still greater revolutionary character —the bloc of the proletariat, the peasantry and the petty town bourgeoisie, while the greater part of the big capitalistic bourgeoisie will be excluded. . . .

6. Parallel to the grouping of the class forces of the revolution the forces of the counterrevolution also take shape. . . .

General Prospects of the Chinese Revolution

7. The general prospects of the Chinese revolution become very clear when the grouping of the classes is considered from this point of view. Although, historically speaking, the Chinese revolution at its present stage of development bears a bourgeois democratic character, it must get the character of a wider social movement. It is essential that the Chinese revolution should not result in the creation of such social-political conditions as would lead to a capitalistic development of the country. The Chinese revolution which is effected in the period of collapse of capitalism, is a part of the general struggle tending to overthrow capitalism and introduce socialism. The structure of a revolutionary state is defined by the class on which it is based. It will not be purely that of a bourgeois-democratic state. The state will be a democratic dictatorship of the proletariat, the peasantry and other classes that are being exploited. It will be a revolutionary anti-imperialistic government up to the time when it will develop into a noncapitalistic (socialistic) one.

The Chinese Communist Party must strain every nerve to realize in the end this revolutionary aim of taking the way to a noncapitalistic development. Otherwise, i.e., if the bourgeoisie obtains victory over the proletariat and the bourgeoisie that leads it, the power in the country will practically fall again into the hands of the foreign imperialists, even though in new forms of domination.

The Line Changes

18/Political Report of the Central Committee at the Fifteenth Congress of the CPSU   *December 1927*

JOSEPH STALIN

The International Policy of Capitalism and the Preparation of New Imperialist Wars

In this connection, the question of redividing the world and spheres of influence, which constitute the basis of foreign markets, is today the principal question in the policy of world capitalism. I have already said that the existing distribution of colonies and spheres of influence brought about as a result of the last imperialist war has already become obsolete. It now fails to satisfy either the United States, which, not being content with South America, is trying to penetrate Asia (primarily China); or Britain, whose dominions and a number of whose most important Eastern markets are slipping from her hands; or Japan, which every now and again is "obstructed" in China by Britain and America; or Italy and France, which have an incalculable number of "points of dispute" in the Danubian countries and in the Mediterranean; and least of all does it satisfy Germany, which is still bereft of colonies. . . .

Have attempts been made during the period under review to bring about a "peaceful settlement" of the maturing military conflicts? Yes, there have been more of them than might have been expected; but they have led to nothing, absolutely nothing. Not only that; those attempts have turned out to be merely a screen for the preparations that the "powers" are making for new wars, a screen intended to deceive the people, to deceive "public opinion." Take the League of Nations, which, according to the mendacious bourgeois press, and the no less mendacious Social-Democratic press, is an instrument of peace. What has all the League of Nations' talk about peace, disarmament, reduction of armaments led to? To nothing, except the deception of the masses, except new spurts in armaments, except a further aggravation of the maturing conflicts. Can it be regarded as accidental that although the League of Nations has been talking about peace and disarmament for three years, and although the so-called Second International has been giving its

Joseph Stalin, *Works* (Moscow: Foreign Languages Publishing House, 1954), Vol. X, pp. 282–298, *excerpts.*

support to this mendacious talk for three years, the "nations" are continuing to arm more and more, expanding the old conflicts among the "powers," piling up new conflicts, and thus undermining the cause of peace? . . .

Is it not obvious that the growth of armaments is dictated by the inevitability of new imperialist wars between the "powers," that the "spirit of war" is the principal content of the "spirit of Locarno"?

I think that the present "peaceful relations" could be likened to an old, worn-out shirt consisting of patches held together by a thin thread. It is enough to pull this thread fairly hard, to break it in some place or other, for the whole shirt to fall to pieces, leaving nothing but patches. It is enough to shake the present "peaceful relations" somewhere in Albania or Lithuania, in China or North Africa, for the whole "edifice of peaceful relations" to collapse.

That is how things were before the last imperialist war, when the assassination in Sarajevo led to war.

That is how things are now.

Stabilization is inevitably giving rise to new imperialist wars.

The State of the World Revolutionary Movement and the Harbingers of a New Revolutionary Upsurge

. . . the revolutionary awakening of the colonial and dependent countries presages the end of world imperialism. The fact that the Chinese revolution has not yet led to direct victory over imperialism cannot be of decisive significance for the prospects of the revolution. Great popular revolutions never achieve final victory in the first round of their battles. They grow and gain strength in the course of flows and ebbs. That has been so everywhere, including Russia. So it will be in China. . . .

The Stabilization of Capitalism Is Becoming More and More Putrid and Unstable

Whereas a year or two ago it was possible and necessary to speak of a period of a certain equilibrium and "peaceful coexistence" between the USSR and the capitalist countries, today we have every ground for asserting that *the period of "peaceful coexistence" is receding into the past,* giving place to a period of imperialist assaults and preparation for intervention against the USSR.

True, Britain's attempts to form a united front against the USSR have failed so far. The reasons for this failure are: the contradiction of interests in the camp of the imperialists; the fact that some countries are interested in economic relations with the USSR; the peace policy of the USSR; the counteraction of the working class of Europe; the imperialists' fear of unleashing revolution in their own countries in the event of war against the USSR. But this does not mean that Britain will abandon her efforts to organize a united front against the USSR, that she will fail to organize such a front. The threat of war remains in force, despite Britain's temporary setbacks.

Hence the task is to take into account the contradictions in the camp of the imperialists, to postpone war by "buying off" the capitalists and to take all measures to maintain peaceful relations.

We must not forget Lenin's statement that as regards our work of construction very much depends upon whether we succeed in postponing war with the capitalist world, which is inevitable, but which can be postponed either until the moment when the proletarian revolution in Europe matures, or until the moment when the colonial revolutions have fully matured, or, lastly, until the moment when the capitalists come to blows over the division of the colonies.

19/The Program of the Communist International

September 1928

The USSR [is] the base of the world movement of all oppressed classes, the center of international revolution, the greatest factor in world history. In the USSR, the world proletariat for the first time acquires a country that is really its own, and for the colonial movements the USSR becomes a powerful center of attraction. Thus, the USSR is an extremely important factor in the general crisis of capitalism, not only because she has dropped out of the world capitalist system and has created a basis for a new socialist system of production but also because she plays an exceptionally great revolutionary role generally; she is the international driving force of proletarian revolution that impels the proletariat of all countries to seize power; she is the living example proving that the working class is not only capable of destroy-

U.S., Congress, House Committee on Foreign Affairs, *The Strategy and Tactics of World Communism,* 80th Cong., 2d sess. (1948), H. Doc. 619, pp. 121–140, *excerpts.*

ing capitalism, but of building up Socialism as well; she is the prototype of the fraternity of nationalities in all lands united in the World Union of Socialist Republics and of the economic unity of the toilers of all countries in a single world socialist economic system that the world proletariat must establish when it has captured political power. . . .

In view of the fact that the USSR is the only fatherland of the international proletariat, the principal bulwark of its achievements and the most important factor for its international emancipation, the international proletariat must on its part facilitate the success of the work of socialist construction in the USSR and defend her against the attacks of the capitalist powers by all the means in its power. . . .

In the event of the imperialist states declaring war upon and attacking the USSR, the international proletariat must retaliate by organizing bold and determined mass action and struggle for the overthrow of the imperialist governments with the slogan of: Dictatorship of the Proletariat and alliance with the USSR.

In the colonies, and particularly the colonies of the imperialist country attacking the USSR, every effort must be made to take advantage of the diversion of the imperialist military forces to develop an anti-imperialist struggle and to organize revolutionary action for the purpose of throwing off the yoke of imperialism and of winning complete independence. . . .

The tasks of the Communist International connected with the revolutionary struggle in colonies, semi-colonies and dependencies are extremely important strategical tasks in the world proletarian struggle. The colonial struggle presupposes that the broad masses of the working class and of the peasantry in the colonies be rallied round the banner of the revolution; but this cannot be achieved unless the closest cooperation is maintained between the proletariat in the oppressing countries and the toiling masses in the oppressed countries. . . .

In order that revolutionary work and revolutionary action may be coordinated and in order that these activities may be guided most successfully, the international proletariat must be bounden by international class discipline. . . . This international Communist discipline must find expression in the subordination of the partial and local interests of the movement to its general and lasting interests and in the strict fulfillment, by all members, of the decisions passed by the leading bodies of the Communist International.

Unlike the Social-Democratic, Second International, each section of which submits to the discipline of "its own" national bourgeoisie and of its own "fatherland," the sections of the Communist International submit to only one discipline, i.e. international proletarian discipline, which guarantees victory in the struggle of the world's workers for world proletarian dictatorship. . . .

The Communists disdain to conceal their views and aims. They openly declare that their aims can be attained only by the forcible overthrow of all the existing social conditions. Let the ruling class tremble at a Communist revolution. The proletarians have nothing to lose but their chains. They have a world to win.

"Workers of all countries, unite!"

1934: The End of an Era

20/Report to the Seventeenth Congress of the CPSU *January 26, 1934*

JOSEPH STALIN

Comrades, more than three years have passed since the Sixteenth Congress. That is not a very long period. But it has been fuller in content than any other period. I do not think that any period in the last decade has been so rich in events as this one.

In the *economic* sphere these years have been years of continuing world economic crisis . . . While formerly people here and there still disputed whether there was a world economic crisis or not, now they no longer do so, for the existence of the crisis and its devastating effects are only too obvious. Now the controversy centers around another question: Is there a way out of the crisis or not; and if there is, then what is to be done?

In the *political* sphere these years have been years of further tension both in the relations between the capitalist countries and in the relations within them. Japan's war against China and the occupation of Manchuria, which have strained relations in the Far East; the victory of fascism in Germany and the triumph of the idea of revenge, which have strained relations in Europe; the withdrawal of Japan and Germany from the League of Nations, which has given a new impetus to the growth of armaments and to the preparations for an imperialist war;

Joseph Stalin, *Works* (Moscow: Foreign Languages Publishing House, 1955), Vol. XIII, pp. 288–312, *excerpts.*

the defeat of fascism in Spain,* which is one more indication that a revolutionary crisis is maturing and that fascism is far from being long-lived—such are the most important events in the period under review. It is not surprising that bourgeois pacifism is breathing its last and that the trend toward disarmament is openly and definitely giving way to a trend towards armament and rearmament.

It is easy to understand how difficult it has been for the USSR to pursue its peace policy in this atmosphere poisoned with the miasma of war schemes. . . .

What did the USSR rely on in this difficult and complicated struggle for peace?

(a) On its growing economic and political might.
(b) On the moral support of the vast masses of the working class of all countries, who are vitally interested in the preservation of peace.
(c) On the prudence of those countries which for one motive or another are not interested in disturbing the peace, and which want to develop trade relations with such a punctual client as the USSR.
(d) Finally—on our glorious army, which stands ready to defend our country against assaults from without.

It was on this basis that we began our campaign for the conclusion with neighboring states of pacts of nonaggression and of pacts defining aggression. You know that this campaign has been successful. As you know, pacts of nonaggression have been concluded not only with the majority of our neighbors in the West and in the South, including Finland and Poland, but also with such countries as France and Italy; and pacts defining aggression have been concluded with those same neighboring states, including the Little Entente (Czechoslovakia, Rumania, and Yugoslavia).

On the same basis the friendship between the USSR and Turkey has been consolidated; relations between the USSR and Italy have improved and have indisputably become satisfactory; relations with France, Poland, and other Baltic states have improved; relations have been restored with the USA, China, etc.

Of the many facts reflecting the successes of the peace policy of the USSR two facts of indisputably material significance should be noted and singled out.

1. I have in mind, firstly, the change for the better that has taken place recently in the relations between the USSR and Poland and between the USSR and France. In the past, as you know, our relations

[* The monarchy had been overthrown in 1931 and a republic set up.—Ed.]

with Poland were not at all good. Representatives of our state were assassinated in Poland. Poland regarded herself as the barrier of the Western states against the USSR. All the various imperialists counted on Poland as their advanced detachment in the event of a military attack on the USSR. The relations between the USSR and France were no better . . . But now those undesirable relations are gradually beginning to disappear. They are giving way to other relations, which can only be called relations of rapprochement . . . the atmosphere of mutual distrust is beginning to be dissipated. This does not mean, of course, that the incipient process of rapprochement can be regarded as sufficiently stable and as guaranteeing ultimate success. Surprises and zigzags in policy, for example in Poland, where anti-Soviet sentiments are still strong, can as yet by no means be regarded as out of the question. But the change for the better in our relations, irrespective of its results in the future, is a fact worthy of being noted and emphasized as a factor in the advancement of the cause of peace.

What is the cause of this change? What stimulates it?

Primarily, the growth of the strength and might of the USSR.

In our times it is not the custom to take any account of the weak—only the strong are taken into account. Furthermore, there have been some changes in the policy of Germany which reflect the growth of revanchist and imperialist sentiments in Germany.

In this connection some German politicians say that the USSR has now taken an orientation towards France and Poland; that from an opponent of the Versailles Treaty it has become a supporter of it, and that this change is to be explained by the establishment of the fascist regime in Germany. That is not true. Of course, we are far from being enthusiastic about the fascist regime in Germany. But fascism is not the issue here, if only for the reason that fascism in Italy, for example, has not prevented the USSR from establishing the best relations with that country. Nor is it a question of any alleged change in our attitude towards the Versailles Treaty. It is not for us, who have experienced the shame of the Brest Peace, to sing the praises of the Versailles Treaty. We merely do not agree to the world being flung into the abyss of a new war on account of that treaty. The same must be said of the alleged new orientation taken by the USSR. We never had any orientation towards Germany, nor have we any orientation towards Poland and France. Our orientation in the past and our orientation at the present time is towards the USSR, and towards the USSR alone. (*Stormy applause*) And if the interests of the USSR demand rapprochement with one country or another which is not interested in disturbing peace, we adopt this course without hesitation.

No, that is not the point. The point is that Germany's policy has changed. The point is that even before the present German politicians came to power, and particularly after they came to power, a contest began in Germany between two political lines: between the old policy, which was reflected in the treaties between the USSR and Germany, and the "new" policy, which, in the main, recalls the policy of the former German Kaiser, who at one time occupied the Ukraine and marched against Leningrad, after converting the Baltic countries into a *place d'armes* for this march; and this "new" policy is obviously gaining the upper hand over the old policy. The fact that the advocates of the "new" policy are gaining supremacy in all things, while the supporters of the old policy are in disfavor, cannot be regarded as an accident. . . .

2. I have in mind, secondly, the restoration of normal relations between the USSR and the United States of America. There cannot be any doubt that this act is of very great significance for the whole system of international relations. . . .

Such are the two main facts which reflect the successes of the Soviet policy of peace.

It would be wrong, however, to think that everything went smoothly in the period under review. . . .

Recall, say, the pressure that was brought to bear upon us by Britain; the embargo on our exports, the attempt to interfere in our internal affairs and to use this as a probe—to test our power of resistance. True, nothing came of this attempt, and later the embargo was lifted; but the unpleasant aftereffect of these sallies still makes itself felt in everything connected with the relations between Britain and the USSR. . . .

Nor must we lose sight of the relations between the USSR and Japan, which stand in need of considerable improvement. Japan's refusal to conclude a pact of nonaggression, of which Japan stands in no less need than the USSR, once again emphasizes the fact that all is not well in the sphere of our relations. . . . It is not difficult to understand that such circumstances cannot but create an atmosphere of uneasiness and uncertainty. Of course, we shall persistently continue to pursue a policy of peace and strive for an improvement in our relations with Japan, because we want to improve these relations. But it does not depend entirely upon us. That is why we must at the same time take all measures to guard our country against surprises, and be prepared to defend it against attack. . . . Those who want peace and seek business relations with us will always have our support. But those who try to attack our country will receive a crushing repulse to teach them in the future not to poke their pig snouts into our Soviet garden. (*Thunderous applause*)

FOR FURTHER STUDY

Angress, Werner T. *Stillborn Revolution: The Communist Bid for Power in Germany, 1921–1923*. Princeton, N.J.: Princeton University Press, 1963.

Beloff, Max. *The Foreign Policy of Soviet Russia, 1929–1936*. Vol. I. New York: Oxford University Press, 1947.

Borkenau, Franz. *World Communism*. Ann Arbor: University of Michigan Press, 1962.

Brandt, Conrad. *Stalin's Failure in China, 1924–1927*. Cambridge, Mass.: Harvard University Press, 1958.

Browder, Robert P. *The Origins of Soviet-American Diplomacy*. Princeton, N.J.: Princeton University Press, 1953.

Carr, Edward Hallett. *German-Soviet Relations Between the World Wars, 1919–1939*. Baltimore: Johns Hopkins Press, 1951.

_____. *Socialism in One Country 1924–1926*. Part 3, vol. II. New York: Macmillan, 1964.

Dallin, David J. *The Rise of Russia in Asia*. New Haven, Conn.: Yale University Press, 1949.

Deutscher, Isaac. *Stalin: A Political Biography*. New York: Oxford University Press, 1949.

Dyck, Harvey L. *Weimar Germany and Soviet Russia 1926–1933: A Study in Diplomatic Instability*. New York: Columbia University Press, 1966.

Eudin, Xenia, and Harold H. Fisher (eds.). *Soviet Russia and the West, 1920–1927*. Stanford, Calif.: Stanford University Press, 1957.

_____, and Robert C. North (eds.). *Soviet Russia and the East, 1920–1927*. Stanford, Calif.: Stanford University Press, 1957.

_____, and Robert M. Slusser (eds.). *Soviet Foreign Policy 1928–1934*. 2 vols. University Park: Pennsylvania State University Press, 1967.

Fischer, Louis. *The Soviets in World Affairs*. 2 vols. New York: Vintage, 1960.

_____. *Russia's Road From Peace to War 1917–1941*. New York: Harper & Row, 1969.

Freund, Gerald. *Unholy Alliance: Russian-German Relations from the Treaty of Brest-Litovsk to the Treaty of Berlin*. New York: Harcourt Brace Jovanovich, 1957.

Hilger, Gustav, and Alfred G. Meyer. *The Incompatible Allies*. New York: Macmillan, 1953.

Kochan, Lionel. *Russia and the Weimar Republic*. Cambridge, Eng.: Bowes and Bowes, 1954.

Kung-po, Ch'en. *The Communist Movement in China.* New York: Columbia University Press, 1960.

Lensen, George A. *Japanese Recognition of the USSR: Soviet-Japanese Relations, 1921–1930.* Tokyo: Sophia University, in cooperation with the Diplomatic Press, Tallahassee, Fla., 1970.

Lerner, Warren. *Karl Radek: The Last Internationalist.* Stanford, Calif.: Stanford University Press, 1970.

McKenzie, Kermit E. *Comintern and World Revolution, 1928–1943.* New York: Columbia University Press, 1964.

North, Robert C. *Moscow and Chinese Communists.* Stanford, Calif.: Stanford University Press, 1953.

Rosenbaum, Kurt. *Community of Fate: German-Soviet Diplomatic Relations, 1922–1928.* Syracuse, N.Y.: Syracuse University Press, 1965.

Schwartz, Benjamin. *Chinese Communism and the Rise of Mao.* Cambridge, Mass.: Harvard University Press, 1951.

Scott, William Evans. *Alliance Against Hitler: The Origins of the Franco-Soviet Pact.* Durham, N.C.: Duke University Press, 1962.

Thornton, Richard C. *The Comintern and the Chinese Communists, 1928–1931.* Seattle: University of Washington Press, 1969.

Whiting, Allen S. *Soviet Policies in China, 1917–1924.* New York: Columbia University Press, 1954.

4 the search for security, 1934–1941

Soviet entry into the League of Nations on September 18, 1934, marked a basic shift in Soviet foreign policy. It was one of the early manifestations of a determined effort to meet the growing threat of an expansionist-minded Germany and Japan and to end the increasing sense of isolation, through a system of collective security. The military resurgence of Germany in particular drew the USSR and the Western democracies closer in the face of the common danger. Cooperation foundered, however, on misunderstandings rooted in past antagonisms and suspicions and on a mutual ideological hostility that virtually precluded politically necessary adjustments. This failure was to bring tragedy to the Soviet Union and to all of Europe.

In the next few years the Soviet government emerged as a leading advocate of united League action. The address of Soviet Foreign Minister Litvinov, before the Assembly on the occasion of the USSR's becoming a member, set the pattern for subsequent Soviet disquisitions on the potential role of the League (reading 21). Litvinov acknowledged the early Soviet fear that the nations of the League "might give collective expression to their hostility towards the Soviet Union and combine their anti-Soviet activities," and he added that many of the League's decisions and activities were not looked upon with favor by the Soviet government. The Soviet Union, however, cognizant of the ominous danger posed by aggressive fascism, appreciated the urgent need to organize an effective collective security system and was convinced that, "with the firm will and close cooperation of all its Members a great deal could be done at any given moment for the utmost diminution of the danger of war."

But though using the League to mobilize resistance to aggressive fascism, the Soviet Union sought, at the same time, to vitalize its bilateral agreement with France. On December 5, 1934, a protocol—preliminary to a more extensive security agreement—was signed.

The departure of Germany from the League of Nations on October 14, 1933, and its unconcealed hostility toward the Soviet Union had forced the Soviet government to revise its previous assumption that only a Germany friendly to the Versailles victors threatened Soviet security.

The rapprochement between the Soviet Union and the Western democracies proceeded promisingly during the spring of 1935, with Anthony Eden's visit to Moscow in March and Pierre Laval's in May. Meanwhile, Hitler's courtship of Poland had added to Soviet fears. Moscow openly acknowledged the seriousness of the deterioration of relations with Germany. To cement the budding alliance system, the Soviet Union signed a Treaty of Mutual Assistance with France on May 2, 1935, and one with Czechoslovakia on May 16. France and the USSR pledged themselves to come to one another's assistance in the event of an unprovoked aggression.

The crucial treaty, on which so much of Europe's subsequent tragic history hinged, was that between the Soviet Union and Czechoslovakia. It contained a provision obligating the Soviet government to come to the aid of Czechoslovakia *only* if France acted similarly in fulfillment of its responsibility. Thus, the Czechoslovak-Soviet agreement stated that "The two Governments recognize that the undertakings to render mutual assistance will operate between them only in so far as the conditions laid down in the present Treaty may be fulfilled and in so far as assistance may be rendered by France to the Party victim of the aggression."[1] In 1938–1939, this escape clause, invoked apparently by France's failure to fulfill its written pledge to Prague, was instrumental in the capitulation and collapse of Czechoslovakia. Legally, the provision freed the Soviet Union from any obligation to aid Czechoslovakia; morally, it placed the burden of shame upon France.

Soviet entry into the League, implying a willingness to conform to the accepted pattern of international politics, required a shift in policy by the Communist International, because Soviet leaders were unwilling to dispense with so valuable an asset. At the Seventh (and last) Comintern Congress, in July and August of 1935, the Soviet Government preserved the Comintern by altering its policy in the interests of expediency and alliance with the Western democracies.

The main report was delivered by Georgi Dimitrov, the Bulgarian communist who had won world renown in 1933 for his courageous defense against the Nazi-manufactured charge that he was responsible for the burning of the Berlin Reichstag. Condemning fascism as the most reactionary and dangerous brand of imperialist capitalism, Dimitrov declared that no techniques should be overlooked in striving for its defeat. He turned to classical literature for an appropriate example of the new tactic of the "Popular Front."

> Comrades, you remember the ancient tale of the capture of Troy. Troy was inaccessible to the armies attacking her, thanks to her impregnable walls. And the attacking army, after suffering many sacrifices, was unable to achieve victory until with the aid of the famous Trojan horse it managed to penetrate to the very heart of the enemy camp.
>
> We revolutionary workers, it appears to me, should not be shy about using the same tactics with regard to our Fascist foe, who is defending himself against the people with the help of the living wall of his cutthroats.

Dimitrov discarded the thesis, adopted in 1928, that fascism and social democracy were twin evils and called for the creation of a Popular Front of all parties opposed to fascism (reading 22)—a radical departure from the previous injunction against cooperation with bourgeois parties. But the growing threat from an aggressive Germany overruled all possible objections, and a collective security system embracing the Soviet Union and the Western democracies was pushed. Dimitrov did emphasize, however, that all communist parties were to maintain their identities within the framework of the various Popular Fronts. The Comintern Congress adopted Dimitrov's report on August 20, 1935, and all communist parties moved to act in concert with antifascist parties, regardless of their ideological or political coloration. The Comintern also sought to blame Hitler's advent to power on the shortsightedness of the German Social-Democrats. Thus, the "big lie" was used to gloss over grievous errors of communist strategy, to nurture the myth of Stalin's infallibility, and to associate the Communist Party with the popular struggle against fascism. But the tactical switch adopted by Moscow in no way repudiated the revolutionary doctrines of the Sixth Comintern Congress of 1928. These remained the accepted tenets of world communism, awaiting new "objective situations" for their further utilization.*

The Popular Front policy and the collective security system were soon tested in the crucible of international politics. Both were found

---

* The Popular Front failed for a variety of reasons: the appeasement policy practiced by France and Great Britain at a time when resistance might have resulted in a meaningful cooperation with the USSR; the legacy of suspicion between the communists and their partners against fascism, which precluded any positive or extensive cooperation; the impact of the Soviet purges; and finally the sellout at Munich.

wanting. In October 1935, Italy invaded Ethiopia, as part of Mussolini's course of expansion. Litvinov called upon the League to punish the aggressor. But the Western democracies, fearful of pushing Italy into an alliance with Germany, refrained from any forceful action. As with Manchuria, the League failed to cope with aggression. Scarcely had the furor over Ethiopia subsided than there was a more direct challenge to the European system of collective security.

On March 7, 1936, Hitler marched into the Rhineland in violation of the Locarno Treaty (1925). That treaty's so-called corollary, the Rhine Pact, granted to France and Great Britain specific authority to act without awaiting League approval. But France was beset with one of its perennial cabinet crises and did nothing, despite offers of support from Britain and Poland. Hitler, with his uncanny political insight and sense of timing, had won his great gamble.* This move not only set Germany firmly upon the path to conquest and war, but also strengthened Hitler's power in Germany. The last potential restraint—the German General Staff—was cowed into silence and submission by his stunning success. The Kremlin undoubtedly viewed the French paralysis with concern, for it highlighted the lack of determination of the West to resist German remilitarization and expansion. Russia may also have begun to reappraise the attractiveness of the alliance with France. There is evidence that Moscow, at the time, surreptitiously renewed its efforts to negotiate a Rapallo-type treaty with Nazi Germany.

Events in Spain soon revealed still further the appalling vacillation and feebleness of the French and British. On July 19, 1936, with the newly formed French Popular Front government of Léon Blum scarcely two months old General Franco rose against the Spanish Republic. The Spanish Civil War of 1936–1939 accelerated the disintegration of the Popular Front, provided the first European battleground for World War II, and split Western European political circles so grievously that the effects are still evident today. It confronted Soviet leaders with a serious dilemma. Another fascist country bordering France might push Paris into more intimate ties with Moscow. On the other hand, though a Loyalist victory achieved with open communist support would undoubtedly enhance Soviet prestige, it might paradoxically frighten

---

* The German General Staff opposed Hitler's march into the Rhineland at this time, fearing French retaliation would lead to a reoccupation of the Ruhr and destroy the new Wehrmacht in its infancy. From captured government documents we know that the German Army had orders to withdraw at once if the French gave any indication of opposition. Paul Otto Schmidt, Hitler's personal interpreter, quotes him as saying that "If the French had marched into the Rhineland then we should have had to retreat with ignominy, for we had not the military resources at our disposal for even feeble resistance." Indeed, if France had acted otherwise, how different might have been the subsequent history of Europe!

France and lead her to view Hitler less belligerently.* Stalin moved cautiously, preferring French, rather than Soviet, involvement.† Furthermore, the Soviet Union was committed to supporting the League of Nations. As in the Manchurian and Ethiopian crises, the League proved unable to agree upon effective countermeasures. France and Britain, beset by serious internal problems, did not assist the Spanish Republic but used the League as a crutch to gain meaningless acceptance for an unenforceable policy of nonintervention in Spain by the major European Powers, the Soviet Union included. But the open secret of German and Italian support of Franco with men and equipment induced Stalin to take measures designed to preserve the Popular Front policy, though he maintained the official pretense of nonintervention. By October 1936, increasingly worried by reports of an impending German-Italian-Japanese alliance, the Soviet Union embarked on a program of limited intervention.

Several interpretations of the Soviet move are possible. According to Germany and Italy, the USSR intervened with the specific intent of establishing a Soviet republic. This view received support in many conservative and reactionary European circles. Other elements, only slightly less suspicious of Kremlin motives, felt that Moscow wanted to involve the Western democracies in a war with the fascist states in order to forestall any Nazi expansion in the East. The procommunists attributed Soviet support of the Loyalists to a desire to strengthen the principle of collective security and thereby halt the spread of fascism.

Each contention contains some validity. However, according to one leading student of the period, the *primary* objective of the Soviet Union at that time was to put up "as strong a resistance against Franco and his allies as possible in order to support Russia's foreign policy of defense against fascism,"[2] and thus forestall any Nazi move against Russia itself.

---

* A quite different interpretation is suggested by General W. G. Krivitsky, at that time Chief of Soviet Military Intelligence in Western Europe. He believed that Stalin wanted to establish a Soviet controlled regime in Spain. "That done he could command the respect of France and England, win from them the offer of a real alliance, and either accept it or—with that as a bargaining point—arrive at his underlying steady aim and purpose, a compact with Germany." *I Was Stalin's Agent* (London: Hamilton, 1939), p. 99.

† According to Franz Borkenau, Stalin's initial reaction was to try to involve France, not the Soviet Union, in the Spanish struggle, for "French intervention on the republican side would have eliminated any possibility of a four-power pact (involving Germany, and Britain, and France and Italy), would have driven France into the arms of Russia, would have sharpened the antagonism between the Axis and the West, while Russia could safely remain outside all serious commitments; and it would have redounded to the glory of the French Communists and would have strengthened their position with the Popular Front." *European Communism* (New York: Harper & Row, 1953), p. 167.

The Spanish Civil War was one of the major tragedies of the twentieth century. Like any civil war it involved great bitterness and bloodshed. The communists took advantage of the situation to increase their influence in Loyalist circles and then initiated a purge of all opposition elements comparable to the one then going on in the Soviet Union. In the final analysis, Soviet intervention intensified the distrust between the Soviet Union and the Western democracies.[3]

By 1938, however, Soviet attention was diverted to matters of more immediate concern. The formation of the Rome-Berlin Axis in October 1936 had been followed by the negotiation of the German-Japanese Anti-Comintern Pact in November. As the danger from Germany and Japan became more acute, Soviet apprehension grew.

Just as fear of Germany motivated the Popular Front policy in Europe, so in the Far East did the specter of an expansionist Japan encourage a rapprochement with China. Soviet-Japanese relations had a checkered history. During the Russian Civil War and the Allied intervention Japan took possession of eastern Siberia, including the Vladivostok region. However, as a result of the Washington Conference (1922) and Russia's gradual recovery, the Japanese withdrew. When Japanese relations with Russia were reestablished in January 1925, Japan agreed to evacuate the northern half of Sakhalin Island. The two nations remained passively friendly during the 1925–1931 period, despite their rivalry in Manchuria and recurring difficulties about Japanese fishing rights in the north Pacific. After the Japanese invasion of Manchuria, on September 18, 1931, and subsequent occupation of it, relations deteriorated. The Soviet Union was confronted with a new challenge to its security. Its initial policy was one of strict neutrality, of watch and wait; it fully expected that the Japanese action was but a prelude to a strike against Siberia.

Soviet relations with China, severed since late 1927 and further strained by the 1929 fighting in Manchuria for control of the Chinese Eastern Railway, took a turn for the better after the Japanese invasion of Manchuria. Diplomatic relations were restored on December 12, 1932. Since none of the difficulties that had originally precipitated the break proved amenable to negotiation, however, their agreement merely affirmed the status quo before 1929.[4]

Throughout 1932, the Soviet Union observed the ineffectiveness of the League and the Lytton Commission, the manifest unwillingness of the Great Powers to resist Japan with anything stronger than a stream of protest notes, and the growing indications of its strategic isolation. Fear of attack by a coalition of capitalists became acute. Accordingly, Moscow tried a direct settlement with Japan. Litvinov proposed a nonaggression pact several times but was repeatedly rebuffed, though the Japanese did evince a strong desire to purchase the northern lines of the Manchurian railroad, which were still controlled by the Soviet Union. Negotiations began in Tokyo in June 1933 and continued intermittently for almost two years until, in March 1935, Moscow finally agreed, over bitter Chinese protests, to sell its interests in the railroad. Though Russian relations with the Western democracies had improved, Chinese weakness, anxiety over Hitler's anti-Bolshevik declarations, and indications of closer collaboration between Japan and Germany led the Russians to settle with Japan. During the negotiations to sell the Chinese Eastern Railway, however, they also strengthened their military position along the Amur River and in Outer Mongolia.

This effort at appeasement did not satisfy Japan's expansionist appetite. Japanese forces soon moved into the Inner Mongolian provinces of Jehol and Chahar, seeking to establish a puppet state—as they had established Manchukuo in Manchuria—and thereby to threaten the Soviet position in Outer Mongolia. A mutual assistance treaty was concluded between the USSR and Outer Mongolia in March 1936, despite Chinese protests that the area was juridically under Chinese sovereignty (though controlled by Russia since 1924). The Soviets replied that the treaty, which was obviously designed to bolster Soviet hegemony in this increasingly crucial area, in no way compromised Chinese sovereignty, which they still claimed to recognize. They further exploited Chinese weakness by extending their influence into the sparsely settled, strategic province of Sinkiang. Meanwhile, relations with Japan continued to deteriorate. Through the maze of fisheries disputes, border incidents, and debt difficulties associated with the Chinese Eastern Railway settlement, two traditional enemies were feeling out each other's strength in preparation for the final test that might come at any moment.

It must not be overlooked that Soviet policy in the Far East is conditioned and even controlled by developments in Europe and by their effect on the security of the Soviet homeland. Indeed, this integral relationship is often neglected in analyses of Soviet foreign policy.

As for the Chinese, their protests against the none-too-subtle extension of Soviet influence gave way to an urgent need for Soviet help following the full-scale Japanese invasion of July 1937. During the preceding year Moscow, concerned over the implications of the Anti-Comintern Pact, had pushed for a Popular Front in China. In December 1936, Chiang Kai-shek was dramatically kidnapped. His captors insisted that he stop the enervating punitive expeditions against the communists, husband his strength, and devote himself to leading the struggle against

Japan.* Reluctantly, he consented. The introduction of the Popular Front policy in China benefited Moscow, for the renewed communist-Kuomintang collaboration strengthened China's capacity to resist Japan. It also helped promote the security of Soviet Far Eastern frontiers from possible Japanese attack at a time when developments in Europe were taking an increasingly ominous course. In addition, it enabled the Chinese communists to consolidate their position in northwest China in preparation for the postwar struggle for power with the Kuomintang.

The Japanese launched their second invasion of China on July 7, 1937. Appreciating the potential threat to its security, yet not fearing any immediate attack, the Soviet Union signed a nonaggression pact with China on August 21, though she well knew that this would adversely affect relations with Japan. In time, the USSR provided China with important, though limited, quantities of military supplies, particularly during the period between the fall of France and Hitler's invasion of the Soviet Union.

China appealed to the League for help against Japan. The signers of the Nine-Power Treaty of 1922 met in Brussels to discuss what action, if any, to take. Russia, having accepted an invitation, was momentarily encouraged by President Roosevelt's speech calling for a quarantine against the aggressors. But the conference ended in failure. The concept of collective security had suffered another blow. Events at Munich were shortly to complete Soviet disenchantment and lead to accord with Hitler.

Meanwhile, Soviet supplies were delivered to China via Sinkiang. And farther to the east, along the Manchurian-Mongolian frontier, an increasing number of border "skirmishes" broke out between Japanese and Soviet troops, often involving half a million men. The clashes at Changkufeng, a pivotal area near the Soviet, Manchurian, and Korean borders, in July 1938, and at Nomonhan, on the Mongolian frontier, in May 1939, were of particular importance. The Soviets repulsed the Japanese in both battles. Not until after the signing of the Nazi-Soviet pact in August 1939, which apparently caught the Japanese by surprise, did an uneasy quiet settle along the entire border as Japanese expansion took a southern course and the USSR concentrated on problems

---

* Some experts on the Far East believe that the Soviet government was instrumental in organizing the plot from the beginning. Or, there may not have been any connection. Rather, the absence of efforts to establish a Popular Front in China immediately after the 1935 Comintern pronouncement may have resulted from Stalin's reluctance to commit himself until it had become an accomplished fact in Europe. It may have also indicated a lack of interest or knowledge of the situation in China, not in itself surprising given the growing threats in Europe and the trials and purges in the Soviet Union, which dominated Stalin's attention.

of expansion and conflict in Europe. To safeguard their northern flank, the Japanese concluded a Neutrality Pact with the Soviet Union in April 1941.

Western writers seeking to understand Stalin's reasons for signing with Hitler have generally overlooked the crucial importance for Soviet leaders of the undeclared war with Japan, particularly the degree to which the massive battles fought with armor and aircraft from May through August 1939 influenced Stalin's policy in Europe.* Emphasizing the momentous events in Europe, these writers have underestimated the role that fear of an imminent major war with Japan played in Soviet thinking. The recent outpouring of Soviet military memoirs and histories provides us with much new information on Soviet Far Eastern developments and should result in Western reevaluations of the factors conditioning Soviet policy in Europe at this time.

Throughout the period before 1941, Soviet policy in the Far East aimed principally at preserving Soviet security by the use of balance-of-power politics. Changes in political alignment were undertaken as they served Soviet national interest. The shift to a policy of expansion in the Far East developed out of the new international situation resulting from the defeat of Japan and the triumph of the Chinese Communists in 1949.

By early 1938 Hitler's activities dominated the international stage. For Russia, Spain had become a diversionary theater, and the immediate threat from Japan had receded as a result of the war in China. After the occupation of Austria on March 12, Hitler turned to Czechoslovakia, the next steppingstone to German conquest of Europe. His ostensible objective was the reincorporation of the Sudetenland into Germany. But Hitler's appetite, increased by Western weakness and retreat, would be satisfied only with the reduction of Czechoslovakia to the status of a German province. Five days after the Austrian anschluss Litvinov held a press conference in which he emphasized that the latest aggression was no longer in a remote area: "this time the violence has been perpetrated in the center of Europe and has created an indubitable menace not only for the eleven countries now contiguous with the aggressor, but also for all European states, and not only European ones." After referring to the Czechoslovak and Polish-Lithuanian crises, he proceeded to outline the Soviet position:

The Soviet Government being cognizant of its share in this responsibility and being also cognizant of its obligations ensuing from the League Cove-

* Western military experts, in assessing the ability of the Soviet Union to resist the Nazi onslaught, chose to take as their point of departure the weakening of the Red Army as a result of the 1936–1938 purges and its poor showing in the winter war against Finland, ignoring its impressive performance against Japan in the Far East.

nant, from the Briand-Kellogg Pact, and from the treaties of mutual assistance concluded with France and Czechoslovakia, I can state on its behalf
that on its part it is ready as before to participate in collective actions, which
would be decided upon jointly with it and which would aim at checking
the further development of aggression and at eliminating the increased
danger of a new world massacre. It is prepared immediately to take up in
the League of Nations or outside of it the discussion with other Powers of
the practical measures which the circumstances demand. It may be too late
to-morrow, but to-day the time for it is not yet gone if all the States, and
the Great Powers in particular, take a firm and unambiguous stand in regard
to the problem of the collective salvation of peace.[5]

Britain and France, however, failed to respond to this Soviet invitation
to organize against Germany. Moscow felt a growing sense of isolation,
which was to reach its peak after Munich. From March to September
the Sudeten crisis continued to mount in intensity. The Western
democracies tried to placate Hitler, while they virtually ignored the
Soviet Union. On June 23, 1938, Litvinov spoke in Moscow on the
ominous international situation, the imminent demise of the League,
and the abjectness of Western diplomacy.

The League of Nations is stricken with paralysis and unless urgent measures be taken to restore it, it will fall to pieces completely at the moment
the conflict begins. With the exception of Czechoslovakia, the Western European Powers have no longer any allies among the middle and small States
of Europe. Some of these States have openly entered the orbit of the aggressor countries, others, for fear of the latter, are mumbling about neutrality. . . .
Such are the results of the "realistic" policy of the Western European
Powers counterposed by them to the system of collective security we up-
hold together with the strengthening of the League of Nations, which might,
perhaps, even now be able to save the situation . . .[6]

By mid-September Hitler's crescendo of invective against Czechoslovakia alarmed the British and French Governments enough to cause
British Prime Minister Chamberlain to fly to Berchtesgaden. There on
September 15, Britain, France, and Germany reached an agreement
calling upon Czechoslovakia to accede to Hitler's demands. At first
Prague refused. But British and French pressure reversed Czech
determination. According to President Eduard Beneš:

We were informed that if we did not accept their plan for the cession of
the so-called Sudeten regions, they would leave us to our fate, which, they
said, we had brought upon ourselves. They explained that they certainly
*would not go to war with Germany just "to keep the Sudeten Germans in
Czechoslovakia."*[7]

On September 30, the dismemberment of Czechoslovakia began. The Munich agreement, ceding the Sudetenland to Germany, was signed without the participation of the victim or of the Soviet Union. A tragic mandate was imposed upon a hapless nation.

Throughout the crisis the Soviet Government affirmed its willingness to support the League in any collective action and to live up to its obligation to come to the aid of Czechoslovakia, provided France did likewise. On September 21, at the Nineteenth Session of the Assembly of the League of Nations, Litvinov stated that:

> . . . the Soviet Union has . . . expressed its readiness to perform all the decisions and even recommendations of the League which were directed to preserving peace and combating the aggressors, irrespective of whether those decisions coincided with its immediate interests as a State. . . .
>
> It was only two days ago that the Czechoslovak Government addressed a formal enquiry to my Government as to whether the Soviet Union is prepared, in accordance with the Soviet-Czech pact, to render Czechoslovakia immediate and effective aid if France, loyal to her obligations, will render similar assistance, to which my Government gave a clear answer in the affirmative.[8]

To what extent were Soviet offers of aid genuine? Were the Soviets prepared to cooperate in good faith in a collective security system designed to halt Nazi aggression? The answers must forever remain matters of controversy and conjecture. Many critics of official British and French policy, such as Churchill and Paul-Boncour, insisted that a unique opportunity was lost when the Soviet offers of cooperation were rebuffed.[9] On the other hand, it may be argued that France and Great Britain were not ready for war.* In addition, in the minds of their leaders "any suspicion that the Soviet Government might be less anxious than they were themselves to avoid war, because the USSR might expect to profit from it, was counterbalanced by the suspicion that the Red Army (weakened by the purge) was in no shape in 1938 to enter

---

* A number of works have appeared, written by insiders at Munich, to support the thesis that the sellout of Czechoslovakia was prompted by a need for time in which to prepare for the coming war. For example, Commander P. K. Kemp, the Admiralty archivist and head of the Historical Section, writes that the Chiefs of Staff warned Prime Minister Chamberlain, at the time of Munich, that "the country was not ready for war, that no measures of force, whether alone or in alliance with other European countries, could now stop Germany from inflicting a crushing defeat on Czechoslovakia, and that any involvement in war with Germany at this stage could well lead to an ultimate defeat, through her unpreparedness, of the country [Great Britain] herself." This bleak report, he states, forced Chamberlain into a position from which there was no escape; "national prestige, national honor, the obloquy of future generations, none of these could weigh against his overriding duty to his country, to gain time." *Key to Victory: The Triumph of British Sea Power in World War II* (Boston: Little, Brown, 1958), p. 26.

upon a war against Germany."[10] In any event, Soviet leaders had legitimate grounds for criticizing the Western policy of appeasement, and given their ideological biases, they drew the worst possible conclusions from Munich (reading 23). Hitler had succeeded at one stroke in securing the betrayal of Czechoslovakia, virtually rupturing relations between the Soviet Union and the Western democracies, and undermining France's entire security system in Eastern Europe. The tragedy of Munich was the tragedy of men of little vision, politically inept and plagued by domestic crises, which rendered them helpless in the surging tide of historic forces over which no one individual or party had any control.

In March 1939, contrary to his solemn declaration at Munich that he had no further territorial demands, Hitler occupied all of Czechoslovakia. A few days earlier, Stalin had delivered a major address on the international situation to the Eighteenth Party Congress (reading 24). Though he flailed both the Western democracies for their uncertain policy of neutrality and nonintervention and Germany for its aggressive posture, Stalin did not elaborate on the future orientation of Soviet foreign policy. Rather, he contented himself with the statement that the USSR must be cautious and not allow itself "to be drawn into conflicts by warmongers who are accustomed to have others pull the chestnuts out of the fire for them." The general tenor of his speech was anti-Nazi, but the price for Soviet agreement with either coalition was left open for negotiation.

At last convinced that Hitler's ambitions could not readily be curbed, the British government belatedly undertook to organize resistance and, quite unexpectedly, extended a unilateral guarantee to Poland on March 31, 1939, which stated that:

. . . in the event of any action which clearly threatened Polish independence, and which the Polish Government accordingly considered vital to resist with their national forces, His Majesty's Government would feel themselves bound at once to lend the Polish Government all support in their power.

Poland, a minor and pathetic villain during the Czech crisis,* found itself without friendly neighbors, sandwiched between an opportunistic, insecure Russia and an aggressive, expansionist Germany. After the absorption of Czechoslovakia, Hitler directed his invective against Poland, demanding that the Polish corridor and the port of Danzig,

---

* At the time of Munich, the Poles had refused to discuss the possible passage of Soviet troops across Polish territory in the event that aid was to be rendered Czechoslovakia; afterward, they participated in the mutilation of Czechoslavkia by occupying the Teschen district in Silesia.

separating Germany from East Prussia, be incorporated into the Greater Reich. Despite the growing German threat, Poland balked at any meaningful cooperation with its historic nemesis, Russia. In view of Stalin's subsequent policy of aggrandizement, it is evident that Polish fears were warranted. Hungary and Romania also refused to cooperate with Moscow. On April 19 a report emanating from Warsaw stated that:

> Poland has informed Great Britain and Russia that she refuses to partici-
> pate in any efforts to draw the Soviet Union into the antiaggression "peace
> front" being organized by Britain, it was announced officially tonight.
> Poland has a "negative attitude" toward permitting Soviet troops or planes
> to march or fly over Polish territory, the announcement said.[11]

At the same time, the German Foreign Office responded favorably to the Soviet ambassador's remark that he saw no reason why relations between their countries might not "become better and better." The Kremlin regarded both Western and fascist coalitions as anathemas, but sought a rapprochement with one or the other, irrespective of ideological or political differences. It maneuvered (a) to prevent either coalition from making possible aggression against the Soviet Union and (b) to obtain the highest price for its support. To this end Moscow was prepared to follow any course.

On May 3, 1939, a date that may be regarded as a turning point for Soviet policy, Molotov succeeded Litvinov as Foreign Minister.* This move signified the abandonment of efforts to promote a collective security system and to rely upon the League of Nations—a policy associated by Western leaders with Litvinov—and the start of active work toward an agreement with Germany. Yet in his first report to the Supreme Soviet on May 31, Molotov acknowledged indications that Britain and France were now prepared to counteract fascist expansion.

> How serious these changes are still remains to be seen. As yet it cannot
> even be said whether these countries are seriously desirous of abandoning
> the policy of non-intervention, the policy of non-resistance to the further
> development of aggression. May it not turn out that the present endeavor of
> these countries to resist aggression in *some* regions will serve as no
> obstacle to the unleashing of oppression in *other* regions?

This scarcely veiled allusion reflected Soviet distrust and the belief

* There have thus far been but seven Foreign Ministers: Leon Trotsky (November 1917–
April 1918); Georgi Chicherin (1918–1929); Maxim Litvinov (1929–1939); Vyacheslav M.
Molotov (1939–1949; 1953–1956); Andrei Vyshinsky (1949–1953); Dimitri Shepilov (1956);
Andrei Gromyko (1957–?).

that the Western democracies were still trying to induce Hitler to expand to the east.*

The events of the next three months are too complex and involved to be recounted here.[12] Hitler, faced with the British guarantee to Poland, unilaterally abrogated the 1934 Polish-German treaty and moved to ensure his eastern flank by an accord with the USSR. Negotiations concentrated on the price of Soviet neutrality. During this period Western concern mounted. The German-Soviet rapprochement became a virtual certainty as a result of discussions on August 2–4, when Germany decided to meet Moscow's terms. A British and French *military* mission, with no formal written powers to make *political* decisions, left for Moscow *by sea* on August 5. This seeming lack of urgency on the part of Britain and France was not lost on the Soviet leaders. By the time discussions opened on August 12, it was too late. The Western democracies were unwilling (and unable) to meet Stalin's price—a free hand in the Baltic states and the right to send troops into Poland in the event of attack by Germany.

On August 19, Germany and the Soviet Union signed a trade agreement. Four days later, Ribbentrop, the German Foreign Minister, flew to Moscow and the fateful ten-year Nonaggression Pact was signed the same day (reading 25). The agreement obligated each partner to absolute neutrality "should one of the High Contracting Parties become the object of belligerent action by a third power." In reality, it gave the green light to Hitler's invasion of Poland. The secret protocol called for the partition of Poland and placed Estonia, Latvia, Finland, and Bessarabia within the Soviet sphere of influence, assigning Lithuania to Germany.

The Nazi-Soviet pact differed in two notable ways from previous nonaggression pacts signed by the USSR.[13] First, it had no stipulation that "if one of the contracting parties should commit an act of aggres-

* For a Soviet interpretation of the British policy of appeasement of Germany, Italy, and Japan, during the pre-Munich (1935–1938) period see *A Short History of the Communist Party of the Soviet Union* (New York: International Publishers, 1939): "The 'democratic' states are, of course, stronger than the fascist states. The one-sided character of the developing world war is due to the absence of a united front of the 'democratic' states against the fascist powers. The so-called democratic states, of course, do not approve of the 'excesses' of the fascist states and fear any accession of strength to the latter. But they fear even more the working class movement in Europe and the movement of national emancipation in Asia, and regard fascism as an 'excellent antidote' to these 'dangerous' movements. For this reason the ruling circles of the 'democratic' states, especially the ruling Conservative circles of Great Britain, confine themselves to a policy of pleading with the overweening fascist rulers 'not to go to extremes,' at the same time giving them to understand that they 'fully comprehend' and on the whole sympathize with their reactionary police policy towards the working class movement and the national emancipation movement." (English edition, 1939), p. 334.

sion against a third party the other contracting party would be entitled to denounce the pact." Second, the last article of the Treaty stated that it was to "enter into force as soon as it is signed," an unusual diplomatic provision. These departures from tradition constituted a tacit Soviet acknowledgment of the character of Nazi intentions—indeed, they openly encouraged Germany's aggressive designs. On August 31, at a special session of the Supreme Soviet convened to ratify the treaty, Molotov delivered a lengthy speech in which he defended the Soviet Union in its negotiations with the Axis Powers (reading 26).

At dawn, on September 1, 1939, Nazi legions rolled into Poland. Two days later, true to their word, Britain and France declared war on Germany. World War II was a reality. The new war was an imperialist one to Moscow, in whose view "international war and peace are not two diametrically opposed and mutually exclusive phenomena, but two equally important means, supplementing each other in the communist's advance toward their final revolutionary goal."[14] It never clearly said so, but it undoubtedly wished a plague on both sides and tended "to view the Second World War through the prism of the first one, and to hope that the working classes of the warring countries could revolt as the Russian working class had done."[15] Stalin hoped to remain a spectator, ready to profit from the mutual exhaustion of the competing coalitions.

With the outbreak of war, the Soviet Union abandoned its previous policy of nonaggression for a course of aggression and territorial expansion. It rationalized its actions in terms of national security, exploiting, in true Machiavellian fashion, the preoccupation elsewhere of the other European powers. Soviet imperialism, by whatever name and however legitimized, was, with the subsequent defeat of Germany, to move Soviet power into the heart of Europe and thus give rise to the Cold War. Meanwhile, on September 17, 1939, Red Army troops marched into eastern Poland; on September 28, Germany and the Soviet Union formally partitioned the country by secret agreement. The protocol also transferred most of Lithuania to the Soviet sphere "in return for the emphatic shift eastward in the Soviet-Polish demarcation line, which now followed the Bug instead of the Vistula for most of its length."[16]

Stalin wasted little time in extending Soviet influence into the Baltic states. Mutual assistance agreements with Estonia, Latvia, and Lithuania were only preliminaries to the formal incorporation of these states into the Soviet Union in August 1940. Finland was next on the Soviet list. Negotiations during October and November (1939) failed to bring about the desired result. Accordingly, on November 29, Soviet troops attacked Finland. Mounting Western sympathy for the Finns developed into unstinting admiration as the numerically superior and better-equipped

Soviet troops were stymied and outmaneuvered on the wintry wastes of the Karelian Isthmus and central Finland. The League of Nations condemned the Soviet aggression and evicted the USSR from the organization on December 14. Western support, however, did not crystallize into material assistance for the beleaguered, gallant Finns, who finally had to capitulate. A treaty of peace was signed on March 12, 1940. Reviewing the reasons for the Finnish campaign in his speech of March 29, Molotov stressed the need to safeguard the northwestern frontiers of the USSR and above all the security of Leningrad.

The successful Nazi blitzkrieg in April and May and the astonishing, unexpected French collapse in June, accelerated Soviet efforts to bolster its position vis-à-vis Germany. Soviet pressure was put on Romania to relinquish Bessarabia and northern Bukovina. With evident reluctance, Germany accepted the Soviet annexation, at the same time taking measures to consolidate its own influence in the rest of Romania. Difficulties also developed over Bulgaria and Yugoslavia; the expansionist appetites of Germany and the Soviet Union sharpened their rivalry in the Balkans and in Finland; other strains appeared in the economic sphere. By September 1940, Hitler became convinced that Russia would have to be subjugated if his conquest of Europe was to be safeguarded.

Portentous Soviet-German conversations were held in Berlin on November 12–13, 1940, concerning the shape of the "new order" wrought by the supposed defeat of the British Empire.[17] Ribbentrop referred to the fruitful results of German-Soviet collaboration and asked "whether in the long run the most advantageous access to the sea for Russia could not be found in the direction of the Persian Gulf and the Arabian Sea, and whether at the same time certain other aspirations of Russia in this part of Asia—in which Germany was comfortably disinterested—could not also be realized." He also supported revision of the Montreux Convention (governing access through the Dardanelles and the Bosporus) to make it more favorable to the Soviet Union. A protocol was drawn up, but never signed, between Germany, Italy, and Japan on the one side and the Soviet Union on the other, by which the USSR was to obtain recognition of its recent territorial acquisitions and a promise of peace with Japan; and a secret protocol, assigning spheres of influence among the four powers, declared that Soviet "territorial aspirations center south of the national territory of the Soviet Union in the direction of the Indian Ocean." Molotov's intransigence and his expressed desire for further expansion in the Balkans, Finland, and the Straits area angered Hitler and confirmed his resolve to subjugate the Soviet Union. It is interesting to note that Molotov's demands were set forth in non-Marxist, openly power-political terms, and clearly coincided with traditional Czarist territorial objectives (reading 27). The limits of compatibility had been exceeded. On December 18, 1940, the Führer issued the order to prepare for the attack on the USSR (Operation Barbarossa). Preparations were to be completed by May 15, 1941.

For the next six months the Soviet Union tried to maintain friendly relations with Germany, honoring all economic agreements scrupulously. Relations with the United States and Great Britain were correct, but little else. In February 1941, German troops completely occupied Romania and, in March, Bulgaria as well, thus outflanking Yugoslavia. Meanwhile, Mussolini's invasion of Greece turned into a rout—of the Italian Army. To extricate his partner and safeguard his own Balkan flank, Hitler invaded Yugoslavia on April 6—two days *after* Molotov had informed the German government of his intention to conclude a non-aggression pact with Belgrade. The Soviet leaders retreated. They did not sign the treaty with Yugoslavia, nor did they make any effort to aid the Yugoslavs, and within two weeks Nazi forces occupied all of Yugoslavia. But Hitler's original date for the invasion of the Soviet Union had to be postponed until June 22. On May 6, Stalin assumed the office of Chairman of the Council of People's Commissars (equivalent to Prime Minister). This, his first formal *government* position since his rise to undisputed leadership in the USSR, revealed the Kremlin's growing concern over German intentions. Outwardly, German-Soviet relations remained unchanged as the Soviet Union tried in every way to appease Hitler. Time, however, had run out on the "unholy alliance."

NOTES

1. Leonard Shapiro, *Soviet Treaty Series* (Washington, D.C.: Georgetown University Press, 1955), Vol. II, p. 131.

2. David T. Cattell, *Communism and the Spanish Civil War* (Berkeley: University of California Press, 1956), p. 211. This provides an excellent account of events in Spain and analyzes the extent to which the communist party affected developments in Spain. He stresses "the importance of the defensive motive rather than the offensive motive in the Soviet Union's intervention in Spain. She was not interested in a satellite in Spain at this time but only in a tool to stop the aggression of the Fascist states against herself." Dr. Cattell's companion volume, *Soviet Diplomacy and the Spanish Civil War* (Berkeley: University of California Press, 1957), gives a valuable account of the relationship between Soviet foreign policy and the Soviet attitude toward events in Spain.

3. Max Beloff, *The Foreign Policy of Soviet Russia, 1936–1941* (New York: Oxford University Press, 1949), Vol. II, p. 38.

4. Harriet L. Moore, *Soviet Far Eastern Policy, 1931–1945* (Princeton, N.J.: Princeton University Press, 1945), p. 19.

5. *Documents on International Affairs, 1938* (London: Oxford University Press, 1942), Vol. I, pp. 314–315.

6. *Ibid.,* p. 322.

7. Dr. Eduard Beneš, *Memoirs of Eduard Beneš: From Munich to New War and New Victory* (Boston: Houghton Mifflin, 1954), p. 43.

8. Maxim Litvinov, *Against Aggression* (New York: International Publishers, 1939), pp. 128–130.

9. *Survey of International Affairs, 1938* (London: Oxford University Press, 1953), Vol. III, p. 408.

10. *Ibid.,* p. 409.

11. *The New York Herald Tribune,* April 20, 1939; quoted by V. A. Yakhontoff, *USSR Foreign Policy* (New York: Coward-McCann, 1945), p. 201.

12. For an excellent treatment of this period see David J. Dallin, *Soviet Russia's Foreign Policy, 1939–1942* (New Haven, Conn.: Yale University Press, 1942), chaps. I–IV.

13. *Ibid.,* pp. 55–56.

14. T. A. Taracouzio, *War and Peace in Soviet Diplomacy* (New York: Macmillan, 1940), p. 295.

15. Isaac Deutscher, *Stalin: A Political Biography* (New York: Oxford University Press, 1949), p. 411.

16. Beloff, *op. cit.,* p. 284.

17. Raymond J. Sontag and James S. Beddie (eds.), *Nazi-Soviet Relations, 1939–1941: Documents from the Archives of the German Foreign Office* (Washington, D.C.: Department of State, 1948), pp. 217–260.

The USSR Tries Collective Security

21/Speech on the Occasion of the Soviet Entry into the League of Nations   *September 18, 1934*

MAXIM LITVINOV

I will speak with that frankness and moderation which many of you, knowing me of old, will, I am sure, grant me, and which can only be helpful to our mutual understanding and our future cooperation.

We represent here a new state—new, not geographically, but new in its external aspects, its internal political and social structure, and its aspirations and ideals. The appearance in the historical arena of a new form of state has always been met with hostility on the part of old state formations. It is not surprising that the phenomenon of a new state with a social-political system radically different from any heretofore known should come up against intense hostility from without and manifested by literally all other countries in the world. This hostility has been not merely theoretical, but has found expression even in military action, assuming the form of prolonged externally organized attempts to interfere in the internal affairs of the new state for the purpose of getting it back to the old lines. At the time when the League of Nations was being formed to proclaim the organization of peace, the people of our country had as yet not been enabled to enjoy the blessings of peace. They still had to defend their internal peace with arms, and to contend for long their right to internal self-determination and their external independence. Even after the most extreme forms of intervention in the affairs of our state were over, the hostility of the outer world continued to be manifested in the most varying degrees and forms . . . people in the Soviet Union naturally feared that these nations united in the League might give collective expression to their hostility towards the Soviet Union and combine their anti-Soviet activities. It can hardly be denied that at that time, and even very much later, there were still statesmen who thought or at least dreamed, of such collective action. . . .

In order to make our position quite clear, I should like further to state that the idea in itself of an association of nations contains nothing theoretically inacceptable for the Soviet state and its ideology . . . The Soviet state has . . . never excluded the possibility of some form or other of

League of Nations, *Official Journal,* Special Supplement No. 125 (September 1934), pp. 66–69, *excerpts.*

association with states having a different political and social system, so long as there is no mutual hostility and if it is for the attainment of common aims. For such an association it considers that the essential conditions would be, first, the extension to every state belonging to such an association of the liberty to preserve what I might call its state personality and the social-economic system chosen by it—in other words, reciprocal noninterference in the domestic affairs of the States therein associated; and, secondly, the existence of common aims. As to the first condition, which we have named the peaceful coexistence of different social-political systems at a given historical stage, we have advocated it again and again at international conferences. . . . The invitation to the Soviet Union to join the League of Nations may be said to represent the final victory of this principle.

For its part, the Soviet Government, following attentively all developments of international life, could not but observe the increasing activity in the League of Nations of States interested in the preservation of peace and their struggle against aggressive militarist elements . . . The organization of peace! Could there be a loftier and at the same time more practical and urgent task for the cooperation of all nations? The words used in political slogans have their youth and their age. If they are used too often without being applied, they wear themselves out and end by losing potency. Then they have to be revived and instilled with new meaning. The sound and the meaning of the words "organization of peace" ought now to be different from their sound and meaning twelve or fifteen years ago. Then, to many Members of the League of Nations, war seemed to be a remote theoretical danger, and there seemed to be no hurry as to its prevention. Now, war must appear to all as the threatening danger of tomorrow. Now, the organization of peace, for which so far very little has been done, must be set against the extremely active organization of war. Then, many believed that the spirit of war might be exorcised by adjurations, resolutions and declarations. Now, everybody knows that the exponents of the idea of war, the open promulgations of the refashioning of the map of Europe and Asia by the sword, are not to be intimidated by paper obstacles. Members of the League of Nations know this by experience. We are now confronted with the task of averting war by more effective means. . . .

We must accept the incontestable fact that, in the present complicated state of political and economic interests, no war of any serious dimensions can be localized, and any war, whatever its issue, will turn out to have been but the first of a series. We must also tell ourselves that sooner or later any war will bring misfortune to all countries, whether belligerents or neutrals. . . .

Finally, we must realize once and for all that no war with political or economic aims is capable of restoring so-called historical justice, and that all it could do would be to substitute new and perhaps still more glaring injustices for old ones, and that every new peace treaty bears within it the seeds of fresh warfare. . . .

I do not consider it the moment to speak in detail about effective means for the prevention of impending and openly promulgated war. One thing is quite clear for me, and that is that peace and security cannot be organized on the shifting sands of verbal promises and declarations. The nations are not to be soothed into a feeling of security by assurances of peaceful intentions, however often they are repeated, especially in those places where there are grounds for expecting aggression or where, only the day before, there have been talk and publications about wars of conquest in all directions, for which both ideological and material preparations are being made. We should establish that any state is entitled to demand from its neighbors, near and remote, guarantees for its security, and that such a demand is not to be considered as an expression of mistrust. Governments with a clear conscience and really free from all aggressive intentions, cannot refuse to give, in place of declarations, more effective guarantees which would be extended to themselves and give them also a feeling of complete security.

Far be it from me to overrate the opportunities and means of the League of Nations for the organization of peace. I realize, better perhaps than any of you, how limited these means are. I am aware that the League does not possess the means for the complete abolition of war. I am however convinced that, with the firm will and close cooperation of all its Members, a great deal could be done at any given moment for the utmost diminution of the danger of war, and this is a sufficiently honorable and lofty task, the fulfillment of which would be of incalculable advantage to humanity.

The Comintern, the Popular Front, and Soviet Policy

22/Report to the Seventh Congress of the Communist International *August 1935*

Comrades, millions of workers and toilers of the capitalist countries ask the question: How can fascism be prevented from coming to power and how can fascism be overthrown after being victorious? To this the Communist International replies: *The first thing that must be done, the thing with which to commence, is to form a united front, to establish unity of action of the workers in every factory, in every district, in every region, in every country, all over the world. Unity of action of the proletariat on a national and international scale is the mighty weapon which renders the working class capable not only of successful defense but also of successful counter-offensive against fascism, against the class enemy* . . . a powerful united front of the proletariat would exert tremendous influence in *all other strata of the toiling people,* on the peasantry, on the urban petty bourgeoisie, on the intelligentsia. A united front would inspire the wavering groups with faith in the strength of the working class.

But even this is not all. The proletariat of the imperialist countries has possible allies not only in the toilers of its own countries but also in the *oppressed nations of the colonies and semi-colonies* . . . [and] if, finally, we take into consideration that international unity of action by the proletariat relies on the *steadily growing strength of a proletarian state, a land of socialism, the Soviet Union,* we see that broad perspectives are revealed by the realization of united action on the part of the proletariat on a national and international scale. . . .

Is it possible to realize this unity of action by the proletariat in the individual countries and throughout the whole world? Yes, it is. And it is possible at this very moment. The Communist International *attaches no conditions to unity of action except one, and that an elementary condition acceptable for all workers, viz. that the unity of action be directed against fascism, against the offensive of capital, against the threat of war, against the class enemy.*

What objections can the opponents of the united front have and how do they voice their objections?

U.S., Congress, House Committee on Un-American Activities, *The Strategy and Tactics of World Communism; The World Congress of the Communist International,* 84th Cong., 2d sess. (1956), pp. 308–313, *excerpts.*

Some say: "To the Communists the slogan of the united front is merely a maneuver." But if it is a maneuver, we reply, why don't you expose the "Communist maneuver" by your honest participation in a united front? We declare frankly: We want unity of action by the working class, so that the proletariat may grow stronger in its struggle against the bourgeoisie, in order that while defending today its current interests against attacking capital, against fascism, the proletariat may be in a position tomorrow to create the preliminary conditions for its final emancipation.

"The Communists attack us," say others. But listen, we have repeatedly declared: We shall not attack anyone, neither persons nor organizations nor parties that stand for the united front of the working class against the class enemy. . . .

"We cannot form a united front with the Communists, since they have a different program," says a third group. But you yourselves say that your program differs from the program of the bourgeois parties, and yet this did not and does not prevent you (Social-Democrats) from entering into coalitions with these parties. . . .

"If we establish a united front with the Communists, the petty bourgeoisie will take fright at the 'Red Danger' and will desert to the fascists," we hear it said quite frequently. But does the united front represent a threat to the peasants, the petty traders, the artisans, the toiling intellectuals? No, the united front is a threat to the big bourgeoisie, the financial magnates, the *junkers* and other exploiters, whose regime brings complete ruin to all these strata.

"Social-Democracy is for democracy, the Communists are for dictatorship, therefore we cannot form a united front with the Communists," say some of the Social-Democratic leaders. But are we offering you now a united front for the purpose of proclaiming the dictatorship of the proletariat? We make no such proposal for the time being.

"Let the Communists recognize democracy, let them come out in its defense, then we shall be ready for a united front." To this we reply: We are adherents of Soviet democracy, the democracy of the toilers, the most consistent democracy in the world. But in the capitalist countries we defend and shall continue to defend every inch of bourgeois-democratic liberties which are being attacked by fascism and bourgeois reaction, because the interests of the class struggle of the proletariat so dictate. . . .

"The Communists act like dictators, they want to prescribe and dictate everything to us." No. We prescribe nothing and dictate nothing. We only make proposals concerning which we are convinced that if realized they will meet the interests of the toiling people. . . .

Thus all these arguments against the united front *will not bear the slightest criticism*. They are rather the flimsy excuses of the reactionary leaders of Social-Democracy, who prefer their united front with the bourgeoisie to the united front of the proletariat. . . .

What is and ought to be the basic content of the united front at the present stage? The defense of the immediate economic and political interests of the working class, the defense of the working class against fascism, must form the *starting point* and *main content* of the united front in all capitalist countries.

Soviet Diplomacy and the Munich Crisis

23/The Soviet View of Munich

Returning from Munich, Chamberlain claimed in one of his public addresses that "henceforth peace was assured for a generation." Churchill appraised the results of Munich quite differently. "England," he said with bitterness and indignation, "had to choose between war and shame. Its ministers chose shame, and thereby received war itself."

. . . [on the eve of Munich] from Paris and London urgent warnings went to Prague: Czechoslovakia must not count on the Soviet Union, which is too far away, does not have a common frontier with Czechoslovakia, and finally, does not want to enter in a war regardless of its treaty obligations concerning aid to Czechoslovakia. In this way the diplomacy of the French and British governments sought to weaken the resolve of the Czechoslovak people and discredit the Soviet Union in the eyes of the democrats of the entire world. It also indicated the other motives of bourgeois diplomacy. To the [bourgeois] leaders, the thought of joint action with the Soviet Union against Hitler was an unpleasant one. The former head of the French military mission in Czechoslovakia, General Foch, expressed this attitude with a soldier's bluntness in conversations with certain politicians in Prague.

Foch declared that France would be unwilling to smash Hitler through

V. P. Potemkin (ed.), *Istoriia Diplomatii* [*History of Diplomacy*] (Moscow: Government Publication of Foreign Literature, 1945), Vol. III, pp. 643–646, *excerpts*. This work, which appeared shortly after the end of the war, was edited by a former member of the Soviet foreign service and represents a rather serious, relatively nonpolemical treatment of the interwar period. Editor's translation.

the help of the Soviet Union. For first of all, world public opinion would accord the honor for this victory to the Red Army. This would painfully affect the national honor of France. But there was still a more important reason.

The destruction of Hitler in cooperation with the Bolsheviks would evoke a stormy wave of sympathy for the Soviet Union. This would promote a dangerous growth in the revolutionary workers' movement. Such a prospect was by no means pleasing to the French government. "In short," concluded General Foch, "we do not want to come out against Hitler, united with the Bolsheviks." By slanderous inventions anti-Soviet diplomacy opposed all known facts. The whole world knew that the Soviet government considered the demands on its honor fulfilled by assuming treaty obligations for itself and by tirelessly struggling for collective security and mutual cooperation by the democratic countries against the inciters of war.

The Soviet Union proved to be the only government that kept faith with its international obligations in relations with Czechoslovakia. . . . At the beginning of September 1938 the French government turned to the USSR government with the question of what its position would be in the event that Czechoslovakia was subjected to attack. The answer of the Soviet government was clear and unequivocal; to convene quickly the governments of the USSR, England, and France; to issue a declaration in the name of these powers that would state that Czechoslovakia will be rendered aid in case of an unprovoked attack on it by Germany; to bring this question to the League of Nations for consideration of the measures to take for its (Czechoslovakia's) defense; finally, to organize a technical consultation among the representatives of the General Staffs of the USSR, France, and Czechoslovakia in order to work out a plan of mutual military cooperation. Such were the proposals of the Soviet government. From this it was shown that the USSR would render Czechoslovakia help by all available means and by all accessible paths, if, as was established by its treaty with Czechoslovakia, France itself came to her defense.

In the middle of September the Czechoslovak government asked the USSR government whether it was prepared to render rapid and effective aid to Czechoslovakia in accordance with the Czech-Soviet pact, if such aid came from the side of France. To this inquiry the Soviet government quickly replied in the affirmative. As is known, the Czech-Soviet pact stipulated that the USSR will render aid to Czechoslovakia only in the event that France does exactly the same thing. At any rate it was understood that, by compelling Czechoslovakia to accept the German-English-French ultimatum, France was in fact breaking its promise of aid to Czechoslovakia, as stipulated by the Czech-French pact.

By that very action the Soviet government was formally freed from the obligation to render aid to Czechoslovakia in accordance with the Czech-Soviet pact. None the less, the Soviet government did not take advantage of its right to leave Czechoslovakia to its fate. The Czech-Soviet pact was not declared inoperative. The USSR was ready as before to provide support to Czechoslovakia if its government wished it. . . .

Between them the reactionary press of Britain and France intensively spread fabrications about the Soviet Union, intimating that it did not intend to fulfill its treaty obligations with respect to Czechoslovakia. The machinations of the slanderers were exposed: in Geneva, in the Assembly of the League of Nations, the reply of the Soviet government to the inquiries of France and Czechoslovakia was announced. So was torn away the provocative intentions of the reactionaries. On the other hand, the USSR appeared before the world as the only country that, in a moment of universal panic, desertion, and treachery, maintained complete calm, demonstrated its unswerving faith to treaty obligations, and showed a strong determination to defend international peace and democracy against the instigators of war. . . . As to the Munich conference and its decision, the USSR government in no way had, nor does it now have, anything to do with it.

24/Report to the Eighteenth Congress of the CPSU

March 10, 1939

JOSEPH STALIN

Comrades, five years have elapsed since the Seventeenth Party Congress. No small period, as you can see. During this period the world has undergone considerable changes. . . . What changes exactly have taken place in this period in the international situation? In what way exactly has the external and internal position of our country changed? . . .

The new imperialist war became a fact.

It is not so easy in our day suddenly to break loose and plunge straight into war without regard for treaties of any kind or for public opinion. Bourgeois politicians know this quite well. So do the fascist rulers. That is why the fascist rulers decided, before plunging into war, to mold public opinion to suit their ends, that is, to mislead it, to deceive it.

Joseph Stalin, *Problems of Leninism* (Moscow: Foreign Languages Publishing House, 1953), p. 746, pp. 751–759, *excerpts.*

A military bloc of Germany and Italy against the interests of Britain and France in Europe? Bless us, do you call that a bloc? "We" have no military bloc. All "we" have is an innocuous "Berlin-Rome axis"; that is, just a geometrical equation for an axis. (*Laughter*)

A military bloc of Germany, Italy, and Japan against the interests of the United States, Britain, and France in the Far East? Nothing of the kind! "We" have no military bloc. All "we" have is an innocuous "Berlin-Rome-Tokyo triangle"; that is, a slight penchant for geometry. (*General laughter*)

A war against the interests of Britain, France, the United States? Nonsense! "We" are waging war on the Comintern, not on those states. If you don't believe it, read the "anti-Comintern pact" concluded between Italy, Germany, and Japan.

That is how Messieurs the aggressors thought to mold public opinion, although it was not hard to see how preposterous this clumsy game of camouflage was; for it is ridiculous to look for Comintern "hotbeds" in the deserts of Mongolia, in the mountains of Abyssinia, or in the wilds of Spanish Morocco. (*Laughter*)

But war is inexorable. It cannot be hidden under any guise. For no "axes," "triangles," or "anti-Comintern pacts" can hide the fact that in this period Japan has seized a vast stretch of territory in China, that Italy has seized Abyssinia, that Germany has seized Austria and the Sudeten region, that Germany and Italy together have seized Spain, and all this in defiance of the interests of the nonaggressive states. The war remains a war; the military bloc of aggressors remains a military bloc; and the aggressors remain aggressors. It is a distinguishing feature of the new imperialist war that it has not yet become a universal, a world war. The war is being waged by aggressor states, who in every way infringe upon the interests of the nonaggressive states, primarily Britain, France, and the USA, while the latter draw back and retreat, making concession after concession to the aggressors.

Thus we are witnessing an open redivision of the world and spheres of influence at the expense of the nonaggressive states, without the least attempt at resistance, and even with a certain connivance, on their part. Incredible, but true. To what are we to attribute this one-sided and strange character of the new imperialist war? How is it that the nonaggressive countries, which possess such vast opportunities, have so easily and without resistance abandoned their positions and their obligations to please the aggressors? Is it to be attributed to the weakness of the nonaggressive states? Of course not! Combined, the nonaggressive, democratic states are unquestionably stronger than the fascist states, both economically and militarily. To what then are we to attribute the systematic concessions made by these states to the aggressors? . . . The chief reason is that the majority of the nonaggressive countries, particularly Britain and France, have rejected the policy of collective security, the policy of collective resistance to aggressors, and have taken up a position of nonintervention, a position of "neutrality." Formally speaking, the policy of nonintervention might be defined as follows: "Let each country defend itself against the aggressors as it likes and as best it can. That is not our affair. We shall trade both with the aggressors and with their victims." But actually speaking, the policy of nonintervention means conniving at aggression, giving free rein to war, and, consequently, transforming the war into a world war. The policy of nonintervention reveals an eagerness, a desire, not to hinder the aggressors in their nefarious work: not to hinder Japan, say, from embroiling herself in a war with China, or, better still, with the Soviet Union; not to hinder Germany, say, from enmeshing herself in European affairs, from embroiling herself in a war with the Soviet Union; to allow all the belligerents to sink deeply into the mire of war, to encourage them surreptitiously in this; to allow them to weaken and exhaust one another; and then, when they have become weak enough, to appear on the scene with fresh strength, to appear, of course, "in the interests of peace," and to dictate conditions to the enfeebled belligerents.

Cheap and easy!

Take Japan, for instance. It is characteristic that before Japan invaded North China (1937) all the influential French and British newspapers shouted about China's weakness and her inability to offer resistance, and declared that Japan with her army could subjugate China in two or three months. Then the European and American politicians began to watch and wait. And then, when Japan commenced military operations, they let her have Shanghai, the vital center of foreign capital in China; they let her have Canton, a center of Britain's monopoly influence in South China; they let her have Hainan, and they allowed her to surround Hongkong. Does not this look very much like encouraging the aggressor? It is as though they were saying: "Embroil yourself deeper in war; then we shall see."

Or take Germany, for instance. They let her have Austria, despite the undertaking to defend her independence; they let her have the Sudeten region; they abandoned Czechoslovakia to her fate, thereby violating all their obligations; and then they began to lie vociferously in the press about "the weakness of the Russian army," "the demoralization of the Russian air force," and "riots" in the Soviet Union, egging on the Germans to march farther east, promising them easy pickings, and prompting them: "Just start war on the Bolsheviks, and everything will be all right." It must be admitted that this looks very much like egging on and encouraging the aggressor. . . .

Far be it from me to moralize on the policy of nonintervention, to talk of treason, treachery, and so on. It would be naive to preach morals to people who recognize no human morality. Politics are politics, as the old, case-hardened bourgeois diplomats say. It must be remarked, however, that the big and dangerous political game started by the supporters of the policy of nonintervention may end in serious fiasco for them. . . .

The war has created a new situation with regard to the relations between countries. It has enveloped them in an atmosphere of alarm and uncertainty. By undermining the basis of the postwar peace regime and overriding the elementary principles of international law, it has cast doubt on the value of international treaties and obligations. Pacifism and disarmament schemes are dead and buried. Feverish arming has taken their place. Everybody is arming, small states and big states, including primarily those which practice the policy of nonintervention. Nobody believes any longer in the unctuous speeches which claim that the Munich concessions to the aggressors and the Munich agreement opened a new era of "appeasement." They are disbelieved even by the signatories to the Munich agreement, Britain and France, who are increasing their armaments no less than other countries.

Naturally, the USSR could not ignore these ominous developments . . . while our country is unswervingly pursuing a policy of maintaining peace, it is at the same time working very seriously to increase the preparedness of our Red Army and our Red Navy. At the same time, in order to strengthen its international position, the Soviet Union decided to take certain other steps. At the end of 1934 our country joined the League of Nations, considering that despite its weakness the League might nevertheless serve as a place where aggressors could be exposed, and as a certain instrument of peace, however feeble, that might hinder the outbreak of war. The Soviet Union considers that in alarming times like these even so weak an international organization as the League of Nations should not be ignored. In May 1935 a treaty of mutual assistance against possible attack by aggressors was signed between France and the Soviet Union. A similar treaty was simultaneously concluded with Czechoslovakia. In March 1936 the Soviet Union concluded a treaty of mutual assistance with the Mongolian People's Republic. In August 1937 the Soviet Union concluded a pact of nonaggression with the Chinese Republic. . . .

The Tasks of the Party in the sphere of foreign policy are:

1. To continue the policy of peace and of strengthening business relations with all countries;
2. To be cautious and not allow our country to be drawn into conflicts by warmongers who are accustomed to have others pull the chestnuts out of the fire for them;
3. To strengthen the might of our Red Army and Red Navy to the utmost . . .

The Unholy Alliance

○25/Treaty of Nonaggression Between Germany and the Union of Soviet Socialist Republics *August 23, 1939*

The Government of the German Reich and the Government of the Union of Soviet Socialist Republics desirous of strengthening the cause of peace between Germany and the USSR, and proceeding from the fundamental provisions of the Neutrality Agreement concluded in April 1926 between Germany and the USSR, have reached the following agreement:

ARTICLE I

Both High Contracting Parties obligate themselves to desist from any act of violence, any aggressive action, and any attack on each other, either individually or jointly with other powers.

ARTICLE II

Should one of the High Contracting Parties become the object of belligerent action by a third power, the other High Contracting Party shall in no manner lend its support to this third power.

ARTICLE III

The Governments of the two High Contracting Parties shall in the future maintain continual contact with one another for the purpose of consultation in order to exchange information on problems affecting their common interests.

ARTICLE IV

Neither of the two High Contracting Parties shall participate in any grouping of powers whatsoever that is directly or indirectly aimed at the other party.

Raymond J. Sontag and James S. Beddie (eds.), *Nazi-Soviet Relations 1939–1941: Documents from the Archives of the German Foreign Office* (Washington, D.C.: Department of State, 1948), pp. 76–78, *excerpts.*

ARTICLE V

Should disputes or conflicts arise between the High Contracting Parties over problems of one kind or another, both parties shall settle these disputes or conflicts exclusively through friendly exchange of opinion, or, if necessary, through the establishment of arbitration commissions.

ARTICLE VI

The present treaty is concluded for a period of ten years, with the proviso that, in so far as one of the High Contracting Parties does not denounce it one year prior to the expiration of this period, the validity of this treaty shall automatically be extended for another five years.

ARTICLE VII

The present treaty shall be ratified within the shortest possible time. The ratifications shall be exchanged in Berlin. The agreement shall enter into force as soon as it is signed.

Done in duplicate, in the German and Russian languages.

Moscow, August 23, 1939

*For the Government
of the German Reich:*

V. Ribbentrop

*With full power of the
Government of the USSR:*

V. Molotov

[SECRET ADDITIONAL PROTOCOL]

On the occasion of the signature of the Nonaggression Pact between the German Reich and the Union of Soviet Socialist Republics the undersigned plenipotentiaries of each of the two parties discussed in strictly confidential conversations the question of the boundary of their respective spheres of influence in Eastern Europe. These conversations led to the following conclusions:

1. In the event of a territorial and political rearrangement in the areas belonging to the Baltic States (Finland, Estonia, Latvia, Lithuania) the northern boundary of Lithuania shall represent the boundary of the spheres of influence of Germany and the USSR. In this connection the interest of Lithuania in the Vilna area is recognized by each party.

2. In the event of a territorial and political rearrangement of the areas belonging to the Polish state the spheres of influence of Germany and the USSR shall be bounded approximately by the line of the rivers Narew, Vistula, and San.

The question of whether the interests of both parties make desirable the maintenance of an independent Polish state and how such a state should be bounded can only be definitely determined in the course of further political developments.

In any event both Governments will resolve this question by means of a friendly agreement.

3. With regard to Southeastern Europe attention is called by the Soviet side to its interest in Bessarabia. The German side declares its complete political disinterestedness in these areas.

4. This protocol shall be treated by both parties as strictly secret.

Moscow, August 23, 1939

For the Government
of the German Reich:

V. Ribbentrop

Plenipotentiary of the
Government of the USSR:

V. Molotov

26/The Meaning of the Soviet-German Nonaggression Pact—Speech to the Supreme Soviet

August 31, 1939

V. M. MOLOTOV

Comrades: Since the third session of the Supreme Soviet the international situation has shown no change for the better. On the contrary, it has become even more tense. The steps taken by various governments to put an end to this state of tension have obviously proved inadequate. They met with no success. This is true of Europe.

Nor has there been any change for the better in East Asia. Japanese troops continue to occupy the principal cities and a considerable part of the territory of China. Nor is Japan refraining from hostile acts against the USSR. Here, too, the situation has changed in the direction of further aggravation.

U.S., Congress, House Committee on Foreign Affairs, *The Strategy and Tactics of World Communism,* 80th Cong., 2d sess. (1948), H. Doc. 619, pp. 158–165, *excerpts.*

In view of this state of affairs, the conclusion of a pact of nonaggression between the USSR and Germany is of tremendous positive value, eliminating the danger of war between Germany and the Soviet Union. In order more fully to define the significance of this pact, I must first dwell on the negotiations which have taken place in recent months in Moscow with representatives of Great Britain and France. As you know, Anglo-French-Soviet negotiations for conclusion of a pact of mutual assistance against aggression in Europe began as far back as April.

True, the initial proposals of the British Government were, as you know, entirely unacceptable. They ignored the prime requisites for such negotiations—they ignored the principle of reciprocity and equality of obligations. In spite of this, the Soviet Government did not reject the negotiations and in turn put forward its own proposals. We were mindful of the fact that it was difficult for the Governments of Great Britain and France to make an abrupt change in their policy from an unfriendly attitude towards the Soviet Union which had existed quite recently to serious negotiations with the USSR based on the condition of equality of obligation.

However, the subsequent negotiations were not justified by their results. The Anglo-French-Soviet negotiations lasted four months. They helped to elucidate a number of questions. At the same time they made it clear to the representatives of Great Britain and France that the Soviet Union has to be seriously reckoned with in international affairs. But these negotiations encountered insuperable obstacles. The trouble, of course, did not lie in individual "formulations" or in particular clauses in the draft of the pact. No, the trouble was much more serious.

The conclusion of a pact of mutual assistance against aggression would have been of value only if Great Britain, France, and the Soviet Union had arrived at agreement as to definite military measures against the attack of an aggressor. Accordingly, for a certain period not only political but also military negotiations were conducted in Moscow with representatives of the British and French armies. However, nothing came of the military negotiations.

They encountered the difficulty that Poland, which was to be jointly guaranteed by Great Britain, France, and the USSR, rejected military assistance on the part of the Soviet Union. Attempts to overcome the objections of Poland met with no success. More, the negotiations showed that Great Britain was not anxious to overcome these objections of Poland, but on the contrary encouraged them. It is clear that, such being the attitude of the Polish Government and its principal ally towards military assistance on the part of the Soviet Union in the event of aggression, the Anglo-French-Soviet negotiations could not bear fruit. After this it became clear to us that the Anglo-French-Soviet negotiations were doomed to failure.

What have the negotiations with Great Britain and France shown? The Anglo-French-Soviet negotiations have shown that the position of Great Britain and France is marked by howling contradictions throughout. Judge for yourselves. On the one hand, Great Britain and France demanded that the USSR should give military assistance to Poland in case of aggression. The USSR, as you know, was willing to meet this demand, provided that the USSR itself received like assistance from Great Britain and France. On the other hand, precisely Great Britain and France brought Poland on the scene, who resolutely declined military assistance on the part of the USSR. Just try under such circumstances to reach an agreement regarding mutual assistance, when assistance on the part of the USSR is declared beforehand to be unnecessary and intrusive.

Further, on the one hand, Great Britain and France offered to guarantee the Soviet Union military assistance against aggression in return for like assistance on the part of the USSR. On the other hand, they themselves displayed extreme dilatoriness and an absolutely light-minded attitude towards the negotiations, entrusting them to individuals of secondary importance who were not invested with adequate powers.

It is enough to mention that the British and French military missions came to Moscow without any definite powers and without the right to conclude any military convention.

More, the British military mission arrived in Moscow without any mandate at all (*general laughter*), and it was only on the demand of our military mission that on the very eve of the breakdown of the negotiations they presented written credentials. But even these credentials were of the vaguest kind, that is, credentials without proper weight. Just try to distinguish between this light-minded attitude towards the negotiations on the part of Great Britain and France and frivolous make-believe at negotiations designed to discredit the whole business of negotiations. . . .

I shall now pass to the Soviet-German Nonaggression Pact. The decision to conclude a nonaggression pact between the USSR and Germany was adopted after military negotiations with France and Great Britain had reached an impasse owing to the insuperable differences I have mentioned. As the negotiations had shown that the conclusion of a pact of mutual assistance could not be expected, we could not but explore other possibilities of ensuring peace and eliminating the danger of war between Germany and the USSR. If the British and French Governments refused to reckon with this, that is their affair. It is our duty to think of the interests of the Soviet people, the interests of the Union of Soviet Socialist Republics. (*Prolonged applause*) . . . it is clear that the commercial and credit agreement [concluded on August 19] with Germany is fully in accord with the economic interests and defense needs of the

Soviet Union. This agreement is fully in accord with the decision of the Eighteenth Congress of our Party, which approved Stalin's statement as to the need for "strengthening business relations with all countries."

When, however, the German Government expressed the desire to improve political relations as well, the Soviet Government had no grounds for refusing. This gave rise to the question of concluding a non-aggression pact. Voices are now being heard testifying to the lack of understanding of the most simple reasons for the improvement of political relations between the Soviet Union and Germany which has begun. For example, people ask with an air of innocence how the Soviet Union could consent to improve political relations with a state of a fascist type. "Is that possible?" they ask. But they forget that this is not a question of our attitude towards the internal regime of another country but of the foreign relations between the two states. They forget that we hold the position of not interfering in the internal affairs of other countries and, correspondingly, of not tolerating interference in our own internal affairs. Furthermore, they forget the important principle of our foreign policy which was formulated by Stalin at the Eighteenth Party Congress as follows:

We stand for peace and the strengthening of business relations with all countries. That is our position; and we adhere to this position as long as these countries maintain like relations with the Soviet Union, and as long as they make no attempt to trespass on the interests of our country.

The meaning of these words is quite clear: the Soviet Union strives to maintain friendly relations with all non-Soviet countries, provided that these countries maintain a like attitude towards the Soviet Union. In our foreign policy towards non-Soviet countries, we have always been guided by Lenin's well-known principle of the peaceful coexistence of the Soviet state and of capitalist countries. A large number of examples might be cited to show how this principle has been carried out in practice. But I will confine myself to only a few. We have, for instance, a nonaggression and neutrality treaty with Fascist Italy ever since 1933. It has never occurred to anybody as yet to object to this treaty. And that is natural. Inasmuch as this pact meets the interests of the USSR, it is in accord with our principle of the peaceful coexistence of the USSR and the capitalist countries. We have nonaggression pacts also with Poland and certain other countries whose semi-fascist system is known to all. These pacts have not given rise to any misgivings either. . . .

August 23, 1939, the day the Soviet-German Nonaggression Pact was signed, is to be regarded as a date of great historical importance. . . .

The art of politics in the sphere of foreign relations does not consist in increasing the number of enemies for one's country. On the contrary, the art of politics in this sphere is to reduce the number of such enemies and to make the enemies of yesterday good neighbors, maintaining peaceable relations with one another. (*Applause*)

History has shown that enmity and wars between our country and Germany have been to the detriment of our countries, not to their benefit. Russia and Germany suffered most of all countries in the war of 1914–1918. Therefore the interests of the peoples of the Soviet Union and Germany stand in need of peaceable relations. The Soviet-German Nonaggression Pact puts an end to enmity between Germany and the USSR and this is in the interests of both countries. The fact that our outlooks and political systems differ must not and cannot be obstacles to the establishment of good political relations between both states, just as like differences are not impediments to good political relations which the USSR maintains with other non-Soviet capitalist countries. Only enemies of Germany and the USSR can strive to create and foment enmity between the peoples of these countries. We have always stood for amity between the peoples of the USSR and Germany, for the growth and development of friendship between the peoples of the Soviet Union and the German people. (*Loud and prolonged applause*)

The importance of the Soviet-German Nonaggression Pact lies in the fact that the two largest states of Europe have agreed to put an end to the enmity between them, to eliminate the menace of war and live at peace one with the other, making narrow thereby the zone of possible military conflicts in Europe. Even if military conflicts in Europe should prove unavoidable, the scope of hostilities will now be restricted. Only the instigators of a general European war can be displeased by this state of affairs, those who under the mask of pacifism would like to ignite a general conflagration in Europe.

The Soviet-German Pact has been the object of numerous attacks in the English, French, and American press. . . . Attempts are being made to spread the fiction that the signing of the Soviet-German Pact disrupted the negotiations with England and France on a mutual assistance pact. In reality, as you know, the very reverse is true. The Soviet Union signed the Nonaggression Pact with Germany, for one thing, in view of the fact that the negotiations with France and England had run into insuperable differences and ended in failure through the fault of the ruling classes of England and France.

Further, they go so far as to blame us because the pact, if you please, contains no clause providing for its denunciation in case one of the signatories is drawn into war under conditions which might give someone an external pretext to qualify this particular country as an aggressor. But they forget for some reason that such a clause and such a reservation is not to be found either in the Polish-German Nonaggression Pact signed in 1934 and annulled by Germany in 1939 against the wishes of Poland, or in the Anglo-German declaration on nonaggression signed only a few months ago. The question arises: Why cannot the USSR allow itself the same privilege as Poland and England allowed themselves long ago?

Finally, there are wiseacres who construe from the pact more than is written in it. (*Laughter*) For this purpose, all kinds of conjectures and hints are mooted in order to cast doubt on the pact in one or another country. But all this merely speaks for the hopeless impotence of the enemies of the pact who are exposing themselves more and more as enemies of both the Soviet Union and Germany, striving to provoke war between these countries.

In all this, we find fresh corroboration of Stalin's warning that we must be particularly cautious with warmongers who are accustomed to have others pull the chestnuts out of the fire for them. We must be on guard against those who see an advantage to themselves in bad relations between the USSR and Germany, in enmity between them and [those] who do not want peace and good neighborly relations between Germany and the Soviet Union.

We can understand why this policy is being pursued by out-and-out imperialists. But we cannot ignore such facts as the especial zeal with which some leaders of the Socialist parties of Great Britain and France have recently distinguished themselves in this matter. And these gentlemen have really gone the whole hog, and no mistake. (*Laughter*) These people positively demand that the USSR get itself involved in war against Germany on the side of Great Britain. Have not these rabid warmongers taken leave of their senses? (*Laughter*) Is it really difficult for these gentlemen to understand the purpose of the Soviet-German Nonaggression Pact, on the strength of which the USSR is not obligated to involve itself in war either on the side of Great Britain against Germany or on the side of Germany against Great Britain? Is it really difficult to understand that the USSR is pursuing and will continue to pursue its own independent policy, based on the interests of the peoples of the USSR and only their interests? (*Prolonged applause*)

If these gentlemen have such an uncontrollable desire to fight, let them do their own fighting without the Soviet Union. We would see what fighting stuff they are made of . . . The Soviet Union signed a pact with Germany, fully assured that peace between the peoples of the USSR and Germany is in the interests of all peoples, in the interests of universal peace. Every sincere supporter of peace will realize the truth of this. This pact corresponds to the fundamental interests of the working people of the Soviet Union and cannot weaken our vigilance in defense of these interests . . .

This pact, like the unsuccessful Anglo-French-Soviet negotiations, proves that no important questions of international relations, and questions of Eastern Europe even less, can be settled without the active participation of the Soviet Union, that any attempts to shut out the Soviet Union and decide such questions behind its back are doomed to failure.

Soviet Strategic Objectives: 1940

⊘27/Molotov's Demands on Hitler   *November 1940*

[The German Ambassador in the Soviet Union (Schulenburg) to the German Foreign Office]

TELEGRAM

VERY URGENT   Moscow, November 26, 1940—5:34 a.m.
STRICTLY SECRET   Received November 26, 1940—8:50 a.m.
No. 2362 of November 25

For the Reich Minister in person.

Molotov asked me to call on him this evening and in the presence of Dekanosov stated the following:

The Soviet Government has studied the contents of the statements of the Reich Foreign Minister in the concluding conversation on November 13 and takes the following stand:

The Soviet Government is prepared to accept the draft of the Four Power Pact which the Reich Foreign Minister outlined in the conversation of November 13, regarding political collaboration and reciprocal economic [support] subject to the following conditions:

(1) Provided that the German troops are immediately withdrawn from Finland, which, under the compact of 1939, belongs to the Soviet Union's sphere of influence. At the same time the Soviet Union undertakes to ensure peaceful relations with Finland and to protect German economic interests in Finland (export of lumber and nickel).

Raymond J. Sontag and James S. Beddie (eds.), *Nazi-Soviet Relations 1939–1941: Documents from the Archives of the German Foreign Office* (Washington, D.C.: Department of State, 1948), pp. 258–259, *excerpts.*

(2) Provided that within the next few months the security of the Soviet Union in the Straits is assured by the conclusion of a mutual assistance pact between the Soviet Union and Bulgaria, which geographically is situated inside the security zone of the Black Sea boundaries of the Soviet Union, and by the establishment of a base for land and naval forces of the U.S.S.R. within range of the Bosporus and the Dardanelles by means of a long-term lease.

(3) Provided that the area south of Batum and Baku in the general direction of the Persian Gulf is recognized as the center of the aspirations of the Soviet Union.

(4) Provided that Japan [renounces] her rights to concessions for coal and oil in Northern Sakhalin.

In accordance with the foregoing, the draft of the protocol concerning the delimitation of the spheres of influence as outlined by the Reich Foreign Minister would have to be amended so as to stipulate the focal point of the aspirations of the Soviet Union south of Batum and Baku in the general direction of the Persian Gulf.

Likewise, the draft of the protocol or agreement between Germany, Italy, and the Soviet Union with respect to Turkey should be amended so as to guarantee a base for light naval and land forces of the U.S.S.R. on [am] the Bosporus and the Dardanelles by means of a long-term lease, including—in case Turkey declares herself willing to join the Four Power Pact—a guarantee of the independence and of the territory of Turkey by the three countries named.

This protocol should provide that in case Turkey refuses to join the Four Powers, Germany, Italy, and the Soviet Union agree to work out and to carry through the required military and diplomatic measures, and a separate agreement to this effect should be concluded.

Furthermore there should be agreement upon:

(a) a third secret protocol between Germany and the Soviet Union concerning Finland (see Point 1 above);

(b) a fourth secret protocol between Japan and the Soviet Union concerning the renunciation by Japan of the oil and coal concession in Northern Sakhalin (in return for an adequate compensation);

(c) a fifth secret protocol between Germany, the Soviet Union, and Italy, recognizing that Bulgaria is geographically located inside the security zone of the Black Sea boundaries of the Soviet Union and that it is therefore a political necessity that a mutual assistance pact be concluded between the Soviet Union and Bulgaria, which in no way shall affect the internal regime of Bulgaria, her sovereignty or independence.

In conclusion Molotov stated that the Soviet proposal provided for five protocols instead of the two envisaged by the Reich Foreign Minister. He would appreciate a statement of the German view.

Schulenburg

FOR FURTHER STUDY

Alexandrov, Victor. *The Tukhachevsky Affair.* Englewood Cliffs, N.J.: Prentice-Hall, 1964.

Beloff, Max. *The Foreign Policy of Soviet Russia, 1929–1941.* 2 vols. New York: Oxford University Press, 1947, 1949.

Blackstock, Paul W. *The Secret Road to World War II: Soviet versus Western Intelligence, 1921–1939.* Chicago: Quadrangle Books, 1969.

Budurowycz, Bohdan B. *Polish-Soviet Relations, 1932–1939.* New York: Columbia University Press, 1963.

Cattell, David T. *Communism and the Spanish Civil War.* Berkeley: University of California Press, 1956.

_____. *Soviet Diplomacy and the Spanish Civil War.* Berkeley: University of California Press, 1957.

Dallin, David J. *Soviet Russia's Foreign Policy, 1939–1942.* New Haven, Conn.: Yale University Press, 1942.

Deakin, F. W., and G. R. Storry. *The Case of Richard Sorge.* London: Chatto & Windus, 1966.

Gafencu, Grigoire. *Prelude to the Russian Campaign.* London: Gollancz, 1945.

Ginsburgs, George. "The Soviet Union as a Neutral, 1939–1941," *Soviet Studies,* Vol. 10 (July 1958).

Jakobson, Max. *The Diplomacy of the Winter War: An Account of the Russo-Finnish Conflict, 1939–1940.* Cambridge, Mass.: Harvard University Press, 1961.

Johnson, Chalmers. *An Instance of Treason: Ozaki Hotsumi and the Sorge Spy Ring.* Stanford, Calif.: Stanford University Press, 1964.

Kennan, George F. *From Prague After Munich: Diplomatic Papers, 1938–1939.* Princeton, N.J.: Princeton University Press, 1968.

Krivitsky, Walter. *In Stalin's Secret Service.* London: Hamilton, 1939.

Krosby, H. Peter. *Finland, Germany, and the Soviet Union, 1940–1941: The Petsamo Dispute.* Madison: University of Wisconsin Press, 1968.

McLane, Charles B. *Soviet Policy and the Chinese Communists, 1931–1946.* New York: Columbia University Press, 1958.

McSherry, James E. *Stalin, Hitler, and Europe, 1933–1941.* 2 vols. Cleveland: World Publishing, 1968, 1970.

Maisky, Ivan. *Who Helped Hitler?* London: Hutchinson, 1964.

Moore, Harriet L. *Soviet Far Eastern Policy, 1931–1945.* Princeton, N.J.: Princeton University Press, 1945.

Presseisen, Ernst L. *Germany and Japan: A Study in Totalitarian Diplomacy, 1933–1941.* The Hague: Nijhoff, 1958.

Rossi, Angelo. *The Russo-German Alliance, 1939–1941.* Boston: Beacon, 1951.

Schapiro, Leonard. *Soviet Treaty Series, 1917–1939.* 2 vols. Washington, D.C.: Georgetown University Press, 1950, 1955.

Sontag, Raymond J., and James S. Beddie (eds.). *Nazi-Soviet Relations: 1939–1941, Documents from the Archives of the German Foreign Office.* Washington, D.C.: Department of State, 1948.

Tanner, Väinö. *The Winter War: Finland Against Russia.* Stanford, Calif.: Stanford University Press, 1950.

Taracouzio, T. A. *War and Peace in Soviet Diplomacy.* New York: Macmillan, 1940.

Tarulis, Albert N. *Soviet Policy Toward the Baltic States, 1918–1940.* Notre Dame, Ind.: University of Notre Dame Press, 1958.

Ulam, Adam B. *Expansion and Coexistence: The History of Soviet Foreign Policy, 1917–1967.* New York: Praeger, 1968.

Wheeler-Bennett, John W. *Munich: Prologue to Tragedy.* New York: Duell Sloan & Pearce, 1948.

_____. *The Nemesis of Power.* New York: St. Martin's, 1953.

5

the wartime alliance

The Nazi-Soviet honeymoon ended on June 22, 1941, as German troops swept into the USSR on an eighteen-hundred-mile front. Later that day, V. M. Molotov, the People's Commissar for Foreign Affairs, made the announcement to the Soviet people:

Citizens of the Soviet Union! The Soviet Government and its head, Comrade Stalin, have instructed me to make the following statement:

Today, at 4 A.M., without any complaints having been presented to the Soviet Union, without a declaration of war, German troops attacked our country, attacked our borders at many points, and bombed from their airplanes our cities of Zhitomir, Kiev, Sevastopol, Kaunas, and some others, killing and wounding over 200 persons. There were also enemy air raids and artillery shelling from Rumanian and Finnish territory.

This unheard of attack upon our country is perfidy unparalleled in the history of civilized nations. The attack on our country was perpetrated despite the fact that a Treaty of non-aggression had been signed between the USSR and Germany, and that the Soviet Government was most faithfully abiding by all the provisions of this Treaty. The attack upon our country was perpetrated despite the fact that during the entire period of the operation of this Treaty the German Government could not find grounds for a single complaint to the USSR concerning observance of the Treaty. The entire responsibility for this brigand attack upon the Soviet Union falls fully and completely upon the German-Fascist rulers.

Twice within a generation were the Bolsheviks engaged in a struggle for survival. This time, however, they were to have powerful allies. A common cause—the destruction of Hitlerism—submerged ideological differences and political antagonisms. Winston Churchill, long an open opponent of Bolshevism, cast aside politics and personal feelings and offered the Soviets friendship and alliance. The day after the Nazi invasion, he made his intentions clear in a broadcast to the British people:

No one has been a more consistent opponent of Communism than I have for the last twenty-five years. I will unsay no word that I have spoken about it. But all this fades away before the spectacle which is now unfolding. The past, with its crimes, its follies, and its tragedies, flashes away. . . .

We have but one aim and one single, irrevocable purpose. We are resolved to destroy Hitler and every vestige of the Nazi regime. From this nothing will turn us—nothing. We will never parley, we will never negotiate with Hitler or any of his gang. We shall fight him by land, we shall fight him by sea, we shall fight him in the air, until, with God's help, we have rid the earth of his shadow and liberated its peoples from his yoke. Any man or state who fights on against Nazidom will have our aid. Any man or state who marches with Hitler is our foe. . . . That is our policy and that is our declaration. It follows, therefore, that we shall give whatever help we can to Russia and the Russian people. . . .

Soon afterward, the British and Soviet governments entered into negotiations and on July 12 signed a protocol in which both agreed not "to negotiate nor conclude an armistice or treaty of peace except by mutual agreement" and "to render each other assistance and support of all kinds in the present war against Hitlerite Germany." On July 18, Stalin replied directly to Churchill. Thus began the forging of "The Grand Alliance" against Hitler.

As Nazi Panzer divisions rolled farther into Russia, Western military experts predicted the collapse of the Soviet Union within a matter of weeks. Their appraisal of Soviet military power was influenced by the known weakening of the Red Army caused by the 1937 purges, the poor performance of Soviet forces in the Finnish winter campaign of 1939–1940, and, perhaps most important of all, the impressive record of Nazi successes in the West and in the Balkans.

On July 3, Stalin made a momentous radio appeal to the Soviet people (reading 28). With rare candor, no doubt dictated by the extreme gravity of the situation, he admitted that the country was in mortal peril, that there was no time for comforting words. Sensing a need to justify his pro-Nazi policy orientation of 1939–1941, he held that this course had afforded the Soviets time to strengthen their defenses. For reasons of his own, Stalin did not mention the territorial acquisitions of that period—the Baltic states, the eastern part of Poland, and Bessarabia. He emphasized instead the initial German advantage from the "treacherous" attack and appealed for the people to unite to defeat the invader as their ancestors before them had triumphed over Napoleon and Kaiser Wilhelm II, both of whom had enjoyed a reputation of invincibility.

Note: Stalin did not tell the Soviet people that he had ignored repeated warnings from Churchill in April and May of the impending German invasion;[2] nor did he assume responsibility for the nation's unprepared-ness. Indeed, if we are to believe Khrushchev's revelations, made at the Twentieth Party Congress in February 1956, about Stalin's shortcomings, it was Stalin's refusal to heed well-founded and persistent intelligence and diplomatic reports of imminent German invasion that cost the Soviets so heavily and facilitated the rapidity and extent of the initial Nazi advances. According to Khrushchev:

Despite these particularly grave warnings, the necessary steps were not taken to prepare the country properly for defense and to prevent it from being caught unawares.

Did we have time and the capabilities for such preparations? Yes, we had the time and capabilities. . . .

Had our industry been mobilized properly and in time to supply the Army with the necessary material, our wartime losses would have been decidedly smaller. Such mobilization had not been, however, started in time. . . .

When the fascist armies had actually invaded Soviet territory and military operations began, Moscow issued the order that the German fire was not to be returned. Why? It was because Stalin, despite evident facts, thought that the war had not yet started, that this was only a provocative action on the part of several undisciplined sections of the German Army, and that our reaction might serve as a reason for the Germans to begin the war.

As you see, everything was ignored: warnings of certain Army commanders, declarations of deserters from the enemy army, and even the open hostility of the enemy. Is this an example of the alertness of the Chief of the Party and of the State at this particularly significant historical moment?[3]

The complete truth may never be known.

As the Nazis penetrated deeper into Russia, even to the outskirts of Leningrad and Moscow, the Soviets relied on their traditional scourges for any would-be conqueror—the vastness of their country and the severity of its winters. They also adopted a "scorched earth" policy, leaving nothing of use to the invader. At first the Germans were greeted as liberators in many *non-Russian* areas of the Soviet Union, such as the Ukraine—an illuminating testament to a generation of communist rule. But the Nazis, themselves captives of their racist ideology, came as self-proclaimed conquerors, intent upon colonizing the country and brutally exploiting its manpower and resources.[4] They thus wasted, politically and psychologically, the strong vein of anti-communist sentiment and by this blunder contributed greatly to their eventual defeat.

While the Nazis continued to advance into Russia, anticipating the victory that would make them masters of the Eurasian land mass, the newly formed Allied coalition sought to establish a firm basis for military cooperation. Churchill had promised to render all possible aid, but obviously only the United States could meet the enormous needs of the Soviet Union. In America, as in Great Britain, all hostility toward the Soviet Union was overshadowed by the resolve to work together in the common interest. President Roosevelt immediately moved to extend lend-lease aid. This aspect of cooperation with the Soviets proved successful, though not without frequent difficulties. Harry Hopkins, President Roosevelt's trusted adviser and trouble-shooter, flew to Moscow in July 1941 to assess the Soviet capacity and determination to resist Hitler. His favorable report helped convince Roosevelt, and shipments to Russia, under an interim lend-lease agreement, began almost immediately. In 1942, though understandably eager to take the offensive against the Japanese, the United States undertook to deliver more than $1 billion worth of war material and supplies to the Soviet Union. Subsequently, other lend-lease agreements were concluded. The USSR's contact with its Allies was effected via Murmansk, Iran, and Vladivostok, particularly the first two. America eventually supplied the USSR with approximately $11 billion in vitally needed goods of every description: trucks, tanks, rolling stock, machine tools, textiles, shoes, oil, and food.

British-Soviet cooperation first developed in Iran, where events impelled them to act in concert. Confronted with an imminent pro-Nazi coup in Teheran, the British and Soviets occupied the country. In its note of August 25, 1941, the Soviet government justified the Allied action on the basis of the pertinent provision of its 1921 treaty with Iran, which held that:

. . . if a third party should attempt to carry out a policy of usurpation by means of armed intervention in Persia, or if such power should desire to use Persian territory as a base for operations against the Russian Socialist Federal Soviet Republic, or if a foreign power should threaten the frontiers of the Russian Socialist Federal Soviet Republic, or those of its allies, and if the Persian Government should not be able to put a stop to such a menace after having been once called upon to do so by the Russian Socialist Federal Soviet Republic, the Russian Socialist Federal Soviet Republic shall have the right to advance its troops into the Persian interior for the purpose of carrying out the military operations necessary for its defense. The Soviet Government undertakes, however, to withdraw its troops from Persian territory as soon as the danger has been removed.

By mid-September 1941, the Shah capitulated and abdicated in favor of his son, the present ruler of Iran. The joint Allied occupation was followed by a Treaty of Alliance with Iran, signed on January 29, 1942, and Iran soon became a main Allied artery of supplies for the Soviet war effort. In addition to outlining Allied prerogatives, including the right to "maintain in Iranian territory land, sea, and air forces in such numbers as they consider necessary," the treaty assured Iran that the Allies would withdraw their forces "from Iranian territory not later than six months after all hostilities between the Allied Powers and Germany and her associates have been suspended by the conclusion of an armistice or armistices, or on the conclusion of peace between them, whichever date is the earlier."[5] Soviet failure to abide by the terms of this provision precipitated one of the early crises of the postwar period—one involving Iran, the Great Powers, and the United Nations.

Meanwhile, the German advance overran the Soviet economic and industrial heartland. It failed, however, to attain its principal strategic objective: the destruction of the Red Army. Moscow and Leningrad held firm, and by the beginning of December it was apparent that Hitler would not winter in the Kremlin. As in 1812, winter providently came early.* Furthermore, the Japanese surprise attack on Pearl Harbor on December 7, 1941, meant that the Soviets no longer had to fear a two-front war. Nonetheless, the danger to the Allied cause was never greater than during the bleak winter of 1941–1942—a winter of successive defeats and disasters—and the summer of 1942. But when the Nazis and the Japanese failed to attain victory by late 1942, their ultimate defeat was assured. Time and resources favored the Allies.

In November 1942, the British and Americans landed in North Africa, while the Soviets engaged the Germans in the epic struggle for Stalingrad. The battle-to-the-death for this vital industrial center on the lower Volga was a symbol of Soviet determination to retreat no further. The grim struggle for the city continued for weeks, fought street by street, house by house. On February 2, 1943, the Nazi forces surrendered. Stalingrad was saved. The defeat was one from which the Nazis never recovered, and the Allied cause received an incalculable boost of morale.

On all fronts 1943 marked the turning of the tide. Now, political differences within the strange alliance between communist Russia and the Western democracies assumed added dimensions. All had shared the resolve to defeat the Axis Powers, subordinating other war aims to this overriding objective. However, as *military* victory approached, the *polit-*

---

* The need to postpone the invasion of Russia from May 15 to June 22, which was occasioned by the resistance of Yugoslavia in April 1941, cost the Germans dearly. One astute observer commenting on this development observed that: "The winter had fallen three weeks earlier than usual; and it is one of the many ironies of the war, that the Yugoslav defiance, which had produced so little immediate impression on the Germans, may have paid compound interest in the end by delaying the onset of the attack on Russia just long enough to permit the Russian winter to intervene decisively. The Russian historic stubbornness, flair for strategy, and enlightened adoption of the mechanical developments of modern warfare, with the appropriate tactical implications, had done the rest." Strategicus, *A Short History of the Second World War* (London: Faber & Faber, n.d.), p. 117.

ical dilemmas and disagreements over the postwar settlement sharpened. The post-1945 Cold War was rooted in the conflicting, incompatible objectives of the Allies. Each understandably sought greater security against a possible German revival. But this meant different things to each. Subsequent Soviet maneuvering for power, position, and economic advantage rendered impossible the task of formulating a postwar settlement. Throughout the war, even during the darkest days of the Nazi invasion, Stalin was more concerned with political issues than were Churchill or Roosevelt. Certainly he had a clearer idea, politically and otherwise, of what he wanted as a victor, but for the time being military necessities overshadowed political differences. Defeat of the Axis Powers took precedence over all other considerations. At the Inter-Allied Conference in London in late September 1941, Soviet Ambassador Maisky pledged his government's adherence to the principles of the Atlantic Charter (drawn up by Churchill and Roosevelt at their mid-Atlantic meeting of August 14, 1941), called for Allied unity in the struggle against Germany, and announced Soviet support for the right of every nation "to establish such a social order and to choose such a form of government as it deems opportune and necessary for the better promotion of its economic and cultural prosperity." As long as specific political questions did not intrude upon the straightforward task of destroying Nazism, Allied unity held firm.

From the first forging of the coalition, the Soviet Union pressed for the launching of a second front in Europe that would draw forty to sixty German divisions away from the East. This demand was repeated again and again and proved a "constant dissonance in the theme of coalition."[6] Stalin broached the issue in his first direct communication to Churchill on July 18, 1941, and many times again (see pertinent sections in readings 29 and 30). Stalin's xenophobia toward the West reflected his uncompromising ideological hostility and his memory of two trying decades of Soviet-Western diplomatic relations. He was particularly critical of what he regarded as Allied unwillingness to make military efforts comparable to those being made by the Red Army and the Soviet people. This remained a sore point in Allied relations. To cement closer ties and to try to overcome such attitudes, the British signed a twenty-year treaty of alliance with the Soviets on May 26, 1942. Molotov had been led by earlier talks, first with Churchill and then with Roosevelt, to expect a second front in France in 1942, and in his speech of June 18, 1942, calling upon the Supreme Soviet to ratify the Soviet-British alliance, he stated this as a promised certainty rather than as an eventual intention. The result was Soviet disappointment, open skepticism of Allied ability, and continued suspicion. At no time during the war did Stalin show a real understanding or appreciation of the unique logistic and military problems involved in a projected invasion across the English Channel—the mammoth amount of shipping required to transport millions of men and many more millions of tons of equipment —or of America's need to fight an additional war against a powerful foe in the Pacific. Patient Allied efforts at compromise with their distrustful partner proved largely futile, for Stalin invariably interpreted such Allied efforts in the worst possible light.

Of the many political problems besetting Soviet-Western wartime relations, none assumed more dramatic proportions or proved more elusive of accord than that of the future of Poland. Since the Nazi-Soviet partition of 1939, there had been no diplomatic relations between the Soviet Union and Poland. As far as the Soviet government was concerned, Poland no longer existed. With the advent of the Nazi attack, however, Stalin adopted a conciliatory position with respect to the Polish question, a gesture designed to strengthen the newly formed bonds of friendship with the West. On July 30, 1941, an agreement was reached in London between the Soviet and Polish governments that was supposed to serve as a basis for future amicable relations (reading 31). In a fundamental reversal of policy, the Soviets conceded that the territorial changes of 1939 were no longer valid. Diplomatic relations between Poland and the USSR were reestablished and plans made for training and equipping a Polish army on Soviet soil from among the thousands of Poles imprisoned after the 1939 partition.

Several days later, a portentous article appeared in *Pravda*. Though applauding the Soviet-Polish pact, it justified Soviet action in the 1939 partition on the grounds that Moscow was "duty bound to give a helping hand to the Ukrainians and Byelorussians who made up most of the population in the eastern regions of Poland."[7] *Pravda* also asserted that although the time was not suitable for discussion of final frontier lines, there was nothing "immutable" in the Polish-Soviet frontier as established by the 1921 Treaty of Riga: "The question of future Soviet-Polish borders is a matter for the future." Thus did the Soviets dilute the sense of their signed word, even as the ink dried on the agreement. Similar occurrences were to mar future Allied unity.

During British Foreign Minister Anthony Eden's visit to Moscow in December 1941, Stalin insisted on recognition for the Soviet frontiers as they existed in June 1941, which would sanction all Soviet territorial acquisitions since September 1939. Though evaded at the time, this frequently repeated demand became, with the change in Allied fortunes, a growing source of discord. The Allies opposed Soviet claims to eastern Poland, as well as any prospective incorporation of the Baltic states into the Soviet Union. Tension between the Polish government-in-exile and the Soviet government reached the breaking point over the Katyn Forest controversy.* On April 13, 1943, the Nazis reported the "discovery" of the mass grave of Polish officers and blamed the Soviets for the atrocity. The Polish government-in-exile proposed an impartial investigation of this allegation. Stalin's reply was quick and harsh: he severed diplomatic relations with the Polish government, holding that Polish belief in the Nazi accusations indicated a lack of faith in the integrity of the Soviet government; he also charged the Poles with exploiting the "Hitlerite slanderous fake" in order to force territorial concessions from the Soviet government. Though the ostensible cause of the breach was the Polish request for an investigation of the German charges, in the background was the continued insistence of the Poles upon a restoration of their 1939 frontier with the Soviet Union. The Poles refused to settle for territorial compensation at the expense of Germany. This Katyn incident was most convenient for Stalin. Eager to ensure a pro-Soviet (communist) regime in postwar Poland, he announced the establishment of an organization known as the "Union of Polish Patriots" a few days later. This group later served as the basis for the Soviet puppet Lublin government. As a postscript to the Katyn Forest controversy, it may be noted that upon reconquering the area, the Soviets conducted their own investigation and "conclusively" placed the blame on the Nazis. The issue was later raised at the Nuremberg war crimes trials, but the Soviet representatives chose neither to refute the German accusation of 1943 nor to take advantage of the opportunity to clear themselves of the widely believed charge. In such circumstances, silence decrees a presumption of Soviet guilt.†

The Soviet-Polish rupture seriously tried Allied unity. The Allies, reluctant to jeopardize the alliance, beset by continual Soviet demands for a second front, and increasingly indignant at Soviet disparagement

* After the partition of Poland the Soviets interned, among others, some 15,000 Polish officers and men, the elite of the defunct Polish army. By the spring of 1940 their whereabouts were a mystery. With the resumption of Polish-Soviet diplomatic relations in July 1941, the Polish government-in-exile repeatedly requested information concerning the fate of these Poles. Soviet officialdom maintained an ominous silence. The Nazis placed the blame for the murder on the Soviet government. Meanwhile, the Polish government-in-exile reacted with honorable intent but little political prudence and requested the International Red Cross to conduct an investigation.

† The House of Representatives Select Committee to Conduct an Investigation and Study of the Facts, Evidence, and Circumstances of the Katyn Forest Massacre concluded, in its *Interim Report of July 2, 1952* (82nd Cong., 2nd sess., H. Rept. 2430) that "the Soviet NKVD committed the mass murders . . . as a calculated plot to eliminate all Polish leaders who subsequently would have opposed the Soviets' plans for communizing Poland." A dispassionate study by J. K. Zawodny, *Death in the Forest* (Notre Dame, Ind.: University of Notre Dame Press, 1962), places the responsibility conclusively on the Soviet Union.

of their war effort and aid, did not wish to press the Polish issue too far. The possibility that Stalin might conclude a sudden and separate agreement with Hitler as in 1939 also concerned Allied leaders.[8] The temper eased noticeably when Moscow announced the dissolution of the Communist International on May 22, 1943. In reply to a question from a British correspondent, Stalin expressed the hope that this action would end all fears that the Soviet Union "intends to intervene in the life of other nations and to 'Bolshevize' them" and that it would promote the unity of all groups fighting Hitlerism. Undoubtedly a dramatic gesture aimed at assuaging Western feelings and at obscuring the Polish question, the announced dissolution of the Comintern seemed to herald the Kremlin's abandonment of its global apparatus designed to subvert existing governments and serve Soviet interests. We now know that the Comintern was never really dissolved; it merely functioned in secret.*

The growing complex of political problems convinced the heads of state that a meeting was necessary. Accordingly, at a preliminary conference of Foreign Ministers—Hull, Eden, Molotov—in Moscow from October 15–30, 1943, an agenda was prepared, and on November 28, 1943, Stalin, Churchill, and Roosevelt met at Teheran. A broad range of topics was discussed: the makeup of the proposed United Nations Organization, Soviet interests in the Far East, the future of Germany, the Polish question, and Soviet objectives in Eastern Europe. Shortly after the conference ended, one of the American participants summed up in a memorandum what the full application of Stalin's desires could mean:

> Germany is to be broken up and kept broken up. The states of eastern, southeastern, and central Europe will not be permitted to group themselves into any federations or association. France is to be stripped of her colonies and strategic bases beyond her borders and will not be permitted to maintain any appreciable military establishment. Poland and Italy will remain approximately their present territorial size, but it is doubtful if either will be permitted to maintain any appreciable military force. The result would be that the Soviet Union would be the only important military and political force on the continent of Europe. The rest of Europe would be reduced to military and political impotence.[9]

Western leaders considered this statement unnecessarily pessimistic.

---

* See Wolfgang Leonhard, *Child of the Revolution* (Chicago: Regnery, 1957). In this personal account of life as a professional Communist Party functionary, the author tells of his assignment to the German section of the Comintern in Moscow after its "dissolution" in May 1943. There he was trained for future political tasks in Germany. The Comintern apparatus was kept intact, merely moving its headquarters to an anonymous section of Moscow.

Meanwhile, the military picture progressively brightened. Soviet offensives drained Nazi strength and drove the Germans from Soviet soil. By January 1944 the Red Army had crossed the former Polish frontier. On January 10, 1944, the Soviet news agency TASS contradicted Polish claims to the 1939 boundary (reading 32) and accused the Polish government of deliberately falsifying the frontier question. The incorporation of the western Ukraine and western Byelorussia, according to TASS, reflected the wishes of the peoples living in these areas. The Soviet government continued to favor the existence of a strong, independent, friendly Polish state, whose western frontier should be extended "through incorporation with Poland of ancient Polish lands previously wrested by Germany."

The intransigence both of the leaders of the Polish government-in-exile and of Stalin, and the fear on the part of the Western Powers of prejudicing postwar cooperation with the Soviets, precluded an acceptable settlement. At the urging of both Churchill and Roosevelt, however, Mikolajczyk, the Polish Prime Minister, journeyed to Moscow in a desperate effort to reach an agreement. He arrived on July 30, 1944, on the eve of the tragic attempt by the Polish underground to expel the Nazis and liberate Warsaw. Four days earlier, the Soviet government had signed an agreement with a puppet creation of the Kremlin, the Committee of National Liberation, which became the core of the postwar communist regime. This Committee declared Lublin the capital of Poland. The Soviet statement only heightened an already tense situation:

> The Soviet Government declares that it considers the military operations of the Red Army on the territory of Poland as operations on the territory of a sovereign, friendly, allied state. In connection with this, the Soviet Government does not intend to establish on the territory of Poland organs of its own administration, considering this the task of the Polish people.
>
> It has decided, in view of this, to conclude with the Polish Committee of National Liberation an agreement on relations between the Soviet Government and the Polish administration.
>
> The Soviet Government declares that it does not pursue aims of acquiring any part of Polish territory or of a change of social structure in Poland, and that the military operations of the Red Army on the territory of Poland are dictated solely by military necessity and by the striving to render the friendly Polish people aid in its liberation from German occupation.[10]

This assertion, that the Soviets had no territorial ambitions nor desire to alter existing institutions, had previously been made by Molotov on April 2, 1944, as the Red Army approached the Romanian frontier. However, he referred specifically to the Soviet-Romanian frontier as it existed in 1941, thus making it indisputably clear that the 1940 Soviet annexation of Bessarabia was not open for negotiation. The full extent of Soviet objectives in Eastern Europe was to become tragically evident in the next few years.

Another source of dissension among the Allies, Finland, had proved particularly embarrassing in the early days of the war. Western sympathy toward Finland was long standing, and Finland's joining (voluntarily or not) the Nazi attack on the USSR had placed American policy-makers in a quandary. Prior to United States entry into the war, the Finns attempted to rationalize their behavior; the Soviet government had acted immediately to refute Finnish contentions. Once America entered the war, its treatment of Finland as a belligerent was but a matter of time. Efforts to induce Finland to disengage itself from German domination failed. By the summer of 1944, Finland stood alone with no prospects of help from any quarter, not even from Germany. On September 19, 1944, an armistice was signed with the Soviet Union, and Finland was out of the war.* Under the final treaty of peace signed in 1947, Finland's independence was preserved, but its foreign policy orientation understandably reflected the prevailing attitudes of its powerful neighbor.

The year 1944 was one of Allied victories. On June 6, Anglo-American-Canadian forces landed in France—the long-awaited second front was a reality. By the end of the year France had been liberated and the final preparations for the invasion of Germany itself were under way. On the Eastern Front Soviet military leaders shifted their offensives "with astonishing regularity, power and circumspection, like a boxer who systematically covers his opponent with telling blows without expecting that one single blow will knock him down."[11] With the approach of victory the unresolved political problems could no longer be evaded. The future of Poland and of all Eastern Europe, the division of Germany, the role of the Soviet Union in the war against Japan, the coordination of the final assault on Germany, and the preparations for the establishment of the United Nations Organization—all had to be discussed and agreements reached. To facilitate solutions to these knotty problems, Roosevelt and Churchill expressed a willingness to meet with Stalin, and so, once again, the Western leaders embarked on a long journey, this time to the Crimea, in an attempt to ensure the

---

* The terms imposed on Finland were harsh, but they did ensure that its independence would be preserved. They provided that: (1) Finland would withdraw her troops behind the Soviet-Finnish frontier line of March 12, 1940. (2) This would continue as the boundary except that in the far north Finland agreed to cede Petsamo to the Soviets and granted them a naval base at Porkkala-Udd; in return, the Soviets agreed to relinquish their previously held lease on the peninsula of Hangoe. (3) Finland would pay a $300 million indemnity in kind in six years. (4) Soviet forces would not occupy Finland; the administration was to remain in control of Finnish authorities.

peace. The Yalta Conference was held in the former Czarist palace of Livadia February 4–10, 1945.

Much has been written about this conference. Some insist that Eastern Europe and China were here "sold out" to the Soviets; others argue that the agreements reached were justifiable under existing circumstances and information known and that they reflected military realities. In any honest effort at appraisal we must remember that differences in the relative weights accorded the same "facts" will result in strikingly different final judgments. Before examining the Yalta deliberations, it is useful to review the military-political picture of February 1945.

Allied troops were at the Rhine; Soviet forces prepared to cross the Oder and launch the final attack on Berlin, some forty miles away. The Red Army already controlled most of Eastern Europe; Tito's Partisans dominated the political scene in Yugoslavia. In the Far East, despite major victories over the Japanese at Iwo Jima and Okinawa, American military experts expected a difficult fight before Japan's final surrender. In November 1944, the Joint Chiefs of Staff had weighed the pros and cons of Soviet participation in the war against Japan and concluded that:

(a) We desire Russian entry at the earliest possible date consistent with her ability to engage in offensive operations and are prepared to offer the maximum support possible without prejudice to our main effort against Japan.

(b) We consider that the mission of Russian Far Eastern Forces should be to conduct an all-out offensive against Manchuria to force the commitment of Japanese forces and resources in North China and Manchuria that might otherwise be employed in the defense of Japan, to conduct intensive air operations against Japan proper and to interdict lines of communication between Japan and the mainland of Asia.[12]

On the eve of the conference most Western leaders firmly believed and hoped that it would be possible to extend the unity forged in wartime to the postwar period.* Suspicion of Soviet intentions did exist among some professional diplomats, but popular sentiment in the West favored continued collaboration with the Soviet Union. Admiration for the courage displayed by the Soviet people and sympathy for their suffering and sacrifice were widespread. It remained for political developments and Stalin's blatant disregard of his pledged word to

* However, it should be noted that on January 8, 1945, Churchill, in writing to Roosevelt about their coming meeting with Stalin, prophetically wrote: "This may well be a fateful Conference, coming at a moment when the Great Allies are so divided and the shadow of the war lengthens out before us. At the present time I think the end of this war may well prove to be more disappointing than was the last." Winston S. Churchill, *Triumph and Tragedy* (Boston: Houghton Mifflin, 1953), p. 341.

bring about a fundamental shift in climate and to trigger the Cold War. But this was still in the future.

The most important political discussions at Yalta focused on the Polish and German questions and on the conditions under which the Soviet Union would later enter the war against Japan.

The discussions between Western and Soviet military staffs gave no evidence of competition or distrust in their planning for the final assault on Germany. According to the eminent historian Herbert Feis:

> Each showed a wish to have the other push its attack with all possible speed and vigor so that the Germans would not be able to transfer troops between east and west and their reserves would the sooner be used up. Thus no attempt was made to reach agreement as to the places or lines along which the armies coming from the east and from the west should stop. Their destination was to be decided by the course of battle; the question of where and how long the armies of each would *remain* was left to the makers of political arrangements.[13]

However, the political issues affecting the fate of postwar Europe did not fare so well. The Polish question figured "at no fewer than seven out of the eight plenary meetings of the Yalta Conference."[14] Attention centered on four key aspects of this perhaps most vexing of all existing questions: (a) a formula for establishing a single provisional government for Poland; (b) how and when to hold free elections; (c) possible solutions to the future of Poland's frontiers, both in the east and the west; (d) steps designed to safeguard the security of the Soviet rear.

The communiqué issued at the end of the Yalta Conference, on February 12, 1945, took note of these and other problems and sketched solutions that, if applied with fidelity and good faith, might have served the interests of all (reading 33). But it was evident, even before the war was won, that Stalin intended to interpret the Yalta Declaration in a manner most apt to enhance Soviet security and power. A prime catalyst in the disintegration of the wartime alliance, the Polish question represented, in a larger sense, a barometer recording the peril points of two incompatible conceptions of security.

Agreement on Germany's immediate future came more readily. All parties agreed that Germany must surrender unconditionally. Upon the termination of hostilities an Allied Control Council was to serve as the top coordinating and policy organ of the occupying powers; three zones of occupation were established, a fourth later being allocated to France from the American and British zones; the Soviets agreed that the Western Powers were to have free and unhampered access to Berlin, which was situated deep inside the Soviet zone of occupation; and the basic principles guiding reparations arrangements were reached. Accord was also achieved on the proposed organization of the United Nations and on the broad approaches determining future political actions in Eastern Europe and the Balkans. The stage was well set at Yalta to sustain concerted military action against Germany until final victory and to manage the German surrender smoothly.

The Far East played no part in the published formal deliberations at Yalta; a secret protocol was drawn up. No mention of it, therefore, appeared in the public statement issued at the end of the conference. Throughout the war the Soviet Union maintained strictly correct relations with Japan in accordance with the five-year neutrality pact of April 13, 1941. Only in the last days of the war did Soviet forces become involved in the Pacific conflict. Moscow had departed slightly from its posture of neutrality and associated itself with the Chinese government by signing the Four Power Declaration of November 1, 1943, under which the United States, Great Britain, China, and the Soviet Union pledged themselves to cooperate against all their common enemies. More significantly, as early as August 1942 Stalin had assured Harriman of Soviet help in the war against Japan at the appropriate time and had specifically repeated this assurance in November 1943 and in September and October 1944. There had been some informal discussion at Teheran of Soviet territorial objectives in the Far East, with Stalin expressing interest in a warm-water port, the return of southern Sakhalin, and the acquisition of the Kuril Islands, but nothing definite was settled at the time. In October 1944 at the Moscow Conference, Stalin reaffirmed to Churchill his willingness to enter the war against Japan three months after the defeat of Germany, subject to certain conditions, which were presented to the American government in December and served as the basis for the secret agreement on the Far East that was concluded at Yalta (reading 34). They provided for the preservation of the status quo in Outer Mongolia (Mongolian People's Republic), the return of southern Sakhalin, the internationalization of the port of Dairen, the annexation of the Kuril Islands, and the restoration of former Russian rights in Manchuria. These stipulations were later accepted by China and incorporated into the Sino-Soviet Treaty of Friendship and Alliance, signed on August 14, 1945, which contained a 'Soviet promise "to render to China moral support and aid in military supplies and other material resources, such support and aid to be entirely given to the National Government as the Central Government of China."

Was the price paid for Soviet participation excessive considering the dividends expected? Would the United States government have accepted Stalin's conditions had it realized the imminence of Japan's surrender? Indeed, in view of traditional Russian Far Eastern objectives, would Stalin not have entered the war even without the Yalta concessions? Ironically, it was the American military experts, with their estimates of another eighteen months of war after the defeat of Germany and anticipated casualties approaching the million mark in any invasion of the Japanese home islands, who influenced the political decision at Yalta to grant Soviet demands; these concessions helped restore the USSR to a position of power in the Far East comparable to that which it held in 1904, on the eve of the Russo-Japanese war.

The intricate and fascinating story of all the controversies, discussions, and deals that marked the Yalta deliberations,[15] and their implications for the postwar period, will long be debated by historians. We who examine the record in retrospect would do well to ponder the afterthoughts on Yalta so eloquently expressed by Sir Winston Churchill:

> It is not permitted to those charged with dealing with events in times of war or crisis to confine themselves purely to the statement of broad general principles on which good people agree. They have to take definite decisions from day to day. They have to adopt postures which must be solidly maintained, otherwise how can any combinations for action be maintained? It is easy, after the Germans are beaten, to condemn those who did their best to hearten the Russian military effort and to keep in harmonious contact with our great Ally, who had suffered so frightfully. What would have happened if we had quarrelled with Russia while the Germans still had three or four hundred divisions on the fighting front? Our hopeful assumptions were soon to be falsified. Still, they were the only ones possible at the time.[16]

With the approach of victory the tide of trust that had flowed at Yalta ebbed fast; "Stalin was giving way to suspicion of the American-British conduct of the war and to resentment at their attempts to maintain influence in any region near Soviet frontiers. To the Western Allies it seemed that under the spell of victory the Russians were becoming indifferent to their wartime vows."[17]

On May 8, 1945, Germany surrendered unconditionally. Japan collapsed quickly thereafter.* The dropping of the atomic bomb on Hiroshima on August 6, 1945, and the entry of the USSR two days later into the war sealed Japan's fate. She capitulated on August 14; the formal signing was aboard the battleship *Missouri* in Tokyo Bay on September 2.

The war was over. The challenge of the peace remained.

---

* During the late spring and early summer the Japanese government sought to enter into surrender negotiations with the West, hopeful that the Soviet government would act as a disinterested intermediary. For an excellent account of these negotiations and Soviet behavior as seen from the Japanese position see Toshikazu Kase, *Journey to the Missouri* (New Haven, Conn.: Yale University Press, 1950).

NOTES

1. Robert E. Sherwood, *Roosevelt and Hopkins* (New York: Harper & Row, 1948), pp. 303–305.

2. Winston S. Churchill, *The Grand Alliance* (Boston: Houghton Mifflin, 1950), pp. 358–361.

3. Nikita S. Khrushchev, *Special Report to the Twentieth Congress of the Communist Party of the Soviet Union* (February 1956).

4. For a superb scholarly account of this phase of Nazi policy see Alexander Dallin, *German Rule in Russia, 1941–1945: A Study of Occupational Policies* (New York: St. Martin's, 1957); also of particular interest is the story of Soviet General Andrei Vlasov, a hero of the battle of Moscow who defected to the Germans, as told by George Fischer in *Soviet Opposition to Stalin* (Cambridge, Mass.: Harvard University Press, 1952). According to the author, General Vlasov organized an army of almost 600,000 from among the captive Soviets and offered to fight under German control. But the Nazis never used this "Russian Liberation Army" to advantage. Fischer believes that Vlasov was not so much pro-Hitler as anti-Stalin.

5. Andrew Rothstein (tr.), *Soviet Foreign Policy During the Patriotic War: Documents and Materials* (New York: Hutchinson, n.d.), Vol. I, p. 129.

6. Herbert Feis, *Churchill-Roosevelt-Stalin* (Princeton, N.J.: Princeton University Press, 1957), p. 15.

7. *Pravda,* August 4, 1941.

8. Sherwood, *op. cit.,* p. 734.

9. Feis, *op. cit.,* p. 275.

10. *USSR Information Bulletin,* Vol. 4, No. 86 (July 29, 1944).

11. Isaac Deutscher, *Stalin: A Political Biography* (New York: Oxford University Press, 1949), p. 512.

12. U.S., Department of Defense, *The Entry of the Soviet Union into the War Against Japan: Military Plans, 1941–1945* (Washington, D.C.: Government Printing Office, 1955).

13. Feis, *op. cit.,* p. 498.

14. Winston S. Churchill, *Triumph and Tragedy* (Boston: Houghton Mifflin, 1953), p. 365.

15. For a full account of the Conference see *Foreign Relations of the United States: The Conferences at Malta and Yalta, 1945* (Washington, D.C.: Government Printing Office, 1955).

16. Churchill, *Triumph and Tragedy,* p. 402.

17. Feis, *op. cit.,* p. 562.

Forging the Alliance

28/Broadcast Speech   *July 3, 1941*

JOSEPH STALIN

Comrades, citizens, brothers, and sisters, men of our Army and Navy! I am addressing you, my dear friends!

The perfidious military attack on our Motherland begun on June 22 by Hitler Germany is continuing. In spite of the heroic resistance of the Red Army, and although the enemy's finest divisions and finest air force units have already been smashed and have met their doom on the field of battle, the enemy continues to push forward, hurling fresh forces into the attack. . . . A grave danger hangs over our country.

How could it have happened that our glorious Red Army surrendered a number of our cities and districts to the Fascist armies? Is it really true that the German-Fascist troops are invincible, as is ceaselessly trumpeted by boastful fascist propagandists? Of course not! History shows that there are no invincible armies and never have been. Napoleon's army was considered invincible but it was beaten successively by Russian, English, and German armies. Kaiser Wilhelm's German army in the period of the first imperialist war was also considered invincible, but it was beaten several times by Russian and Anglo-French forces and was finally smashed by the Anglo-French forces. The same must be said of Hitler's German-Fascist army today. This army has not yet met with serious resistance on the continent of Europe. Only on our territory has it met serious resistance. . . .

As to part of our territory having nevertheless been seized by German-Fascist troops, this is chiefly due to the fact that the war of Fascist Germany on the USSR began under conditions favorable for the German forces and unfavorable for the Soviet forces. The fact of the matter is that the troops of Germany, as a country at war, were already fully mobilized, and the 170 divisions hurled by Germany against the USSR and brought up to the Soviet frontiers were in a state of complete readiness, only awaiting the signal to move into action, whereas the Soviet troops had still to effect mobilization and to move up to the frontiers. Of no little importance in this respect is the fact that Fascist Germany suddenly and treacherously violated the nonaggression pact

Soviet War Documents, USSR Information Bulletin, Special Supplement (Washington, D.C.: USSR Embassy, December 1943), *excerpts.*

she concluded in 1939 with the USSR, disregarding the fact that she would be regarded as the aggressor by the whole world. Naturally, our peace-loving country, not wishing to take the initiative in breaking the pact, could not resort to perfidy.

It may be asked: how could the Soviet Government have consented to conclude a nonaggression pact with such treacherous fiends as Hitler and Ribbentrop? Was this not an error on the part of the Soviet Government? Of course not! Nonaggression pacts are pacts of peace between two states. It was such a pact that Germany proposed to us in 1939. Could the Soviet Government have declined such a proposal? I think that not a single peace-loving state could decline a peace treaty with a neighboring state, even though the latter was headed by such fiends and cannibals as Hitler and Ribbentrop. But that, of course, only on the one indispensable condition, namely, that this peace treaty did not infringe, either directly or indirectly, on the territorial integrity, independence and honor of the peace-loving state. As is well known, the nonaggression pact between Germany and the USSR was precisely such a pact.

What did we gain by concluding the nonaggression pact with Germany? We secured our country peace for a year and a half and the opportunity of preparing its forces to repulse Fascist Germany should she risk an attack on our country despite the pact. This was a definite advantage for us and a disadvantage for Fascist Germany.

What has Fascist Germany gained and what has she lost by treacherously tearing up the pact and attacking the USSR? She has gained certain advantageous positions for her troops for a short period, but she has lost politically by exposing herself in the eyes of the entire world as a bloodthirsty aggressor. There can be no doubt that this shortlived military gain for Germany is only an episode, while the tremendous political gain of the USSR is a serious and lasting factor that is bound to form the basis for the development of decisive military successes of the Red Army in the war with Fascist Germany.

29/Speech to the Moscow Soviet on the Anniversary of the October Revolution *November 6, 1941*

JOSEPH STALIN

What are the causes of the temporary military reverses of the Red Army?

One of the causes of the reverses is the absence of a second front in Europe against the German Fascist armies. The fact is that at the present time there are on the continent of Europe no armies of Great Britain or of the United States which could wage war against the German Nazi troops. Therefore, the Germans do not have to split their forces and wage war on two fronts—in the west and in the east. This situation means that the Germans, considering their rear in the West secure, are free to move all their troops and the troops of their European allies against our country. The situation is now such that our country is waging the war of liberation alone, without anybody's assistance, against the combined forces of the Germans, Finns, Rumanians, Italians, and Hungarians. . . .

We have not nor can we have such war aims as the seizure of foreign territories or the conquest of other peoples, irrespective of whether European peoples and territories or Asiatic peoples or territories, including Iran, are concerned. . . . We have not nor can we have such war aims as the imposition of our will and regime on the Slavic and other enslaved peoples of Europe who are waiting for our help. Our aim is to help these peoples in their struggle for liberation from Hitler's tyranny, and then to accord them the possibility of arranging their lives on their own land as they think fit, with absolute freedom. No interference of any kind with the domestic affairs of other nations!

USSR Information Bulletin, No. 127, Special Supplement (December 13, 1941), *excerpts.*

The Second Front and the Turning of the Tide

30/Report on the Occasion of the Twenty-fifth Anniversary of the October Revolution   *November 6, 1942*

JOSEPH STALIN

[Stalin started his speech by outlining the activities undertaken to strengthen the economy and armed forces. After presenting an analysis of military operations on the Soviet-German front, he proceeded to raise the question of the Second Front in Europe.]

. . . How are we to explain the fact that the Germans this year were still able to take the initiative of operations into their hands and achieve substantial tactical successes on our front?

It is to be explained by the fact that the Germans and their allies succeeded in mustering all their available reserves, hurling them onto the Eastern Front and creating a big superiority of forces in one of the directions. There can be no doubt that but for these measures the Germans could not have achieved any success on our front.

But why were they able to muster all their reserves and hurl them onto the Eastern Front? Because the absence of a second front in Europe enabled them to carry out this operation without any risk to themselves. Hence the chief reason for the tactical successes of the Germans on our front this year is that the absence of a second front in Europe enabled them to hurl onto our front all their available reserves and to create a big superiority of forces in the southwestern direction.

Let us assume that the second front existed in Europe as it existed in the first World War, and that the second front diverted, let us say, sixty German divisions and twenty divisions of Germany's allies. What would have been the position of the German troops on our front then?

It is not difficult to guess that their position would be deplorable. More, it would have been the beginning of the end of the German-Fascist troops, for in that case the Red Army would not be where it is now, but somewhere near Pskov, Minsk, Zhitomir, and Odessa. That means that in the summer of this year the German-Fascist army would already have been on the verge of disaster. If that has not occurred,

USSR Information Bulletin, No. 135 (November 12, 1946), *excerpts.*

it is because the Germans were saved by the absence of a second front in Europe.

Let us examine the question of a second front in Europe in its historical aspect. In the first World War Germany had to fight on two fronts: in the west chiefly against Great Britain and France, and in the east against the Russian troops. Thus in the first World War there existed a second front against Germany. Of the 220 divisions which Germany had then, not more than 85 German divisions were stationed on the Russian front. If to this we add the troops of Germany's allies then facing the Russian front, namely 37 Austro-Hungarian divisions, 2 Bulgarian divisions, and 3 Turkish divisions, we get a total of 127 divisions facing the Russian troops. The rest of the divisions of Germany and her allies chiefly held the front against the Anglo-French troops, while a part of them performed garrison service in the occupied territories of Europe. Such was the position in the first World War.

What is the position now, in the second World War, in September of this year, let us say? According to authenticated information which is beyond all doubt, of 256 divisions which Germany now has, not less than 179 German divisions are on our front. If to this we add 22 Rumanian divisions, 14 Finnish divisions, 10 Italian divisons, 13 Hungarian divisions, 1 Slovak and 1 Spanish division, we get a total of 240 divisions which are now fighting on our front. The remaining divisions of Germany and her allies are performing garrison service in the occupied countries of France, Belgium, Norway, Holland, Yugoslavia, Poland, Czechoslovakia, etc. while part of them are fighting in Libya or Egypt against Great Britain, the Libyan front diverting in all 4 German divisions and 11 Italian divisions.

Hence, instead of the 127 divisions as in the first World War, we are now facing on our front no less than 240 divisions, and instead of 85 German divisions we now have 179 German divisions fighting the Red Army. There you have the chief reason and foundation for the tactical success of the German-Fascist troops on our front in the summer of this year.

The German invasion of our country is often compared to Napoleon's invasion of Russia. But this comparison will not bear criticism. Of the 600,000 troops which began the campaign against Russia, Napoleon scarcely brought 130,000 or 140,000 as far as Borodino. That was all he had at his disposal at Moscow.

Well, we now have over 3,000,000 troops facing the front of the Red Army and armed with all the implements of modern warfare. What comparison can there be here?

The German invasion of our country is also sometimes compared to the German invasion of Russia at the time of the first World War. But neither will this comparison bear criticism. First, in the first World War there was a second front in Europe which rendered the German position very difficult, whereas in this war there is no second front in Europe.

Secondly, in this war, twice as many troops are facing our front as in the first World War. Obviously the comparison is not appropriate. You can now conceive how serious and extraordinary are the difficulties confronting the Red Army, and how great is the heroism displayed by the Red Army in its war of liberation against the German-Fascist troops.

The Problems of Poland and the Future of Eastern Europe

31/Agreement Between the Government of Poland and the Union of Soviet Socialist Republics

London, July 30, 1941

ARTICLE 1

The Government of the USSR recognizes the Soviet-German treaties of 1939 as to territorial changes in Poland as having lost their validity. The Polish Government declares Poland is not bound by any agreement with any third power which is directed against the USSR.

ARTICLE 2

Diplomatic relations will be restored between the two Governments upon the signing of this agreement, and an immediate exchange of Ambassadors will be arranged.

ARTICLE 3

The two Governments mutually agree to render one to another aid and support of all kinds in the present war against Hitlerite Germany.

USSR Information Bulletin, No. 123 (December 6, 1941), *excerpts.*

ARTICLE 4

The Government of the USSR expresses its consent to the formation on territory of the USSR of a Polish Army under a commander appointed by the Polish Government in agreement with the Soviet Government, the Polish Army on territory of the USSR being subordinated in an operational sense to the Supreme Command of the USSR, in which the Polish Army will be represented. All details as to command, organization and employment of this force will be settled in a subsequent agreement.

ARTICLE 5

This agreement will come into force immediately upon signature and without ratification. The present agreement is drawn up in two copies in the Russian and Polish languages. Both texts have equal force.

The Soviet Government grants amnesty to all Polish citizens now detained on Soviet territory either as prisoners of war or on other sufficient grounds, as from the resumption of diplomatic relations.

32/Declaration on Soviet-Polish Relations— TASS Communiqué *January 10, 1944*

On January 5 in London was published a declaration of the émigré Polish Government on Soviet-Polish relations which contains a number of incorrect assertions, including an incorrect assertion about the Soviet-Polish frontier.

As is well known, the Soviet Constitution established the Soviet-Polish frontier in conformity with the will of the population of Western Ukraine and Western Byelorussia, as expressed through a plebiscite conducted on a broad democratic basis in 1939. Then the territories of the Western Ukraine in which Ukrainians form the overwhelming majority of the population were incorporated with the Soviet Ukraine,

USSR Information Bulletin, Vol. 4, No. 7 (1944), p. 1.

and the territories of Western Byelorussia in which Byelorussians form an overwhelming majority of the population were incorporated with Soviet Byelorussia. The injustice committed by the Riga Treaty of 1921, which was imposed upon the Soviet Union, in regard to the Ukrainians inhabiting the Western Ukraine and the Byelorussians inhabiting Western Byelorussia, was thus rectified.

The incorporation of Western Ukraine and Western Byelorussia with the Soviet Union not only did not violate the interests of Poland, but on the contrary created a reliable foundation for stable and permanent friendship between the Polish people and its neighbors—the Ukrainian and Byelorussian and Russian peoples.

The Soviet Government has repeatedly stated that it stands for the reestablishment of a strong and independent Poland and for friendship between the Soviet Union and Poland. The Soviet Government declares again that it seeks to establish friendship between the USSR and Poland on the basis of stable, good neighborly relations and mutual respect and, if the Polish people will so desire—on the basis of an alliance for mutual assistance against the Germans as the chief enemies of the Soviet Union and Poland. . . .

At present the possibility is opening for the rebirth of Poland as a strong and independent state. However, Poland must be reborn not through the seizure of Ukrainian and Byelorussian lands, but through the restoration to Poland of lands which belonged to Poland from time immemorial and were wrested by the Germans from her. Only in this way trust and friendship could be established between the Polish, Ukrainian, Byelorussian and Russian peoples.

The eastern frontiers of Poland can be established by agreement with the Soviet Union. The Soviet Government does not regard the frontiers of 1939 as unalterable. These frontiers can be modified in Poland's favor so that the areas in which the Polish population forms a majority be turned over to Poland. In this case the Soviet Polish frontier could pass approximately along the so-called Curzon line, which was adopted in 1919 by the Supreme Council of the Allied Powers, and which provides for inclusion of the Western Ukraine and Western Byelorussia into the Soviet Union.

The western frontiers of Poland must be extended through incorporation with Poland of ancient Polish lands previously wrested by Germany, without which it is impossible to unite the whole Polish people in its state, which thereby will receive a needed outlet to the Baltic Sea.

The just aspiration of the Polish people for its full reunion in a strong and independent state must receive recognition and support.

The émigré Polish government, isolated from its people, proved incapable of establishment of friendly relations with the Soviet Union. It also proved incapable of organizing active struggle against the German invaders within Poland herself. Furthermore, by its incorrect policy it not infrequently plays into the hands of the German occupationists.

However, the interests of Poland and the Soviet Union consist in that stable, friendly relations be established between our countries and that the people of Poland and the Soviet Union unite in struggle against the common external enemy, as demanded by the common cause of all the Allies.

The Yalta Conference

33/Report of the Crimea Conference   *February 12, 1945*

For the past eight days, Winston S. Churchill, Prime Minister of Great Britain, Franklin D. Roosevelt, President of the United States of America, and Marshal J. V. Stalin, Chairman of the Council of Peoples' Commissars of the Union of Soviet Socialist Republics have met with the Foreign Secretaries, Chiefs of Staff and other advisors in the Crimea. . . .

The Defeat of Germany

We have considered and determined the military plans of the three Allied Powers for the final defeat of the common enemy. The military staffs of the three Allied nations have met in daily meetings throughout the Conference. These meetings have been most satisfactory from every point of view and have resulted in closer coordination of the military effort of the three Allies than ever before. The fullest information has been interchanged. The timing, scope, and coordination of new and even more powerful blows to be launched by our armies and air forces into the heart of Germany from the East, West, North, and South have been fully agreed and planned in detail . . . Nazi Germany is doomed. The German people will only make the cost of their defeat heavier to themselves by attempting to continue a hopeless resistance.

Foreign Relations of the United States: The Conferences at Malta and Yalta, 1945 (Washington, D.C.: Government Printing Office, 1955), pp. 968–975, *excerpts.*

The Occupation and Control of Germany

We have agreed on common policies and plans for enforcing the unconditional surrender terms which we shall impose together on Nazi Germany after German armed resistance has been finally crushed. These
terms will not be made known until the final defeat of Germany has
been accomplished. Under the agreed plan, the forces of the Three
Powers will each occupy a separate zone of Germany. Coordinated
administration and control has been provided for under the plan
through a central Control Commission consisting of the Supreme Commanders of the Three Powers with headquarters in Berlin. It has been
agreed that France should be invited by the Three Powers, if she should
so desire, to take over a zone of occupation, and to participate as a
fourth member of the Control Commission. The limits of the French
zone will be agreed by the four governments concerned through their
representatives on the European Advisory Commission.

It is our inflexible purpose to destroy German militarism and Nazism
and to ensure that Germany will never again be able to disturb the
peace of the world. We are determined to disarm and disband all German armed forces; break up for all time the German General Staff that
has repeatedly contrived the resurgence of German militarism; remove
or destroy all German military equipment; eliminate or control all
German industry that could be used for military production; bring all
war criminals to just and swift punishment and exact reparation in kind
for the destruction wrought by the Germans; wipe out the Nazi Party,
Nazi laws, organizations and institutions, remove all Nazi and militarist
influences from public office and from the cultural and economic life of
the German people; and take in harmony such other measures in Germany as may be necessary to the future peace and safety of the world.
It is not our purpose to destroy the people of Germany, but only when
Nazism and militarism have been extirpated will there be hope for a
decent life for Germans, and a place for them in the comity of nations.

Reparation by Germany

We have considered the question of the damage caused by Germany
to the Allied Nations in this war and recognized it as just that Germany
be obliged to make compensation for this damage in kind to the greatest
extent possible. . . .

United Nations Conference

We are resolved upon the earliest possible establishment with our Allies of a general international organization to maintain peace and security. . . .

Declaration on Liberated Europe

We have drawn up and subscribed to a Declaration on Liberated Europe. This Declaration provides for concerting the policies of the Three Powers and for joint action by them in meeting the political and economic problems of liberated Europe in accordance with democratic principles. The text of the Declaration is as follows:

. . . The establishment of order in Europe and the rebuilding of national economic life must be achieved by processes which will enable the liberated peoples to destroy the last vestiges of Nazism and Fascism and to create democratic institutions of their own choice . . . the three governments will jointly assist the people in any European liberated state or former Axis satellite state in Europe . . . (a) to establish conditions of internal peace; (b) to carry out emergency measures for the relief of distressed people; (c) to form interim governmental authorities broadly representative of all democratic elements in the population and pledged to the earliest possible establishment through free elections of governments responsive to the will of the people; and (d) to facilitate where necessary the holding of elections. . . .

Poland

We came to the Crimea Conference resolved to settle our differences about Poland. We discussed fully all aspects of the question. We reaffirm our common desire to see established a strong, free, independent, and democratic Poland. As a result of our discussions we have agreed on the conditions in which a new Polish Provisional Government of National Unity may be formed in such a manner as to command recognition by the three major powers.

The agreement reached is as follows:

A new situation has been created in Poland as a result of her complete liberation by the Red Army. This calls for the establishment of a Polish Provisional Government which can be more broadly based than was possible before the recent liberation of western Poland. The Provisional Government which is now functioning in Poland should therefore be reorganized on a broader democratic basis with the inclusion of democratic leaders from Poland itself and from Poles abroad. . . . This Polish Provisional Government of National Unity shall be pledged to the holding of free and unfettered elections as soon as possible on the basis of universal suffrage and secret ballot. In these elections all democratic and anti-Nazi parties shall have the right to take part and to put forward candidates. . . .

The three Heads of Government consider that the eastern frontier of Poland should follow the Curzon Line with digressions from it in some regions of five to eight kilometres in favor of Poland. They recognize that Poland must receive substantial accessions of territory in the north and west. They feel that the opinion of the new Poland Provisional Government of National Unity should be sought in due course on the extent of these accessions and that the final delimitation of the western frontier of Poland should thereafter await the Peace Conference.

34/Secret Agreement Regarding the Entry of the Soviet Union into the War Against Japan

February 11, 1945

Agreement

The leaders of the three Great Powers—the Soviet Union, the United States of America, and Great Britain—have agreed that in two or three months after Germany has surrendered and the war in Europe has terminated the Soviet Union shall enter into the war against Japan on the side of the Allies on condition that:

1. The *Status Quo* in Outer Mongolia (The Mongolian People's Republic) shall be preserved;

2. The former rights of Russia violated by the treacherous attack of Japan in 1904 shall be restored, viz.:

Foreign Relations of the United States: The Conferences at Malta and Yalta, 1945 (Washington, D.C.: Government Printing Office, 1955), p. 984, *excerpts.* This top-secret document was made public by the Department of State on February 11, 1946.

(a) the southern part of Sakhalin as well as the islands adjacent to it shall be returned to the Soviet Union,
(b) the commercial port of Dairen shall be internationalized, the preeminent interests of the Soviet Union in this port being safeguarded and the lease of Port Arthur as a naval base of the USSR restored,
(c) the Chinese-Eastern Railroad and the South-Manchurian Railroad which provides an outlet to Dairen shall be jointly operated by the establishment of a joint Soviet-Chinese Company, it being understood that the preeminent interests of the Soviet Union shall be safeguarded and that China shall retain full sovereignty in Manchuria;

3. The Kuril Islands shall be handed over to the Soviet Union.

It is understood, that the agreement concerning Outer Mongolia and the ports and railroads referred to above will require concurrence of Generalissimo Chiang Kai-shek. The President will take measures in order to obtain this concurrence on advice from Marshal Stalin.

The Heads of the three Great Powers have agreed that these claims of the Soviet Union shall be unquestionably fulfilled after Japan has been defeated.

For its part the Soviet Union expresses its readiness to conclude with the Nationalist Government of China a pact of friendship and alliance between the USSR and China in order to render assistance to China with its armed forces for the purpose of liberating China from the Japanese yoke.

J. Stalin
Franklin D. Roosevelt
Winston S. Churchill

FOR FURTHER STUDY

Butow, Robert J. C. *Japan's Decision to Surrender.* Stanford, Calif.: Stanford University Press, 1954.

Churchill, Winston S. *The Second World War.* 6 vols. Boston: Houghton Mifflin, 1948–1953.

Clark, Alan. *Barbarossa: The Russian-German Conflict, 1941–1945.* New York: Morrow, 1964.

Clemens, Diane Shaver. *Yalta.* New York: Oxford University Press, 1970.

Dallin, Alexander. *German Rule in Russia, 1941–1945: A Study of Occupation Policies.* New York: St. Martin's, 1957.

Dawson, Raymond H. *The Decision to Aid Russia, 1941.* Chapel Hill: University of North Carolina Press, 1959.

Deane, John R. *The Strange Alliance: The Story of Our Efforts at Wartime Cooperation with Russia.* New York: Viking, 1947.

Djilas, Milovan. *Conversations with Stalin.* New York: Harcourt Brace Jovanovich, 1962.

Feis, Herbert. *Churchill-Roosevelt-Stalin.* Princeton, N.J.: Princeton University Press, 1957.

_____. *Between War and Peace: The Potsdam Conference.* Princeton, N.J.: Princeton University Press, 1960.

Gallagher, Matthew P. *The Soviet History of World War II: Myths, Memories, and Realities.* New York: Praeger, 1963.

Higgins, Trumbull. *Hitler and Russia: The Third Reich in a Two-Front War, 1937–1943.* New York: Macmillan, 1966.

Jones, Robert Huhn. *United States Lend-Lease to the Soviet Union.* Norman: University of Oklahoma Press, 1969.

Kase, Toshikazu, *Journey to the Missouri.* New Haven, Conn.: Yale University Press, 1950.

Kot, Stanislaw (ed.). *Conversations with the Kremlin and Dispatches from Russia.* New York: Oxford University Press, 1963.

Lundin, Charles L. *Finland in the Second World War.* Bloomington: Indiana University Press, 1957.

McNeill, William H. *America, Britain, and Russia: Their Cooperation and Conflict, 1941–1946.* New York: Oxford University Press, 1954.

Neumann, William L. *After Victory: Churchill, Roosevelt, Stalin and the Making of Peace.* New York: Harper & Row, 1967.

Petrov, Vladimir. *June 22, 1941: Soviet Historians and the German Invasion.* Columbia: University of South Carolina Press, 1968.

Rozek, Edward J. *Allied Wartime Diplomacy: A Pattern in Poland.* New York: Wiley, 1958.

Sharp, Samuel. *Poland, White Eagle on a Red Field.* Cambridge, Mass.: Harvard University Press, 1953.

Snell, John L. (ed.). *The Meaning of Yalta.* Baton Rouge: University of Louisiana Press, 1956.

Stettinius, Edward R. *Roosevelt and the Russians: The Yalta Conference.* Garden City, N.Y.: Doubleday, 1949.

Strik-Strikfeldt, Wilfred. *Against Stalin and Hitler, 1941–1945.* London: Macmillan, 1970.

Umiastowski, Roman. *Poland, Russia, and Great Britain, 1941–1945.* London: Hollis & Carter, 1946.

Werth, Alexander. *Russia at War: 1941–1945.* New York: Dutton, 1964.

Xydis, Stephen G. *Greece and the Great Powers, 1944–1947: Prelude to the "Truman Doctrine."* Thessaloniki: Institute for Balkan Studies, 1963.

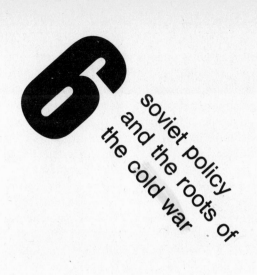

6 soviet policy and the roots of the cold war

The inability of the victors to maintain their wartime cooperation—and the consequent division of the world into two hostile camps—overshadowed all else in the immediate postwar period. Within months after the defeat of the Axis Powers this failure was revealed by fundamental disagreements over Eastern Europe, Germany, Iran, and the Far East. Pre-1939 power relationships significantly changed: Germany and Japan had been defeated; Britain and France were seriously weakened; and Soviet forces occupied all Eastern Europe. The sharply delineated bipolarity of world power soon exacerbated the situation.

The investigation into the "causes" of the Cold War involves several factors, each important as a historical determinant, though its relative significance is subject to disagreement. First, there are these constants: the enduring legacy of Soviet-Western suspicion, only partially mitigated by wartime collaboration;* the quest of the Soviet Union for security, which, though understandable, required an extension of its frontier and sphere of influence westward into the center of Europe where it conflicted with the security interests of the Western Powers; the tendency of Soviet leaders, reared in the Marxist-Leninist tradition, to regard the West again as an enemy once the common foe had been beaten; and, above all, the theme of territorial expansion so manifest in Czarist, as well as in Bolshevik, foreign policy.

Second, there are the fortuitous and unpredictable components of

* Distrust was a continuing feature of the alliance. Muted during the war, it crystallized clearly after victory and revealed its deep-rooted character. For manifestations of wartime distrust among the Big Three see *Stalin's Correspondence with Churchill, Attlee, Roosevelt and Truman, 1941–1945* (New York: Dutton, 1958).

historical events. Thus, there may have been a strong Soviet expectation, based on remarks of American officials at Yalta, of a rapid American military withdrawal from Europe. Soviet leaders could and did "treat with contempt American protests, even President Roosevelt's personal appeals to Stalin, concerning the open and frequent violations of the Yalta agreement on eastern Europe."[1] One may also muse over the probable effect on the Kremlin of the sudden American decision in August 1945 to end all lend-lease aid. Coming so soon after the military victory, it may have dispelled any Soviet hopes of basing its recovery and reconstruction at least partially on continued American assistance. This, in turn, may have lessened the possibility of a more moderate policy toward the West and the problems of postwar settlement.* Coupled with the fresh disclosure of America's monopoly possession of the atom bomb (a factor in itself having enormous military-political implications), this may have magnified Soviet suspicions of American intentions—particularly when viewed through the prism of Marxist-Leninist assumptions.

Finally, the inexorable drift in the 1945–1947 period toward a bipolarity of power and politics must also be attributed to the xenophobia, imperial ambitions, and sense of insecurity of Joseph Stalin and to his resolve to ensure Soviet security by establishing Moscow's hegemony over all of Europe east of the Stettin-Trieste line. At Yalta Stalin had expressed particular concern over the orientation of postwar Poland's government and politics. In response to Churchill's assertion that for Britain the matter of Polish independence was a question of honor, Stalin replied that:

> Throughout history, Poland has been the corridor through which the enemy has passed into Russia. Twice in the last thirty years our enemies, the Germans, have passed through this corridor. It is in Russia's interest that Poland should be strong and powerful, in a position to shut the door of this corridor by her own force. . . . it is necessary that Poland should be free, independent in power. Therefore, it is not only a question of honor but of life and death for the Soviet state itself.[2]

The line between legitimate security needs and openly expansionist objectives is not easily drawn. C. E. Black, appraising Soviet aims in Europe, has stated that:

* Certainly, subsequent events added to the Soviet impression of Western antagonism. For example, on December 6, 1945, the United States Government wrote off $25 billion of lend-lease aid to Britain and the Commonwealth and agreed to lend the British Government $4.4 billion. A few months later France received $1.4 billion. An earlier Soviet request for a loan remained unanswered by the State Department; it supposedly "got lost" in the department. While too much need not be made of such incidents, they must, nonetheless, be weighed in the balance.

What is important is that regardless of whether Soviet Russia merely wants friendly states on her border or in fact desires to use eastern Europe as a springboard of aggression, the same revolutionary method will be employed. The theoretical basis of this policy is that only countries as fully sovietized as Russia itself can be regarded as safe neighbors and reliable friends.[3]

Certainly, the post-World War II expansion of Soviet power into the heart of Europe exceeded the wildest dreams of the most imperialistic Czar. For the first time in European history one Great Power dominated the entire area between the Soviet Union and Western Europe, an area extending from the Baltic to the Black Sea (reading 35; and see map). The Western Powers, on the other hand, regarded this expansion of Soviet influence as a lasting threat to their safety. The roots of the Cold War lay in this fundamental conflict between incompatible concepts of national security.

The difficulties of the postwar period may conveniently be dated from the Potsdam Conference of July 1945. Relations between the USSR and the Western Powers had deteriorated noticeably since Yalta. Discord developed over the reconstitution of the Polish government, the heavy-handedness of Soviet rule in Bulgaria and Romania, the disposition of Trieste, the reparations issue, and the Allied administration of Germany.* The Conference failed to dispel the bitterness resulting from the Soviet Union's installation in Eastern Europe of governments in which communists were assured strategic posts (such as control of the all-important Ministries of Interior and of the Courts). While conflicting interpretations of what constituted "democratic" government aggravated suspicion and augured ill for the future, America's rapid demobilization encouraged Stalin to act without fear of effective resistance.

The Council of Foreign Ministers met formally for the first time in London from September 11 to October 2, 1945, primarily to draft peace treaties with Finland, Italy, and the Balkan countries. But the old problems remained unsolved, and new ones appeared, such as Soviet demands for a trusteeship over one of the former Italian colonies and for the establishment of an Allied Control Council in Japan, comparable to the one operating in Germany, which would have given the Soviet government a veto over American occupation policy. The Foreign Ministers adjourned without reaching agreement on any substantive

---

* On June 5, 1945, the United States, France, Great Britain, and the Soviet Union negotiated an agreement calling for the division of Germany into separate zones that were to be administered by each of the Great Powers. Berlin was treated as a separate zone and similarly partitioned. Finally, responsibility for policy decisions affecting Germany as a whole was vested in the Allied Control Council.

ARCTIC OCEAN

• Murmansk

NORWEGIAN SEA

NORWAY

SWEDEN

FINLAND

• Leningrad

UNION OF SOVIET SOCIALIST REPUBLICS

ESTONIA

LATVIA

• Moscow

LITHUANIA

NORTH SEA

DENMARK

BALTIC SEA

GREAT
BRITAIN

NETHER-
LANDS

Berlin

Oder-Neisse Line

Warsaw

BELGIUM

EAST
GERMANY

POLAND

LUXEMBOURG

WEST
GERMANY

CZECHOSLOVAKIA

FRANCE

BESSARABIA

SWITZER-
LAND

AUSTRIA

HUNGARY

ROMANIA

BLACK SEA

YUGOSLAVIA

ADRIATIC SEA

BULGARIA

ITALY

ALBANIA

TURKEY

GREECE

MEDITERRANEAN   SEA

The Soviet Union in Europe

///// Recovered by the Soviet Union in Its Westward Expansion: Northern and
Southern Border Regions in Finland (1940 and 1944); Estonia, Latvia, and
Lithuania (1940); and Part of Former East Prussia from Germany, Eastern Poland,
Ruthenia from Czechoslovakia, and Bessarabia from Romania (All After World War II)

------ Boundaries of Soviet Union Before Expansion

——— Present Boundaries of Soviet Union

0 _____ 300 miles

issue. They convened again in late December, this time in Moscow, at the behest of Secretary of State Byrnes, who had been informed by Ambassador Harriman that "the breakdown of the London Conference had been stimulated by the Russians' belief that they were not being consulted adequately by our [American] officials in Japan"[4] —a cogent example, if this was the actual cause of the impasse, of the hypersensitivity of the Soviets to imagined slights in the diplomatic arena.

As a compromise, the Soviet Union was made a member of the Far Eastern Commission (meeting in Washington) and the Allied Control Council for Japan (Tokyo). However, since these organs had only advisory functions, the Soviet government could not interfere with the conduct of American occupation policy. A breakthrough was also achieved on other issues, and the Foreign Ministers agreed to convene a peace conference in Paris not later than May 1, 1946. The question of free elections in Bulgaria, Poland, and Romania, however, and the character of the governments established there under Soviet aegis, continued to plague the discussants. Finally before the conference ended, controversy flared up over Iran.

Amid this rising tide of dissension, suspicion, and frustration, Premier Stalin delivered a preelection speech on February 9, 1946, that presaged a resurgence of Marxist-Leninist orthodoxy in domestic affairs as well as in official Soviet pronouncements on international matters. Again he emphasized the Leninist thesis that the uneven development of capitalism leads to war. He noted:

. . . that group of capitalist countries which considers itself worse provided than others with raw materials and markets usually [makes] attempts to alter the situation and repartition the "spheres of influence" in its favor by armed force. The result is a splitting of the capitalist world into two hostile camps and war between them.

In reaffirming the fundamental postulates of communist theory on the causes and nature of capitalist wars, Stalin blamed the West for World War II. He insisted that the defeat of Germany did not necessarily eliminate the danger of war and, lauding the superiority of the Soviet system, called for a "new mighty upsurge in the national economy" that would treble prewar production and guarantee the Soviet Union against another invasion. His gloomy outlook on relations with the capitalist world dominated Soviet behavior and hastened the Cold War. Stalin spoke six weeks before the Iranian crisis reached its critical phase and almost a month *before* Churchill, at Fulton, Missouri, on March 5, 1946, called for a strengthening of Anglo-American ties in the face of growing Soviet expansion. Churchill pointed out that:

From Stettin in the Baltic to Trieste in the Adriatic an iron curtain has descended across the Continent. All these famous cities and the populations around them lie in the Soviet sphere and are subject, in one form or another, not only to Soviet influence but to a very high and increasing degree of control from Moscow.

Stalin termed Churchill a "warmonger" and compared him to Hitler. Quite surprisingly, a number of students of Soviet affairs have echoed this theme, intimating that Churchill's speech helped intensify East-West hostility. But they ignore the implications of Stalin's speech made some four weeks earlier.[5]

By early 1946, Soviet power was entrenched in Eastern Europe and was threatening in the Middle East, especially in Iran. Occupied by the Allies during the war in order to safeguard the flow of supplies to the Soviet Union, Iran now could not obtain the promised evacuation of Soviet troops. During their occupation of northern Iran, Soviet authorities denied the central government in Teheran access to the area and at the same time strengthened the local communist (Tudeh) party. In September 1945, the Tudeh party sought increased autonomy for Azerbaijan, the Iranian province bordering on the Soviet Union. The central government refused Tudeh demands, for fear of augmenting communist influence elsewhere in Iran. In December 1945 the communists announced the creation of a new government in Tabriz, capital of Azerbaijan, under Ja'far Pishevari, a veteran communist and Comintern agent; proclaimed a "Kurdish People's Republic," with its capital in Mahabad, in western Azerbaijan; and intensified their efforts to kindle an irredentist movement among the Kurdish tribes of northern Iraq and eastern Turkey. This hastened the deterioration of Turkish-Soviet relations.* Meanwhile Iranian troops seeking to reenter Azerbaijan were turned back by the Red Army.

Despite Stalin's statement "that the Soviet Union had no designs, territorial or otherwise, against Iran and would withdraw its troops as soon as they felt secure about the Baku oil fields"[6] (a rather specious excuse for retaining troops in Iran in view of the obvious disparity of military power of the two countries), Soviet troops continued to occupy the northern provinces. Iran appealed to the United Nations on January 19, 1946, charging the Soviet Union with interference in its internal affairs and with endangering the peace. American efforts to effect a

---

* The Soviet government had terminated its 1925 treaty of friendship with Turkey in March 1945 and applied pressure for a revision of the Montreux Convention that would accord it military control over the Straits. The Soviets also demanded the return of Kars and Ardahan, provinces ceded to Turkey in 1918. Soviet pressure on Turkey sharpened, and by late 1946 Bulgarian and Greek communists were active in stirring up trouble along Turkey's exposed frontier. These activities were instrumental in the promulgation of the Truman Doctrine in March 1947.

withdrawal of all foreign troops by January 1, 1946, were rejected by the Soviet government, which reminded the Western Powers that under the Iranian-Soviet-British treaty of 1942 it was entitled to remain in Iran until March 2, 1946. During the often acrimonious negotiations in the Security Council, a cabinet crisis in Teheran led the Shah to appoint Qavam Saltaneh, generally regarded by Western officials as pro-Tudeh, as Premier. Qavam began direct talks with Soviet leaders and spent almost a month in Moscow attempting to negotiate a settlement. In the United Nations Soviet tactics thwarted every constructive effort at a solution—a portent of future behavior in the world organization. As the date for the departure of Soviet troops under the 1942 agreement came and went with no visible change in Soviet attitude, Western leaders grew profoundly disturbed, particularly in view of Stalin's speech of February 9, 1946. Churchill's speech at Fulton reflected this increasing anxiety over Soviet ambitions.

On April 4, the Soviet government agreed to evacuate Iran in return for Iranian concessions, including the formation of a joint-stock Soviet-Iranian oil company and a degree of autonomy for Azerbaijan. Westerners viewed this as a Soviet triumph and glumly awaited Iran's early disappearance behind the Iron Curtain, a view undoubtedly shared, but with more pleasure, by the Kremlin. Though the final decision of the Soviet government to withdraw from Iran by May 9 is usually attributed primarily to pressure by the UN Security Council and world public opinion, some specialists credit it mainly to the astuteness and shrewdness of Premier Qavam. Richard N. Frye states that:

The Soviet evacuation of northern Iran was the result of a number of factors; probably the most important was the belief on the part of the Russians that Qavam had been won over to their side. He had suppressed the anti-Soviet elements and had agreed to a joint oil company, subject to ratification of parliament. The rebel government in Azerbaijan was growing in strength and there was every reason to suppose that it would maintain its position and even gain at the expense of the Teheran government. The pressure of world opinion and the debates in the United Nations, although they may have been responsible in influencing the Soviet government to evacuate Iran earlier than had been planned, were probably of much less significance than the factors mentioned above. When the Soviet government did announce that it had evacuated all its troops on May 9, 1946, it seemed as though Iran had fallen on the Soviet side of the curtain.[7]

Late that year, the Iranian parliament rejected the proposed economic treaty with the USSR. Qavam had actually outfoxed Moscow, and by the end of 1946 the immediate threat of a communist coup had passed. Azerbaijan was once again under the control of the central government.[8] Shortly after, in one of the ironies for which Middle

Eastern politics are noted, Qavam was replaced as Premier and all but exiled.

Meanwhile, preparations for the Peace Conference dragged on through the spring of 1946. Not until the end of July did representatives of twenty-one nations meet in Paris. Though no agreement was reached over Germany or Austria, the Soviet Union yielded sufficiently on a number of peripheral issues and seemed willing enough to accept compromises on others to permit the conclusion of peace treaties with Italy, Finland, Hungary, and Romania in February 1947. The West had the treaties it so coveted, but time quickly revealed how hollow they were. The Soviet government soon repudiated its concessions and moved to complete its political domination of Eastern Europe. Stalin not only had an acute appreciation of the revolutionary conditions in Eastern Europe, but he pursued his principal political and strategic objectives in the area with a singleness of purpose that had become only too clear to the Western Powers by early 1947. He sought, first, to eliminate all Western influence from Eastern Europe and, concomitantly, to establish Soviet hegemony. These objectives superseded all others. The quest for control of Eastern Europe culminated in the setting up of "People's Democracies" in all these countries by the end of 1948. Though the pattern and the pace varied from country to country, the result was the same: complete Sovietization.*

Soviet diplomacy in microcosm may be seen in the approach to one aspect of the peace treaties: the provision affecting the free navigation of the Danube. Since 1815, with certain modifications, an international commission whose members included Europe's Great Powers had maintained the principle and practice of free navigation of this vital commercial artery. Russia, not a member of the commission, had traditionally sought to control the Danube valley and to deny any voice in Danubian affairs to states not bordering on the river. Therefore, as a necessary first step toward itself becoming a riparian state, Russia had long coveted Bessarabia. Having annexed it in 1940, the USSR insisted in 1945 on the exclusion of nonriparian powers from membership. At Paris the Soviets agreed, after lengthy negotiation, to specific clauses in the peace treaties assuring the international character of the Danube. Once the treaties were signed, however, they

* An outstanding account of the Soviet take-over in Eastern Europe, perhaps the best single volume in English on the subject, is Hugh Seton-Watson's *The East European Revolution* (New York: Praeger, 1956). Mr. Seton-Watson distinguishes three distinct stages in the Soviet pattern of satellitization: the genuine coalition, the bogus coalition, and the communist-controlled monolith. Each of these stages is traced in the various countries of Eastern Europe during the 1945–1949 period. Another excellent work on this topic is Robert Lee Wolff's *The Balkans in Our Time* (Cambridge, Mass.: Harvard University Press, 1956), chaps. 9 and 10.

promptly proceeded to ignore their obligations in this matter. The denouement came with startling finality at the Belgrade Conference of July-August 1948—the most significant postwar incident in the international control of the Danube. Outnumbering the Western, nonriparian powers, the Soviet Union and its satellites arbitrarily and easily changed membership requirements to allow only riparian states on the commission. Through its annexation of Bessarabia, the USSR became the only Great Power on the commission. Its voice became dominant. This episode further diminished the West's fading influence in the Balkans and helped the USSR consolidate its Eastern European empire.

Throughout 1946 and 1947, the Soviet government deliberately sought to curb all Eastern European contact with the noncommunist world, even excluding United Nations personnel from the area. Addressing the General Assembly on December 8, 1946, Soviet Foreign Minister Molotov proposed "that all states represented in the General Assembly should present information on their troops stationed in foreign territories belonging to other United Nations"—an effort to obtain data on United States forces in Western Europe. He fought, however, the American counterproposal that information be given "about troops stationed not only in territories of the United Nations *but in the territories of former enemy states as well,*" for this would have required the Soviets to reveal their troop dispositions in Bulgaria, Hungary, East Germany, and Romania.

Of all postwar problems, none contributed more to East-West hostility than that of the future of Germany. In a sense, the German problem is *the* European problem. Economic, political, strategic, and technological power factors all coalesce in the struggle over Germany; and the present unchallenged position of the Soviet Union in Eastern Europe cannot be permanently assured as long as Germany, with its reservoir of skilled manpower, scientific tradition, and industrial strength, remains a potential opponent. International politics has frequently seen the victors disagree among themselves and end by courting the former enemy. Since 1946, this has been true with respect to Germany.

The Soviets at first had favored an exploitative policy, designed to weaken Germany industrially, aid Soviet reconstruction, and encourage instability in Western Europe. Excessive Soviet reparations demands ruined efforts to negotiate the German question. However, the Kremlin soon realized the folly of this course and shifted to a more accommodating, conciliatory policy toward Germany—though not toward Western attitudes on the issue of Germany. This Soviet policy was first expressed by Molotov at the July 1946 Paris meeting of Foreign Ministers (reading 36). Asserting that the spirit of revenge could not underlie negotiations with Germany, he acknowledged that it would be folly to seek to destroy Germany as a state or to agrarianize her and destroy her major industries. Molotov suggested instead that Germany be permitted to become "a democratic and peace-loving state which alongside of agriculture, would have its own industry and foreign trade, but which would be deprived of the economic and military potentiality to rise again as an aggressive force." He also proposed that the Ruhr, the key to German industrial power, be placed under inter-Allied control and that a single German government be set up, willing to fulfill all its obligations, particularly those concerning reparations. Secretary of State Byrnes responded to this bid for German favor by making similar comments in his Stuttgart speech of September 6, 1946. He also, significantly, threw American support behind Germany in the question of a return of the "eastern territories." It will be remembered that before the Potsdam Conference, the Soviet Union had unilaterally transferred all German territory east of the Neisse River to Poland, thus strengthening Poland's claim to the area. This territory has served, to this day, to compensate Poland for the 180,000 square kilometers of eastern Poland taken over by the USSR and to bind her to the Soviet Union. According to Barrington Moore, Jr.,

This pair of speeches by Byrnes and Molotov might be regarded as the unofficial funeral of the Potsdam agreement and the overt beginning of a race for Germany between the Western Powers and the USSR, though the roots of the split can be traced back to the divergent policies of the various powers from the first days of the occupation.[9]

Byrnes' strategy forced the Soviets to choose between the Poles and the Germans, thus deflating Soviet prestige in Western Germany.

The long succession of Soviet vetoes in the Security Council in 1946–1947 also indicated the growing cleavage between the West and the Soviet Union. The Soviet representative cast his first veto on February 16, 1946, and cast eight more before the year was over. Most early Soviet vetoes dealt with the admission of new members, a recurring issue throughout the first decade of the United Nations. Though the proposal to amend the UN Charter and abolish the veto is often raised, there is little likelihood that any great power would support such a change. Molotov justified the veto right in a speech before the UN on September 14, 1946 (reading 54), and the defense has subsequently been reiterated.*

* An added source of antagonism was the Soviet veto in August 1947 of a report submitted by the UN Commission of Investigation which had been set up to investigate guerrilla fighting in northern Greece. The General Assembly, however, established a UN Special Commission on the Balkans, boycotted by the USSR, which helped confine hostilities in the area (along the Greek-Yugoslav-Bulgarian frontier). The Titoist defection in June 1948 and Truman Doctrine aid finally restored the peace.

In Poland ill-disguised communist manipulations of the general elections of January 19, 1947, convinced the West that the Soviets had no intention of permitting free elections as pledged at Yalta and Potsdam. The Polish Peasant Party of Mikolajczyk waged a hopeless struggle,[10] and the Democratic Bloc (composed of the communists and their allies) not unexpectedly emerged victorious. Official British and American protests were futile.

After a year and a half of following a policy of "patience with firmness," the United States prepared to assume Western leadership and embark upon a positive program of checking Soviet expansion. In 1947 a fateful chain of policy decisions by the Soviet Union and the United States irrevocably decided their political estrangement and led from a period of simulated accord to the one of protracted hostility that still endures with varying degrees of intensity.

On March 12, 1947, President Truman announced the decision of the American government to extend economic and military assistance to Greece and Turkey.[11] The immediate impetus behind this move was the expressed inability of Great Britain to continue the responsibility for the defense of these areas. British power in the eastern Mediterranean was replaced by that of the United States. Quite possibly, the Truman Doctrine came at an inopportune moment in international diplomacy, two days after the Moscow Conference of Foreign Ministers had convened to discuss a number of key questions, including the Soviet demand for reparations. Western rejection of these demands, coupled with the apparent American willingness to aid liberally two small, strategically located nations, seriously undermined any prospects the conference may have had, and it ended in failure (March 10–April 24).

Moscow promptly denounced the Truman Doctrine as "but a smokescreen for expansion" (reading 37). The criticisms against it were sharp and varied: it was characterized as an example of America's postwar policy of imperialism; the Soviets also insisted that it deliberately circumvented the UN, thereby undermining the world organization. The Soviet journal, *New Times,* held that:

The proposed measures for Greece and Turkey cannot be taken as a demonstration of the will of the American Government for international cooperation within the framework of the UN Charter. On the contrary, they confirm the suspicion of a desire to convert the United Nations Organization into a tool of American policy, and, since that does not succeed, to reduce its importance virtually to naught. The reference to the UNO in the [Truman] message cannot but serve as a reminder that the only lawful and sensible way to assist Greece and Turkey, if the need for that has arisen, is by action undertaken through the UNO.[12]

Once committed to recognizing Europe's vital relationship to American national interest, the United States supplemented the Truman Doctrine with a more permanent and far-reaching program of assistance. On June 5, 1947, Secretary of State Marshall, speaking at Harvard University, expressed America's willingness to help rebuild Europe and invited the European nations to draw up a list of their needs and to prepare the necessary machinery for the implementation of American assistance. Under the leadership of British Foreign Secretary Ernest Bevin and French Foreign Minister Georges Bidault a conference of all European nations, including the Soviet Union, was convened in Paris on June 27. Discussions were at first secret. Then Moscow unexpectedly issued a statement on June 29 presenting its views and criticisms of the conference and of the British and French proposals. The ostensible bases of the Soviet attack were then largely economic. To the Soviets, Western proposals seemed to entail an all-encompassing program of integration of the various national economies. They felt that this would have required abandonment of their plan to industrialize Eastern Europe and incorporate it in the Soviet Five Year Plans. They also intimated that Marshall Plan aid was to be used to promote the economic, and hence political, expansion of American influence. This soon became a dominant theme of Soviet propaganda. Molotov's suspicions on this point "were accentuated when he learnt that Marshall aid was not to be administered through any machinery set up by the United Nations but through an independent medium, in which—he assumed—American influence would be unchallenged."[13] By July 2 Moscow withdrew from the conference.

For several days after the Soviet departure, the question of Eastern European participation remained open. Indeed, as late as July 8, the Czechoslovak government indicated its willingness to attend the Paris meetings. However, this acceptance was soon withdrawn as a result of Soviet pressure.*

The Soviet refusal to participate in the Marshall Plan program accelerated the East-West estrangement. Many attempts have been made to explain the Soviet decision. Since it is unlikely that American aid would have been forthcoming had Moscow remained one of the proposed recipients, continued Soviet participation might well have sounded the death knell for the Marshall Plan and for European recovery. The Kremlin, however, committed a blunder, and the West benefited. Several interpretations may be noted at this time. They also represent the general policy alternatives available to the Kremlin in 1945, when cooperation with the West was still a distinct, if fading, possibility.

* At the time, Czechoslovak Prime Minister Klement Gottwald, an old-guard communist, was in Moscow negotiating a new trade agreement. He ordered Czechoslovakia's withdrawal at Stalin's order. Gottwald's refusal, as well as those of most of the Eastern European governments, was first announced by Moscow radio.

First, the Soviet leaders probably believed in an impending severe economic crisis in the United States. Early postwar Soviet periodicals stressed this theme. If Soviet leaders did indeed anticipate such a crisis, they could scarcely be expected, with their ideology and objectives, to join any plan specifically designed to stabilize the capitalist world. After Stalin's speech of February 9, 1946, Soviet society moved toward increased orthodoxy and conformity in all areas. Of particular pertinence was the denunciation, in May 1947, of Eugen Varga, a prominent Soviet economist, for asserting that a capitalist crisis was not imminent and that capitalism was entering an era of stabilization and expansion.

Second, Stalin's preoccupation with Sovietizing Eastern Europe and with integrating that area into a Soviet-controlled economic and political system may have precluded any cooperation with Western Europe that would have interfered with this paramount strategic objective. Soviet leaders held that to have permitted these countries to maintain any but the most unavoidable economic ties with the West would have politically strengthened the pro-Western elements still operating in the coalition governments of Eastern Europe.

Third, Soviet lack of interest in European recovery was apparent early in the postwar period. This is logical economically, in view of the Soviet need to attend its own wounds; it is also logical politically, since an unstable Europe gave added promise of succumbing to communism. This promise was particularly evident in Italy and France, countries whose communist parties had emerged from the war with enhanced prestige and with a broad base of voted support. More significantly, the perpetuation of unstable conditions in Western Europe decreased the likelihood of any Western interference with Stalin's policies in Eastern Europe. Thus, discouraging Europe's recovery would not only keep the West from challenging Soviet hegemony in Eastern Europe, but also would facilitate the spread of communism in Western Europe itself.

Fourth, Soviet mistrust of American motives may have underlain Stalin's reluctance to make any concessions in order to obtain American financial assistance. According to one analyst:

It [the Soviet Union] fears that this country, by offering loans to Russia's neighbors for the purchase of American goods, will not only make it difficult for the Russians to obtain the goods they need, but that the flag will follow, and American political influence will penetrate in the wake of loans and goods.[14]

Finally, an interpretation of a quite different stripe held that the Soviets chose not to participate because they then would have been required to divulge vital statistical data concerning their needs and shortages, information of military significance that the Kremlin preferred not to reveal.

Though there is wide disagreement over what motivated Soviet policy, there is no question that during the summer and fall of 1947 East-West relations steadily deteriorated. Prospects for an over-all European political settlement disappeared as Soviet attacks on the Marshall Plan intensified. The growing egocentricity of Stalinist policy can be seen in an editorial in *Izvestia* (September 3, 1947) that attributed the Allied victory in the Far East "primarily through the efforts of the Soviet people and its armies, led by the great Stalin." On September 18, 1947, Andrei Y. Vyshinsky, the Soviet delegate to the United Nations, set the general tenor for official policy in a speech before the General Assembly (reading 38):

As is now clear, the Marshall Plan constitutes in essence merely a variant of the Truman Doctrine adapted to the conditions of postwar Europe.

. . . Moreover, this Plan is an attempt to split Europe into two camps and, with the help of the United Kingdom and France, to complete the formation of a *bloc* of several European countries hostile to the interests of the democratic countries of Eastern Europe and most particularly to the interests of the Soviet Union.

Stalin now moved to complete the breach by establishing a rival grouping of states controlled by the Soviet Union. The Comintern was resurrected as the Cominform (Communist Information Bureau) at a special conference of communist parties in Wiliza Gora (Upper Silesia) on September 22–23, 1947. Communist strategy changed significantly. The Kremlin formally revived the thesis of the capitalist menace, and policy statements emphasized the enduring and irreconcilable antagonism between the capitalist and communist systems.*

Andrei Zhdanov's speech at the founding conference of the Cominform must be regarded as the most significant effort since the Comintern program of 1928 to formulate the position of international communism in the world and to integrate it into a unified whole[15] (reading 39). The speech was important not only because of its ambitious scope, but also because of the powerful position of the man charged with its presentation.† It represented the most comprehensive postwar statement of Soviet policy and tactics yet delivered.

* In his speech of September 9, 1945, Stalin had indicated that the Soviet Union considered itself liberated from the capitalist menace. Two years later, this old thesis was revived. A. W. Just, "Moskaus neue These," *Aussenpolitik*, Vol. I (July 1950), 103–109.

† Andrei Zhdanov ranked high in the upper echelons of the Soviet hierarchy. Indeed, many observers of the Soviet scene regarded him as second only to Joseph Stalin. Zhdanov, however, died in 1948.

Zhdanov began by announcing that the war had wrought fundamental changes in world power relationships.

A new alignment of political forces has arisen. The more the war recedes into the past, the more distinct become two major trends in postwar international policy, corresponding to the division of the political forces operating on the international arena into two major camps: the imperialist and antidemocratic camp, on the one hand, and the anti-imperialist and democratic camp, on the other.

Identifying the United States as the principal antagonist, he proceeded to interpret the economic, ideological, and military bases of its foreign policy. Expansionism was the theme common to all these factors. Zhdanov justified Soviet opposition to the Marshall Plan and, defending Soviet policy, made clear Moscow's determination to control Eastern Europe. In concluding, he called for concerted and active opposition by all communist parties to the Marshall Plan. In effect, Zhdanov's speech declared a permanent Cold War against the West. The tactical ramifications of this militant policy soon became apparent in France and Italy, where general strikes, accompanied by labor violence, were instigated in November 1947 in an attempt to paralyze the nascent Marshall Plan program, and in Southern Asia, where communist parties split with bourgeois-nationalist movements and attempted to subvert existing regimes by direct revolutionary means.

In addition to mobilizing communist parties against the Marshall Plan and Western policy, the Cominform served manifold purposes. Ideologically, it demanded unquestioning adherence to the Moscow line. Organizationally, it facilitated the consolidation of communist power, as purges swept the East European satellites. The Cominform became an instrument for ensuring a monolithic control over the various European communist parties. It was also a nucleus for future intra-Eastern European economic planning and integration. Politically, as a focal point for international communism, it not only crystallized opposition to Western policy, but symbolized communist unity and cooperation. Whether Soviet motivation was primarily defensive or offensive, the establishment of the Cominform was a turning point in postwar international relations. Cooperation, accommodation, and collaboration with the noncommunist world—the official line in the early postwar period—were now dropped. Henceforth, Stalin concentrated on preserving the Soviet empire in Eastern Europe.

NOTES

1. Philip E. Mosely, "Soviet-American Relations Since the War," *Annals* (May 1949), p. 207.

2. James F. Byrnes, *Speaking Frankly* (New York: Harper & Row, 1947), pp. 31–32.

3. C. E. Black, "Soviet Policy in Eastern Europe," *Annals* (May 1949), p. 153.

4. Byrnes, *op. cit.,* p. 108.

5. For example, such useful works as Georg von Rauch, *A History of Soviet Russia* (New York: Praeger, 1957); Frederick L. Schuman, *Russia Since 1917* (New York: Knopf, 1957); and an otherwise particularly skillful presentation of the 1945–1947 period by Kenneth Ingram, *History of the Cold War* (New York: Philosophical Library, 1955).

6. Byrnes, *op. cit.,* p. 119.

7. Lewis V. Thomas and Richard N. Frye, *The United States and Turkey and Iran* (Cambridge, Mass.: Harvard University Press, 1951), pp. 239–240.

8. For an excellent account of this period see George Lenczowski, *Russia and the West in Iran, 1918–1948: A Study in Big Power Rivalry* (Ithaca, N.Y.: Cornell University Press, 1949), chap. XI.

9. Barrington Moore, Jr., *Soviet Politics—The Dilemma of Power* (Cambridge, Mass.: Harvard University Press, 1950), p. 378.

10. Stanislaw Mikolajczyk, *The Rape of Poland: The Pattern of Soviet Domination* (New York: McGraw-Hill, 1948). See chapter XIV for a description of the appalling difficulties devised by the communists to deprecate and destroy the Peasant party.

11. U.S., Department of State, *Bulletin,* 16 (March 23, 1947), 534–537.

12. "American Foreign Policy," *New Times,* March 21, 1947, p. 3.

13. Ingram, *op. cit.,* p. 61.

14. Vera M. Dean, "Russia's Foreign Economic Policy," *Foreign Policy Reports,* 22 (February 1, 1947), 267.

15. G. I., "The Evolution of the Cominform, 1947–1950," *World Today,* 6 (May 1950), 213–214.

Structural Changes in Postwar Europe

35/The Geopolitics of the Peace Settlement

HUEY LOUIS KOSTANICK

Soviet power has been extended westward through creation of a large bloc of satellite states and through Soviet military occupation of Eastern Germany and Eastern Austria. In conjunction with Soviet expansion has come a major Slavic westward movement, which has wiped out a thousand years of Germanic expansion.

The impact of Soviet power applies in almost as strong a measure in other countries of Eastern and Central Europe outside the Soviet sphere of influence, as it applies to the Soviet satellite states themselves. In the immediate postwar period, Greece was faced not only with the problems of postwar rehabilitation but also with the problems of Communist guerrilla warfare which threatened to split Greece through loss of the fertile plains of Macedonia and western Thrace. . . . Similarly, Turkey has been disquieted by Soviet demands for participation in military defense of the Turkish straits. These pressures have created severe drains on the economies of Greece and Turkey. As a direct result, the United States undertook the task of supplying economic and military aid to these countries and thus became the other major power actively participating in Eastern European affairs. . . .

Politically, the Soviet bloc has been formed of Poland, Czechoslovakia, Hungary, Rumania, Bulgaria, and Albania, while Estonia, Latvia, and Lithuania have been directly annexed to the USSR. The satellite countries are dominated by Communist governments, which have made political, economic, and military agreements with the Soviet Union and among themselves. . . .

Alliance with the Soviet Union has also reversed the traditional pattern of trade with Western Europe. Eastern Europe has, essentially, an agricultural economy, which must export agricultural commodities. . . . In the interwar period, Germany, which in turn needed agricultural products, became the major trader with almost all of the countries of the area. The Danube River played a major role in this trade and, in addition, northwestern European ports served as outlets for Eastern

Huey Louis Kostanick, "The Significance of Geopolitical Changes in Eastern Europe," *Education,* 72 (February 1952), 381–387, *excerpts.* Reprinted with the permission of the author and the Palmer Publishing Company.

European exports to other areas of the world. In the postwar period, the trade of the satellites was reoriented toward the Soviet Union, whose economy could be bolstered by the valuable supplies of foods and industrial crops as well as Rumanian petroleum and other minerals. . . .

A basic realignment of Eastern Europe both politically and demographically has been created by the loss of German and Italian territories and the subsequent westward expansion of the Soviet Union and of other Slavic states. This expansion has taken place in different zones and in different fashions. The Soviet Union has advanced westward territorially through annexation of areas from each of the countries that bordered her on the West, and politically through creation of the Soviet bloc and through military occupation of Eastern Germany and of Eastern Austria. Poland and Yugoslavia have also gained territory at the expense of their western neighbors.

This westward expansion is most evident in the reversal of previous German expansion into Eastern Europe. Viewed broadly, this reversal may be expressed in terms of three successive "axes" having Trieste as the southern pivot. In 1939, the axis between Germanic and Slavic control extended roughly from Trieste to Königsberg (Kaliningrad) in German East Prussia. In the postwar period, through German losses of territory to Poland the line of German-Slav territorial and ethnic division swung westward to extend from Trieste to Stettin (Szczecin). But the ultimate Slavic political advance is more realistically marked by the western border of Soviet military occupation as represented by the Trieste-Lubeck axis, although the occupied territory is still German populated. . . .

Since 1939, approximately 187,000 square miles of territory with an estimated population of nearly 23 million have been annexed by the USSR. These territories are now administered as integral parts of the Soviet Union. . . . This expansion represents the greatest territorial change resulting from World War II, and was achieved at the expense of a number of East European countries.

In the Arctic zone, the Soviet Union gained from Finland the ice-free port of Petsamo, west of the Soviet port of Murmansk which in winter is kept open only by icebreakers. . . . Another zone of Soviet advance was the vital Baltic lowland, a portion of the North European Plain which has served as the invasion route to Western Europe for centuries. . . . [The] Baltic "window to the West" has been widened by the inclusion of Estonia, Latvia, and Lithuania in the USSR. Although their annexation is not recognized by the United States, they are Soviet republics, and their transportation facilities and ports form an additional link between the producing areas of western Russia and the Baltic Sea. . . .

The greatest loss of territory was by Poland, from whom the USSR annexed the entire eastern zone. Part of this territory, the Vilno area, was ceded to Lithuania, which had contested Polish possession of this historic Lithuanian capital. The annexation of southeastern Poland, of Ruthenia from Czechoslovakia, and of Northern Bucovina from Rumania gave control of strategic Carpathian passes, and, of greater importance, extended Russian territory over the Carpathians into the Danubian basin of Central Europe. A common border with Hungary was also secured.

In the Balkans, control of the northern distributory channel of the Danube was secured through the return of Bessarabia by Rumania, thus making the USSR a Danubian and Balkan power.

Through these territorial gains, the Soviet Union won an ice-free Arctic port, increased access to the Baltic Sea and the North European Plain, advanced into the Danubian basin, and secured a control point at the mouth of the Danube, as well as extending frontiers to Norway and Hungary. These are indeed significant geopolitical gains. . . .

Poland has been "moved" bodily westward in comparison to its prewar position. In the east, Poland had ceded to the USSR a 70,000 square-mile zone, thus placing its capital, Warsaw, only a hundred miles from the new eastern border. As compensation, Poland gained control of the southern portion of German East Prussia and of the international port of Danzig. Of even greater importance to Poland was the addition of 39,000 square miles of eastern Germany, which included the valuable industrial district of German Silesia. Thus, although Poland decreased from a total area of 150,000 to 121,000 square miles, its economy has been strengthened by additions of fertile agricultural land, a major industrial district, and the Baltic port of Stettin. Through this westward shift, a new position has been secured on the North European Plain. Expulsion of Germans and resettlement of Poles in the new areas poses a future problem should Germany seek the return of these territories. . . .

Axis defeat resulted in the elimination of Germany and Italy as Eastern European powers. Axis defeat also created another aspect of the new geopolitical situation—Soviet military occupation of Eastern Germany and of Eastern Austria. Under the division of Germany into four Allied occupational zones, Eastern Germany and Eastern Austria were placed under Soviet administration. Within these zones, the Berlin and Vienna enclaves were similarly subdivided. The western borders of these zones have come to mark the real frontiers of Soviet expansion. They are within the "Iron Curtain" of Europe, which separates differing ideologies, because in the Soviet zones Communist governments have come into power. In both countries, valuable agricultural land and industrial districts are included in the Soviet zones, and, from a strategic point of view, the Soviet position on the North European Plain has been extended westward to the Elbe River and further control of the Danubian gateway has been secured. . . .

The geopolitical changes that have taken place since the opening of

World War II are indeed broad and sweeping and are evident in diverse aspects of the East European scene. Their scope ranges from the new political power of both the Soviet Union and of the United States and the new political and economic patterns to territorial shifts and population displacement. Through these changes, a new phase of the history of Eastern Europe has been created, a phase in which the Soviet Union has played a dominant role. The Axis defeat set the stage for the westward expansion of Eastern Europe and for new political and demographic alignments.

The Struggle for Germany

36/The Future of Germany and the Peace Treaty with Germany *July 10, 1946*

V. M. MOLOTOV

The time has come for us to discuss the future of Germany and the peace treaty with that country.

The Soviet Government has always held that the spirit of revenge is a poor counsellor in such affairs. Nor would it be correct to identify Hitler Germany with the German people, although the German people cannot divest themselves of responsibility for Germany's aggression and for its dire consequences.

The Soviet people experienced the unparalleled suffering of enemy occupation, as a result of the invasion of the Soviet Union by the German armies. Our losses are great and inestimable. Other peoples of Europe, and not of Europe alone, will long feel the heavy losses and hardships caused by the war which Germany imposed.

It is, therefore, understandable that the problem of Germany's future should be agitating the minds not only of the German people, who are anxious to safeguard themselves for the future and prevent a renewal of

V. M. Molotov, *Problems of Foreign Policy: Speeches and Statements, April 1945– November 1948* (Moscow: Foreign Languages Publishing House, 1949), pp. 63–68, *excerpts.* This statement was made at the July 10, 1946, meeting of the Council of Foreign Ministers.

German aggression. . . . Nor can one forget that more than once this industrial might has served as the base for the arming of aggressive Germany.

Such are the premises from which we must draw our conclusions.

I proceed from the consideration that, in the interests of world economy and tranquility in Europe, it would be incorrect to adopt the line of annihilating Germany as a state, or of agrarianizing her, with the destruction of her main industrial centers.

Such a line would undermine the economy of Europe, dislocate world economy, and lead to a chronic political crisis in Germany, which would spell a threat to peace and tranquility.

I think that, even if we were to adopt such a line, historical development would impel us subsequently to renounce it as abortive and groundless.

I think, therefore, that our purpose is not to destroy Germany, but to transform her into a democratic and peace-loving state which alongside of agriculture, would have its own industry and foreign trade, but which would be deprived of the economic and military potentiality to rise again as an aggressive force. . . .

It has of late become fashionable to talk about dismembering Germany into several "autonomous" states, federalizing her, and separating the Ruhr from her. All such proposals stem from this same line of destroying and agrarianizing Germany, for it is easy to understand that without the Ruhr Germany cannot exist as an independent and viable state. But I have already said that the destruction of Germany should not be our objective, if we cherish the interests of peace and tranquility. . . .

If the world is to be made safe against possible German aggression, Germany must be completely disarmed, militarily and economically; and as to the Ruhr, it must be placed under inter-Allied control exercised by our four countries, with the object of preventing the revival of war industries in Germany.

The program of complete military and economic disarmament of Germany is not something new. The decisions of the Berlin conference deal with it in detail. And it is natural that the Ruhr, as the main base of Germany's war industry, should be kept under the vigilant control of the principal Allied Powers. The aim of completely disarming Germany militarily and economically should also be served by the reparations plan. The fact that until now no such plan has been drawn up, in spite of the repeated demands of the Soviet Government that the relevant decision of the Berlin conference should be carried out, and the fact that the Ruhr has not been placed under inter-Allied control, on which the Soviet Government insisted a year ago, is a dangerous thing from the point of view of safeguarding future peace and the security of nations.

We hold that it is impossible to put off the accomplishment of these tasks without running the risk of frustrating the decision to effect the complete military and economic disarmament of Germany. . . .

In order that the development of Germany's civilian industries may benefit other nations that need German coal, metal, and manufactured products, Germany should be granted the right to export and import and, if this right to engage in foreign trade is realized, we should not hinder Germany from increasing her output of steel, coal, and manufactured products for peaceful needs, naturally within certain bounds, and with the indispensable proviso that inter-Allied control is established over German industry, and over the Ruhr industries in particular.

As we know, the Control Council in Germany recently fixed the level which German industry should attain in the next few years. Germany is still a long way from this level. Nevertheless, it should be recognized now that her civilian industries must be given the opportunity to develop more widely, provided only that this industrial development is really used to satisfy the peaceful needs of the German people and for the promotion of trade with other countries. All this calls for the establishment of proper inter-Allied control over German industry and over the Ruhr industries in particular, responsibility for which cannot rest upon any one Allied country alone.

Soviet Perceptions of American Foreign Policy

37/Soviet Views on the Truman Doctrine

Izvestia, *March 13, 1947*

On March 12, President Truman addressed a message to the US Congress asking for 400 million dollars to be assigned for urgent aid to Greece and Turkey, and for authority to send to those countries American civil and military personnel, and to provide for the training by Americans of specially picked Greek and Turkish personnel.

Greece, said Truman, was in a desperate economic and political situation. Britain was no longer able to act as trustee for the Greeks. Turkey

Quoted from *Soviet News,* March 15, 1947, *excerpts.*

had requested speedy American aid. Turkey, unlike Greece, had not suffered from the Second World War, but she needed financial aid from Britain and from the USA in order to carry out that modernization necessary for maintaining her national integrity. Since the British Government, on account of its own difficulties, was not capable of offering financial or other aid to the Turks, this aid must be furnished by the USA.

Thus Congress was asked to do two "good deeds" at once—to save Greece from internal disorders and to pay for the cost of "modernizing" Turkey. . . .

British troops have been on Greek territory since 1944. On Churchill's initiative, Britain took on herself the responsibility for "stabilizing" political conditions in Greece. The British authorities did not confine themselves to perpetuating the rule of the reactionary, antidemocratic forces in Greece, making no scruple in supporting ex-collaborators with the Germans. The entire political and economic activities under a number of short-lived Greek governments have been carried on under close British control and direction.

Today we can see the results of this policy—complete bankruptcy. British troops failed to bring peace and tranquillity to tormented Greece. The Greek people have been plunged into the abyss of new sufferings, of hunger and poverty. Civil war takes on ever fiercer forms.

Was not the presence of foreign troops on Greek territory instrumental in bringing about this state of affairs? Does not Britain, who proclaimed herself the guardian of Greece, bear responsibility for the bankruptcy of her charge?

The American President's message completely glosses over these questions. The USA does not wish to criticize Britain, since she herself intends to follow the British example. Truman's statement makes it clear that the USA does not intend to deviate from the course of British policy in Greece. So one cannot expect better results.

The US government has no intention of acting in the Greek question as one might have expected a member of UNO, concerned about the fate of another member, to act. It is obvious that in Washington they do not wish to take into account the obligations assumed by the US government regarding UNO. Truman did not even consider it necessary to wait for the findings of the Security Council Commission specially sent to Greece to investigate the situation on the spot.

Truman, indeed, failed to reckon either with the international organization or with the sovereignty of Greece. What will be left of Greek sovereignty when the "American military and civilian personnel" get to work in Greece by means of the 250 million dollars brought into that country? The sovereignty and independence of Greece will be the first victims of such singular "defense."

The American arguments for assisting Turkey base themselves on the existence of a threat to the integrity of Turkish territory—though no one and nothing actually threatens Turkey's integrity. This "assistance" is evidently aimed at putting this country also under US control.

Some American commentators admit this quite openly. Walter Lippmann, for example, frankly points out in the *Herald Tribune* that an American alliance with Turkey would give the USA a strategic position, incomparably more advantageous than any other, from which power could be wielded over the Middle East.

Commenting on Truman's message to Congress, the *New York Times* proclaims the advent of "the age of American responsibility." Yet what is this responsibility but a smokescreen for expansion? The cry of saving Greece and Turkey from the expansion of the so-called "totalitarian states" is not new. Hitler used to refer to the Bolsheviks when he wanted to open the road for his own conquests. Now they want to take Greece and Turkey under their control, they raise a din about "totalitarian states". . . .

We are now witnessing a fresh intrusion of the USA into the affairs of other states. American claims to leadership in international affairs grow parallel with the growing appetite of the American quarters concerned. But the American leaders, in the new historical circumstances, fail to reckon with the fact that the old methods of the colonizers and die-hard politicians have outlived their time and are doomed to failure. In this lies the chief weakness of Truman's message.

38/Soviet Interpretation of the Marshall Plan—
Speech to the UN General Assembly *September 18, 1947*

ANDREI Y. VYSHINSKY

The so-called Truman Doctrine and the Marshall Plan are particularly glaring examples of the manner in which the principles of the United Nations are violated, of the way in which the Organization is ignored.

As the experience of the past few months has shown, the proclamation of this doctrine meant that the United States Government has

United Nations General Assembly, *Official Records,* Plenary Meetings, Verbatim Record, September 18, 1947, pp. 86–88, *excerpts.*

moved toward a direct renunciation of the principles of international collaboration and concerted action by the great Powers and toward attempts to impose its will on other independent states, while at the same time obviously using the economic resources distributed as relief to individual needy nations as an instrument of political pressure. This is clearly proved by the measures taken by the United States Government with regard to Greece and Turkey which ignore and by-pass the United Nations as well as by the measures proposed under the so-called Marshall Plan in Europe. This policy conflicts sharply with the principle expressed by the General Assembly in its resolution of 11 December 1946, which declares that relief supplies to other countries "should . . . at no time be used as a political weapon."

As is now clear, the Marshall Plan constitutes in essence merely a variant of the Truman Doctrine adapted to the conditions of postwar Europe. In bringing forward this plan, the United States Government apparently counted on the cooperation of the Governments of the United Kingdom and France to confront the European countries in need of relief with the necessity of renouncing their inalienable right to dispose of their economic resources and to plan their national economy in their own way. The United States also counted on making all these countries directly dependent on the interests of American monopolies, which are striving to avert the approaching depression by an accelerated export of commodities and capital to Europe. . . .

It is becoming more and more evident to everyone that the implementation of the Marshall Plan will mean placing European countries under the economic and political control of the United States and direct interference by the latter in the internal affairs of those countries.

Moreover, this Plan is an attempt to split Europe into two camps and, with the help of the United Kingdom and France, to complete the formation of a *bloc* of several European countries hostile to the interests of the democratic countries of Eastern Europe and most particularly to the interests of the Soviet Union.

An important feature of this Plan is the attempt to confront the countries of Eastern Europe with a *bloc* of Western European States including Western Germany. The intention is to make use of Western Germany and German heavy industry (the Ruhr) as one of the most important economic bases for American expansion in Europe, in disregard of the national interests of the countries which suffered from German aggression.

I need only recall these facts to show the utter incompatibility of this policy of the United States, and of the British and French Governments which support it, with the fundamental principles of the United Nations.

Stalinism and Bipolarism

39/Soviet Policy and World Politics

ANDREI ZHDANOV

The end of the Second World War brought with it big changes in the world situation. The military defeat of the bloc of fascist states, the character of the war of liberation from fascism, and the decisive role played by the Soviet Union in the vanquishing of the fascist aggressors sharply altered the alignment of forces between the two systems—the socialist and the capitalist—in favor of socialism.

What is the essential nature of these changes?

The principal outcome of World War II was the military defeat of Germany and Japan—the two most militaristic and aggressive of the capitalist countries. . . .

[Second], the war immensely enhanced the international significance and prestige of the USSR. . . .

[Third], the capitalist world has also undergone a substantial change. Of the six so-called great imperialist powers (Germany, Japan, Great Britain, the USA, France, and Italy), three have been eliminated by military defeat. France has also been weakened and has lost its significance as a great power. As a result, only two great imperialist world powers remain—the United States and Great Britain. But the position of one of them, Great Britain, has been undermined. The war revealed that militarily and politically British imperialism was not so strong as it had been. . . .

[Fourth], World War II aggravated the crisis of the colonial system, as expressed in the rise of a powerful movement for national liberation in the colonies and dependencies. This has placed the rear of the capitalist system in jeopardy. The peoples of the colonies no longer wish to live in the old way. The ruling classes of the metropolitan countries can no longer govern the colonies on the old lines. . . .

Of all the capitalist powers, only one—the United States—emerged from the war not only unweakened, but even considerably stronger economically and militarily. The war greatly enriched the American capitalists. . . . But the end of the war confronted the United States with a number of new problems. The capitalist monopolies were anxious to maintain their profits at the former high level, and accordingly pressed

Andrei Zhdanov, *The International Situation* (Moscow: Foreign Languages Publishing House, 1947), *excerpts*.

hard to prevent a reduction of the wartime volume of deliveries. But this meant that the USA must retain the foreign markets which had absorbed American products during the war, and moreover, acquire new markets, inasmuch as the war had substantially lowered the purchasing power of most of the countries [to do this] . . . the United States proclaimed a new frankly predatory and expansionist course. The purpose of this new, frankly expansionist course is to establish the world supremacy of American imperialism. . . .

The fundamental changes caused by the war on the international scene and in the position of individual countries have entirely changed the political landscape of the world. A new alignment of political forces has arisen. The more the war recedes into the past, the more distinct become two major trends in postwar international policy, corresponding to the division of the political forces operating on the international arena into two major camps; the imperialist and antidemocratic camp, on the one hand, and the anti-imperialist and democratic camp, on the other. The principal driving force of the imperialist camp is the USA. Allied with it are Great Britain and France. . . . The cardinal purpose of the imperialist camp is to strengthen imperialism, to hatch a new imperialist war, to combat socialism and democracy, and to support reactionary and antidemocratic pro-fascist regimes and movements everywhere.

The anti-fascist forces comprise the second camp. This camp is based on the USSR and the new democracies. It also includes countries that have broken with imperialism and have firmly set foot on the path of democratic development, such as Rumania, Hungary and Finland. . . .

Soviet foreign policy proceeds from the fact of the coexistence for a long period of the two systems—capitalism and socialism. From this it follows that cooperation between the USSR and countries with other systems is possible, provided that the principle of reciprocity is observed and that obligations once assumed are honored. Everyone knows that the USSR has always honored the obligations it has assumed. . . .

The strategical plans of the United States envisage the creation in peacetime of numerous bases and vantage grounds situated at great distances from the American continent and designed to be used for aggressive purposes against the USSR and the countries of the new democracy. . . .

Economic expansion is an important supplement to the realization of America's strategical plan. American imperialism is endeavoring like a usurer to take advantage of the postwar difficulties of the European countries, in particular of the shortage of raw materials, fuel, and food in the Allied countries that suffered most from the war, to dictate to them extortionate terms for any assistance rendered. With an eye to the impending economic crisis, the United States is in a hurry to find new monopoly spheres of capital investment and markets for its goods.

American economic "assistance" pursues the broad aim of bringing Europe into bondage to American capital. The more drastic the economic situation of a country is, the harsher are the terms which the American monopolies endeavor to dictate to it. . . .

Lastly, the aspiration to world supremacy and the antidemocratic policy of the United States involve an ideological struggle. The principal purpose of the ideological part of the American strategical plan is to deceive public opinion by slanderously accusing the Soviet Union and the new democracies of aggressive intentions, and thus representing the Anglo-Saxon bloc in a defensive role, and absolving it of responsibility for preparing a new war. . . .

The unfavorable reception which the Truman doctrine was met with accounts for the necessity of the appearance of the Marshall Plan which is a more carefully veiled attempt to carry through the same expansionist policy. The vague and deliberately guarded formulations of the Marshall Plan amount in essence to a scheme to create a bloc of states bound by obligations to the United States, and to grant American credits to European countries as recompense for their renunciation of economic, and then of political, independence. . . .

The dissolution of the Comintern, which conformed to the demands of the development of the labor movement in the new historical situation, played a positive role . . .

In the course of the four years that have elapsed since the dissolution of the Comintern (1943), the Communist Parties have grown considerably in strength and influence in nearly all the countries of Europe and Asia. . . . But the present position of the Communist Parties has its shortcomings. Some comrades understood the dissolution of the Comintern to imply the elimination of all ties, of all contact, between the fraternal Communist Parties. But experience has shown that such mutual isolation of the Communist Parties is wrong, harmful and, in point of fact, unnatural. The Communist movement develops within national frameworks, but there are tasks and interests common to the parties of various countries. We get a rather curious state of affairs . . . the Communists even refrained from meeting one another, let alone consulting with one another on questions of mutual interest to them, from fear of the slanderous talk of their enemies regarding the "hand of Moscow." . . . There can be no doubt that if the situation were to continue it would be fraught with most serious consequences to the development of the work of the fraternal parties. The need for mutual consultation and voluntary coordination of action between individual parties has become particularly urgent at the present junction when continued isolation may lead to a slackening of mutual understanding, and at times, even to serious blunders.

FOR FURTHER STUDY

Alperovitz, Gar. *Atomic Diplomacy: Hiroshima and Potsdam.* New York: Simon and Schuster, 1965.

Barghoorn, Frederick C. *The Soviet Image of the United States.* New York: Harcourt Brace Jovanovich, 1950.

Betts, R. R. (ed.). *Central and South East Europe, 1945–1948.* London: Royal Institute of International Affairs, 1950.

Blackett, P. M. S. *Fear, War, and the Bomb.* New York: Whittlesey House, 1949.

Byrnes, James F. *Speaking Frankly.* New York: Harper & Row, 1947.

Djilas, Milovan. *Conversations with Stalin.* New York: Harcourt Brace Jovanovich, 1962.

Druks, Herbert. *Harry S Truman and the Russians, 1945–1953.* New York: Speller, 1966.

Eagleton, William. *The Kurdish Republic of 1946.* New York: Oxford University Press, 1963.

Ebon, Martin. *World Communism Today.* New York: McGraw-Hill, 1948.

Feis, Herbert. *From Trust to Terror: The Onset of the Cold War, 1945–1950.* New York: Norton, 1970.

Fleming, D. F. *The Cold War and Its Origins, 1917–1960.* 2 vols. Garden City, N.Y.: Doubleday, 1961.

Gardner, Lloyd C., Arthur Schlesinger, Jr., and Hans J. Morgenthau. *The Origins of the Cold War.* Boston: Ginn, 1970.

Gluckstein, Yagael. *Stalin's Satellites in Europe.* London: Allen & Unwin, 1952.

Herz, Martin F. *Beginnings of the Cold War.* Bloomington: Indiana University Press, 1966.

Ingram, Kenneth. *History of the Cold War.* New York: Philosophical Library, 1955.

Kennan, George F. *Memoirs 1925–1950.* Boston: Atlantic-Little, Brown, 1967.

Kirk, George E. *Survey of International Affairs: The Middle East 1945–1950.* London: Oxford University Press, 1954.

Lane, Arthur B. *I Saw Poland Betrayed.* Indianapolis: Bobbs-Merrill, 1948.

Lenczowski, George. *Russia and the West in Iran, 1918–1948: A Study in Big Power Rivalry.* Ithaca, N.Y.: Cornell University Press, 1949.

Lukacs, John. *The Great Powers and Eastern Europe.* New York: American Book, 1953.

_____. *A New History of the Cold War.* 2d ed. Garden City, N.Y.: Doubleday, 1966.

Mikolajczyk, Stanislaw. *The Rape of Poland: Pattern of Soviet Aggression.* New York: McGraw-Hill, 1948.

Nagy, Ferenc. *The Struggle Behind the Iron Curtain.* New York: Macmillan, 1948.

Paterson, Thomas G. *Cold War Critics: Alternatives to American Foreign Policy in the Truman Years.* Chicago: Quadrangle Books, 1971.

Rieber, Alfred J. *Stalin and the French Communist Party, 1941–1947.* New York: Columbia University Press, 1962.

Seton-Watson, Hugh. *The East European Revolution.* New York: Praeger, 1956.

Smith, Walter Bedell. *My Three Years in Moscow.* Philadelphia: Lippincott, 1950.

Truman, Harry S, *Memoirs.* 2 vols. Garden City, N.Y.: Doubleday, 1955–1956.

stalinization and empire, 1948–1953

The imperialist nature of Stalinist political and military objectives in Eastern Europe and the renewed emphasis upon Marxist-Leninist orthodoxy at home and abroad, with its implication of uncompromising hostility, led inexorably to the institutionalization of the Cold War. Soviet intransigence sharpened in the United Nations, in Germany, and in Austria. By February 1948, when the Communist Party effected a coup d'état and Czechoslovakia disappeared behind the Curtain, the conquest of Eastern Europe was completed. The fall of Prague had far-reaching consequences. More than any other single Soviet-inspired move, it dispelled remaining Western illusions concerning Soviet intentions, heightened anxiety over the Soviet threat, and hastened Western rearmament. In the early postwar period, democratic Czechoslovakia had represented a tenuous link between the Soviet Union and its former allies; it had symbolized the possibility of compromise and cooperation. The disappearance of Czechoslovakia as a middle ground ended such hopes. The lines of conflict were now clearly drawn.

Stalin next proceeded to end the last vestiges of coalition government in Eastern Europe—a process noticeably accelerated after the split with Tito—and to consolidate his empire. Through an intricate network of alliances, trade and economic agreements, joint-stock companies,* and Communist Party ties, Soviet hegemony was entrenched

---

* According to the Soviets "the Joint Stock Company, half of whose capital belongs to the Soviet Union, and the other half to the Governments of the People's Democracies, is a new form of economic collaboration between the countries of the socialist camp based on the principle of equality and mutual economic advantage; all expenses and profits of the Joint Stock Company are shared equally." M. Paramov, "Forms and

throughout the area. Cultural and political ties with the West were eliminated, and economic transactions reduced to an insignificant minimum. Previously negotiated political agreements were either ignored or so interpreted by the Kremlin as to accord with its expansionist aims (reading 40). By June 1948 the Soviet Union had seemingly succeeded in establishing a monolithic structure extending from the Baltic to the Black Sea. To the West it appeared that America's monopoly of atomic weapons constituted the only bar to Soviet domination of all Europe.

Two dramatic developments occurred in June 1948: the Berlin blockade and the expulsion of Tito from the Cominform. Each had an effect far beyond its immediate frame of reference. In retrospect, they constitute two of Stalin's major postwar miscalculations (the aggression in Korea might be considered a third), setting in motion a chain of events unfavorable to the consolidation and expansion of Soviet power.

On June 24, 1948, the Soviet Union imposed a blockade on the Western sectors of Berlin, deep inside the Soviet zone of Germany. During the previous months Soviet authorities had periodically interfered with Western access to Berlin, but had hesitated before imposing a full blockade. Several considerations motivated the Soviets. First, by forcing the Western Powers out of Berlin and bringing the entire city under their control, the Soviets expected to enhance their prospects of controlling Germany, the ultimate prize in the Cold War. Second, they hoped to undermine efforts then being made to establish West Germany as a united and independent country within the Western camp. Third, an Allied surrender in Berlin would have strengthened Communist Party prestige in the weakened countries of Western Europe, further softening them for future subversion by local communist parties. However, once the Berlin airlift started, the Soviets were committed to a lengthy test of strength. Western determination was on trial. The stakes were high, particularly for the West. Moscow mentioned none of these factors in its stated version of the reasons for imposing the blockade (reading 41). Moscow's statement dwelt on legalisms and split hairs, but bore little relation to power realities or political considerations.

Allied willingness to pay the price of the airlift convinced Stalin of the futility of this tactic, and a settlement was finally reached in May 1949, after months of trying negotiation. The Kremlin had suffered its

Methods of Economic Cooperation Between the U.S.S.R. and the People's Democracies," *Voprosy Ekonomiki,* 3 (December 1950), 46.

Through a convenient interpretation of the provision in the peace treaties dealing with "German assets," the Soviet Union acquired extensive holdings in Bulgaria, Hungary, Romania, and Poland. These preempted assets gave the Soviets a position of economic importance without the actual outlay of any funds. Soviet managers controlled the enterprises.

first postwar defeat in Europe. The blockade failed not only to drive the Western Powers out of Berlin, but also to prevent the establishment of the West German Federal Republic on May 23, 1949. Moscow retaliated in kind by setting up the German Democratic Republic in October 1949. This formalized partition of Germany has endured to the present, exacerbating fear and insecurity and serving as an ever-present reminder of the division between West and East and of the deep-rooted incompatibility of Soviet-Western objectives in Europe.

The Berlin blockade exposed Western vulnerability to Soviet pressure: whenever Moscow wants to create a crisis atmosphere it need only move to isolate West Berlin, which lies 110 miles inside communist East Germany. As long as the West lacks guaranteed land access to West Berlin, it is captive to Soviet and East German initiatives. Berlin is the open sore in the East-West relations, easily irritated and quickly swollen to international crisis proportions.

The world first learned of the deep fissure within the supposedly solid edifice of international communism on June 28, 1948. The Cominform announced the expulsion of the Yugoslav Communist Party for "anti-Party and anti-Soviet views, incompatible with Marxism-Leninism." The Yugoslav leaders, the announcement stated:

> . . . have placed themselves in opposition to the Communist Parties affili-
> ated to the Information Bureau [Cominform], have taken the path of seced-
> ing from the united socialist front against imperialism, have taken the path
> of betraying the cause of international solidarity of the working people, and
> have taken up a position of nationalism.[1]

Though the split was less one of principle than of power and personality, it had important ideological ramifications. The Soviet leadership resorted to a variety of pressures short of war to topple Tito and make Yugoslavia a compliant satellite. In 1951, fearful of a Soviet attack and desirous of gaining international support, the Yugoslav government published a detailed account of Soviet efforts to destroy it (reading 42).

Stalin refused to accept Tito as an equal and grew dissatisfied with Yugoslav intransigence in commercial and political negotiations. He insisted upon unchallenged and absolute economic and political control by the Kremlin and upon a privileged position for Soviet diplomats and advisers stationed in Yugoslavia. The Yugoslavs resisted Sovietization. Irritated by failure either to dominate the Yugoslav Communist Party, to infiltrate it and the Yugoslav governmental apparatus with agents loyal to the Kremlin, or to reduce Yugoslavia to a subservient satrapy comparable to that of the other nations of Eastern Europe, Stalin invoked the "ultimate" weapon of excommunication against his former protégé. He expected to overthrow Tito by waging an intensive propaganda campaign through the Cominform and by utilizing Soviet prestige to alienate Yugoslav public opinion away from Tito. This Stalin assumed would bring to power a pro-Soviet, anti-Tito faction. However, in considering that the highest loyalty of all "good" communists was to the Soviet Union and not to any particular national communist party, Stalin underestimated the broad bases of Tito's strength, as well as the force of Yugoslav nationalism. Aided by the fortunate circumstance of geography, the loyalty of party and military associates whose bonds had been forged in the crucible of a common struggle against the Germans, and the undoubted popularity of Tito as a national hero, the Yugoslav leadership withstood the Cominform assault.

"Titoism" signifies more than a reaction against Soviet domination; it represents a fusion of nationalism and communism into an ideology and a movement having a variety of forms and connoting a measure of independence not acceptable to Moscow.* No single formula can account for the phenomenon of Titoism. Rather, it must be viewed within a particular framework of historical circumstances, as in Yugoslavia and Poland. In the case of Yugoslavia, national support of Tito, coupled with generous infusions of Western economic and military aid, enabled it to withstand Stalin's attempt at subversion. Since then, the Yugoslavs have insisted that it is they who are the true interpreters of the Marxist-Leninist tradition and that Stalinism represented a perversion of this tradition.

Titoism poses a permanent dilemma for Soviet leaders: under what circumstances should the Kremlin use "diplomacy," as opposed to "compulsion," in order to eliminate threats to its established hegemony and leadership? Events of the post-Stalin period (e.g., in Poland and Hungary in 1956 and Czechoslovakia in 1968) have shown that any acceptance by Moscow of the "many roads to socialism" doctrine may well result in the release of those pent-up forces of frustration and opposition that the Kremlin seeks either to curb through an easing

---

* During the early postwar years a few leading East European communists—notably Tito in Yugoslavia and Dimitrov in Bulgaria—entertained the age-old vision of a Balkan Federation. The two met at Bled, Yugoslavia, in the summer of 1947 and discussed the possibility of setting up a Yugoslav-Bulgarian customs union that would serve as the nucleus for such a federation. Independent, it was to be closely associated with the Soviet Union. However, Moscow had some second thoughts on the subject. It feared that a Balkan Federation might prove too difficult to control. Therefore, on January 28, 1948, *Pravda* declared that: "The countries of Eastern Europe do not need a problematic and invented federation or customs union but a strengthening of their independence and sovereignty through the organization of internal popular and democratic forces as had been stated in the Cominform declarations." To Moscow, Titoism and a "Third Force" in Eastern Europe are equally an anathema.

of political and economic controls or to crush through the use of military force.

After 1948, Stalin initiated a series of purges of possible "Titos" and intensified the pace of Sovietization. Thus, leading communists were swept from power—Gomulka in Poland, Rajk in Hungary, Kostov in Bulgaria, Slansky in Czechoslovakia. Stalin moved to ensure the absolute obedience of the party organizations to Moscow. Though the purges were rationalized in terms of faulty ideological attitudes on the part of the purged, the verbalisms merely camouflaged Byzantine intrigue and primitive power considerations. The Stalinist pattern of organization was imposed upon Eastern Europe. Industry, foreign trade, and transportation were nationalized; centralized economic control and planning were introduced; and heavy industrialization was emphasized. Stalin sought to guarantee the permanence and stability of his empire by remaking the economic, social, and political fabric of Eastern European society. Operating through pro-Moscow local communists, the Soviet Union asserted its unchallenged hegemony over the area. Stalin stopped short of military measures in his efforts to overthrow Tito, but the intensified Sovietization of Eastern Europe, the Soviet pressure on Berlin, and the outbreak of communist-engineered rebellions in India, Indonesia, Indochina, Malaya, and the Philippines all heightened Western insecurity and led to the establishment of a more formalized system of military alliance.

The North Atlantic Treaty Organization (NATO) was established on April 4, 1949. It represented the West's military response to the Sovietization of Eastern Europe, the Soviet threat to Berlin, Moscow's global effort to subvert Western and pro-Western governments, and the enormous military disparity in conventional forces existing between the two camps in Europe. Only America's nuclear monopoly was considered to stand between the Red Army and the English Channel. Western Europe was weak, war-weary, defenseless. NATO served as a trip-wire, a reminder to the Soviet Union that any military move westward on its part would meet with an American nuclear response.

NATO was intended primarily as a defense against any possible Soviet aggression; only secondarily was it concerned with promoting economic and political cooperation among its members. Its founders regarded NATO as a legitimate exercise of the "inherent right of individual or collective self-defense" granted under Articles 51 and 52 of the UN Charter, designed to compensate for the inability of the fledgling United Nations to guarantee the peace. British Foreign Secretary Ernest Bevin, championing the NATO Treaty and emphasizing its defensive character, argued that Soviet duplicity and threatening behavior had left the Western democracies with no choice. "The pact," he held,

does not seek to interfere, but equally it does resist the right of any Powers with aggressive intentions to upset our institutions, to bring us into bondage, or to create a situation which will enable them to introduce the police state, or carry out devices which have been applied in so many other countries.

The Soviets, on the other hand, regarded NATO in a completely different light (reading 43). Denying that their treaties with the Eastern European countries could be interpreted "as treaties which are in any degree aimed against the allies of the USSR in the late war," they declared that Western rearmament and establishment of NATO could "in no way be justified by the interests of self-defense." Rather, "the North Atlantic Pact is designed to intimidate the states which do not agree to obey the dictates of the Anglo-American grouping of Powers that lay claim to world domination." Indeed, continued the Soviet memorandum, it undermines the very foundations of the UN and, "far from corresponding to the aims and principles of the United Nations Organization, runs counter to the Charter of this organization."

The Soviet government considered NATO the newest expression of an aggressive capitalism that could perpetuate itself only by embarking on imperialist ventures. Ideologically, its interpretation reflected the hostile tradition of Marxism-Leninism. Politically, the Soviets saw their expansion in Europe halted and watched with concern and surprise the unexpectedly rapid revival of Japan and Germany and their shift from passivity to active adherence to the Western bloc. To supplement its diplomatic activity, the Kremlin intensified its anti-Western propaganda campaign. Operating through a variety of organizations, the most important being the Partisans of Peace, it attempted to preempt the theme of peace and undermine Western influence in Asia and the Middle East. Militarily, the Soviets seemed to feel at a disadvantage with the West, despite their spectacularly improved postwar strategic position. However, by late 1949, two developments did much to affect advantageously the Soviet power position: the announcement that a Soviet atom bomb had been successfully produced and detonated and the victory of the Chinese communists on the mainland of China, which meant that domination of the Eurasian land mass had passed to the communist world. As the lines of hostility froze in Europe, events in the Far East attracted increasing attention.

The Chinese People's Republic was proclaimed in Peking on October 1, 1949. An era of Far Eastern history had come to an end. For the first time in more than a century all of (mainland) China was controlled by one elite, a Chinese elite. China's destiny was no longer decided in Europe. The century of civil wars, unequal treaties, forced concessions to foreign powers, and progressively weakened central authority was now past. Out of this crucible emerged a harsh, dedicated, disciplined leadership—the Calvinists of Asia—ruthlessly intent on creating a powerful, industrialized, totalitarian China. This development inevitably affected great power relationships in Asia, relationships already greatly altered as a consequence of World War II and the confused 1945–1949 interregnum.

There is no question that World War II was won in Europe. But the postwar peace has experienced its severest stresses in Asia, a trend apt to continue for the foreseeable future. On the eve of victory over Nazi Germany, a spirit of optimism prevailed in Washington concerning postwar Soviet objectives in the Far East and particularly in China. But it was by no means universal. A brilliant analysis of probable Soviet objectives in the Far East was developed in a memorandum cabled by George F. Kennan, then Chargé d'Affaires in Moscow, to Ambassador Harriman, in Washington at the time for consultation:

Actually I am persuaded that in the future Soviet policy respecting China will continue what it has been in the recent past: a fluid resilient policy directed at the achievement of maximum power with minimum responsibility on portions of the Asiatic continent lying beyond the Soviet border. This will involve the exertion of pressure in various areas in direct proportion to their strategic importance and their proximity to the Soviet frontier. I am sure that within the framework of this policy Moscow will aim specifically at: (1) reacquiring in substance, if not in form, all the diplomatic and territorial assets previously possessed on the mainland of Asia by Russia under the Czars; (2) domination of the provinces of China in central Asia contiguous to the Soviet frontier. Such action is dictated by the strategic necessity of protecting in depth the industrial core of the USSR; (3) acquiring sufficient control in all areas of North China now dominated by the Japanese to prevent other foreign powers from repeating the Japanese incursion. This means, to the Russian mind, the maximum possible exclusion of penetration in that area by outside powers including America and Britain. . . .

It would be tragic if our natural anxiety for the support of the Soviet Union at this juncture, coupled with Stalin's use of words which mean all things to all people and his cautious affability, were to lead us into an undue reliance on Soviet aid or even Soviet acquiescence in the achievement of our long term objectives in China.[2]

Soviet aims in the Far East were realized at Yalta. Western agreement to restore the sphere of influence controlled by Russia in 1904 at the time of the Russo-Japanese war fulfilled Stalin's most ambitious territorial objectives. Stalin had regained Czarist Russia's patrimony in Asia. Quite remarkably, Nationalist China quickly accepted the accords on Asia reached at the Yalta Conference, to which it had not been invited. Like Sun Yat-sen in 1923, Chiang Kai-shek was prepared to acquiesce to Soviet demands for hegemony over portions of imperial China in return for support against a domestic rival—in Chiang's case, Mao Tse-tung and the Chinese communists. Such was Chiang Kai-shek's eagerness that Washington on several occasions had to caution the Chinese against granting too many concessions, as for example, agreeing to an unsupervised plebiscite in Mongolia. China recognized the "independence" of Outer Mongolia and agreed to Soviet participation in the operation of the Chinese Changchun Railway* (thus affording Moscow an entering wedge into Manchuria); to joint Sino-Soviet use of the naval base of Port Arthur; and to the internationalization of the port of Dairen. These Soviet gains were formally acknowledged by Nationalist China in the Sino-Soviet Treaty of Friendship and Alliance, signed on August 14, 1945. In return, the Soviet government recognized the government of Chiang Kai-shek as the legitimate government of China and pledged itself "to render to China moral support and aid in military supplies and other material resources, such support and aid to be entirely given to the Nationalist Government as the central government of China." Soviet leaders quickly broke this pledge.

Our knowledge of the relations between the Soviet and Chinese communist leaders during the 1945–1949 period is meager. Reliable data are lacking. As far as can be determined, Soviet contact with the Chinese communists was not extensive until early 1946, notwithstanding the common ideological heritage. We do know that the takeover by the Chinese communists of the key province of Manchuria was facilitated by Soviet authorities (then still occupying the area after the Japanese surrender), who prevented Nationalist Chinese troops from entering the main cities and who stacked quantities of captured Japanese weapons in places convenient for Mao's communist troops to collect. Despite this, there is reason to believe that Stalin did not expect Mao to emerge the victor from the Chinese civil war, certainly not as quickly as he did. For example, in late 1945, shortly before the Chinese communist guerrilla armies took over, the Soviets stripped Manchuria of all usable industrial equipment and rolling stock; the USSR clearly did not expect to have to establish formal state-to-state relations with the Chinese communists within four years. Possibly Stalin was as surprised as the West at the shocking deterioration of the well-equipped, well-supplied Kuomintang forces and at the dramatic communist military advances in 1947–1948. According to a Yugoslav

* The Japanese had combined the Chinese Eastern Railway with the South Manchurian Railway into one unified system—the Chinese Changchun Railway.

communist official, Stalin recommended that Mao reach an agreement with Chiang Kai-shek and enter into a coalition government. Supposedly, Mao agreed, but on returning home went his own way and won. Stalin is also alleged to have had doubts about the extent to which the Chinese communists were genuine communists: he called them "Radish Communists—red on the outside, but white on the inside."

The outcome of the Chinese civil war was not determined in Moscow. At best, Soviet leaders contributed in marginal fashion to the Chinese communist victory. The Kuomintang failure to cope effectively with China's myriad administrative, economic, and social ills; the venality of Kuomintang officials; the insensitivity of Chiang Kai-shek to the peasants' desire for an end to war all served to enhance the political appeal of the communists. Mao adroitly exploited the spreading discontent with Kuomintang incompetence and corruption, the legacy of communist resistance against the Japanese, the deep-rooted desire of the peasantry for fundamental agrarian reforms, and the appeal that a strong and united China had for students, intellectuals, and even middle-class elements.

American efforts to mediate the Chinese civil war proved futile. Indeed, it is doubtful that they ever enjoyed the faintest prospect of success. Meanwhile, Moscow pursued a policy of ambiguity with the Kuomintang, though taking care to maintain outwardly "correct" diplomatic relations. But these rapidly deteriorated with the approaching victory of Mao Tse-tung. Throughout the 1945–1949 period Stalin concentrated mainly on recovery at home and the consolidation of the Soviet empire in Europe. Only after the rise to power of the Chinese communists and the Sovietization of Eastern Europe did Soviet interests shift markedly to the Far East. The communist victory in China raised Soviet hopes, as well as Western fears, that communism might sweep all Asia.

In December 1949 Mao went to Moscow and for two months negotiated the future of Sino-Soviet relations. On February 14, 1950, three agreements were signed (reading 44). They provided: (1) a military alliance clearly directed against the United States; (2) the renunciation by Moscow of all rights in Manchuria except in Dairen (Dalny), though the changes this involved were not to be implemented before "the conclusion of a peace treaty with Japan, but not later than the end of 1952"; (3) a five-year, $300 million Soviet credit to Peking. These agreements were modified in 1954 to the further advantage of China. Even in 1950, however, they reflected the Kremlin's awareness that Mao, like Tito, had come to power under circumstances completely unlike those leading to the establishment of communist regimes in Eastern Europe. Traditional Russian policy had dealt with a weak China that had sought security in a pro-Western orientation. This situation, Stalin recognized, no longer existed. And, though he tried to get as much as possible from Mao, he did not overreach himself in trying to retain a privileged position for the Soviet Union. Mao, commanding his own army and controlling a vast land mass, was accorded a partnership in the communist world, albeit a junior partnership. Stalin apparently had learned the lesson of Tito well. Besides, Mao's victory presented Stalin with the opportunity of improving his power position in Asia.

Within a few months the alliance was tested by conflict in Korea. American and Soviet troops had withdrawn from Korea by mid-1949, leaving that country divided at the 38th parallel "between two rival authorities, each bent on the elimination of the other and on the unification of Korea after its own pattern."[3] All prospects for a peaceful unification vanished on June 25, 1950, when North Korean communist troops invaded South Korea in a calculated attempt to resolve the issue by force. Well-equipped, having the advantage of surprise, and encouraged by the signs of widespread discontent with the Syngman Rhee regime that appeared in the May election, they came very close to victory. As the conflict assumed global significance, it threatened to turn the Cold War into an all-encompassing conflagration.

In New York the Security Council convened in emergency session on the very day of invasion in response to a request by the United States government. The Soviet Union was not represented at this or any of the subsequent meetings of the Council, having undertaken a boycott of the United Nations in January 1950 because of the exclusion of Chinese communist representatives. Not until August 1 did the Soviet delegate return. With the Soviet delegate absent, the Security Council passed a resolution calling for the immediate cessation of hostilities and the withdrawal of the North Korean forces to their side of the border. It also requested all UN members to help in implementing this resolution. President Truman, noting the failure of the North Korean government to heed the Security Council's injunction, announced the intention of the United States to provide air and naval support for the South Koreans in accordance with the Council's request, despite previous indications by Washington that it regarded Korea as indefensible and beyond the area strategically necessary for America's defense. On June 27, the Security Council called upon the United Nations to "furnish such assistance to the Republic of Korea as may be necessary to repel the armed attack and to restore international peace and security in the area." American (and UN) forces came to the support of South Korea.

In a note to the Soviet government, the United States sought Soviet assistance in securing the withdrawal of North Korean forces. The Soviet reply placed the blame on South Korea and maintained that the

Security Council was not competent to act in the absence of one of its permanent members (reading 45). Soon afterward, the Soviets set their vast propaganda apparatus in motion, attacking the United States for intervening in a civil war, for carrying on an aggression, and for practicing bacteriological warfare and assorted atrocities. Meanwhile, UN forces counterattacked and advanced toward the Yalu River—and the Manchurian border. Once across the 38th parallel, they were no longer merely repelling aggression; they were seeking to unify all Korea by force of arms. This decision was never explicitly sanctioned by the General Assembly, nor the Security Council. Its wisdom and legality remain debatable. In early November the Chinese communists, apprehensive over the approach of a hostile army and insecure enough to fear invasion of the mainland by Kuomintang troops, entered the struggle. A new dimension had been added to the conflict. General MacArthur stated that "we face an entirely new war."

After much bitter fighting, a stalemate developed roughly along the 38th parallel. Convinced that victory was impossible, anxious to localize the conflict, and disturbed by the acceleration of Western rearmament resulting from the Korean attack, Stalin pressured the North Koreans and Chinese to enter into truce negotiations in July 1951. These dragged on for almost two years, but an armistice agreement was finally signed in July 1953, and today an uneasy truce prevails in a divided Korea.

Why did Stalin order the invasion of South Korea? Indeed, did he? Though hypotheses abound, conclusive historical evidence is lacking for any objective assigning of responsibility. The North Korean invasion remains shrouded in uncertainty. The reasons usually advanced depend, in great measure, upon which set of assumptions one is disposed to accept. For example, most Western observers hold the Soviet Union solely responsible. They cite the elaborate preparations obviously required for the attack and the fact that the North Korean Communist party was at the time unquestionably Kremlin-controlled and could not have launched such an effort without Moscow's prior knowledge and approval. Only after the Chinese intervention in Korea in November 1950 did Peking expand its influence and begin to compete with Moscow for a position of dominance in Pyongyang. Other observers suggest that the invasion was actually planned with Mao during his stay in Moscow. The experts all believe that the Soviets expected a quick victory and were surprised by the American decision to fight. Statements by Secretary of State Acheson in January and May (1950) encouraged the belief that the United States considered the defense of Korea as untenable. Also, all the experts interpret the continued Soviet absence from the Security Council as a grievous Soviet miscalculation. For, whereas Stalin may have expected the Security Council to pass some resolutions of admonition as the League of Nations had done in similar circumstances in the 1930s, he did not expect a vigorous American military response to a local aggression. A decidedly minority view goes so far as to hypothesize that Moscow was not directly to blame, that indeed the North Korean attack came as a total surprise. They concede that the Kremlin favored the elimination of South Korea as a separate state, but they maintain that there is evidence to indicate that the North Koreans acted on their own. Once the die was cast, however, Moscow had no choice but to support its satellite and prevent any unfriendly forces from coming too close to Soviet industrial centers in Siberia.

Though thwarted militarily, the Soviets benefited politically in two important ways: first, the West was required to commit a large part of its limited strength-in-being to a remote, strategically peripheral area, thereby weakening Western Europe's defenses and forcing it to undertake a massive program of rearmament that it could economically ill afford. In a sense, the West fought "the wrong war, at the wrong time, in the wrong place." Second, the Korean war "confirmed the breach between Communist China and the Western World," thus emphasizing to the Chinese communists their heavy dependence upon Soviet economic and military support.[4] The existence of a common enemy (the United States) further strengthened the bonds linking the colossi of the communist world. Under such circumstances, Stalin could well be confident that China would not readily develop into a second Yugoslavia.

In 1951–1952, Stalin continued the Sovietization of Eastern Europe and its economic and military integration into the Soviet empire, operating through such organizations as the Council for Mutual Economic Aid—the Soviet version of the Marshall Plan—and an elaborate network of interlocking military treaties. Indeed, Stalin went so far as to place Soviet Marshal Rokossovsky in command of the Polish army in order to ensure its reliability. The growing strength of the Soviet Union and its satellites, coupled with the overt aggression in Korea, spurred Western rearmament and intensified the Cold War. The threat of a Soviet attack in Europe still loomed large in Western thinking.

In retrospect, however, we can discern Stalin's innate conservatism in foreign policy. He did not seek to overwhelm the West by force; he probably never intended to do so. He sought rather to undermine Western power and prestige and to enhance correspondingly the strength and stability of his empire. In October 1952, at the Nineteenth Party Congress, Stalin outlined an approach to international tensions notable for its long-range perspective. In his view the revival of Germany and Japan would sharpen the contradictions *within* the capitalist world, and the ensuing struggle for markets would cause wars among the capitalists, rather than between the mutually irreconcilable camps of socialism and capitalism. Aware of the undercurrents of discontent in the satellites, as well as in the Soviet Union, Stalin moved with caution. But he took advantage of every opportunity to expand Soviet power. His strategy of protracted conflict with capitalism, however, halted short of war.

The year 1953 was a fateful one. Stalin had ruled the Soviet Union for a generation. One of history's most ruthless tyrants, he had transformed a backward, underdeveloped country into one of the world's great industrial-military powers and had created an empire dwarfing those of Genghis Khan and Tamerlane. He bequeathed an empire and an approach to power. Both continue to threaten world peace. Though Soviet expansion has been greatest in Europe, Stalin appreciated the importance of Asia. Undistinguished as a theorist, he insisted upon a confining orthodoxy in ideological and party affairs. He seldom deluded himself with fervent expectations of imminent world revolution, but he was quite willing to use revolutions abroad to spread Soviet power. He understood the nature of power and used it to advantage to expand the Soviet empire, fusing in the process the needs of national security with his imperialist ambitions. He ruled in the autocratic tradition of Peter the Great and westernized the economy of the Soviet Union; in the realm of foreign policy, he followed in the footsteps of the most expansionist of Czars. His successors have sought to maintain his tradition.

On March 5, 1953, Moscow announced the death of Stalin. An era had come to an end.

NOTES

1. *The Soviet-Yugoslav Dispute* (New York and London: Oxford University Press and the Royal Institute of International Affairs, 1948), pp. 68–69.
2. U.S., Department of State, *United States Relations with China* (Washington, D.C.: Government Printing Office, 1949), p. 97.
3. Peter Calvocoressi, *Survey of International Affairs, 1949–1950* (New York: Oxford University Press, 1953), p. 466.
4. Max Beloff, *Soviet Policy in the Far East, 1944–1951* (New York: Oxford University Press, 1953), p. 255.

Background Data on Stalin's Imperialist Expansion

40/Soviet Violations of Treaty Obligations

A. Germany

1. *Agreement:* The final delimitation of German-Polish frontier should await the peace settlement (Potsdam protocol, VIII, B).

Violations: USSR has repeatedly maintained that the Oder-Neisse line constitutes the definitive German-Polish frontier and has approved incorporation of territory east of this line into Poland.

2. *Agreement:* Payment of reparations to leave enough resources to enable the German people to subsist without external assistance. Reparation claims of USSR to be met by removals of capital goods and appropriation of external assets (Potsdam protocol, II, B, 15, 19).

Violations: USSR has taken large amounts of reparations from current production, has absorbed a substantial part of German industry in Soviet zone into Soviet state-owned concerns, and has otherwise exploited and drained German resources in a manner not authorized by Potsdam protocol or other agreements.

3. *Agreement:* Economic Directorate of Allied Control Authority agreed, May 24, 1946, that each member would submit report on reparations from its zone.

Violation: USSR has refused to submit report on any reparations removals from its zone.

4. *Agreement:* Germany to be treated as a single economic unit (Potsdam protocol, II, B, 14).

Violation: USSR has consistently obstructed all four-power attempts to implement this principle and has carried out a unilateral economic policy in its own zone.

5. *Agreement:* All democratic political parties to be allowed and encouraged throughout Germany (Potsdam protocol, II, A, 9).

Violations: Soviet authorities have restricted the freedom of action of non-Communist parties by depriving them of equal facilities with the SED (the Communist-dominated coalition), interfering in their internal affairs, coercing their leaders, dictating party actions, and in general denying them the autonomy essential to democratic political organizations. They have denied the Social Democratic Party the right to operate in the Soviet zone as an independent organization.

U.S., Department of State, *Bulletin*, 18 (April 4, 1948), 738–742, *excerpts.*

B. Eastern and Southeastern Europe

POLAND

1. *Agreement:* "This Polish Provisional Government of National Unity shall be pledged to the holding of free and unfettered elections as soon as possible on the basis of universal suffrage and secret ballot. In these elections all democratic and anti-Nazi parties shall have the right to take part and to put forward candidates" (Crimea Conference, February 12, 1945).

"The Three Powers (US, USSR, UK) note that the Polish Provisional Government in accordance with the decisions of the Crimea Conference has agreed to the holding of free and unfettered elections as soon as possible on the basis of universal suffrage and secret ballot in which all democratic and anti-Nazi parties have the right to take part and to put forward candidates" (Potsdam Agreement, August 2, 1945).

Violations: On several occasions prior to the elections and following persistent reports of reprehensible methods employed by the Government against the democratic opposition, this (US) Government reminded the Polish Provisional Government of its obligations under the Yalta and Potsdam agreements and was joined on these occasions by the British Government. On January 5, 1947, the British and Soviet Governments were asked to associate themselves with this Government in approaching the Poles on this subject, and the British Government made similar representations to the Soviet Government reiterating the request that the Soviet Government support the British and American Governments in calling for a strict fulfillment of Poland's obligations. The Soviet Government refused to participate in the proposed approach to the Polish Government. The British and American representations were summarily rejected by the Polish Government as "undue interference" in the internal affairs of Poland.

Of the 444 deputies elected to the parliament in the elections of January 19, 1947, the Polish Peasant Party (reliably reported to represent a large majority of the population) obtained only 28 places, thus demonstrating the efficiency with which the Government had prepared the ground. . . .

RUMANIA

1. *Agreement:* The three heads of Government of the USSR, the USA, and UK declared their mutual agreement to concert during the temporary period of instability in liberated Europe the policies of their three governments in assisting the peoples of the former Axis satellite states

of Europe to solve by democratic means their pressing political and economic problems (Yalta agreement on liberated Europe, February 1945).

Violations: Contrary to its agreement at Yalta, the USSR, acting through the Rumanian Communist Party and its own agencies and armed forces in Rumania, systematically and unilaterally subverted the democratic will of the Rumanian people to totalitarianism in negation of their fundamental freedoms. For example:

(a) Unilateral intervention by Soviet occupation authorities and by Vyshinsky (February–March 1945) in effecting the overthrow of Premier Radescu's interim representative government and the installation of a Communist-controlled regime.

(b) Direct and indirect unilateral interference by the Soviet occupation authorities in the election campaign of 1946, extending to the use of Soviet troops to break up meetings of the opposition and the arbitrary exercise of censorship.

(c) Exploitation of the Rumanian economy . . . through the establishment of Soviet-controlled joint companies covering the principal economic activities of Rumania, and through commercial agreements the knowledge of whose terms was repeatedly refused to the other two Yalta powers. . . .

C. Manchuria

1. *Agreements:* "The high contracting parties agree to render each other every possible economic assistance in the postwar period with a view to facilitating and accelerating reconstruction in both countries and to contributing to the cause of world prosperity" (*Sino-Soviet Treaty* of August 14, 1945, art. VI).

Violations: "Industry (in the three eastern provinces, also known as Manchuria) . . . was directly damaged to the extent of $858,000,000 during Soviet occupancy . . . the greatest part of the damage to the Manchurian industrial complex . . . was primarily due to Soviet removals of equipment" (Department of State press release No. 907 of December 13, 1947).

2. *Agreements:* ". . . in accordance with the spirit of the aforementioned treaty, and in order to put into effect its aims and purposes, the Government of the USSR agrees to render to China moral support and aid in military supplies and other material resources, such support and aid to be entirely given to the National Government as the central government of China."

Violations: The Chinese Government has failed to receive from the

USSR since August 14, 1945, the promised military supplies and other material resources. But when Russian troops withdrew from Manchuria, "Chinese Communists in that area appeared with Japanese arms in very substantial quantities . . . the natural assumption is that they were taken with the acquiescence, at least, of the Russians."

3. *Agreement:* "The administration of Dairen shall belong to China" (Agreement concerning Dairen of August 14, 1945).

Violation: Chinese Government troops attempting to enter Manchuria subsequent to the Japanese surrender were denied the right to land at Dairen by the Soviet authorities there and were forced to utilize less advantageous landing points.

Due in large part to Soviet obstructionism, China has up to the present time been unable to establish a Chinese Government administration at Dairen.

The Berlin Crisis

41/Reply of the Soviet Government to the United States Note of July 6 Which Protested Against the Blockade of Berlin   *July 14, 1948*

Firstly, the Soviet Government has acquainted itself with the note of the Government of the United States of America of July 6, this year, in which the situation that has at present arisen in Berlin is ascribed to measures taken by the Soviet side. The Soviet Government cannot agree with this declaration of the Government of the United States and considers the situation that has arisen in Berlin has arisen as a result of the violation by the Governments of the United States of America, Great Britain, and France of an agreed decision adopted by the four powers in relation to Germany and Berlin, expressed in carrying out a separate currency reform, the introduction of special currency notes for the Western sectors of Berlin and a policy of dismembering Germany. . . .

The decisions adopted at the Yalta and Potsdam conferences, as well

The New York Times, July 15, 1948.

as the agreement of the four powers on the control machinery in Germany, set as their aim the demilitarization and democratization of Germany, undermining the very basis of German militarism, and prevention of the revival of Germany as an aggressive power, and hence, the conversion of Germany into a peace-loving and democratic state. These agreements stipulate Germany's obligation to pay reparations and thus, even if only partially, to compensate for the damage done to countries that suffered from German aggression.

In accordance with these agreements, the governments of the four powers accepted the responsibility for administering Germany and undertook to determine jointly the status of Germany or of any areas, including Berlin, that are part of the German territory, and conclude a peace treaty with Germany which should be signed by a democratic government of Germany adequate for the purpose.

The highly important agreements by the four powers in relation to Germany have been violated by the Governments of the United States of America, Great Britain, and France. Measures for the demilitarization of Germany have not been completed and such an important center of German war industry as the Ruhr region has been removed from the control of the four powers. Fulfillment of the decision on reparations from the Western zones of occupation of Germany has been disrupted by the Governments of the United States of America, Great Britain, and France. The quadripartite council has ceased to function.

Since the London conference of the three powers with the participation of the Benelux countries, measures are being carried out by the Governments of the United States of America, Great Britain, and France aimed at splitting and dismembering Germany, including the preparation now taking place for the appointment of a separate government for the Western zones of Germany and the separate currency reform carried out June 18 of this year for the Western zones of occupation. . . .

The Soviet Government must reject as altogether unfounded the declaration of the Government of the United States of America to the effect that measures for restricting transport and communications between Berlin and the Western zones of occupation of Germany, introduced by the Soviet command to protect the economy of the Soviet zone from disorganization, allegedly constitute a violation of existing agreements relating to the administration of Berlin.

The Government of the United States declares that it occupies its sector of Berlin by a right deriving from the defeat and surrender of Germany, referring in this connection to the agreement between the four powers in relation to Germany and Berlin. . . .

When the United States, Great Britain, and France, by their separate actions in the Western zones of Germany, destroyed the system of quadripartite administration in Germany and began to create in Frankfort-on-Main a capital for the Government of Western Germany, they thereby undermined also the legal basis on which rested the right to participate in the administration of Berlin. . . .

The Government of the United States declares that temporary measures introduced by the Soviet command for restricting transport and communications between Berlin and the Western zones created difficulties in the supply of the Berlin population in the Western sectors.

It cannot, however, be denied that these difficulties were caused by the actions of the Governments of the United States, Great Britain, and France and, above all, by their separate actions in introducing a new currency in the Western zones of Germany and a special currency in the Western sectors of Berlin.

Berlin is in the center of the Soviet zone and is part of that zone.

The interests of the Berlin population do not admit to a situation where there has been introduced into Berlin, or even only into the Western sectors of Berlin, a currency that is not in circulation in the Soviet zone. Moreover, the introduction of a separate currency reform in the Western zones of Germany placed Berlin, and with it the entire Soviet zone of occupation, in a position where the entire mass of currency notes invalidated by the Western zones threatened to pour into Berlin and into the Soviet occupation zone of Germany.

The Soviet command was compelled, therefore, to adopt urgent measures to safeguard the interest of the population as well as the economy of the Soviet zone of occupation and the area of "Greater Berlin."

The Soviet-Yugoslav Split: The Origins of Titoism

42/White Book on Aggressive Activities by the Governments of the USSR, Poland, Czechoslovakia, Hungary, Romania, Bulgaria, and Albania Towards Yugoslavia

From the very moment inter-State relations were established, the Soviet Government began organizing espionage against the existing socialist order in Yugoslavia and against the independence of the Yugoslav peoples. The primary aim of these actions was to create a network of secret agents which would be a tool of the Soviet Government for undermining the Yugoslav Government. By a whole series of steps and acts which it undertook even before the Cominform Resolution of June, 1948, the Soviet Government attempted to impose unequal relations on Yugoslavia and to interfere in its internal affairs. Until the dispute broke out, however, the Yugoslav Government did not lodge any formal protest against any one of these acts although it did point out, in a friendly and well-meaning way, that there were certain short-comings in these relations. It proceeded in this way because it was convinced that all the differences which might arise between the two countries in the course of their cooperation would be settled through friendly and democratic agreement. When the Soviet Government realized that its attempts to impose its will upon Yugoslavia were in vain, it determined to undertake measures that would forestall any complaints and opposition to the imposition of unequal relations.

In that way, it came about that the Central Committee of the Communist Party of the Soviet Union (Bolsheviks) then sent its well-known letters to the Central Committee of the Communist Party of Yugoslavia in the first half of 1948. Under the guise of "party criticism" these letters were to conceal the attack of the Soviet Government on Yugoslavia before its essence became known to the world public. At the same time the letters from the Central Committee of the Communist Party of the Soviet Union (Bolsheviks) were also a warning to all those who might dare to seek equal relations between the USSR and

Ministry of Foreign Affairs of the Federal People's Republic of Yugoslavia, *White Book on Aggressive Activities by the Governments of the USSR, Poland, Czechoslovakia, Hungary, Romania, Bulgaria, and Albania Towards Yugoslavia* (Belgrade, Yugoslavia, 1951), pp. 14–37, *excerpts.*

their country, that they would in such a case be proclaimed the bitterest opponents of the USSR.[1]

The letters from the Central Committee of the Communist Party of the Soviet Union, although appearing to be an exchange of letters between two political parties, are not in essence documents having such a character nor can they be considered as mere mutual criticism between Parties on an equal footing. These letters must be regarded as documents in inter-State relations which are typical as an expression of the policy of imposition of a foreign will on Yugoslavia which the Soviet Government began to pursue by the arbitrary withdrawal of all Soviet specialists from Yugoslavia in March, 1948, and by the unilateral breach of the Agreement on Consultation in April, 1948. Various passages in these letters, which are particularly characteristic from the aspect of international relations, are clear illustrations of the undemocratic principles today underlying Soviet foreign policy towards Yugoslavia. For instance, the Soviet Government considers that its diplomatic and other representatives in a friendly country should have a special privileged status and that they have the right of insight into all State and Party affairs without the knowledge of the Government of that country. At the same time, the movements of the Yugoslav diplomatic representatives in the USSR were very restricted while there could be no question of any possibility of their gaining insight into the Soviet State and Party system. In implementing this "theory," according to which the Soviet Government considers itself a super-Government in another socialist country, the Soviet representatives did not hesitate to inveigle the citizens of that country into their intelligence service, taking as a point of departure the concept that Communists owe allegiance to the Soviet Government first and then to the leadership of their own

[1] The Central Committee of the Communist Party of the Soviet Union (Bolsheviks) sent the first letter to the Yugoslav Communist Party's Central Committee on March 27, 1948. At the same time, copies of the letter were also forwarded to the leaderships of the Communist Parties that are members of the Cominform, although the Central Committee of the Yugoslav Communist Party was not informed of this. A short time later, the Yugoslav Communist Party's Central Committee received a letter from the Hungarian Communist Party's Central Committee, sent through the Central Committee of the Soviet Communist Party, in which agreement was expressed with the latter's stand. After that, the Central Committee of the Yugoslav Communist Party received similar letters from the other leaderships of the Communist Parties of the Eastern European countries whose governments are under the control of the Soviet Government. All these leaderships adopted the stand of the Soviet Communist Party toward Yugoslavia although they had heard no arguments whatsoever from the Central Committee of the Communist Party of Yugoslavia. On May 2 and 23, 1948, the Central Committee of the Soviet Communist Party sent two more letters to the Yugoslav Communist Party's Central Committee. The contents of these letters were along the same lines as the first.

socialist State. This destructive work was especially directed towards engaging certain high-ranking State and Party officials for traitorous activities aimed at disrupting the highest State and military organs and overthrowing the legal Yugoslav Government. . . .

The Central Committee of the Communist Party of the Soviet Union (Bolsheviks) rejected the endeavours of the Yugoslav Government to have Yugoslavia and the USSR localize and settle the controversy without extending it artificially to the other countries and Governments with which Yugoslavia had until that time been enjoying the friendliest relations and with which it had been cooperating closely. Instead of that there came another openly hostile step against Yugoslavia—the adoption of the Cominform Resolution entitled "On the Situation in the Communist Party of Yugoslavia" of June, 1948, in which the citizens of Yugoslavia were openly called upon to overthrow their legal Government and to provoke a civil war. This Cominform Resolution says in part:

It is the task of the healthy elements inside the Communist Party of Yugoslavia *to compel* their present leaders to recognize their mistakes openly and honestly and to rectify them . . . or, should the present leaders of the Yugoslav Communist Party prove to be incapable of doing this, their job is to replace them and to advance a new internationalist leadership of the Party.

The Information Bureau *does not doubt* that the Communist Party of Yugoslavia will be able to fulfill this honorable task.*

. . .

In its Note of June 29, 1948, that is, a day after the Cominform Resolution was published, the Bulgarian Government informed the Yugoslav Government that the Cominform Resolution would in no way affect and that it "in no way alters the existing friendly relations between the People's Republic of Bulgaria and the Federal People's Republic of Yugoslavia." This, hence, is the way in which certain circles in the Bulgarian leadership understood the question of "party criticism." However, despite this, Bulgaria's foreign policy toward Yugoslavia began to deteriorate rapidly. When the Yugoslav Ambassador in Sofia sought an explanation for this change in the Bulgarian Government's attitude and brought out the discrepancy between the words in the Bulgarian Government's Note and its policy in practice, the Bulgarian Deputy Foreign Minister, Savo Ganovski, was forced to declare, only a few months after the Cominform Resolution, that it was impossible for the Bulgarian Government to separate Party from State issues. The Bulgarian Government did not maintain its original position because the Cominform Resolution had the precise purpose of increas-

* [Original editors' italics.—Ed.]

ing foreign political pressure on Yugoslavia, not only by the Soviet Government but by other Governments dependent on it as well.

The Cominform Resolution was in effect a signal for the launching of the unprecedented campaign against Yugoslavia, aimed at forcing the Yugoslav Government and peoples, by way of political, diplomatic, economic, propagandistic, military and other kinds of pressure and threats, to renounce their rights to sovereignty and independence, their right to be the master in their own home. . . .

The principle of economic cooperation with all countries, regardless of their internal systems, which the Governments of the USSR and the Eastern European countries support in words, has actually been transformed into an economic war which the Governments of those countries are waging against Yugoslavia in the most varied forms, including cancellation of regularly concluded contracts; the circumvention, violation and breach of trade agreements; the complete cessation and breaking off of all economic exchanges; the stoppage of reparations payments, issuing from the Peace Treaty, by Hungary; the obstruction and cessation even of transport and postal connections; the impeding of free navigation on the Danube, etc., etc.

In what manner, however, did the Soviet representatives appraise some far milder forms of economic discrimination in international relations? Following are the words pronounced by the Soviet representative in the League of Nations on November 4, 1931, at the Session of the Special Committee for the Study of the Pact on Economic Non-Aggression:

It is necessary to say openly that discrimination, taken as a collection of measures aimed against one specific country, can in no case be a means of defence or preservation; it will always be a method of attack . . .

Sudden and simultaneous cessation of credit to a country and analogous measures in the field of financial policy, if undertaken in an aggressive spirit, are obvious forms of economic aggression . . .

The first country to introduce measures of economic discrimination should be considered as the aggressor.

. . .

The Governments of the USSR and the Eastern European countries directly or indirectly circumvented, actually violated or broke off all trade agreements they had concluded with Yugoslavia. Since they considered it embarrassing to break off trade agreements with Yugoslavia publicly and formally because of international public opinion, they resorted to methods of circumvention, to actual cancellation of these agreements by the refusal to fix new short-term quota lists within the designated period, quota lists which represented a component part of the trade agreements. In this manner, the Soviet Government, followed by the other Governments of Eastern Europe, first reduced all trade and economic relations with Yugoslavia to a minimum and then broke them off altogether so that today these countries do not have even the slightest economic ties with Yugoslavia. . . .

The mixed Yugoslav-Soviet companies known as JUSTA (Yugoslav-Soviet Stock Company for Civil Air Transport) and JUSPAD (Yugoslav-Soviet Danube Shipping Stock Company), had a special place and role in the economic relations between Yugoslavia and the Soviet Union.

These mixed companies were founded in 1946 with the avowed purpose of serving the acceleration of, and facilitating, the economic development of Yugoslavia. This form of economic cooperation with the USSR was to have secured capital goods and the necessary technical assistance for Yugoslavia, and thereby to have helped its backward economy to develop as rapidly as possible. It should be emphasized, and this was confirmed by the experience of running these companies, that mixed companies are not and cannot be a form of economic cooperation guaranteeing equal relations between their partners. The formal parity (paid-up capital on a 50–50 basis, parity distribution of profits, etc.) was only a screen to conceal direct exploitation and appropriation of profits by the utilization of Yugoslavia's natural resources and of the value created by the labour of the Yugoslav working people. For this reason, in 1947, when the question arose of founding new mixed companies, the Yugoslav representatives said in Moscow that no more such companies should be founded. However, even after the complete breaking off of all economic relations with Yugoslavia, the Soviet Government undertook no measures for the liquidation of the existing mixed companies through which it was reaping economic benefits and attempting to gain control over Yugoslav river shipping and civil air transport. On the contrary, it described the Yugoslav demand for their liquidation as a hostile gesture. These companies became a brake to the economic development of Yugoslavia; they were not a means of assistance but of exploitation and economic subjugation.

Soviet Opposition to NATO

43/Memorandum of the Soviet Government on the North Atlantic Treaty   *March 31, 1949*

On March 18 the State Department of the United States published the text of the North Atlantic Treaty which the Governments of the United States of America, Great Britain, France, Belgium, the Netherlands, Luxemburg, and Canada intend to sign within the next few days.

The text of the North Atlantic Treaty fully confirms what was said in the declaration of the USSR Ministry of Foreign Affairs of January 29 this year, which is being attached hereto, both as regards the aggressive aims of this Treaty and the fact that the North Atlantic Treaty contradicts the principles and aims of the United Nations Organization and the commitments which the Governments of the United States of America, Great Britain, and France have assumed under other Treaties and Agreements. The statements contained in the North Atlantic Treaty, that it is designated for defense and that it recognizes the principles of the United Nations Organization, serve aims which have nothing in common either with the tasks of self-defense of the parties to the Treaty or with real recognition of the aims and principles of the United Nations Organization. Such great Powers as the United States, Great Britain, and France are parties to the North Atlantic Treaty. Thus the Treaty is not directed either against the United States of America, Great Britain, or France. Of the Great Powers only the Soviet Union is excluded from among the parties to this Treaty, which can be explained only by the fact that this Treaty is directed against the Soviet Union. The fact that the North Atlantic Treaty is directed against the USSR as well as against the countries of people's democracy was definitely pointed out also by official representatives of the United States of America, Great Britain, and France.

To justify the conclusion of the North Atlantic Treaty, references are being made to the fact that the Soviet Union has defensive treaties with the countries of people's democracy. These references, however, are utterly untenable.

All the treaties of the Soviet Union on friendship and mutual assistance with the countries of people's democracy are of a bilateral nature, and they are directed solely against a possible repetition of German aggression, the danger of which not a single peace-loving state

The New York Times, April 1, 1949.

can forget. The possibility of interpreting them as treaties which are in any degree aimed against the allies of the USSR in the late war, against the United States or Great Britain or France, is absolutely precluded.

Moreover, the USSR has similar treaties against a repetition of German aggression not only with the countries of people's democracy, but also with Great Britain and France.

In contradistinction to this, the North Atlantic Treaty is not a bilateral, but a multilateral Treaty, which creates a closed grouping of states and, what is particularly important, absolutely ignores the possibility of a repetition of German aggression, consequently not having as its aim the prevention of a new German aggression. And inasmuch as of the Great Powers which comprised the anti-Hitlerite coalition only the USSR is not a party to this Treaty, the North Atlantic Treaty must be regarded as a Treaty directed against one of the chief allies of the United States, Great Britain, and France in the late war, against the USSR. . . .

The North Atlantic Pact is designed to intimidate the states which do not agree to obey the dictate of the Anglo-American grouping of Powers that lay claim to world domination, though the bankruptcy of such claims was once again affirmed by the Second World War, which ended in the debacle of Fascist Germany which also had laid claim to world domination.

Among the participants in the North Atlantic Treaty are also countries whose governments expect to benefit at the expense of richer parties to the Treaty and make various plans with regard to obtaining new credits and other material advantages.

At the same time one cannot but see the groundlessness of the anti-Soviet motives of the North Atlantic Treaty, inasmuch as it is known to all that the Soviet Union does not intend to attack anyone and in no way threatens the United States of America, Great Britain, France, or the other parties to the Treaty.

The conclusion of the North Atlantic Treaty and the establishment of the new grouping of Powers is motivated by the weakness of the United Nations Organization. It is perfectly evident, however, that the North Atlantic Treaty does not serve the cause of strengthening the United Nations Organization, but on the contrary leads to undermining the very foundations of this international organization, because the establishment of the above grouping of Powers, far from corresponding to the aims and principles of the United Nations Organization, runs counter to the Charter of this organization.

The parties to the North Atlantic Treaty maintain that this Treaty allegedly represents a regional arrangement envisaged by Article 52 of the United Nations Charter. But such references are utterly groundless and untenable. There can be no question whatsoever of any regional character of this Treaty, inasmuch as the union provided for by this Treaty embraces settlement of any regional issues. This is also confirmed by the fact that, as has already been announced, states which are not members of the United Nations Organization (Italy, Portugal) are being drawn into participation in the North Atlantic Treaty, whereas Article 52 of the United Nations Charter has in view the conclusion of regional arrangements only among members of the United Nations Organization.

Nor can the establishment of the North Atlantic grouping of states be justified by the right of each member of the United Nations to individual or collective self-defense in conformity with Article 51 of the Charter. Suffice it to say that such a right under the Charter of the United Nations can arise only in the case of armed attack against a member of the organization, whereas, as is known to all, neither the United States of America, Britain, France, nor the other parties to the Pact are threatened by any armed attack. . . .

On the basis of all the above, the Soviet Government arrives at the following conclusions:

1. The North Atlantic Treaty has nothing in common with the aims of the self-defense of the states who are parties to the Treaty, who are threatened by no one, whom no one intends to attack. On the contrary, this Treaty has an obviously aggressive character and is aimed against the USSR, which fact is not concealed even by official representatives of the states who are parties to the Treaty in their public pronouncements.
2. The North Atlantic Treaty not only does not contribute to the consolidation of peace and international security, which is the duty of all members of the United Nations Organization, but runs directly counter to the principles and aims of the United Nations Charter and leads to undermining the United Nations Organization.
3. The North Atlantic Treaty runs counter to the Treaty between Great Britain and the Soviet Union signed in 1942, under which both states assumed the obligation to cooperate in the maintenance of peace and international security and "not to conclude any alliances and not to participate in any coalitions directed against the other High Contracting Party."
4. The North Atlantic Treaty runs counter to the Treaty between France and the Soviet Union signed in 1944, under which both states assumed the obligation to cooperate in the maintenance of peace and international security and "not to conclude any alliance and not to take part in any coalition directed against one of the High Contracting Parties."

5. The North Atlantic Treaty runs counter to the agreements between the Soviet Union, the United States of America, and Great Britain concluded at the Yalta and Potsdam Conferences, as well as at other conferences of the representatives of these Powers held both during and after the Second World War, under which the United States of America and Great Britain, like the Soviet Union, assumed the obligation to cooperate in the consolidation of general peace and international security and to contribute to the consolidation of the United Nations Organization.

The Moscow-Peking Axis

44/The Sino-Soviet Treaty *February 14, 1950*

(A) The Treaty

The Presidium of the Supreme Soviet of the Union of Soviet Socialist Republics and the Central People's Government of the People's Republic of China;

Filled with determination jointly to prevent, by the consolidation of friendship and cooperation between the Union of Soviet Socialist Republics and the People's Republic of China, the rebirth of Japanese imperialism and a repetition of aggression on the part of Japan or any other State which should unite in any form with Japan in acts of aggression;

Imbued with the desire to consolidate lasting peace and universal security in the Far East and throughout the world in conformity with the aims and principles of the United Nations Organization;

Profoundly convinced that the consolidation of good neighborly relations and friendship between the Union of Soviet Socialist Republics and the People's Republic of China meets the fundamental interests of the peoples of the Soviet Union and China;

Resolved for this purpose to conclude the present Treaty and appointed as their plenipotentiary representatives:

The Presidium of the Supreme Soviet of the Union of Soviet Socialist Republics—Andrei Yanuaryevich Vyshinsky, Minister of Foreign Affairs of the Union of Soviet Socialist Republics;

The Central People's Government of the People's Republic of China
—Chou En-lai, Prime Minister of the State Administrative Council and
Minister of Foreign Affairs of China;

Who, after exchange of their credentials, found in due form and
good order, agreed upon the following:

ARTICLE I

Both High Contracting Parties undertake jointly to take all the necessary measures at their disposal for the purpose of preventing a repetition of aggression and violation of peace on the part of Japan or any
other State which should unite with Japan, directly or indirectly, in
acts of aggression. In the event of one of the High Contracting Parties
being attacked by Japan or States allied with it, and thus being involved
in a state of war, the other High Contracting Party will immediately
render military and other assistance with all the means as its disposal.

The High Contracting Parties also declare their readiness in the
spirit of sincere cooperation, to participate in all international actions
aimed at ensuring peace and security throughout the world, and will
do all in their power to achieve the speediest implementation of these
tasks.

ARTICLE II

Both the High Contracting Parties undertake by means of mutual agreement to strive for the earliest conclusion of a peace treaty with Japan,
jointly with the other Powers which were allies during the Second
World War.

ARTICLE III

Both High Contracting Parties undertake not to conclude any alliance
directed against the other High Contracting Party, and not to take part in
any coalition or in actions or measures directed against the other High
Contracting Party.

ARTICLE IV

Both High Contracting Parties will consult each other in regard to all
important international problems affecting the common interests of the
Soviet Union and China, being guided by the interests of the consolidation of peace and universal security.

ARTICLE V

Both the High Contracting Parties undertake, in the spirit of friendship and cooperation and in conformity with the principles of equality, mutual interests, and also mutual respect for the State sovereignty and territorial integrity and noninterference in internal affairs of the other High Contracting Party—to develop and consolidate economic and cultural ties between the Soviet Union and China, to render each other every possible economic assistance, and to carry out the necessary economic cooperation.

ARTICLE VI

The present Treaty comes into force immediately upon its ratification; the exchange of instruments of ratification will take place in Peking.

The present Treaty will be valid for 30 years. If neither of the High Contracting Parties gives notice one year before the expiration of this term of its desire to denounce the Treaty, it shall remain in force for another five years and will be extended in compliance with this rule.

Done in Moscow on February 14, 1950, in two copies, each in the Russian and Chinese languages, both texts having equal force.

Signed: By Authorization of the Presidium of the Supreme Soviet of the Union of Soviet Socialist Republics—A. Y. Vyshinsky.

By Authorization of the Central People's Government of the People's Republic of China—Chou En-lai.

(B) An Agreement on the Chinese Changchun Railway, Port Arthur, and Dalny

The Presidium of the Supreme Soviet of the Union of Soviet Socialist Republics and the Central People's Government of the People's Republic of China state that since 1945 radical changes have occurred in the situation in the Far East, namely: Imperialist Japan suffered defeat; the reactionary Kuomintang Government was overthrown; China has become a People's Democratic Republic, and in China a new, People's Government was formed which has united the whole of China, carried out a policy of friendship and cooperation with the Soviet Union and proved its ability to defend the State independence and territorial integrity of China, the national honor and dignity of the Chinese people.

The Presidium of the Supreme Soviet of the Union of Soviet Socialist

Republics and the Central People's Government of the People's Republic of China maintain that this new situation permits a new approach to the question of the Chinese Changchun Railway, Port Arthur, and Dalny.

In conformity with these new circumstances, the Presidium of the Supreme Soviet of the Union of Soviet Socialist Republics and the Central People's Government of the People's Republic of China have decided to conclude the present agreement on the Chinese Changchun Railway, Port Arthur, and Dalny.

ARTICLE I

Both High Contracting Parties have agreed that the Soviet Government transfers gratis to the Government of the People's Republic of China all its rights in the joint administration of the Chinese Changchun Railway, with all the property belonging to the Railway. The transfer will be effected immediately upon the conclusion of a peace treaty with Japan, but not later than the end of 1952.

Pending the transfer, the now existing position of the Soviet-Chinese joint administration of the Chinese Changchun Railway remains unchanged; however, the order of filling posts by representatives of the Soviet and Chinese sides, upon the coming into force of the present Agreement, will be changed, and there will be established an alternating filling of posts for a definite period of time (Director of the Railway, Chairman of the Central Board, and others).

As regards concrete methods of effecting the transfer, they will be agreed upon and determined by the Governments of both High Contracting Parties.

ARTICLE II

Both High Contracting Parties have agreed that Soviet troops will be withdrawn from the jointly utilized naval base of Port Arthur and that the installations in this area will be handed over to the Government of the People's Republic of China immediately upon the conclusion of a peace treaty with Japan, but not later than the end of 1952, with the Government of the People's Republic of China compensating the Soviet Union for expenses incurred in the restoration and construction of installations affected by the Soviet Union since 1945.

For the period pending the withdrawal of Soviet troops and the transfer of the above installations, the Governments of the Soviet Union and China will appoint an equal number of military representatives for organizing a joint Chinese-Soviet Military Commission which will be in charge of military affairs in the area of Port Arthur; concrete measures in this sphere will be determined by the joint Chinese-Soviet

Military Commission within three months upon the coming into force of the present Agreement and shall be implemented upon the approval of these measures by the Governments of both countries.

The civil administration in the aforementioned area shall be in direct charge of the Government of the People's Republic of China. Pending the withdrawal of Soviet troops, the zone of billeting of Soviet troops in the area of Port Arthur will remain unaltered in conformity with the now existing frontiers.

In the event of either of the High Contracting Parties being subjected to aggression on the part of Japan or any State which should unite with Japan and as a result of this being involved in military operations, China and the Soviet Union may, on the proposal of the Government of the People's Republic of China and with the agreement of the Soviet Government, jointly use the naval base of Port Arthur in the interests of conducting joint military operations against the aggressor.

ARTICLE III

Both High Contracting Parties have agreed that the question of Port Dalny must be further considered upon the conclusion of a peace treaty with Japan.

As regards the administration in Dalny, it fully belongs to the Government of the People's Republic of China.

All property now existing in Dalny provisionally in charge of or under lease to the Soviet side, is to be taken over by the Government of the People's Republic of China. For carrying out work involved in the receipt of the aforementioned property, the Governments of the Soviet Union and China appoint three representatives from each side for organizing a joint commission which in the course of three months after the coming into force of the present agreement shall determine the concrete methods of transfer of property, and after approval of the proposals of the Joint Commission by the Governments of both countries will complete their implementation in the course of 1950.

ARTICLE IV

The present agreement comes into force on the day of its ratification. The exchange of instruments of ratification will take place in Peking.

Done in Moscow on February 14, 1950, in two copies, each in the Russian and Chinese languages, both texts having equal force.

Signed: By Authorization of the Presidium of the Supreme Soviet of the Union of Soviet Socialist Republics—A. Y. Vyshinsky. By Authorization of the Central People's Government of the People's Republic of China—Chou En-lai.

(C) An Agreement on the Granting of Credits by the USSR to China

In connection with the consent of the Government of the Union of Soviet Socialist Republics to grant the request of the Central People's Republic of China on giving China credits for paying for equipment and other materials which the Soviet Union has agreed to deliver to China, both Governments have agreed upon the following:

ARTICLE I

The Government of the Union of Soviet Socialist Republics grants the Central People's Government of the People's Republic of China credits, calculated in dollars, amounting to 300 million American dollars, taking 35 American dollars to one ounce of fine gold.

In view of the extreme devastation of China as a result of prolonged hostilities on its territory, the Soviet Government has agreed to grant credits on favorable terms of 1 per cent annual interest.

ARTICLE II

The credits mentioned in Article I will be granted in the course of five years, as from January 1, 1950, in equal portions of one-fifth of the credits in the course of each year, for payments for deliveries from the USSR of equipment and materials, including equipment for electric power stations, metallurgical and engineering plants, equipment for mines for the production of coal and ores, railway and other transport equipment, rails and other material for the restoration and development of the national economy of China.

The assortment, quantities, prices and dates of deliveries of equipment and materials will be determined under a special agreement of the Parties; prices will be determined on the basis of prices obtaining on the world markets.

Any credits which remain unused in the course of one annual period may be used in subsequent annual periods.

ARTICLE III

The Central People's Government of the People's Republic of China repays the credits mentioned in Article I, as well as interest on them, with deliveries of raw materials, tea, gold, American dollars. Prices for raw materials and tea, quantities and dates of deliveries will be determined on the basis of prices obtaining on the world markets.

Repayment of credits is effected in the course of ten years in equal annual parts—one-tenth yearly of the sum total of received credits not later than December 31 of every year. The first payment is effected not later than December 31, 1954, and the last on December 31, 1963.

Payment of interest on credits, calculated from the day of drawing the respective fraction of the credits, is effected every six months.

ARTICLE IV

For clearance with regard to the credits envisaged by the present agreement the State Bank of the USSR and National Bank of the People's Republic of China shall open special accounts and jointly establish the order of clearance and accounting under the present agreement.

ARTICLE V

The present agreement comes into force on the day of its signing and is subject to ratification. The exchange of instruments of ratification will take place in Peking.

Done in Moscow on February 14, 1950, in two copies, each in the Russian and Chinese languages, both texts having equal force.

Signed: By Authorization of the Government of the Union of Soviet Socialist Republics—A. Y. Vyshinsky.

By Authorization of the Central People's Government of the People's Republic of China—Chou En-lai.

Aggression in Korea

45/Exchange of Views Between the United States and the Soviet Union Regarding the Invasion of South Korea

(A) Aide-Memoire from the United States Government Delivered to the Soviet Deputy Foreign Minister by the United States Ambassador, June 27, 1950

My Government has instructed me to call to your attention the fact that North Korean forces have crossed the 38th parallel and invaded the territory of the Republic of Korea in force at several points. The refusal of the Soviet Representative to attend the United Nations Security Council meeting on June 25, despite the clear threat to peace and the obligations of a Security Council member under the Charter, requires the Government of the United States to bring this matter directly to the attention of the Union of Soviet Socialist Republics. In view of the universally known fact of the close relations between the Union of Soviet Socialist Republics and the North Korean regime, the United States Government asks assurance that the Union of Soviet Socialist Republics disavows responsibility for this unprovoked and unwarranted attack, and that it will use its influence with the North Korean authorities to withdraw their invading forces immediately.

(B) The Soviet Reply, June 29, 1950

1. In accordance with facts verified by the Soviet Government, the events taking place in Korea were provoked by an attack by forces of the South Korean authorities on border regions of North Korea. Therefore, the responsibility for these events rests upon the South Korean authorities and upon those who stand behind their back.

2. As is known, the Soviet Government withdrew its troops from Korea earlier than the Government of the United States and thereby confirmed its traditional principle of noninterference in the internal affairs of other states. And now as well the Soviet Government adheres

U.S., Department of State, *United States Policy in the Korean Crisis* (Washington, D.C.: Government Printing Office, 1950), pp. 63–64, *excerpts.*

to the principle of the impermissibility of interference by foreign powers in the internal affairs of Korea.

3. It is not true that the Soviet Government refused to participate in meetings of the Security Council. In spite of its full willingness, the Soviet Government has not been able to take part in the meetings of the Security Council inasmuch as, because of the position of the Government of the United States, China, a permanent member of the Security Council, has not been admitted to the Council, which has made it impossible for the Security Council to take decisions having legal force.

FOR FURTHER STUDY

Adler-Karlson, Gunnar. *Western Economic Warfare 1947–1967: A Case in Foreign Policy.* Stockholm: 1968.

Armstrong, Hamilton F. *Tito and Goliath.* New York: Macmillan, 1951.

Bader, William B. *Austria Between East and West, 1945–1955.* Stanford, Calif.: Stanford University Press, 1966.

Beloff, Max. *Soviet Policy in the Far East, 1944–1951.* New York: Oxford University Press, 1953.

Boorman, H., A. Eckstein, P. Mosely, and B. Schwartz. *Moscow-Peiping Axis.* New York: Harper & Row, 1957.

Davison, W. Phillips. *The Berlin Blockade: A Study in Cold War Politics.* Princeton, N.J.: Princeton University Press, 1958.

Dedijer, Vladimir. *The Battle Stalin Lost: Memoirs of Yugoslavia, 1948–1953.* New York: Viking, 1971.

Feis, Herbert. *Contest Over Japan.* New York: Norton, 1967.

Halle, Louis J. *The Cold War as History.* New York: Harper & Row, 1967.

Hellmann, Donald C. *Japanese Foreign Policy and Domestic Politics: The Peace Agreement with the Soviet Union.* Berkeley: University of California Press, 1969.

Kennedy, Malcolm. *A History of Communism in East Asia.* New York: Praeger, 1957.

Kertesz, Stephen D. *The Fate of East Central Europe: Hopes and Failures of American Foreign Policy.* Notre Dame, Ind.: University of Notre Dame Press, 1956.

Korbel, Josef. *The Communist Subversion of Czechoslovakia.* Princeton, N.J.: Princeton University Press, 1959.

Lattimore, Owen. *Pivot of Asia: Sinkiang and the Inner Asian Frontiers of China and Russia.* Boston: Little, Brown, 1950.

MacVicker, Charles P. *Titoism: Pattern for International Communism.* New York: St. Martin's, 1957.

Melby, John F. *The Mandate of Heaven, Record of a Civil War, China 1945–1949.* Toronto: University of Toronto Press, 1968.

Nettl, J. P. *Eastern Zone and Soviet Policy in Germany.* New York: Oxford University Press, 1951.

Seton-Watson, Hugh. *The East European Revolution.* New York: Praeger, 1956.

Shepherd, Gordon. *Russia's Danubian Empire.* London: Heinemann, 1954.

Shulman, Marshall D. *Stalin's Foreign Policy Reappraised.* Cambridge, Mass.: Harvard University Press, 1963.

Ulam, Adam B. *Titoism and the Cominform.* Cambridge, Mass.: Harvard University Press, 1952.

Whiting, Allen S. *China Crosses the Yalu: The Decision to Enter the Korean War.* New York: Macmillan, 1960.

————, and General Shen Shih-ts'ai. *Sinkiang: Pawn or Pivot?* East Lansing: Michigan State University Press, 1958.

Wolff, Robert Lee. *The Balkans in Our Time.* Cambridge, Mass.: Harvard University Press, 1956.

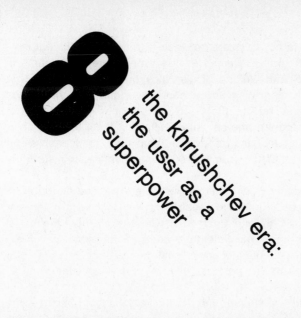

8 the khrushchev era: the ussr as a superpower

The Soviet Union emerged as a superpower during the Khrushchev era (1954–1964). It was Nikita S. Khrushchev who benefited from Stalin's concentration on heavy industry and research in nuclear and missile technology; it was Khrushchev who sought to reform Soviet society and adjust Soviet policy to the nuclear age; and it was under Khrushchev that the Soviet Union embarked on a global course commensurate with its new power and status.

Major changes in Soviet foreign policy began soon after Stalin's death. Three developments, in particular, strengthened Soviet power: the effective stabilization of empire in Eastern Europe; a steady economic and military growth; and the dramatic penetration into the politically vulnerable developing areas of the Third World. The global balance of power (in Soviet terms "the correlation of world forces") shifted perceptibly toward the Soviet world and made coexistence more than ever the prerogative of the Kremlin. Though the extent of the Soviet imperial system did not increase after the death of Stalin, the international position of the Soviet Union improved considerably.

First, the Kremlin began to decentralize its Eastern European empire during the 1953–1956 period. This tentative easing of Moscow's iron grip reflected the struggle for power then being waged within the Soviet leadership. But the Polish and Hungarian revolutions of October–November 1956, confronting Soviet leaders with the prospective disintegration of their empire, forced them to reimpose their control. Soon thereafter, aware that further nationalist, anticommunist, anti-Russian eruptions might jeopardize the entire Soviet military position in Eastern Europe, Moscow acceded to the demands of communist "nationalists" and agreed to ever-larger measures of local autonomy. Additional concessions have been granted since 1961 in order to retain support in the sharpening rift with Peking. Thus, Moscow overcame the first serious threat of disintegration and separatism within Eastern Europe by relinquishing, albeit reluctantly, much of its former imperial control over the domestic affairs of the satellites—allowing them to settle their own intra-party struggles and to evolve their road to socialism—in return for recognition of the primacy of Soviet military and strategic interests in the area.

Second, Soviet economic and military strength expanded enormously. The increased nuclear and missile capabilities were particularly impressive; with Sputnik in 1957 and Cosmonaut Gagarin in 1961, the USSR launched the space age. The diplomatic implications of these military achievements were evident: Moscow's confident approach to international problems reflects, in part, its growing sense of superiority in military technology.

Third, Soviet influence mushroomed in the regions lying south of the Soviet Union—the developing areas of the Middle East, Southern Asia, and Africa. The death of Stalin hastened the injection of flexibility, imagination, and vigor into Soviet foreign relations. This new diplomacy, foreshadowed by Stalin's last public statement at the Nineteenth Party Congress in October 1952, was nowhere more evident, or successful, than in the uncommitted areas of the world. Soviet interest in these areas—and, conversely, the significance of these regions for Soviet foreign policy—must now be regarded as a permanent feature of the continuing Cold War (a detailed treatment of this phase of Soviet policy is given in Chapter XIII).

Stalin left no obvious successor. To effect an orderly transition of power, the Soviet leaders revived the principle of "collective leadership." Except in the Beria affair, shifts at the top have thus far been accomplished without recourse to the terror of the Stalinist period. Rather, the struggle for power remains bloodless, a reflection of the changing, more sophisticated nature of Soviet totalitarianism.

During the 1953–1956 period, the Soviet leaders, eager to establish the "legitimacy" of their rule, reassured the various privileged groups (such as the Party, the military, and the technocracy) whose support is essential for the stability of the regime, that their status and security would remain unimpaired—would indeed be enhanced. Further, a series of "involuntary" economic, demographic, social, and political pressures arising out of the nature of contemporary Soviet society itself impelled the leadership to disengage itself from the oppressive, inefficient aspects of the Stalinist legacy. In Eastern Europe this took the form of removing "Stalinists" from power, of granting limited autonomy within the framework of Soviet control, and of seeking a rapprochement with Tito.

Stalin's postwar objectives had been relatively clear-cut: to eliminate Western influence from Eastern Europe and, concomitantly, to establish Moscow's dominion over the area; to undermine Western recovery through the manipulation of local communist parties; and finally, to weaken NATO, forestall West Germany's entrance into the Western coalition, and effect a withdrawal of American power from Europe. Except for the first, which admittedly was most important at the time, Stalin failed to achieve these objectives.

His successors, however, were faced with more subtle challenges: to preserve yet decentralize the Soviet empire, to obtain Western acceptance of the permanence of Soviet domination over Eastern Europe, and to expand Soviet power where possible without jeopardizing the security of the USSR. They were also confronted with the formidable task of coordinating strategy and maintaining the alliance with Communist China. They soon discovered that to preserve an empire is more difficult than to acquire one. Not only do the techniques of rule differ from those of revolution, but the price of empire may prove so exorbitant that it weakens the structure of power within the metropolitan country itself. To avoid this, Soviet leaders sought to perpetuate their Eastern European empire within a moderately decentralized framework designed to increase the economic productivity and political-military reliability of their satellites. They granted varying degrees of local autonomy, revised Soviet-satellite economic relations along less exploitative lines, and encouraged modest improvements in living standards.

The first satellite challenge to Soviet rule broke out in June 1953: a wave of riots swept East Berlin and parts of Soviet-occupied Germany. The West was unable or unwilling to hazard the consequences of intervention. Accordingly, the Soviets quickly and brutally suppressed the outbreaks. The danger of the situation, however, was not lost on Moscow. The Kremlin understood that in East Germany, as elsewhere in Eastern Europe, the problem was to chart a course between the Scylla of Stalinism on the one hand and the Charybdis of widespread convulsions stemming from a too rapid easing of controls on the other. In Moscow, Beria was purged, and Soviet leaders adopted a series of measures designed to mollify the undercurrents of discontent.

Through most of 1953 and 1954 intra-communist-bloc problems preoccupied the Kremlin. To decrease the likelihood of effective pressure from the West and to sow discord among the NATO nations, Soviet leaders held out prospects of a respite from the Cold War. They also moved to make the Korean conflict less incendiary, thereby extricating themselves from an uncomfortable position and at the same time gaining favorable international response to the "new look" in Soviet policy. A truce agreement was concluded on July 27, 1953. Thus began an effort to liquidate the liabilities bequeathed by Stalin. It enabled the Soviet Government to reduce the economic-military drain on its economy, return the East-West conflict to the political arena, and provide the Chinese communists with time to consolidate their power on the mainland. It also permitted the Kremlin to placate its people and strengthen the unity of the communist world.

On August 9, 1953, Premier Malenkov announced the government's intention to allocate more resources to satisfy consumer needs. His foreign policy statement also hinted at a departure from the uncompromising hostility of Stalin. Changes were soon perceptible in the satellites. Though varying in degree and scope from country to country, the innovations followed a similar pattern: forced collectivization was halted; prices of staples were cut; the more oppressive features of the labor and criminal codes were changed; and most of the joint-stock companies were dissolved. Modest concessions to satellite discontent in the political sphere were also noticeable: communist leaders too closely identified as "Stalinists" were removed; the omnipotence of the party seemed to be subtly deemphasized in favor of greater governmental authority and attention to "socialist legality"; and the attacks on Tito subsided.

In another important policy reversal, Moscow started to court Tito in earnest. A barter agreement was concluded in September 1954, ending the Cominform's economic blockade. The Khrushchev-Bulganin-Mikoyan visit to Belgrade in May 1955 highlighted the Soviet effort to "normalize" relations. Khrushchev appealed for a full resumption of relations between Yugoslavia and the Soviet Union, blithely blaming the rift on Beria and avoiding any allusion to continuing ideological-political differences. Upon the signing of a joint governmental declaration a few days later, a rapprochement appeared well under way—though significantly a comparable statement on party accord was not agreed upon until Tito's visit to the USSR in June 1956. At that time Moscow formally subscribed to the concept that there were "many roads to socialism." Another trade agreement was negotiated in September 1955, and the Soviet government also granted Yugoslavia a $54 million credit for the purchase of Soviet goods, as well as a $30 million credit.

The errant Tito's return to the fold was a necessary step for the Kremlin in the reconstitution of the formal unity of the communist world. It hoped thereby to blunt the appeal of "Titoism" in Eastern Europe and to reduce that potentially disruptive force to relative impotence. Moscow further sought to reconcile loyalty to the Soviet Union with the desire of many Eastern European communists for greater national autonomy.

Short of this goal, the Soviet leaders hoped to weaken Yugoslav ties with the West, eliminate the military usefulness of the Balkan Pact (with Greece and Turkey), and gain more opportunities for increasing Soviet influence over the regime. The rapprochement also harmonized with the then current Soviet policy of attaining cooperation with the respectable socialist parties of the West, demonstrating to the world Moscow's reasonableness and flexibility, and of encouraging neutralist tendencies in the free world by demonstrating that the USSR was not a threat against which an unaligned country needed to seek protection by joining the other bloc.[1]

The rapprochement was also consistent with the general pattern developing in the Soviet Union during this period. But this promising restoration of Yugoslav-Soviet unity lasted only until late 1956, when the aftermaths of the Hungarian revolution, the support by Communist China of Moscow's line in Eastern Europe, and the introduction of neo-Stalinism in the USSR again alienated Belgrade from Moscow.

In the spring of 1955, Soviet leaders also reversed their position on Austria. Their previous insistence that an Austrian peace treaty be linked with settlement of the German question had accounted, in part, for the failure of the 1954 Berlin Foreign Ministers Conference. However the Soviet government in March 1955 unexpectedly dropped its demand for a German treaty and reinstituted negotiations to end the occupation of Austria. The result, the Austrian treaty signed on May 15, 1955, committed Austria to a policy of nonalignment with either bloc. In return, Austria's "neutral" status was to be recognized and guaranteed by the Great Powers.

The treaty was significant because it marked the first voluntary postwar withdrawal by the Soviet leaders from an established position in the center of Europe. Moscow's policy of amiability extended to other areas. For example, the Soviet Union renounced all claims against Turkey, attempted to promote closer relations with Greece, moved to settle its differences with Iran, and began to participate actively in the economic development and technical assistance operations of the various United Nations specialized agencies and economic commissions. The West's hopes for a settlement of the major Cold War issues rose, as a meeting of the heads of state of the Soviet Union, the United States, Great Britain, and France was called in Geneva in July 1955.

Meanwhile, in Asia, the Kremlin was especially attentive to Communist China. In October 1954, Khrushchev and Bulganin visited Peking and negotiated a series of new economic and political agreements that more accurately reflected China's independence and growing stature within the communist world. The accords of October 11, 1954, led to the withdrawal of Soviet military forces from the naval base of Port Arthur in May 1955 and to the transference without compensation of the military installations in that area to the Chinese government. They also led to Soviet acknowledgment of Chinese hegemony in Manchuria and Sinkiang and to the dissolution of the four mixed Soviet-Chinese companies, thereby signifying the end of visible Soviet economic influence in China. Trade and technical assistance arrangements were expanded, but the Soviets were now in China on sufferance, not on the basis of power. Though Moscow was still the senior partner of the alliance, Peking began to play a more active role in international communist affairs. China also acquired added prestige as a result of the stalemate and subsequent armistice in Korea, the defeat of the French in Indochina (Vietnam) in 1954, and the brilliant diplomacy displayed by Foreign Minister Chou En-lai at the Bandung Conference of Afro-Asian states in April 1955. The growing importance of China in Asian and international affairs was a trend that the Soviets were quick to notice and for a time willing to accept.

At the Geneva Summit Conference (July 1955) Khrushchev offered to institutionalize the status quo in Europe and to enter into "competitive coexistence" with the West in the developing areas. He agreed to push the search for agreement on disarmament (see Chapter XI). To lessen international tension, the Soviet Union offered minor compromises in marginal areas—the return of the Porkkala naval base to Finland and the withdrawal from eastern Austria. But it was not ready seriously to negotiate any of the major questions of the Cold War; it was not prepared to yield any of its Eastern European empire, nor to compromise on German unification. In fact, it wanted mainly time in order to expand its program of domestic development and to delay Germany's rearmament and effective integration into the NATO alliance. In another maneuver, Moscow sought to undermine the Western alliance system by suggesting that NATO and the nations of the Warsaw Pact—the communist counterpart of NATO established in May 1955—be fused into an overall European security system. It is questionable whether Soviet leaders ever expected the West seriously to entertain such a proposal. But they did succeed in nurturing the image of Soviet "reasonableness" and in starting a series of diplomatic exchanges. Thus, in September 1955, West German Chancellor Adenauer visited Moscow and agreed to establish diplomatic relations between Bonn and Moscow; in March 1956 Malenkov visited Great Britain, followed the next month by Bulganin (who had succeeded Malenkov as Premier in February 1955) and Khrushchev.

Soviet "manners" might have changed; however, Soviet objectives had not. The rapprochement with Tito and the conciliatory attitude toward the European and Asian socialists paved the way for another diplomatic offensive, this time aimed southward and eastward. The Soviet sale of arms to Egypt in September 1955 dispelled much of the good will cultivated at Geneva and signaled an intensified Soviet effort to undermine the Western position in the Middle East. An unsettling variable had been introduced into an already delicate equation. This Soviet initiative, combined with the continued refusal to accept the principle of free German elections or the right of a unified Germany to order its own international relations and choose its own allies, doomed the October–November Foreign Ministers Conference to failure. The stalemate in Europe persisted. But in Southern Asia, the prestige of the USSR soared as Khrushchev and Bulganin toured the region. Their visits dramatized the increased post-Stalinist awareness of the important role these countries (Afghanistan, Burma, India) could play in improving the international position of the Soviet Union. An area once dominated by the West was now to be used to weaken it. As Soviet diplomacy acquired a more dynamic orientation, the dimensions of the Cold War increased.

Perhaps the most spectacular incident of the post-Stalin period occurred at the Twentieth Party Congress of the CPSU in February 1956: in a "secret" speech Khrushchev denounced Stalin for his "crimes" and self-deification. Yet even as the assault on the former demigod of international communism spread and "de-Stalinization" gathered momentum, a chain of events was under way that threatened not only the Soviet empire, but the structure of power in the Soviet Union itself, and that led to a partial return to Stalinism before the year was over.

In his discussion of foreign policy, Khrushchev introduced several significant doctrinal shifts affecting the Kremlin's approach to world affairs (reading 4). First, while affirming the Leninist dogma of the irreconcilability of capitalism and socialism, he stated that *war* between the two systems is not inevitable. According to Khrushchev, the changed balance of world power and the influence of the developing areas made it possible for peace to be preserved and the "schemes of war-makers" thwarted. Second, Khrushchev accepted the Titoist contention that there are several roads to socialism, thereby creating a theoretical basis for closer cooperation not only with Yugoslavia but also with the socialist parties of Western Europe. Perhaps even more important, the Kremlin hoped to cultivate better relations between the Soviet Union and the nationalist movements of Asia, Africa, and the Middle East. Third, communists were encouraged to seek power, where and when possible, through peaceful, parliamentary means in Western countries. Khrushchev's landmark denunciation of Stalin was linked to the succession struggle being waged within the Soviet hierarchy, but it also heralded eight years of frenetic internal reforms, as Khrushchev tried to "rationalize" the Soviet economic system. In foreign policy, the new doctrinal formulations greatly disturbed the Chinese and precipitated the split between Moscow and Peking. In Khrushchev's off-and-on-again efforts to effect a limited détente with the United States (in part, to reduce the arms burden and devote more resources to domestic needs), Mao saw a downgrading of the Sino-Soviet alliance, a shift in Soviet foreign policy priorities, and a possible danger to Chinese interests in Asia. For his part, Khrushchev turned to the tasks of preserving the Soviet imperial system and extending Soviet influence globally as part of the growing strategic interaction with the United States.

Eastern Europe

The period in 1956 between the Twentieth Party Congress in February and the revolutions in Poland and Hungary in the summer and fall marked the high point of the post-Stalinist "thaw" in Soviet domestic and foreign policy. An unwary Kremlin, intent on de-Stalinization, sanctioned a modest program of "liberalization" in the satellites and thus unwittingly released turbulent anti-Russian, nationalistic currents. The result was the most massive uprising against Soviet rule ever witnessed. Shaking the very foundations of the Soviet empire in Eastern Europe, it led to a neo-Stalinist revival and to some serious second thoughts by Soviet leaders on the permanence of their position in Eastern Europe.

Riots broke out in Poznan, Poland, in June 1956. Smoldering resentment over a decade of economic privation and Soviet domination, sparked by Khrushchev's "revelations," flared into widespread denunciations of the Moscow-controlled government and secret police. The Poles' traditional hatred of Russia erupted. The Kremlin realized the gravity of the situation and grudgingly made concessions. It permitted the ouster of many known Stalinists from the Central Committee of the Polish United Workers' (Communist) Party and in October 1956 accepted the Polish communists' choice of Wladyslaw Gomulka, a national communist who had spent several years in prison for his opposition to Stalin, as Party Secretary. Moscow also publicly reaffirmed Poland's "sovereignty and independence," agreed not to interfere in Polish domestic affairs, and withdrew Soviet Marshal Rokossovsky as head of Poland's armed forces. Trade and financial relations were adjusted to Poland's advantage, and Soviet troops were "permitted" by special agreement to remain in Poland pending a settlement of the German question. Yet despite this greater independence in internal affairs, Poland remains inevitably influenced in important foreign policy decisions by its powerful communist neighbor. The Soviet troops in East Germany (and in Poland itself), as well as Poland's deep-rooted fear of the claims of a revived, expansionist Germany to the territories east of the Oder-Neisse line, which are now incorporated into Poland, are levers to assure the continued adherence of Poland to the Soviet bloc. Indeed, the possibility of another Soviet-German "understanding" at the expense of Poland, as in 1939, is a pervasive, though rarely voiced, Polish phobia.

Meanwhile, events in Hungary took a tragic turn. Matyas Rakosi, a confirmed Stalinist and long-time ruler of Hungary, had been deposed in June 1956, but his successor, Ernö Gerö, refused to compromise sufficiently to lessen the mounting popular pressure for change. On October 23, revolution erupted in Budapest. Anticommunist and anti-Soviet, it threatened the entire Soviet position in Central Europe. Moscow tried to maintain communist rule, but it could not resolve this challenge as it had the one in Poland. The Hungarians wanted too much, too quickly. They sought to withdraw from the Warsaw Pact, end the political monopoly of the communist party, and liquidate all vestiges of Soviet rule. Confronted with the imminent loss of Hungary and disintegration elsewhere in Eastern Europe, Moscow hurled 250,000 troops and 5,000 tanks against the Hungarians on November 4, after a ruse had betrayed key Hungarian military leaders into Soviet hands. Though the Hungarians resisted valiantly, they were no match for Soviet power.

The United Nations General Assembly called upon the Soviet government "to desist from its intervention in the internal affairs of Hungary, to withdraw its forces from Hungary, and to cease its repression of the Hungarian people." The Soviets ignored UN and Western protests. The coincidence of the Suez and Hungarian crises was unfortunate. Though the UN was able, through the temporary coalescence of Soviet-American policy on Suez, to end the Middle Eastern hostilities, no similar power and prestige could be marshaled on behalf of Hungary. As the Soviets ruthlessly overwhelmed the Hungarians, the West watched, helpless to intervene for fear of precipitating World War III. This "moment of truth" for the West tragically emphasized what Raymond Aron has described as "the unwritten law of the atomic age": that the Soviet Union can do as it pleases within its sphere of influence without fear of retaliation. And Hungary is part of that sphere.

But the Kremlin learned several bitter lessons. First, Soviet control in Eastern Europe can be preserved only if backed by the Red Army. Second, nationalism remains strong, even among avowed communists. Third, authority once weakened cannot easily be reimposed. Fourth, a sine qua non for the continued political and military adherence of East European countries to the Warsaw Pact is acceptance of a substantial measure of economic and cultural diversity and autonomy. Eastern Europe can no longer be considered an unquestioned asset to the

Soviets. Strategically, it remains important; Moscow will undoubtedly resist any attempt, either by the West or by the satellites themselves, to dislodge Soviet influence and control. On the other hand, the area represents a material and military drain on Soviet resources; the reliability of East European troops remains a continual question mark; and East European nationalism, a force too often slighted, increases the strains of Moscow rule. Finally, Soviet prestige, especially among influential Western European intellectuals, suffered a sharp setback as a consequence of the Hungarian episode. The nations of the Afro-Asian bloc also expressed varying degrees of disappointment and alarm at Soviet policy, though generally they were far more sensitive and outraged over the British-French attack on Egypt, a country only recently emerged from colonial bondage, with which they felt close emotional ties. The "remoteness" of Hungary blunted their concern and indignation. Still, the 1956 crises in Eastern Europe (and the 1968 crisis in Czechoslovakia) have shown that the USSR regards the area as vital to its security and is prepared to use force if necessary to preserve its dominance.

The Soviet government took advantage of tensions in the Middle East and of disagreements within NATO over Suez (as well as over Cyprus and North Africa) to undertake an extensive diplomatic and propaganda campaign aimed at promoting Soviet prestige in the developing countries of the world and at undermining Western unity. While acting with a belligerency reminiscent of the Stalinist era, Moscow continued to play upon the theme of peaceful coexistence. During 1957–1958, and particularly after the launching of Sputnik in October 1957, it sent a series of notes to the various NATO nations warning them of the dangers of permitting American atomic and missile bases on their territory. In the UN Disarmament Commission, Soviet delegates raised the possibility of a military "disengagement" in Central Europe, proposing a demilitarized zone of 400 kilometers on either side of the Elbe, complete with aerial and other inspection procedures. Several variants of this proposal have been suggested: in October 1957 Polish Foreign Minister Rapacki called for the establishment of a nuclear-free area that would include Poland, East and West Germany, and Czechoslovakia. The West has thus far opposed such plans on the grounds that nuclear weapons constitute the first line of defense against Soviet attack, that inspection would be too uncertain in the present political situation, and that such an arrangement avoids a solution of the key European problem— the future of Germany.

In November 1957, on the occasion of the fortieth anniversary of the Bolshevik revolution, the leaders of international communism met in Moscow to repair the damage of 1956. A "Declaration of Unity" was issued that reaffirmed the solidarity of the socialist camp "headed by the Soviet Union," "the first and mightiest socialist power" in the communist world. It implicitly acknowledged the disruptive consequences of national communism, emphasized the unity of the communist world, and attacked "revisionism" (the sin of going further than Moscow in internal innovativeness or in improving relations with the West). The Chinese, uneasy over Khrushchev's de-Stalinization and doctrinal "creativeness" in foreign affairs, made formal obeisance to Soviet leadership for the last time and tried to nudge the Soviet Union back to Stalinism, especially as it related to the United States.

Tito, who absented himself from the gala get-together, refused to sign the declaration—an indication of the brittleness of the Moscow-Belgrade accommodation. He had supported Khrushchev's policy in Hungary partially out of fear that the "counterrevolutionary fever" might spread elsewhere in Eastern Europe, even to Yugoslavia, but primarily out of a desire to bolster Khrushchev in curbing the influence of the "Stalinists" in the Kremlin and to retain a measure of influence on Soviet policy in Eastern Europe. The November declaration disillusioned Tito, as did the abrupt dismissal of Marshal Zhukov from the CPSU Presidium in October, immediately following his visit to Yugoslavia. In December 1957, the Soviet press initiated an intensive antirevisionist campaign designed to restore ideological conformity in the communist world. Pressure against the Yugoslavs mounted, particularly after publication of their new program in April 1958.

During the 1958–1961 period, the Soviet-Yugoslav controversy centered on four main points: first, the Yugoslavs insisted that the Kremlin as well as NATO was responsible for the Cold War; second, they maintained that each communist state should be free to determine its own course toward socialism; third, they asserted that the Soviet Union was continuing to evolve along Stalinist lines and had developed into a bureaucratic state that keeps "strengthening in all fields of social life" rather than withering away in accord with Marxist-Leninist theory; fourth, the 1958 Yugoslav Party Program (reaffirmed by the December 1964 Party Congress) claimed for Yugoslavia democratic developments that constituted a challenge to Moscow's ideological leadership of the communist camp. The Kremlin denounced the Yugoslav assertions. It subsequently applied economic and political pressure but avoided any open split along 1948 lines. At the same time, Moscow moved to expand economic integration and planning through the Council for Mutual Economic Assistance (COMECON). (However, after 1961, as relations between Moscow and Peking progressively worsened, the Soviet Union muted its quarrel with Yugoslavia, and relations between the two improved, though regressions were frequent—a function of continuing Soviet repressiveness in Eastern Europe.)

Khrushchev, concerned over the evident disunity in the communist world, convened another international conference of Communist and Workers' Parties in November 1960, particularly to pressure the Chinese into closing ranks behind the Soviet line that had been established at the Twentieth Congress in 1956. This failing, Khrushchev delivered a major report on January 6, 1961, in which he presented a comprehensive analysis of Soviet accomplishments, aims, and strategic outlook (reading 46). The report exuded confidence in Soviet military prowess and growing influence abroad. It reaffirmed the necessity to struggle militantly against Western (i.e., United States) imperialism, but signified a willingness to negotiate differences where possible. A new emphasis was placed on developing the unity of the socialist camp. Finally, Khrushchev's attention to the various types of wars, especially his focus on wars of national liberation, caused much uneasiness in the new Kennedy administration, which became obsessed with the danger of Communist-led guerrilla movements overthrowing pro-American governments, especially after the abortive Bay of Pigs adventure in April 1961 had failed to topple Castro.

Soviet policy toward Eastern Europe underwent a number of important changes after the tumultuous events of 1956. First, Moscow accommodated to East European nationalism by granting substantial domestic autonomy to local communist elites. In Hungary, Janos Kadar, placed in power by the Soviet Union after the Hungarian revolution was suppressed, successfully implemented far-reaching economic reforms and a degree of internal liberalization unrealized elsewhere in Eastern Europe. In Romania, the national communists ousted the pro-Muscovites and weakened Soviet influence over domestic decision making. Second, Moscow readjusted economic relationships with Eastern Europe.

Khrushchev was aware of the attraction of Western Europe's Common Market for the East European countries, of the widening technological gap between Western and Eastern Europe, and of the need to improve the economic viability of the socialist camp, and he sought to strengthen COMECON by pushing for the economic integration of the "socialist community," or commonwealth. His blueprint for a socialist community that would advance the economic integration of the Soviet bloc was included in the first new CPSU Party Program since 1919— adopted at the Twenty-second Congress in October 1961 (reading 47). However, there has been tenacious opposition to Soviet proposals for coordinated planning, trade, and a "socialist international division of labor," in large part because the East European countries are sensitive to infringements on their national sovereignty. Though there are sound economic reasons for bloc integration, memories of the Stalin period and of Brezhnev's intervention in Czechoslovakia in August 1968 linger and engender resistance to Moscow's ambitions.

A third policy change toward Eastern Europe was Moscow's acceptance of some expansion of economic and cultural links with the West, although bloc members were cautioned against using "their relations with capitalist countries at the expense of other fraternal countries." The issue did not become critical again until the late 1960s, when Khrushchev's grand design faltered on the intractable phenomenon of East European nationalism.

The Sino-Soviet Rift

Of central importance to the USSR is its relationship with Communist China. As senior member of the alliance, Moscow's leadership was acknowledged during the Stalin period. Stalin's successors were diligent in maintaining close relations with Peking. In late 1956 China played, for the first time, a brief but not unimportant role in East European affairs. Originally a sympathetic supporter of increased autonomy for the Poles and Hungarians, it grew apprehensive over the unexpectedly sharp opposition not only in Eastern Europe but also in China as a consequence of "de-Stalinization." It quickly perceived the danger involved in even a limited "decompression" and came out uncompromisingly hostile toward all "revisionist" manifestations, a policy that made it bitterly critical of the Yugoslavs. Peking opposed any détente with the United States—against which it has major political and territorial grievances—preferring to keep East-West tensions high in order to obtain more economic and military aid from the USSR and to justify the perpetuation of ideological and political orthodoxy within the bloc. It also opposed summit conferences and any arms control or disarmament agreement that might retard its development as a great power.

There is convincing evidence to indicate that during the 1957–1960 period Moscow was frequently constrained by Chinese objections against moving too far in the direction of a détente with the West. For example, the Soviet government appeared eager for a conference "at the summit" in late 1957 and early 1958. At the time of the Lebanese crisis (July 1958), a Khrushchev visit to the United Nations and a meeting with President Eisenhower seemed a certainty. However, Khrushchev made a sudden visit to Peking in August, and soon thereafter the Quemoy crisis broke out in the Taiwan Straits and the Soviets lost interest in top-level talks with Western leaders.

Moscow found itself increasingly pressured by Peking to act more militantly in furtherance of revolutionary wars in Asia, Africa, and Latin America, particularly after the USSR had launched its Sputnik in October 1957 and claimed missile superiority over the United States. Moscow's inability or unwillingness to extend China large-scale credits for imports of machinery, industrial plants, and metals, which were necessary for the success of China's ambitious 1958 "great leap forward" program of internal transformation and agricultural reorganization, constituted an additional irritant. Indeed, by late 1960 Soviet aid to China dropped sharply, leading the Chinese to charge subsequently that Moscow had deliberately sought to impede China's economic development.

Efforts were made throughout 1959 and 1960, and in particular at the November 1960 Moscow conference of eighty-one communist parties, to close the growing policy and ideological rift between Moscow and Peking and to reach agreement on a unified strategy toward both the West and intra-communist bloc developments. By 1961 the seriousness of the rift became a matter of public record, as Moscow and Peking exchanged charges and countercharges. At the Twenty-second Party Congress of the CPSU in October 1961, Khrushchev criticized the Albanian communists for their espousal of "Stalinism" and reiterated his contention that war with the capitalist powers could and should be avoided. Peking promptly declared its friendship for Albania, condemned "revisionism," and averred its hostility toward the United States and all "lackeys of imperialism." At the Congress Chinese Premier Chou-en-lai implicitly castigated Khrushchev, observing that "If there are quarrels in the socialist camp, we consider that they should be settled through bilateral contacts and that a public denunciation does not contribute to the cohesion of the socialist camp."

The crescendo of condemnatory attacks rose throughout the remaining years of the Khrushchev era. Moscow assailed the "dogmatists" (Chinese communists) "who have learned by heart the general formula about imperialism and stubbornly turn their eyes away from life." A high-level meeting of representatives of the CPSU and Communist Party of China (CPC) was held in Moscow July 5–20, 1963, in an effort to mediate the dispute, but it failed abjectly. In a major statement on July 14, 1963, *Pravda* published an Open Letter from the Central Committee of the CPSU to all party organizations and members in which were presented the main lines of the Soviet position (reading 48). During the following year, Moscow sought to gain support for an international communist congress, which many Western analysts believed was intended to bring about a final showdown with Peking. In July 1964, the CPSU sent invitations to twenty-five communist parties to attend a conference in Moscow on December 15. Soviet-Chinese relations seemed on the brink of an open and formal rupture when Khrushchev was suddenly deposed on October 14, 1964. At the heart of the Sino-Soviet dispute was Khrushchev's policy (which has been basically accepted by his successors) of seeking a limited accommodation with the United States. This approach, outlined by Foreign Minister Andrei

Gromyko soon after the Cuban missile crisis, continues to reflect Soviet policy (reading 49).

Though the Sino-Soviet dispute is often cast within an ideological framework, it is fundamentally a rivalry over power and mirrors the divergent strategies, interests, and objectives of the two countries. Briefly, the main sources of discord center on the following five issues. First, Moscow believes that as the senior and most powerful member of the international communist community it should be accorded the authority to interpret Marxist-Leninist doctrine and establish basic strategy for the bloc and in particular to decide on the best way to deal with the capitalist world. It resents Chinese pretensions to leadership and feels that the Chinese are newcomers not familiar with global realities, that they seriously underestimate the strength of the United States, and that they do not appreciate the extent to which imperialism can be weakened by nonmilitary means. Second, there is disagreement over priorities: the areas and issues that are most important to Moscow are least important to Peking, and vice versa. For example, if for no other reason than that the main *military* threat to the USSR in the past and at present comes from the West, Moscow's primary political attention is drawn to European developments, for example, centrifugal communist tendencies in Eastern Europe, the resurgence of West Germany, the impact of the Common Market. A satisfied power territorially, the Soviet Union is not prepared to go to war against the United States over the Taiwan question, an issue that is paramount in Chinese thinking. Thus do geography, history, and economics shape the perception of political priorities. Third, Moscow and Peking differ in their approach to developing countries. While these differences are not as clear-cut as the West sometimes imagines, they do connote a readiness on the part of China to advocate militant policies that inevitably would exacerbate relations between the Soviet Union and the United States. For example, the Chinese criticism of the Soviet retreat at the time of the Cuban missile crisis moved Soviet leaders to denounce the Chinese for their "recklessness" and "irresponsibility" (reading 48). The Chinese sought to profit politically from the failure of Khrushchev's reckless gamble, but they themselves have, in practice, yet to precipitate any such dramatic showdowns with the United States. A major source of discord between Moscow and Peking has been the Soviet courtship of India, particularly the Soviet military buildup after 1963. Another is Moscow's program of extending extensive economic and military aid to nonaligned countries, whereas aid to China was ended in 1961. By emphasizing the revolutionary path to power and opposing (in principle but not in practice) cooperation between local communist parties and bourgeois-nationalist parties, China is directly challenging the

Soviet strategy for spreading communist influence in the Third World. Fourth, Moscow's unwillingness after 1959 to assist China to develop a nuclear capability and its signing of the limited nuclear test-ban treaty in 1963 signified to China a Soviet desire to keep its communist ally a second-rate military power. Once China acquires its own "credible" nuclear capability, it is likely to become even more independent and truculent toward the USSR. Fifth, China has long-standing frontier grievances against the USSR. Under treaties imposed on Imperial China by Czarist Russia in 1858, 1860, and 1881, China was forced to cede almost one million square miles of territory in Central Asia and the Maritime Provinces of Siberia. Peking does not recognize the validity of these treaties and has called for the revision of existing borders, a demand that has been rejected by Moscow.

Officially, alliance with Peking remains the cornerstone of Soviet foreign policy. However, Moscow recognizes that the mushrooming disagreements of recent years, coupled with China's immense population, intensified program of industrialization, and ambitious aims, constitute a long-range threat to Soviet national interests in the Far East and Central Asia and a challenge to Moscow's preeminent position within the communist movement.

The Poles say with bitter humor: "Thank God for the Soviet Union. We are lucky to have a buffer state between us and the Chinese." The Soviets are not so fortunate; they must deal with the developing colossus of communism. The extent to which China and the Soviet Union cooperate or clash will greatly affect the future of world communism. Events of the past decade indicate that a formal split is a possibility, though for the present the alliance remains intact.

Germany and the Berlin Question

The foremost of European problems attracting Soviet attention is that of Germany. The remilitarization of West Germany is a cause of constant Soviet concern. In 1954 an article in *Kommunist*, the authoritative journal of the CPSU, contended that the United States, to realize its "aggressive plans," needed "a powerful, well-trained land army in Europe equipped with the latest weapons" and, accordingly, initiated German rearmament in order to make West Germany "into an obedient instrument of its aggressive policy, into a mailed fist that would be directed against the Soviet Union and the People's Democracies and at the same time be used to subject NATO to United States control." This Soviet interpretation has not changed.

Moscow bitterly attacked the Paris Agreements of 1954, which brought West Germany into NATO and sanctioned its rearmament. It further insisted that the integration of West Germany into NATO complicated the solution of the German problem. Since 1958, Soviet apprehensions have heightened as they see an increase in the possibility of West Germany's obtaining missiles and nuclear weapons. To Soviet leaders, the United States proposal for a multilateral nuclear force (MLF) was a step in this direction.

As the Chinese Communists eased their pressure on Quemoy and the offshore islands, the Soviet Union provoked a new crisis with the West over Berlin on November 27, 1958. In a belligerent note Khrushchev threatened to abrogate all existing agreements on Berlin and transfer Soviet rights as an occupying power to the East Germans. He insisted that West Berlin be set up as a "free city," guaranteed by the four former occupying powers and the two existing German states, and that the Western Powers withdraw from the city. Unless the West initiated negotiations within six months, Khrushchev indicated, the administration of East Berlin and the regulation of Western access routes to the city would be turned over to the East German government.

The immediate aim of the Kremlin was probably to obtain Western diplomatic recognition of the East German regime, but the Berlin crisis reopened the entire question of Germany's future. By calling for a conference to draw up a German peace treaty, Moscow appeared also to seek anew attainment of its long-term objectives in Europe—the acceptance by the West of the status quo in Europe and the weakening of NATO.

The Khrushchev "ultimatum" was extended for almost three years, as the Soviet government avoided any precipitous action. During a meeting with President Kennedy in Vienna June 3–4, 1961, Premier Khrushchev declared that the Berlin problem must be settled before the end of the year or the Soviet Union would sign a separate peace treaty with East Germany. On August 13, 1961, without warning, the Berlin Wall was put up, physically sealing off the two sectors of the city. The precise reason for Khrushchev's intensifying the Berlin crisis was obscure. Perhaps it was pressure from the Chinese to adopt a more aggressive attitude toward the West, an effort to exploit Western preoccupation with Laos and the Congo and American embarrassment over Castro's communist Cuba, a desire to bolster the East German regime by sealing off the major remaining escape route of East Germans to the West. Or perhaps Khrushchev felt that after almost three years he had to show something or face rising opposition among his Party colleagues.

On September 1, 1961, the USSR ominously resumed nuclear testing and the specter of Sarajevo loomed over an anxious Europe as the Berlin crisis deepened. Tensions eased in the ensuing months, only to erupt with dramatic intensity in October 1962 in Cuba. The removal of Soviet missiles and the signing of the test-ban treaty ten months later marked an upturn in Soviet-American relations, though the Berlin problem continued to fester. On June 12, 1964, the Soviet Union signed a twenty-year Treaty of Friendship, Mutual Assistance, and Cooperation with East Germany that, to the great disappointment of the puppet Pankow regime, merely served to reaffirm the status quo character of the German and Berlin problems. This diplomatic gesture was a far cry from the dire threats inherent in Khrushchev's "ultimatum" of November 1958. East Germany was further jarred by the Soviet announcement in late July 1964 of Khrushchev's acceptance of an invitation to visit West Germany. This startling move indicated that Khrushchev was prepared to discuss the issue of German reunification with Bonn. Peking thereupon accused Khrushchev of preparing to "sell out" the Ulbricht East German regime. The removal of Khrushchev in October shelved for the time being the prospect of a serious Soviet initiative to settle the issue of Germany.

Khrushchev in Perspective

The Khrushchev record is a bundle of contradictions, a combination of achievements and failures as difficult to categorize as the man himself. Khrushchev pushed the development of an awesome nuclear and missile capability that made the Soviet Union a superpower. But he was unable to Americanize the Soviet economy—to make it businesslike, innovative, efficient—and therein lay a major cause of his fall. A dedicated communist who believed in the inherent superiority of communism as a social system, he sired de-Stalinization and inadvertently set in motion disruptive, divisive currents in the Soviet empire and society that have yet to run their course. Not since the 1860s and the reign of Czar Alexander II had a Russian leader tried so to reform national institutions and practices only to be frustrated by the forces of tradition, bureaucratism, and reaction.

Khrushchev's foreign policy was a reflection of his temperament: activist, ambitious, pragmatic, bold, occasionally reckless. He was not averse to bullying, but desisted in the face of determination and strength. Proud of Soviet achievements, he also understood the unwritten law of the nuclear age—that war between the superpowers must be avoided—and pushed limited détente with the United States, at the cost of friendship with Communist China. Heir to Moscow's imperial tradition, he had no intention of relinquishing the Soviet empire in Eastern Europe. Still, he was pressed to eliminate the excesses of the Stalin period and to establish a more equitable basis for the relationship, despite the impetus this gave to anti-Russian nationalism. He committed the Soviet Union to a forward policy in the Third World as much for psychological as for strategic reasons, even though the dividends are less than obvious. An inveterate traveler, he was the first to expose Kremlin leaders to public scrutiny in the noncommunist world and to bring back personal impressions that affected Soviet decision making —as to how much, we can only speculate. He was a "cracker-barrel" communist: folksy, shrewd, brash, and uncultured (*nekulturni*), as epitomized by the shoe-thumping incident at the United Nations; he was also a tough-minded and ruthless leader. On one thing perhaps agreement is unanimous: we shall not soon see the like of Khrushchev again in the Kremlin.

NOTE

1. U.S., Department of State, *Soviet Affairs Notes,* No. 224 (Washington, D.C.: Government Printing Office, July 28, 1958), p. 3.

Moscow's Strategic Assessment for the 1960s

46/Speech to the Higher Party School of the Institute of Marxism-Leninism of the Central Committee of the CPSU   *January 6, 1961*

N. S. KHRUSHCHEV

The analysis of the world situation at the beginning of the sixties can only evoke in every fighter in the great Communist movement feelings of profound satisfaction and legitimate pride. Indeed, comrades, life has greatly surpassed even the boldest and most optimistic predictions and expectations. . . .

The question of the character of the era is by no means an abstract or a narrow theoretical question. The general strategic line and tactics of world communism, of each Communist Party, are closely related to it. . . . We must determine correctly the correlation of forces, to exploit new possibilities which the present era opens up for the further advancement of our great cause. . . . Our era, whose essence is the transition from capitalism to socialism begun by the great October Socialist revolution, is an era of the struggle of two diametrically opposed social systems, an era of Socialist revolutions and national liberation revolutions; an era of the collapse of capitalism and of liquidation of the colonial system; an era of the change to the road of socialism by more and more nations; and of the triumph of socialism and communism on a world scale. . . .

The principal distinguishing feature of our time is the fact that the world Socialist system is becoming a decisive factor in the development of human society . . . For the first time in history, the present balance of power in the world arena enables the Socialist camp and other peace-loving forces to pursue the completely realistic task of compelling the imperialists, under the threat of the downfall of their system, not to unleash a world war.

In connection with the possibility of averting a world war, I should like to dwell on the question concerning the prospects for a further development of the general crisis of capitalism. It is generally known that both World War I and World War II exerted enormous influence on the emergence and deepening of the general crisis of capitalism. Does

U.S., Congress, Senate Committee on the Judiciary, Subcommittee to Investigate the Administration of the Internal Security Act and Internal Security Laws, *Hearings (June 16, 1961)*, 87th Cong., 1st sess. (1961), pp. 53–78, *excerpts.*

it follow from this that a world war is a necessary condition for a further intensification of the general crisis of capitalism? Such a conclusion would be profoundly incorrect, since it distorts the Marxist-Leninist theory of the Socialist revolution and conflicts with the real reasons for revolution. A proletarian revolution does not result from military cataclysms; it is first of all a consequence of the development of the class struggle and of the internal contradictions of capitalism. . . .

The primary task of Socialist countries is to exploit possibilities inherent in socialism to outstrip, as soon as possible, the world capitalist system in absolute volume of industrial and agricultural production, and then to overtake the most developed capitalist countries in per capita production and living standards. . . . The victory of the USSR in economic competition with the United States, the victory of the whole Socialist system over the capitalist system, will be the biggest turning point in history, will exert a still more powerful, revolutionizing influence on the workers' movement all over the world. . . . To win time in the economic contest with capitalism is now the main thing. The quicker we increase economic construction, the stronger we are economically and politically, the greater will be the influence of the Socialist camp on historical development, on the destiny of the world. . . .

In modern conditions the following categories of wars should be distinguished: World wars, local wars, liberation wars, and popular uprisings. This is necessary to work out the correct tactics with regard to these wars. Let us begin with the question of world wars. Communists are the most determined opponents of world wars, just as they are generally opponents of wars among states. These wars are needed only by imperialists to seize the territories of others, and to enslave and plunder other peoples. . . . In present conditions, the most probable wars are wars among capitalist and imperialist countries, and this too should not be ruled out. Wars are chiefly prepared by imperialists against Socialist countries, and in the first place against the Soviet Union as the most powerful of the Socialist states. Imperialists would wish to undermine our might and thus reestablish the former domination of monopolistic capital. The task is to create impassable obstacles against the unleashing of wars by imperialists. We possess increasing possibilities for placing obstacles in the path of the warmongers. Consequently, we can forestall the outbreak of a world war. Of course, as yet we are unable to completely exclude the possibility of wars, for the imperialist states exist. However, the unleashing of wars has become a much more complicated business for the imperialists than it was before the emergence of the mighty Socialist camp. Imperialists can unleash a war, but they must think hard about the consequences. . . .

A word or two about local wars . . . There have been local wars and they may occur again in the future, but opportunities for imperialists to unleash these wars too are becoming fewer and fewer. A small imperialist war, regardless of which imperialist begins it, may grow into a world thermonuclear rocket war. We must therefore combat both world wars and local wars. As an example of a local war unleashed by the imperialists, we may take the Anglo-French-Israeli aggression against Egypt. They wanted to strangle Egypt and thus intimidate the Arab countries struggling for independence, and also to frighten the other peoples of Asia and Africa. . . . This was in 1956, when the balance of power between the countries of socialism and the countries of imperialism was not the same as it is today. We were not as mighty then as we are today. . . .

Now a word about national liberation wars. The armed struggle by the Vietnamese people or the war of the Algerian people, which is already in its 7th year, serve as the latest examples of such wars. These wars began as an uprising by the colonial peoples against their oppressors and changed into guerrilla warfare. Liberation wars will continue to exist as long as imperialism exists, as long as colonialism exists. These are revolutionary wars. Such wars are not only admissible but inevitable, since the colonialists do not grant independence voluntarily. . . .

Or let us take Cuba's example. A war took place there too. But it also started as an uprising against the internal tyrannical regime supported by U.S. imperialism. Batista was a protégé of the United States. The latter rendered active assistance to him. However, the United States did not interfere in that war directly with its Armed forces. The Cuban people, under the leadership of Fidel Castro, have won.

Can such wars flare up in the future? They can. Can there be such uprisings? There can. But these are wars which are national uprisings. In other words, can conditions be created where a people will lose their patience and rise in arms? They can. . . . The Communists fully support such just wars and march in the front rank with the peoples waging liberation struggles. . . .

Vladimir Ilich Lenin, with his usual perspicacity, stated that the struggle with the evil of nationalism, with the most deep-rooted national petty-bourgeois prejudices, moves more and more urgently into the foreground as a task of turning the dictatorship of the proletariat from a national one—one existing in a single country and incapable of determining world policy—into an international one—a dictatorship of the proletariat in at least several leading countries and capable of having a decisive influence on all world policy.

The struggle with revisionism in all its forms still remains today an important task of the Communist Party. As long as the bourgeois order exists, there will be a nutritive medium for the ideology of revisionism too. Therefore, we must always keep our powder dry and wage implacable war on revisionism which tries to wipe out the revolutionary essence of Marxism-Leninism, white-wash modern capitalism, undermine the solidarity of the Communist movement, and encourage Communist Parties to go their separate national ways.

The Communist movement has another danger: Dogmatism and sectarianism. At the present time, when a rallying of all forces for the struggle against imperialism, for the prevention of war, and for the overthrow of the monopolies is required, dogmatism and sectarianism can do great harm to our cause. Leninism is uncompromising toward dogmatism. Lenin wrote: "It is essential to learn the indisputable truth that a Marxist must take account of life, of the exact facts of reality, and not go on clinging to yesterday's theory, which, like all theory, at best outlines fundamentals, generalities, and only approximates a total comprehension of the complexities of life."

Dogmatism nourishes sectarian stodginess which hinders the rallying of the working class and all progressive forces around the Communist Parties. Dogmatism and sectarianism are in irreconcilable contradiction to the creative development of revolutionary theory and its creative application in practice. They lead to the isolation of Communists from the broad strata of the workers; they condemn them to passive temporizing or leftist adventurist activities in the revolutionary struggle. . . .

The CPSU in reality does not exercise leadership over other parties. In the Communist movement there are no parties that are superior or subordinate. All Communist Parties are equal and independent . . . The role of the Soviet Union does not lie in the fact that it leads other Socialist countries but in the fact that it was the first to blaze the trail to socialism, is the most powerful country in the world Socialist system, has amassed a great deal of positive experience in the struggle for the building of socialism, and was the first to enter the period of comprehensive construction of communism. It is stressed in the statement [of the Moscow Conference] that the universally acknowledged vanguard of the world Communist movement has been and still remains the CPSU. . . . as is well known, the CPSU does not give directives to any other parties. The fact that we are called the leader gives no advantages either to our party or to other parties. On the contrary, it only creates difficulties.

Socialist Integration and the Soviet Imperium

47/The World Socialist System   *October 31, 1961*

PROGRAM OF THE COMMUNIST PARTY
OF THE SOVIET UNION

The world socialist system is a new type of economic and political relationship between countries. The socialist countries have the same type of economic basis—social ownership of the means of production; the same type of political system—rule of the people with the working class at their head; a common ideology—Marxism-Leninism; common interests in the defense of their revolutionary gains and national independence from encroachments by the imperialist camp; and a great common goal—communism. This socio-economic and political community constitutes the objective groundwork for lasting and friendly inter-governmental relations within the socialist camp. The distinctive features of the relations existing between the countries of the socialist community are complete equality, mutual respect for independence and sovereignty and fraternal mutual assistance and cooperation. In the socialist camp or, which is the same thing, in the world community of socialist countries, none have, nor can have, any special rights or privileges.

The experience of the world socialist system has confirmed the need for the *closest unity* of countries that fall away from capitalism, for their united effort in the building of socialism and communism. The line of socialist construction in isolation, detached from the world community of socialist countries, is theoretically untenable because it conflicts with the objective laws governing the development of socialist society. It is harmful economically because it causes waste of social labour, retards the rates of growth of production and makes the country dependent upon the capitalist world. It is reactionary and dangerous politically because it does not unite, but divides the peoples in face of the united front of imperialist forces, because it nourishes bourgeois-nationalist tendencies and may ultimately lead to the loss of the socialist gains. . . .

All the socialist countries make their contribution to the building and development of the world socialist system and the consolidation of its might. The existence of the Soviet Union greatly facilitates and acceler-

The Road to Communism: Documents of the Twenty-second Congress of the Communist Party of the Soviet Union (Moscow: Foreign Languages Publishing House, 1961), pp. 464–469, *excerpts.*

ates the building of socialism in the People's Democracies. The Marxist-Leninist parties and the peoples of the socialist countries proceed from the fact that the successes of the world socialist system as a whole depend on the contribution and effort made by each country, and therefore consider the greatest possible development of the productive forces of their country an internationalist duty. The cooperation of the socialist countries enables each country to use its resources and develop its productive forces to the full and in the most rational manner. *A new type of international division of labour* is taking shape in the process of the economic, scientific and technical cooperation of the socialist countries, the coordination of their economic plans, the specialization and combination of production. . . .

The experience of the peoples of the world socialist community has confirmed that their fraternal *unity and cooperation* conform to the supreme national interests of each country. The strengthening of the unity of the world socialist system on the basis of proletarian internationalism is an imperative condition for the further progress of all its member countries. The socialist system has to cope with certain difficulties, deriving chiefly from the fact that most of the countries in that system had a medium or even low level of economic development in the past, and also from the fact that world reaction is doing its utmost to impede the building of socialism. . . .

Nationalism is the chief political and ideological weapon used by international reaction and the remnants of the domestic reactionary forces against the unity of the socialist countries. Nationalist sentiments and national narrow-mindedness do not disappear automatically with the establishment of the socialist system. Nationalist prejudice and survivals of former national strife are a province in which resistance to social progress may be most protracted and stubborn, bitter and insidious.

The Communists consider it their prime duty to educate working people in a spirit of internationalism, socialist patriotism, and intolerance of all possible manifestations of nationalism and chauvinism. Nationalism is harmful to the common interests of the socialist community and, above all, the people of the country where it obtains, since isolation from the socialist camp holds up that country's development, deprives it of the advantages deriving from the world socialist system and encourages the imperialist powers to make the most of nationalist tendencies for their own ends. Nationalism can gain the upper hand only where it is not consistently combated. The Marxist-Leninist internationalist policy and determined efforts to wipe out the survivals of bourgeois nationalism and chauvinism are an important condition for the further consolidation of the socialist community.

The Soviet Case Against China

48/Open Letter from CPSU Central Committee to Party Organizations and All Communists of the Soviet Union   *July 14, 1963*

What is the gist of the differences between the Communist Party of China (C.P.C.) on the one hand and the C.P.S.U. and the international communist movement on the other? . . . .

Take, for instance, such cardinal problems as war and peace . . . The C.P.S.U. central committee believes it to be its duty to tell the party and the people with all frankness that in questions of war and peace the C.P.C. leadership has cardinal differences, based on principle, with us and with the world communist movement. The essence of these differences lies in a diametrically opposite approach to such vital problems as the possibility of averting thermonuclear world war, peaceful co-existence between states with different social systems and the interconnection between the struggle for peace and the development of the world revolutionary movement.

Our party, in the decisions of the 20th and 22nd Congresses, and the world communist movement, in the Declaration and Statement [of November 1960], set before communists as a task of extreme importance the task of averting a thermonuclear world catastrophe. We appraise the balance of forces in the world realistically, and from this draw the conclusion that, though the nature of imperialism has not changed, and the danger of the outbreak of war has not been averted, in modern conditions the forces of peace, of which the mighty community of socialist states is the main bulwark, can, by their joint efforts, avert a new world war.

We also soberly appraise the radical, qualitative change in the means of waging war and, consequently, its possible aftermaths. The nuclear rocket weapons which have been created in the middle of our century change the old notions about war. These weapons possess an unprecedented devastating force. Suffice it to say that the explosion of only one powerful thermonuclear bomb surpasses the explosive force of all the ammunition used during all previous wars, including the First and Second World Wars. And many thousand such bombs have been accumulated!

Soviet News, No. 4872 (July 16, 1963), *excerpts.*

Do communists have the right to ignore this danger? Do we have to tell the people all the truth about the consequences of thermonuclear war? We believe that, without question, we must. This cannot have a "paralyzing" effect on the masses, as the Chinese comrades assert. On the contrary, the truth about modern war will mobilize the will and energy of the masses in the struggle for peace and against imperialism—the source of military danger. . . .

To prevent a new world war is a real and quite feasible task. The 20th Congress of our party came to the extremely important conclusion that in our times there is no fatal inevitability of war between states. This conclusion is not the fruit of good intentions, but the result of a realistic, strictly scientific analysis of the balance of class forces on the world arena; it is based on the gigantic might of world socialism. . . .

The Chinese comrades obviously underestimate the whole danger of thermonuclear war. "The atomic bomb is a paper tiger"; "it is not terrible at all," they contend . . . We would like to ask the Chinese comrades who suggest building a bright future on the ruins of the old world destroyed by a thermonuclear war whether they have consulted the working class of the countries where imperialism dominates? The working class of the capitalist countries would certainly tell them: are we asking you to trigger off a war and destroy our countries while annihilating the imperialists? Is it not a fact that the monopolists, the imperialists, are only a comparatively small group, while the bulk of the population of the capitalist countries consists of the working class, working peasantry, and working intelligentsia?

The nuclear bomb does not distinguish between the imperialists and working people: it hits great areas, and therefore millions of workers would be destroyed for one monopolist. The working class, the working people, will ask such "revolutionaries"; what right have you to decide for us the questions of our existence and our class struggle? We also are in favor of socialism; but we want to gain it through the class struggle and not by unleashing a thermonuclear world war. . . .

The deep difference between the views of the C.P.S.U. and other Marxist-Leninist Parties on the one hand and the C.P.C. leaders on the other, on the questions of war, peace and peaceful co-existence was demonstrated with particular clarity during the 1962 crisis in the Caribbean Sea. It was a sharp international crisis: never before did mankind come so close to the brink of a thermonuclear war as it did in October [1962].

The Chinese comrades allege that in the period of the Caribbean crisis we made an "adventurist" mistake by introducing rockets into Cuba and then "capitulated" to American imperialism when we removed the rockets from Cuba. Such assertions utterly contradict the facts.

What was the actual state of affairs? The C.P.S.U. central committee and the Soviet government possessed trustworthy information that an armed aggression by United States imperialism against Cuba was about to take place. We realized with sufficient clarity that the most resolute steps were needed to rebuff the aggression and to defend the Cuban revolution effectively. Curses and warnings—even if they are called "serious warnings" and repeated two and a half hundred times over—have no effect on the imperialists.

Proceeding from the need to defend the Cuban revolution, the Soviet government and the government of Cuba reached agreement on the delivery of missiles to Cuba, because this was the only effective way of preventing aggression on the part of American imperialism. The delivery of missiles to Cuba meant that an attack on her would meet with a resolute rebuff and the use of rocket weapons against the organizers of the aggression. Such a resolute step on the part of the Soviet Union and Cuba was a shock to the American imperialists, who felt for the first time in their history that if they were to undertake an armed invasion of Cuba, a shattering retaliatory blow would be dealt against their own territory. Inasmuch as the point in question was not simply a conflict between the United States and Cuba, but a clash between the two major nuclear powers, the crisis in the Caribbean Sea area would have turned from a local into a world war. A real danger of thermonuclear world war arose.

There was one alternative in the prevailing situation: either to follow in the wake of the "madmen" (this is how the most aggressive and reactionary representatives of American imperialism are dubbed) and embark upon a course of unleashing a world thermonuclear war or, profiting from the opportunities offered by the delivery of missiles, to take all steps to reach an agreement on a peaceful solution of the crisis and to prevent aggression against the Republic of Cuba.

As is known, we chose the second path and are convinced that we did the right thing. . . . Agreement to remove the missile weapons in return for the United States government's commitment not to invade Cuba and to keep its allies from doing so, and the heroic struggle of the Cuban people and the support rendered to them by the peace-loving nations, made it possible to frustrate the plans of the extreme adventurist circles of American imperialism, which were ready to go the whole hog. As a result it was possible to defend revolutionary Cuba and to save peace.

The Chinese comrades regard our statement that the Kennedy government also displayed a certain reasonableness and a realistic approach in the course of the crisis around Cuba as "embellishing imperialism." Do they really think that all bourgeois governments lack all reason in everything they do? . . . The Chinese comrades argue that the imperialists cannot be trusted in anything, that they are bound to cheat; but this is not a case of faith, but rather a case of sober calculation. Eight months have passed since the elimination of the crisis in the Caribbean Sea area, and the United States government is keeping its word—there is no invasion of Cuba. We also assumed a commitment to remove our missiles from Cuba, and we have fulfilled it. . . .

The next important question on which we differ is that of the ways and methods of the revolutionary struggle of the working class in the capitalist countries, the struggle for national liberation, the paths of the transition of all mankind to socialism. . . . The Chinese comrades, in a haughty and abusive way, accuse the Communist Parties of France, Italy, the United States, and other countries of nothing less than opportunism and reformism, of "parliamentary cretinism," and even of slipping down to "bourgeois socialism." On what grounds do they do this? On the grounds that these Communist Parties do not put forward the slogan of an immediate proletarian revolution, although even the Chinese leaders must realize that this cannot be done without the existence of a revolutionary situation.

Every knowledgeable Marxist-Leninist realizes that to put forward the slogan of an armed uprising, when there is no revolutionary situation in the country, means condemning the working class to defeat. It is common knowledge how exceedingly serious was Lenin's approach to this question, with what political perspicacity and knowledge of the concrete situation he approached the question of choosing the time for revolutionary action. On the very eve of the October Revolution, Lenin pointed out that it would be too early to start on October 24, too late on October 26—everything might be lost—and, consequently, power had to be taken, at whatever cost, on October 25. Who determines the intensity of class contradictions, the existence of a revolutionary situation, and chooses the moment for the uprising? This can be done only by the working class of each given country, by its vanguard—the Marxist-Leninist party. . . .

The Chinese leaders regard as a mortal sin of the Communist Parties of the developed capitalist states the fact that they see their direct tasks in the struggle for the economic and social interests of the working people, for democratic reforms, feasible even under capitalism and easing the living conditions of the working class, the peasantry and the petty bourgeois sections of the population, and contributing to the formation of a broad anti-monopoly front, which will serve as a basis for further struggle for the victory of the socialist revolution, that is to say, the fact that they are doing precisely what is recorded in the Moscow Statement of 1960. . . .

Yet another important question is that of *the relationship between the struggle of the international working class and the national liberation movement of the peoples of Asia, Africa, and Latin America.* The international revolutionary working-class movement, represented today by the world system of socialism and the Communist Parties of the capitalist countries and the national liberation movement of the peoples of Asia, Africa, and Latin America—these are the great forces of our epoch. Correct coordination between them constitutes one of the main prerequisites for victory over imperialism.

How do the Chinese comrades solve this problem? This is seen from their new "theory," according to which the main contradiction of our time is, you see, the contradiction, not between socialism and imperialism, but between the national liberation movement and imperialism. The decisive force in the struggle against imperialism, the Chinese comrades maintain, is not the world system of socialism, not the struggle of the international working class, but again the national liberation movement. In this way the Chinese comrades, apparently, want to win popularity among the peoples of Asia, Africa, and Latin America by the easiest possible means. But let no one be deceived by this "theory." Whether the Chinese theoreticians want it or not, this theory in essence means isolating the national liberation movement from the international working class and its creation—the world system of socialism. Yet this would constitute a tremendous danger to the national liberation movement itself.

Indeed, could the many peoples of Asia have been victorious, in spite of all their heroism and selflessness, if the October Revolution, and then the formation of the world system of socialism, had not shaken imperialism to its very foundations, if they had not undermined the forces of the colonialists? And now that the liberated peoples have entered a new stage in their struggle, concentrating their efforts on the consolidation of their political gains and economic independence, do they not see that it would be immeasurably more difficult, if not altogether impossible, to carry out these tasks without the assistance of the socialist states? . . .

The question arises: What is the explanation for the incorrect propositions of the C.P.C. leadership on the basic problems of our time? It is either the complete divorcement of the Chinese comrades from actual reality, a dogmatic, bookish approach to problems of war, peace, and the revolution, their lack of understanding of the concrete conditions of the present epoch, or the fact that behind the rumpus about the "world revolution," raised by the Chinese comrades, there are other goals, which have nothing in common with revolution. . . .

The erroneous views of C.P.C. leaders on the paramount political and theoretical questions of our time are inseparably linked with their practical activities aimed at undermining the unity of the world socialist camp and the international Communist movement. In words Chinese comrades recognize that the unity of the U.S.S.R. and the People's Republic of China is a mainstay of the entire socialist community, but in actual fact they are undermining contacts with our party and with our country in all directions. The C.P.C. leadership often speaks of its loyalty to the commonwealth of socialist countries, but the attitude of the Chinese comrades to this commonwealth refutes their high-sounding declarations. The statistics show that in the course of the past three years the People's Republic of China cut the volume of its trade with the countries of the socialist community by more than 50 per cent. Some socialist countries felt the results of this line of the Chinese comrades particularly keenly . . .

Parallel with the line directed towards curtailing economic contacts, the leadership of the C.P.C. took a number of measures aimed at worsening relations with the Soviet Union. The Chinese leaders are undermining the unity, not only of the socialist camp, but also of the entire world communist movement, trampling underfoot the principles of proletarian internationalism and flagrantly violating the standards governing the relations between fraternal parties. The leadership of the C.P.C. is organizing and supporting various anti-party groups of renegades who are coming out against the Communist Parties in the United States, Brazil, Italy, Belgium, Australia and India . . . Comrades of the C.P.C. are making particular efforts to conduct subversive activities in the Communist and Workers' Parties in the countries of Asia, Africa, and Latin America . . .

And in its letter of June 14, 1963, the leadership of the C.P.C. sinks to insinuations that the C.P.S.U., too—so it alleges—"comes out in the role of a helper of imperialism." No one but Trotskyites has so far dared, in view of the obvious absurdity of this, to level such slanderous accusations against the great party of Lenin! . . .

One of the clear examples of the special line in the leadership of the C.P.C. in the socialist camp and the international communist movement is its position on the Albanian question. As is well known, in the second half of 1960 the Albanian leaders openly came out with a left opportunist platform on the main questions of our day and began to promote a hostile policy in relation to the C.P.S.U. and other fraternal parties. The Albanian leadership started an anti-Soviet campaign in the country, which led to a rupture of political, economic, and cultural ties with the Soviet Union . . . It is now known that the Chinese comrades openly pushed them on to the road of open struggle against the Soviet Union . . .

A Soviet-American Accommodation: A Soviet Perspective

49/Some International Implications of the Cuban Missile Crisis *December 13, 1962*

ANDREI GROMYKO

Resolutely casting off the burden of Stalin's mistaken views on a number of international questions and his fallacious methods of conducting foreign relations, the Central Committee of our Party is now displaying an increasingly greater energy and initiative in the struggle for peace among nations.

Has cooperation between the USSR and the United States, whose strength was well demonstrated during the struggle against fascist Germany and militarist Japan, really become less necessary and less valuable than it was during the war? No, the Soviet government is convinced that such cooperation is today at least as much more necessary as a new war is much more dangerous, because of up-to-date means of extermination. Either international disputes are settled at the conference table or we slip into war—there is no other choice either for the United States or for us. Now, too, the Soviet government sees no insurmountable obstacle to the establishment and development of cooperation between the Soviet Union and the United States, if the Americans also want this. . . .

There are deep ideological differences between the Soviet Union and the United States, because the social systems of the two states are different. But the Soviet Union has no territorial claims on the United States, or anything else of the kind. It is to be assumed that the U.S.A. can have no such claims on us either. There are no reasons for an economic clash between the Soviet Union and the United States: the Soviet Union has truly fabulous natural resources, incalculable material and spiritual values created by the work and genius of our people. In other words, we have everything necessary to fulfill the program of communist construction which was set by the 22nd Congress of the CPSU and whose scope staggers even the most vivid imagination.

The United States of America is also a rich country, though the Soviet people know who, in effect, takes advantage of the wealth created by the business-like and vigorous American people. . . .

Soviet News, No. 4785 (December 17, 1962), pp. 178–179, *excerpts.*

Both United States officials and the American people are now posing the questions, as is happening everywhere: what developments are likely in the world, and how will Soviet-American relations develop? The questions are understandable and legitimate. There are sober voices calling for an adjustment of relations with the Soviet Union, and for a policy which takes the interests of the Soviet Union and other socialist countries into consideration. But there are also leaders who have learned little, especially from the crisis in the Caribbean. They are ready to deny almost any possibility of improving relations between the USSR and the United States and of establishing confidence between them, stating specifically that the United States did not know about the weapons installed by the Soviet Union in Cuba at the request of the Cuban government. Reproaches are hurled at the Soviet Union alleging that it shipped offensive weapons to Cuba and did this secretly. All these statements by U.S. leaders are unfounded.

Even before the events in the Caribbean, the head of our government, Nikita Khrushchev, said that all our weapons sent to Cuba were for the defense of the Cuban Republic and for deterring the aggression with which it was constantly menaced. Consequently, they were weapons for defense, defensive weapons. There could be no question of any deliveries of weapons for offensive purposes, i.e., offensive weapons. I, too, stated this, in the name of the Soviet government in a talk with President Kennedy at the White House on October 18, and in a talk with the U.S. Secretary of State Rusk on the same day. . . .

Yes, some American statesmen say, but there were intermediate range missiles in Cuba. Well, what of it? If the U.S.A. did not know of the existence of such rockets on Cuba, does this mean that somebody had deluded them? By the way, the United States government did not ask the Soviet government whether or not there were intermediate range rockets on Cuba. And since they did not ask, the Soviet government could not give a reply about the presence or absence of Soviet rockets in Cuba. Neither President Kennedy nor Secretary of State Rusk asked this question in our talks with them in Washington. It follows that United States statesmen consider that something was concealed from them though they did not ask anything about it.

Besides, since when does the United States consider that it has the right to learn or receive information from the Soviet Union about what weapons it has and where they are? What right can the United States have to declare that the Americans were deceived in practice since they were not notified of the installation of Soviet rocket weapons in Cuba? Does the U.S. government inform the Soviet government of what weapons the U.S. has at the numerous American military bases scattered throughout Europe, Asia, and Africa, including regions adjoining the frontiers of the Soviet Union? The Soviet government cannot recall having received such information from the United States. And if we are to talk of exchanging such information, then this exchange is unthinkable without reciprocity. Why then does the U.S. demand more? The U.S. government is, of course, itself well aware that such pretensions are completely unfounded.

One thing is necessary if there is to be trust in the relations between the two largest powers, and it is that the U.S. construct its foreign policy on the only realistic basis of peaceful coexistence between states and observance of the United Nations Charter, which it has grossly violated more than once, and specifically with regard to Cuba.

It can be said with full confidence that if there is cooperation and trust between the Soviet Union and the United States, there will be peace.

FOR FURTHER STUDY

Brzezinski, Zbigniew K. *The Soviet Bloc: Unity and Conflict.* Rev. ed. Cambridge, Mass.: Harvard University Press, 1967.

Cheng, Chu-Yuan. *Economic Relations Between Peking and Moscow, 1949–1963.* New York: Praeger, 1964.

Crankshaw, Edward. *The New Cold War: Moscow and Pekin.* Baltimore: Penguin, 1963.

Dallin, Alexander, Jonathan Harris, and Grey Hodnett (eds.). *Diversity in International Communism: A Documentary Record, 1961–1963.* New York: Columbia University Press, 1963.

Dallin, David J. *Soviet Foreign Policy After Stalin.* Philadelphia: Lippincott, 1961.

Feld, Werner. *Reunification and West German-Soviet Relations.* The Hague: Nijhoff, 1963.

Floyd, David. *Mao Against Khrushchev.* New York: Praeger, 1963.

Freund, Gerald. *Germany Between Two Worlds.* New York: Harcourt Brace Jovanovich, 1961.

Griffith, William E. *Albania and the Sino-Soviet Rift.* Cambridge, Mass.: M. I. T. Press, 1963.

_____. *The Sino-Soviet Rift.* Cambridge, Mass.: M. I. T. Press, 1964.

_____ (ed.). *Communism in Europe.* Vol. I. Cambridge, Mass.: M. I. T. Press, 1965.

Grzybowski, Kazimierz. *The Socialist Commonwealth of Nations.* New Haven, Conn.: Yale University Press, 1964.

Hayter, William. *The Kremlin and the Embassy.* New York: Macmillan, 1967.

Ionescu, Ghita. *The Breakup of the Soviet Empire in Eastern Europe.* Baltimore: Penguin, 1965.

Kennan, George F. *Russia, the Atom and the West.* New York: Harper & Row, 1957.

Kertesz, Stephen D. (ed.). *East Central Europe·and the World: Developments in the Post-Stalin Era.* Notre Dame, Ind.: University of Notre Dame Press, 1962.

Laqueur, Walter Z. *Russia and Germany.* Boston: Little, Brown, 1965.

London, Kurt (ed.). *Unity and Contradiction: Major Aspects of Sino-Soviet Relations.* New York: Praeger, 1962.

Lowenthal, Richard. *World Communism: Disintegration of a Secular Faith.* New York: Oxford University Press, 1964.

Luard, Evan (ed.). *The Cold War: A Reappraisal.* New York: Praeger, 1964.

Lukacs, John. *A New History of the Cold War.* 2d ed. Garden City, N.Y.: Doubleday, 1966.

Mehnert, Klaus. *Peking and Moscow.* New York: Putnam, 1963.

Neal, Fred Warner. *War and Peace and Germany.* New York: Norton, 1962.

North, Robert C. *Moscow and Chinese Communists.* 2d ed. Stanford, Calif.: Stanford University Press, 1963.

Speier, Hans. *Divided Berlin.* New York: Praeger, 1961.

Szaz, Zoltan M. *Germany's Eastern Frontiers: The Problem of the Oder-Neisse Line.* Chicago: Regnery, 1960.

Vali, Ferenc A. *Rift and Revolt in Hungary.* Cambridge, Mass.: Harvard University Press, 1961.

Zagoria, Donald S. *The Sino-Soviet Conflict, 1956–1961.* Princeton, N.J.: Princeton University Press, 1962.

Zinner, Paul. *Revolution in Hungary.* New York: Columbia University Press, 1962.

9
the brezhnev period: competitive coexistence and imperial consolidation

The duumvirate of Brezhnev and Kosygin altered the style but not the substance of Khrushchev's foreign policy. The years 1965 and 1966 were characterized by cautious inconclusiveness in foreign policy: the acrimonious exchanges with Communist China were largely suspended, though the differences remained unsolved; the hints of change toward West Germany were dropped, and the specter of German revanchism was dramatized as Soviet leaders groped for ways of stimulating bloc cohesion; the escalation of American involvement in Vietnam was sharply condemned, but behind-the-scenes exploratory talks with the United States tried to find a basis for systematic discussions to curb the nuclear and missile race and limit the introduction of new weapons systems; the level of new commitments to Third World countries was tightly controlled and, with the exception of the effective intervention in the Indo-Pakistan war of 1965, diplomatic initiatives were modest; and the theme of peaceful coexistence was repeated, as the new rulers consolidated their position. Internal economic reforms and the mending of intra-communist-bloc divisions overshadowed involvement and influence building abroad. The Twenty-third Congress of the CPSU, held in March 1966, was distinguished by its uneventfulness. The ebullience of Khrushchev was replaced by the circumspection of Brezhnev. The new managers of the Soviet system adopted the anonymity of the bureaucrat.

From 1967 on, however, international developments thrust foreign policy into the foreground. The Arab-Israeli war of June 1967 resulted in enormously expanded Soviet commitments and a massive military presence in the United Arab Republic, an open naval challenge to the

United States, and a greater involvement in Middle Eastern affairs than ever before in Soviet history (see Chapter XIII). In early 1968 the democratic impulse in Czechoslovakia was destroyed by Moscow, and new uncertainties entered Soviet–East European and East-West relations. In 1969 the eruption of serious fighting along the Sino-Soviet border further aggravated tensions between the two communist mammoths and may well have prompted Chinese leaders to reevaluate their attitude toward the United States and to agree in July 1971 to a precedent-shattering visit by President Richard M. Nixon. The introduction of new weapons systems led the superpowers to inaugurate the Strategic Arms Limitation Talks (SALT) in late 1969 (see Chapter XI). And the European policy of the USSR acquired a new impetus with the election in October 1969 in West Germany of the Social Democratic Party (SPD), under the leadership of Willy Brandt, who staked his prestige on the success of his new Eastern policy—the establishment of improved relations with the Soviet Union and reconciliation with Poland and Czechoslovakia. These complex and interconnected developments compelled Soviet leaders to confront policy options whose consequences are an ambivalent mixture of promise and danger.

One of the features of the Brezhnev period has been the advancement of seemingly incompatible policies: repression in Czechoslovakia and rapprochement with Western Europe; significant increments in nuclear and missile capability and SALT talks with the United States; ambitious expansionism in the Middle East, South Asia, and Latin America with dexterous maneuvering to avoid open confrontations with the United States; pressure on China with attempts to restore unity in the international communist movement; neo-Stalinism at home and imports of Western technology and technicians. Many analysts see only indecisiveness and weakness in such behavior and do not adequately value the short-term dividends of a policy of ambiguity and chameleonic adaptation to concrete situations, with little concern for the niceties of a cohesive global design. Far from being indecisive, Brezhnev's policy has realized or come within reach of a number of long-term aims: the stabilization of the Soviet imperial system in Eastern Europe; the recognition by the Western powers of the territorial status quo; the exclusion of West Germany from any access to nuclear weapons; the exploitation, through diplomatic initiatives and economic agreements, of intra-Western rivalry, both between Western Europe and the United States, and West Germany and France; the weakening of NATO; and the cultivation of respectability for the Soviet Union and, not incidentally, for local communist parties.

Eastern Europe

As Sino-Soviet rivalry dispelled the myth of international communist solidarity and as nationalism intensified in Eastern Europe, Soviet leaders sought a formula for reasserting their authority within the bloc. Romania's obstructionism within COMECON and establishment of diplomatic ties with West Germany, and Czechoslovakia's and Hungary's expanding economic and cultural contacts with Western Europe, whose markets, tourists, and technology they coveted, exacerbated Soviet uneasiness. In April 1967, Moscow convened a meeting of European communist parties at Karlovy Vary, Czechoslovakia. Brezhnev devoted most of his attention to East-West relations and the continuing threat from NATO and only in passing alluded to China. He outlined the essential Soviet aims in Europe (reading 50). But the meeting failed to reconcile the differences between Moscow and the nationalist communist parties on the issue of how much autonomy for Eastern Europe was consonant with Soviet security and ideological control.

At the celebrations in Moscow for the fiftieth anniversary of the Bolshevik Revolution, Soviet leaders persuaded eighteen communist parties to cosponsor a "consultative" meeting in Budapest in late February 1968 to plan a world conference of communist parties, the first since November 1960. In this effort to restore Soviet centralizing authority, Moscow found its staunchest supporters among the East Germans. The campaign for orthodoxy and struggle against "revisionism" came at a time when events in Czechoslovakia were moving the Kremlin toward a moment of truth.

In January 1968 a combination of disgruntled Stalinists and reformers ousted Antonin Novotny—Moscow's man in Prague—as General Secretary of the Czechoslovak Communist party and brought in Alexander Dubcek. Long a loyal party bureaucrat, Dubcek became the rallying symbol for all factions and groups seeking to liberalize Czechoslovak society and to assert a greater autonomy in domestic affairs. By mid-February, the skepticism among the population at large changed to hopeful anticipation. By late spring, the air of freedom intoxicated the country: Dubcek and the reformers spoke of a parliament free from party control; they rehabilitated the victims of the Stalinist past, began to rid the party and trade unions of the front men for Moscow, and eliminated censorship. Ludvik Svoboda replaced Novotny as President. In the Central Committee, the Dubcek group was in control. Democratization flowered. From early February to August 1968, Czechoslovakia experienced a rebirth of political, cultural, and social freedom. The secret police were stripped of their arbitrary powers; links to the Soviet secret police apparatus were exposed; criticisms of the past and proposals for the future were aired with a candor and passion that disturbed the oligarchs of Byzantine communism in Moscow. The "Prague spring" lasted until August 21.

In the early hours of August 21, 1968, Soviet troops invaded Czechoslovakia. As in Hungary in 1956, Moscow responded with overwhelming force to a perceived threat to its imperial hegemony. Joined by Polish, East German, Hungarian, and Bulgarian divisions (but not Romanian), the Red Army quickly occupied the country. From the very beginning, the Soviet Union was exposed and discredited by its own lies: it said Soviet troops were sent at the request of party and government officials, but Svoboda, Dubcek, and other leaders denied this allegation; it claimed to have acted to forestall an insidious effort at counterrevolution, but the collapse of its initial efforts in late August to install pro-Soviet puppets showed that what was in jeopardy in Czechoslovakia was Soviet domination, not socialism; it resorted to anti-Semitism to tarnish all Czech reformers, a few of whom were Jewish, but dropped these charges when they became counterproductive. But inexorably Moscow eliminated the patriots and replaced them with puppets.

The Soviet justification for the intervention in Czechoslovakia appeared in *Pravda* on September 26, 1968 (reading 51). Quickly dubbed the "Brezhnev Doctrine," it proclaimed the inherent right of the Soviet Union to intervene anywhere in the "socialist" world to preserve "socialism." It warned other communist regimes in Eastern Europe that, while Moscow would tolerate a degree of autonomy, it would be the sole judge and jury of when the limits of the permissible had been exceeded.

Soviet leaders used force to solve the Czechoslovak problem, even though such action might have jeopardized many of their policy goals: for example, a limited rapprochement with the United States, including prospects for an arms limitation agreement; the steady erosion and possible demise of NATO; the support of foreign communist parties, many of which publicly condemned the Soviet aggression against an ally and fellow-communist country; and the propaganda advantage of castigating the United States for its policy of force in Vietnam. Several reasons may be advanced for the invasion.

The first is the domestic situation in the Soviet Union, which may have been the most important single determinant. The ethnic and racial diversity of the USSR has a profound effect on Soviet politics and policy making. The Russians, who constitute no more than 52 percent of the approximately 250 million Soviet population, have had trouble for more than 300 years with the 45 million Ukrainians, the second largest nationality group. Of all the peoples in Eastern Europe, the Czechs and Slovaks are regarded by Ukrainians as the nearest to them in tradition and culture. The rulers of the CPSU may well have been afraid that the virus of Czechoslovak liberalization would find a congenial breeding ground in the national consciousness of the Ukrainians and stimulate demands in the Ukrainian SSR for greater autonomy and liberalization. After all, if the Slavs and fraternal communists of Czechoslovakia were permitted democratization, why not those of the Soviet Union? Ethnic nationalism is a perennial nightmare for Moscow. Soviet leaders proclaim abroad the notion of "proletarian internationalism" (i.e., unswerving acceptance by all communists of the primacy of defending the homeland of socialism—the Soviet Union) (see Chapter XII) to justify Soviet claims to leadership of the international communist movement; but ironically, they may be more concerned with its acceptance *internally* as ideological justification for Great Russian domination over the non-Russian nationalities of the Soviet Union.

Reinforcing this hypothesis of the salience of nationality considerations is the post-Khrushchev trend toward neo-Stalinism and repression in the Soviet Union. There is a general tightening of Party control by Soviet leaders, whose fundamental approach to social dissonance is defensive, provincial, and repressive. The present oligarchs in the Kremlin are anxious authoritarians. They are suspicious of arguments for decentralization of the Soviet imperial system, for greater autonomy and encouragement of innovation, and prefer to tinker with familiar institutions and procedures rather than introduce new ones, an attitude as clearly evident in their approach to COMECON and Eastern Europe as to internal problems.

A second major factor in the Soviet decision to invade Czechoslovakia was the pressure of the military to safeguard the Soviet strategic military position in Central Europe. The Czech suggestion in July 1968 that the Warsaw Pact should be revised raised the ghost of another Hungarian crisis. The military no doubt argued that Czechoslovakia was too important geographically to allow its political neutralism or instability. The military favored intervention because they opposed any weakening of their advantageous strategic position in Eastern Europe. Furthermore, it is also possible that Soviet intelligence assured the political leadership that the Czechs would not fight and that the affair could be handled swiftly and satisfactorily if overwhelming force were applied. As it was, Warsaw Pact maneuvers in 1966 had exposed glaring weaknesses along the Czechoslovak-West German border; and Prague's unwillingness to agree to the permanent stationing of Soviet troops on Czech soil was an objection the Soviet military wished to override. East German leaders supported the Soviet military, arguing that if Czechoslovakia opened her economy to Western investment and technology and established diplomatic relations with West Germany, as Romania and Yugoslavia had, the net result would be a severe weakening of

East Germany, Moscow's dependable ally and most important economic partner.

So for both domestic and strategic reasons Moscow acted in Czechoslovakia as it had in Hungary twelve years earlier. Preservation of its sphere of influence was of overriding importance. Spheres of influence are a fact of international politics. By its action, the USSR showed that its policy in Europe is based on the axiom: "What's mine is mine; what's yours is negotiable." The Soviet Union considers Eastern Europe nonnegotiable. It said, in effect, that any American policy of "building bridges" to Eastern Europe would have to be cleared with Moscow; but that Moscow felt free to seek a rapprochement with any West European country, independent of any consideration of American interests or attitudes. It would not, out of a desire for improved relations with the United States, passively tolerate what it perceived as a threatening erosion of its political and strategic hold over a contiguous communist country. Moscow also demonstrated once again that it would not be deterred from harsh suppression of liberal communists by considerations of prestige among foreign communist parties. In Moscow's indifference to the opinion of foreign communists we see again the dominance of Russian national and imperial interests over the needs and wishes of communist parties abroad.

The limits of Soviet tolerance are clear. Hungary in 1956 and Czechoslovakia in 1968 show that the Soviet Union will use force to preserve intact its sphere of influence in Eastern Europe. Different political constellations in control in the Kremlin at any given time are prepared to accept lesser or greater measures of autonomy, but the determination of what is permissible is subject to Moscow's continual redelineation and restraint. Eastern Europe cannot divest itself completely of Soviet influence. Geography, shared ideological goals, the close dependency of the "new class" in Eastern Europe on the power of the Soviet Union, and the realities of international power preclude such a situation. By keeping alive fears of German "revanchism" among the Poles and East Germans, particularly, Moscow ensures their military dependence. Should any of the East European regimes show signs of assuming an anti-Soviet, anticommunist coloration, Moscow would presumably feel impelled to act, as it did in 1956 and 1968, to safeguard its national interests. To paraphrase what the Mexican dictator, Porfirio Diaz, once said of Mexico and the United States: "Poor Eastern Europe, so far from God—so close to the Soviet Union."

The world conference of Communist and Workers' Parties, scheduled for November 1968, was postponed, while Moscow purged the Czechoslovak Communist Party, imposed a status-of-forces agreement that legalized an indefinite Soviet military occupation, and pressured other communist parties to close ranks behind the Soviet Union. When held in June 1969, the conference accepted, over dissonant voices, the "Brezhnev Doctrine"; but it did not give Moscow the unequivocal backing it sought for condemnation of the Chinese, who did not attend.

Since then Moscow has directed considerable attention to improving bloc economic relationships. It has tried to infuse COMECON with new purpose. On January 1, 1971, COMECON's Investment Bank commenced operations. In late July 1971, COMECON announced the adoption of measures intended to promote voluntary economic cooperation and technological sharing among member states during the next two decades. It called for a freely convertible "collective currency" by the end of the 1970s and for greater East European participation in the development of those Soviet natural resources needed by Eastern Europe for its internal economic growth. For example, all member countries have agreed to take part in the construction in Siberia of a cellulose plant. Meaningful economic cooperation would benefit the region, but Moscow has yet to dispel the suspicions of the East Europeans that greater integration would be more likely to strengthen the Soviet imperium than to redound to the genuine benefit of all parties concerned.

Western Europe

Concurrent with the revival of neo-Stalinism at home and the suppression of Czechoslovakia was Moscow's effort to ease tensions with the NATO countries, with a view toward sharpening intra-NATO differences and weakening American influence. It encouraged De Gaulle's downgrading of NATO in French foreign policy, inviting him to the Soviet Union in 1966 and agreeing to closer Franco-Soviet political consultation; it negotiated major trade agreements with Italy and West Germany and held out prospects for even more, though making clear that its purchases would entail machinery kept on the embargo list of strategic goods at United States insistence; and it played on French and British uneasiness over the growing economic influence of West Germany in the Common Market. NATO's embarrassed vacillation must have been very reassuring to the Politburo: not only would the West do nothing at all to interfere with Moscow's rule in Eastern Europe, but it apparently could not even generate enough lasting concern about its own safety to increase military expenditures or improve alliance cohesion. Prosperity, a pervasive belief that any war fought between the two blocs in Europe would be nuclear and hence it was futile to spend more on conventional forces, and West European acceptance of its dependency on the protection of the American nuclear umbrella inhibited action. However, French-inspired talk of further weakening NATO was dropped.

The United States government did, with great reluctance, cancel the talks on limiting strategic weapons that were to begin with the Soviet Union; but beyond that the Western countries could scarcely wait to sweep Czechoslovakia under the rug and to resume pre-Czechoslovakia efforts at a rapprochement with the USSR.

While using fear of West Germany to keep Eastern Europe in line, Brezhnev began by 1966 to explore possible ways of improving relations. The Berlin problem had been quiescent since 1964, the Khrushchev-manufactured crisis of 1958 having eased with the signing of the Soviet–East German Treaty of June 12, 1964, and Soviet assurances that it would not abolish Western rights in Berlin or access privileges across East Germany to the city. At the Twenty-third Congress of the CPSU in March–April 1966, Foreign Minister Gromyko declared that "the normalization and improvement of relations with the Federal Republic of Germany" depended, in effect, on the Bonn government's renouncing nuclear weapons and accepting the existing frontiers of all states in Europe. At its March 17, 1969, meeting in Budapest, the Political Consultative Committee of the Warsaw Pact reiterated the oft-made Soviet proposal for "the holding of a general European conference on questions of security and cooperation in Europe." It referred to a similar proposal that had been suggested in Bucharest in 1966 by the committee and said that such a conference could lead to the end of the division of Europe into military blocs and the beginning of genuine cooperation among the European states. The formula was multifaceted but familiar:

One of the main preconditions for safeguarding European security is the inviolability of the frontiers existing in Europe, including the frontiers of the Oder and Neisse and also the frontiers between the German Democratic Republic and the Federal Republic of Germany, renunciation by the Federal Republic of Germany of its claims to represent the entire German people, and renunciation of the possession of nuclear weapons in any form. West Berlin has a special status and does not belong to West Germany.

Developments in West Germany since October 1969 have provided the Soviet Union with a golden opportunity to realize most of these goals.

The rise to power of the Social Democratic party (SPD) in West Germany—first as junior partner in a coalition government, then, in October 1969, as the principal party—ushered in a new readiness by West Germany to offer concessions, in return for an improvement in relations with the Soviet Union and Eastern Europe. SPD Chancellor Willy Brandt offered the assurances Moscow sought against possible West German military ambitions: on November 28, 1969, the West German government signed the Non-Proliferation Treaty (NPT) renouncing nuclear weapons; on December 7, 1969, talks began in Moscow, on Brandt's initiative, on an agreement to renounce the use or threat of force between the two countries; and on February 1, 1970, the Soviet Union and West Germany signed a new trade and credit treaty under which West Germany agreed to provide steel pipes and industrial credits in return for 52 billion cubic meters of natural gas for twenty years, starting in 1973. In addition, on March 26, 1970, the four powers (the United States, the Soviet Union, France, and Great Britain) resumed talks on Berlin at the ambassadorial level for the first time in eleven years. Most important of all from the Soviet standpoint was the signing, on August 12, 1970, of a treaty in Moscow between West Germany and the USSR under which they agreed to settle their disputes by peaceful means only and to refrain from the threat or use of force. This Moscow Treaty also stipulates that:

(a) They undertake to respect without restriction the territorial integrity of all States in Europe within their present frontiers;
(b) They declare that they have no territorial claims against anybody nor will assert such claims in the future;
(c) They regard today and shall in future regard the frontiers of all States in Europe as inviolable such as they are on the date of signature of the present Treaty, including the Oder-Neisse line which forms the western frontier of the People's Republic of Poland and the frontier between the Federal Republic of Germany and the German Democratic Republic.

By this treaty, West Germany agrees to virtually all of Moscow's desires in Europe. Willy Brandt has made clear that he will not offer the Moscow Treaty (or the NPT) to the West German parliament for ratification until there is a satisfactory settlement of the Berlin problem, including Soviet recognition of the special ties between West Berlin and West Germany and guarantees of undisturbed access to the city. Since August 12, 1970, the ball has been in Moscow's court.

On September 3, 1971, the governments of the United States, the Soviet Union, Great Britain, and France signed an agreement governing the status of Berlin. The main provisions are: (1) the assurance by the Soviet Union that transit traffic "of civilian persons and goods between the Western sectors of Berlin and the Federal Republic of Germany will be unimpeded," expedited, and accorded preferential treatment; (2) the Soviet assurance that communications and traffic between "the Western sectors of Berlin and areas bordering on these sectors [a euphemism for East Berlin] and those sectors of the German Democratic Republic which do not border on these sectors will be improved"; (3) the commitment of the Western Powers to maintain their control and to continue governing West Berlin, which is not to be considered part of

West Germany and "not to be governed by it"; (4) the Soviet Union is to be permitted to open a consulate in the Western sectors of Berlin; (5) the Four Powers assume responsibility for seeing that the agreements are carried out. The task of working out the concrete details implementing the agreement rests with the West German and East German governments. Their negotiations have been difficult and slow. In December 1971 East and West German negotiators agreed to new terms regulating the status of Berlin. If implemented, the agreement would go a long way toward improving the condition of Berliners and of eliminating many of the day-to-day tensions occasioned by the division of Germany.

Moscow has moved slowly, the Four-Power ambassadorial agreement of September 3, 1971, notwithstanding. There are several possible explanations. First, Moscow may be adopting a tough position in order to improve its bargaining position and to pay the minimum price for the treaty. The reputation of the Soviet government as a tough, shrewd, skillful negotiator is well-deserved. Reasoning that time is on its side, it sees no need to make concessions at this juncture. (Its reluctance to move quickly has proved a boon to NATO, which at its meeting in December 1970 said that acceptance of the Soviet proposal for an East-West conference on European security was contingent upon a satisfactory conclusion of the Four-Power talks on Berlin.) Second, the USSR may be constrained by its links to East Germany. East Germany has diligently pushed for strengthening COMECON and restricting East European economic contacts with the capitalist countries. By supporting Moscow on the necessity of promoting bloc cohesion within COMECON, the East Germans are deliberately buttressing the position of those Soviet leaders who fear the unanticipated consequences of the expanded East-West economic, cultural, and political contacts that would ensue from ratification of the treaty. Third, Moscow believes that it can obtain the credits and technology that it wants from the West without weakening its stranglehold on Berlin. It expects Western business interests, in their eagerness to expand trade with the Soviet bloc, to override the political and strategic reservations of Western diplomats. Fourth, Moscow needs the specter of German revanchism to justify its political and military domination of Eastern Europe. Nationalism is on the rise everywhere in Eastern Europe, and any normalization of Moscow's relations with West Germany is bound to generate additional demands for autonomy. A reconciliation between the Soviet Union and West Germany would encourage Poland and Czechoslovakia to follow suit, to the detriment of East Germany's international position, and would throw into question the need for Soviet troops in Eastern Europe. Finally, improvement of the atmosphere in Europe entails risks for the Soviet Union. Moscow is not unhappy over the present division of

Germany and, though it would like to obtain diplomatic recognition of the legitimacy of the East German state, it would not want East Germany to emerge as a strong, independent country. Freezing the status quo may suit Moscow best of all, especially if this can be achieved with a large dose of economic assistance from West Germany, which has been forthcoming despite Bonn's nonratification of the treaty.

Brezhnev has opened new possibilities for Soviet diplomacy in Western Europe. Soviet President Nikolai V. Podgorny made a state visit to Italy in 1967 and had an audience with Pope Paul VI, thus reaping the benefits of Khrushchev's conciliatory policy toward the Vatican. Two French presidents—Charles de Gaulle in 1966 and Georges Pompidou in 1970—visited the Soviet Union and were regally received. Brezhnev was received in Paris in October 1971. Franco-Soviet relations improved noticeably, as Moscow catered to French pretensions to diplomatic status as a Great Power by agreeing, under the joint accord of October 13, 1970, "to extend and deepen political consultations on major international problems of mutual interest." By drawing closer to Paris and Bonn, Moscow aims at creating the illusion of a détente in Europe, while encouraging intra-Western rivalries.

And Brezhnev managed to play on the restiveness in the United States Senate over the continued deployment of 310,000 American troops in Western Europe, when in May 1971 he called for negotiations on reductions of military forces and armaments in Central Europe and tried to revive interest in a European security conference. So Moscow flits from issue to issue: it makes proposals, raises hopes for negotiations, and relinquishes nothing, but succeeds in sowing dissension in the Western camp.

Sino-Soviet Relations

After toppling Khrushchev, Brezhnev acted quickly to suspend the vituperative exchanges with the Chinese, a priority second only to the reintegration of the Communist Party, which Khrushchev had divided in two in 1962. In the hope of encouraging exploratory discussions with the Chinese, the conference scheduled for December 1964 (which Khrushchev had organized) was postponed until March 1, 1965. Though the new Soviet leadership stressed the consultative character of the meeting and disclaimed any intention of excommunicating any communist party from the international movement, the Chinese communists and their adherents boycotted it. The March meeting did little more than highlight the depth of the Sino-Soviet rift and reaffirm the desirability of holding a world conference of communist parties. For a time the Soviets shelved their polemics and refrained from responding to

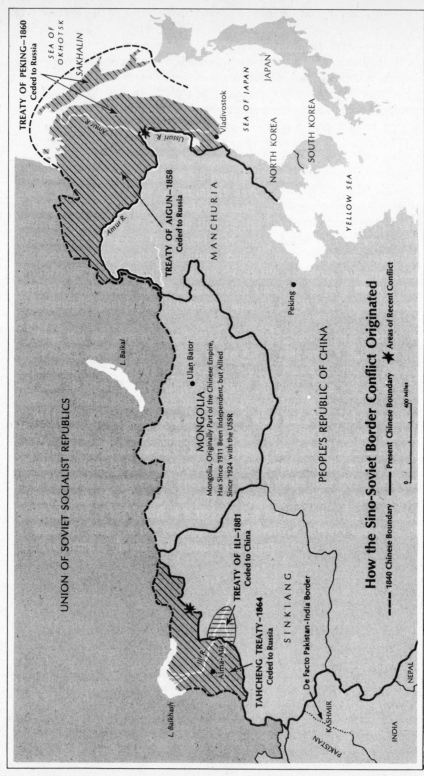

How the Sino-Soviet Border Conflict Originated

---- 1840 Chinese Boundary   —— Present Chinese Boundary   ★ Areas of Recent Conflict

0   400 Miles

TREATY OF PEKING—1860
Ceded to Russia

TREATY OF AIGUN—1858
Ceded to Russia

TREATY OF ILI—1881
Ceded to China

TAHCHENG TREATY—1864
Ceded to Russia

UNION OF SOVIET SOCIALIST REPUBLICS

PEOPLE'S REPUBLIC OF CHINA

MANCHURIA

MONGOLIA
Mongolia, Originally Part of the Chinese Empire,
Has Since 1911 Been Independent, but Allied
Since 1924 with the USSR

SINKIANG

SEA OF OKHOTSK

SAKHALIN

SEA OF JAPAN

JAPAN

NORTH KOREA

SOUTH KOREA

YELLOW SEA

Vladivostok

Amur R.

Ussuri R.

Amur R.

L. Baikal

Ulan Bator

Peking

Ili R.

Alma-Ata

L. Balkhash

De Facto Pakistan-India Border

KASHMIR

PAKISTAN

INDIA

NEPAL

Chinese gibes that they were practicing "Khrushchevism without Khrushchev." However, within the international communist movement, Moscow strengthened its ties: for example, it concluded a new treaty of alliance with the Mongolian People's Republic, which had long depended on Moscow and feared Peking's ambitions; it supported the establishment of a rival communist party in Japan to compete with the entrenched pro-Chinese one; and, in February 1965, Premier Kosygin visited North Korea and North Vietnam, which generally followed China's lead in intrabloc politics for geographical strategic reasons but which were noncommittal in the dispute itself.

By late 1966 the grievances between the Soviet Union and Communist China were unchanged. In October, Moscow ordered all Chinese students to return home, in retaliation for expulsion of Soviet students from China; in November, it resumed open attacks on Peking, charging that "experience shows that success is achieved by Communist Parties that guide themselves unswervingly by Marxism-Leninism, while those espousing pseudo-revolutionary phraseology and dogmas inevitably suffer a fiasco." In March 1967, *Kommunist*, the authoritative organ of the CPSU, accused Mao Tse-tung of following a policy of "splittism" that "undermined the unity of world revolutionary forces, greatly damaged the national liberation movement, and is playing into the hands of the imperialists, primarily the U. S. imperialists." Events in Eastern Europe and the Middle East, the restiveness of many nonruling communist parties over Moscow's centralist aims, the jubilee celebration in Moscow in November 1967, and the turmoil in China arising out of the "Cultural Revolution" (which was neither "cultural" nor "revolution," but a struggle for power), diverted Moscow's attention for a while. At a consultative meeting in Budapest in late February 1968, again boycotted by the Chinese, Moscow engineered enough support to convene an international conference of communist parties (originally scheduled for November 1968, but postponed until June 1969 because of the Soviet invasion of Czechoslovakia).

On March 2, 14, and 15, 1969, border clashes erupted along the Ussuri River in the vicinity of Damansky Island. In a diplomatic note delivered to the Chinese embassy on March 29, the Soviet government accused the Chinese of deliberate armed provocations and dismissed as untenable Peking's irredentist claims to 800,000 square miles of Soviet territory (reading 52; and see map). It noted that, as a result of the Soviet initiative of May 17, 1963, discussions on border questions had started in Peking in February 1964, but had been broken off soon thereafter. The two governments had agreed to resume the talks in Moscow on October 15, 1964, but the overthrow of Khrushchev resulted in their postponement. However, the seriousness of the situation in the spring and early summer of 1969 and veiled Soviet threats of a preemptive strike against Chinese nuclear installations in Sinkiang led Chinese leaders to reopen the talks on October 20, 1969; they have been carried on in Peking intermittently ever since, with no apparent progress.

Conceivably, no final solution is possible because the border issue is largely symbolic of the general state of Sino-Soviet relations. There is enough circumstantial evidence to indicate that Moscow was as responsible as Peking for the fighting in 1969, intent as it was on mobilizing support at the June conference of communist parties in Moscow for condemnation and isolation of China. Western governments and opinion makers were intensively briefed by Soviet officials on the background of the Damansky incidents, with a view toward engendering anew doubts about the wisdom of extending diplomatic recognition to Communist China. At the conference, Brezhnev sought to isolate China, as was clear from his proposal to create a "system of collective security in Asia," in which inclusion of China was conspicuously absent.

Despite relentless recriminations at the party to party level, there have been efforts at "normalizing" the relationship at the government to government level: in September 1969, Premier Kosygin made a quick visit to Peking, after attending Ho Chi Minh's funeral in Hanoi; in late 1970, ambassadors were exchanged after a hiatus of three years; and in November 1970, the Soviet Union and Communist China signed a trade and payments agreement in Peking (trade between the two countries, which had exceeded $2 billion annually in 1959, dropped below $50 million in 1970).

However, relations remain tense and bitter. The accusations leveled by each against the other are unprecedented in modern diplomacy. For example, on the occasion of the centenary of Lenin's birth, Communist China broadcast the following:

Brezhnev and his like extort exorbitant taxes in total disregard of the lives of the people, follow Hitler's policy of "guns instead of butter" and accelerate the militarization of the national economy to meet the needs of social-imperialism for arms expansion and war preparation. . . .

Now the Soviet revisionist new Czars have restored the old Czars' policy of national oppression, adopted such cruel measures as discrimination, forced migration, splitting and imprisonment to oppress and persecute the minority nationalities and turned the Soviet Union back into the "prison of nationalities" [Lenin's term for Czarist Russia]. . . . One can just as well compare the rule of the Soviet revisionist renegade clique with the Czarist system castigated by Lenin. It talks glibly about practicing "international-ism" toward its so-called fraternal countries, but in fact it imposes fetter upon fetter, such as the "Warsaw Treaty Organization" and the "Council for Mutual Economic Assistance," on a number of East European countries and the Mongolian People's Republic, thereby confining them within its barbed-wire "socialist community" and freely ransacking them. It has adopted the most despotic and vicious methods to keep these countries under strict control and stationed massive numbers of troops there, and it has even openly dispatched hundreds of thousands of troops to trample Czechoslovakia underfoot and install a puppet regime at bayonet point. Brezhnev's theory of "limited sovereignty" is nothing but an echo of imperialist ravings. . . .

In exposing Czarist Russia's policy of aggression a hundred years ago, Marx pointed out: "Its methods, its tactics, its maneuvers may change, but the guiding star of this policy—world hegemony—will never change." Czar Nicholas I once arrogantly shouted: "The Russian flag should not be taken down wherever it is hoisted." Czars of several generations cherished the fond dream, as Engels said, of setting up a vast "Slav empire" extending from the Elbe to China, from the Adriatic Sea to the Arctic Ocean. They even intended to extend the boundaries of this vast empire to India and Hawaii. To attain this goal, they "are as treacherous as they are talented."

The Soviet revisionist new Czars have completely taken over the old Czars' expansionist tradition, branding their faces with the indelible stigma of the Romanov dynasty.

Moscow's retort and denunciation came soon after:

Imperialist propagandists are echoed in Peking, which repeats their concoctions about the "aggressiveness" of the USSR, about the "crisis" of the Soviet economy. It galvanizes Trotskyite ideas about some sort of "a bourgeois degeneration of Soviet power" and puts a sign of equality between the United States imperialism and the Soviet Union, which is labeled "social imperialism". . .

By their actions the Peking leaders leave no doubt that they strive to use the heroic freedom struggle of peoples in their global intrigues that stem from the Great Han dreams of becoming new emperors of "the Great China" that would rule at least Asia, if not the whole world. . . . "Superrevolutionaryism" in words and betrayal of the class interests of working people in deeds—such is the genuine essence of Maoism in the field of international relations.

A new variable was introduced into the Sino-Soviet equation in April 1971, occasioned by Peking's unexpected invitation to a group of American Ping-Pong players to come for a visit. In July 1971 the White House announced that President Nixon had accepted an invitation to visit Communist China. The intimation of improved Sino-American relations must inevitably have consequences for Sino-Soviet and Soviet-American relations. In the meantime, the military build-up continues along the 4,500 mile Sino-Soviet border; Communist China presses ahead with its military-industrial development; and the two communist giants wage their rivalry over divergent national interests, festering grievances, and ideological authority within the international communist movement. Regardless of Moscow's short-term response to the Chinese problem in the light of tentative Sino-American initiatives, the Soviet Union is unlikely soon to alter its view of China as an ambitious country that seeks to acquire Great Power status, expand its influence, and challenge Soviet interests in the years ahead, as a recent study published by the Institute of Far Eastern Studies of the USSR Academy of Sciences makes unmistakably clear (reading 53).

Concluding Comments

Soviet foreign policy under Khrushchev and Brezhnev has been characterized by its essential continuity. The basic aims remain: the preservation of the Soviet imperial system; the weakening of NATO; the cultivation of a limited détente with the United States; the importation of Western technology and expertise; the isolation of China within the international communist movement; and the consolidation of Soviet influence in the Third World.

Brezhnev cannot indefinitely avoid decisions on relations with West Germany; with the United States, especially as they relate to strategic arms limitations; and with Communist China. Hard decisions also face the Soviet leadership on the Middle East, South Asia, and Japan. What can be said at this juncture is that Brezhnev's diplomacy is Russian to the core: patient, probing, ambitious, shrewd, and tough-minded.

Soviet Aims in Europe

50/Speech at the Conference of Communist and Workers' Parties of Europe in Karlovy Vary, Czechoslovakia *April 24, 1967*

LEONID BREZHNEV

It might be asked: Why do we sharply pose the question of military danger in Europe today? Is the threat so serious? Yes, comrades, there are grounds for this. We do not want to exaggerate the danger of war, but neither do we wish to underestimate it.

Where and in what do we see the threat to European security today? We answer: The threat to peace in Europe is borne by the aggressive forces of American and West German imperialism. What is the increasingly close partnership of these forces built upon? For American imperialism, collusion with the ruling circles of the Federal German Republic is the chief means, convenient for the United States and in essence not very expensive, of preserving its military-strategic positions in Europe. And this gives the United States significant levers for pressuring the policy and economics of the West European countries. As far as West German politicians are concerned, in their calculations partnership with the United States opens up for them real opportunities for implementing revanchist plans. . . .

For our part, we have stated more than once and state again: The Soviet Union is not against improving relations with the Federal Republic and is ready to do everything necessary to this end. If the present Federal Government displays sobriety in its approach to the existing situation in Europe, if it does not encroach upon the interests of other states and people, and demonstrates by deeds its desire to strengthen peace on our continent, then we shall be among those who support such a course. . . .

The West German imperialists, of course, do not have the power to achieve revanchist aims. The Soviet Union and other socialist countries have sufficient military might to strike a crushing blow at an aggressor who would dare start a war. But the revanchists could plunge the

U.S., Congress, Senate Committee on Government Operations, Subcommittee on National Security and International Operations, *"The Soviet View of NATO," speech by Leonid I. Brezhnev, April 24, 1967*, 90th Cong., 1st sess. (1967), pp. 5–13, *excerpts*.

European countries, and eventually the whole world, into the horrors of another war, and this danger must be clearly recognized. . . . The basic instrument of U.S. policy in Europe has been and still is the NATO bloc. From the beginning, this pact has been maintained on the artificially fabricated myth of "the danger of communist aggression," of the "threat from the East." The peace-loving policy of the Soviet Union and other socialist countries, the entire course of events in Europe and throughout the world, have destroyed this myth. . . .

As is known, at their conference in Bucharest the socialist Warsaw Pact countries proposed a program for security and peaceful cooperation in Europe. This program finds more and more supporters in Europe and elsewhere. In particular, the Warsaw Pact countries put on the agenda the idea of convoking an all-European conference of states to discuss questions of insuring security in Europe and of arranging all-European cooperation. This proposal has found a positive response from many West European states.

The central question of European security is the inviolability of the frontiers of the European countries in the form established as a result of, and after, World War II. Any attempt to break up these frontiers would cause countless suffering for the peoples. This is also true of the German Federal Republic's frontiers in east and west, north and south. A very important prerequisite for security in Europe is recognition of the existence of two German states with different social systems. The shortsighted policy of "nonrecognition" of the GDR [East Germany], which in effect serves only the interests of the West German revanchists, conflicts irreconcilably with European reality and serves as a serious source of international tension. The GDR has been living and flourishing for almost two decades, and the Soviet Union and the other socialist countries of Europe consider the strengthening of the GDR's international position as an important aim of their policy.

In the age of the atom and rockets, new problems have arisen connected with insuring European security. The people of Europe can well imagine what the appearance of nuclear weapons would mean in the hands of a state advocating the revision of European frontiers. Therefore, the inadmissibility of further proliferation of nuclear weapons is not only a general world problem but also one of the key questions of European security. . . .

Overcoming the division of the world and Europe into military blocs or alliances is part of the general struggle of the peoples to limit and completely end the arms race, to check militarism, and to clean the political atmosphere in Europe and throughout the world. From this point of view, there would be considerable significance in partial measures to reduce military tension in Europe, from the establishment of nuclear-free zones in separate regions of the continent to the liquidation of foreign military bases. There is no justification whatever for the constant presence of the U.S. fleet in waters washing the shores of southern Europe. One would like to ask: What are the grounds, 20 years after the end of World War II, for the U.S. Sixth Fleet to cruise the Mediterranean and to use military bases, ports, and supply bases in a number of Mediterranean countries? . . .

The CPSU, for its part, is willing to develop contacts with those social democratic parties which wish to march with us in the interests of [the] struggle against aggressors, for peace, and for the security of the peoples of Europe. We proceed from the fact that in the struggle for European security there is also the possibility of unity of action with other European political forces. They include trade union movements of all orientations, as well as peasant parties and associations. We are aware of the fruitful work of the fraternal parties aimed at establishing closer contacts with the working people who are members of different Christian parties and organizations. . . .

Our conference is the first meeting in history of communist parties of both parts of Europe—those effecting state leadership of society in socialist countries and those selflessly struggling for the cause of the working class in capitalist states. The convocation of the conference convincingly bears witness to the growing tendency toward unity of the world communist movement, toward unanimous joint actions by Marxist-Leninist parties.

All our parties are united by the common Marxist-Leninist ideology, by common ultimate aims. We know that the fraternal parties work under different conditions and therefore take different tactical steps, the result of the specific conditions of their work. But all this does not prevent our parties from cooperating closely, from drawing up agreed positions, from striving for unity of action in the struggle for the common end. And we are convinced that the solidarity of communists will continue to grow. In this respect, our conference is the best reply to those bourgeois politicians who maintain that communism has split along national lines.

The Brezhnev Doctrine: The Ideological Basis of the Soviet Imperial System

51/Sovereignty and the International Duties of Socialist Countries   *September 26, 1968*

S. KOVALEV

The question of the correlation and interdependence of the national interests of the socialist countries and their international duties has acquired particularly topical and great importance in connection with the events in Czechoslovakia. The measures taken by the Soviet Union, jointly with other socialist countries, in defending the socialist gains of the Czechoslovak people, are of great importance for strengthening the socialist community, which is the main achievement of the international working class.

We cannot ignore the allegations heard in some places that the actions of the five socialist countries are contrary to the Marxist-Leninist principle of sovereignty and the right of nations to self-determination. The unfounded nature of such reasoning lies primarily in the fact that it is based on an abstract, nonclass approach to the question of sovereignty and the right of nations to self-determination.

The peoples of the socialist countries and the Communist Parties certainly do have and should have freedom to determine the roads of advance for their respective countries. However, none of their decisions should do harm either to socialism in their own country or to the fundamental interests of other socialist countries and of the entire working-class movement which is striving for socialism. This means that each Communist Party is responsible not only to its own people but also to all the socialist countries and to the entire communist movement. Whoever forgets this, stressing only the independence of the Communist Parties, takes a one-sided attitude; he departs from his international duty.

Marxist dialectics are opposed to one-sidedness. They demand that each phenomenon be examined concretely, in general connection with other phenomena and with other processes. Just as, in Lenin's words, a man, living in a society, cannot be free from that society, so this or

Sergei Kovalev, "Sovereignty and the International Duties of Socialist Countries," *Pravda*, September 26, 1968, as published in *Soviet News*, No. 5458 (October 1, 1968), pp. 5–6, *excerpts*.

that socialist state, existing in the system of other states making up the socialist community, cannot be free from the common interests of that community. The sovereignty of each socialist country cannot be set up in opposition to the interests of the socialist world and the interests of the world revolutionary movement. Lenin demanded that all communists "fight against small-nation narrow-mindedness, seclusion and isolation, consider the whole and the general, subordinate the particular to the general interest." . . .

Every Communist Party is free to apply the basic principles of Marxism-Leninism, of socialism in its own country, but it cannot depart from these principles (always provided, naturally, that it remains a Communist Party). Concretely, this means, first of all, that in its activity every Communist Party cannot fail to take into account such a decisive fact of our times as the struggle between two opposing social systems —capitalism and socialism. This is a struggle, an objective fact which does not depend on the will of people and which follows from the circumstances that the world is split into two opposing social systems. Lenin said: "Each man must choose between joining our side or the other side. Any attempt to avoid taking sides in this issue must end in fiasco."

It must be emphasized that when a socialist country seeks to adopt a "non-affiliated" attitude, it, in actual fact, retains its national independence precisely thanks to the strength of the socialist community, and above all the Soviet Union as its central force, which also includes the might of its armed forces. The weakening of any of the links in the world socialist system directly affects all the socialist countries, which cannot look on indifferently when this happens. Thus, with talk about the right of nations to self-determination the anti-socialist elements in Czechoslovakia actually covered up a demand for so-called neutrality and Czechoslovakia's withdrawal from the socialist community. However, the implementation of "self-determination" of that kind or, in other words, the detaching of Czechoslovakia from the socialist community would have come into conflict with Czechoslovakia's vital interests and would have been detrimental to the other socialist states. Such "self-determination," as a result of which NATO troops would have been able to come up to the Soviet borders, while the community of European socialist countries would have been rent, would have encroached, in actual fact, upon the vital interests of the peoples of these countries and would be in fundamental conflict with the right of these peoples to socialist self-determination. In discharging their internationalist duty to the fraternal peoples of Czechoslovakia and defending their own socialist gains, the USSR and the other socialist states had to act decisively, and they did act, against the anti-socialist forces in Czechoslovakia. . . .

People who "disapprove" of the actions of the allied socialist states are ignoring the decisive fact that these countries are defending the interests of the whole of world socialism, the interests of the entire world revolutionary movement. The socialist system exists in concrete form in some countries, which have their own definite state frontiers. This system is developing, with account being taken of the specific features existing in each of these countries. Furthermore, no one interferes in the specific measures taken to improve the socialist system in the various socialist countries. The picture changes fundamentally, however, when a danger arises to socialism itself in this or that country. As a social system, world socialism is the common gain of the working people of all countries. It is indivisible and its defense is the common cause of all communists and all progressive people in the world, and in the first place the working people of the socialist countries. . . .

What the right-wing anti-socialist forces set out to achieve in recent months in Czechoslovakia had nothing to do with the specific features of socialist development or the application of the principles of Marxism-Leninism to the concrete conditions existing in that country, but constituted an onslaught on the foundations of socialism, on the basic principles of Marxism-Leninism. . . . Under the guise of "democratization" those elements were little by little undermining the socialist state, seeking to demoralize the Communist Party and befog the minds of the masses, step by step arranging a counter-revolutionary coup, and inside the country they were not repulsed in a proper way.

Naturally the communists of the fraternal countries could not allow the socialist states to remain inactive for the sake of sovereignty, interpreted in an abstract way, when they saw that the country was in danger of anti-socialist degeneration. The actions of the five allied socialist countries in Czechoslovakia are also in keeping with the vital interests of the people of Czechoslovakia themselves. . . .

Formal observance of the freedom of self-determination of a nation in that concrete situation which arose in Czechoslovakia would mean freedom of "self-determination," not for the masses of the people, the working men and women, but for their enemies. The anti-socialist path, the "neutrality" towards which the Czechoslovak people were being pushed, would have led their country into the den of the West German revanchists and would have brought it to the loss of its national independence. . . .

The troops of the allied socialist countries who are now in Czechoslovakia, are proving by their actions that they really do have no tasks other than the task of defending the socialist gains in that country. They are not interfering in the country's internal affairs; they are fighting for the principles of the self-determination of the peoples of Czechoslovakia, not in words but in deeds. . . . Those who talk about the "illegal" actions of the allied socialist countries in Czechoslovakia forget that in a class society there is not, and there cannot be, law that is independent of class. Laws and legal standards are subject to the laws of the class struggle, to the laws of social development. These laws are clearly formulated in the Marxist-Leninist teaching and in documents jointly adopted by the Communist and Workers' Parties.

One must not lose a class approach beneath arguments of a formal juridical character. Anyone who does that, thereby losing the class criterion (the only correct one) in assessing legal standards, begins to measure events with the yardstick of bourgeois law. Such an approach to the question of sovereignty means that, for example, the progressive forces of the world would not be able to come out against the revival of neo-Nazism in the Federal Republic of Germany, against the actions of the butchers Franco and Salazar, or against reactionary, arbitrary actions of the "black colonels" in Greece, because these are the "internal affairs" of "sovereign states." . . .

The interests of the socialist community and of the whole revolutionary movement, and the interests of socialism in Czechoslovakia demand that the reactionary forces in that country be exposed and politically isolated, that the working people be strengthened and that the Moscow Agreement between the Soviet and Czechoslovak leaders be consistently carried out.

The Soviet Case on the Border Clashes with China

52/Note on the Situation on the Soviet-Chinese Frontier   *March 29, 1969*

Armed border incidents provoked by the Chinese side have taken place recently on the River Ussuri in the area of Damansky Island . . . In their statements, the Chinese authorities are now trying to escape responsibility for the armed clashes. They contend that it was not the Chinese, but Soviet frontier guards, who violated the state border and they claim that this island does not belong to the Soviet Union. The Chinese side does not deny that its military personnel acted in accord-

Soviet News, No. 5483 (April 1, 1969), pp. 3–4, 14, *excerpts.*

ance with a prepared plan but, resorting to a false statement, it tries to present the use of arms by the Chinese violators as a "forced measure." It follows from the Chinese statements that the question of Damansky Island is only a part of some territorial problem, allegedly inherited from the past, which has yet to be solved and which is connected with the recarving of state frontiers. Moreover, the Chinese government refuses to take into consideration the treaties that exist between China and the USSR, ignores the long-standing practice of Soviet-Chinese inter-state relations and distorts history to suit its territorial claims. . . .

As is known, Chinese official propaganda questions the present borders of China's neighboring states, where a historical community of the peoples populating them has long taken form. The claims to neighboring territories are made on the pretext that they were once the subjects of dispute between some feudal chiefs, emperors and tsars, or that Chinese conquerors or merchants once set foot there. History is full of examples of those who claimed foreign territories, describing some feudal conquerors of the past as "just" and others as "unjust." Such an approach to conquerors and oppressors of the peoples is alien to Leninist policy.

The Soviet-Chinese border in the Far East, as it exists now, took shape many generations ago and passes along natural boundaries dividing the territories of the Soviet Union and China. This border was given legal status by the Aigun (1858), Tientsin (1858) and Peking (1860) treaties. . . . After the victory of the Great October Socialist Revolution in Russia, the Soviet Republic solemnly proclaimed its repudiation of the unequal and secret treaties with China and renunciation of tsarist Russia's spheres of influence, extra-territorial rights and consular jurisdiction in China. . . . The repudiation of these treaties was given legal status by the Agreement on the General Principles of Settling Questions between the Soviet Union and China of May 31, 1924.* This agreement did not refer to the Russian-Chinese treaties determining the state borders as unequal or secret ones. There was no question of annulling or revising them. . . . Speaking at the Seventh Congress of the Communist Party of China in 1945, Mao Tse-tung noted that "the Soviet Union was the first to repudiate the unequal treaties and conclude new, equal treaties with China." Mao Tse-tung repeated this statement in Moscow on December 16, 1949.

The question of some unequal treaties in Soviet-Chinese relations which is now being so pressingly brought up by Chinese propaganda is thus a concoction from beginning to end. . . .

[The] good-neighborly cooperation, which embodied the principles of socialist internationalism, has been wrecked as a result of a change in

---

* [This Chinese government was overthrown by Chiang Kai-shek in 1927.—Ed.]

the Chinese government's domestic and foreign policies in the early 1960s. It was then that the situation on the frontier began to worsen. At first there were minor, insignificant violations of the existing frontier regulations which were committed, as a rule, by civilians, or, at any rate, by people not wearing military uniform. On certain sections Chinese servicemen pointedly tried to violate the state frontier of the Soviet Union. At the same time the construction of airfields, roads, barracks and military depots was started in districts bordering on the Soviet Union.

Official Chinese propaganda openly began to glorify the aggressive raids of Genghis Khan, who was described as "Emperor of China," against the peoples of Asia and Europe, and to glorify the Manchu Emperor Kanghsi and Chinese emperors and feudal chiefs who pursued a policy of conquest. In the same vein, school textbooks and other publications in China were revised and maps published in which vast territories of the Soviet Union were marked as Chinese areas. On certain maps showing China "at the height of its might," the border line was drawn in such a way as to incorporate within China lands in which almost all peoples of Asia and even many European peoples now live. . . .

The armed provocation of the Chinese authorities on the River Ussuri in the area of Damansky Island are, therefore, not accidental. These actions, as well as the engineering of general tension on the Soviet-Chinese frontiers, are doing great harm to the cause of socialism and peace, to the common front of the anti-imperialist struggle and to friendship between the Soviet and Chinese peoples. . . . The Soviet government has stated, and considers it necessary to repeat, that it resolutely rejects any encroachments by anyone on Soviet territory and that any attempts to talk to the Soviet Union and the Soviet people in the language of weapons will be firmly repulsed.

Soviet Perceptions of China

53/Maoism and Chinese Expansionism

USSR ACADEMY OF SCIENCES,
INSTITUTE OF FAR EASTERN STUDIES

The facts concerning the activities of the Chinese leadership in the international arena during the recent period prove that the characteristic trait of the foreign policy of the Chinese People's Republic today is not proletarian internationalism but petty-bourgeois militant nationalism. The nationalism of the Chinese leaders emerges in its crudest and most aggressive form in the shape of great power chauvinism, in the shape of great power ambitions to rule the whole world.

In essence, these ambitions represent the revival in a new form of the great Han ambitions of the Chinese emperors for the political and ideological subordination of all neighboring peoples. At the heart of these ambitions, in the past as well as now, were and continue to be racist representations concerning the alleged superiority of the Chinese race as the superior race over all the peoples of the world. To these hallucinatory, medieval representations, the Chinese leaders attempt to give a contemporary form. In using leftist ultrarevolutionary slogans, popular in petty-bourgeois circles, the Maoists seek to represent themselves, and the Chinese as a nation, as the most consistent revolutionaries and anti-imperialists. On this basis they claim the leadership of the world revolutionary movement. The Maoists strive to impose their political and ideological hegemony on the world socialist community, on the international communist movement, and on the national-liberation movement, hoping to use the power of world revolutionary forces and of the most advanced social system in their great power aims of conquest by China, first in Asia and then in all the world. . . .

At the end of 1962 and the beginning of 1963 the Maoists openly passed to an anti-Soviet, antisocialist position and adopted the course aimed at splitting the socialist community and utilizing the petty-bourgeois elements in the international communist and national-

G. V. Astaf'ev, M. I. Makarov, A. M. Dubinskii, B. N. Zanegin (eds.), *Vneshniaia Politika KNR: O Sushchnosti Vneshnepoliticheskogo Kursa Sovremennogo Kitaiskogo Rukovodstva* [*The Foreign Policy of the CPR: The Essence of the Foreign Policy Course of the Contemporary Chinese Leadership*] (Moscow: International Relations Publishing House, 1971), pp. 175–179, *excerpts*. Editor's translation.

liberation movements for the fulfillment of their great power aims. With this in mind, Mao Tse-tung presented new "theories" designed to attract the petty-bourgeois forces and to subordinate them to the leadership of the Maoists. These are "theories" concerning the leading role of the national-liberation movement and the peasantry in the anti-imperialist struggle; armed struggle in the form of "people's war" as the only form of struggle; and the "excellent revolutionary situation" in all the developing countries—allegedly allowing the generation of a military struggle in any country and the creation of many centers of war of the Vietnam type to destroy imperialism. . . .

In subsequent years, especially after the "Cultural Revolution," the Chinese leaders, while continuing to rely on the national-liberation movement and attempting to draw new developing nations into the Chinese sphere of influence, began to broaden their contacts with the capitalist countries, expanding them as early as the 1960s. To achieve these goals, the Maoists not only deal in anti-Sovietism, but they are not squeamish about also using the most reactionary slogans and methods, such as racism, the principle of blood, unity, etc. . . . Peking appeals to such arguments as Pan-Asianism and the unity of the yellow race and praises the former imperialist conquests by Japan in order to develop mutual understanding with the leaders of the Japanese Liberal-Democratic party on the basis of the joint struggle for domination in Asia. . . .

The Soviet Union is being regarded as an enemy only because it is the main obstacle to the realization of the great power plans of the Maoists.

FOR FURTHER STUDY

Blackmer, Donald L. M. *Unity in Diversity: Italian Communism and the Communist World.* Cambridge, Mass.: M.I.T. Press, 1968.

Brzezinski, Zbigniew K. *Alternative to Partition.* New York: McGraw-Hill, 1965.

Clubb, O. Edmund. *China and Russia: The "Great Game."* New York: Columbia University Press, 1971.

Collier, David, and Kurt Glaser (eds.). *Elements of Change in Eastern Europe.* Chicago: Regnery, 1968.

Fejto, Francois. *The French Communist Party and the Crisis in International Communism.* Cambridge, Mass.: M.I.T. Press, 1967.

Garthoff, Raymond L. *Sino-Soviet Military Relations.* New York: Praeger, 1966.

Gittings, John (ed.). *Survey of the Sino-Soviet Dispute.* New York: Oxford University Press, 1968.

Griffith, William E. (ed.). *Communism in Europe: Continuity, Change, and the Sino-Soviet Dispute.* Vol. II. Cambridge, Mass.: M.I.T. Press, 1966.

Halpern, Morton H. (ed.). *Sino-Soviet Relations and Arms Control.* Cambridge, Mass.: M.I.T. Press, 1967.

Littell, Robert (ed.). *The Czech Black Book.* New York: Praeger, 1969.

London, Kurt (ed.). *Eastern Europe in Transition.* Baltimore: Johns Hopkins Press, 1966.

Remington, Robin A. (ed.). *Winter in Prague: Documents on Czechoslovak Communism in Crisis.* Cambridge, Mass.: M.I.T. Press, 1969.

Salisbury, Harrison E. *War Between Russia and China.* New York: Norton, 1969.

Strong, John W. (ed.). *The Soviet Union Under Brezhnev and Kosygin.* New York: Van Nostrand Reinhold, 1971.

Sugar, Peter F., and Ivo J. Lederer (eds.). *Nationalism in Eastern Europe.* Seattle: University of Washington Press, 1969.

Vali, Ferenc A. *The Quest for a United Germany.* Baltimore: Johns Hopkins Press, 1967.

Whelan, Joseph G. *World Communism, 1967–1969: Soviet Efforts to Re-Establish Control.* Washington, D.C.: Government Printing Office, 1970.

Wolfe, Thomas. *Soviet Power and Europe, 1945–1970.* Baltimore: Johns Hopkins Press, 1970.

Zartman, I. William (ed.). *Czechoslovakia: Intervention and Impact.* New York: New York University Press, 1970.

10
the united nations in soviet diplomacy

The Soviet Union joined the United Nations as an act of accommodation and self-preservation, not out of conviction. A number of unpromising determinants shaped the Soviet attitude toward the United Nations: Moscow's previous, bitter experience with the League of Nations; its fundamentally hostile attitude toward international organizations, rooted in the ideological belief that they are controlled and manipulated "by monopoly capital" for the perpetuation of Western bourgeois influence; Stalin's xenophobia; and the imperial nature of Soviet objectives in Eastern Europe. Nonetheless, the Soviet Union joined to ensure that the United Nations would not be converted into a militant, anti-Soviet coalition. Its participation was predicated on the assumptions that the United Nations would function primarily as an instrument to handle specific political and security problems, and that the ultimate responsibility for the maintenance of international peace and security would devolve upon the permanent members of the Security Council—the five Great Powers: the USSR, the United States, Great Britain, France, and China. In effect, Moscow envisaged a peacetime extension of the wartime condominium of the United States, Great Britain, and the Soviet Union. As the price for its acceptance of the UN Charter, the USSR insisted on the inclusion of the veto power in the Security Council and the provision that amendments to the Charter be subject to the approval of the five permanent members. (To keep Soviet behavior in the United Nations in perspective, it is important to recall that inclusion of the veto power was absolutely essential for the United States Senate's ratification of the UN Charter.) As a consequence of the diplomatic bargaining that accompanied the drafting of the Charter, the Soviets acquiesced to the establishment of the Economic and Social Council (ECOSOC) as one of the integral UN bodies and to the UN's assumption of economic and social responsibilities, which have over time become as prominent—even more so, argue the Soviets—as the political and security activities of the United Nations.

Soviet behavior in the United Nations has evolved in response to changes in the perceptions and policies of the Soviet leaders and to changes in the international system and in the United Nations itself. Soviet interest has focused on a number of areas: (a) political and security questions, including UN peacekeeping and peace observation activities; (b) disarmament (see Chapter XI); (c) decolonization; (d) economic development; and (e) organizational questions.

Political and Security Questions

Central to any understanding of the Soviet position during the 1945–1953 period is full appreciation of the bipolarizing impact that intensifying Cold War animosities had on international alignments. From the First Session of the Security Council in January 1946 when the USSR was severely criticized for its failure to withdraw Soviet troops from Iranian territory in accordance with the treaty signed in January 1942 between Iran and the Allied powers, Moscow felt its isolated minority position in the United Nations. It directed its main attention to issues directly affecting Soviet interests and used the veto extensively as a political corrective to American-organized, overwhelming anti-Soviet majorities. The Soviet representative cast his first veto on February 16, 1946, and cast eight more before the year was over. Most early Soviet vetoes dealt with the admission of new members, a perennial issue throughout the first decade of the United Nations. A noted Soviet scholar, G. I. Morozov, dismissed Western criticisms of the Soviet Union for allegedly "abusing the right of veto":

In the past, the Soviet Union used its right of veto most in connection with the vote on the admission of new members. This was due to the unfair approach to this issue by the Western powers which for many years opposed the admission to the U.N. of certain socialist states, although this militated against the principles of the U.N. Charter and the interests of international cooperation which can be promoted by the U.N. only if it is a truly universal organization. The Soviet Union's efforts finally led at the Tenth General Assembly [1955] to the simultaneous admission of sixteen states, including a number of socialist countries.

The proposal to abolish the veto is often heard in the West, but there is no likelihood that the Soviet Union (or any Great Power) would sanction such a change. Soviet Foreign Minister V. M. Molotov justified the veto right in a speech before the United Nations on September 14, 1946 (reading 54), and the defense has subsequently been repeated on many occasions.

Stalin's main interest in the activities of the United Nations was making sure that they would not be directed against the USSR or its satellites. Intent on Sovietizing Eastern Europe, Moscow thwarted all UN efforts to extend economic recovery to Eastern Europe as part of its policy of eliminating Western influence; it denounced UN reports implicating the communist governments of Bulgaria, Albania, and Yugoslavia for their role in abetting the Greek civil war; it refused to permit any UN investigation of violations of human rights in Hungary, Romania, and Bulgaria; and it tried to keep the UN's authority to act in any sphere narrowly defined. Stalin, however, was unable to prevent the West from using UN instrumentalities to achieve the resolutions that it favored in the crises in Iran, Indonesia, and Greece. He underestimated, in a way his successors have not, the capacity of the United Nations for effective intercession in international crises.

In January 1950, the USSR abruptly walked out of the Security Council, the General Assembly, and the other UN bodies over the question of Chinese representation; it argued that the Chinese People's Republic, not the Kuomintang regime of Chiang Kai-shek, was the legitimate government of China and should be seated in the Security Council, and it declared a boycott of the UN until Communist China's admission was procured. The resultant absence of the Soviet Union at the time of the North Korean aggression on June 25, 1950, enabled the Security Council to pass resolutions calling for the cessation of hostilities, the withdrawal of North Korean forces from South Korea, and the rendering of all possible assistance to South Korea by UN members. Caught off guard by the energetic American leadership and UN response—no doubt because of reliance on historical analogy with the League of Nations' ineptness in handling instances of aggression—the Soviet Union returned to the UN on August 1, 1950, too late to block UN authorization of a police action to repel the aggression and "restore international security in the area."

The Western powers, however, realized that the Security Council's decisiveness had been possible only because of the absence of the Soviet delegate and obtained approval in the General Assembly on November 3, 1950, for the Uniting for Peace Resolution. This stipulates that if the Security Council fails, because of the lack of unanimity of its five permanent members, to act in a situation threatening international peace and security, the General Assembly itself may discuss the problem and recommend appropriate measures, including the use of armed forces. The effect of this American proposal was a de facto amendment of the Charter that thrust the General Assembly more prominently into the sphere of security affairs. The Soviet Union condemned the resolution on the ground that the Security Council is the sole body responsible under the Charter for initiating and implementing peacekeeping measures and that the assumption of such authority by the General Assembly is illegal.

The Soviet Union has not been averse to the implementation of the Uniting for Peace Resolution in practice, though in principle it deplores the allegedly unconstitutional assumption of authority. At the time of the combined British, French, and Israeli attack on Egypt in late October 1956 and the paralysis of the Security Council because of the British and French veto, the Soviet government supported the General Assembly's intervention and the creation of the United Nations Emergency Force (UNEF), though it objected to the financing of the peacekeeping operation by assessments on all UN member-states. The Soviet Union, however, bitterly opposed the General Assembly's attempted interjection into the Hungarian crisis of November 1956. It argued that the fighting in Hungary was purely an internal affair, despite the presence of 5,000 Soviet tanks and 250,000 Soviet troops, and came under the domestic jurisdiction of the Hungarian government. Accordingly, Moscow invoked Article 2, paragraph 7, of the UN Charter, which says that the United Nations shall not "intervene in matters which are essentially within the domestic jurisdiction of any state" nor shall it "require members to submit such matters to settlement." Moscow does not consider developments in Eastern Europe as coming within the UN's sphere of competence. For a brief period in the early summer of 1960 the USSR approved of the United Nations Peacekeeping Operation in the Congo (ONUC), but reversed itself when the possibility of acquiring a foothold in the Congo disappeared. It does not oppose the existence of a United Nations Force in Cyprus (UNFICYP), created in March 1964 to keep the Greek and Turkish Cypriots separated, in part because the operation has been financed by voluntary contributions and in part because the USSR has been trying to improve relations with Greece, Turkey, and Cyprus.

The attitude of the Soviet Union, in particular, on the financing of peacekeeping operations precipitated a major financial crisis in the UN. At issue was the Soviet conception of what should be the outer limits to political and economic commitments by UN organizations. Specifically, the USSR has refused to pay its assessed share of the UNEF and ONUC operations on the ground that they are not legal because the expenditures were authorized by the General Assembly and not the Security Council. It holds that the Charter invests the Security Council with the sole responsibility for defining the terms, including the financial terms, under which armed forces may be employed by the

United Nations to maintain international peace and security; to substitute the General Assembly or the UN Secretariat for the Security Council is to undermine the principle of Great Power unanimity that is embodied in the Charter and that must be controlling in situations involving the use of armed forces on behalf of the United Nations. Moscow dismissed the July 1962 advisory opinion of the International Court of Justice, which held that the UNEF and ONUC operations were legitimate expenses of the United Nations and thus subject to the budgetary authority of the General Assembly, as devoid of legal value (since advisory opinions are not binding) and as improperly effecting a fundamental change in the Charter. In company with other countries, for example, France and the Arab countries, the USSR has insisted that full financial responsibility for the Middle East and Congo operations must be borne by the countries most directly responsible for their having been undertaken by the United Nations.

The financial difficulties assumed crisis proportions in late 1964, at the nineteenth session of the General Assembly, when the United States delegation contended that Article 19 of the UN Charter should be invoked against delinquent countries. Under this Article a nation that falls two years behind in paying its assessments "shall have no vote in the General Assembly." With Moscow threatening withdrawal from the United Nations—having refused to pay its assessment in the regular UN budget for activities it considers "illegal"—the General Assembly adjourned in February 1965 without debating the issue. The crisis passed soon thereafter because the United States, sensing the reluctance of the membership to implement Article 19, decided not to press the issue. From time to time, Moscow has indicated that it would make a "voluntary contribution" to help ease the UN deficit caused by peacekeeping expenditures, but has yet to do so. A Special Committee of Thirty-three nations has been at work since 1964 trying to find a way out of the impasse on financing peacekeeping operations. Moscow shows no signs of any willingness to modify its position, which was set forth in a memorandum on March 16, 1967 (reading 55).

The future of United Nations peacekeeping operations has been thrown into question by the events of 1967. In 1957, in the aftermath of the Suez crisis of October 1956, UNEF forces were stationed in Gaza and the Straits of Tiran and, for one decade, maintained an uneasy truce between the Egyptians and the Israelis; but Egypt's summary termination of the UNEF presence in mid-May 1967 set in motion the chain of events that triggered the Arab-Israeli war of June 5–10, 1967. Thus far, attempts to find a new mediatory role for the United Nations in this volatile area have failed. Moscow's pro-Egyptian partisanship makes it politically unlikely that Israel will accept any plan involving the use of Soviet troops; and Moscow's unyielding opposition to financing peacekeeping forces by regular assessments further weakens the UN's potential for effective action.

Moscow is not interested in a strong United Nations. Under Khrushchev and Brezhnev it has become an adroit participant in many UN activities with the aim of advancing Soviet interests. The Soviet penchant for making noble proposals with little regard for their implementation ties in with Moscow's tactics of politicizing the United Nations, of polarizing alignments, and of isolating the West from the developing countries of Africa, Asia, and Latin America. The USSR encourages tendentious proposals on anticolonialism, but refuses to support their implementation with increased authority, money, or arms for relevant UN bodies. Seeking to mobilize international opinion against the United States in Vietnam, it urged the General Assembly's adoption in 1966 of a Declaration on the Inadmissibility of Intervention in the Domestic Affairs of States, but in August 1968 ruthlessly invaded Czechoslovakia, indifferent to world opinion and undeterred by possible criticism in the United Nations. It has long called for a definition of aggression; in 1952 it declared in the United Nations that the establishment of a blockade should be deemed an act of aggression on the part of the initiator of the blockade—but it demanded that the UN declare Israel the aggressor in the June 1967 war, overlooking the fact that the UAR by its imposition of a blockade of the Straits of Tiran on May 21, 1967, had precipitated an Israeli response. The Soviet Union declaims the need for safeguarding human rights, but brought pressure on Secretary-General U Thant to order UN Information Centers abroad (specifically, the Center in Moscow) to stop accepting individual petitions to the United Nations for redress of discriminatory treatment. It calls for strengthening international security, but will not support a stronger UN.

The Soviet Union opposes the expansion of UN activities and insists that the present Charter is flexible enough for any necessary modifications (reading 56). It apparently intends the UN to remain a forum in which it can advance Soviet views, render support to non-aligned countries on issues not affecting the Soviet Union, and embarrass the West. However, with the admission of Communist China to the UN in November 1971 a change in strategy may be required. The Soviet Union can no longer keep intra-Communist world differences from being aired in the United Nations: Communist China has already attacked Moscow for its "collusion" with the United States to arrange a settlement of the Middle East conflict; and in December 1971 it denounced the Soviet Union for vetoing resolutions designed to halt the Indo-Pakistani war and for thereby protecting the "Indian aggressors." The Soviet Union will find Communist China a formidable opponent in the UN.

Decolonization

The process of decolonization has now been virtually completed, but in the early postwar years the issue of independence for colonial areas occupied a central place in UN deliberations. From the beginning Moscow staked out a position in the UN debates that placed it in the vanguard of the anticolonialist movement. Such ambitions as it had in 1945 to become the administering authority for one of the trusteeships that were to be established for former Italian colonies were blocked by the United States. Nonetheless, the Soviet Union joined the new nations in bringing pressure through the United Nations for the dismantling of the remainder of Western Europe's overseas empires. During the 1945–1955 period, when countries such as India, Burma, Ceylon, Pakistan, and Indonesia became independent, the Soviets were passive observers. They were precluded from immixing themselves in the decolonization process by geographical distance, ignorance of local conditions, isolation in the UN, and the absence of meaningful contacts with Asian national-liberation leaders, most of whom were educated in Paris and London. They could and did offer moral support, rhetorical encouragement, and unsolicited advice, but little else.

By the late 1950s, as the anticolonial movement became increasingly militant, Moscow initiated its policy of expanding Soviet influence in the Afro-Asian world, with a view toward hastening the end of Western domination and establishing a permanent Soviet presence. It was quick to offer aid to Guinea and Algeria, which were particularly receptive because of the difficult circumstances under which they obtained their independence from France. In 1960, seventeen new nations, sixteen of them from Africa, joined the United Nations. Premier Khrushchev shrewdly utilized this situation to propose a declaration—subsequently adopted in a modified version—calling for the granting of independence to all colonial countries and peoples. The abstention by the Western powers enhanced the political impact of the Soviet proposal among the Afro-Asian leaders.

In 1961 the Soviet Union again lay claim to a bold initiative, subsequently approved in revised form by the General Assembly, namely, the establishment of a Special Committee of Twenty-four (formally known as the Special Committee on the Situation with Regard to the Implementation of the Declaration on the Granting of Independence to Colonial Countries and Peoples) to bring decolonization to a successful completion. Decolonization efforts now center on Southern Africa. Under the leadership of the African states, the Committee has militantly pressed for an end to apartheid in South Africa and for the independence of the

Portuguese colonies, Rhodesia (Zimbabwe) and South-West Africa (Namibia). With Soviet bloc encouragement, the Committee has, at various times, called on Britain to use military force to overthrow the white-minority Rhodesian government (which proclaimed itself independent of Britain on November 11, 1965); demanded the dismantlement of military bases in all colonial territories; and engaged in abusive attacks on the United States and Great Britain, resulting in the withdrawal of the two Western powers from the Committee in January 1971. Moscow votes for the most radical Afro-Asian resolutions in the General Assembly (where they are recommendatory only), but in the Security Council shies away from upholding the demands of the militants for action under the Uniting for Peace Resolution. It cultivates its image as an ardent anticolonialist power, but opposes any broadening of UN operational responsibilities and, coincidentally, any increase in the financial demands on member-states. For Moscow, a residual colonial issue can go a long way politically.

Economic Development

During the Stalin period, the Soviet Union did not contribute "one red ruble" to UN programs designed to promote the development of the new nations. Soviet delegates criticized the Western emphasis on agriculture and light industry, insisting, oblivious of the resource base of developing countries, that only heavy industry could make the countries truly independent. They opposed all forms of direct investment, saying that it led inevitably to political interference, but refused to support the creation of a fund that would instead disburse loans and credits, allegedly because the amounts contemplated were inadequate to the task. Stalin's policy of deliberate isolation of the East from the West dictated Soviet policy of nonparticipation in any of the UN economic and technical assistance operations.

In July 1953 Soviet leaders ended this damaging legacy and began to contribute to UN technical assistance programs. They sought thereby to make Soviet bilateral aid, which they were then starting to dangle before developing countries, respectable and desirable. Their courtship of developing countries, in turn, led them to pay more attention to UN discussions of how best to assist the development programs of Afro-Asian nations. However, Moscow is more interested in image building than in nation building. It opposed the view favored by developing countries that aid should be given primarily in the form of grants and insisted that the problem "could not be solved by the creation of a charitable society": what was required was "an organization capable of development, which could renew and expand its resources." But neither the establishment of the Special Fund in 1959 nor the UN Capital Development Fund in 1966 brought forth any generous Soviet response. Judging by its niggardliness toward UN development programs, Moscow is interested merely in conveying an impression of concern for developing countries and in dominating the proceedings and headlines of international organizations with its proposals and resolutions. Soviet voluntary contributions (most UN development programs are financed by contributions, not assessments) are minimal, the price Moscow pays to play power politics in the United Nations.

From the earliest discussions in UN organs, Soviet delegates have argued to sympathetic delegates that "the principal source of means for the economic development of underdeveloped countries should be their own exploitation of their natural resources and natural wealth." The elites of these countries find the Soviet diagnosis of their economic backwardness plausible, sufficiently familiar in essentials to be readily accepted, and comforting to believe, as it relieves them of any responsibility for their present malaise and blames instead imperialist rule, exploitation of national wealth by foreign monopolies, forced dependence upon a single crop, and lack of industry. However, after almost two decades of interaction with the Soviet Union, there are few non-aligned leaders today who are prepared to accept uncritically Soviet assurances that an emphasis on heavy industry, nationalization of all foreign-controlled enterprises, and central planning will produce the desired economic "takeoff."

The Soviet delegation also stressed the importance of the expansion of international trade and the stabilization of primary commodity prices, upon which the developing countries rely for most of their export earnings. In 1954 it supported, over American opposition, the establishment of an eighteen-nation UN Commission on International Commodity Trade to explore possibilities of stabilizing prices of raw materials; and in 1955, in an important reversal of an earlier policy, Moscow came out in favor of creating a UN agency for trade cooperation. With developing countries understandably anxious over their growing foreign trade predicament and the unsettling effects of fluctuations in international commodity prices, Moscow had a field day.

At the initiative of the developing countries, the United Nations convened a Conference on Trade and Development (UNCTAD) in 1964 and again in 1968. The conferences were intended to promote foreign trade, lower tariffs to the advantage of developing countries, stabilize commodity prices, and obtain more favorable terms of trade for the new nations. For all its oft-declared sympathy for the plight of the developing countries, the Soviet Union has not altered its commercial practices: Soviet foreign trade organizations exact high prices for their products (except where political considerations are controlling and they are ordered to sell at a low price); they buy primary products at the lowest possible prices and will not increase their purchases (e.g., of cocoa beans or coffee) to assist the producing countries in disposing of large surpluses; and the terms of trade are often less favorable to the developing countries than those offered by the Western countries. By its behavior the Soviet Union has been moved from the sympathetic spectators' box and placed squarely in the dock with the other wealthy, highly developed industrialized nations.

The contrast between Soviet declarations and Soviet deeds has not been lost on most Afro-Asian countries. On the one hand, since 1955 the Soviets have pressed for the establishment of an international organization that would promote regional and interregional trade; on the other hand, they have preferred, in practice, that developing countries negotiate bilateral agreements with the Soviet Union and other bloc countries, on the grounds that long-term bilateral agreements "ensured stability, certainty, and reliability in trade relations and contributed to the implementation of economic development plans." A number of developing countries have had sobering trade experiences with the Soviet bloc and would prefer markets in the West. But as long as their alternative to bilateral agreements with the Soviet bloc is no trade at all, they will sell and buy where they can.

Along with others, the Soviet government has recognized that contamination and pollution of the environment—the unanticipated consequences of industrialization and economic development—have reached crisis proportions. It favors forms of cooperation for improving the environment, but contends that they "should not be supranational, an approach many Western proposals actually suggest"; and it repeatedly cautions against turning the United Nations into "some kind of philanthropic society." At the Twenty-fifth Session of the General Assembly, in a speech assessing the achievements and challenges of the UN (reading 57), Foreign Minister Andrei Gromyko mentioned merely in passing, in one paragraph, the need to promote economic and social progress in the Third World. Clearly, these functions are of secondary importance in the Soviet view of what UN priorities should be.

Organizational Issues

With the exception of its expressed hostility to Secretary-General Trygve Lie during the early stages of the Korean war, the USSR paid little attention to the Secretariat during the Stalin period. Until 1960 Moscow assigned few Soviet nationals to the secretariats of international organizations, a reflection of its general depreciation and lack of understanding of their value in advancing Soviet interests. Not until

Khrushchev's troika proposal at the 1960 session of the General Assembly did Moscow begin to assign more of its nationals to a wide range of policy-making posts in international organizations.

The failure of the Soviet Union to gain a foothold in the Congo during the unrest that accompanied independence (June 1960) turned Khrushchev against Secretary-General Dag Hammarskjold, for his allegedly partisan handling of the ONUC peacekeeping mission. Speaking before the General Assembly on September 23, 1960, Premier Khrushchev attacked the Office of the Secretary-General and the entire concept of an impartial international civil service. He recommended replacement of the Secretary-General by a three-man directorate, representing the three political blocs—Western, communist, and non-aligned—and justified the proposal in terms of the UN's need to reflect the changed alignment of political forces in the world. The Afro-Asian nations, however, saw that the troika would give the USSR a veto over Secretariat activities with which it disagreed and refused to back the Soviet stand.

The Soviet government does not accept the validity of the concept of an impartial international civil service nor the assumption that men can act independently and impartially in the interest of the United Nations. Soviet leaders, conditioned by their ideological outlook, do not believe that individuals will make decisions that contravene their class or political interests. On one occasion Khrushchev said that he "would never accept a single neutral administrator. Why? Because while there are neutral countries, there are no neutral men."

The Soviet Union has long espoused the principle of universality of membership in the United Nations, including of course the seating of Communist China. It also has generally favored accreditation of all nongovernmental organizations to all international organizations, but there have been exceptions. For example, since the 1967 Middle East war, it has joined with Arab delegations in trying to deprive Jewish nongovernmental organizations of accreditation with the UN Economic and Social Council. Parliamentary in-fighting and tactical maneuvering are the stuff of which Cold War skirmishes are made in UN organizations.

On organizational issues, the Soviet Union has usually tailored its position to the sentiments prevailing among the developing countries. But no hard and fast generalizations should be made, as is clear from the opposition of most developing countries to radical Soviet demands for the restructuring of international secretariats. Moscow also incurred the annoyance of the African states for its intransigence on the issue of expanding the membership of the Security Council (from 11 to 15) and the Economic and Social Council (from 18 to 27). From 1955 to 1965 action on increasing the membership of these bodies foundered on

Soviet insistence that changes in the size of either body required amendment of the UN Charter and approval by the five permanent members of the Security Council; since Communist China was not represented, no steps, said the Soviets, could be taken. (The Western powers, too, dragged their feet on this issue, though for different reasons.) In late 1963, the Afro-Asians approved two draft amendments to the Charter and submitted them to the Security Council. After almost two years of effective lobbying, they persuaded the Great Powers to go along, and the expansion of the two organs went into effect in the fall of 1965.

Evolving Soviet Policy

Eschewing the negativism of the Stalin period, Moscow has adapted to the UN pattern of bloc politics by siding with the nonaligned nations against the West and by actively cultivating their support for Soviet resolutions and policies. But, as in Stalin's day, the USSR opposes expansion of UN authority in the economic, financial, and social realms and insists upon concentration on political and security issues, with decisional authority vested in the Security Council. It uses the United Nations for establishing contacts with officials from developing countries and for gaining a wide audience for Moscow's views. As one Soviet writer observed, "The UN General Assembly is the world's highest political rostrum. . . . Everything said in the Assembly goes round the world and is commented upon everywhere, generating fresh currents of thought among men and working on their frame of mind." Moscow uses UN forums to promote its version of peaceful coexistence, but is not inclined to use the UN as an instrument for settling Great Power disputes. On major questions, Moscow (like Washington) prefers to negotiate bilaterally with its superpower rival.

The USSR, the UN, and the Veto

54/Soviet Defense of the Veto Power   *September 14, 1946*

V. M. MOLOTOV

An international organization, confronted with the serious tasks of struggling for the peace and security of nations, was for the first time founded at the San Francisco Conference. This organization is built on the unity of all peace-loving Powers with the purpose of protecting universal peace.

It is precisely the right of the veto which was granted to the five Great Powers in the Security Council that is the chief element of the principle of this organization. According to the United Nations Organization's Charter, the veto means that in all important questions concerning the interest of peace, the United States of America, Great Britain, the Soviet Union, France, and China must act in accord, and the Security Council cannot adopt any decisions on those questions with which any of these powers may not be in accord. That means that the veto prevents a situation in which two or three or even four Powers could agree among themselves and act against one or another of the five chief states.

The veto stimulates the Great Powers to joint work, hampering intrigues of some against others, which undoubtedly conforms to the interests of all the United Nations and to the interests of universal peace.

It goes without saying that this does not eliminate the present disagreements and disputes; however, free and open discussion on disputed questions, when there is the right of veto, provides in the long run a better way for understanding and concessions, for cooperation and agreements. Thus the veto is aimed at benefiting all peace-loving states, large and small, by the actions of the Great Powers.

There was no right of veto vested in the Great Powers in the League of Nations. The League was formally built on the principles of equality of large and small states. Those who now advocate the abolition of the veto are dragging us back from the United Nations Organization to something of the sort of the League of Nations. But it is precisely this which determines the political meaning of those actions as well.

We must recall something concerning the developments of the prewar

Speech by V. M. Molotov, Minister for Foreign Affairs of the USSR, delivered September 14, 1946, at the session of the Committee on Political and Territorial Questions of the Peace Treaty with Italy of the Paris Peace Conference, *excerpts*.

years. The League of Nations was created after the World War of 1914–1918. It was the first experiment in setting up an international organization, and it cannot be recognized as successful. In fact, the League of Nations failed to play a substantial part in defending the cause of peace. The League of Nations failed to become an efficient organization to protect the security of the peoples, and, moreover, it failed to defend even the security of the countries of the Anglo-French group, which enjoyed a dominating influence in that first international organization. How it ended—we know. . . .

In the course of the last war a bloc of Great Powers sprang up, and they took the lead of the democratic countries and routed the aggressor in the West and in the East. As a result of this, it was recognized as necessary to set up a new international organization to defend the peace and security of the peoples. The United Nations Organization appeared, as well as the Security Council and the right of veto. Thereby, an attempt was made to create at last an efficient organization to ensure universal security.

It is precisely the veto that plays the leading part in this. The principle of the veto demands that all the Great Powers display attention with regard to their common interests and the interests of universal peace, hindering the creation of narrow blocs and groups of some Powers against other Powers, and still more hampering opportunity for anyone's bargaining with an aggressor behind the backs and contrary to the interests of peace-loving countries.

What can refusal of the right of veto in the United Nations Organization mean? It is not difficult to guess that it can untie someone's hands for certain actions. Refusal of the right of veto would facilitate, of course, the setting up of narrow groups and blocs among the Great Powers, and in any case would untie the hands of those who oppose a united front of the United Nations in defending the cause of peace.

But we have already tried that path. Along that path we reached the Second World War. That path promises nothing but a disgraceful collapse of the United Nations Organization.

Such plans meet the desires of reactionary circles alone, and help the camp of unbridled imperialists only. They do not conceal that they feel uncomfortable about collaboration with the Soviet State. There are no few people in these circles, of course, who are inclined toward cooking up ever-new anti-Soviet projects. . . .

In our time it is dangerous to ignore the Soviet Union, to forget the importance of its support in matters of peace. This path could be taken only by those who, instead of collaboration with the Soviet Union, prefer to build their calculations on bargains and agreements with a future aggressor, which, of course, has nothing in common with the interests of peace and international security. . . .

A new organization to defend the peace has sprung up after the Second World War. The Security Council has now been authorized to ensure the collaboration of all the Great Powers and at the same time to display undeviating care for the interests of universal peace. No such organization existed in the nineteenth century, nor on the eve of the First or on the eve of the Second World Wars. An international organization has been created which is built on the principle of not allowing neglect, not only of the Soviet Union, but of other peace-loving states as well.

The right of veto is precisely intended for this purpose. Of course the veto is no panacea. Blocs and groups occur now, too, and yet the principle of the veto furnishes a certain basis for the development of collaboration among the Powers in defending the security of nations, no matter how great are the difficulties in this respect. If we really stand for peace and security, we must value this weapon, which is intended to serve such important aims. Among the Powers there are no few differences, of course, on these or other questions, and disputes are inevitable.

Yet we have already more than once found ways of solving disagreements. These ways are not barred to us in the future, either, and especially if we all understand that attempts to dictate the will of one Power or of one group of Powers to other Powers are inconsistent and out of place. We must look ahead and not permit ourselves to be dragged back to a broken trough—the League of Nations.

In this international organization created after the war, we must strive to set up a united front of peace-loving states which will not permit the ignoring of any Power, and which will be aimed against any attempts to resurrect aggressors.

Soviet Policy on UN Peacekeeping Activities

55/Memorandum on United Nations Operations for the Maintenance of International Peace and Security   *March 16, 1967*

Recently the United Nations has been actively discussing the question of United Nations operations for the maintenance of international peace and security with the use of armed forces. One of the major aims of the United Nations, laid down in its Charter, is, as everyone knows, to save succeeding generations from the scourge of war, i.e., the maintenance of international peace and security. Therefore, the interest shown in the way in which the United Nations carries out its tasks in this field is very understandable.

However, there are some powers which, acting under cover of a desire to strengthen the effectiveness of the United Nations in maintaining international peace and security, are actually infringing on the provisions of the U.N. Charter regulating actions taken on behalf of the United Nations for the preservation and restoration of international peace, and especially actions connected with the use of armed forces. What is being referred to is an outright intention to press for proposals to be worked out aimed at revising the most important provisions of the United Nations Charter according to which all questions connected with taking action for the maintenance of international peace and security can be settled only by the Security Council. . . .

The present discussion in the United Nations . . . shows that some of the states [that] are threatened by the encroachment of imperialist powers on their independence and sovereignty feel apprehension lest the United Nations may not be able properly to ensure their security, if the General Assembly is not vested with powers to take decisions, binding on all the member-states of the United Nations, on operations for the maintenance of peace and for the defense of victims of imperialist aggression—operations including the dispatch of armed forces to various areas on behalf of the United Nations. At the same time, the idea is occasionally being expressed that the western powers would not be able to interfere with the adoption of such decisions by the General Assembly, since in the Assembly those powers do not have the right of veto, whereas in the Security Council they do have that right and can therefore thwart the adoption of the aforementioned decisions.

Soviet News, No. 5381 (April 11, 1967), pp. 15–17, *excerpts*.

The Soviet government considers it necessary, in this connection, to declare its stand on this question, so important for the United Nations, of United Nations actions connected with the use of armed force. To begin with, a warning should be given against certain dangerous delusions that the ensuring of the security of lesser countries with the assistance of the United Nations can be based on some foundation other than strict observance of the provisions of the U.N. Charter regulating the use of force on the organization's behalf. In reality, only unswerving observance of the Charter constitutes a real guarantee that the use of armed forces for purposes having nothing in common with the aims and principles of the U.N. Charter or with the intentions of states that would like to make use of those forces to safeguard their security, will be precluded. . . .

The principle of the unanimity of the permanent members of the Security Council in taking decisions concerning the preservation of international peace is important not only, and not so much, for the Soviet Union, which is capable of defending itself from any outside danger, as for the young independent states which are not yet strong enough to do so. The Soviet Union cannot agree to the Charter being wrecked or to having questions connected with the use of force on the United Nations' behalf, settled by a mechanical majority of votes in the General Assembly, and having this happen, above all, because the imperialist forces can make use of it in their own interests. The right of veto which the Soviet Union has is an important guarantee of the defense of the independence and sovereignty of lesser states. The Arabs and other independent countries know from their own experience how, in the Security Council, the Soviet Union repels the onslaught of imperialist states against young independent countries. Had there been no rule concerning the unanimity of the permanent members of the Security Council, the imperialists could, without difficulty, have used the United Nations for suppressing the national liberation movement of the peoples. . . .

It is common knowledge that, according to the Charter, all decisions connected with the dispatch of United Nations armed forces can be taken only by the Security Council with the consent of all its permanent members. This is a reliable guarantee against armed forces being used, in the name of the United Nations, in the narrow interests, of some state or group of states. If, for instance, there had been no rule concerning the unanimity of the permanent members of the Security Council and the implementation of measures for the maintenance of peace had been decided by a majority vote, then the attempts of certain of the Security Council's permanent members to use armed forces contrary to the interests of other permanent members could in practice have led only to one result—war. Naturally, no international intergovernmental organization can be or should be the initiator of a new war, and thereby its own grave-digger. The sponsors of the United Nations realized this full well as long ago as 1944–1945, when they were working out the United Nations Charter, and, having exerted immense efforts in their attempts to reach a mutually acceptable decision, they found a way out in providing the permanent members of the Security Council with the right of "veto." . . .

There is another important aspect of this question. The adoption by the General Assembly of decisions concerning the use of armed forces on the United Nations' behalf presupposes that the carrying out of corresponding military operations would take place, not under the guidance of the Security Council and its military staff committee, as is stipulated by the United Nations Charter, but under the guidance of the United Nations secretariat. It is not hard to imagine what this could lead to, and has already led to, when corresponding attempts have been made, and this regardless of who has held the post of secretary-general. Even a most authoritative and objective statesman cannot solve problems which should be solved by the states themselves and their governments, in keeping with the Charter.

Everyone remembers, for instance, the negative consequences for the Congo which resulted from the fact that, owing to the efforts of western powers, the United Nations' guidance of the operations in that country was placed in the charge of the U.N. secretariat, instead of the Security Council. As can be seen from the book written by [Conor Cruse] O'Brien, the former U.N. representative in Katanga, all matters connected with the Congo were handled in the United Nations, after that, by the so-called Congo Club, consisting of United States citizens working as officials in the secretariat and grouped around Hammarskjold. In that situation, says O'Brien, it was in fact the United Nations secretariat that took the disgraceful decision which turned the United Nations troops in the Congo into actual accomplices in the murder of Prime Minister Patrice Lumumba, at whose request those troops had been sent to the Congo. As a result of such violations of the United Nations Charter in carrying out the U.N. operations in the Congo, the only forces that benefited from the Congolese tragedy were foreign monopolies. . . .

That is why the Soviet Union has come out, in connection with the question of United Nations armed forces, in favor of increasing the effectiveness of this organization in the maintenance of international peace and security on the basis of strict observance of the U.N. Charter and of use being made of the opportunities latent in that Charter. This stand was expressed in the "Memorandum of the Government of the USSR Regarding Certain Measures to Strengthen the Effectiveness of the United Nations in the Safeguarding of International Peace and Security of July 10, 1964.". . .

The Soviet Union's proposals . . . offer other opportunities, latent in the U.N. Charter, for strengthening the organization's machinery for maintaining and restoring international peace. They provide, among other things, for the Security Council to have an extensive choice of methods of financing, when it is taking decisions concerning the financial aspects of this or that operation. The Council, for instance, can take a decision making the aggressor meet the expenditures for a particular operation, or it can decide to distribute such expenditures among the U.N. member-states, to cover the expenditures by voluntary donations, or to have them paid directly by the parties concerned, etc. . . .

. . . the Soviet government considers it necessary to emphasize once again that any attempts to revise the provisions of the Charter dealing with the use of armed forces on behalf of the United Nations or with the conditions governing the financing of such operations, will come up against a negative attitude on the part of the Soviet Union. The Soviet Union will not remain a passive witness to the United Nations Charter being violated so that certain western powers may be provided with the opportunity to impose upon the General Assembly decisions detrimental to the fundamental interests of the United Nations member-states. Should the U.N. member-states set out on such a path, a situation would develop in which the Soviet Union would be compelled to revise its attitude towards the activity of the United Nations.

A Soviet Critique of "Revisionism" in the UN

56/Against Utilitarianism and Charter Revision

November 1970

V. ISRAELYAN

An unquestionable contribution to the prevention of a new world war has been made by the United Nations. In a number of instances the UN was instrumental in the resolution of certain international conflicts, and it has been a convenient place for conducting bilateral and multilateral consultations on urgent problems of world politics. The UN provides a rostrum for its member states to give a full presentation of their position on virtually all problems of international relations. The organisation

V. Israelyan, "International Security and the United Nations," *International Affairs* (Moscow), No. 11 (November 1970), pp. 72–76, *excerpts.*

played a substantial role in eliminating the shameful system of colonialism, and also in developing international cooperation in various fields and condemning the aggressive policy of imperialism. . . .

Unfortunately the UN plays what is obviously too small a role in the most important area—in the strengthening of international security. The major part of the organisation's activity is in the economic, social, scientific and technical fields. . . .

Some scientists, politicians and ideologists are now saying that it won't be long before the problems of unregulated population growth and increasing pollution will pose an even greater threat to mankind than the arms race. And they use statistics to back up their theses. They point out, for example, that the population of the world had reached 1,000 million only by the year 1830, but that it took only another 100 years for it to increase by another 1,000 million, and then only 30 years to grow to 3,000 million. It is estimated that it will reach 4,000 million by 1975 and about 6,000 million by the year 2000.

Similar uncontrolled processes are predicted in regard to the pollution of man's natural environment. It is estimated that by the middle of the 1980s, air pollution will reduce by half the amount of sunlight reaching the Earth, and the increase in the amount of carbon dioxide in the atmosphere will change the climate. This, in turn, will lead either to a gigantic flood resulting from a polar ice thaw, or to a new ice age.

In view of all this, it is proposed that the UN concentrate its attention primarily on these problems.

At the same time, the representatives of a number of countries have been frankly stating that they view the organisation chiefly from the standpoint of how it can help solve their various economic and social problems. There has even been a tendency to try to grab as much economic aid as possible through the UN and its specialised agencies. An attempt is being made to proclaim the UN's Second Development Decade programme as almost the key issue of UN activity for the 1970s.

This kind of utilitarian-consumption approach to the UN taken by some countries only helps the imperialist forces to distract the organisation from considering urgent political problems and to turn it into a kind of philanthropic agency in arranging aid to the "poor" from the "beneficent rich."

There has been a noticeable increase in recent years in the number of subdivisions and services in the UN Secretariat dealing with economic and social problems. The natural result of this excessive and totally unjustified overloading of the UN with problems far removed from its basic aims and tasks has been an uncontrollable inflation of the organisation's bureaucratic apparatus, duplication and parallelism in the activity of its separate agencies, an avalanche of published documentation, endless logomachy, a steady growth of the budget, etc. For example, in the year 1968 alone, the various bodies of the UN and its specialised agencies held over 6,000 meetings and published over 700,000,000 pages of protocols and documents. The organisation's budget over the years of its existence has increased from $21 million to $168 million.

No one questions the urgency of many social and economic problems for a large group of countries. It would be naive, however, to suppose that these problems, which reflect the complex processes of the socio-economic development of different states, can be solved in some UN committee or sub-committee. They can be solved only on the basis of the general laws of the development of human society discovered by Marxist-Leninist science. Nor is there any doubt concerning the importance to mankind of such pressing problems as overpopulation, pollution, exploration of the ocean floor, etc. International cooperation in these areas is unquestionably important and promising. Yet, unless a lasting peace is assured, international cooperation in any sphere cannot develop successfully. It should be obvious to anyone that if mankind had not been able to prevent a new world war involving the use of thermonuclear weapons and other means of mass destruction, all the other problems, including overpopulation and pollution, would have lost all meaning.

Only when it has achieved a stable peace on earth and strengthened international security, can mankind successfully solve the other problems as well. It is no accident, therefore, that those who want to draw the organisation away from considering effective measures to halt the imperialist policy of aggression and to settle pressing international problems, seek to exaggerate certain other problems in the present development of mankind, particularly those connected with the development of science and technology. The United States and other imperialist powers reckon that if attention is concentrated on the problems indicated, the UN will get even further away from solving the fundamental problems of present-day world politics.

The Soviet Union strongly opposes having the United Nations concentrate its activity on relatively minor issues, thus weakening its efforts in tackling the major problems of the times. To seek to give the UN this orientation means to undermine its prestige as a political organisation. . . .

The Soviet government urges that the UN, whose aims and principles are clearly and precisely stated in its Charter, be strengthened, that its prestige in international affairs be augmented, that its structure be unimpaired, and that its political mechanism be made to function more effectively. Certain other countries, however, bring up with increasing persistence the question of revising the Charter under the pretext of "improving" it, "bringing it up to date," etc.

For many of the representatives who take such a position it has become virtually "good form"—a peculiar fashion—to criticise the Charter and demand its revision. These people bend over backwards to think up all kinds of additions, changes and corrections to the Charter, whereupon each tries to outdo the other in the "originality" of his proposal. In studying these proposals it is hard to say what they reflect more—the absence of an elementary sense of reality in assessing current international relations, or a deliberate wish to undermine the foundations of the United Nations.

A case in point is the report of the American commission to study the organisation of peace published in November 1969, and given wide distribution among the UN member states' missions. The report in essence advocates limiting the sovereign rights and independence of the UN member nations, and agitates for the interference of this organisation in their internal affairs. The authors of the report propose that the General Assembly be vested with the right to adopt declarations in developing the standards of so-called world law, and that the dominant position of the UN Charter be stressed not only over other international agreements, but also over the corresponding constitutional and legislative principles of individual states. It is also proposed to broaden the jurisdiction of the International Court and the International Law Commission.

The authors of the report also consider it necessary to create a whole series of new UN organs: a standing conciliatory committee, a permanent international court of justice, a council on planning and coordination of social development, a scientific research agency and others—to complicate the organisation's already cumbersome structure.

The representatives of a number of countries come out in favour of establishing the post of UN Supreme Commissioner on Human Rights and of making the relevant amendments to the Charter. Of interest in this connection are the records of the US Congress Foreign Affairs Committee devoted to the discussion of UN activity on the occasion of its silver jubilee. It was frankly stated at one of the meetings of this Committee that the establishment of such a post would make it possible to gain access to any region of any country and to conduct negotiations with the corresponding government. There is no doubt that certain imperialist circles connect the establishment of the proposed post with anti-Soviet and anti-socialist propaganda and subversive activity.

A number of states have come up with arguments in favour of re-examining the principle of big power unanimity in the Security Council; they feel that it establishes "dominance of the big powers over the small countries" and "obstructs the UN in the fulfilment of its basic function." According to the above-mentioned American committee on the study of the organisation of peace, the permanent members of the Security Council should be approached with a proposal to limit the right of veto. Being widely discussed in the lobbies of the UN is a proposal to increase the number of members in the Security Council by establishing the institution of "semi-permanent members," or increasing the number of permanent Council members.

Thus, there is no shortage of proposals aimed at revising the UN Charter under the pretext of adapting this basic document to the current international situation. To be sure, cardinal changes have taken place in the international situation since the founding of the UN. But the historical processes that have developed have certainly also been reflected in the activity of the UN. In the past 25 years, the position and influence of the socialist and developing states have been substantially strengthened in the UN. The changes in the correlation of forces in the international arena have affected both the nature of the questions taken up in the UN and the decisions that have been adopted in recent years.

Thus, in line with the substantial increase in the overall number of UN member states, the Security Council and the Economic and Social Council were enlarged, drawing new members primarily from the developing countries. Whenever any acute situations or new problems have arisen, special organs have been formed to consider the specific concrete issues. In the last two years alone, for example, three special organs were created within the Security Council . . . a committee to consider the effectiveness of sanctions against Rhodesia, a subcommittee on Namibia [South-West Africa], and a committee of experts on the question of admitting small states to the UN. Working actively are organs dealing with problems of space, the peaceful use of the sea-bed and the ocean floor and a large number of other problems.

All this refutes any assertions that the UN does not reflect the realities of current international life and that its Charter somehow impedes the organization's effectiveness. The shortcomings and ineffectiveness of the organization, especially in questions of maintaining peace, do not stem from any so-called imperfections of its Charter, but from the fact that the imperialist powers grossly violate the high aims and principles expressed in it.

A characteristic example . . . Both the General Assembly and the Security Council have adopted a number of resolutions on the question of eliminating the remnants of colonialism in the southern part of Africa. But here again as a result of non-compliance with these resolutions by the colonial racialist regimes of Portugal, South Africa and Rhodesia, and the support of the racialists on the part of Britain, the USA and other imperialist states, colonialism has still not been liquidated in the southern part of the African continent. And here again we have a case of gross violation of the aims and principles of the UN by a number of the organisation's members, including certain of the permanent members of the Security Council.

It would be at least illusory, therefore, to suppose that such measures as amending the UN Charter or increasing the number of permanent members on the Security Council will act as some kind of panacea helping to resolve all acute international problems. Such a position can be taken only by those who either ignore the realities of present international life or seek to make political capital.

It must not be forgotten that the UN is an inter-governmental organisation based on the idea of the sovereign equality of states. For this reason, the actual events of world politics and the positions taken by the states on specific concrete international problems are inevitably reflected in the work of the organisation. U Thant noted in one of his statements that when the world is divided, such division has a great impact on the UN, which obviously cannot exist independently of the will of its member nations. It is not through revisions of the Charter that improvement in the organisation's functioning should be sought, but through a strict adherence to the Charter by all members of the organisation, above all the permanent members of the Security Council. Contrived and artificial additions and amendments to the Charter will not strengthen the United Nations. What is required is for all the member states to act in strict accordance with the provisions of the Charter.

In connection with the 25th anniversary of the UN there is broad discussion of the question: what path will the organisation take in the next quarter century? What will be the predominant trends in its activity? In other words, what kind of development will the UN undergo in the future? Forecasts of the most diverse nature are being made, from the extremely utopian, predicting that the UN will become a kind of "super-government" having unlimited rights and powers, to the extremely pessimistic, predicting the organisation's collapse in the near future. Many of the prognosticators commit one basic error: they view the prospects for the UN's development in isolation from the main trends in the development of present-day international relations; they approach the question as if international life and the United Nations Organisation each is going to go its own separate way.

Such an approach cannot withstand criticism. The UN will continue, as it has done in the past, to reflect the correlation of political forces in the international arena, a correlation which, in conformity with the deep socio-economic processes taking place throughout the world in the present epoch, will continue to develop in favour of the forces of peace, democracy and socialism. The influence of these forces on the entire manifold activities of the UN will also grow progressively with time. This circumstance will, in turn, have its effect on increasing the role and the prestige of the UN in all aspects of international relations.

Whither the UN?

57/Speech at the Twenty-fifth Session of the UN General Assembly   *October 21, 1970*

ANDREI GROMYKO

It goes without saying that the UN is not and cannot be above states. It presents the sum total of states and, consequently, the degree of its effectiveness depends on the foreign policies of its members. An organization cannot be better than the policy pursued by its participants. If some states strictly observe in their foreign-policy actions the obligations they have undertaken under the UN Charter while others whose signatures are also attached to the same obligations ignore or even violate them, this cannot but affect the outcome of the organization's work. Whenever the principles of the UN Charter are not observed, the United Nations proves to be incapable of finding a solution of the respective problem, or its resolution lacks authority. But every time the United Nations members direct their joint efforts for promoting peace, the UNO makes an important contribution to improving the international situation.

The UNO has adopted a great many beneficial resolutions. These include the well-known resolutions of the General Assembly in favor of restricting the arms race and of disarmament, the UN Declaration on the Granting of Independence to the Colonial Countries Peoples, the resolutions on recognizing the lawful nature of the struggle of the peoples of colonies for their liberation and on rendering them moral and material support in this struggle, the UN Declaration on the Impermissibility of Interference in Internal Affairs of States . . . The list of wise decisions passed by different UN organs can be continued. . . .

Comparing the UNO successes in the quarter of a century with the instances when it suffered failures, we may draw the conclusion that the greater part of its activity is, on the whole, favorable. Such is the opinion of our country, and it was recently expressed by L. I. Brezhnev, General Secretary of the CPSU Central Committee. He pointed out: "In spite of all its shortcomings and weaknesses, the United Nations Organization has made a useful contribution to the realisation of the goals and principles proclaimed in its Charter. It helped to overcome

Andrei Gromyko, "To Justify the Hopes of Nations," Speech at the Twenty-fifth Session of the UN General Assembly on October 21, 1970 (Moscow: Novosti Press Agency, 1970), pp. 18–22, *excerpts.*

a number of grave international crises. We consider this result an important success for the foreign policy of the Soviet Union, the other socialist countries and all the peaceloving forces of our globe."

We do not close our eyes to the difficulties which the UNO comes up against. But speaking about difficulties, we are not inclined to follow the example of those who are ready to fold their arms and adopt the pose of an outside observer. Neither do we agree in principle with those who propose to revise the UN Charter as a means of overcoming the difficulties. No, this way could only lead to the destruction of the UN structure. The UN Charter has passed the test for strength, and it should not be allowed to be destroyed.

In order to consolidate the United Nations, the Soviet Union deems it proper to proceed differently, to multiply the efforts of all its member-countries, to seek to make it more effective. . . . The development of events in the world today imposes great responsibility upon states and their leaders. In this connection, coordination of the program of con-solidating international security acquires particular significance. . . . The Soviet Union and other socialist states submitted for discussion at the current session of the Assembly a Draft Declaration on Consolidating International Security, in which due account has been taken of the considerations and wishes of many states. Our proposals provide for a whole number of practical steps, ranging from commitments by states to adhere to the principle of the impermissibility of territorial acquisitions through wars to the discontinuance of all military and other acts con-nected with oppression of the liberation movements of colonial peoples and expediting work on defining aggression. Taken together, these measures may considerably improve the international situation.

FOR FURTHER STUDY

Butler, William E. *The Soviet Union and the Law of the Sea*. Baltimore: Johns Hopkins Press, 1971.

Claude, Inis L. *Swords Into Plowshares: The Problems and Progress of International Organization*. 4th ed. New York: Random House, 1971.

Dallin, Alexander. *The Soviet Union at the United Nations*. New York: Praeger, 1962.

Fernbach, Alfred P. *Soviet Coexistence Strategy*. Washington, D.C.: Public Affairs Press, 1960.

Gordenker, Leon. *The United Nations and the Peaceful Unification of Korea: The Politics of Field Operations*. The Hague: Nijhoff, 1959.

Grzybowski, Kazimierz. *Soviet Public International Law: Doctrines and Diplomatic Practice.* Leyden: Sijthoff, 1970.

Higgins, Roslyn (ed.). *United Nations Peacekeeping, 1946–1967: Documents and Commentary.* Vol. I: *The Middle East;* Vol. II: *Asia.* London: Oxford University Press, 1969, 1970.

Jacobson, Harold K. *The USSR and the UN's Economic and Social Activities.* Notre Dame, Ind.: University of Notre Dame Press, 1963.

James, Alan. *The Politics of Peacekeeping.* New York: Praeger, 1969.

Kay, David A. *The New Nations in the United Nations, 1960–1967.* New York: Columbia University Press, 1970.

Kramish, Arnold. *The Peaceful Atom in Foreign Policy.* New York: Harper & Row, 1963.

Lall, Arthur. *The UN and the Middle East Crisis, 1967.* New York: Columbia University Press, 1968.

Lie, Trygve. *In the Cause of Peace.* New York: Macmillan, 1954.

Morozov, G. *International Organization: Some Theoretical Problems.* Moscow: Mysl, 1969.

Ramundo, Bernard A. *Peaceful Coexistence: International Law in the Building of Communism.* Baltimore: Johns Hopkins Press, 1967.

Rubinstein, Alvin Z. *The Soviets in International Organizations: Changing Policy Toward Developing Countries, 1953–1963.* Princeton, N.J.: Princeton University Press, 1964.

_____, and George Ginsburgs (eds.). *Soviet and American Policies in the United Nations.* New York: New York University Press, 1971.

Russell, Ruth B. *United Nations Experience With Military Forces: Political and Legal Aspects.* Washington, D.C.: Brookings Institution, 1964.

Sewell, James Patrick. *Functionalism and World Politics.* Princeton, N.J.: Princeton University Press, 1966.

Shkunaev, V. G. *The International Labor Organization: Past and Present.* Moscow: International Relations, 1969.

Slusser, Robert M., and Jan F. Triska. *A Calendar of Soviet Treaties, 1917–1957.* Stanford, Calif.: Stanford University Press, 1959.

_____. *The Theory, Law, and Policy of Soviet Treaties.* Stanford, Calif.: Stanford University Press, 1962.

Stoessinger, John C. *The United Nations and the Superpowers.* 2d ed. New York: Random House, 1970.

Tornudd, Klaus. *Soviet Attitudes Towards Non-military Regional Cooperation.* Helsinki: Censraltryckeriet, 1963.

11 soviet policy and the dilemma of disarmament

Since 1945 no problem has occupied the attention of the superpowers and the United Nations more than that of disarmament. Concern exists over the population explosion, the pollution of our environment, and the ecological despoliation accompanying industrial progress, but the specter of nuclear annihilation overshadows all else. Efforts to initiate disarmament and establish a viable system of arms control and inspection continue to founder on the divisive realities of international politics. However, a start has been made to contain the more immediate threats inhering in unrestricted nuclear testing and nuclear proliferation. And in response to escalating defense expenditures, domestic pressures, uncertainty arising from new technological advances in weapons systems, the emergence of Communist China as a nuclear power, and pressures from the Afro-Asian and Latin American countries, the Soviet Union and the United States have undertaken Strategic Arms Limitation Talks (SALT) in an attempt to stabilize their strategic arms relationship and prevent a runaway armaments race.

The term "disarmament" is a misnomer. Very little of what goes under the heading of disarmament actually entails a planned and ascertainable reduction of weaponry or armed forces. Rather, most of the issues under discussion relate to the stabilization of arms levels and the limiting of the use and acquisition of nuclear weapons. Conventional forces no longer constitute an important item on the agenda of superpower discussions.

The disarmament question is a combination of interdependent problems, and it cannot be fully understood except against the background of changing power relationships and foreign policy goals. Thus, that the Soviet Union agreed to the SALT talks presumably meant it was satisfied that it had at last caught up with the United States and had achieved an approximate parity in missiles and nuclear weapons; and Soviet policy on nuclear nonproliferation must be seen in the context of its goals in Europe, especially as they relate to preventing West Germany from acquiring nuclear weapons. The specific issues that compose the overall disarmament package can be isolated and analyzed. For instance, there has been discussion of the deployment of an antiballistic missile (ABM) system—that is, a missile designed to intercept and destroy an incoming nuclear warhead before it approaches the target—and of the technical feasibility of detecting Soviet underground nuclear explosions from points outside the USSR. However, any agreement on these issues must rest upon political accommodation, compromise, and trust—elements conspicuously absent from postwar discussions. There exist among national leaders on both sides of the Iron Curtain legitimate differences of opinion over the extent to which national security would be adversely affected by political concessions and over the importance to be attributed to the various components of power: the rate and level of economic development, military strength, the percentage of defense expenditures allotted for research and defense-oriented technological innovation, and so forth. But too rigid an interpretation of the military needs of national security may in time prove to be as unrealistic as the visionary proposals for immediate and universal disarmament.

In the present structure of international power, what kind of disarmament is feasible? Indeed, what is meant by disarmament? Are the differing Soviet and Western plans capable of meaningful negotiation? How will technology affect the possibility of stability in the nuclear weapons balance between the United States and the Soviet Union? What role does Communist China play in the Soviet position on disarmament? What kinds of domestic pressures are felt by Soviet leaders, and how do those pressures influence the range and choice of options that the Kremlin might select in its bargaining with the United States? Does the doctrine of strategic nuclear superiority, which dominated American policy until 1969 when President Nixon substituted the concept of "sufficiency," motivate Soviet policy-makers? These questions are not easily answered, but it is important to reflect upon them.

It is a truism that wars do not happen, they are made by men. Similarly, it is true that though any arms race tends to exacerbate existing tensions, thus adding to the probability of war, the *causes* of war must usually be sought elsewhere. They are rooted in economics, politics, and the *Weltanschauung* of the ruling elite. In this respect, the attitude of a potential aggressor toward its own people, its neighbors, and the international community is invariably more a determinant of war than is the level of armaments. The economic, military, and political condition of a country may be exploited to justify the ambitions of an expansionist-minded elite. To such rulers disarmament negotiations are mere exercises in deception. Has not the diplomat been described as "one who is sent abroad to lie for his country"? However, we must proceed on the assumption, tenuous though it may seem, that national leaders will not resort to all-out nuclear war to attain political objectives as long as acceptable alternatives are available.

Underlying the 1946–1950 period were the American monopoly of atomic weapons and the Soviet preponderance in mobilized military manpower and conventional weapons. During these years Soviet leaders repeatedly called for prohibition of the production and use of nuclear weapons, though refusing to accept Western demands for a suitable system of international control and inspection. A stalemate also developed over establishing limitations on conventional armaments. All these discussions took place against a background of progressively deteriorating relations. As political conflicts sharpened, national positions hardened.

The disarmament question became a prominent issue in UN proceedings at a very early stage. A comprehensive proposal for controlling the atom was offered by the United States at the first meeting of the UN Atomic Energy Commission, in June 1946. Commonly known as the Baruch Plan, it called for the establishment of an international agency to control, own, and operate all nuclear facilities "from the mine to the finished product." The agency's officials were to be international civil servants, standing above politics and having the power to conduct continuous inspection of all phases of the production of fissionable materials, to carry on research in nuclear weapons, and to promote the peaceful uses of atomic energy. The Baruch Plan provided for the eventual destruction of existing nuclear weapons, but *only after* an adequate international inspection system had been set up and an effective system of sanctions free from the veto of any power had been organized by the Security Council. The plan was endorsed in principle by the General Assembly, but Soviet objections prevented any further action.

The Soviets responded along markedly different lines. At the autumn 1946 session of the General Assembly, Foreign Minister V. M. Molotov reversed the American pattern of priorities and called first for the abandonment by the United States of its preeminent nuclear position, the destruction of all nuclear weapons, and the prohibition of their further manufacture or use. Under the Soviet Plan a system of inspection would be established only after these conditions had been met, and the proposed international agency would have only a limited authority to inspect national atomic establishments. It would also be regulated by the Security Council, where the veto power would be operative on all substantive decisions. Molotov attacked the Baruch Plan for its lack of vision and its national egoism:

The American plan, the "Baruch plan," unfortunately suffers from a certain degree of egoism. It is based on the desire to guarantee the United States monopoly possession of the atomic bomb. At the same time, it demands the immediate establishment of control over the production of atomic energy in all countries—a control so shaped as, on the surface, to appear international, while in reality it is designed to secure a veiled monopoly for the United States in this field. Projects of this type are obviously unacceptable, for they are dictated entirely by the narrowly conceived interests of one country, by an impermissible negation of the equality of states and of their legitimate interests.

Moreover, this plan suffers from a number of illusions. Even in the sphere of atomic energy, no single country can count on retaining a complete monopoly. Science and its exponents cannot be shut up in a box and kept under lock and key. It is about time illusions on that score were discarded. Another illusion is the hope that the atomic bomb will have a decisive effect in war. . . . Excessive enthusiasm over the atomic bomb as a decisive factor in future war may lead to political consequences that will bring tremendous disappointment, first and foremost, to the authors of such plans. And finally, it must not be forgotten that atomic bombs on one side may draw a reply in atomic bombs, and perhaps something else to boot, from the other side.

It is impossible to analyze in detail here the statements of the American and Soviet spokesmen at the United Nations or to trace the nuances and shifts in national policy they reflected. However, intensive research casts doubt upon the willingness of the Great Powers to establish in 1946 a workable system of disarmament. Two incidents are ignored by most studies on the disarmament negotiations of this period. First, on November 20, 1946, Molotov, in proposing a comprehensive program of disarmament, did not specifically insist upon a prohibition of atomic weapons, as he had several weeks earlier in his original arms-limitation proposals. This seemed an important preliminary concession that should have invited further exploration. UN delegates regarded this speech as one of the most constructive made by any Soviet spokesman. Western representatives, however, did not comment on Molotov's revised resolution, nor did the Soviets press the issue. Neither party chose to test the intentions of the other.

Second, and perhaps even more intriguing, Molotov stated, on December 4, 1946, that the Soviet Union did not envisage Security Council control (or veto) over the day-to-day operations of inspection commissions that might be established to verify compliance with an adopted program of arms limitation or nuclear disarmament. In his speech before the UN Political and Security Committee of the General Assembly, he held that:

> ... the question of the well-known principle of unanimity operating in the Security Council has no relation at all to the work of the commissions themselves. Consequently, it is entirely wrong to consider the matter in the light that any government possessing the "right of veto" will be in a position to hinder the fulfillment of the control and inspections.
>
> The control commissions are not the Security Council, and, therefore, there are no grounds whatsoever for saying that any power making use of the "right of veto" will be in a position to obstruct the course of control. Every attempt to obstruct the control or inspection carried out in accordance with the decisions taken by the Security Council will be nothing other than a violation of the decisions of the Security Council. That is why talk about a "veto" in connection with control and inspection is devoid of foundation. Such talk cannot be understood as anything other than an attempt to substitute one question for another, as an attempt to evade a straight answer to the question raised regarding the general reduction of armaments.

This speech by Molotov was regarded as a major concession and some agreement appeared possible. But nothing materialized. Indeed, the proposal was ignored by *both* parties. A number of questions remain unanswered. If the Soviets were sincere in their proposal, why did they not elaborate upon it at subsequent UN meetings? Or did Moscow have serious second thoughts about its implications? Why did the Western Powers fail to investigate the Soviet proposal more fully? Had international developments made national policies on disarmament completely rigid by late 1946?

In general, Soviet arms proposals were designed to accord military and psychological advantages to the Soviet Union. First, they enabled the USSR to capitalize on the universal desire for peace. Second, the proposals would have vastly improved the Soviet military position. They demanded, in reality, unilateral disarmament on the part of the United States, which would have relinquished the most powerful weapon in its protective armor without any corresponding decrease in Soviet conventional weapons. Also, they failed to provide a way of checking Soviet technological efforts in the nuclear field because the Soviets refused to submit to an international inspection authority. The trend within the Soviet Union was again toward isolation and secrecy. The years 1946–1947 were characterized by an intensification of cultural conformity, labor discipline, and ideological orthodoxy—a rapid return to the Stalinist excesses of the 1930s, only temporarily eased under the pressure of war.

By early 1947 disarmament prospects faded. The nature of Stalin's objectives in Eastern Europe became clearer and more ominous. Intemperate Soviet attacks on Western proposals were a regular feature of UN sessions. To obtain support abroad for their policies, the Soviet Government launched a global propaganda campaign, calling "for the unconditional abolition of atomic weapons and the branding of any government which first used such weapons against another as guilty of war crimes against humanity." The Soviet-instigated "Stockholm Peace Campaign" of 1950, for example, circulated petitions in virtually every nation in an attempt to exploit Western differences in approach to the disarmament problem. In June the North Korean communists moved across the 38th parallel. Rearmament now overshadowed disarmament proposals.

In October 1950, speaking before the General Assembly, President Truman indicated a willingness to treat as a unit two issues the United States had previously considered as separate and distinct problems, and which the Soviet Union had held to be but phases of the same problem: the control of nuclear weapons and the regulation of conventional weapons. (To add to the confusion, the Soviets reversed their attitude in 1956 and stated there were no cogent reasons for linking the two problems.) However, the tense atmosphere engendered by the aggression in Korea precluded any follow-up until 1952 when, on the eve of armistice in Korea, the UN established a twelve-man Disarmament Commission, consisting of the eleven members of the Security Council and Canada, to replace the separate Commissions on Conventional Armaments and Atomic Energy. The Soviet Union boycotted the Disarmament Commission and its subcommittee in 1957, soon after launching Sputnik, on the ground that they contained a pro-Western majority. To meet Soviet objections and revitalize disarmament talks, the General Assembly expanded the Disarmament Commission in November 1958 to include all members of the United Nations. It was evident from the start that so unwieldy a commission could not negotiate the delicate and complex issues affecting the policies and alliances of the Great Powers. The full commission convened briefly in 1960 and again in 1965. However, the brunt of the negotiations has been handled, first, by a subordinate ten-nation Disarmament Committee, which met from March to June 1960 and was disbanded after the Soviet Union abruptly walked out of the conference on June 27, 1960; and then by a reconstituted seventeen-nation Disarmament Committee (membership was originally planned for eighteen but France refused to participate) which was convened in March 1962 and has since met frequently for prolonged periods. In July 1969 the United States and the Soviet Union agreed, without even consulting other members, to expand to twenty-six the size of the Committee, now referred to as the Conference of the Committee on Disarmament.

America's nuclear monopoly ended in September 1949, when the Soviets exploded their first atomic bomb. On November 1, 1952, the United States detonated the first hydrogen bomb. The USSR followed with a similar success in August 1953. But for over a decade thereafter the United States possessed a commanding superiority in strategic weapons. Many Western experts believe this was the crucial factor in Khrushchev's decision to back down during the Cuban missile crisis of October 1962. Soon afterward, pressed by the military establishment, the Soviet government determinedly pushed its build-up to the point that in early 1969 it achieved a basic parity with the United States in strategic weapons. Today each superpower is deterred by the knowledge that the other has an assured destruction capability (ADC) of between 50 and 80 percent, that is, the ability to destroy from 50 to 80 percent of both the population and productive capacity of the other. A "balance of terror" has been reached.

After Stalin's death, the Soviet leadership, absorbed with internal problems, adopted a more conciliatory approach toward the West. This "thaw" in the Cold War raised expectations in the disarmament field. However, the two sides were far apart. The Soviets insisted that the inspection authority have only "the right to demand of states the necessary information concerning the execution of measures for the curtailing of armaments and armed forces." In other words, no UN inspection team was to be granted access to the Soviet Union. The West, on the other hand, insisted that a carefully supervised inspection system be established *prior* to any actual limitation of nuclear or conventional weapons and that the prohibition of atomic weapons be part of a comprehensive plan of control and inspection.

At the fall 1954 session of the General Assembly, the Soviet delegate, Andrei Y. Vyshinsky, called for the reduction of conventional arms by 50 percent, the establishment of a temporary commission under the Security Council to study methods of controlling atomic energy, and an end to the manufacture of atomic weapons. These proposals provided a basis for negotiation because they avoided an a priori demand for the immediate prohibition of nuclear weapons. Perennially hopeful, the General Assembly revived the activities of the Disarmament Subcommittee. Closed sessions were held in London in the spring of 1955, and the periodic communiques reflected a restrained optimism.

On May 10, 1955, the Soviet Government presented a new series of proposals. Concrete and detailed, they encouraged hopes for the success of the forthcoming Big Four Conference. The proposals called for a gradual reduction of armed forces to fixed levels, the destruction of nuclear weapons after these levels had been reached, and the institution of measures designed to prevent surprise attack. Though recommending the establishment of "control posts at the big ports, railway junctions, motor roads, and in airfields . . . to see that no dangerous concentrations of land, air, or naval forces are effected," they failed to provide the mechanics of an actual inspection system. They also would have subjected to the veto power any decision to use atomic weapons defensively. The Soviet proposals were, nevertheless, important for two reasons: first, they recognized the need to account for nuclear stockpiles and guard against surprise attack; second, they afforded a basis for further negotiation. The stage was set for the Geneva "Summit" Conference of the heads of government in July.

President Eisenhower's "open skies" proposal was the highlight of the Geneva Conference. Its main purpose was to enable the Great Powers to detect and thereby to discourage any concentration of military forces that might be used to launch a surprise attack. Under the proposal each country would carry out a systematic aerial photographing of the other. The Soviet leaders ignored the potentialities of the President's plan because they interpreted it as an entering wedge for United States intelligence-gathering activities and because they were more interested at the time in spreading Soviet influence in the Middle East through shipments of arms to Egypt.

During the Suez and Hungarian crises of October–November 1956, the Soviet government expressed a willingness "to consider the question of using aerial photography in the area in Europe where basic military forces of the North Atlantic Pact are located and in countries participating in the Warsaw Pact to a depth of 800 kilometers to the East and West from the line of demarcation of the above-mentioned military forces, if there is agreement of the appropriate state." The offer of mutual aerial inspection narrowed national positions to a point where a preliminary accord seemed within grasp.

At the 1957 sessions of the Disarmament Subcommittee, the Soviet delegates dropped their demands for the elimination of nuclear weapons and the liquidation of American overseas bases and discussed means of setting up a limited, first-phase arms control plan. Their approach seemed serious and in good faith. Western observers, conditioned by more than a decade of futile negotiating with the Soviet Union, were surprised by the sudden shift in attitude. They speculated that Khrushchev needed a respite from the onerous armament burden, with its drain on manpower and resources, in order to consolidate his position at home, that the Soviet leaders genuinely feared an accidental nuclear conflagration, and that they desired to limit the number of powers possessing nuclear weapons, though they could not openly admit this for fear of antagonizing Communist China. On the other hand, there were many Western experts who regarded the Soviet stand as a tactical maneuver designed to sow political dissension among the NATO powers and bring about the realization of the main Soviet objective in Europe—the disintegration of the NATO defense structure. Whatever the reasons, agreement proved as elusive as ever.

After the failure of the 1957 negotiations, which were the longest and most intensive up to that time, prospects for any accord plummeted. There were too many areas where considerations of national security conflicted with proposals for arms limitation, and there was no consensus among the Great Powers as to what would be feasible, politically acceptable, and militarily secure—all "must" prerequisites for a minimal agreement. Protracted discussions continued in UN disarmament meetings. In 1959, Premier Khrushchev, speaking before the General Assembly, issued his call for general and complete disarmament (GCD)—a theme the Soviet government has propounded ever since. But GCD was a giant step no nation was prepared to take in the current international environment, least of all the Soviet Union, notwithstanding its proposal. With the persistence of political discord in crucial areas, the ability to reach agreement on some initial "confidence-building measures" seemed a precondition for progress in arms control and disarmament. Accordingly, during the 1958–1963 period the superpowers concentrated upon the negotiation of a treaty ending nuclear tests—an aspect of the overall disarmament complex that both had a stake in, if only to halt contamination of the atmosphere by harmful radioactive fallout.

Each side has periodically made concessions, and a number of treaties have come into force: for example, in 1959 the Antarctic Treaty, which contains inspection provisions, forbidding militarization or testing of weapons in Antarctica; in 1963 the Limited Nuclear Test-Ban Treaty, prohibiting nuclear testing in the atmosphere, underwater, or in outer space; in 1967 the Outer Space Treaty, barring the testing or placement of nuclear weapons in space, on the moon, or on other celestial bodies; and in 1970 the Non-Proliferation Treaty (NPT), seeking to limit the number of countries possessing nuclear weapons. Though it was agreement between the superpowers that made these treaties possible, the United Nations, too, contributed to their realization. It must not be forgotten that from the outset the impetus for establishing some degree of arms control came from the smaller states, while the main contenders for world supremacy seemed bent on piling up the largest possible storehouses of sophisticated weaponry. It was also the United Nations that undertook to educate the global constituency to the dangers of what former Secretary of Defense Robert S. McNamara described as "a kind of mad momentum intrinsic to the development of all new nuclear weaponry."

Since the late 1950s diplomatic efforts have concentrated on five issues: (1) limiting nuclear testing, (2) protection against surprise attack, (3) restricting the use of outer space to peaceful purposes, (4) halting the proliferation of nuclear weapons, and (5) since November 1969, limitations on strategic weapons. A brief review of these issues will serve to illustrate the complexities of negotiating disarmament.

Limiting Nuclear Testing

The Soviet Government has been a vocal advocate of a nuclear test ban since it was first proposed by India in 1954. In March 1958, having completed a series of experimental nuclear explosions, Moscow went so far as to announce its unilateral renunciation of further tests. (It was aware at the time of the West's intention to conduct tests during the summer.) By October the Soviets resumed testing, as military considerations apparently outweighed the propaganda advantage accruing from the ban. Prior to March 1958, the United States had rejected proposals calling for a cessation of nuclear tests unless they included a ban on the *production* of nuclear weapons. Moscow countered with the demand that the *use* of nuclear weapons be outlawed. It also stated that linking a test ban with an end to bomb production was not practical, for, while a cessation of tests could be verified, a production cutoff could not. The United States subsequently modified its position and came out in favor of a nuclear test ban for one year, subject to renewal, "provided that the Soviet Union would do the same, that the agreed inspection system is installed and working effectively, and that satisfactory progress is being made in reaching agreement on and implementing major and substantive arms control measures." A one-year moratorium on nuclear testing was agreed upon, effective October 31, 1958, and lasted almost three years.

During the protracted discussions at the Geneva Conference on the Discontinuance of Nuclear Weapon Tests, which opened on that date, national positions differed, *inter alia,* on the voting procedures to be followed by the proposed control commission, the composition and functions of the international observation teams, and the threshold below which underground nuclear explosions could be accurately detected. Both sides made important concessions, and agreement often seemed close at hand. However with the downing of an American U-2 reconnaissance plane over Soviet territory on May 1, 1960, and the subsequent collapse of the Paris Summit Conference, the test-ban negotiations bogged down.

On August 31, 1961, amid mounting tensions over Berlin, Laos, and the Congo, the Soviet government abrogated the informal moratorium without warning and resumed testing in the atmosphere the next day. This was done despite Khrushchev's statement to the Supreme Soviet on January 14, 1960, that the "Soviet Government, prompted by the desire to provide the most favorable conditions for the earliest possible drafting of a treaty on the discontinuance of tests, will abide by its commitment not to resume experimental nuclear blasts in the Soviet Union unless the Western Powers begin testing atomic and hydrogen weapons" and despite the convocation in Belgrade of the first summit conference of nonaligned Afro-Asian countries, a group long opposed to all testing and the target of intensive Soviet attention since the mid-1950s. Khrushchev justified breaking the moratorium on several grounds: for example, the requirements of Soviet security, the inability to agree on the conditions of a treaty, and the testing by France during the time of the moratorium, allegedly with NATO's blessing (reading 58). What Khrushchev did not mention was the intense pressure of the Soviet military to test nuclear weapons. The political leadership could not withstand the arguments by the military that testing was essential to overcome the American lead and to develop a reliable and varied arsenal of tactical nuclear weapons. In other words, the same arguments were probably used in the Soviet Union as in the United States, though in the Soviet Union the individual advocates of testing and resistance to any détente with the West cannot be easily identified.

In the negotiations following the Soviet resumption of nuclear testing, Moscow at first insisted that a nuclear test-ban treaty be made part of a comprehensive agreement on general and complete disarmament along the lines advanced by Premier Khrushchev in his 1959 UN speech. This condition was dropped once the USSR decided that a limited test ban was in its interest. At the last moment the negotiations faltered on the questions of the number of on-site inspections, the composition of the inspection teams, the area where there could be drilling, etc.

But finally, on August 5, 1963, the Treaty Banning Nuclear Weapon Tests in the Atmosphere, in Outer Space, and Under Water was signed in Moscow. This was the *first* concrete result to emerge from post–World War II disarmament negotiations. The treaty does not cover underground nuclear testing because of the inability to agree on an acceptable system of international on-site inspections. The Soviet position is that such inspections are unnecessary because adequate seismographic equipment exists to permit detection and identification from a distance and that on-site inspections would be a front for espionage. The treaty is self-executory: its effectiveness rests on observance by each signatory. In the event of a violation, "each Party shall in exercising its national sovereignty have the right to withdraw from the treaty . . ."

Why did the Soviet Union sign the limited test-ban treaty? According to Khrushchev, the following considerations were controlling: to end the contamination of the atmosphere, to decrease international tension and pave the way for a settlement of the German problem, to slow down the arms race and permit a freezing or reduction of military budgets and a greater attention to domestic problems, and to facilitate the negotiation of an agreement on measures to prevent surprise attack. Four other factors may have been important: first, the urgency, dramatized by the Cuban missile crisis of October 1962, of reaching a détente before accelerating tensions deprived national leaders of control over their own policy actions; second, realization by Moscow (and Washington) that further atmospheric testing was not necessary for national security, that essential military requirements could be met with existing weapons and with expanded underground testing, which is not forbidden by the treaty; third, the rift between Moscow and Peking that led Soviet leaders to place a greater premium on easing tensions with the United States; and fourth, the hope that the treaty might forestall the proliferation of nuclear weapons to other countries, especially to West Germany.

Improved seismological methods in the late 1960s and early 1970s have led former high-ranking United States government officials, such as Dr. Jerome B. Weisner (science adviser to President Kennedy), to suggest that the United States could "with very little risk" to its national security agree to a ban on underground nuclear testing without any on-site inspections. They consider that the potential gains from any clandestine tests below the detection threshold are "sufficiently marginal that any risks on a comprehensive test ban appear slight compared to the risks of proliferation and an ever-escalating arms race supported by massive underground testing."*

Opposed to this view are those American planners who argue for continued testing to ensure the reliability of nuclear weapons on the ground that inadequate knowledge of how weapons perform could have destabilizing consequences for the strategic relationship between the United States and the Soviet Union. Another purpose of testing is to develop a warhead for an ABM system, which is intended to protect the permanent Minutemen missile silos—an essential component of America's nuclear deterrent against any massive Soviet first strike attack. The military consider it essential to have additional underground tests such as the one in October 1971 on Amchitka Island,

* They add that through the use of reconnaissance satellites flying over the Soviet Union at heights of 50 to 100 miles photographs can detect increased radioactivity that would signify secret testing. Advocates of a comprehensive ban insist that with improved detection methods it is now possible to differentiate between very low yield nuclear explosions—of the 1–10 kiloton range (a kiloton is the equivalent of 1,000 tons of TNT) —and natural earthquakes.

Alaska.* Finally, the military insist that nuclear explosions of less than 10 kilotons (equivalent to half the explosive power of the atomic bombs dropped on Hiroshima and Nagasaki in August 1945) can be successfully tested in secret. The scientific arguments are part and parcel of the political and military considerations that influence decision makers.

Protection Against Surprise Attack

Since 1955 various conferences have been convened to study measures for reducing the danger of surprise attack, but have failed to reach any agreement. As the military capability of the Great Powers increases, fear of a crippling first strike looms ever larger in national chancelleries. Advances in military technology give rise to conflicting assessments of areas of possible compromise; in some instances they make agreement less imperative, in others, even more so. Thus, on the one hand, fear of surprise attack has been allayed by the development of space satellites and high altitude photography, which enables each superpower to gather reliable intelligence information about the troop dispositions, missile emplacements, and military testing of the other. These national means of open, though unofficial, verification of the military movements of the adversary reduce the urgency for international inspection. On the other hand, technological developments such as FOBS and MOLS only engender new anxieties over national security. FOBS (Fractional Orbital Bombardment System) refers to a missile with a nuclear warhead that can be placed in a very low earth orbit and released before it completes one orbit around the earth; FOBS allow for much less warning time and do not technically violate the Outer Space Treaty (forbidding the use of weapons of mass destruction in outer space) because they do not make one complete orbit of the earth. MOLS (Manned Orbiting Laboratories) would give the country able to establish such space stations decided military advantages.

A corollary of the concern over surprise attack is the attention given to preventing misunderstandings and inadvertent miscalculations in moments of crisis. A pioneering agreement establishing a direct com-

* The five megaton explosion (equivalent to five million tons of TNT) was designed to help develop an effective ABM system, by testing the effect of energy output "in various forms such as thermal radiation, neutrons, fission products, X-rays, gamma rays, and shock waves" on incoming missiles and nuclear warheads and by helping to devise ABM warheads that would have maximum X-ray output (which would damage the heat shield of the incoming missile and, if strong enough, even cause the shield to disintegrate so that the nuclear warhead would burn on reentry into the earth's atmosphere) and a low fission output of radioactivity to reduce radar blackout effects that would hamper radar units guiding the ABM to their targets—the incoming ICBMs.

munications link between Moscow and Washington was signed in Geneva on June 20, 1963, and became operational on August 30, 1963. This "hot line" teletype link is intended for use only in situations requiring immediate and direct communications between the top political leaders of the two countries. It was used for the first time on June 5, 1967, when the Soviet Government wanted to ascertain American intentions regarding the Arab-Israeli war.

The first agreements to crystallize from SALT dealt with measures to lessen the fear of surprise attack and the danger of nuclear war through inadvertence. The two agreements were signed on September 30, 1971, by the United States and the Soviet Union. One agreement calls on each party to notify the other immediately "in the event of an accidental, unauthorized or any other unexplained incident involving a possible detonation of a nuclear weapon"; it calls for advance notification of planned missile launches "if such launches will extend beyond its national territory in the direction of the other party." What is intended is prevention of an overreaction by one side to an accidental launch of a nuclear weapon by the other side. The second agreement improves on the June 20, 1963, hot line arrangement by providing for a direct communications link via communications satellites. Special communications stations will be constructed in each country, probably by 1973, and used exclusively for the emergency voice and teletype transmissions between the two governments.

Restricting Outer Space to Peaceful Purposes

In an age when man has walked on the moon, lived in space for weeks at a time, and launched unmanned probes to Venus and Mars, the military implications of peaceful explorations of outer space are never out of mind. Each superpower fears technological breakthroughs by the other that could upset the current relationship in the neck-and-neck missile race. A decided military advantage would accrue to the first nation developing a reliable ABM defense or constructing missile-mounted space platforms that would reduce even further the number of minutes required to deliver a thermonuclear weapon thousands of miles.

Former UN Secretary-General Dag Hammarskjold expressed the hope that the General Assembly would "find the way to an agreement on a basic rule that outer space, and the celestial bodies therein, are not considered as capable of appropriation by any state, and that it would further affirm the overriding interest of the community of nations in the peaceful and beneficial use of outer space and initiate steps for an international machinery to further this end." Accordingly, an eighteen-nation Committee on the Peaceful Uses of Outer Space was established in December 1958 and held its first meeting in May 1959. However, Soviet opposition, ostensibly on the ground that the Committee was not sufficiently representative, prevented any discussion of substantive issues and led to a recasting of the Committee in late 1961 and its expansion to twenty-eight members.

The Soviet Union and the United States established a "cold line" in October 1963 to exchange weather data and have cooperated in the use of satellites to map the earth's magnetic field. They joined, through the United Nations in December 1966, in adopting a treaty prohibiting weapons in outer space and providing for free access to space installations on celestial bodies. The Soviet Union proposed a treaty in June 1971 calling for international cooperation on the moon and barring any country from establishing military bases there. All of the agreements on outer space are welcome preliminaries, but they should not be mistaken for arms control or disarmament.

Halting the Proliferation of Nuclear Weapons

One hopeful aspect of the new Cold War between the superpowers has been their cooperation in limited but not unimportant areas. On the assumption that any increase in the number of powers possessing nuclear weapons would further complicate the negotiation of agreements and would add to international tension, the Soviet government advocated a treaty under which "countries not possessing nuclear weapons should enter into an understanding not to manufacture such weapons, not to acquire them from powers which do possess them, and not to permit them in their territory."

The issue first acquired urgency in the early 1960s when Moscow attacked the American proposal to provide NATO with a multilateral nuclear force (MLF), which was intended to satisfy West German interest in acquiring an independent nuclear capability by providing it with a voice in a collective nuclear arrangement. Moscow assailed this plan to give West Germany a finger on the nuclear trigger and played on European fears of a revival of German militarism. China's entry into the nuclear club in October 1964, and the acquisition by other countries such as Sweden, India, Japan, and Israel of the technological capability for manufacturing nuclear weapons, made the issue even more immediate. By 1965 the United States, too, had had second thoughts; by 1968 the two superpowers co-sponsored a UN resolution proposing the Non-Proliferation Treaty (NPT). For its part, the Soviet Union has emphasized the tension-reducing consequences of a regional variant of

NPT, that is, the establishment of geographical areas from which nuclear weapons would be barred altogether (reading 59).

The NPT was approved in 1968 and went into effect in 1970, even though not all nations have ratified it—notably, France, Communist China, India, Israel, and West Germany—and even though many less developed countries had strenuous objections. Brazil, for example, said NPT would perpetuate "a status of permanent technological dependence," and India deprecated the security guarantees offered by the nuclear powers to the nonnuclear powers, asserting that "there can be no imposition of a Pax Nuclearia on non-nuclear weapon states." The Soviet Union has continued to pressure nonsigners, especially West Germany and Israel, into ratifying NPT, arguing that it reduces the danger of nuclear war and enables the superpowers to proceed to the next stage of the disarmament process, namely, eliminating all nuclear-weapons testing and limiting the deployment of delivery systems. In actuality, however, neither objective is contingent upon NPT. Along with the United States and Great Britain, the Soviet Union pledged itself in the UN "to seek immediate Security Council action to provide assistance, in accordance with the Charter, to any nonnuclear-weapon state party to the treaty on the nonproliferation of nuclear weapons that is a victim of an act of aggression or an object of a threat of aggression in which nuclear weapons are used."

On the occasion of Moscow's signing of NPT on July 1, 1968, the Soviet government listed its priorities for future disarmament efforts in a memorandum distributed to all governments (reading 60). The list may be regarded as the disarmament agenda for the next decade.

Another step to curtail nuclear proliferation centered on barring the "emplanting or emplacing" of nuclear weapons on the ocean floor more than 12 miles offshore. The issue was originally raised in 1967 by Ambassador Arvid Pardo of Malta, who urged the United Nations to demilitarize the seabed "beyond the limits of present national jurisdiction and to internationalize its resources in the interest of mankind." The superpowers pushed the military aspect, but showed little interest in the economic one. On February 11, 1971, the USSR, the United States, and Great Britain signed a treaty prohibiting "any nuclear weapons and launching installations or any other facilities specifically designed for storing, testing, or using such weapons" from the ocean seabed beyond a 12-mile coastal zone.

The treaty does not ban nuclear-armed submarines or the emplacement of submarine detection devices, which the Soviet Union tried to include, but which the United States forestalled because of the difficulties of verification and the military's interest in perfecting anti-submarine defenses. To the unhappiness of the small nations, which are less than enchanted with the NPT and Seabed Treaties, neither superpower has been active in exploring ways of exploiting the resources of the ocean for the benefit of mankind. The treaties have in no way diminished the arms race; they may act as confidence-building measures that will make possible some tangible accord in the substantive SALT talks; however, if not supplemented by actual disarmament, they are merely instances of trivial superpower collaboration in nonvital areas and are likely to widen still further the gap between the nuclear haves and havenots.

Limitations on Strategic Weapons

The most important of all postwar disarmament discussions began in Helsinki on November 17, 1969. The initiative for the Strategic Arms Limitation Talks (SALT) came from the United States on January 10, 1967, with an invitation to the Soviet Union to enter into talks aimed at curtailing the arms race in strategic defensive weapons, that is, ABMs. Moscow did not assent until June 27, 1968. The reasons for the prolonged delay are obscure: we can only surmise that they were due to the combination of sharp differences within the Politburo; the calculation that a delayed response would encourage political cleavages in the United States and occasion a postponement of a "thin" ABM system; the desire to have offensive weapons included as well; and the determination to overcome the United States lead in strategic weapons before agreeing to talks. The Soviet invasion of Czechoslovakia then intervened, prompting the United States to cancel the start of SALT. Another year passed before the new Nixon administration was ready. Since then SALT, which seeks to reach agreement on mutually acceptable levels for all kinds of strategic arms, has been carried on intermittently in Helsinki and Vienna and is expected to continue for years. While conducting SALT, each superpower has been simultaneously pressing ahead with the development and deployment of qualitatively improved, as well as completely new, weapons systems. This brings regular changes in national positions in response to each country's changed evaluations of its own security needs and of the adversary's capability.

The overwhelming superiority in strategic weapons that the United States enjoyed since 1945 ended in 1969. Its replacement by a measure of strategic parity was inevitable given the Soviet determination to increase its strategic nuclear forces to levels that would provide it with an assured destruction capability (ADC) of its own. Thus in 1967 the Soviet Union more than doubled its ICBM force, from 340 to 720, while the United States kept its force at 1,054. The United States did not expand the number of ICBMs, because the existing level was deemed sufficient for strategic deterrence. By 1971 the Soviet Union had surpassed the United States, with 1,500 ICBMs. However, barring a technological breakthrough that would render existing delivery systems obsolete—an unlikely prospect in the near future, according to most specialists—the exact ratio of forces is relatively unimportant, since each superpower possesses an ADC capable of deterring any possible first strike attack.

For the first time both superpowers are in a relationship of approximate strategic parity. They realize that failure to agree on levels of mutual restraint will entail a sharp escalation of the arms race, bringing in its wake heightened international tension and astronomical defense expenditures. Each superpower fears that the other may acquire an offensive edge or an improved defensive system of ABMs. Either eventuality could have a destabilizing effect on superpower relations.

In late 1970 Soviet negotiators sought to limit talks to defensive weapons only, while the Americans insisted that offensive forces also be included, thus reversing their 1967 positions. In May 1971 they agreed to concentrate on an agreement to limit ABM systems,* but also to take "certain measures" to limit the number of offensive weapons.

It is easier to limit ABMs than ICBMs, since there are fewer of them in operational use and each nation can use its own reconnaissance satellites to check on adherence to any agreement. The key to regulating ABMs is in limiting radars, which are essential for speedy and successful interception of incoming ICBMs by ABMs. (An agreement that did not curb radars would not be worth its salt!) It is argued that if the permissible ABM system were kept "thin," this would serve to slow down the arms race because it would allay anxiety over the possible erosion of the existing offensive capability of the ICBM force and obviate the need for an increasingly larger offensive capability.

However, the advocates of strengthening ABM systems in both camps say that recent developments in offensive weaponry intensify the need to protect a first-strike capability. A major breakthrough in offensive weaponry came with development of the MIRVs (Multiple Independently Targeted Reentry Vehicles), which make it possible for one missile to carry not only one nuclear warhead, but as many as six,

* Since the mid-1960s, the Soviet Union has had an ABM system (GALOSH) installed around Moscow, Leningrad, and other major industrial centers in European Russia; it also has a system known as TALLINN, which is assumed to operate only against airplanes. In 1969 the United States embarked on the construction of Safeguard, a limited ABM system intended to protect the hardened ICBM silos essential to United States deterrent strategy rather than any industrial or population centers. This difference of emphasis makes comparability of ABM systems very difficult.

perhaps even more. The Soviets have developed the SS-9, a giant ICBM powerful enough to carry one nuclear warhead of 8 to 10 megatons or as many as six warheads in the 1 to 2 megaton range. Both superpowers have MIRVs in operation. The fear is that with a quantum increase in operational MIRVs, the adversary could overwhelm both a "thin" ABM system and the first-strike force and thus effectively carry out a preemptive attack. Here we have a classic example of technological change rendering political positions obsolete. With the arms race moved to a new level, the promise of SALT has diminished greatly.

Observations

What, then, are Soviet intentions in the field of disarmament? Now that the Soviet Union has achieved strategic parity with the United States will it be more amenable to meaningful arms limitation agreements? Is the Soviet Union bent on strategic superiority? According to Leonid Brezhnev, it is not; but it does insist that any agreement provide for "equal security" (reading 61). On the other hand, many American analysts cite evidence that the USSR is busily constructing dozens of new underground silos to house SS-9 missiles and contend that the presumption must be that it seeks a first-strike capability. Can capabilities be frozen in an era of accelerating technological change, in an era that has seen weapons systems become obsolete on an average of every five years? Can incentives outpace innovations? Can mutual interests transcend mutual fears? How important is the China factor in Soviet strategic planning? Though an all-encompassing arms control agreement is unattainable, Soviet spokesmen maintain that useful agreements can be reached in various areas and that the arms race can be reversed (reading 62).

The Soviet-American strategic weapons competition has reached a temporary stalemate. An easing of political tensions and the promotion of confidence-building measures could infuse vigor into the current SALT negotiations. But neither side seems willing to take any really big step, such as, for example, declaring a moratorium on all missile testing, which by its very nature would be a self-executing agreement like the limited test-ban treaty and readily verifiable through the use of reconnaissance space satellites. A moratorium on missile testing would freeze weapons development. The truth is that the overcoming of deeply ingrained national anxieties will not soon or readily be managed. Most national leaders are reconciled to an indefinite continuation of the present "balance of terror." Yet, it is possible that negotiating out of fear may in the long run bring results as effective and enduring as negotiating from a sense of trust. Toward the end of his active political life as Prime Minister, Sir Winston Churchill observed in the House of Commons that "it may well be that we shall, by a process of sublime irony, have reached a stage in this story where safety will be the sturdy child of terror, and survival the twin brother of annihilation."

A far-reaching agreement between the Soviet Union and the United States on strategic weapons is unlikely, not only because of misunderstandings and suspicions engendered by different outlooks and perceptions of reality—though these are major inhibitory elements—but also because in a changing world man does not behave according to predictable and rational formulas. To change the attitudes of leaders and to dispel their legitimate as well as irrational anxieties, indeed, to bring them to a stage where they will be prepared to introduce extensive policy changes, requires a fundamental restructuring of national and international institutions. Until such an evolution of attitudes and institutions occurs, the negotiation of peace and security will continue to be a piecemeal, untidy, and uncertain venture in the regulation of human behavior.

Breaking the Nuclear Test Ban

58/The Soviet Justification for the Resumption of Nuclear Testing in the Atmosphere   *August 31, 1961*

The peoples are witnessing the ever-increasing aggressiveness of the policy of the NATO military bloc. The United States and its allies are spinning the flywheel of their military machine ever faster, fanning up the arms race to unprecedented scope, increasing the strength of armies, making the tension of the international situation red-hot. Things have reached a point that the leading statesmen of the United States and its allies are resorting to threats to take to arms and to unleash war as a countermeasure to the conclusion of a peace treaty with the German Democratic Republic.

Being faced with these facts, which cannot but cause anxiety, the Soviet Government considers it its duty to take all measures so that the Soviet Union should be completely prepared to render harmless any aggressor if he tried to launch an attack. The tragedy of the first months of the great patriotic war when Hitler attacked the U.S.S.R., having ensured for himself superiority in military equipment, is too fresh in the memory of people to allow this to happen now.

This is the reason why the Soviet Government has already taken a number of serious measures for strengthening the security of the U.S.S.R. For the same reason, after a thoughtful and comprehensive consideration of this question, it has made a decision to carry out experimental explosions of nuclear weapons. . . .

The main thing in our days is disarmament, general and complete, and an agreement on such disarmament would cover the question of nuclear testing. Indeed, when the arms race is stopped and the stock-piled weapons are destroyed, there will be no stimulus for its perfection and consequently for the need to carry out our experimental nuclear tests but, on the contrary, merely an agreement to stop nuclear weapons tests cannot by itself put an end to the arms race.

The states that already possess atomic weapons will inevitably feel tempted to act violating such an agreement, to seek new ways and loopholes for perfecting weapons, to say nothing of the fact that the tests carried out by three-four powers are quite sufficient for unlimited stockpiling of the most dangerous thermonuclear weapons of the existing types.

TASS statement, issued August 31, 1961, *excerpts.*

The states which do not yet possess thermonuclear weapons will in their turn try to create them despite the agreement that prohibits atomic tests. . . .

The Governments of the Western powers have persistently advanced and continue to advance the demand that a treaty on the discontinuance of nuclear tests should not provide for the prohibition of underground nuclear explosions. Meanwhile, it is obvious to every informed person that the carrying out of such explosions, even if it is claimed that they are conducted for peaceful purposes, is nothing else but a hidden form of perfecting the existing nuclear weapons or putting finishing touches to its new types. If a nuclear explosive device is effective, for example, for moving ground—and the Western powers want to secure for themselves the right of carrying out such explosions—the same explosive device will also be effective for military purposes . . .

The entire course of the negotiations in Geneva proves that the Western powers pursue the aim of actually legalizing those types of nuclear tests in which they are interested and of establishing an international control body which would be an obedient tool in their hands and in fact would be an appendage of the general staffs of Western powers. . . .

It is an open secret that the United States is standing at the threshold of carrying out underground nuclear explosions and only waits for the first suitable pretext to start them. However, it is clear to everybody that since the U.S. Government has the intention to resume nuclear weapons tests, it is only a matter of time.

The Soviet Government cannot ignore the fact that France, the ally of the United States in NATO, has been carrying out nuclear tests already for a long time. While the Soviet Union refrained from nuclear tests, trying to achieve agreement with the United States and Great Britain at the table of negotiations on their complete discontinuance, France conducted explosions of nuclear devices one after another. It continues to do so in spite of the appeal of the United Nations to all states to refrain from such tests, in spite of the protests of broad public circles in all countries of the world, in spite of the warnings of the Soviet Union that it will be forced to resume tests if France does not stop its experiments with nuclear weapons.

Curbing the Spread of Nuclear Weapons

59/Non-nuclear Zones

M. PETROV

In its proposals for reducing conventional armaments and armed forces placed before the U.N. Sub-Committee of the Disarmament Commission in 1956, the Soviet Union suggested the establishment of a zone free from atomic and hydrogen weapons. This first introduced into international usage the entirely new concept including a number of measures to keep nuclear weapons in any form out of one area of the world or another. Since then, the idea of establishing non-nuclear zones has developed and has become one of the most important components in the set of measures aimed at limiting the arms drive and easing international tensions.

It would be no exaggeration to say that the non-nuclear zone idea has now been widely accepted in many parts of the globe and has been winning increasing support. The reason why it is popular is that the peoples of the world regard it as a realistic and concrete means of limiting the danger of nuclear war and slowing down the arms race. . . .

The establishment of non-nuclear zones is of especial importance now that the question of halting the spread of nuclear weapons is on the international agenda. The emergence of such zones in various parts of the world would restrict the sphere of nuclear weapons territorially, and, hence, ultimately reduce the objective possibilities of a nuclear conflict. It would also help to improve relations between states.

There are now several projects and plans for establishing non-nuclear zones in various parts of the world, including Central Europe, Northern Europe, the Mediterranean, the Balkans, Africa and Latin America. Some practical steps have also been taken in that direction. Under the 1959 treaty, which was signed by 12 states, the vast area of the Antarctic was excluded from the sphere of nuclear weapons and practically made a non-nuclear zone. But if it has proved possible to make a non-nuclear zone out of the Antarctic, whose population is no more than a few hundred Polar explorers, it is all the more important to provide guarantees against the possible use of nuclear weapons in Europe, Africa and Latin America, with their millions of inhabitants. That something

M. Petrov, "Non-Nuclear Zones: A Pressing Demand," *International Affairs* (Moscow), No. 6 (June 1967), pp. 12–15, *excerpts.*

practical is being done towards that end will be seen from the efforts of a number of Latin American countries which culminated last February 14 in the signing of a treaty banning the stockpiling, use and manufacture of nuclear weapons in Latin America. . . .

But so far, the establishment of non-nuclear zones has come up against great practical difficulties, the main obstacle being the attitude of the United States and other Western Powers, who are opposed to the idea, especially for Europe. They argue that wherever the armed forces of the Great Powers are confronting each other, the establishment of non-nuclear zones would upset the balance of forces in favour of the Soviet Union. Actually, however, non-nuclear zones are most needed where there are concentrations of considerable quantities of nuclear weapons, and where the armed forces of the NATO and the Warsaw Treaty Powers are in direct confrontation. Central Europe is such an area, and that is why the Soviet Union and other Socialist countries attach such great importance to the establishment of non-nuclear zones in Europe, for, as was stated in the Declaration on Strengthening Peace and Security in Europe adopted by the Bucharest Conference of the Warsaw Treaty's Political Consultative Committee on July 5, 1966, they regard the establishment of such zones as an effective partial measure designed to bring about a military détente on the European continent. . . .

The idea of setting up a zone free from atomic and nuclear weapons in Central Europe was proposed by the Polish People's Republic and is known as the Rapacki Plan, after her Foreign Minister, who first formulated the proposal. Adam Rapacki told the 12th General Assembly on October 2, 1957, that if "both German states were to express their agreement to ban the manufacture and stockpiling of atomic and thermonuclear weapons on their territory, the Polish People's Republic was prepared to do the same on its territory at the same time."

On February 14, 1958, the Polish Government sent a memorandum to the states concerned setting forth the details of its proposal for a non-nuclear zone in Central Europe. It was to cover the territory of Poland, Czechoslovakia, the German Democratic Republic and the Federal Republic of Germany, with the states inside the zone undertaking not to manufacture, stockpile or import nuclear weapons of any kind for their own purposes, or to allow their deployment on their own territory, and also not to allow to be installed on their territory any equipment or devices servicing nuclear weapons, including missile launchers.

For their part, the United States, Britain, France and the U.S.S.R. would undertake not to have any nuclear weapons or devices servicing nuclear weapons as equipment for their troops stationed on the territory of the states within the zone, and not to transfer those weapons or means of servicing them to governments or other agencies on that territory. The four nuclear Powers would undertake not to use such weapons against the zone or installations within it. In order to ensure the fulfilment of these proposals, the Polish Government suggested the establishment of appropriate effective international control. It was proposed that the details and forms of control were to be worked out by agreement between the Powers concerned. . . .

The Western reaction to the Polish proposal was a negative one. A note of the U.S. State Department, for instance, asserted that Poland's proposal was too limited in scope to reduce the threat of nuclear war or to provide a sound basis for security in Europe. The Western Powers' main line of argument was that the ban on the manufacture and possession of nuclear weapons in Central Europe would deprive the NATO forces of their "nuclear shield," and that with the superiority of the Warsaw Treaty Powers in conventional armaments this would "upset the balance of forces" in Central Europe. This is clearly a specious line of argument. . . .

The Soviet Union, wishing to safeguard other parts of Europe, too, from any nuclear threat, has proposed that the whole Mediterranean area should be turned into a zone free from nuclear missiles. A Soviet Government note to the governments of the United States, Britain, France, Italy, Turkey, Greece, Algeria, Israel, Cyprus, the Lebanon, Libya, Morocco, the U.A.R., Syria, Tunisia and Spain on May 20, 1963, said that if a non-nuclear zone was established in the Mediterranean area, the U.S.S.R. was prepared "to undertake not to station nuclear weapons and means of their delivery in the waters of this sea, on the assumption that the other Powers would contract similar commitments." It stressed that the U.S.S.R. was prepared to provide (jointly with the U.S.A. and other Western Powers) "reliable guarantees that in the event of any military complications, the Mediterranean area would be regarded as lying outside the sphere of use of nuclear weapons."

The Soviet initiative met with understanding on the part of a number of Mediterranean states, particularly the U.A.R., Syria and Algeria. But the United States, whose missile-equipped ships have been plying the Mediterranean, and its NATO allies rejected the Soviet proposal, again arguing the need to preserve the balance of forces. . . .

Moscow's Disarmament Priorities for the 1970s

60/Soviet Memorandum on Disarmament   *July 1, 1968*

Following the conclusion of the treaty on the nonproliferation of nuclear weapons, the Soviet government proposes that an understanding be reached on the implementation, in the near future, of the following urgent measures for an end to the arms race and for disarmament:

1. A Ban on the Use of Nuclear Weapons

Ever since the emergence of nuclear weapons, the Soviet Union has consistently stood for a ban on these weapons of mass annihilation and the complete destruction of such weapons. The conclusion of an international agreement banning the use of nuclear weapons would be an important advance towards the solution of this problem and towards the removal of the danger of nuclear war. Such an agreement would be a serious deterrent for all those who might like to use nuclear weapons. This agreement would help to improve the international atmosphere by dispelling the suspicions of some powers concerning the intentions of others to use nuclear weapons. . . .

2. Measures to End the Manufacture of Nuclear Weapons and to Reduce and Destroy Stockpiles of Such Weapons

Seeking to rid mankind of the threat of nuclear war, the Soviet government proposes that all nuclear powers should immediately open talks on the ending of the manufacture of nuclear weapons, the reduction of the stockpiles of those weapons and a subsequent total ban on, and destruction of, nuclear weapons under appropriate international control. . . .

3. Limitation and Subsequent Reduction of Means of Delivery of Strategic Weapons

The Soviet government proposes that an understanding be reached on concrete steps for the limitation and subsequent reduction of strategic

Soviet News, No. 5444 (July 2, 1968), pp. 2, 15, *excerpts.*

means of delivery of strategic nuclear weapons. In so doing, the Soviet government proceeds on the basis of the assumption that the destruction of the entire arsenal of means of strategic delivery and, in any case, the reduction of this arsenal to the absolute minimum, with the retention, and this only temporarily, of only a strictly limited quantity of such means, would be a measure leading to the removal of the danger of nuclear war. . . .

4. Ban on Flights of Bombers Carrying Nuclear Weapons Beyond National Frontiers. Limitation of the Zones of Voyages of Submarines Carrying Missiles

The Soviet government has more than once drawn the attention of the governments of other states and of world opinion to the danger of flights of bombers carrying nuclear weapons beyond the limits of national frontiers. The increasing number of crashes of American bombers carrying nuclear weapons beyond the territory of the United States arouse the legitimate anxiety of many countries. There is no guarantee that the next crash of a bomber carrying nuclear weapons will not lead to a nuclear explosion with all the ensuing consequences. . . .

5. Ban on Underground Tests of Nuclear Weapons

The Soviet Union has been and continues to be a firm supporter of a ban on all tests of nuclear weapons and believes that a ban on all tests would promote the strengthening of peace and the slowing down of the arms race. The Soviet Union is prepared to reach an immediate understanding on the banning of underground tests of nuclear weapons on the basis of using national means of detection to control this ban.

6. Ban on the Use of Chemical and Bacteriological Weapons

The Soviet government has more than once drawn the attention of states to the danger to mankind from the use of chemical and bacteriological weapons. Reflecting the common anxiety of the peoples in view of that danger, the 21st session of the United Nations General Assembly passed a resolution calling for strict observance by all states of the principles of the Geneva Protocol of 1925 on the prohibition on the use of chemical and bacteriological weapons. . . . However, this important decision of the General Assembly is not being fulfilled by some countries, and in the first place, by the United States. Moreover the United States is using chemical weapons in its aggressive war in Vietnam. . . .

7. Dismantling of Foreign Military Bases

Military bases on foreign territories create a serious threat to peace. Such bases serve as a source of the outbreak of military conflicts and threaten the freedom and independence of the peoples. This is convincingly borne out by the United States' continuing war of aggression in Vietnam and by the tension and conflicts in other parts of the world where foreign bases are situated. . . .

8. Measures for Regional Disarmament

The Soviet government supports the establishment of nuclear-free zones in various parts of the world. In so doing, it proceeds on the basis of the assumption that the formation of such zones would effectively limit the sphere of deployment of nuclear weapons and fully accord with the task of preventing the direct or indirect proliferation of such weapons. . . .

9. Peaceful Uses of the Sea Bed and Ocean Floor

. . . This would ban, specifically, the establishment of fixed military installations on the sea bed, and also any other military activity . . .

The Soviets on Strategic Parity

61/Speech Dealing with the Stabilization of International Peace   *June 11, 1971*

LEONID BREZHNEV

It goes without saying that the struggle for disarmament is a difficult matter. Here, just as in many other problems of foreign policy, one comes up against the stubborn resistance of the imperialist forces. Nevertheless, we regard the slogans put forward by the 24th Congress of the CPSU, not as propaganda slogans, but as slogans for action reflecting political goals which are becoming increasingly attainable in our epoch.

What precisely permits us to present the matter in this way? First and foremost, the changed balance of forces in the world—both socio-political and military. Even a few years ago, the imperialists, and above all the U.S. imperialists, really hoped to strengthen their positions on the world arena with the help of the arms race and hoped, at the same time, to weaken the economy of the USSR and other socialist countries and frustrate our plans for peaceful construction. Now, the failure of such schemes of those who wish us ill has become perfectly obvious. Now everyone sees that socialism is sufficiently strong to ensure both reliable defenses and economic development, although it is true that without the great expenditure on defense we would have ensured a much faster advance of our economy. On the other hand, the imperialists, including those of the richest capitalist country—the United States of America—increasingly sense the negative economic and political consequences of an unrestrained arms race. The tremendous military expenditures give rise to chronic inflation in the capitalist countries, cause systematic monetary and financial crises and prevent the solution of worsening domestic problems. At the same time, the working peoples' indignation over the militarist and aggressive policy is growing. In the United States the anti-war movement is assuming an increasingly mass scale and is bringing strong pressure to bear on the government. Resistance to the increase in military spending is growing in other NATO countries, too. As a result, even some members of the ruling circles of the western states are ceasing to regard the arms race as an undoubted blessing. All this, of course, facilitates, to a certain extent,

Soviet News, No. 5592 (June 15, 1971), p. 162, *excerpts.*

the struggle of the socialist and other peace-loving countries against the arms race. That struggle is becoming a more realistic proposition than it was in the past.

In this situation, growing importance is undoubtedly acquired by the Soviet-American strategic arms limitation talks, a favorable outcome for which would, in our opinion, accord with the interests of the peoples of both countries and with the task of strengthening world peace. *I have already said that the decisive factor for the success of these talks is strict observance of the principle of equal security for both sides, renunciation of attempts to secure any unilateral advantages at the expense of the other side.** It is to be hoped, therefore, that the United States administration will also take a constructive stand.

The principle of equal security is recognized in words by Washington, too. In actual fact, however, the American side simply cannot bring itself to carry this out consistently in practice. In the United States, time and time again, for instance, a hue and cry is raised about the Soviet defense programs—particularly on the eve of adopting a new military budget in Washington. The measures we take to strengthen our defenses are presented at the same time as something well nigh amounting to "treachery," as a direct threat to the success of the talks. But what grounds, we are entitled to ask, has Washington for expecting us to abandon programs that have already been adopted† if the U.S. administration itself, during the period of the talks, has taken a number of very important decisions on building up its strategic forces?‡ It is high time to get rid of this double yardstick, this double standard in assessing one's own actions and the actions of the other side.

And this does not only apply to missiles. The U.S. propaganda machine has launched an extensive campaign concerning the Soviet Navy. Washington, if you please, sees a threat in the fact that our warships appear in the Mediterranean, the Indian Ocean, and other seas. But at the same time, U.S. politicians regard it as normal and natural for their Sixth Fleet to be constantly present in the Mediterranean, hard by the side of the Soviet Union, as it were, and for the Seventh Fleet to be stationed off the coasts of China and IndoChina. . . .

---

* [Author's italics.—Ed.]

† [In particular, an ABM system around key cities in the USSR.—Ed.]

‡ [President Nixon's decision to build an ABM system protecting U.S. underground missile sites.—Ed.]

Prospects for Disarmament

62/Cautious Optimism: Utopian or Utilitarian?

A. SHEVCHENKO

Despite the fairly modest results yielded by the disarmament talks over the last 25 years, it would be quite wrong to assume that it is utopian to hope to end the arms race and achieve disarmament. On the contrary, disarmament is a pressing problem that can be solved. Of course, there are serious difficulties involved in finding a solution, for this requires consent and a willingness, even if reluctant, on the part of more than one or two states—in fact, of an overwhelming majority of states, above all those with a considerable military potential. There is an objective possibility of reaching an understanding on disarmament measures . . .

This means that in order to assess how real and practicable the plans for disarmament are one has to consider the social forces behind them, and their growth and development. This view of the concrete historical conditions today shows that development is heading in a direction favorable for disarmament. The fundamental realignment of forces in favor of those who want peace has given the struggle for disarmament a real basis. . . . Since the Second World War, the social forces that want to put a stop to the arms race and work for further disarmament have grown immensely. Instead of being confined to the diplomatic conference table, the struggle for disarmament has become a broad field of public activity. Whereas in the period between the two world wars the Soviet Union stood virtually alone against the looming danger of war and the arms race, because the progressive social forces in other countries were disunited and poorly organized, today not only individuals and small groups but millions of people of various convictions, including many in the imperialist countries, are backing their genuine desire to see an end to the arms race by active participation in the movement for disarmament. . . .

A struggle over disarmament has also been going on among the ruling circles in the imperialist states, between those who speak on behalf of the most aggressive forces and the military-industrial complex, and those who see the contradictions between the grossly inflated military machine

A. Shevchenko, "Disarmament: A Problem That Can Be Solved," *International Affairs* (Moscow), No. 5 (May 1971), pp. 70–72, *excerpts*.

of imperialism and the possibilities of its practical use for the purposes of war. The imperialist powers have failed in their attempt to achieve technical-military superiority by means of an arms race. The USA, the bulwark of imperialism, has lost its relative strategic invulnerability, while socialism has become so strong militarily that any aggressor who dared to attack the socialist community would go down in crushing defeat. . . . As a result, the more sober-minded and far-sighted Western statesmen have realized the absurdity and imprudence of any attempts to solve the historical argument between socialism and capitalism by means of war, and have had to admit that in the present conditions world war is madness, and that steps have to be taken to limit the nuclear-missile race.

That does not reflect a change in the aggressive nature of imperialism, but a tilting of the world balance in favor of socialism, which has forced the imperialist powers to accept the idea of some understanding in the nuclear sphere. Hence the recent agreements, although none of these abolishes or even reduces nuclear armaments, but only puts some limits on the sphere of their deployment. However, their importance lies not so much in these limitations, but in the fact that each is something of a springboard in the struggle for disarmament and all of them together pave the way for further advance. With several such springboards now in existence, the offensive can be carried on with more confidence and on a wider front. A broad and resolute offensive by all peaceloving forces can make the opponents of disarmament retreat still farther and ensure worldwide implementation of actual disarmament measures. . . .

As for the Soviet Union, it does not regard the first few nuclear treaties as an end in itself. It does not want an arms race, however well controlled, but real prerequisites for serious, business-like talks on disarmament, and above all nuclear disarmament with a view to stopping the arms race. . . .

It is also becoming more and more evident that it will take joint efforts by all the nuclear powers to achieve success in disarmament. Otherwise, nuclear, let alone complete, disarmament is impossible. That is why the Soviet government's memorandum of July 1, 1968, suggested that all the nuclear powers should begin talks without delay on measures in the sphere of nuclear disarmament.

FOR FURTHER STUDY

Barnet, Richard. *Who Wants Disarmament?* Boston: Beacon, 1961.

Bechhofer, Bernhard G. *Postwar Negotiations for Arms Control.* Washington, D.C.: Brookings Institution, 1961.

Bloomfield, Lincoln C., Walter C. Clemens, Jr., and Franklyn Griffiths. *Khrushchev and the Arms Race: Soviet Interests in Arms Control and Disarmament 1954–1964.* Cambridge, Mass.: M.I.T. Press, 1966.

Clemens, Walter C., Jr. *The Arms Race and Sino-Soviet Relations.* Stanford, Calif.: Hoover Institution, 1968.

Dallin, Alexander (ed.). *The Soviet Union and Disarmament: An Appraisal of Soviet Attitudes and Intentions.* New York: Praeger, 1965.

Dougherty, James E., and John F. Lehman (eds.). *Arms Control for the Late Sixties.* New York: Van Nostrand Reinhold, 1967.

Garthoff, Raymond L. *Soviet Strategy in the Nuclear Age.* New York: Praeger, 1958.

_____. *Soviet Military Policy: A Historical Analysis.* New York: Praeger, 1966.

Halperin, Morton H. (ed.). *Sino-Soviet Relations and Arms Control.* Cambridge, Mass.: M.I.T. Press, 1967.

Horelick, Arnold L., and Myron Rush. *Strategic Power and Soviet Foreign Policy.* Chicago: University of Chicago Press, 1966.

Kintner, William R. *Peace and Strategy Conflict.* New York: Praeger, 1967.

_____, and Harriet Fast Scott (eds.). *The Nuclear Revolution in Soviet Military Affairs.* Norman: University of Oklahoma Press, 1968.

Kissinger, Henry A. *Nuclear Weapons and Foreign Policy.* New York: Harper & Row, 1957.

Kolkowicz, Roman, et al. *The Soviet Union and Arms Control: A Superpower Dilemma.* Baltimore: Johns Hopkins Press, 1970.

Lapp, Ralph E. *The Weapons Culture.* New York: Norton, 1968.

Larson, Thomas B. *Disarmament and Soviet Policy, 1964–1968.* Englewood Cliffs, N.J.: Prentice-Hall, 1969.

Levine, Robert A. *The Arms Debate.* Cambridge, Mass.: Harvard University Press, 1963.

Nogee, Joseph L. *Soviet Policy Toward International Control of Atomic Energy.* Notre Dame, Ind.: University of Notre Dame Press, 1961.

Schelling, Thomas C. *The Strategy of Conflict.* Cambridge, Mass.: Harvard University Press, 1960.

Sokolovskii, V. D. (ed.). *Soviet Military Doctrine.* Translated, analyzed and annotated by H. S. Dinerstein, L. Gouré, and Thomas W. Wolfe. Englewood Cliffs, N.J.: Prentice-Hall, 1963.

Spanier, John W., and Joseph L. Nogee. *The Politics of Disarmament: A Study in Soviet-American Gamesmanship.* New York: Praeger, 1962.

Stone, Jeremy J. *Containing the Arms Race.* Cambridge, Mass.: M.I.T. Press, 1966.

_____. *Strategic Persuasion: Arms Limitation Through Dialogue.* New York: Columbia University Press, 1967.

Voss, E. H. *Nuclear Ambush: The Test-Ban Trap.* Chicago: Regnery, 1963.

Wolfe, Thomas W. *Soviet Strategy at the Crossroads.* Cambridge, Mass.: Harvard University Press, 1964.

12 the role of developing areas in soviet ideology

Since World War I and especially since 1945 nationalism has been the motive force underlying the unrest and instability in the two-thirds of the world often referred to as the "developing areas." Soviet leaders have long appreciated the significance of these areas, though it is only in the post–World War II period that communism has succeeded in making important political advances there. The victory of the Chinese communists is the most notable example of this phenomenon. A statement characterizing the role developing areas play in Soviet thought, often erroneously attributed to Lenin, holds that "the road to Paris lies through Calcutta and Bombay." This sentiment has certainly epitomized Soviet expectations and attitudes for more than half a century.

The essence of the Soviet approach to developing areas can be traced to the Leninist theory of imperialism—that capitalist countries, in their search for raw materials, cheap labor, and potential markets, seized the less developed areas, thus forestalling their own eventual decay and disintegration. The struggle against imperialism must be waged on two fronts: first, the developing nations must break colonial rule, thereby weakening the global structure of capitalism; second, the proletariat of the imperialist countries must strive to defeat capitalism from within. This two-fold struggle will ensure the ultimate collapse of capitalism.

The ideological appeal of communism for colonial and dependent areas stems from its advocacy of national self-determination and from its promise of a better future. To nations long subject to foreign control and confronted with massive problems of poverty, economic backwardness, and burgeoning populations, communism offers a seemingly simple, direct, and effective path to economic development and political power. "Did not the Soviet Union transform itself from a backward nation to one of the world's most powerful industrial states in a generation?" ask the often myopic nationalists of the developing countries. The quest for simple solutions to complex problems has often led well-intentioned leaders astray, to their subsequent sorrow. But the evidence of Soviet industrial development is incontrovertible, and the formula *does* appear deceptively easy to apply elsewhere. Also, in many of these societies, the reformers, intellectuals and newly educated, covetous of position, prestige, and power, are too often denied these fruits by reactionary, venal, inbred cliques, who rule without regard for the needs of their peoples. It is among these frustrated, ambitious, idealistic, alienated, and suppressed groups, insistent upon rapid change and intent upon discarding the past for a more promising future, that communism makes its greatest inroads.

Lenin realized the political potential of the underdeveloped areas and made it an integral concern of Soviet ideology. Whereas Marx predicted the downfall of capitalism through the proletariat of the industrialized nations, Lenin understood that this defeat could be hastened by detaching the underdeveloped areas from the control of the colonial powers. He wove the twin themes of national self-determination and internationalism* into a common policy fabric and tailored it to the situations existing in underdeveloped areas. Subsequent Soviet leaders have expanded and modified these concepts, varying the emphasis to accord with contemporary need. They are in a sense two aspects of the same problem: the national question, which is concerned with the relationships between the colonial powers and the subjugated peoples and between the majority nationality and the national minorities within a particular nation. Lenin held that all nations were equal, a concept with enormous appeal, and that they had the right to determine their own future. He predicted that all nations would

---

* Lenin defined "internationalism" as follows: "There is one, only one kind of internationalism in deed: working wholeheartedly for the development of the revolutionary movement and the revolutionary struggle *in one's own country,* and supporting (by propaganda, sympathy and material aid) *such and only such a struggle* and such a line in *every* country without exception."

Ideally, internationalism united the workers of all nations in the struggle against imperialism; once independence was attained, it would act to diminish national differences and bring about a communist world. As applied to developing areas, internationalism and national self-determination are closely interrelated. On the one hand, the proletariat of the advanced countries must work both for revolution in their own countries and for the liberation and national independence of all colonial and semicolonial areas. This alliance of the proletariat of the developed countries and the peoples of the developing areas transcends national allegiance. They have in common the goal of overthrowing capitalism and eventually establishing a global system of communist states.

in time be united in a common bond of brotherhood—communism. However, since they first had to be free from the domination of "imperialist" powers, national self-determination for all nations had to be supported. To weaken imperialism, Lenin proposed an alliance between the proletarian forces in the advanced countries and the revolutionary forces in the colonial and semicolonial areas. Internationalism aids both and constitutes the bond that links them in common cause.

Declaration of the right of national self-determination was a principal contribution of the first Congress of the Russian Social Democratic-Labor Party, which met in March 1898. (At its second congress in 1903 this party split into the Menshevik and Bolshevik wings.)

Lenin's views on national self-determination were not formulated in detail until the 1913–1914 period. Before that Lenin had not defined the right of nations to national self-determination as meaning the right of political secession and establishment of a separate state, though he later insisted that such was his intention. His approach to the problem had been more in terms of internationalism and the unity of the proletariat of all nations. During the Czarist oppression preceding World War I the problem of nationalities became increasingly aggravated. Aware of the growing disillusionment and discontent among the non-Russian nationalities, especially in the Caucasus, Lenin suggested that a young Georgian then visiting him undertake to write an essay setting forth the Bolshevik position on the entire problem of national minorities. The result was Stalin's essay *Marxism and the National Question.*

Stalin's analysis became accepted Bolshevik doctrine and was incorporated in the party platform at the seventh All-Russian Conference of the Russian Social Democratic-Labor Party in May 1917 (reading 63). It encompassed national self-determination (if desired) for national minorities in the Russian empire and freedom for minority nationalities residing in a country controlled by a dominant nationality. After 1917 it was expanded to include freedom for the colonial and semicolonial countries ruled by a Great Power. In his report Stalin declared:

. . . our views on the national question can be reduced to the following propositions: (a) recognition of the right of nations to secession; (b) regional autonomy for nations remaining within the given state; (c) special legislation guaranteeing freedom of development for national minorities; (d) a single, indivisible proletarian body, a single party for the proletarians of all the nationalities of the given state.

Bolshevik doctrine on the national question has undergone several changes, always in the interest of political expediency. For example, during the period of War Communism the Bolsheviks found it profitable to espouse the principle of national self-determination, including the right of secession. At that time they encouraged national minorities to oppose the White armies, thus promoting Bolshevik prospects of survival. However, with victory assured, the Bolsheviks forcibly reincorporated these minority groups into the Russian state. In another situation, the policy of "national-cultural autonomy," long opposed by Lenin* and rejected as a solution to the national question by the Party resolution of May 1917, was in large measure the same solution subsequently adopted by Stalin, as Commissar of Nationalities, in the early 1920s.

National self-determination, in its usual implication of *political* freedom to establish and function as an independent nation, had but a brief and almost exclusively tactical significance in Russia. However, *outside* of the Soviet Union, the Leninist stress on political freedom is still used. As part of the Soviet ideological baggage abroad, it seeks to portray the Soviet Union as an advocate of liberation for all peoples from colonial rule and as a firm opponent of imperialism. Soviet leaders today see national self-determination as an effective instrument for undermining Western political and economic power. The "myth" of Soviet support of national-liberation movements has acquired a growing power and appeal in developing areas. Thus a double standard is effectively used.

Earlier, Lenin had found it a useful expedient. Not only did national-liberation movements weaken imperialism and strengthen the indigenous communist parties working with these bourgeois-nationalist elements, but they could also be used to establish a global system of Soviet republics. On the other hand, as interpreted *within* the Soviet Union, national self-determination "was to be the exclusive prerogative of the workers; and the national bourgeoisie was to have no voice in the matter." That is to say, national self-determination was to be granted only to the proletariat and its spokesman, the Communist Party, which, in the case of the USSR, had no "desire" to secede.

Such an approach would obviously have little appeal for the peoples of developing areas. Therefore, while *within* the USSR the right of national self-determination has been narrowly construed, in *non-Soviet* areas, a broader, more flexible interpretation has been developed.

During the period of War Communism, 1917–1921, the Bolsheviks

* In late 1913 Lenin declared that: "National-cultural autonomy implies the most refined and therefore the most pernicious kind of nationalism; it means that the workers are corrupted by the slogan 'national culture,' and by propaganda for a thoroughly harmful and even anti-democratic division of the educational system according to nationalities. In a word, this programme, which satisfies the ideals only of the nationalistic petty-bourgeois, is in absolute contradiction with the internationalism of the proletariat."

were occupied with their survival in European Russia. However, the political significance of the East was very much in Lenin's thoughts. Shortly after the Bolsheviks came to power, Lenin and Stalin made their famous appeal "To All the Toiling Moslems of Russia and the East." There was no mistaking their attempt to incite revolution in the Moslem-populated areas of Russia, the Middle East, and India. This active interest waned under the impact of more pressing concerns, but appreciation of the importance of these areas did not. Of the Bolshevik leaders only Stalin remained continually involved in Asian and non-European affairs. His interest in the potential of the East persisted during the post-armistice period, at a time "when every Soviet leader had his eyes fixed on Berlin and on the incipient German revolution."[1] In November 1918 Stalin wrote several articles, including "Don't Forget the East" (reading 64), in which he called attention to the revolutionary ferment spreading throughout the East. He feared that the Bolsheviks, in their intense focus on the expected revolution in Germany and Western Europe, would neglect vital interests in the East.

At the founding Congress of the Communist International in March 1919, the colonial question received relatively little attention. However, as the situation in Russia stabilized, Lenin shrewdly perceived that the East could be used to improve Russia's military-political position. Accordingly, he proceeded to assign colonial areas a more significant role in communist strategy. In July 1920, at the Second Comintern Congress, Lenin's "Preliminary Draft of Theses on the National and Colonial Questions" was adopted and incorporated into Soviet ideology.* These theses reflected the dominant theme of the Congress which was "to apply the principles of world revolution to the Eastern peoples, to develop the doctrine of a common struggle in which all the workers of the world, West and East, had their part to play, and, in particular, to strengthen the revolt under the leadership of the RSFSR against British imperialism."[2]

Lenin's double-edged program aimed at cutting off the West from the resources and labor supply of the East and at expanding the influence of the Communist Party in the developing areas. Stressing the fundamental hostility between the capitalist and socialist (Soviet) systems and the division of the world into oppressing and oppressed

---

* A set of theses was also introduced by Manabendra Nath Roy, the Indian delegate, an able, well-educated, independent-minded individual who split with Moscow in 1929. Roy recommended that the proletariat operate independently of the bourgeois national-liberation groups in developing its revolutionary movement. He also placed inordinate emphasis, the Congress thought, upon the theme that the success of revolution in Europe depended upon the *prior* success of revolution in Asia. Though adopted unanimously, Roy's theses were rarely referred to afterwards by the Comintern, which proceeded to regard Lenin's theses as its guide.

nations, Lenin called upon the Comintern to promote the alliance between the proletariat of the advanced countries and the peoples of the developing areas. As natural allies, the two would work toward the defeat of capitalism; the proletariat weakening imperialist power at its home base and the colonial peoples weakening imperialist power by driving out the European rulers. According to Lenin, the cornerstone of Comintern policy in the national and colonial question must be:

> . . . to pursue a policy that will bring about the closest alliance of all the national and colonial liberation movements with Soviet Russia; the form of this alliance is to be determined by the degree of development of the Communist movement among the proletariat of each country, or of the bourgeois-democratic liberation movement of the workers and peasants in backward countries or among backward nationalities.[3]

Lenin acknowledged that nationalist movements in developing areas would usually have a bourgeois character initially. Nevertheless, he enthusiastically endorsed temporary cooperation with them, provided that the proletarian movement, however rudimentary, maintain its sense of identity and independence of action. Furthermore, the Comintern must not permit itself to be overshadowed by any of these bourgeois-national movements.

> . . . the Communist International must support bourgeois-democratic national movements in colonial and backward countries only on the conditions that the elements of future proletarian parties existing in all backward countries, which are not merely Communist in name, shall be grouped together and trained to appreciate their special tasks, *viz.,* the tasks of fighting the bourgeois-democratic movements within their own nations; the Communist International must enter into a temporary alliance with bourgeois democracy in colonial and backward countries, but must not merge with it, and must unconditionally preserve the independence of the proletarian movement even in its most rudimentary form.[4]

The first Soviet experiment with such a coalition was tried in China in the 1923–1927 period, with disastrous results. Lenin also stressed the need "to fight against the clergy" and against "Pan-Islamism and similar tendencies which strive to combine the liberation movement against European and American imperialism with the strengthening of the positions of the Khans, the landlords, the mullahs, etc." This position was later to prove embarrassing to Khrushchev and Brezhnev in their dealings with Arab and Moslem countries.

Thus while the Comintern was aiding national-liberation movements, it was also supposed to advance the interests of communism, defend the Soviet Union, strengthen the bonds between the Russian proletariat and the developing areas, and stimulate the revolutionary character of the agrarian movement, linking it with the revolutionary proletariat in Western Europe. Lenin emphasized the leading role of the Soviet Union. The relationship between the Soviet Union and the less developed countries "is to be determined by the degree of development" of the area involved; similarly, the relationship between the Soviet Union and the national-liberation movements will depend upon the strength of these movements, and particularly of their proletarian components. Lenin's theses became the accepted ideological and tactical basis of Soviet policy toward the developing areas. Though later Congresses expanded his views, the essentials of his program were retained: to promote nationalist revolutions that in their advanced stage were to be captured by communists and converted into socialist revolutions; to encourage cooperation between the proletariat of the advanced countries and the peoples of the colonial and semicolonial areas; to accept temporary alliances with bourgeois-nationalist groups, provided the proletariat could maintain its position as an "independent revolutionary factor in the anti-imperialist front as a whole."[5]

Soviet leaders did not wait long to link their foreign policy objectives with bourgeois efforts to foment nationalist revolutions. Under Comintern aegis, the first "Congress of the Peoples of the East" met in Baku on September 1, 1920. It openly and uncompromisingly espoused the doctrine of world revolution and tried to enlist Moslem support for an all-out crusade against the West. Soviet objectives were clear: to undermine British and French power in the Middle East by embroiling them in debilitating wars in colonial areas, to associate Soviet Russia with the aspirations of these areas, to penetrate, and eventually to dominate, the national-liberation movements.

The Baku Conference never fulfilled Comintern expectations. But it did illustrate two things: Soviet awareness of the politically important role the East could play in the struggle against the West and the persistence of the Czarist tradition of an alternating Western and Eastern foreign policy orientation. Finally, the propaganda invective of Baku dismayed the colonial powers. Britain, for example, was clearly aware of the potentially disruptive impact of Bolshevik appeals in its Middle Eastern and South Asian possessions. Accordingly, one condition they insisted upon in their trade agreement with the Soviets of March 16, 1921—an agreement important to the Soviets in terms of ending their diplomatic isolation and obtaining needed material from abroad—stated the following:

That each Party refrains from hostile action or undertakings against the other and from conducting outside of its own borders any official propaganda direct or indirect against the institutions of the British Empire or the

Russian Soviet Republic respectively, and more particularly that the Russian Soviet Government refrains from any attempt by military or diplomatic or any other form of action or propaganda to encourage any of the peoples of Asia in any form of hostile action against British interests or the British Empire, especially in India and in the Independent State of Afghanistan.[6]

The Soviets never abided by these provisions, nor apparently had they ever intended to do so. Subsequent Soviet agreements with other nations usually contained a similar provision, just as frequently violated. Throughout its history, the Soviet government has persisted in the convenient fiction that the Comintern (and between 1947–1956, the Cominform) operated independently of Kremlin control, and therefore its propaganda and subversive activities were not the responsibility of the Soviet government. More recently, it has dismissed on similar grounds official Indian protests against the abusive attacks made by Radio Tashkent on anticommunist political leaders.

The colonial question continued to occupy an important position in Comintern deliberations. At the Fourth Congress (November 1922) the Leninist position was reaffirmed by Zinoviev in his "Theses on the Eastern Question," and the Comintern agreed to support "every national revolutionary movement against imperialism." The agrarian question and the nascent labor movements in the less developed areas received particular attention. But, though propounding the theory that the revolutionary movement in these areas could not be successful without peasant participation, the Comintern relied, in practice, principally upon the urban proletariat. Not until the rise to power of Mao Tse-tung and the Chinese communists did communist strategy *and practice* in the East accord the peasantry a significant role in the struggle for political power. The "united front from above" strategy—characterized by a friendly attitude toward bourgeois-democratic parties seeking liberation from imperialist rule—dominated Comintern policy until 1928. Zinoviev developed the outlines of this anti-imperialist strategy for the as-yet weak party organizations in the developing areas, stating that "The Communist Parties of the colonial and semi-colonial countries of the East, which are still in a more or less embryonic stage *must take part in every movement which gives them access to the masses*" (italics are the author's); and that "the working class acknowledges that it is permissible and necessary to make partial and temporary compromises in order to win a breathing space in the revolutionary struggle for liberation against imperialism." In keeping with Leninist tradition, he maintained that communists should become prominent in bourgeois-nationalist political parties but at the same time bind the peasants and the workers into a revolutionary force. Finally, the necessity for the international proletariat to remain allied with Soviet Russia was made unmistakably clear; indeed, a precondition for a genuine revolutionary movement was its acknowledged subordination to Soviet authority. This set the pattern for future Kremlin policy.

On January 21, 1924, after a prolonged illness, Lenin died. The struggle for succession, already well under way behind the scenes, assumed major proportions. All the aspiring heirs sought to associate themselves with the Leninist tradition and assume the mantle of legitimacy. In April 1924, at Sverdlov University, Stalin delivered a series of lectures on *The Foundations of Leninism.* In his speech on "The National Question" (reading 65) he embraced Lenin's position on the intimate connection between the vitality of national-liberation movements, the success of the proletarian revolution in Europe, and the preservation of socialism in the Soviet Union. Stalin lauded Lenin for expanding the national question to include all the oppressed peoples of Asia and Africa, and he expressed the view that, though it was but one aspect of the world proletarian revolution, "the road to the victory of the revolution in the West lies through the revolutionary alliance with the liberation movement of the colonies and dependent countries against imperialism."

Stalin also enunciated a series of principles on the national question, which he elaborated in his speech of May 18, 1925, on "The Political Tasks of the University of the Peoples of the East" (reading 66). Taken together, these two speeches constitute a comprehensive statement of his thinking on the tasks of the revolutionary movement in the colonies. Stalin stressed the need:

1. To win over the best elements of the working class to the side of communism and to create independent communist parties.
2. To form a national-revolutionary bloc of workers, peasants, and the revolutionary intelligentsia against the bloc of the compromising national bourgeoisie and imperialism.
3. To ensure the hegemony of the proletariat in that bloc.
4. To fight to free the urban and rural petty bourgeoisie from the influence of the compromising national bourgeoisie.
5. To ensure that the liberation movement be linked with the proletarian movement in the advanced countries.

In his general appraisal, Stalin held that though capitalism was entering a period of stabilization, the national revolutionary movements in the colonies precluded the restoration of capitalism's former unity and strength. Accordingly, indigenous communist parties would support national-liberation movements, provided the *class* interest (of the proletariat) was not overshadowed in the process. The "revolutionary internationalism" of the proletariat acts to reduce the importance and the length of the period of national self-determination and accelerates the trend toward "the subsequent fusion of all nations." Above all, said Stalin, the Soviet Union represents the example of a country that is the "living prototype of the future amalgamation of nations in a single economic system" and exemplifies true internationalism. All developing nations were invited to emulate the Soviet experience. Stalin elaborated this theme in a piece commemorating the tenth anniversary of the Bolshevik Revolution. Three months earlier, in August 1927, he had also stated that internationalism required proletarians of all countries to support the Soviet Union, since an internationalist is one who "unhesitatingly, unconditionally, without vacillation, is ready to defend the USSR because the USSR is the basis of the world revolutionary movement, and it is impossible to defend and to advance (this movement) unless the USSR is defended."[7] These manifestations of growing Soviet egocentrism were further emphasized in the program adopted by the Sixth Comintern Congress on September 1, 1928, which stated in part that:

In view of the fact that the USSR is the only fatherland of the international proletariat . . . [it] must on its part facilitate the success of the work of Socialist construction in the USSR and defend her against the attacks of the capitalist powers by all the means in its power.

Thus, Soviet national policy shaped proletarian internationalism in such a way that the two became increasingly synonymous.

The 1928 Comintern program constituted the clearest single statement on the general aims of communism made between the Communist Manifesto of 1848 and Andrei Zhdanov's speech to the first meeting of the Cominform in 1947. It became a guide for Communists throughout the world. The Comintern described its revolutionary objectives, the role of the proletariat, of bourgeois-national movements, and of the Soviet Union. It also revised one aspect of Leninist strategy operative in less developed areas since its Second Congress in 1920, namely, the policy of communist collaboration with bourgeois-nationalist groups.

The new line—the "united front from below" or anticapitalist strategy—regarded these groups as "lackeys" of imperialism who had sold out and deserted the revolution. Therefore, the Comintern now held that only communists could lead the liberation movements. All cooperation with the noncommunist nationalists was abandoned, and the communists sought to build up their following at the expense of the bourgeois-nationalist elements. Revolutionary agitation was encouraged, with the main stress placed on the urban proletariat; the peasantry was largely ignored. This left (anticapitalist) strategy remained in effect until the Comintern's adoption of the Popular Front tactic in 1935, when there was not only a return to the Leninist accommodation and cooperation with bourgeois-nationalist parties, but even a collaboration with the colonial powers themselves. Confronted with the pressing threat of fascism, the Kremlin curbed its revolutionary activities and advanced the theme of coexistence with capitalism. The two basic strategies (right and left)—"united front from above" (anti-imperialist) and "united front from below" (anticapitalist)—have since been incorporated into the broader framework of Soviet foreign policy, with emphasis on one or the other, according to the tactical dictates of the moment.

With the rise of Hitler in 1933 the Soviet government took steps to improve relations with both the West and Japan. Mounting domestic and international tensions forced the Soviets to reappraise their relations with the capitalist world. Thus, in 1933 Molotov reported to the Central Committee that "in the Far East the Soviet Government consistently pursues a policy of nonintervention and strict neutrality in regard to other countries"; furthermore, Soviet foreign policy was "not only cautious but deliberate, since here too the Soviet Government proceeds, before all, in the interests of peace and of consolidating peaceful relations with other countries."[8] Soviet protests against Mussolini's invasion of Ethiopia in 1935 were designed primarily to foster collective security arrangements with Britain and France, though they also added to the image of the USSR as the leading opponent of imperialist ventures.

During the 1935–1945 period, with the exception of the brief Nazi-Soviet honeymoon, Stalin pursued a moderate policy in the developing areas. Because of the growing Hitlerian danger, he wanted to develop a security system with the colonial powers and was hence quite circumspect about Comintern activities in the colonial countries. Soviet national interest demanded accommodation and cooperation with the West. Generally speaking, the entire 1922–1945 period was one in which major Soviet efforts centered on European and Far Eastern (Japanese and Chinese) developments. Interest in the developing areas understandably remained secondary to the paramount problem of ensuring the security of the Soviet Union. The troubles within the Soviet Union itself (such as the intra-Party struggle for power after Lenin's death, the agricultural crisis occasioned by Stalin's decision to industrialize rapidly and collectivize agriculture, and the pervasive purges of the mid-1930s), further diluted Soviet interest in the developing areas. But with the end of World War II and the emergence of the Soviet Union as one of the superpowers, a new era opened in Soviet policy toward developing areas.

Two policy principles emerge from the pre-1945 Soviet experience with developing areas. First, these areas have long played an important role in Soviet thinking, as a means of undermining Western power as well as of improving the international situation of the Soviet Union. Second, all nationalist movements are considered useful insofar as they weaken imperialism; yet they must not be permitted to monopolize popular sentiment nor overshadow for long the communists themselves. Temporary alliances with bourgeois parties are permissible provided they serve the greater interests of communism. However, only communist leadership of national-liberation movements can be deemed satisfactory in the long run.

Adapting to the changed international environment, Soviet leaders since Stalin have demonstrated flexibility in adjusting doctrine to socioeconomic and political developments in the Third World. Nikita S. Khrushchev, particularly, was responsible for radically renovating Soviet ideological and political attitudes toward developing countries. Indeed, his ideological free-wheeling may have been a factor in his deposal. For example, during Khrushchev's visit to Cairo in May 1964 he warmly endorsed Nasser's regime as one moving along "the path of socialist construction," thereby incurring the disapproval of other Politburo members who were unhappy over what they considered fulsome praise for a government that had not instituted radical social and political reforms and that was persecuting local communists.

Khrushchev's ideological innovations and encouragement of fresh Soviet interpretations of Third World developments did much to modernize Marxist-Leninist thought on developing areas. A few examples may be cited. First, Stalin's bipolar "two-camp" thesis was superseded by Khrushchev's "zone of peace" concept, which heralded a fundamental shift in Soviet policy toward developing countries (reading 71). This ideological recognition of the independent existence of former Afro-Asian colonies came shortly after Moscow's political appreciation of the promising opportunities for weakening Western influence and introducing a major Soviet presence into countries such as India, Egypt, and Syria.

Second, Lenin's thesis that imperialist nations must go to war over the division of the spoils of colonialism was discarded, giving way to a contemporary variant of his view on imperialism. Recognizing that the decolonization process and the disintegration of Western overseas empires had gone too far to be reversed, Moscow propounded the view that many of the Afro-Asian and Latin American countries are still the *economic* vassals of the Western powers, even though formal *political* independence has been achieved. The term "collective colonialism," which became part of the Soviet lexicon after Khrushchev coined it on February 26, 1960, during a visit to Indonesia, is now used to describe the cooperative attempts of the Western powers to preserve their foothold in the Third World (reading 67). Thus Moscow regards the Common Market's granting of associate membership to many African countries as disguised neocolonialism, the maintenance of Western influence through economic leverage.

Third, Soviet leaders devised an ideological justification for their assistance to noncommunist developing countries through the concept of the "national democratic state." Originally advanced at the November 1960 Moscow Conference of Communist and Workers' Parties and later modified in the party program adopted at the Twenty-second Congress of the CPSU in late 1961, the "national democratic state" refers to radically oriented, noncommunist developing countries that adhere to nonalignment, adopt anti-Western foreign policies, and pursue domestic programs aimed at building socialism through a "noncapitalist path of development." They are also countries that Moscow regards, because of their favorable orientation toward the socialist camp, as promising candidates for eventual transition to the status of "People's Democracies"—the Soviet descriptive for the countries of Eastern Europe—(reading 68). The Soviets see the "national democratic state" as a stage in the consolidation of the anti-imperialist, antifeudal, democratic revolution, as a "temporary transitional" form for developing countries desiring to move toward socialism.

Fourth, the notion of a "revolutionary democratic state" was advanced, apparently to distinguish radical Third World regimes that were both implementing many of the programmatic demands of the local communist party and tolerating its active functioning from regimes that persecuted communists. On December 21, 1963, in a prepared interview with journalists from Algeria, Ghana, and Burma, Khrushchev noted that "the revolutionary democratic leaders of a number of liberated countries are seeking methods and forms for the transition to a noncapitalist path of development." To distinguish the above-mentioned governments, which were then considered particularly progressive by Moscow, from others that were less tolerant of communists, Khrushchev held that:

socialism . . . cannot be introduced by decrees, stages of development cannot be skipped and measures cannot be effected for which the necessary social and economic conditions have not been created and which do not have the support of the masses . . . There is another thing that is not open to doubt. Socialism cannot be built on positions of anti-communism, by opposing the countries in which socialism is victorious, by persecuting communists.

Soviet officials have lauded "revolutionary democratic" regimes, for example, Guinea, Congo (Brazzaville), Syria, and Tanzania, for accelerating the struggle against "imperialism" by curtailing the private sector and expanding the public sector and for drawing on the experience of the Soviet Union to pioneer a "socialist orientation." On occasion, however, Moscow has criticized them for inadequate understanding and for failing to permit the communist party to play an active role in leading the revolutionary forces. The overthrows of Kwame Nkrumah of Ghana in March 1966, Modibo Keita of Mali in November 1968, and Milton Obote of Uganda in January 1971 were keen disappointments to the USSR. In response Soviet writers emphasized the importance of a communist party to regimes seeking to build socialism and cautioned communist analysts against overoptimism in assessing the prospects for socialism in the Third World (reading 69).

In contrast to Khrushchev, Brezhnev has shied away from ideological innovation. At the moment, there are more than enough doctrinal formulations available for attempting to reconcile theory with reality. To the extent that doctrine complicates the shaping of policy, Soviet leaders continue to face dilemmas in their approach to developing countries. What should be the attitude toward the national bourgeoisie? How far can the USSR go in supporting a developing country that is anti-Western and committed to pursuing a "noncapitalist path of development," on the one hand, but that suppresses communists and communism on the other? What should Moscow's attitude be toward military regimes? Objectively, the military may be the only effective political force capable of introducing revolutionary changes, but subjectively it is suspect by virtue of its nonproletarian origins and anticommunist attitudes. How far should Moscow go in supporting the various brands of national socialism emerging in the Third World?

Growing Soviet involvement in the affairs of the Third World enhances the importance of those aspects of Marxism-Leninism which deal with developing areas. Correct theory is considered essential for socioeconomic analysis of diverse trends and developments; it is needed for internal justification for Soviet support of noncommunist regimes; it provides guidance to foreign communist parties; and it is one dimension of the rivalry with the Chinese communists for the leadership of the international communist movement. The revision of outmoded doctrinal assumptions within the broad framework of Marxism-Leninism testifies also to the Soviet leaders' continuing belief in the usefulness of ideology and its relevance as a guide for analyzing contemporary international phenomena.

NOTES

1. Edward Hallett Carr, *The Bolshevik Revolution* (New York: Macmillan, 1953), Vol. III, p. 234.

2. *Ibid.*, p. 251.

3. V. I. Lenin, *Selected Works* (New York: International Publishers, 1938), Vol. X, p. 233.

4. *Ibid.*, p. 237.

5. Jane Degras, *The Communist International, 1919–1943* (New York: Oxford University Press, 1956), Vol. I, p. 390.

6. Leonard Shapiro, *Soviet Treaty Series* (Washington, D.C.: Georgetown University Press, 1950), Vol. I, p. 102.

7. Jane Degras, *Soviet Documents on Foreign Policy* (New York: Oxford University Press, 1952), Vol. II, p. 243.

8. Jane Degras, *Soviet Documents on Foreign Policy* (New York: Oxford University Press, 1953), Vol. III, pp. 4–5.

Bolshevik Policy and National Self-determination

63/Resolution on the National Question

*Adopted by the All-Russian Conference of the Russian
Social Democratic Labor Party on May 12, 1917*

To the extent that the elimination of national oppression is achievable
at all in capitalist society, it is possible only under a consistently democratic republican structure and state administration that guarantee complete equality of status for all nations and languages.

The right of all the nations forming part of Russia freely to secede and
form independent states must be recognized. To negate this right, or to
fail to take measures guaranteeing its practical realization, is equivalent
to supporting a policy of seizure and annexation. The recognition by the
proletariat of the right of nations to secede can alone bring about complete solidarity among the workers of the various nations and help to
bring the nations closer together on truly democratic lines . . .

The question of the right of nations freely to secede must not be
confused with the question whether it would be expedient for any given
nation to secede at any given moment. This latter question must be
settled quite independently by the Party of the proletariat in each particular case, from the standpoint of the interests of the social development as a whole and of the class struggle of the proletariat for Socialism.

The Party demands wide regional autonomy, the abolition of tutelage
from above, the abolition of a compulsory state language and the determination of the boundaries of the self-governing and autonomous
regions by the local population itself, based on economic and social
conditions, the national composition of the population, and so forth.
The Party of the proletariat decisively rejects what is known as
"national cultural autonomy," under which education, etc., is removed
from the competence of the state and placed within the competence of
something in the nature of National Diets. National cultural autonomy
artificially divides the workers living in one locality, and even working
in the same industrial enterprises, in accordance with their adherence
to a particular "national culture"; in other words it strengthens the ties
between the workers and the bourgeois culture of individual nations,
whereas the aim of Social-Democracy is to strengthen the international
culture of the proletariat of the world.

Lenin-Stalin, 1917: Selected Writings and Speeches (Moscow: Foreign Languages
Publishing House, 1938), pp. 118–119, *excerpts.*

64/Don't Forget the East   *November 24, 1918*

JOSEPH STALIN

At a time when the revolutionary movement is rising in Europe, when old thrones and crowns are tumbling and giving place to revolutionary Soviets of Workers and Soldiers, and the occupied regions are ejecting the creatures of imperialism from their territories, the eyes of all are naturally turned to the West. It is there, in the West, that the chains of imperialism, which were forged in Europe and which are strangling the whole world, must first of all be smashed. It is there, first of all in the West, that the new, socialist life must vigorously develop. At such a moment one "involuntarily" tends to lose sight of, to forget the far-off East, with its hundreds of millions of inhabitants enslaved by imperialism.

Yet the East should not be forgotten for a single moment, if only because it represents the "inexhaustible" reserve and "most reliable" rear of world imperialism.

The imperialists have always looked upon the East as the bases of their prosperity. Have not the inestimable natural resources (cotton, oil, gold, coal, ores) of the East been an "apple of discord" between the imperialists of all countries? That, in fact, explains why, while fighting in Europe and *prating* about the West, the imperialists have never ceased to *think* of China, India, Persia, Egypt, and Morocco, because the East was always the real point at issue. It is this that chiefly explains why they so zealously maintain "law and order" in the countries of the East—without this, imperialism's far rear would not be secure.

But it is not only the wealth of the East that the imperialists need. They also need the "obedient" manpower which abounds in the colonies and semi-colonies of the East. They need the "compliant" and cheap "labor power" of the Eastern peoples. They need, furthermore, the "obedient" "young lads" of the countries of the East from whom they recruit the so-called "colored" troops which they will not hesitate to hurl against "their own" revolutionary workers. That is why they call the Eastern countries their "inexhaustible" reserve.

It is the task of communism to break the agelong sleep of the oppressed peoples of the East, to infect the workers and peasants of these countries with the emancipatory spirit of revolution, to rouse them

Joseph Stalin, *Works* (Moscow: Foreign Languages Publishing House, 1953), Vol. IV, pp. 174–176, *excerpts.*

to fight imperialism, and thus deprive world imperialism of its "most reliable" rear and "inexhaustible" reserve.

Without this, the definite triumph of socialism, complete victory over imperialism, is unthinkable. . . .

It is the duty of the Communists to intervene in the growing spontaneous movement in the East and to develop it further, into a conscious struggle against imperialism.

Stalin and the Colonial Question

65/The National Question   *April 1924*

JOSEPH STALIN

During the last two decades the national question has undergone a number of very important changes . . . Formerly, the national question was usually confined to a narrow circle of questions, concerning, primarily, "civilized" nationalities. The Irish, the Hungarians, the Poles, the Finns, the Serbs, and several other European nationalities—that was the circle of unequal peoples in whose destinies the leaders of the (Socialist) Second International were interested. The scores and hundreds of millions of Asiatic and African peoples who are suffering national oppression in its most savage and cruel form usually remained outside their field of vision. . . . Now we can say that this duplicity and half-heartedness in dealing with the national question has been brought to an end. Leninism laid bare this crying incongruity, broke down the wall between whites and blacks, between Europeans and Asiatics, between the "civilized" and "uncivilized" slaves of imperialism, and thus linked the national question with the question of the colonies. The national question was thereby transformed from a particular and internal state problem into a general and international problem, into a world problem of emancipating the oppressed peoples in the dependent countries and colonies from the yoke of imperialism.

Joseph Stalin, *Works* (Moscow: Foreign Languages Publishing House, 1953), Vol. VI, pp. 143–152, *excerpts*.

Formerly, the principle of self-determination of nations was usually misinterpreted, and not infrequently it was narrowed down to the idea of the right of nations to autonomy. . . . As a consequence, the idea of self-determination stood in danger of being transformed from an instrument for combating annexations into an instrument for justifying them. Now we can say that this confusion has been cleared up. Leninism broadened the conception of self-determination, interpreting it as the right of the oppressed peoples of the dependent countries and colonies to complete secession, as the right of nations to independent existence as states. This precluded the possibility of justifying annexations by interpreting the right to self-determination as the right to autonomy . . .

Formerly, the national question was regarded from a reformist point of view, as an independent question having no connection with the general question of the power of capital, of the overthrow of imperialism, of the proletarian revolution. It was tacitly assumed that the victory of the proletariat in Europe was possible without a direct alliance with the liberation movement in the colonies, that the national-colonial question could be solved on the quiet, "of its own accord," off the highway of the proletarian revolution, without a revolutionary struggle against imperialism. Now we can say that this anti-revolutionary point of view has been exposed. Leninism has proved, and the imperialist war and the revolution in Russia have confirmed, that the national question can be solved only in connection with and on the basis of the proletarian revolution, and that the road to victory of the revolution in the West lies through the revolutionary alliance with the liberation movement of the colonies and dependent countries against imperialism.

. . . Are the revolutionary potentialities latent in the revolutionary liberation movement of the oppressed countries *already exhausted,* or not; and if not, is there any hope, any basis, for utilizing these potentialities for the proletarian revolution, for transforming the dependent and colonial countries from a reserve of the imperialist bourgeoisie into a reserve of the revolutionary proletariat, into an ally of the latter?

Leninism replies to this question in the affirmative, i.e., it recognizes the existence of revolutionary capacities in the national liberation movement of the oppressed countries, and the possibility of using these for overthrowing the common enemy, for overthrowing imperialism. . . . Hence the necessity for the proletariat of the "dominant" nations to support—resolutely and actively to support—the national liberation movement of the oppressed and dependent peoples.

This does not mean, of course, that the proletariat must support *every* national movement, everywhere and always, in every individual concrete case. It means that support must be given to such national movements as tend to weaken, to overthrow imperialism, and not to strengthen and preserve it. Cases occur when the national movements in certain

oppressed countries come into conflict with the interests of the development of the proletarian movement. In such cases support is, of course,
entirely out of the question. . . .

The same must be said of the revolutionary character of national
movements in general. The unquestionably revolutionary character of
the vast majority of national movements is as relative and peculiar as is
the possible reactionary character of certain particular national movements. The revolutionary character of a national movement under the
conditions of imperialist oppression does not necessarily presuppose the
existence of proletarian elements in the movement, the existence of a
revolutionary or a republican program of the movement, the existence of
a democratic basis of the movement. The struggle the Emir of Afghanistan is waging for the independence of Afghanistan is objectively a
revolutionary struggle, despite the monarchist views of the Emir and his
associates, for it weakens, disintegrates and undermines imperialism;
whereas the struggle waged by . . . democrats and "Socialists" . . .
during the imperialist war was a *reactionary* struggle, for its result was
the embellishment, the strengthening, the victory of imperialism. . . .
There is no need to mention the national movement in other, larger,
colonial and dependent countries, such as India and China, every step
of which along the road to liberation, even if it runs counter to the
demands of formal democracy, is a steamhammer blow at imperialism,
i.e., is undoubtedly a *revolutionary* step.

66/The Political Tasks of the University of the Peoples of the East   *May 18, 1925*

JOSEPH STALIN

Let us pass to . . . the question of the tasks of the Communist University
of the Toilers of the East in relation to the colonial and dependent
countries of the East. What are the characteristic features of the life
and development of these countries, which distinguish them from the
Soviet republics of the East?

Firstly, these countries are living and developing under the oppression
of imperialism.

Joseph Stalin, *Works* (Moscow: Foreign Languages Publishing House, 1954), Vol.
VII, pp. 146–154, *excerpts*.

Secondly, the existence of a double oppression, internal oppression (by the native bourgeoisie) and external oppression (by the foreign imperialist bourgeoisie), is intensifying and deepening the revolutionary crisis in these countries.

Thirdly, in some of these countries, India for example, capitalism is growing at a rapid rate, giving rise to and molding a more or less numerous class of local proletarians.

Fourthly, with the growth of the revolutionary movement, the national bourgeoisie in such countries is splitting up into two parts, a revolutionary part (the petty bourgeoisie) and a compromising part (the big bourgeoisie), of which the first is continuing the revolutionary struggle, whereas the second is entering into a bloc with imperialism.

Fifthly, parallel with the imperialist bloc, another bloc is taking shape in such countries, a bloc between the workers and the revolutionary petty bourgeoisie, an anti-imperialist bloc, the aim of which is complete liberation from imperialism.

Sixthly, the question of the hegemony of the proletariat in such countries, and of freeing the masses of the people from the influence of the compromising national bourgeoisie, is becoming more and more urgent.

Seventhly, this circumstance makes it much easier to link the national-liberation movement in such countries with the proletarian movement in the advanced countries of the West.

From this at least three conclusions follow:

1. The liberation of the colonial and dependent countries from imperialism cannot be achieved without a victorious revolution: you will not get independence gratis.
2. The revolution cannot be advanced and the complete independence of the capitalistically developed colonies and dependent countries cannot be won unless the compromising national bourgeoisie is isolated, unless the petty-bourgeois revolutionary masses are freed from the influence of that bourgeoisie, unless the policy of the hegemony of the proletariat is put into effect, unless the advanced elements of the working class are organized in an independent Communist Party.
3. Lasting victory cannot be achieved in the colonial and dependent countries without a real link between the liberation movement in those countries and the proletarian movement in the advanced countries of the West.

The main task of the Communists in the colonial and dependent countries is to base their revolutionary activities upon these conclusions. What are the immediate tasks of the revolutionary movement in the colonies and dependent countries in view of these circumstances?

The distinctive feature of the colonies and dependent countries at the present time is that there no longer exists a single and all-embracing colonial East. Formerly the colonial East was pictured as a homogeneous whole. Today, that picture no longer corresponds to the truth. We have now at least three categories of colonial and dependent countries. Firstly, countries like Morocco, which have little or no proletariat, and are industrially quite undeveloped. Secondly, countries like China and Egypt, which are underdeveloped industrially, and have a relatively small proletariat. Thirdly, countries like India, which are capitalistically more or less developed and have a more or less numerous national proletariat.

Clearly, all these countries cannot possibly be put on a par with one another.

In countries like Morocco, where the national bourgeoisie has, as yet, no grounds for splitting up into a revolutionary party and a compromising party, the task of the Communist elements is to take all measures to create a united national front against imperialism. . . .

In countries like Egypt and China, where the national bourgeoisie has already split up into a revolutionary party and a compromising party, but where the compromising section of the bourgeoisie is not yet able to join up with imperialism, the Communists can no longer set themselves the aim of forming a united national front against imperialism. In such countries the Communists must pass from the policy of a united national front to the policy of a revolutionary bloc of the workers and the petty bourgeoisie. . . . The tasks of this bloc are to expose the half-heartedness and inconsistency of the national bourgeoisie and to wage a determined struggle against imperialism. Such a dual party is necessary and expedient, provided it does not bind the Communist Party hand and foot, provided it does not restrict the freedom of the Communist Party to conduct agitation and propaganda work, provided it does not hinder the rallying of the proletarians around the Communist Party, and provided it facilitates the actual leadership of the revolutionary movement by the Communist Party. . . .

The situation is somewhat different in countries like India. The fundamental and new feature of the conditions of life of colonies like India is not only that the national bourgeoisie has split up into a revolutionary party and a compromising party [i.e., Gandhi's Congress Party] but primarily that the compromising section of this bourgeoisie has already managed, in the main, to strike a deal with imperialism. Fearing revolution more than it fears imperialism, and concerned more about its money bags than about the interests of its own country, this section of the bourgeoisie, the richest and most influential section, is going over entirely to the camp of the irreconcilable enemies of the revolution, it is forming a bloc with imperialism against the workers and peasants of its own country. The victory of the revolution cannot be achieved unless this bloc is smashed. But in order to smash this bloc, fire must be concentrated on the compromising national bourgeoisie, its treachery exposed, the toiling masses freed from its influence, and the conditions necessary for the hegemony of the proletariat systematically prepared . . .

In this connection it is necessary to bear in mind two deviations in the practice of the leading cadres in the colonial East, two deviations which must be combated if real revolutionary cadres are to be trained.

The first deviation lies in an underestimation of the revolutionary potentialities of the liberation movement and in an overestimation of the idea of a united, all-embracing national front in the colonies and dependent countries, irrespective of the state and degree of development of those countries. That is a deviation to the Right, and it is fraught with the danger of the revolutionary movement being debased and of the voices of the Communist elements becoming drowned in the general chorus of the bourgeois nationalists. It is the direct duty of the University of the Peoples of the East to wage a determined struggle against that deviation.

The second deviation lies in an overestimation of the revolutionary potentialities of the liberation movement and in an underestimation of the role of an alliance between the working class and the revolutionary bourgeoisie against imperialism. . . . That is a deviation to the Left, and it is fraught with the danger of the Communist Party becoming divorced from the masses and converted into a sect.

The "New Imperialism"

67/The Essence of Collective Colonialism

V. BOGOSLOVSKY

The Suez crisis, the war in Algeria, and the intervention of the Belgian colonialists in the Congo have proved that *separate colonial powers are now unable to suppress, as they did before, the national-liberation movement of the peoples single-handed.*

The new alignment of forces in the world in favour of the anti-imperialist front has made the imperialists change their political and economic approach to the exploitation of the Asian, African, and Latin American countries. Aware that the imperialist Powers are today no longer able to cope singly with the national-liberation movement, the colonialists have started to apply the policy of collective colonialism. This policy signifies *joint* participation of the imperialist countries in suppressing the liberation movement (Algeria, the Congo, etc.), *joint* exploitation of the natural wealth of the Asian and African countries (activities of international companies), *joint* action of the colonialists in the United Nations and other international organizations against the legitimate demands of the Asian, African, and Latin American peoples.

Today, as never before, the imperialists are giving priority to the active defence of their common class interests because the abolition of colonialism means the collapse of the hinterland of imperialism, the loss of their reserves, and far-reaching economic consequences which they are most unwilling to see . . .

Today there is hardly any underdeveloped but formally independent country which is under the exclusive influence of one "metropolitan country" or in which only one group of monopoly capital operates. The exception is some Latin American countries which to this day remain the predominant sphere of American companies. But in Latin America, too, the imperialist monopolies of various countries are frequently entering into all kinds of combinations. . . .

Collective colonialism stands out most vividly in the form of various monopoly and state alliances of the Eurafrica type. . . .

A Government which concludes an agreement with monopoly associations deals not with one metropolitan country, as was the case in the

V. Bogoslovsky, "The Essence of Collective Colonialism," *International Affairs* (Moscow), No. 12 (December 1960), pp. 20–24, *excerpts*.

past, but with a number of imperialist Powers. On the other hand, the United States, Britain, France, and the other capitalist countries are doing everything to bring collective pressure to bear on any under-developed country to direct its economy and policies into the channel they want . . .

What new factors are compelling the colonialists frenziedly to form alliances to exploit the peoples of Asia, Africa, and Latin America? The main thing is growing fear for the future of their raw material markets and cheap labour. The winning of state sovereignty by Asian and African countries first of all deprived the metropolitan countries of the means of non-economic exploitation, that is, all the forms of colonial enslavement directly associated with the control of the state machine by the imperialists . . .

The recovery by the Asian, African, and Latin American countries of their raw material resources through nationalization threatens to reduce the fabulous profits which still flow into the coffers of the imperialist companies operating in these countries, both in the sphere of production (mining companies, industrial enterprises, plantations, transport facilities) and in the sphere of circulation (banks, insurance, and trading companies).

As a result of the widespread movement for nationalization of the natural resources in Asia, Africa, and Latin America, the imperialists are no longer confident that their investments are "safe." They see a guarantee of such "safety" in collective colonialism.

Uniting in monopolistic alliances, sometimes enlisting in these alliances local capital and placing it in a subordinate position, American, French, West German, and British monopolies expect to preserve and perpetuate the exploitation of the Afro-Asian countries, to deprive them of the chance of independent industrial development.

On the one hand, the system of collective colonialism serves as a sort of "shield," raised by the colonialists in face of the Asian, African, and Latin American peoples who demand the nationalization of their wealth; on the other hand, the imperialists have utilized it as a weapon for reinforcing the colonialist positions in Asia and Africa and attacking the rights of the peoples . . .

As we see, on the economic plane collective colonialism is a system of colonial exploitation which is being introduced and consists of joint actions by the colonialists, whose aim is to suppress the national-liberation movement of the Asian and African peoples and at the same time secure large dividends for the monopolists.

The collective colonialism of the imperialist Powers is strikingly manifested in international organizations, the United Nations in particular. Ever since the United Nations was established the colonial Powers belonging to it have been using the flag of this international organization for their expansionist policy. The imperfect structure of the leading UN bodies enables the Western monopoly forces in a number of cases to dictate their will to, and direct the activities of, the United Nations for the promotion of their selfish interests. The actions of the UN Secretary-General in the Congo provide a concrete example of the United Nations being used as a tool of neo-colonialism . . .

In an attempt to undermine the national-liberation movement, Western monopoly capital is employing against the Asian, African, and Latin American countries not only international organizations but its economic strength as well. Above all, it seeks to unite the capitalist camp on a military basis . . .

It is not for "defence" against the non-existent "Communist danger" that the system of military blocs in the Middle East and Asia has been whipped together. By building up this system and inveigling some Asian countries into it, the imperialists are trying to save the remnants of the colonial system, to block the road to social progress for the Asian peoples, and, on the pretext of fighting Communism, to stem the mighty drive of the Asian peoples for national liberation.

Afro-Asian Radical Nationalism in Soviet Strategy

68/Concerning the National Democratic State

B. PONOMAREV

The peoples of the former colonial countries won their independence both through armed struggle and by nonmilitary means. But in all instances independence was attained as the result of an anti-imperialist, antifeudal, democratic, national-liberation struggle. . . . All these goals [i.e., to end imperialism and feudalism] can be successfully achieved by the creation and development of a national democratic state. . . .

The policy of the national bourgeoisie is contradictory. It participates in the struggle against colonialism, attempts to weaken the control of

B. Ponomarev, "O Gosudarstve Natsional'noi Demokratii" ["Concerning the National Democratic State"], *Kommunist,* No. 8 (May 1961), pp. 41–47, *excerpts.* Editor's translation.

foreign monopolies over the national economy, and at the same time supports ties with the imperialist powers and provides the opportunity for the continued flow of their capital. Trying to restrain and weaken feudalism, the national bourgeoisie simultaneously makes concessions to the landowners, upholding an alliance with them against the democratic forces. . . .

National-liberation revolutions can be brought to completion only by a resolute struggle against imperialism and internal reactionary forces. Only through the struggle of the masses is the question of the creation of a national democratic state decided. . . .

What are the characteristics of a national democratic state? A national democratic state is a state that is consistently defending its political and economic independence, that is struggling against imperialism and the military blocs and against having military bases on its territory.

Without ensuring political and economic independence, there cannot even be talk of genuine sovereignty of a country. Political independence makes it possible for a people to drive the imperialists completely out of their country, to choose a path of further development that will make it possible to ensure a national rebirth in a historically short period, and to establish a national economy and raise the standard of living and culture of the population.

The imperialists . . . are trying in every way to restrict the national sovereignty of the liberated countries, to keep them in economic dependence, and to draw them into military blocs. In Pakistan, Thailand, Malaya, and the Philippines the actual masters are the United States imperialists. In many other countries—Tunisia, Libya, Kenya, Morocco, Liberia—the imperialist countries have established military bases. The imperialists exercise a strong ideological influence on these liberated countries through the dissemination of tendentiously selected literature and through special radio and television broadcasts. . . .

Facing the newly liberated, economically underdeveloped countries are a series of common tasks that characterize the goals and content of the present stage of the national-liberation revolutions: the consolidation and strengthening of political independence in the struggle against imperialism; the elimination of the dominance of foreign capital in the economy and the liquidation of unequal economic relations with developed capitalist countries; the rapid development of productive forces by means of the elimination of the remnants of the Middle Ages; the development of national industry and agriculture and the liquidation of the one-sided economic structure; and the decisive improvement of the material conditions of life and a rapid rise in the cultural level of the population. . . .

The establishment of a state sector of industry is an effective means of ensuring economic independence; such a sector plays a progressive role in the liberated countries. It helps to concentrate efforts on the development of crucial branches of the national economy, to accelerate significantly the rate of economic development, and to undermine the positions of the imperialist monopolies. The development of a state sector by means of a national democratic system and the transformation of it into a determining factor in the economy of a country can prepare the material basis for the gradual transition to a noncapitalist path of development.

A national democratic state is a state that is struggling against both the old and the new forms of colonialism and against the penetration of imperialist capital. In conditions where the imperialists are inventing new forms and methods of colonial exploitation, it is necessary for the people to maintain high vigilance in relations with the colonialist intriguers. . . .

A national democratic state is a state that rejects dictatorial and despotic methods of government. Historical experience shows that after the attainment of national independence, the leadership of the local bourgeoisie and the landowners try to establish reactionary, antidemocratic institutions in the country. The danger of the establishment of despotic regimes is a real one in many countries, and in a number of them such regimes have already been set up. . . .

By resorting to the establishment of dictatorial regimes, the reactionary leadership of the bourgeoisie weakens the nation's solidarity in the struggle against imperialism, dealing a blow to national interests. Such a policy leads to a contraction of the social base in the struggle against foreign imperialists and, in the long run, to loss of national independence. . . .

A national democratic state is a state in which the people are guaranteed broad democratic rights and freedoms and the possibility of achieving agrarian reform and of satisfying other demands in the sphere of democratic and social transformations. A decisive aspect of the development of the national democratic revolution, the strengthening of its successes and the development of a higher stage, is the granting to the people of democratic rights and freedoms—freedom of speech, press, assembly and petition—and the right to establish political parties and public organizations and to participate in the formulation of state policy. . . .

The establishment of a national democratic state, its development, and its realization of progressive reforms can take place only through the struggle of the working masses and through their solidarity in parties and organization. Reactionary circles are violently attacking the freedom to establish progressive political parties and public organizations, portraying this as detrimental to the unity of the nation. . . .

The communists have always been in the front ranks of fighters for national independence; thousands of them have died the death of heroes in the struggle against colonialism. However, even now, communist parties are underground in the majority of newly liberated countries. Is this just? By no means. The communists express the interests of the working class and the peasant masses and the highest interests of the nation. To ban their parties means in effect to ban the struggle of the workers and peasants and of the entire people for their rights. But it is impossible to stop the struggle of the masses for their rights by any draconic measures. Those who adopt an antidemocratic course and ban the activity of progressive parties and organizations hurt the fundamental interests of their nations, willingly or unwillingly contribute to the loss of all gains, and possibly create the conditions for a return of foreign imperialists. . . .

National democracy makes it possible for each country that has attained political independence, regardless of the level of its productive forces, to weaken the influence of, and then break away from, the world capitalist economic system—to go forward along the path ensuring not only political but also economic independence and the comprehensive flourishing of material and spiritual forces.

This fact, that the idea of the national democratic state was propounded by communists, again shows that communists are the most ardent defenders of national interests and are selfless patriots of their own countries. . . .

There is no doubt that the national democratic state provides the possibility, as the objective and subjective prerequisites mature and depending on the struggles of the peoples of these countries, for a transition to a higher form of social structure. The achievement of a socialist system requires revolutionary change in one form or another. However, the possibility is not excluded that for some countries the way to a noncapitalist path of development will lie through a national democratic state.

69/The Diplomacy of the Developing States

V. NIKHAMIN

The diplomacy of the countries with a socialist orientation is most consistent in promoting social progress. . . . The diplomatic activity of the young national states where the bourgeoisie is in power, is also largely aimed at strengthening their independence and eliminating the consequences of colonial domination. Now and again it resists imperialist moves. But it is vacillating and inconsistent, and is frequently prepared to compromise with the Western powers. Another group of developing countries is ruled by the pro-imperialist circles of local exploiting classes, and their diplomacy is frequently used to promote neocolonialist plunder and acts as an accomplice of imperialism in international affairs, that is, blocks social progress.

This classification is purely relative, of course. More and more often the government of a Latin American or Asian country, which is a member of a pro-imperialist bloc, and had but recently blindly followed in the wake of the imperialist powers, takes an independent stand in international affairs.

The struggle of the diplomacy of the young states for social progress has run along two main lines: first, promoting stronger national sovereignty, forming the national economy, carrying out pressing change, and doing away with the domination of the imperialist monopolies at home; second, creating a situation in the world which favors the solution of these tasks. . . .

The struggle for social progress is the main line in the diplomatic activity of most developing countries, but is not the only one, because it has also shown the opposite tendencies which spring from the self-seeking interests of the exploiting classes, the instability of the petty bourgeoisie, inadequate organization of the masses, economic backwardness, and dependence on Western monopolies. On some occasions, their spokesmen declare the imperialist and the socialist countries to be equally responsible for mounting international tension, talk about "rich" and "poor" nations and an equally "neutral" attitude to imperialism and to socialism, and demand that the socialist countries and the liberation movement make unwarranted concessions to the imperialists on the plea of "promoting a settlement."

As the class struggle sharpens within the developing countries and

V. Nikhamin, "The Diplomacy of the Developing States," *International Affairs* (Moscow), No. 3 (March 1971), pp. 19–20, *excerpts.*

internationally the differentiation of their diplomatic activity is bound to increase. The states taking the socialist orientation will, as their non-capitalist changes deepen, make more resolute use of diplomacy to promote social progress and beat back the moves of the colonialists. By contrast, advance along the capitalist way is bound to weaken the importance of diplomacy as an instrument of social progress.

The possibility that the diplomacy of some young bourgeois governments may lose all its progressive principles should not be ruled out, and this may run along two lines. First, transition to imperialist-type diplomacy, where the developing country concerned may join the united front of the Western powers, with all the consequences this entails. This may happen only if this country becomes a developed bourgeois state dominated by powerful monopolies. Second, repudiation of its independent line and complete subservience to imperialist dictates in diplomatic activity. The latter alternative is the more likely one, because experience has shown the futility of trying to overcome semi-colonial and semi-feudal backwardness along the capitalist way.

As a result of the imperialist intervention, shifts to the right among the ruling sections, and reactionary coups, Western control over their foreign affairs and the domination of foreign monopolies within the country may be reestablished in some instances. But this turn of events would signify a loss of positions already gained, and this would in turn intensify resistance by all forces standing for independence.

FOR FURTHER STUDY

Aspaturian, Vernon V. *The Union Republics in Soviet Diplomacy: A Study of Soviet Federalism in the Service of Soviet Foreign Policy.* Geneva: Droz, 1960.

Boersner, Demetrio. *The Bolsheviks and the National and Colonial Questions, 1917–1928.* New York: Lounz, 1957.

Caroe, Olaf. *Soviet Empire.* London: Macmillan, 1953.

Carr, Edward Hallett. *The Bolshevik Revolution, 1917–1923.* Vols. I, II, III. New York: Macmillan, 1951, 1952, 1953.

Cobban, Alfred. *National Self-Determination.* New York: Oxford University Press, 1945.

Klinghoffer, Arthur Jay. *Soviet Perspectives on African Socialism.* Rutherford, N.J.: Fairleigh Dickinson University Press, 1969.

Lichtheim, George. *Imperialism.* New York: Praeger, 1971.

Low, Alfred D. *Lenin on the Question of Nationality.* New York: Twayne, 1958.

Meyer, Alfred G. *Leninism.* Cambridge, Mass.: Harvard University Press, 1957.

Pipes, Richard. *The Formation of the Soviet Union, 1917–1923.* 2d ed. Cambridge, Mass.: Harvard University Press, 1964.

Thornton, Thomas P. *The Third World in Soviet Perspective.* Princeton, N.J.: Princeton University Press, 1964.

Ulam, Adam B. *The Unfinished Revolution.* New York: Random House, 1960.

13
soviet policy in the third world

The Third World has become a key arena of superpower rivalry because it enables the Soviet Union and the United States to engage in a low-cost, low-risk, highly intensive pattern of sub-strategic inter-action. Unlike Europe or East Asia, where relatively stable political-military constellations coincide generally with territorially delineated spheres of influence, Southern Asia, the Middle East, Sub-Saharan Africa, and Latin America are characterized by transient alignments and systemic instability. This encourages the superpowers to offer the full range of their wares in order to acquire short-term advantages. In an age of nuclear and missile "sufficiency" it is primarily in the Third World that the Soviet Union and the United States can wage their global struggle, through proxies, with minimal risk of direct military confrontation. For these areas of contention are usually not vital to the security of either superpower, and setbacks there are not likely to affect the fundamental balance of power in significant fashion in the short run.

Developing countries have long occupied an important place in Soviet ideological formulations and long-range calculations. With the crumbling of former European overseas empires in the wake of World War II and the emergence of the Soviet Union as a superpower, these countries acquired an operational significance as well. Communism has made advances in them as both a creed and a political movement. The appeal of communism in these undeveloped, preindustrial, tradition-bound, weak societies is stronger, paradoxically, than in countries living under Communist rule. The Soviet Union has succeeded in foster-ing the belief that only communism represents change and in encourag-

405

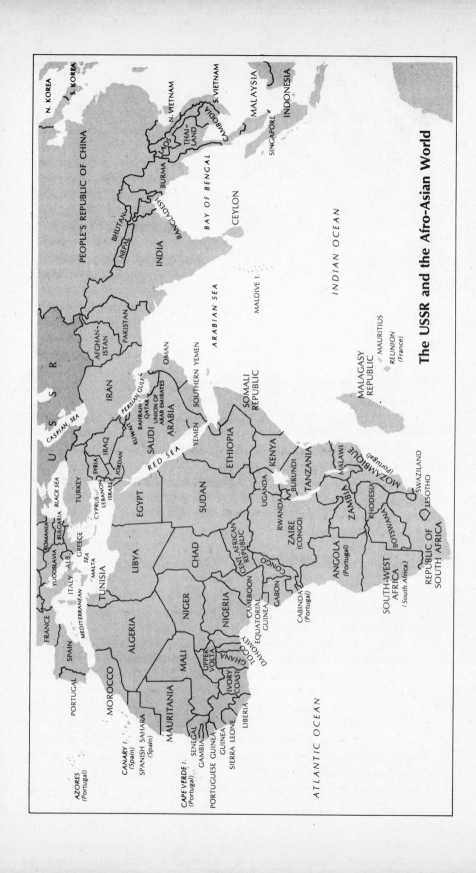

The USSR and the Afro-Asian World

ing the uncritical acceptance of this image among influential segments of the educated elites of the developing countries. Communism offers a facile explanation for past poverty and present weakness, as well as a formula for future growth and strength. Though not primarily responsible for the ferment and turmoil pervading these areas, the communists have exploited it. And Soviet policy has increasingly maneuvered to influence the economic and political development of the "gray" areas between the Western and communist worlds (see map).

Despite such a politically promising environment the Kremlin was slow to use its opportunities, for several reasons. Stalin was absorbed during the post-1945 period with the imperatives of economic reconstruction and recovery, the consolidation of the Soviet empire in Eastern Europe, and the need to modify intra-communist-bloc power relationships as a consequence of Yugoslavia's excommunication and the rise to power of Communist China. Moscow's approach was also tailored to Stalin's rigid, antagonistic attitude toward the noncommunist world. Regarding the emerging Cold War as a global phenomenon, he lumped all noncommunist countries together, regardless of their political orientation, and classified them as "hostile."

Stalin also misperceived the role that developing areas might play in promoting the international position of the Soviet Union. At a time when struggles for national independence were on the threshold of success, communist parties in such countries as India, Burma, and Indonesia adopted policies that isolated them from political reality and alienated them from the national struggle for freedom. In general, this period may be divided into two phases: from 1945 through 1947 and from 1948 through 1953.

During the first phase, when Soviet-Western hostility had not yet hardened completely, local communist parties were instructed to infiltrate national-liberation movements, to support anticolonial, antiimperialist themes, and to exploit agrarian discontent and agitation for land reform. Soviet propaganda blamed the West for the backwardness and poverty of the developing areas, while lauding the "progressive" role of the Soviet Union in championing national-liberation movements and economic developments. These themes, reaffirming Marxist-Leninist orthodoxy, were widely proclaimed by the Soviet Press. An article in *Pravda* by E. Zhukov, a leading Soviet authority on underdeveloped areas, typified the official Soviet line (reading 70).

Moscow permitted, though it did not explicitly encourage, local communist parties to cooperate with bourgeois-nationalist elements during these early, uncertain postwar years. It did direct them to acquire strategic positions in the new governments, labor movements, political parties, and student organizations in order to be advantageously situated to channel the anti-Western struggle along lines favored by Moscow. But no detailed, uniformly applicable, Moscow-drawn plan seemed to exist. Communist tactics varied from area to area and from country to country. Thus, in Southern Asia, communist parties at first openly supported nationalist movements for independence, whereas, in the Middle East, their activity was secretive, conditions there being unsuitable for overt political operations.

The second phase was initiated by the establishment of the Cominform in September 1947 and the adoption of the Zhdanov "two-camp" thesis. The Kremlin adopted a revolutionary strategy that dictated the rupture of communist cooperation with bourgeois-nationalist elements in favor of a program of armed insurrection: This "hard" line had been formulated primarily with Europe in mind. However, it was applied to Asia, and communist revolts were attempted in India, Indonesia, Burma, Malaya, and the Philippines. But in most cases they bore little relevance to existing political conditions in these countries and were quickly suppressed. Having thus placed themselves in open opposition to mass-supported nationalist revolutions and movements, the Soviet Union and the local communist parties declined disastrously in prestige and influence. Moscow's lack of a sure grasp of political reality in many Third World countries compounded local communist blunders. Thus, the 1948 revolution in India was begun mainly at the instigation of leftist Cominform circles and may not have had Stalin's considered approval. But once it started, the Soviet leadership was willing, apparently on the basis of an exaggerated belief in Communist capabilities, to let it continue. Moscow evidently anticipated that India would be fragmented by the clash between Nehru and the princely states and that the communists would be able to establish secure political bases in various parts of the country.

Nowhere was Moscow's ignorance of the Indian scene more obvious than in the Soviet attitude toward Gandhi and Nehru. Gandhi's hold upon the Indian masses transcended party, caste, and class. He was the bridge between the essentially middle-class, educated Congress Party leadership and the poverty-bound, illiterate millions. Moscow interpreted Gandhism as "the most important ideological weapon in the hands of the Indian bourgeoisie for keeping the masses under its influence"; it criticized Gandhi for preaching class peace and social harmony. Gandhi's policy for attaining India's independence, *satyagraha* (nonviolent direct action), contrasted with Moscow's insistence upon class struggle and violence. Stalin's bipolarism forced all communists to condemn Gandhism as a reactionary movement. Jawaharlal Nehru, a Brahmin aristocrat, educated in England, held a place in the hearts of the Indian people second only to Gandhi. Moscow attacked him as a "lackey of British imperialism." After Stalin's death, Nehru's autobiography, *Discovery of India,* was translated into Russian on the occasion of his visit to Moscow in June 1955, signifying Moscow's "discovery" of Nehru the great nationalist leader and renowned statesman. Gandhi, too, was eventually recast in a more positive light in keeping with the Soviet policy of improving relations with India.

Stalin maintained that countries such as India, Burma, Ceylon, and Indonesia, which had obtained their independence under noncommunist leaderships, were not really free—they were puppets, exercising the formal prerogatives of sovereignty, but in reality controlled by a combination of Western capitalists and indigenous wealthy elements. Stalin regarded these governments as agents of "Anglo-American imperialism in Southeast Asia," and acted accordingly. For example, the Soviet government did not contribute either in the United Nations or on a bilateral basis, toward the economic development of these countries.

Brief mention must be made of the related policy of Communist China. With Mao Tse-tung's victory in China, communist strategy in Southern Asia shifted. Recognizing Mao's "National Front" strategy as the proper road for Asian communism, Moscow accepted cooperation with bourgeois parties in broadly based nationalist, anti-imperialist coalitions as a tactical necessity. Though this line of approach was openly acknowledged as "correct" during the last three years of the Stalinist era, it was not actively implemented until the post-Stalinist period. Stalinist doctrine, which insisted upon a *leading* role for the Communist Party in the struggle against foreign imperialism and indigenous capitalism, has since given way to the more flexible Maoist view that encourages cooperation with bourgeois-nationalist groups against foreign domination and with the "progressive" elements of the national bourgeoisie against the "big" bourgeoisie and the native capitalist class. Once independence has been achieved, Maoist strategy calls for an all-out communist effort to seize the leadership of the nationalist movement from the bourgeois parties and assume control of the entire revolutionary struggle, with heavy reliance upon the peasantry as the base upon which to build the revolutionary movement. However, neither the Soviet Union nor Communist China has uniformly applied the Maoist line. Each has adapted its strategy in the interest of maximizing its own prospects for influence-building among bourgeois-nationalist elites in developing countries. Both have repeatedly cooperated with and supported the national bourgeoisie in countries where the communist party is weak, where the regime is neutralist or anti-Western, and where friendly diplomatic ties are deemed more in the national interest than the promotion of internal revolutions. Formulation of the "correct" strategy involves identification of the main enemy and the ranking of political priorities. In recent years, the differences between Moscow and Peking over the question of "wars of national-liberation"—

the communist term for armed efforts to overthrow pro-Western regimes by force and establish communist control—reflect the inability of the two to agree upon a common strategy.

Since 1954 Soviet courtship of the Third World, with few exceptions, has been a skillful blend of opportunism, largesse, and salesmanship. Through a readiness to provide military equipment, economic assistance, and diplomatic support, the USSR has established itself as an indispensable benefactor of such key countries as India and Egypt and as a welcome participant in the nation-building activities of such countries as Afghanistan, Syria, Iraq, Algeria, Guinea, and the Sudan. Soviet ideologists continually try to cluster recipients and targets of Moscow's attention into ideologically conceptualized typologies for reasons appertaining to the dynamics of communist world politics and the methodological schemas of Soviet Marxist-Leninist analysis; but Soviet leaders approach opportunities and dilemmas in piecemeal, pragmatic fashion, ever alert to pitfalls and rewards and with an incisive understanding of *Realpolitik*.

Perceiving openings for penetrating the Third World and for exploiting the flaws in the Western network of alliances, Soviet leaders embarked on a bold course. Stinting neither on economic aid nor military equipment, they took advantage of Western bungling and the systemic realignments in the Third World. Two purposes underlay Soviet policy: (1) to undermine the Western international system and (2) to satisfy imperial ambitions in areas that previously had been outside the realm of Soviet capabilities.

A number of promising circumstances favored the Soviet Union in its overtures to Third World countries. First, the newly independent nations, though not unaware of the danger of communist subversion, were motivated by domestic political considerations to avoid military alliances with the West and to establish their independence of former colonial masters. Democratic forces in the new nations are weak, and in the struggle to survive these countries often chose a policy of non-involvement in what they regarded as merely a Great Power conflict.

Second, Soviet imperialism was not apparent in Southern Asia, the Middle East, or Africa, as it was in Europe and the Far East. These areas have never known Russian rule, and the postwar experience of Eastern Europe and the Baltic States has meant little to them.

Third, an intense preoccupation with domestic problems led many new nations to look to the Soviet industrialization experience as a possible model for their own development. They found the Soviet emphasis on nationalization of key industries, heavy public sector investment, and central economic planning congenial to their own aspirations.

Finally, Moscow's offer of trade and economic credits for purchasing

Soviet equipment and goods on a low-interest, long-term basis came at an opportune time.

Khrushchev gave ideological sanction to this new Soviet policy toward developing countries at the Twentieth Congress of the CPSU in February 1956. He emphasized the importance of the uncommitted, developing countries in international politics and the political significance of the fact that "a vast 'peace zone,' including both socialist and non-socialist peace-loving states in Europe and Asia has emerged in the world arena. This zone embraces tremendous expanses of the globe, inhabited by nearly 1,500,000,000 people, that is, the majority of the population of our planet" (reading 71).

During the 1956–1971 period the Soviet Union extended to Third World countries approximately $7 billion in economic credits, of which only $4 billion were actually delivered. These credits are loans that must be repaid; outright grants play a negligible role in Soviet international economic relations. Virtually all Soviet aid is "tied" (can only be spent in the donor country) and concentrated on specific projects (e.g., factories and dams). More than 50 percent has gone to India and Egypt; and almost 85 percent to the group of nine countries comprising India, the UAR, Indonesia, Turkey, Syria, Iran, Iraq, Afghanistan, and Pakistan. (Cuba is regarded as a communist country, and Soviet assistance to it is treated apart from assistance to Third World countries.) The Soviet Union has also become a major purveyor of military aid. By 1972 it had extended more than $9 billion in military credits to noncommunist countries, the overwhelming bulk of it to Egypt and India.

In general, Moscow has courted three categories of developing countries: first, those that adhere to nonalignment but maintain friendly, even dependent, relations with the USSR; second, the swing states that are formally nonaligned but that have shifted, as a result of the vagaries of internal leadership convolutions, to a pro-West leaning and can one day swing as quickly back to Moscow; and third, those countries whose formal alignment to the West is weakening, in ways assiduously encouraged by Moscow. Congenial neutralization rather than communization is Moscow's goal in the 1970s. In this the Soviet Union is motivated more by traditional balance-of-power considerations than by ideologically engendered drives, more by its needs as the hub of an established but restive imperial system than by any compulsion to spread communism. Gradualism, not revolution, typifies the present Soviet style.

The chameleon-like character of many nonaligned leaderships makes them poor material for building sustained political relationships. Moscow has never been comfortable with nonalignment and has, in practice, treated it with reserve and suspicion. There are a number of reasons for this. Moscow does not believe in the abolition of blocs or alliances; it sees nonaligned countries as a vast potential strategic reserve in the global struggle with the United States, rather than as intrinsically autonomous entities capable of playing an independent role in world affairs; and it has yet to accept the proposition that a country can be both "socialist" (in its parlance, pro-Soviet and with a communist vanguard) and nonaligned. Nonetheless, Soviet leaders readily modify their tactical relationships with those nonaligned countries whose internal political inconstancies require frequent adjustment. Moscow sustains a modicum of assistance to ensure that they remain committed to an essentially nonaligned course. Calculating that such countries as Ghana, Indonesia, and the Sudan may again become more pro-Soviet, it aims to safeguard as much of the Soviet stake as possible and to lessen the likelihood that a pro-Chinese orientation will develop.

Soviet policy toward Indonesia is illustrative. When Sukarno moved closer to Peking during the 1961–1965 period, relations between Djakarta and Moscow cooled. After the abortive communist coup in September 1965 and Sukarno's subsequent deposal, Indonesia turned to the West, although remaining nonaligned. Attempts to improve relations with Moscow languished in the wake of Indonesian criticisms of the Soviet occupation of Czechoslovakia. But by August 1970 Moscow and Djakarta agreed on an economic protocol that called for a rescheduling of Indonesia's indebtedness on terms as generous as those offered by the Western countries. There are even signs that Moscow may reinstitute a program of limited economic assistance to encourage Indonesia to maintain her nonaligned status and to afford itself some political access and leverage.

Notwithstanding the considerable attention that has been devoted to Soviet policy toward nonaligned India and the Arab Republic of Egypt, from Moscow's point of view its greatest strategic-political triumph in the Third World has been the changed policies of Iran, Turkey, and Pakistan—countries still formally aligned with the West but increasingly pursuing a de facto policy of nonalignment, including a conscious effort to improve ties with the USSR. In the mid-1950s Moscow vaulted over the alliance system organized by John Foster Dulles to penetrate the Arab world, in part to undermine the West's predominance there, but even more importantly to outflank and weaken the network of Western military bases along its "southern tier." Its successes here must be acknowledged as in themselves amply repaying Soviet efforts in the 1960s.

The détente with Iran, for example, began in 1962, when the Shah indicated that he would not permit the United States to establish military bases or missile installations on Iranian territory, even though Iran would remain formally a member of CENTO. In 1963 Brezhnev visited Iran, and in 1965 the Shah visited the Soviet Union. A long-term economic agreement between the two countries was concluded in April 1966 and modified upward in April 1967. Under its terms, Iran agreed to provide the USSR with deliveries of oil and natural gas and to build the Trans-Iranian Gas Trunkline (IGAT) from the Agha Jari field in south Iran to Astara on the Soviet border; in return Moscow undertook to build a $350 million steel complex at Isfahan, a $200 million machine tool plant, several grain storage elevators, and 250 miles of the natural gas pipeline. Iran has also started to purchase sophisticated Soviet weaponry. Political suspicions remain, but the USSR has astutely promoted a degree of nonalignment in Iran's diplomatic stance and a level of economic cooperation that would have been deemed inconceivable ten years ago. Though less pronounced, tangible measures of Soviet achievement can also be discerned in the cases of Turkey and Pakistan.

A closer look at the Soviet record in four key geographic regions— Southern Asia, the Middle East, Sub-Saharan Africa, and Latin America —may illumine the nature of Soviet objectives, the reasons for Soviet influence among the nonaligned countries, and the possible future sources of discord between them and Moscow.

Southern Asia

The Soviet campaign to cultivate developing nations began in Southern Asia. The prime target is India, the most populous, strategically situated, and by virtue of its leading role among other nonaligned nations, politically important. Interesting case studies could also be made of Afghanistan, Burma, Indonesia, Ceylon, and Pakistan.

Nowhere else in noncommunist Asia has Soviet foreign policy achieved so much so rapidly as in India. Stalin's successors were quick to appreciate the role a friendly India could play in enhancing the international position and prestige of the Soviet Union. The shift in Soviet policy toward India may be dated from September 1953, with the appointment as ambassador of Mikhail A. Menshikov, who immediately initiated discussions aimed at closer economic relations. The first dramatic success was the signing of an agreement on February 2, 1955, under which the Soviet government obligated itself to construct and finance a million-ton steel mill in the Bhilai region of Central India. This agreement marked the debut of the USSR as a lender of investment capital to noncommunist countries. (Similar agreements with other nations have become familiar features of post-1955 Soviet diplomacy.) And Soviet amiability was soon supplemented by increased trade, cultural exchanges, and a steady flow of technical assistance.

Soviet economic credits to India have exceeded $2 billion, placing the Soviet Union second only to the United States in helping India implement its program of economic development and industrialization. Psychologically, Soviet aid may be reaping disproportionate rewards because of the manner in which it is expended. Whereas American aid has concentrated on helping India meet its pressing food requirements and pushing the vital Community Development program, Soviet credits are used to build easily identifiable, economically necessary, and much publicized plants and industries. In addition to the Bhilai steel plant, the Soviet government financed a $300 million program to expand the manufacture of heavy machinery, which included the construction of a major machine-building plant at Ranchi (Bihar); cooperated in the financing and construction of India's pharmaceutical industry; and conducted an extensive geological survey of India's oil resources. The discovery of oil in the Punjab and on the west coast by Soviet and Romanian geologists in 1958 and the construction of a refinery in Assam in 1961 received much publicity in oil-poor India. Of particular importance to India is a second steel plant built by the Soviet Union in the public sector: the agreement to construct the Bokaro plant was signed on January 23, 1965, and the USSR extended initial credits of $211 million for the project.

To carry out such projects, increasing numbers of Soviet engineers and technicians are being employed in India. There has also been a notable increase in Soviet-Indian trade, with the Soviet bloc as a whole now accounting for about 18 percent of India's total foreign trade. In return for Soviet machinery and materials for complete installations, oil products, and cereals, India exports tea, spices, jute products, handicrafts, and processed steel products. Soviet willingness to accept repayment of economic loans in rupees and in Indian goods is of special significance to a country burdened by a chronic shortage of hard currency. In recent years, some Indian dissatisfaction with Soviet technology, terms of trade, and business practices has surfaced in Parliament and the press. However, political considerations and growing dependency constrain Indian officials from pressing grievances too far.

Under Khrushchev, Soviet policy unequivocally supported India on Kashmir, that is, in its dispute with Pakistan. In the UN Security Council the Soviet Union could be counted on to block any resolution India deemed unfriendly. Moscow repeatedly endorsed the Indian-approved concepts contained in the *panch shila* ("The Five Principles" of peace: mutual respect for territorial integrity and sovereignty, nonaggression, noninterference in internal affairs, equality and mutual benefit, and peaceful coexistence). It upheld India's policy of nonalignment and opposition to Western military blocs, to Western colonialism in Africa, and to United States involvement in Vietnam. During the Goa affair of December 1961, the Soviet Union alone among the Great Powers fully upheld India's use of force to liquidate the Portuguese enclave on India's west coast. Moscow's benevolent neutrality on the Sino-Indian border dispute was especially appreciated. However, when China attacked India in October 1962, Moscow straddled the fence; it was reluctant to condemn its communist ally and thereby preclude any possibility of a reconciliation, yet it wanted to retain its expensively cultivated stake in Asia's leading nonaligned nation. Providentially for the Soviets, the Chinese did not press their advantage and the Western Powers immediately came to India's defense with military assistance. The crisis passed, and Moscow ingratiated itself with offers of jet fighters, guided missiles for air defense, and other military equipment, as with its neutrality on the border dispute. In 1964 Khrushchev agreed to sell India a factory for producing MIG fighters; Brezhnev reaffirmed this commitment with ancillary agreements in 1966–1967. Though most of the plane is manufactured and assembled in Indian plants, New Delhi depends on the USSR for certain essential parts, a situation that provides Moscow with added political leverage. The Soviet Union has become India's largest supplier of sophisticated weaponry.

In the undeclared war that erupted between India and Pakistan in September 1965, Moscow was instrumental in persuading the two disputants to cease hostilities and sign the Tashkent Declaration of January 1966. India was less than pleased with what it viewed as Soviet "evenhandedness" on Kashmir. During the 1966–1970 period Moscow undertook to improve relations with Pakistan, in order to offset Chinese influence there. Its limited sale of arms to Pakistan in 1968 stirred up a hornet's nest in India and strained Soviet-Indian relations. However, India's dependence on Soviet support and the pervasive pro-Soviet sentiments in Prime Minister Indira Gandhi's entourage muted New Delhi's criticisms, never more noticeably than during the Soviet invasion of Czechoslovakia. The Soviet goal in trying to draw closer to Pakistan and to encourage a gradual normalization of relations between India and Pakistan was to realize its dream of a land route linking Soviet Central Asia to India via Afghanistan and Pakistan that could enhance its penetration of the subcontinent and coincidentally, after June 1967, eliminate the inconveniences and expenses incurred by the closing of the Suez Canal. This would also help to isolate China in Asia.

Soviet prestige soared with the signing, on August 9, 1971, of a twenty-year Treaty of Friendship that presumably commits the Soviet Union to help India in the event that Communist China decided to help Pakistan during any war between India and Pakistan. India's desire for the treaty arose out of the Pakistan government's suppression, starting on March 25, 1971, of the separatist movement in East Pakistan.

As millions of refugees were driven from East Pakistan into India and militants on both sides talked of war, Prime Minister Indira Gandhi sought a security guarantee from the Soviet Union to offset the China factor. By responding positively, Moscow consolidated its influential position in India, though at the cost of its Pakistani policy. When war erupted between India and Pakistan in December 1971, the treaty proved its value: Communist China kept out, limiting its support of Pakistan to verbal denunciations of India, while India's armed forces, well supplied with Soviet planes, tanks, and weapons, crushed Pakistani forces in East Pakistan. And in the UN Security Council the Soviet Union vetoed all resolutions calling for an immediate cease-fire, thus enabling India to complete its military campaign in East Pakistan. By recognizing the independence of East Pakistan (Bangla Desh), India has irreparably weakened Pakistan, eliminating it as a credible military threat. By its actions the Soviet Union has emerged as India's closest ally, an ironical twist of fate in the light of 1962.

Friendship with India serves Moscow well in its drive for influence in Southern Asia. It demonstrates to the nonaligned countries that closer relations with the Soviet bloc can bring them tangible economic, military, and political dividends; it encourages India's policy of non-alignment and estrangement from the West; it serves as a long-term hedge against an ambitious Chinese expansionism; and it provides the Communist Party of India with increased respectability, which could make the Moscow-oriented CPI an important force in Indian political life in the decades ahead.

In Vietnam, Moscow's policy evolved in response to America's massive intervention after 1964. The Soviet Union extended the military and economic aid necessary for Hanoi to continue to wage war: aid rose from approximately $40 million in 1964 to a peak of more than $800 million in 1967 and 1968; Soviet assistance included jet aircraft, missiles, ammunition, and food. At stake was not only Soviet credibility as an ally, but Soviet influence with Asian communists, especially in the context of the Sino-Soviet rivalry.

Moscow's aims in Vietnam have been ambivalent since 1945, when Stalin refused to support Ho Chi Minh's bid for Vietnamese independence in order to avoid antagonizing the French and compromising the strong position of the French Communist Party. Moscow established diplomatic relations with Ho Chi Minh's Democratic Republic of Vietnam (DRV) on January 30, 1950, soon after the communist victory in China, but gave little attention or aid to Hanoi. It served as co-chairman of the 1954 Geneva Conference, which formally ended French rule in Indochina and recognized the two Vietnams. Despite a limited involvement in the 1961 Laotian crisis, Moscow did not urge intensification of "wars of national liberation" in Indochina; it considered Vietnam a minor area and did not want a communist insurgency there to hamper its efforts to improve relations with Indonesia, Burma, India, and Ceylon. However, Ho Chi Minh had ambitions, which inexorably drew Moscow into the Vietnam conflict.

In the early stages of the American military escalation in 1965, Soviet leaders may have been concerned over United States intentions, the DRV's capability, and China's response. But the limited effectiveness and aims of American policy soon revealed unanticipated benefits for Moscow. Anti-Americanism, nurtured by Soviet propaganda, rose sharply in Africa, India, and Europe. Domestic strife intensified in the United States and bred an incipient neo-isolationism. America's economy was beset by serious inflation, unemployment, and a growing deficit in the United States international balance of payments, leading to a de facto devaluation of the dollar in August 1971—all of which exacerbated strains in the Western alliance system and reinforced American domestic pressures for a retrenchment of foreign policy commitments. United States military power was squandered in a war without end and United States prestige plummeted.

Moscow has neither opposed nor extended itself to promote a negotiated settlement. It accepts Hanoi's strategy and seeks primarily to forestall any pronounced increase of Chinese influence. Notwithstanding statements by Soviet leaders that relations with the United States are "in a frozen state" as long as the war goes on, Moscow has entered into the SALT talks, negotiations on Berlin, and efforts to contain Middle East tensions. It is sensitive to Chinese charges that it is "an accomplice" of the United States, but relies on harsh anti-American propaganda and Hanoi's dependence on Soviet aid to counter them. Soviet interests in Vietnam are served by Hanoi's stalemating of American power, Washington's dissipation of power and prestige, and Peking's limited influence. At minimum cost, Moscow has reaped rich dividends.

The Middle East

In the Middle East, Moscow followed a "hands-off" policy after efforts in 1945–1946 to pressure Turkey and Iran and to acquire a trusteeship over Tripolitania failed dismally. It did support the partition plan for Palestine in the United Nations in late 1947 and recognized Israel in 1948 in order to weaken British power in the area. The Soviet sale of arms to Israel in 1948–1949—ironically, a period of virulent anti-Semitism in the Soviet Union—was a crucial factor in the Israeli victory. But aside from this, during the Stalin period Moscow was a sideline observer of the political controversies plaguing the Middle

East. This marked absence of direct Soviet involvement redounded to Moscow's advantage in the mid-1950s.

Since 1955, Egypt (renamed the United Arab Republic at the time of its first union with Syria in 1958) has been the main target of Soviet policy in the Middle East. With the arms deal of September 1955, Moscow became Egypt's arsenal. By agreeing to accept cotton in repayment, the USSR set the stage for closer economic and political ties. It welcomed Gamal Abdel Nasser's anti-Westernism and opposition to the Western-sponsored Baghdad Pact (established in 1955 and reorganized as CENTO in 1959, following the revolution in Iraq that brought in an anti-Western regime). Nasser's "positive neutralism" undermined the West's strategic position in the Middle East—a prime Soviet objective. When Washington's precipitate withdrawal of an offer to assist Egypt in building the Aswan Dam provoked Nasser to nationalize the Suez Canal in July 1956, the Soviet government supported the Egyptian action.

The coordinated Israeli-Anglo-French invasion of Egypt in October 1956 afforded the Soviet Union a golden opportunity to champion the Arabs, though it was American pressure on the invaders that actually forced their withdrawal and saved Nasser. Moscow's prestige rose spectacularly in the Arab world as it replaced Egyptian arms lost to the Israelis in Sinai, lent Egypt and Syria several hundred million dollars for economic development, and agreed to participate in the construction of the Aswan High Dam, the most impressive man-made achievement in the Middle East since the Pyramids. Soviet-Egyptian trade has multiplied many times since 1955, and since 1967 the bulk of Egypt's foreign trade has been with the Soviet bloc.

Soviet-Egyptian relations have been periodically strained because of conflicting ambitions. In July 1958, Nasser's jubilation over the military coup in Iraq turned to bitter opposition as it became apparent that General Kassem had no intention of accepting his leadership. Communist influence in Iraq flourished under Kassem and brought generous Soviet support. Nasser's enmity toward Kassem was accompanied by a crackdown on communists within the United Arab Republic that brought sharp criticism from Khrushchev. But Soviet resentment over Cairo's harsh treatment of Egyptian communists did not jeopardize diplomatic ties nor decrease the flow of economic and military aid to the UAR. Once again we see that when the international position of the Soviet Union is strengthened, Moscow often disregards the interests of local communist parties.

A similar situation developed in Iraq, on February 8, 1963, when a coup d'état overthrew Kassem. The new regime, which was pro-Nasser, arrested and executed hundreds of local communists. Soviet relations with Baghdad deteriorated for a short time, but Moscow, reluctant to jeopardize the $400 million economic and military investment that it had made during the 1959–1962 period, soon improved relations with the new regime. During Khrushchev's May 1964 visit to Cairo, Nasser effected a further reconciliation between the Soviet Union and Iraq. In March 1965 Moscow promised to provide aid for a dam on the Euphrates River, although the situation of the local communists remained precarious.

Soviet-UAR relations improved during 1964–1966. Cairo released several hundred local communists from jail, and the Soviet bloc promised more than $500 million in economic credits for the UAR's second five-year plan, which began in July 1965. Coupled with Moscow's financing of the Aswan Dam, this pledge of aid established the Soviet Union as the major foreign aid contributor to the Nasser regime. Moscow also promoted the military build-up of the Egyptian army.

The political-strategic changes resulting from the third Arab-Israeli war in June 1967 concern us here only insofar as they relate to Soviet policy. In the spring of 1967 Moscow feared for the future of the pro-communist Syrian government. To rally support behind its Syrian client, it spread reports of an impending Israeli attack against Syria. Nasser mobilized his army in Sinai and terminated the United Nations peacekeeping operation, which had kept the Egyptians and Israelis apart since 1957. His support for the Syrians was in keeping with the mutual-defense pact the two had signed in November 1966, at the behest of the Soviets. Nasser did not check on the Soviet intelligence reports, which were false: to prove that there was no military build-up, the Israeli Prime Minister offered to tour the Israeli-Syrian border with the Soviet ambassador, who refused. At this point Nasser went beyond Soviet expectations. Instead of settling for the political triumph of liquidating UNEF, the last vestige of Israel's 1956 gains, he closed the Straits of Tiran, blocking Israel's outlet to the Red Sea and Indian Ocean, and moved the mass of his army into position for battle with Israel. Israeli air superiority proved decisive, and in a lightning campaign June 5–10, 1967, the Israelis defeated the Egyptians in Sinai and the Gaza strip, the Jordanians in Jerusalem and the West Bank region, and the Syrians on the Golan Heights.

Since the June war, the Soviet Union not only has reequipped and retrained Egypt's armed forces, but it has committed its own pilots against the Israelis in the fighting along the Suez Canal. Soviet military personnel also man the air defense system and SAM-3 (surface-to-air) missile sites. The Soviet navy freely uses Egyptian facilities and has become a major military force in the Mediterranean. Moscow's pervasive military and economic presence in the UAR is undisputed; what is unknown is the extent of its political influence.

The death of Nasser in September 1970 brought to the fore a struggle for power within Egypt. In early May 1971 Anwar Sadat outmaneuvered the other claimants to Nasser's position. Moscow does not appear to want a major outbreak of hostilities in the Middle East; yet, as 1967 demonstrated, its ability to restrain its Arab clients is limited. On May 27, 1971, the Soviet Union signed a fifteen-year Treaty of Friendship with the UAR—the first time it legally bound itself to a military commitment in the Third World. Article 7 of the treaty holds, "In the event of development of situations creating, in the opinion of both sides, a danger to peace or violation of peace, they will contact each other without delay in order to concert their positions with a view to removing the threat that has arisen or reestablishing peace."

Soviet-Egyptian difficulties remain: Cairo wants more offensive weaponry than Moscow has thus far been prepared to deliver; the Egyptian military is restive over the expanding role of Soviet "advisers"; now that the Aswan Dam has been completed, Egypt seeks new major economic commitments from the USSR, which is reluctant to assume additional economic burdens; Sadat has annoyed the Soviets by his crackdown on local communists, in the wake of the abortive communist coup in the Sudan in July 1971; and Moscow distrusts Cairo's independent efforts to deal with the United States and to "neutralize" its support of Israel. Moscow and Cairo both seek to use the other to promote their own aims, which may not really be compatible. Moscow is not uncomfortable with a condition of "no war, no peace." Its presence in Arab countries rests on dependence, not shared values or aspirations—as Egyptian leaders well know. Soviet analyses mirror Arab views and cleverly feed entrenched intransigence (reading 72).

Soviet objectives in the Middle East are primarily political and strategic, not economic. Moscow seeks (1) to undermine Western influence; (2) to expand Soviet influence through exploitation of Arab-Western and Arab-Israeli tensions; (3) to acquire a foothold in the Mediterranean, the Red Sea, and the Persian Gulf; (4) to disrupt Arab-Western oil relationships, with a view toward weakening Western Europe; and (5) to have a commanding voice in the management of Middle Eastern settlements, as befits the status of a superpower.

Sub-Saharan Africa

Soviet penetration of Black Africa is in its initial phase. Moscow is adapting its tactics to the distinctive conditions of Africa. There are no African proletariats (except in South Africa), no well-organized communist parties, and no divisive class antagonisms. African societies are largely agrarian and rural, rent by tribal and religious animosities, economically undeveloped, and politically unstable. In such a setting Soviet policy gropes for guidelines.

The primary task of the late 1950s and 1960s, of establishing diplomatic relations and some trade with most of the African countries, has been achieved. With few prizes to be won, Moscow has spread its stake-money over a broad range of countries: Ethiopia, Somalia, Ghana (until 1966), Mali (until 1968), Guinea, Tanzania, Sierra Leone, Congo (Brazzaville), and Nigeria. It engages in psycho-political warfare, flails the remnants of European colonialism, and exploits African grievances. After an initial animus against "African socialism," Soviet officials differentiated between the positive variants, which embarked on the noncapitalist path of development under "revolutionary democrats" and which share a common ground with "scientific socialism" (Moscow's brand), and the negative ones, which favor close links with the metropolitan powers and promote "bourgeois" values.

Soviet diplomacy has on a number of occasions blundered. In September 1960 it overplayed a good hand in the Congo with its heavy-handed support of Lumumba in the internal struggle for power, thus facilitating an alliance of noncommunist elements to bring about his deposal. An attempt in late 1961 by the Soviet ambassador to Guinea to interfere in local politics and force President Sekou Touré to accept communists in his government resulted in the ambassador's unceremonious expulsion and a hasty visit by Kremlin trouble-shooter Anastas Mikoyan to repair the damage. In early 1965, Kenya embarrassed Moscow by rejecting a shipment of Soviet arms as "old and second-hand" and by abruptly closing the Soviet-financed Patrice Lumumba Ideological Institute for subversive activities.

In the 1960s Moscow lavished aid and attention on the "revolutionary democratic states": Ghana, Mali, Guinea, Congo (Brazzaville), and Tanzania. Ghana and Guinea, in particular, were to be made into Soviet showpieces. But Nkrumah's overthrow in March 1966 and Touré's unpleasant experience with Soviet interference, coupled with Moscow's growing appreciation of the complexities and pitfalls of African politics and development, dampened Soviet enthusiasm. Under Brezhnev more attention has been paid to the moderate, bourgeois-nationalist countries.

During the Nigerian Civil War (1967–1969) Moscow gave the military government in Lagos modern weapons for use against the secessionist Biafrans. In 1968 it concluded a $140 million economic and technical assistance agreement with Nigeria and agreed to construct an iron-and-steel complex, the first in West Africa. Population, size, and oil make Nigeria potentially one of the most important countries in Africa and, as such, a prime target for Soviet diplomacy. Moscow's more sophisticated approach was also evident in November 1968 in Mali with its restrained response to the deposal of Modibo Keita, long a proponent of pro-Soviet policies. Realizing that conditions in Africa are not ripe for communism, Soviet leaders are tooling for the long haul, focusing their diplomatic efforts on a few key countries and their recruitment on the "progressive" intellectuals and alienated quasi-educated, who are impatient with the rate of progress in their countries.

Latin America

Of all the regions of the Third World none seemed to Moscow a less promising target for influence building than Latin America. Prior to 1959 Soviet writings reflected an assumption of American overlordship in the Western Hemisphere. The success of Fidel Castro's guerrilla-generated revolution in 1959 and his early self-proclaimed "conversion" to communism opened new vistas to Soviet diplomacy (reading 73). Castro's revolution and successful defiance of the United States alerted Moscow to Latin America's revolutionary potential.

Realizing that closer diplomatic relations were a necessary pre-liminary to the ambitious design of encouraging Latin American non-alignment and thereby of weakening United States influence in the hemisphere, the USSR quickly acted to improve its relations with the few Latin American states with which it had formal diplomatic ties. It also sought to obtain diplomatic recognition from and exchange am-bassadors with the other countries of the hemisphere—many of which have thus far refused to deal with it. Some success was achieved, how-ever, notably the reestablishment of diplomatic relations with Brazil in 1962, Chile in 1964, Colombia in 1970, and Costa Rica in 1971.

Castro's "conversion" to Marxism-Leninism gave Moscow a foothold in the Western Hemisphere. Through the Castro revolution, the USSR hopes to promote strong communist movements in other Latin Amer-ican countries. The abortive American-engineered effort to overthrow Castro in April 1961 provided Moscow with a convenient cudgel with which to flail the United States and denounce the Monroe Doctrine; it also led Moscow to expand its economic and military commitments to Cuba. Early in 1962, the Soviet government decided to introduce mis-siles into Cuba and develop it as a military base. On September 2, 1962, Moscow announced an expansion of arms deliveries and the sending of unspecified "technical specialists" to help Cuba meet "the threats" from "aggressive imperialist quarters." On September 11 the Soviet Government, in a major policy statement, asserted that "the armaments and military equipment sent to Cuba are designed exclusively for defensive purposes" and warned that "if war is unleashed," the Soviet Union will render assistance to Cuba "just as it was ready in 1956 to render military assistance to Egypt at the time of the Anglo-

French-Israeli aggression in the Suez Canal region." It deliberately played down the extent of its military commitment to Cuba and maintained that Soviet rocket power made it unnecessary "to search for sites . . . beyond the boundaries of the Soviet Union."

On October 22, 1962, President Kennedy startled the world with the information that Soviet missile installations were being constructed in Cuba. The dramatic account of the "eyeball-to-eyeball" Soviet-American confrontation in the Caribbean is well-known. At no time in the Khrushchev period was there a greater danger of nuclear war. Behind Moscow's gamble there were a number of bold calculations. First, by this "adventurist" course Soviet leaders sought to upset the power balance of the Cold War. They no doubt reasoned that the establishment of a nuclear-weapons capability in Cuba would provide a profound military advantage, which could be used to exact major concessions in Berlin. Second, Soviet leaders gambled that, once the missiles were introduced into Cuba under the guise of "defensive weapons," the United States would not respond resolutely, particularly in light of the Soviet warning of September 11. Third, the success of the Soviet maneuver would force the Chinese to recognize the superiority of Soviet strategy and reestablish Moscow's preeminent authority in the bloc.

Though forced to back down, Khrushchev subsequently defended the Soviet action by asserting that he had removed the missiles only in return for a United States pledge not to invade Cuba and that since Cuba had not been invaded, his policy had been vindicated (readings 48 and 49). Since 1963 Cuba's dependence on the Soviet Union has kept Castro tied to Moscow, though Peking's militant calls for "wars of national-liberation" find a sympathetic audience in Havana and Castro's mistrust of local communists often places him at odds with Moscow. For its part, Moscow's heavy commitment to subsidize Cuba's economic development and national security costs the Soviet Union more than $300 million a year, a price it is prepared to pay for a Cuba that remains an irritant to the United States, a base for anti-American propaganda, and a source of encouragement for revolutionary groups in the Western Hemisphere.

Notwithstanding Moscow's deep involvement in Cuba, Latin America is at present low on the list of Soviet priorities. Heavily committed elsewhere in the Third World and faced with stiff demands upon its resources at home and within the bloc, the Soviet Union does not seem capable of undertaking a massive aid program to many Latin American countries. Encouraged by the anti-American nationalist upheaval in Peru and by the socialist policies of Dr. Salvador Allende in Chile, it seeks to establish normal diplomatic and trade relations with as many countries as possible and to counter the anticommunism promoted by the United States and entrenched conservative interests (reading 74). Citing the national front in Chile—made up primarily of socialists and communists—as a model for Latin America, Soviet officials urge pro-Moscow elements to build similar alliances. Meanwhile, they use UN forums to advertise the benefits of trade with the USSR. Holding out the olive branch and the checkbook, one Soviet delegate asserted that if the Latin American governments were receptive, "the socialist countries would certainly be willing to grant them credits and loans on worthwhile terms."

Observations

Soviet penetration of developing areas is a permanent feature of Soviet foreign policy. Careful not to offend needlessly, the Soviet government has developed an approach generally marked by shrewd planning and timing. It entered into diplomatic relations with most of the new nations, aligned itself with anti-Western and anticolonial movements, launched an ambitious foreign aid program, expanded trade, promoted cultural exchanges, and courted intellectuals and opinion-molders. The Soviet Union came to Afro-Asia with "clean hands," without the taint of a colonial legacy. It experienced an intoxicating initial accumulation of diplomatic influence and goodwill.

Yet in coming decades Soviet diplomacy will be forced to adapt to an environment quite different from the one into which it adroitly moved in the mid-1950s and early 1960s. Moscow is no longer unknown or unblemished. The next stage—the preservation and extension of influence and the transference of economic and military aid into political advantage—is a more trying, expensive, capricious affair, as other Great Powers have already learned. In its relations with developing countries, the Soviet Union is becoming more pragmatic, less doctrinaire, and less abrasive. As a Great Power, its interests have become global, and, paradoxically, it may be less preoccupied with the instigation of revolutions and more interested in the extension of its influence along the traditional paths of diplomacy.

The Stalinist Period, 1945-1953

70/The Colonial Question After the Second World War

E. ZHUKOV

Thirty years ago, overthrowing the landowners and capitalists, the Great October Socialist Revolution smashed the means of national oppression, freed without exception all the oppressed peoples of Russia, and opened in front of them the broad possibility of free national development. The Soviet multinational government showed to all the world and confirmed in practice that it is possible to effect a voluntary union of equal peoples into one socialist family. Mutual trust and national equality, peaceful existence, and fraternal cooperation of peoples are characteristics of the triumph of Leninist-Stalinist national policy in the USSR.

The nations in the capitalist world are found in a completely different situation. Imperialism, teaches Comrade Stalin, can bring nations together only forcibly, by means of predatory war and by the forcible retention of colonies in the framework of "one system." The imperialists, in essence, did not solve the national question, they did not establish relations of mutual trust and friendship among peoples. Capitalism cannot and does not want to eliminate the division between, on the one hand, nations that are suppressed, dependent, and unequal, and, on the other, those [nations] which oppress, exploit, and possess all the rights. Such a division exists and deepens "in the contradictions of the bourgeois-democratic lies, which hide what is characteristic in the epoch of finance capitalism and imperialism, the colonial and financial enslavement of the great majority of the population of the earth by the insignificant minority of wealthy advanced capitalist countries."

Only Leninism offers a solution of the national-colonial problem. In spite of the apologists of the bourgeoisie, who attempt by different means to excuse and to institutionalize the inequality of peoples, in spite of reformers, who carry on, in essence, the same bourgeois policy on the national question, Marxism-Leninism calls all the oppressed peoples to the struggle for their complete liberation, binding the national-liberation movement of the oppressed peoples of the colonies and dependent countries with the revolutionary struggle of the proletariat. The great teach-

Pravda, August 7, 1947, *excerpts*. Editor's translation.

ers—Lenin and Stalin—revealed profoundly and exhaustively in their works the existence of the national-colonial question and worked out the theoretical methods of its solution. Leninist-Stalinist nationality policy found complete fulfillment in the USSR, where the problem of cooperation of nations, and the national question were solved better than in any other state. The brotherhood of peoples seems to be the wellspring of power of the Soviet state.

The colonial question belongs to the group of the most crucial problems of world politics. During the course of many decades the domination of some countries over others, the rivalry of the colonial powers and their struggle for the partition of the dependent and colonial countries, were among the main sources of international conflict and military clashes.

The colonial question continues to disturb world public opinion even after World War II, when it was further intensified. . . .

World War II could not help influencing profoundly the situation in the colonial countries. In the struggle against the Fascist slaveholders, all the democratic forces of the world combined with the Soviet Union as the leader. The victory over Hitlerite Germany and militaristic Japan marked the ruin of the plans of the German and Japanese imperialists, who attempted to expand the sphere of national-colonial slavery. . . .

Even in the course of World War II a significant rise of the national-liberation movement appeared in several colonial and dependent countries. The anti-imperialist struggle in the Arab East, in Syria, Lebanon, and Egypt, intensified remarkably. The forms of struggle against English control in India and Burma also intensified. The masses of Indochina rose, cast off the yoke of Japanese and French imperialists, and declared their independence. The wide anti-imperialist movement that spread in British Malaya, in Indonesia, in the Philippines, assumed in these countries the form of armed partisan struggle against the Japanese seizure. The peoples of the colonial countries could not help declaring themselves against fascism, which was the most blatant form of racial and national oppression. . . .

The war caused serious economic dislocations throughout the world. It affected the economic situation of the colonial countries. . . .*

The Maneuvers and Methods of Disguising Imperialism in the Colonies

The postwar period is characterized by the serious maneuvers of the imperialist states in the colonies. These maneuvers have for their task

* [The article then develops the economic changes wrought in the pattern of colonial-metropolitan relations.—Ed.]

the strengthening of the shaken position of imperialism by means of the establishment of more flexible and experienced disguised forms of domination in the colonies. This is done by granting partial concessions to the national needs of the colonial countries. Among the ruling circles of the colonial empires a theory has received great popularity. It says that the backward peoples in their development undoubtedly have to go through successive stages of dependence on, or trusteeships by, the more developed, advanced states. This theory is extremely suitable for the imperialists and helps them preserve old colonial regimes under the supposedly benevolent suggestion that the peoples of this or that colonial country are not yet ready for independent existence. No wonder this theory received particular popularity in the classical colonial empire—in England. It is necessary to remark that the colonial policy of the British Labour government, as well as its foreign policy, is in essence no different from the policy of the Conservatives. . . .

It was not in vain that Churchill could not hide his delight at the adroitness with which the Labour government "solved" the sensitive problem of India. The partition of India into two dominions, which was effected on the religious-communal basis, along with the preservation of the principalities as an important supplementary factor of English pressure, was satisfactory from the point of view of English imperialism for the national-liberation movement in India. The significance of this measure for English imperialism consisted in the fact that, viewed from the outside, it seemed an important concession, but at the same time it affords the possibility of using, in the future, the traditional English tactic of artificially inflaming and utilizing national, religious, and other internal antagonisms in India in the interests of preserving British domination. Parallel with this is the development of one of the characteristic features of postwar policy of the imperialistic countries in relation to the colonies, namely, the creation of new forms of "unity" of the colonies and metropolis (mother country) under the guise of the establishment of "federation" or "union." Those "unions" consist in principle of nominally equal colonial and metropolitan states, which with the latter's other colonies are granted larger or smaller degrees of internal autonomy. . . .*

The grant of formal independence to the colonies by no means guarantees their actual independence. Many instances exist of strong capitalist states clearly and unceremoniously pressing their will on the weak, but formally "independent" countries. The grant in 1946 of "independence" to the Philippines did not free them from the domination of American imperialism. . . .

* [The article then proceeds to condemn French policy in Indochina and Dutch policy in Indonesia.—Ed.]

The Imperialism of the U.S.A. and the Colonial Question

One of the peculiarities of the postwar period is the increased number of governments that find themselves dependent on American imperialism in greater or lesser degree. As a result of the increased American expansion, the lines between independence and a semicolonial state for many of the formerly independent countries became largely indeterminate and difficult to discern. . . . Earlier the main policing of the colonial system was carried out by England, which, as the most important colonial power, invariably took upon itself the initiative for suppressing the national-liberation struggles of the peoples of the colonial and dependent countries. Now this role of England's is disputed by the United States of America. This is manifested both by the straightforward support by the U.S.A. of the reactionary, feudal elements in many of the semicolonial, dependent countries, and by the immediate willingness of the U.S.A. to lead the intervention for the suppression of the peoples of Southeast Asia—of Indonesia and Indochina, who are throwing off by themselves the yoke of foreign imperialism.

Khrushchev and the Third World

71/The Disintegration of the Imperialistic Colonial System—Report of the Central Committee of the CPSU to the Twentieth Party Congress   *February 14, 1956*

N. S. KHRUSHCHEV

The arms race, the "positions of strength" policy, setting up aggressive blocs, and the "cold war"—all this cannot but aggravate the international situation, as indeed it has. This has been one trend of world events . . .

But other processes have also taken place in the international arena

N. S. Khrushchev, *Report of the Central Committee of the CPSU to the Twentieth Party Congress* (Moscow: Foreign Languages Publishing House, 1956), *excerpts.*

during these years, processes showing that in the world today by no means everything is under the thumb of the monopolist circles. The steady strengthening of the forces of socialism, democracy, and peace and of the forces of the national liberation movement is of decisive importance . . .

The forces of peace have been considerably augmented by the emergence in the world arena of a group of peace-loving European and Asian states which have proclaimed nonparticipation in blocs as a principle of their foreign policy. The leading political circles of these states rightly hold that to participate in closed military imperialist alignments would merely increase the danger to their countries of becoming involved in the aggressive forces' military gambles and being drawn into the ruinous maelstrom of the arms race.

As a result, a vast "peace zone," including both socialist and non-socialist peace-loving states in Europe and Asia, has emerged in the world arena. This zone embraces tremendous expanses of the globe, inhabited by nearly 1.5 billion people—that is, the majority of the population of our planet.

The vigorous work for peace by the broadest masses has greatly influenced international events. In scope and organization of the masses' struggle against the war danger, the present period has no comparison in history.

The Communist Parties have shown themselves to be the most active and consistent fighters against the war danger and reaction . . . At the same time many other social circles are also opposing war. The effectiveness of their activity would naturally be greater should the various forces upholding peace overcome a certain disunity. Unity of the working class, of its trade unions, unity of action of its political parties, the Communists, the Socialists and other workers' parties, is acquiring exceptional importance . . .

Life has placed on the order of the day many questions which not only demand rapprochement and cooperation among all workers' parties, but also create real possibilities for this cooperation. The most important of these problems is that of preventing a new war. If the working class comes out as a united, organized force and acts with firm resolution, there will be no war . . . Cooperation is possible and essential with those circles of the socialist movement which have different views from ours on the forms of transition to socialism. Among them are many who are honestly mistaken on this question, but this is no obstacle to cooperation. . . .

The position of the imperialist forces is growing weaker, not only because the peoples of their countries reject their aggressive policy but also because in the past ten years imperialism has been defeated in the East, where the centuries-old mainstays of colonialism are crumbling and the peoples themselves are, with increasing boldness, beginning to decide their own destinies. . . .

The defeat of fascist Germany and imperialist Japan in the Second World War was an important factor stimulating the liberation struggle in the colonies and dependent countries. The democratic forces' victory over fascism instilled faith in the possibility of liberation in the hearts of the oppressed peoples. The victorious revolution in China struck the next staggering blow at the colonial system; it marked a grave defeat for imperialism. India, the country with the world's second biggest population, has won political independence. Independence has been gained by Burma, Indonesia, Egypt, Syria, Lebanon, the Sudan, and a number of other former colonial countries. More than 1.2 billion people, or nearly half of the world's population, have freed themselves from colonial or semi-colonial dependence during the last ten years.

The disintegration of the imperialist colonial system now taking place is a postwar development of history-making significance. Peoples who for centuries were kept away by the colonialists from the high road of progress followed by human society are now going through a great process of regeneration. . . . The new period in world history which Lenin predicted has arrived, and the peoples of the East are playing an active part in deciding the destinies of the whole world, are becoming a new mighty factor in international relations. In contrast to the pre-war period, most Asian countries now act in the world arena as sovereign states or states which are resolutely upholding their right to an independent foreign policy. International relations have spread beyond the bounds of relations between the countries inhabited chiefly by peoples of the white race and are beginning to acquire the character of genuinely world-wide relations.

The winning of political freedom by the peoples of the former colonies and semi-colonies is the first and most important prerequisite of their full independence, that is, of the achievement of economic independence . . . These countries, although they do not belong to the socialist world system, can draw on its achievements to build up an independent national economy and to raise the living standards of their peoples. Today they need not go begging for up-to-date equipment to their former oppressors. They can get it in the socialist countries, without assuming any political or military commitments.

The very fact that the Soviet Union and the other countries of the socialist camp exist, their readiness to help the underdeveloped countries in advancing their industries on terms of equality and mutual benefit, are major stumbling blocks to colonial policy. The imperialists can no longer regard the underdeveloped countries solely as potential sources for making maximum profits. They are compelled to make concessions to them.

The Soviet Union on the Middle East

72/On Settling the Arab-Israeli Problem

I. BELYAEV

There is now an imperative necessity to force Israel to renounce the pursuit of a policy of armed provocations and to act in such a way that a stable peace will be established in the Middle East. For this purpose effective use could be made of consultations, including four-power consultations between the USSR, the USA, Britain and France within the framework of the Security Council. . . .

The US proposals, often called the "Rogers Plan" in the Western press, boil down to the following: the occupied Arab territories must be freed; the principle of freedom of navigation will be implemented in the Suez Canal and the Strait of Tiran; the status of Jerusalem must be finally defined in negotiations between Jordan and Israel, but some kind of joint administration of the city is already thought of in advance; the problem of the Palestine refugees must be settled by their being granted the choice between remaining where they are now and receiving compensation, or returning to Israel (the number of those returning being left to Israel's discretion); some "adjustment" of Israel's borders should be carried out at the expense of the Arab countries; and, finally, the "Rhodes formula" should be applied to reach an acceptable agreement between the Arab countries and Israel.

On the surface, we see, these proposals differ somewhat from the plans previously advanced by Washington. But they are just as conflicting as earlier proposals, and their contradictions expose the real aims of their authors. . . .

On more than one occasion American diplomats and journalists have maintained that the Arabs must yield part of their land to Israel simply because they lost the "six-day war." But on what standards of international law can such claims be based? It was Israel that made an unprovoked attack on the UAR, Syria and Jordan, and not the other way round.

It may be argued that the closure of the Strait of Tiran was a *casus belli* justifying Israel's actions. That, indeed, was the "argument" put forward by Tel Aviv on the eve of June 5, 1967, when it cried "aggression," "economic blockade," and the like.

I. Belyaev, "Middle East Crisis and Washington's Maneuvers," *International Affairs* (Moscow), No. 4 (April 1970), pp. 30–34, *excerpts*.

This interpretation of the events that took place in the second half of May 1967 was a deliberate attempt to distort the facts. In reality, there has never been to this day any international agreement regulating navigation in the Strait of Tiran. And since this strait is narrow and is part of the territorial waters of the UAR, the Egyptian government alone had the right to regulate the conditions for its use. . . .

Washington is quoting without any justification the formula contained in the November Resolution* calling for the establishment of secure and agreed Israeli-Arab boundaries. The resolution does, indeed, contain such a clause. But it in no way gives Israel the right to expect any addition to its territory at the expense of neighbouring countries. . . .

As for Jerusalem, the suggestion is to preserve the Israeli character of the city and, at the same time, give it international status. . . .

It is useful to recall that, in the first days of June 1967, the Israeli government tried to make Jordan close its eyes to the Israeli aggression. In that event, Jordan was to be guaranteed territorial integrity. Thus, East Jerusalem was by no means the objective of the "six-day war" as Israeli politicians and religious figures now affirm. This version cropped up when Israeli soldiers were already in East Jerusalem. It has become current only because it now seems convenient to pretext the urgency of "reunifying" Jerusalem. But in this case the slogan of "reunification" has been made a means of annexation and an open play on the religious feelings of Jews living in Israel and other countries.

The latest American proposals call for the free navigation in the Strait of Tiran and the Suez Canal. It should be remembered that the UAR, whose sovereignty extends to these waterways, is prepared to carry out this provision. But what commitments will Israel assume in this regard? No clear answer to this question can be heard in Washington. Meanwhile, the UAR has repeatedly stressed that freedom of navigation in the Strait of Tiran, and particularly through the Suez Canal, can be realised only on condition that the Palestine refugee problem is resolved.

It may be pointed out that the American proposals also refer to this complex problem. But how? What they speak of is not the implementation of the well known UN decisions regarding the Palestine refugees, but limited alternatives. . . .

. . . Israeli politicians and military men have been speaking of the need for direct negotiations with the Arab countries. Only such talks, they say, can bring peace. But what peaceful and direct negotiations between Israel and the Arab countries can there be when Israeli forces occupy a significant part of the territory of the UAR, Syria and Jordan, and as long as armed provocations by Israel against these three coun-

* [November 22, 1967, United Nations.—Ed.]

tries continue? Such "negotiations" would immediately be used by Israel to dictate its own terms. Israel would try to impose on the Arab countries a kind of "peace" that would be profitable only to Israel and its imperialist, primarily American, patrons.

In an effort to make the proposals for direct negotiations more acceptable, Washington is now insistently advertising the so-called "Rhodes formula."

As soon as the "Rhodes formula" was mentioned, Tel Aviv emphasised that it regarded it as a formula for direct, and no other, negotiations. Obviously, Tel Aviv, this time with Washington's support, is trying to impose its own approach to a settlement. The position of the Arab countries, who reject all attempts to compel them to negotiate a settlement "from positions of strength," is fully understandable and reasonable....

A question that cannot fail to suggest itself is: why does the US jeopardise its relations with the Arab countries by continuing to pursue its one-sided Middle East policy of supporting Israel and its annexationist aspirations?...

The tremendous upsurge in the national liberation and anti-imperialist movement and the strengthening of progressive national regimes in the UAR, Syria, Algeria and Iraq, have clearly complicated the US military-oil complex's position in the Middle East. The American-British oil empire in this region has turned out to be vulnerable. Hoping to strengthen their shaken positions in the Middle East, the bosses of the US military-oil complex have gone over to open alliance with international Zionism, which has Israel as its fulcrum, and reactionary Arab circles. And Israel has become the strike force of this alliance....

... talk about an alleged arms race imposed on the Middle East by the Soviet Union is but a hackneyed and cheap way of laying the blame at someone else's door. The Middle East conflict can be liquidated only by peaceful settlement and not by war or an arms race. For this, Tel Aviv must abandon its absurd plans of creating a greater Israel from the Nile to the Euphrates; it must carry out the Security Council's November Resolution strictly and without delay. This, it goes without saying, necessarily includes the unconditional recognition of the principle that it is inadmissible to acquire territory by war or military pressure.

The Soviet Union and Latin America

73/The Soviet Image of Latin America

The fundamental instrument of expansion of the U.S.A. into the countries of the Western Hemisphere after World War II was the so-called Inter-American system, which was intended to mask the imperialistic policy of the U.S.A. and to paralyze the struggle of the peoples of the Latin American countries for national independence and economic liberation. The reactionary, cosmopolitan doctrine of Pan-Americanism is based on the ideology of American imperialism, which alleges an existent community of interests of the countries of the Western Hemisphere, one based on their geographical closeness and on an affinity of political ideals and systems. In essence, however, Pan-Americanism is a new edition of the renowned Monroe Doctrine, certifying the domination of the U.S.A. in the Western Hemisphere. . . .

With the help of and under the cover of the Inter-American organs, the U.S.A. unfolded a wide expansion into Latin America in the postwar period. . . . Controlling the economy of the Latin American countries, the monopolies of the U.S.A. stimulate the development only of those branches of industry and agriculture that do not compete with the American ones. . . .

The ruling circles of the U.S.A. considered as one of the main tasks of their policy in Latin American countries the struggle against national-liberation movements, which in the first postwar years were found on the increase. Under the pressure of the U.S.A. in Chile, Brazil, Venezuela, Colombia, Paraguay, Peru, and many other countries, communist parties were declared illegal, thousands of communists and other progressive agents were thrown into prisons. American imperialism, nevertheless, could not frighten, nor buy off the freedom-loving peoples of Latin America. In spite of repressions and defamation, they continued their struggle for independence, peace, and democracy. . . .

Nevertheless, national-liberation movements of the peoples of Latin American countries spread; the idea of a united national front in the struggle against imperialism, which the communists consistently upheld, received wider support among the masses. In 1954–1960, a massive

F. G. Zuev, I. F. Ivashin, V. P. Nikhamin (eds.), *Mezhdunarodnye Otnosheniia i Vneshniaia Politika SSSR, 1917–1960* [*International Relations and Foreign Policy of the USSR, 1917–1960*] (Moscow: State Publishing House of the Higher Party School of the Central Committee of the CPSU, 1961), pp. 506–518, *excerpts.* Editor's translation with the assistance of Mrs. Xenia Sochor-Parry.

protest movement swelled in Latin America ... peasant unrest grew, and democratic organizations strengthened themselves ...

The overthrow of reactionary regimes in countries that were considered patrimonial estates of American capital, for example, Colombia and Venezuela, was met with exultation by the national masses of Latin America and evoked among them a new upsurge of national-liberation movements, particularly in Cuba.

For seven years the Cuban nation fought against the reactionary dictator Batista, who, having come to power in 1952 as a result of a government upheaval that had been organized through the active cooperation of the U.S.A., expansively opened the doors of the country to American monopolies and soldiery.

In December 1956, a group of Cuban patriots, headed by the lawyer Fidel Castro, landed in Cuba and carried on an armed fight for the overthrow of the Batista regime. Castro's appearance marked the beginning of the creation of guerrilla detachments, which consequently formed the revolutionary insurrectionary army. Through the active support of the masses, this army destroyed the government army that had been equipped and trained by the U.S.A. On January 1, 1959, Batista fled from Cuba and hid in the Dominican Republic. . . .

Command passed into the hands of the revolutionary government headed by Fidel Castro, who initiated a radical program of democratic reform. The old government apparatus, which had been serving the interests of the monopolies, Cuban landed magnates, and the large bourgeoisie connected with them, was destroyed; revolutionary armed forces were created; and the military mission of the U.S.A. was sent out of the country. The new government presented the nation with extended democratic rights and began a program of agrarian reform, leading to a liquidation of *latifundia* American sugar monopolies and Cuban landlords.

The triumph of the revolution in Cuba dispelled the myth of the omnipotent power of American imperialism in Latin America. It showed that the U.S.A. in the present international situation cannot undertake armed intervention in the countries of Latin America with her former ease. The Cuban revolution demonstrated that even a small country has the possibility of overthrowing a dictatorial regime that relies on U.S. support and of following an independent policy.

74/Anti-communism in the Latin American Policy of the U.S.A.

K. KHACHATUROV

As it cultivates anti-communism, US propaganda develops and spreads various theories, which, under the pretext of taking into account the peculiarities of Latin America, are actually designed to help strengthen US imperialist hegemony in the Western Hemisphere. The first among these theories that should be mentioned is the theory of *"Pan-Americanism,"* or the theory of *"continental solidarity,"* which stems from an alleged community and unity of economic, political, ideological, cultural and military interests and goals of all the countries of the Western Hemisphere, among which the US plays the leading role.

The idea of "continental solidarity" gives rise to a whole series of propaganda postulates. First of all, it is an advertisement for the Organization of American States, which is portrayed as an instrument for achieving peace and social progress in the countries of the Western Hemisphere. The Alliance for Progress has at the same time been advertised heavily as the most effective channel through which Latin American countries can supplement their "own efforts" to overcome economic and cultural backwardness and carry out reforms within the framework of "representative democracy." Particular emphasis here is given to the thesis of "stability as a necessary prerequisite to development." In other words, it is a call to shun radical reforms and to preserve the existing socio-economic structure in the Latin American countries and its accompanying political superstructure.

Co-authors of such theories are often the ideological lackeys of the latifundists, of the big local capitalists closely connected with US imperialism, of the upper strata of the Catholic hierarchy and the reactionary military cliques. One example is the *"theory of complementarism,"* which claims that the Latin American raw material resources and US industrial potential should form a single production complex. . . . Just as clearly imperialist is the *"theory of ideological frontiers,"* which advocates removal of all national boundaries between the Latin American countries . . . [it] proclaims the dependence of most of the countries of the continent not only on the USA, but also on their largest Latin American neighbors. . . .

The notorious "communist threat" remains as the main criterion for the mass information media in Latin American countries in assessing the

K. Khachaturov, "Anti-communism in the Latin American Policy of the USA," *International Affairs* (Moscow), No. 6 (June 1970), pp. 52–55, *excerpts.*

foreign policy of socialist states. Anti-communist propagandists make a special effort to instill distrust of the Soviet Union's policies, hoping thereby to keep the Latin American countries isolated from the world socialist system. . . .

Today, when the Latin American peoples show an increasing desire to normalize and develop political, economic and cultural ties with the socialist countries—the Soviet Union above all—monopoly propaganda has increased its efforts tenfold to discredit the theory and practice of scientific communism. The main thrust is made, as usual, against the USSR and its foreign policy. The Soviet Union is accused of fictitious "subversive activities" and blamed for developing the class anti-imperialist struggle in Latin American countries; it is blamed for the political demonstrations, strikes, peasant unrest, student riots and even armed struggle. The absurdity of such "exposals" is self-evident. For more than 40 years, the Soviet Union has maintained normal diplomatic relations with Mexico and Uruguay—countries that are free of armed struggle. But no sooner had the USSR established relations with Colombia—where there had been peasant unrest many years ago—than American propaganda hastened to accuse the Soviet Union of "fomenting guerrilla warfare." Although such fabrications are obvious nonsense, they are repeated day in and day out by US propaganda, and this inevitably poisons the minds of certain segments of public opinion.

However, despite the scheming of the reactionaries and their US instigators, contacts with the USSR and other socialist countries are developing, expressing the objective necessity for strengthening allround international cooperation in accordance with the cherished interests of the Latin American states. The Soviet Union has long had diplomatic relations with Mexico, Uruguay, and Argentina. In recent years, relations with Brazil, Chile, and Colombia have been resumed. Early last year, the USSR first exchanged diplomatic representatives with Peru, and at the end of the year a similar exchange was agreed upon with Ecuador and Bolivia. In April [1970] diplomatic relations with Venezuela were resumed.

FOR FURTHER STUDY

Brzezinski, Zbigniew K. (ed.). *Africa and the Communist World.* Stanford, Calif.: Stanford University Press, 1963.

Carter, James Richard. *The Net Cost of Soviet Foreign Aid.* New York: Praeger, 1971.

Dagon, Avigdor. *Moscow and Jerusalem: Twenty Years of Relations.* New York: Abelard-Schuman, 1970.

Dinerstein, Herbert S. *Intervention Against Communism.* Baltimore: Johns Hopkins Press, 1967.

Fic, Victor M. *Peaceful Transition to Communism in India: Strategy of the Communist Party.* Bombay: Nachiketa, 1969.

Goldman, Marshall I. *Soviet Foreign Aid.* New York: Praeger, 1967.

Gupta, Bhabani Sen. *The Fulcrum of Asia: Relations Among China, India, Pakistan and the USSR.* New York: Pegasus, 1970.

Hindley, Donald. *The Communist Party of Indonesia, 1951–1963.* Berkeley: University of California Press, 1964.

Jackson, D. Bruce. *Castro, the Kremlin, and Communism in Latin America.* Baltimore: Johns Hopkins Press, 1969.

Joshua, Wynfred, and Stephen P. Gibert. *Arms for the Third World: Soviet Military Aid Diplomacy.* Baltimore: Johns Hopkins Press, 1969.

Kautsky, John H. *Moscow and the Communist Party of India.* New York: Wiley, 1956.

Kaznacheev, Aleksandr. *Inside a Soviet Embassy.* Philadelphia: Lippincott, 1962.

Laqueur, Walter Z. *Nationalism and Communism in the Middle East.* New York: Praeger, 1956.

_____. *The Soviet Union and the Middle East.* New York: Praeger, 1959.

_____. *The Struggle for the Middle East: The Soviet Union in the Mediterranean, 1958–1968.* New York: Macmillan, 1969.

Legvold, Robert. *Soviet Policy in West Africa.* Cambridge, Mass.: Harvard University Press, 1970.

London, Kurt (ed.). *New Nations in a Divided World.* New York: Praeger, 1963.

McLane, Charles B. *Soviet Strategies in Southeast Asia.* Princeton, N.J.: Princeton University Press, 1966.

Müller, Kurt. *The Foreign Aid Programs of the Soviet Bloc and Communist China: An Analysis.* New York: Walker, 1969.

Overstreet, Gene, and Marshall Windmiller. *Communism in India.* Berkeley: University of California Press, 1959.

Poppino, Rollie E. *International Communism in Latin America, 1917–1963.* New York: Free Press, 1964.

Ra'anan, Uri. *The USSR Arms the Third World.* Cambridge, Mass.: M.I.T. Press, 1969.

Rubinstein, Alvin Z. *Yugoslavia and the Nonaligned World.* Princeton, N.J.: Princeton University Press, 1970.

Seale, Patrick. *The Struggle for Syria: A Study of Postwar Arab Politics 1945–1958.* New York: Oxford University Press, 1965.

Spector, Ivar. *The Soviet Union and the Muslim World: 1917–1958.* Seattle: University of Washington Press, 1959.

Stein, Arthur. *India and the Soviet Union: The Nehru Era.* Chicago: University of Chicago Press, 1969.

Suárez, Andrés. *Cuba: Castroism and Communism 1959–1966.* Cambridge, Mass.: M.I.T. Press, 1967.

Tansky, Leo. *U.S. and U.S.S.R. Aid to Developing Countries: A Comparative Study of India, Turkey, and the U.A.R.* New York: Praeger, 1966.

Walters, Robert S. *American and Soviet Aid: A Comparative Analysis.* Pittsburgh: University of Pittsburgh Press, 1970.

Zabih, Sepehr. *The Communist Movement in Iran.* Berkeley: University of California Press, 1966.

14 problems and prospects

We are moving toward an uncertain tomorrow. No other single factor will so shape the character of the next decade as will the foreign policy of the Soviet Union. The issues of war or peace and, more specifically, the scope and intensity of the new Cold War will be decided largely in Moscow. With undoubted effectiveness the Soviet Union has exploited Western disunity and penetrated the Third World. It holds out the promise of détente, but wages unceasing psychopolitical warfare; it condemns colonialism and imperialism, but is itself engaged in the preservation and extension of a vast imperium. Moscow constantly adjusts its policies to derive maximum tactical advantage from changing world conditions. It believes in the politics of incrementalism, that is, that marginal gains can cumulatively contribute to the weakening of enemy alliances and established relationships. Hence there is a continuing need to reevaluate soberly the Kremlin's almost bewildering effusion of ultimatums, offers to negotiate, denunciations, and assurances of goodwill.

Attempts to interpret Soviet behavior become more important as Soviet power grows. For, in great measure, any effective foreign policy depends upon an accurate appraisal of the strengths and weaknesses, the ambitions and fears, of one's opponent. In the formulation and analysis of foreign policy it is indisputably evident that facts do not speak for themselves, that they are ordered and acted upon by well-intentioned men who seek, not unreasonably, to rely on evidence and interpretations that conform to and buttress their own predilections. Given the arcane character of Soviet policy making and the paucity of reliable data, it is essential that the assumptions underlying foreign policy analysis be made explicit and that the salience of the data, the suitability of the methods, and the rigor of the logic be scrutinized. We must be wary of the emotional, the superfluous, and the fanciful, for the stakes are peace and survival. It is also essential to appreciate the manifold difficulties involved in the actual process of negotiating with the Soviets on specific issues. According to Philip E. Mosely, an eminent specialist on Soviet affairs, the negotiator must be patient, resourceful, and tough-minded. He must thoroughly understand the peculiarities of the Soviet system, with its highly centralized, conspiratorial tradition. He must allow for the distorted image of the outside world held by its leaders and their inflated confidence in the "inevitability" of communism. Above all, he must be prepared for interminable bargaining sessions and seemingly futile discussions. Another close student of Western negotiations with communist powers, Fred Charles Ilke, cautions against distorting past and present trends, either from ingenuousness or guilt, so as to see them as conforming to an alleged symmetry of American and Soviet behavior:

Fudging these fundamental differences [between American policy toward Cuba and Soviet policy toward Czechoslovakia] will not help international reconciliation in the long run, it will merely reduce the pressures toward greater independence among Communist countries and make Soviet imperialism seem legitimate and accepted. Many American officials ably expound the urgency of discovering and cultivating common interests in negotiations with Communist powers and of healing the fissures of conflict. This is all to the good. Yet, successful long-term bargaining requires not only flexibility but also perseverance, not only conciliation but also counter-offensives, not only understanding for the opponent's fears but also understanding of his bad sides. American negotiators are great conciliators in working with allies (far better than Communist negotiators), but they sometimes lack perseverance in pursuing their cause against a hostile environment. The world is not so kind to us that we are likely to succeed where we lack the will to win. The difference between American behavior in "our sphere of influence" and the Brezhnev Doctrine must not be lost.[1]

Summit conferences have value, but only if held after lengthy preliminary discussions have narrowed particular areas of discord to well-defined, explicitly formulated issues for negotiation. Even then, too much must not be expected. They will not result in any sudden end to the Cold War. As George F. Kennan, an American authority on Soviet affairs and formerly ambassador to the Soviet Union, once remarked, "There is nothing that could be said to the Soviet leaders in the space of a few days that would change their corrupted mentality."[2] However, top-level meetings can sometimes play a positive role in paving the way for serious talks on outstanding problems. In dealing with the Soviet government, principle must at all times be supported by power. Moscow may ignore the former, but it will respect the latter. In general, the present rivalry between the West and the Soviet Union must be regarded as transcending the tensions of particular areas. What are involved are incompatible concepts of national security and of the future shape of the international community. Time and changing historical conditions may mitigate the intensity of the antagonism and, indeed, induce a measure of limited collaboration, but they cannot negotiate the rivalry out of existence.

The hostility between the Soviet Union and the Western world need not be further documented here. It is enough to note that since 1917 the USSR has systematically sought to undermine noncommunist governments and to introduce Soviet influence wherever possible. No early departure from this pattern of behavior can be expected. Soviet leaders are committed to unceasing struggle against the Western system of values and institutions. Khrushchev's much-quoted statement —"We will bury you"—was not meant literally in any apocalyptic sense, but signified both a challenge and a belief: a challenge to compete for global supremacy and a belief that communism as a social system would inevitably supersede the Western sociopolitical system. This belief in the inevitable triumph of Soviet diplomacy over Western diplomacy was attributed by Georgi Chicherin, Soviet Foreign Minister from 1918 to 1929, to the fact that "our [Soviet] calculation shows that it is more correct. And that is not because they [the Western powers] do not have any people who can think correctly—on the contrary, they have more than we do—but because it is impossible to draw the right conclusions when one is on the way to one's destruction." Robert Strausz-Hupé has termed the Soviet approach the strategy of "protracted conflict" and emphasizes its all-embracing, continuing character. It is a strategy "for annihilating the opponent over a period of time by limited operations, by feints and maneuvers, psychological manipulations and diverse forms of violence."[3] It involves a total conflict of cultures and precludes any enduring settlement between the Soviet and non-Soviet worlds. Soviet enmity toward the West, argues Adam B. Ulam, is imbedded, for various reasons, in the outlook of Soviet leaders (reading 75).

On the other hand, the image of intractable and unrelieved Soviet hostility is an oversimplification of the reality of Soviet behavior. In recognition of the awesome destructiveness of nuclear weapons, Soviet leaders have revised their ideology and insist that nuclear war is not "fatalistically inevitable." They are therefore not committed by doctrine to attaining global dominance by military means. Furthermore, the Soviet Union has recognized areas in which it has a parallel interest with the United States in curbing trends that, if left uncontrolled, might pose even graver threats than the existing conflictive superpower relationship. It has proven possible to reach agreement to end nuclear testing in the atmosphere, to try to limit the number of countries possessing nuclear weapons, and to prevent the occurrence of war through inadvertence. In this there is ground for guarded optimism. The current SALT talks and the attempt to minimize tension in Europe are steps in the right direction.

The achievements that made the Soviet Union a global power have also given it a vital and growing stake in regularizing and stabilizing certain facets of the international environment. Writing of Moscow's interest in such a world in the twilight of the Khrushchev period, one Western analyst observed that:

Khrushchev's Russia emerges as a conservative state fending off the pressures for a policy of uncompromising hostility to the West, uncompromising support of Communist against capitalist, and uncompromising support of so-called national-liberation movements. What primarily motivates the Soviet Union are the material and technical demands of its own society, which in international terms requires peace, not revolution, accommodation not adventurism.[4]

This evaluation has much to commend it in the present period as well.

Even if we acknowledge the institutionalization of Soviet hostility, the questions of the motivations behind Soviet foreign policy and of its principal objectives during the coming decade must be considered. Is peaceful coexistence possible for any prolonged period? What are the Kremlin's specific objectives in Europe, in Asia, in Africa, in the Middle East, in Latin America? Can the West cope for an indefinite period with the unrelenting pressures from the Soviet camp without sacrificing its strength and vitality and the very structure of its society?

The West and the Soviet Union often use the same phrases, but with different meaning. For example, to the Western Powers, peaceful coexistence implies a willingness to accept an essentially status quo situation, a kind of peace without friendship. To Soviet leaders, it has only a transitory and tactical relevance, to be discarded at their convenience; it affords them time to increase their power, expand the struggle to new areas while preserving their own imperium, and undermine Western unity and resolve. "Peaceful coexistence" is not only subordinate to "proletarian internationalism," but it assumes the continuation of "ideological conflict," as G. A. Arbatov, a top Soviet analyst and foreign-policy adviser to the Kremlin, makes clear (reading 76). There is no recognition in Soviet analyses of the fact that the resolution of political tensions is seriously hampered by the intensification of ideological conflict or that the Soviet perception of current military and political problems is distorted by a priori views and assumptions.

On the one hand, Soviet writers contend that international tensions can be resolved without discarding the ideological struggle because Cold War tensions are not a matter of ideology; on the other hand, *all* Soviet analyses of Western policies are presented in Marxist-Leninist terms and rest, as far as can be determined, on assumptions that stem from the ideology. They dismiss as "unscientific" and "evasive" the Western view that ideological conflicts can contribute significantly to the outbreak of war, or at least to a condition of no peace. Marshall D. Shulman has suggested an apt descriptive for the Soviet-Western relationship, namely, that of "limited adversary." The Soviet-Western rivalry will continue, waxing and waning according to circumstances and the power relationship between them. It will be exacerbated by conflictual perceptions shaped by domestic pressures, technological imbalances, and competing national ambitions. The new Cold War will be a compound of extensive conflict and selective cooperation.

Before hazarding a few speculative remarks about the probable pattern of Soviet foreign policy during the coming decade, we must consider the question of whether there are forces operating within Soviet society "that by themselves, and independent of the balance of power" impel the Soviet Union along an expansionist course. According to Barrington Moore, Jr., there are a number of factors to be considered—the nature of Soviet totalitarianism, the power drive of the Soviet leaders, the lines of continuity linking Czarist and Soviet foreign policies, and the messianism implicit in Marxism-Leninism (reading 77). As the social structure of the Soviet Union undergoes important transformations, the relative significance of these factors may be expected to change. But there is little evidence to justify the hope that changes in the structure of Soviet society (for example, the increase in the number of educated people) will materially affect the character of Soviet foreign policy in the foreseeable future. Indeed, the increasingly formidable Soviet challenge stems precisely from the fact that Soviet leaders have shown an amazing capacity to make the necessary economic and social adjustments without in any way sacrificing the monopolistic power of the Communist Party or their own unquestioned and absolute control of foreign policy. Soviet society, despite its many economic, educational, and social changes, is as autocratic as ever. The autocracy has merely grown more subtle and, correspondingly, more effective. In addition, Soviet leaders have developed a broad base of support for their foreign policy, rooted as it is in an intense, traditional Russian patriotism.

What, then, of the coming decade? Soviet-Western relations face a difficult future. First, of paramount importance to Soviet leaders is concern for the integrity and security of the Soviet state. An immense thermonuclear capability goes a long way toward assuring the *military* security of the USSR, toward insulating it from possible attack. But as long as the Cold War exists, accelerating arms expenditures—especially for research and development of new weapons systems and new defenses—will be mandatory, and these limit the ability of Soviet leaders not only to achieve greater security, but also to improve the standard of living of their people. A détente with the United States, however, would give rise in Eastern Europe to expectations of still greater independence and would thereby congeal the Soviet leadership in a neo-Stalinist policy toward this strategic sector of its empire. It would throw into question Soviet leadership of the non-European wings of the international communist movement—where the Chinese call to militancy and revolution offers to foreign communists the prospect of seizing power. It would open Moscow to Peking's charges that the Soviet Union is indifferent to the cause of world revolution and is prepared to discard it in the interest of an accommodation with the United States.

Second, Soviet leaders still believe that "all roads lead to communism." In their view the transition period will be a long and difficult one. And though the process may be advanced by national revolutions, diplomatic maneuver, and economic crises, the Soviet home base must not be jeopardized by any act likely to provoke an all-out war. Accordingly, no major war involving nuclear weapons will be attempted by Moscow during the next decade. Rather, the Cold War will continue to dominate the international scene, with alternate periods of crisis and relaxation. The "balance of terror" will forestall any precipitate Soviet military action in Europe or in any area the West has clearly committed itself to defend. A mutually destructive nuclear war is a totally unacceptable alternative for attaining coveted political objectives. Besides, there is little warrant for the belief that the Soviet leaders intend to overwhelm their Western opponent by military means. But Soviet strength and imperial ambitions caution against too heavy a reliance solely on the nuclear deterrent to guarantee international peace. The West must be prepared to cope with limited wars and overseas challenges, political and military; it must be strong enough to cope with Soviet-inspired and -nurtured conflict in vital areas such as the Caribbean, the Mediterranean, and the Western Pacific.

Third, the principal Soviet objectives in Europe will continue to be to preserve its Eastern European empire, to weaken NATO, and to prevent West Germany from acquiring nuclear weapons. Germany will remain divided. Moscow has no interest in a unified Germany. Khrushchev once told some visitors, "Understand us: what imbeciles we should be if we accepted the unification of Germany within NATO and thus found ourselves confronted by a single capitalist and militarist Germany in the West and had against us both Germanies united." There is no reason for Moscow to alter this position, now that West Germany has become economically and militarily the strongest European member of NATO. Not even the withdrawal of American power from the continent—supposedly an inducement highly attractive to the USSR—would tempt Moscow very much. The risks would be too great. Moscow cannot with equanimity contemplate the loss of East German technological and economic resources, the sharply reduced leverage for controlling Eastern Europe, or the emergence of a unified Germany as a potential superpower in Europe.

For reasons inhering in its policy toward Eastern Europe, Moscow prefers to remain closely enmeshed with East Germany. To do otherwise might encourage opposition to its authority in Eastern Europe. Control of East Germany assures Moscow of a compliant and communist Poland and Czechoslovakia. Indeed, it may be expected to intensify its efforts to strengthen East Germany internationally, possibly offering some minor concessions on Berlin as bait for Western recognition of two Germanies. The territorial status quo in Europe suits Moscow. Not even a severe succession crisis within the Kremlin is apt to reverse this policy and precipitate a withdrawal of Soviet power from the heart of Europe.

Fourth, the Brezhnev Doctrine signifies that Moscow will not tolerate any anticommunist or noncommunist regime in Eastern Europe. Even though the Eastern European countries are becoming more of an economic, military, and political liability and the military strategy of a nuclear age makes possession of Eastern European real estate a defensive anachronism, Soviet hegemony there does provide Moscow with added military options for dealing with the West. Perhaps even more important, loss of this hegemony would endanger control over the diverse non-Russian nationality groups within the USSR itself. The Kremlin fears that liberalization in Eastern Europe will spread to the Soviet Union and revive nationality particularism.

A critical question for Moscow is how far it can permit the nationalist and independent manifestations to proceed without endangering its political authority. Moscow talks a great deal about the "fraternal" ties among the communist countries. It would like a big brother relationship: the Eastern European countries should be weak enough to take orders, but strong enough to carry them out. Moscow has accepted and will continue to accept decentralization as a formula for preserving its imperium, but too much decentralization might trigger uncontrollable centrifugal tendencies and unprofitable economic relationships. Cognizant of the growing technological gap between Western and Eastern Europe and disturbed by the inability of COMECON to prosper as the Common Market does, the Soviet leadership presses for greater bloc integration, which looks as elusive as ever. It also faces the problem of coming to terms with the Common Market politically and economically.

Fifth, like Humpty Dumpty, Sino-Soviet amity cannot be put back together again. Their mutual grievances, which brought them to the brink of an open rupture, show no signs of abatement. Incompatible and competing Soviet and Chinese objectives toward Japan, the Mongolian People's Republic, and most of the Third World, remain active ingredients in their embittered relationship, which is even less likely to improve if the recent explorations in Sino-American relations are in any way productive.

Sixth, there is every reason to assume that the Soviet Union will pursue a forward strategy in the Third World in the 1970s. The developing countries contiguous or nearly contiguous to the underbelly of the USSR are militarily more salient to the calculations of planners in Moscow than they are to those in Washington. A belt of friendly states on its "southern tier" is not a marginal goal for the Soviet Union.

Moreover, the Soviet navy has begun to play a political role in Soviet diplomacy, and it could be used to advantage in establishing a greater Soviet presence in the Persian Gulf, the Red Sea, and Indian Ocean. In the Mediterranean it has already limited American options for intervention. It is also a valuable prop for shaky clients, serving to stiffen the resolve of anti-Western elites who may be emboldened to pursue radical courses they would have been deterred from had Western power predominated in the area. Certainly, Soviet propaganda has made much of the benefits to the Arabs of the Soviet naval presence: "What is the reason," asked Radio Moscow in Arabic, "for this clamor among the ranks of the imperialist naval sharks? The fact is that they know the presence of Soviet ships in the Mediterranean will paralyze the attempts of the United States Sixth Fleet to carry out its designs against the Arabs." In a word, the Soviet Union is using sea power in the classic way, as an arm of diplomacy, to attain political goals.

Seventh, disarmament, about which so much has been written and so little done, will prove impossible to achieve during the coming decade. Nuclear arsenals will grow. SALT talks will go on, but no major agreement on weapons systems, testing missiles, or curbing research and development of even more advanced (and exorbitantly expensive) military hardware is likely.

Shortly before his assassination, John F. Kennedy cautioned against exaggerating the significance of the progress symbolized by the Limited Nuclear Test-Ban Treaty in curbing the arms race: "a pause in the Cold War is not a lasting peace, and a détente does not equal disarmament . . ." He concluded on a sobering note of idealistic realism:

We have achieved new opportunities, which we cannot afford to waste. We have concluded with the Soviets a few limited, enforceable agreements or arrangements of mutual benefit to both sides and to the world. But a change in atmosphere and emphasis is not a reversal of purpose. . . . The United States and the Soviet Union still have wholly different concepts of the world, its freedom, its future. And so long as these basic differences continue, they cannot and should not be concealed; they set limits to the possibilities of agreement; and they will give rise to further crises large and small, in the months and years ahead, both in the areas of direct confrontation—Germany and the Caribbean—and in areas where events beyond our control could involve us both—areas such as Africa, and Asia, and the Middle East.[5]

Eighth, the concept of "disengagement," a subtle and engaging variation on the disarmament theme, has attracted considerable attention as a possible formula for easing tensions in Central Europe. In essence it calls for a thinning out of Soviet and American military power from the area. The projected all-European Security Conference would have this as a major agenda item. There are many modifications of "disengagement" and as many disagreements over its military and political implications for the balance of power in Europe. Since isolationism is anathema to Moscow and loosening its grip on Eastern Europe entails unnecessary risks, the probable Soviet response is not apt to produce any drastically changed relationships in Europe.

Finally, no major transformation of the Soviet political system is in prospect. The bureaucratic authoritarianism of the CPSU elite holds sway and will continue to rule the Soviet empire unchallenged in harshly conservative, highly regulated, rigidly institutionalized fashion. There are pressing economic problems, but Soviet leaders are unwilling to effect major reforms of existing institutions. The military establishment will command greater influence and national resources. The notion of convergence of social systems seems as chimerical as that of an industrially mature and productive Soviet Union gradually democratizing its society and softening its foreign policy. Historically, brief periods of liberalism in Russia have been followed by far longer periods of repression.

Beyond all of this, we must accept the fact that we live in a time of troubles from which there is no promise of a respite. In this we are not unique. Each generation has tended to regard its own challenges and dangers as particularly difficult and has wistfully envied previous generations their comparative security and tranquility. The dilemmas of yesterday invariably seem uncomplicated and manageable when viewed from the perspective of today. Time passes, and the seemingly insurmountable ills of man somehow find solutions that, in turn, give rise to new problems and new challenges. We may draw hope from this recurring pattern and reassure ourselves that it will continue in the future.

NOTES

1. U.S., Senate, Committee on Government Operations, Subcommittee on National Security and International Operations, "International Negotiation: American Shortcomings in Negotiating with Communist Powers," *Memorandum,* 91st Cong., 2nd sess. (1970), p. 15.

2. *The New York Times,* November 18, 1957.

3. Robert Strausz-Hupé, "Protracted Conflict: A New Look at Communist Strategy," *Orbis,* 2 (Spring 1958), 25.

4. Bernard S. Morris, "Ideology and American Policy," *The Virginia Quarterly Review,* 40, 4 (Autumn 1964), 539.

5. *The New York Times,* October 20, 1963.

Communist Doctrine and Soviet Diplomacy

75/Observations on Dealing with the Soviet Union

ADAM B. ULAM

This doctrine of the outside capitalist world as mainly hostile has obvious politico-psychological advantages: it preserves the image of the Soviet Union as a beleaguered fortress, thus justifying the sacrifices and vigilance the state requires from the citizen whether on the production line or in abjuring the tempting example of the West with its comforts and freedoms. The doctrine justifies interventions in the affairs of other Communist states on the order of the one in Czechoslovakia in 1968. Even to themselves the Soviet leaders probably could not fully admit that they were really afraid of the *example* of Czechoslovakia: that demands for similar freedoms and eventually for a multiparty system would be raised in Poland, East Germany, etc., and, if tolerated there, perhaps even in the Soviet Union. It was easier to allege a capitalist plot to overthrow socialism in a fellow Communist country, and even to hint at the possibility of armed intervention by NATO.

Realistically, no student of world affairs, nobody reading what's happening in the United States and in other states of the West, could have for at least the last fifteen years credited the West with the ability or desire to overthrow Communism by force. But for the Soviet regime, the thesis of the West's basic hostility and evil designs is a necessary psychological crutch. In employing it the regime has had at the same time to avoid unduly alarming its own people. It reconciles these contradictory requirements by the formula that while the "ruling circles" in the West (and it is seldom made clear whether this is supposed to mean the actual governments or the capitalists and their agents within governments) are unremitting in their hostility, the strength and vigilance of the Soviet Union on the one hand, and opposition to war by the people even within capitalist countries on the other, keep aggressive forces in check.

The notion of basic enmity of capitalism is thus welded into the Soviet creed (and much more so into the Chinese Communist one) and

U.S., Congress, Senate, Committee on Government Operations, Subcommittee on National Security and International Operations, "Communist Doctrine and Soviet Diplomacy: Some Observations," *Memorandum*, 91st Cong., 2nd sess. (1970), pp. 2–12, *excerpts*.

it cannot be dispelled even by the most patently peaceful policies of the West, even by periods of collaboration of the West and Russia for attainment of mutually desirable objectives such as the avoidance of an all-out war in the Near East or a reduction of the burden of armaments. . . .

Compared with Russians, the Americans tend to view international problems from either a too large or a too small perspective. For the American public—and this has rubbed off even on the most hard-boiled statesmen and diplomats—there have been questions like how to make "Russia collaborate for peace," or on the contrary the "Berlin problem," or "nuclear proliferation." For the Russians, on the other hand, the underlying nature of international negotiations is, to borrow a legal term, an antagonistic one. In the *very* long run the interests of the two superpowers are antagonistic, not only because of their ideological differences but because of the fact that they are rivals for primacy. This does not mean that they cannot reach a mutually profitable and long-lasting accommodation, but not in the sense that they would ever be able to relax their guard completely or to base their relations on the, say, Canadian-American pattern. Negotiations in the American view are occasions for the interested parties to state their respective positions and to convince their antagonists of their goodwill and reasonability. The Soviet approach is essentially the traditional one of European diplomacy (with some variations, to be discussed below): diplomatic negotiations are a bargaining procedure in which you assess your opponent's strengths and weaknesses and test his endurance.

The Soviet approach to specific points of international disputes is often more elaborate and indirect than is realized on the other side. We speak of the Berlin crisis of 1948–49 and of the crisis of the 1958–62 period. Yet from the Soviet point of view pressure on Berlin during those periods was but the means of securing much longer objectives.

The threat to the Western position in Berlin in 1948–49 was thought in Moscow to be the most efficacious means of making the West abandon or postpone its plans to set up the West German state. When this pressure proved unavailing and a continuation of the blockade threatened dangerous complications, the Soviets simply discontinued it without securing any concessions or declaring what had been on their mind in the first place.

The war of nerves over the same city in 1958–62 was motivated by similar but even wider objectives: the Russians were eager for a German peace treaty, and especially for a guarantee that Bonn would be prohibited from owning or manufacturing nuclear weapons. The most convenient means for extracting from the United States and its allies pledges to that effect was thought again to be to threaten the West in its most vulnerable spot: its rights and access to West Berlin. To appreciate the comprehensive nature of Soviet diplomatic maneuvers, one has to recall that the threat to Berlin was lifted not on account of anything happening there or elsewhere in Germany but as a byproduct of the Cuban missile crisis. In the wake of a genuine scare over the nuclear confrontation it was thought too risky and uncontrollable to keep up the pressure, and, on the contrary, it was thought desirable to lower the level of international tension. To seize West Berlin was never a Soviet aim in itself, though the cutting off of communications between the two segments of the city had a place, though not a very high one, on the Soviet list of priorities. West Berlin was simply thought of as one area where pressure on the West may extract concessions of much greater importance—and Berlin may again become considered such an area.

This example shows that sometimes Soviet policies become over-subtle. It seems like common sense, especially in the nuclear age, to be more straightforward about one's fears and objectives and to negotiate more directly, rather than to employ the circuitous route of veiled advances, veiled to the point of being incomprehensible to the other side, and of threats which taken at face value might lead to a confrontation with incalculable consequences. In a rebuttal, the Russians might echo the argument of defenders of militancy on the contemporary American scene: appeals for change and for solutions which seem reasonable from their point of view are seldom heeded unless accompanied by threats and *faits accomplis.*

Without discussing the merits of this position in either case, it is important to draw attention to another and more important reason for this circuitous approach by Soviet diplomacy. In general the Russians feel it is a mistake to divulge fully the nature of your real fears and the full extent of your weakness. Had the Western policy makers realized in 1948 how deeply concerned the Soviets then were over the prospect of the West German army would they not have (1) speeded up its creation, and (2) used it as a bargaining counter to wrest concessions from the Soviet Union? Wasn't the West deeply impressed how *apparently* unconcerned the Soviet leaders were between 1945–49 about the American monopoly of the atom bomb; how they seemed to ignore the dangerous and decisive character of nuclear weapons in any future war? Had the real extent of Soviet fears on this count been realized at the time, would the United States have acquiesced as readily in Soviet policies in Eastern Europe and in the Far East?

The ability to engage in diplomatic feints and threats is, of course, a natural advantage any totalitarian regime possesses over a democratic one which has to explain and justify its policies to public opinion at home and to its allies, and which seldom can engage in forceful policies without alarming its own people and allies, as much as its opponents. . . .

What has been true of Soviet foreign policy in the recent past will continue to be true in the foreseeable future: it conceives of international relations mainly in terms of power politics. It gauges the strength of its opponents and rivals not only by their military effectives and industrial potential but also by their social cohesion and the strength of their leadership. Except in terms of propaganda, the ideological character of the government of non-Communist countries with which they deal remains a matter of indifference to the Russians. They will not be inhibited if they think it desirable to seek a rapprochement with Greece by the fact that parliamentary institutions have been suspended there; their policies towards the German Federal Republic will not be appreciably different whether a Socialist or a Christian Democratic party is in power. They fashion their policies according to the specific dangers and opportunities they see and not according to the party allegiance of the governments they have to deal with.

The exigencies of the nuclear age have, of course, deeply affected the character of Soviet policies, even if this is not always apparent in statements of the leaders. The earlier disregard of the fundamental change brought to world politics through the atom bomb was, as we suggested above, largely a pose. Later on, with both superpowers equipped with a stock of nuclear weapons, Khrushchev still intermittently behaved as if he believed that a nuclear war would be catastrophic to capitalism and not to the world as a whole. It was only the Cuban crisis, and then the Chinese Communists' (undoubtedly also pretended) disregard of the cataclysmic consequences of a nuclear conflict, which made him acknowledge the imperative necessity of peaceful coexistence between the world's leading powers. But both he and his successors have held on to the notion that this coexistence still offers an ample scope for the Soviet Union to adjust the power relationship vis-à-vis the United States in its favor.

Although they are determined to prevent the outbreak of a major war, Soviet leaders seem as yet insufficiently aware of the need to evolve techniques for preventing small crises from escalating into major ones. On the contrary, they see such small crises as offering opportunities for the Soviet Union to improve its diplomatic and power position. The world, in other words, is for the Kremlin still the stage for a competition of the two systems, and for the struggle for primacy between the US and the USSR. The general tendency of the forces of history, as well as their own superior skill in international maneuvering, afford the Soviet Union, they believe, an opportunity to win those small conflicts while avoiding a major and disastrous one.

The Psychological Roots of the Soviet "Cold War" Mentality

76/Ideological Struggle and Political Conflict

G. A. ARBATOV

The policy of peaceful coexistence is the only possible alternative not only to a world war but to the Cold War. Its aim is to create firm foundations of peace and to put in good order the entire system of international relations... . The policy of peaceful coexistence cannot be reduced simply to the absence of a state of war at any given moment; it envisages a decisive struggle against imperialist aggression. The struggle is for the liquidation of all sources of danger of a new world war, for the settlement by means of negotiation of quarrels and conflicts that increase tension, for the halting of the arms race, for the creation of an effective international mechanism for preventing aggression, and for the development of economic, scientific, and cultural ties among states. . . .

The reasons that lead communist parties to proclaim as their goal the normalization of international relations but at the same time to regard as inevitable and necessary the ideological struggle against imperialism and bourgeois ideas are quite evident.

The essence of the Leninist concept of peaceful coexistence consists in the very fact that it addresses itself to the parallel coexistence not only of different states, but of states belonging to contradictory social systems. From this it already follows that relations between such systems cannot be exhausted by normal diplomatic relations, no matter how important they may be in themselves. The existence of two systems has also another side to it. Each one of the systems personifies the domination of a class—in one instance, the class of capitalists, in the other, the working class; between these classes there is irreconcilable struggle that constitutes the essence of our epoch. The struggle of these classes began long before the emergence of the first communist party, and it was not Marx who brought it into existence.

From the standpoint of the Marxist-Leninists, the struggle can end only in the full victory of communism. The victory of socialism in the countries that now constitute the world socialist system is an important

G. A. Arbatov, *Ideologicheskaia Bor'ba v Sovremennykh Mezhdunarodnykh Otnosheniakh* [*Ideological Struggle in Contemporary International Relations*] (Moscow: State Publishing House for Political Literature, 1970), pp. 304–308, *excerpts.* Editor's translation with the assistance of Dr. Oles Smolansky.

stage on the road to this goal. But this success does not mean and cannot mean the end of the class struggle. Between the workers and the bourgeoisie the struggle continues and will continue, inside the various countries as well as in the international arena, where side by side with the clash of political and economic interests the great historical controversy of the two social systems continues. This controversy, unfolding in the economic, political, and ideological spheres, began more than half a century ago, and it will not end until there is complete victory of the more progressive social system. Such is the inevitable fact of social development, established not by someone's ill will but by objective existence.

No one government and no one political party can "abolish" this fact, can "abolish" the class struggle. But the choice of the kind of historically inevitable struggle depends to a large extent on the governments, ruling classes, and political parties. In offering peaceful coexistence, communists proceed from the assumption that it is possible and necessary to avoid the transformation of this struggle into armed conflict among states and to direct it into channels that would not threaten peoples or civilization with horrible consequences.

In this the communists see the advantages and the necessity of peaceful coexistence, which signifies rejection of a military form of struggle between states and substitution of such a form of struggle as the *competition of social systems*. This competition is designed to demonstrate in practice the historical advantages of the most advanced of them [the two social systems] and in so doing to secure for it the support of the people. This form of struggle corresponds more than any other to the interests of mankind. . . .

But such a form of struggle between the two social systems inevitably presupposes ideological struggle. Insofar as capitalism and socialism will compete with each other for the support of peoples, the struggle of ideas is inevitable.

Is this a good perspective for mankind? Undoubtedly. Indeed, it may be considered the best possible perspective in contemporary conditions.

Only notorious falsifiers can pretend that prior to the emergence of socialism there existed in the world an idyll of fraternity and friendship, some sort of kingdom of universal love, and that the communists came and demanded competition and ideological struggle between the two systems. The real history of international relations was far from such an idyll—it was full of bloody wars, colonizing campaigns, never-ending attempts by the powerful to profit at the expense of the weak. Today also the world does not face the choice between universal brotherhood and prosperity or ideological struggle and the competition of the two systems, on which the communists insist. The latter represents an alternative, not to universal brotherhood and prosperity—they do not exist and cannot exist in the world where imperialism exists—but to a world war, to military conflicts, and to the Cold War. It is clear that to accept this challenge would represent not a step backward, or standing still, but tremendous progress in the matter of putting international relations into good working order.

Continuity and Change in Soviet Policy

77/The Pressures Behind Soviet Expansionism

BARRINGTON MOORE, JR.

Has Soviet expansion during the past decade been primarily defensive, and would it come to rest if external threats were removed? Or is the world now witnessing a special variety of expansionism: Communist imperialism? The same general questions would have to be answered about the United States, but the analysis in this study must necessarily be confined to the Russian side of the equation.

Four considerations enter into the conclusion advanced by many that the Soviet system contains a number of internal expansionist forces impelling it to seek one conquest after another. It is often said that, because the USSR is an authoritarian state, its rulers need a continuous series of triumphs in order to maintain their power. The rulers of a dictatorship, it is claimed, cannot afford to rest on their laurels. Occasionally this type of argument is supported by a neo-Freudian chain of reasoning. It is asserted that the frustrations imposed upon the individual in modern society, especially under a dictatorship, tend to produce socially destructive impulses that have to be channeled outward against an external enemy if the society is not to destroy itself. The second line of argument, at a different level of analysis, emphasizes the indications of a strong power drive in Stalin's personality.* Parallels can be drawn on this basis between his urge for new worlds to conquer and the political aspirations of Napoleon, Hitler, and others. A third

---

* [Professor Moore wrote this article in 1950.—Ed.]

Barrington Moore, Jr., *Soviet Politics—The Dilemma of Power* (Cambridge, Mass.: Harvard University Press, 1950), pp. 394–401, *excerpts.* Reprinted with permission of the author and publisher.

line of reasoning points to various indications in Soviet statements and actions of an old-fashioned interest in territorial expansion that shows strong resemblances to traditional Tsarist policy. The latter argument draws its reasoning from the facts of geography and history, emphasizing traditional Russian interest in warm water ports, the long drive to the South and East, and similar matters. Under the fourth type of argument, Marxist-Leninist ideology is selected as a separate expansionist force. Persons who hold this view point out the Messianic qualities of Marxist doctrine and the continuous need for struggle and victory that it generates.

Each of these arguments and hypotheses represents some portion of the truth. . . .

Concerning the first point, that authoritarian states tend to be expansionist ones, it is necessary to express reservations and doubts on both general and specific grounds. The connection between the internal organization of a society and its foreign policy is a complex question that cannot yet be answered on the basis of simple formulas. Athens engaged in foreign conquest perhaps more than did warlike Sparta, and the Japanese, despite the militaristic emphasis of their society, lived in isolation for centuries until the time of their forced contacts with the West. To show that the authoritarian structure of any state is a source of expansionist tendencies, one would have to show the way in which these pressures make themselves felt upon those responsible for foreign policy. At this point the argument often breaks down, though there are cases where it can be shown that the rulers have embarked on an adventurous policy to allay internal discontent. But those at the apex of the political pyramid in an authoritarian regime are frequently freer from the pressures of mass discontent than are the responsible policymakers of a Western democracy. They can therefore afford to neglect much longer the dangers of internal hostilities. Furthermore, modern events reveal the weakness of the argument that a warlike policy is the result of hostilities toward outsiders among the individuals who make up the society. In the days of total war it is necessary to use all sorts of force and persuasion, from propaganda to conscription, to make men and women fight. To regard war as primarily the expression of the hostilities of rank-and-file citizens of various states toward one another is to fly in the face of these facts.

In the case of the Soviet Union, the Nazi-Soviet Pact of 1939 shows that the rulers of modern Russia had no difficulty in disregarding the hostilities to Nazism that had been built up during preceding years, and that in this respect they enjoyed greater freedom for prompt adjustment of disputes than did other countries. Both totalitarian partners were able to keep mass hostility under control as long as it suited purposes and plans based on the configuration of international power relationships. . . .

An acceptable modification of the argument that the authoritarian nature of the present Soviet regime is a source of an aggressive and expansionist foreign policy may be found along the following lines. It is probable that a certain amount of hostility toward the outside world is an essential ingredient in the power of the present rulers of Russia. Without the real or imagined threat of potential attack, it would be much more difficult to drive the Russian masses through one set of Five Year Plans after another. Yet it does not seem likely that this hostility is in turn a force that reacts back on the makers of Russian foreign policy. Their power can be more easily maximized by the threat of war than by war itself—a precarious enough situation. Nor is there evidence that mass hostility is in any way cumulative or sufficient to force the Soviet leaders into an aggressive policy. There are a number of devices for draining off internally generated hostility into channels other than those of external expansion. Military and combative sentiments, aroused for specific purposes, can be and have been directed into the socially productive channels of promoting a conquest of the physical environment.

There are good grounds for concurring in the conclusion that a drive for power in Stalin's personal make-up has been and will remain a very significant element in Soviet policy as long as his leadership is maintained. . . .*

Those who emphasize the continuity of the Russian historical tradition and the importance of Russia's geographical position in the determination of Soviet foreign policy are correct insofar as Russia's place on the globe and her past relations with her neighbors set certain limitations and provide certain readily definable opportunities for Russian foreign policy. In other words, an expansionist Soviet foreign policy can follow only certain well-defined lines of attack. It may have Persia, China, or Germany as its major object of infiltration, but Latin America and the Antarctic are much more remote objectives.

The reappearance of old-fashioned Russian territorial interests in various parts of the globe has been associated with the revival of Russian strength from the low ebb of revolution, intervention, and civil war. It may be suspected that the early idealist statements of the Bolshevik leaders about the abandonment of Tsarist imperialism were inspired not only by Marxist doctrine but were also made on the grounds that they were the only possible tactics to follow in Russia's weak condition. Now that the proletarian revolution has a territorial base, it is understandable that attempts should be made to combine the interests of the two, and

---

* [Given the nature of political selection in the Soviet Union, we may assume that any individual who climbs to the pinnacle of power would also possess a strong urge for power.—Ed.]

that some of the results should show marked similarities to Tsarist policy. Furthermore, the possibility may readily be granted that the present rulers of Russia are somewhat influenced by the model of Tsarist diplomacy. But the driving forces behind any contemporary Soviet expansionism must be found in a contemporary social situation. Historical and geographical factors may limit the expression of an expansionist drive. They cannot be expansionist forces in their own right.

Turning to the ideological factor, it has already been noted that the Messianic energies of Communism can be, and at times in the past have been, very largely directed toward tasks of internal construction. The "creative myth of Leninism," to use Sorel's suggestive term, involves the building of factories in desert wastes and the creation of a more abundant life for the inhabitants of the Soviet Union. One must agree, however, that a creative myth, if it is effective, is usually an article for export as well as for domestic consumption. Those who really believe in socialism usually believe it is necessary for the world as a whole, just as do the more emotional believers in the virtues of democracy and the four freedoms. There remains, however, another important aspect of Soviet doctrine, which sets at least temporary limits to its expansionist qualities. It is a cardinal point in the Leninist-Stalinist doctrine that a retreat made in good order is not a disgrace. The Soviet myth does not have a "victory or death" quality—there is no urge to seek a final dramatic showdown and a *Götterdämmerung* finale. When faced with superior strength, the Soviets have on numerous occasions shown the ability to withdraw with their forces intact. Although the withdrawal may be followed by a renewal of pressures elsewhere, it may be repeated once more if superior forces are again brought to bear.

The foregoing considerations are enough to suggest the complexity of the problem of interpreting the expansionist forces contained in the Soviet system. They should make us wary of dramatically pessimistic conclusions to the effect that the Soviet leaders, propelled by forces beyond their control, are marching to a world holocaust. But they give many more grounds for pessimism than for optimism concerning the probability of preventing a further increase in tension in the power relationships of Moscow and Washington. Even though Soviet expansionism of the past decade may be explained as primarily an adaptation to the changing balance of power, such an explanation by no means precludes the possibility, perhaps even the probability, that the series of adaptations and "defensive" measures taken by the United States and the USSR may culminate in war.

FOR FURTHER STUDY

Aspaturian, Vernon V. *The Soviet Union in the World Communist System.* Stanford, Calif.: Hoover Institution, 1966.

Barnet, Richard J., and Marcus G. Raskin. *After 20 Years: Alternatives to the Cold War in Europe.* New York: Random House, 1965.

Brzezinski, Zbigniew K. *Between Two Ages: America's Role in the Technetronic Age.* New York: Viking, 1971.

Gamson, William A., and Andre Modigliani. *Untangling the Cold War: A Strategy for Testing Rival Theories.* Boston: Little, Brown, 1971.

Goodman, Elliot R. *The Soviet Design for a World State.* New York: Columbia University Press, 1960.

Halle, Louis J. *The Cold War as History.* New York: Harper & Row, 1967.

Herrick, Robert Waring. *Soviet Naval Strategy: Fifty Years of Theory and Practice.* Annapolis, Md.: United States Naval Institute, 1968.

Kennan, George F. *On Dealing With the Communist World.* New York: Harper & Row, 1964.

Lindsay, Michael. *Is Peaceful Coexistence Possible?* East Lansing: Michigan State University Press, 1960.

Morris, Bernard S. *International Communism and American Policy.* New York: Atherton, 1966.

Pisar, Samuel. *Coexistence and Commerce: Guidelines for Transactions Between East and West.* New York: McGraw-Hill, 1970.

Rapoport, Anatol. *The Big Two: Soviet-American Perceptions of Foreign Policy.* New York: Pegasus, 1971.

Rock, Vincent P. *A Strategy of Interdependence: A Program for Control of Conflict Between the U.S. and the Soviet Union.* New York: Scribner, 1964.

Shub, Anatole. *An Empire Loses Hope: The Return of Stalin's Ghost.* New York: Norton, 1970.

Shulman, Marshall D. *Beyond the Cold War.* New Haven, Conn.: Yale University Press, 1966.

Strausz-Hupé, Robert, *et al. Protracted Conflict.* New York: Harper & Row, 1959.

Strong, John W. (ed.). *The Soviet Union Under Brezhnev and Kosygin.* New York: Van Nostrand Reinhold, 1971.

Ulam, Adam B. *The Rivals: America and Russia Since World War II.* New York: Viking, 1971.

Weeks, Albert L. *The Other Side of Coexistence: An Analysis of Russian Foreign Policy.* New York: Pitman, 1970.

Welch, William. *American Images of Soviet Foreign Policy.* New Haven, Conn.: Yale University Press, 1970.

Index